The Snail and the Ginger Beer

The Singular Case of Donoghue *v* Stevenson

Matthew Chapman

WILDY, SIMMONDS & HILL PUBLISHING

The Snail and the Ginger Beer: The Singular Case of Donoghue v Stevenson

ISBN 9780854900497

First published in Great Britain 2010 by Wildy, Simmonds & Hill Publishing

Website: www.wildy.com

British Library Cataloguing-in-Publication Data:
A catalogue record for this book is available from The British Library

First published in 2010 by
Wildy, Simmonds & Hill Publishing
58 Carey Street, London WC2A 2JB
England

Printed and bound in Great Britain by
CPI Antony Rowe, Chippenham, Wiltshire

For Benjamin, Matthew and Poppy

CONTENTS

LIST OF ILLUSTRATIONS

Baron Atkin of Aberdovey (1867 – 1944)

By permission of the Treasurer and the Masters of the Bench of the Honourable Society of Gray's Inn.

Viscount Buckmaster (1861 – 1934)

By permission of the National Portrait Gallery.

Baron Macmillan of Aberfeldy (1873 – 1952)

By permission of the National Portrait Gallery.

Wellmeadow Street, Paisley in the early 1900s.

By permission of the Paisley Museum and Art Gallery.

Wellmeadow Street, Paisley in the early 1900s.

By permission of the Paisley Museum and Art Gallery.

Mrs May Donoghue holding her twin granddaughters in June 1952.

By permission of Margaret (Maggie) Tomlin

Extract from *Paisley Daily Express*, 31 August 1988.

By permission of the *Paisley Daily Express*.

Donoghue v Stevenson Memorial Park and Garden: August 2008.

Author's collection

Donoghue v Stevenson Memorial Tablet: August 2008

Author's collection

NOTES AND ACKNOWLEDGEMENTS

This book could not have been written without the assistance of a large number of other people. I am grateful to the librarians at the Parliamentary archive for their assistance in my use of the Appeal papers in *Donoghue v Stevenson*. I would also like to thank Andrew Mussell, the Archivist at Gray's Inn, for arranging access to Lord Atkin's papers and for permitting me to see again the magnificent portrait which hangs in the Hall of the Inn (and which now graces this book – for which I am grateful to the Treasurer and Masters of the Bench of the Inn). Emma Butterfield at the National Portrait Gallery archive was very helpful and efficient in arranging reproduction rights for the portraits of Lords Buckmaster and Macmillan which also appear in this book. David Roberts at the Paisley Museum and Art Gallery was tolerant of my repeated requests for assistance with the photographic archive held by the Museum. I am very grateful to the helpful librarians at the Institute of Advanced Legal Studies who patiently and uncomplainingly responded to many requests to collect material from the closed basement of the library. Faber & Faber Ltd and the literary executors of Ted Hughes and Philip Larkin kindly gave permission for the quotations with which the Prologue and Chapter 3 commence. Finally, I am particularly grateful to Margaret (Maggie) Tomlin. Ms Tomlin, who now lives in Dorset, is Mrs Donoghue's granddaughter and was kind enough to permit me to reproduce the photograph of her grandmother which appears in these pages. The photograph was originally located by Evelyn Blair, and so I record my thanks to her as well.

Nicholas Mercer kindly agreed to read a large section of the unfinished manuscript and made a number of helpful editorial and other corrections. I would also like to express my gratitude to Andrew Riddoch and to Wildy, Simmonds & Hill Publishing who provided the opportunity to write on this subject. Finally, I should thank the late Professor RFV Heuston who, as I hope this book makes clear, first fired my interest in this subject and my parents whose home on the south coast provided a quiet place to complete the final chapters.

I have, throughout this book, used the present English/Welsh procedural terms 'claimant' and 'defendant' to refer to the parties to litigation. I am well aware that this will grate horribly for any readers north of the border (and, perhaps, for those who pre-date the Civil Procedure Rules), but seemed to me, for reasons of consistency, preferable to the interchangeable use of 'pursuer', 'plaintiff' and 'defender'. I should make it clear that, in spite of the assistance which is acknowledged in these notes, any errors in the material which follows are all my own work.

Matthew Chapman

1 Chancery Lane

20 August 2009

PROLOGUE

'The Cabbage murmurs:
"I feel something's wrong!"
The Snail says: "Shhh!
I am God's tongue."

The Rose shrieks out:
"What's this? Oh, what's this?"
The Snail says: "Shhh!
I am God's kiss."'

Ted Hughes, 'Snail' from *Collected Animal Poems*

'There are only four cases you need to know in order to pass your torts exam'. This was, it had to be admitted, a good start. More than a hundred undergraduates craned forward in the crowded lecture theatre. On the rostrum stood our guest lecturer: RFV Heuston (some time Regius Professor of Laws at Trinity College, Dublin, Professor of Legal Science at Cambridge, Fellow of Pembroke College, Oxford and bencher of the King's Inns and Gray's Inn). The students were, for the most part, 18 and 19 year olds. Professor Heuston was approaching his seventh decade, but, in his pin-striped three piece suit, seemed even older. He was, however, sufficiently attuned to the thought processes of the average undergraduate to know that what we wanted to hear was how we could pass our exams with the minimum of conscious effort. Decades of lecturing had equipped him with the tricks needed to grab an 18 year old's attention. I can now remember only two of the cases to which Heuston referred, although I could probably make an educated guess at the other two. I remember *Anns v Merton London Borough Council*.[1] The other case was, of course, what I shall call, and what Professor Heuston referred to as, *Donoghue v Stevenson*.[2]

---

1 [1978] AC 728.
2 [1932] AC 562 (HL(Sc)).

Heuston went on to tell us the story of *Donoghue v Stevenson*. How, on an August evening in 1928, May Donoghue, a shop assistant, entered the Wellmeadow café in Paisley, Scotland. She was with a friend who ordered an ice cream and a ginger beer; Mrs Donoghue wanted to make an ice cream float. The proprietor of the café poured some of the ginger beer into a glass containing the ice cream. Mrs Donoghue drank some of the float. Her friend poured out the remainder of the ginger beer. Along with the drink, a decomposed snail tumbled into the glass. May Donoghue claimed that she suffered nervous shock and severe gastro-enteritis as a result of drinking an ice cream float with a snail unexpectedly swimming in it. She could not sue the café proprietor. Her friend had ordered and paid for the drink and Mrs Donoghue therefore had no contract with the café. Instead, she sued the manufacturer of the ginger beer. She alleged that the manufacturer had been negligent because its manufacturing processes had enabled the snail to enter the bottle and had not detected the snail once it was there. The question whether Mrs Donoghue had, in law, a claim against the manufacturer went from the Scottish Court of Session to the House of Lords. The House of Lords' decision made legal history. There is not a corner of the common law world that has not been touched by it.

As our tutors were later keen to emphasise, Professor Heuston was wrong to tell us that we only needed to know four cases to pass the exam, but the lecture that he delivered after his arresting opening line was lively, learned and, in the best sense, gossipy. His lecturing style was eccentric. He recited the lines that he wanted us to write down at dictation speed, but punctuated these staccato bursts of seriousness with lengthy digressions that were rich in anecdote and enlivened with biographical sketches. Each digression was introduced with the word, 'Commentary': a signal that we could put down our pens and listen (something that we were unaccustomed to doing in torts lectures). He repeatedly emphasised the significance of *Donoghue v Stevenson* having been decided by a 'Scottish House of Lords'. While researching this book I discovered that Professor Heuston had, in some lecture notes, referred to Lord Atkin as the leader of 'the celtic majority' in the House of Lords:[3] perhaps a source of pan-celtic pride to the Irish Professor. He produced, like a holy relic, a photograph of a ginger beer bottle similar to that purchased by Mrs Donoghue's friend. He told us stories about the judges who decided the case. At the time I neither knew nor appreciated the scholarship which informed Professor Heuston's lecture: the professional interest that, for decades, he had shown in the significance of *Donoghue v Stevenson*[4] and the biography of Lord Buckmaster (the most powerful dissenting voice in the House of Lords) of which he was the author. However, his students that morning did recognise his sure-footed ability to tell a story and to inform and educate at the same time. Heuston knew that, on some level, every decision taken by a court contains a narrative (or narratives) and has real protagonists. The facts of *Donoghue v Stevenson* are, even if one is unaware of its importance in the history of our law, intriguing. Who was Mrs Donoghue? Who was the friend? Where was the Paisley café and is it still there? Was there ever, in fact, a snail in the ginger beer? It was against the background of these factual issues – the sort of questions that one might naturally ask a friend recounting the events – that Professor Heuston sought to illuminate the legal significance of the case. If it can be said that every non-lawyer, and even every undergraduate law student, should be required to read at least one law report in its original and complete form then there is a good case for arguing that *Donoghue v Stevenson* should be the selected case.

3 Heuston, RFV *The Law of Torts in 1960* (Lecture Notes from 1960 Conference of British, Canadian and American Law Teachers). In a 1957 article, Professor Heuston credited Landon ((1942) 58 LQR 181) with inventing this phrase. There were two Scottish Law Lords in *Donoghue v Stevenson*: Lord Thankerton and Lord Macmillan. Lord Atkin (of Aberdovey) was born in Brisbane, Australia, but raised in Merionethshire, Wales. Much of his ancestry was Irish, but he always considered himself a Welshman.

4 See, for example, Heuston, RFV '*Donoghue v Stevenson* in Retrospect' (1957) 20 MLR 1; Heuston, RFV *Salmond on the Law of Torts* (Sweet & Maxwell, 11th ed, 1953), p 496; Heuston, RFV *Lives of the Lord Chancellors 1885 – 1940* (Clarendon Press, 1964), Chapter 1.

At the heart of *Donoghue v Stevenson's* importance to the development of the common law lies Lord Atkin's famous 'neighbour principle'. His speech contains the following much-quoted passage:

> 'The liability for negligence, whether you style it such or treat it as in other systems as a species of "culpa," is no doubt based upon a general public sentiment of moral wrongdoing for which the offender must pay. But acts or omissions which any moral code would censure cannot in a practical world be treated so as to give a right to every person injured by them to demand relief. In this way rules of law arise which limit the range of complainants and the extent of their remedy. The rule that you are to love your neighbour becomes in law, you must not injure your neighbour; and the lawyer's question, Who is my neighbour? receives a restricted reply. You must take reasonable care to avoid acts or omissions which you can reasonably foresee would be likely to injure your neighbour. Who, then, in law is my neighbour? The answer seems to be – persons who are so closely and directly affected by my act that I ought reasonably to have them in my contemplation as being so affected when I am directing my mind to the acts or omissions which are called in question.'[5]

The 'lawyer's question' to which Lord Atkin referred was, 'And who is my neighbour?' which the clever lawyer puts to Jesus in St Luke's Gospel and which introduces the parable of the Good Samaritan.[6] The story of the man who fell among thieves explicitly and clearly informs Lord Atkin's neighbour principle. One distinguished Christian writer has observed that the point of the Good Samaritan parable, involving as it does a priest and a Levite who pass the injured stranger, rather than risk infringing the rules of their religion,[7] is to teach us that, 'Compassion should overrule code'.[8] One reading of Lord Atkin's speech might lead us to the conclusion that this also underpins his conclusions in *Donoghue v Stevenson*. Lord Atkin's answer to the question, 'Who is my neighbour', is more 'restricted'

5 [1932] AC 562, 580.
6 Luke (10: 25 – 37).
7 The priest and Levite's religious code forbade contact with a stranger who might be morally and religiously unclean to them.
8 Holloway, R *Introduction to the Gospel According to Luke* (Canongate Pocket Canons, 1998), p xii.

than the answer given in St Luke's Gospel, but also discards precedent and tradition ('code') in the pursuit of compassion. In this regard, as in others, *Donoghue v Stevenson* is about more than simply the tort of negligence and its development; it stands at the junction of wider themes which concern the meaning and content of moral and legal duties of care. Mrs Donoghue's unfortunate encounter with the ginger beer bottle and its alleged occupant led the House of Lords to a complex enquiry into what it means to owe another person a duty of care. This was an important question in the 1930s and is no less important now when tabloid headlines and moral panic about the perceived problem of the 'compensation culture' periodically arise.

The genesis of this book lies in Professor Heuston's entertaining lecture (and the serious scholarship which informed it), but this is not an academic textbook. While there is commentary on the legal significance of *Donoghue v Stevenson*, both in the UK jurisdictions and overseas, it does not seek exhaustively to chart the development of the neighbour principle through the decisions of the appellate courts. I have tried to avoid lengthy analysis of the leading case law; there are many other places where interested readers can find that sort of material. Instead, the intention of this book is to tell the story of the decision and its protagonists, to unearth the wider context of the case and to emphasise its enduring importance. The House of Lords has now been abolished as a Court of Appeal, but the 1932 decision of this tribunal is not the fossilised offspring of a now extinct court; twenty-first century lawyers continue to discuss Mrs Donoghue's case and it continues to exert an influence on the jurists of the common law world. Something important was decided by the House of Lords in *Donoghue v Stevenson*. It remains a good, and an important, story. It is still worth telling.

1. MRS DONOGHUE TRAVELS TO PAISLEY

Yepikhodov: '… let's say you pick up your *kvas*, you go to drink it down, and you look, and there's something positively indecent in it, like a cockroach.'

Anton Chekhov, *The Cherry Orchard*

In 1928 the twenty-sixth of August was a Sunday. This weekend fell during the annual Glasgow Trades Holiday when the working men and women of the city were permitted some brief respite from their work. Trains from Glasgow's austere Central Station served the holiday crowds fanning out west to the sea at Ayr; they still do, although these days the railway line from Glasgow Central also delivers package holidaymakers to Prestwick Airport. In August 1928 May Donoghue, a shop assistant then aged 30 years, was living with her brother in a flat at 49 Kent Street in Glasgow. The building in which she lived has been demolished, but Kent Street is still there. It lies just beyond the commercial centre of the city in the heart of the Barras market area where, on the August Saturday that I visited, corrugated iron sheds sheltered trestle tables crowded with toys and cheap clothes. A smell of cigarettes and fried food hung in the air; the area is busy, even commercial, but it is clear that even now (as in 1928) Kent Street is relatively poor and lies just beyond the reach of Glasgow's recent development projects.

Paisley, where Mrs Donoghue travelled on the August Sunday of her day off work is a large town (a Burgh) situated 7 miles to the west of Glasgow. In 1928 there were still fields and some open countryside between Paisley and the city. There is no longer green space of any significance; the train from Glasgow to Paisley rattles through suburbs and commercial developments. Paisley has a proud and ancient municipal history. A great Abbey Church still stands at the site of a pre-Reformation monastery associated with the Irish missionary saint: Mirin (now better known for lending his name to a local football team). By the early twentieth century Paisley's history was inextricably linked to the industrial revolution and to the Empire that industrial Britain funded. The town's principal trade was in textiles (bleaching and printing) and its fame in this industry was such that it gave its name to a Kashmiri-influenced swirling pattern of curved shapes that was printed on silk and cotton fabrics. Paisley's industries served it well. The town grew rich and when May Donoghue travelled there from Glasgow she would have seen Victorian municipal architecture to rival the best in the city. By1928 the ancient Abbey was faced by a magnificent Town Hall standing on the banks of the White Cart river. From Gilmour Street station her route would have taken her along the High Street and past the town's central Library. From there she would have passed the museum, housed behind a sleek and elegant neo-classical façade, which was stuffed full of the treasures that Paisley's wealthy nineteenth-century citizens had brought back from overseas. At the point where the High Street runs into Wellmeadow Street the road is overlooked by the Thomas Coats Memorial Church: an imposing (if rather grim-faced) red-brick Baptist chapel constructed in 1894. Almost opposite the Church, on the corner of Wellmeadow Street and Lady Lane, was Mrs Donoghue's destination on the evening of 26 August 1928: the Wellmeadow Café.

The Wellmeadow Café

The café occupied part of a tenement building probably constructed at the end of the eighteenth or the beginning of the nineteenth century. A photograph taken just after 1900 (in the collection of the Paisley Museum) shows the front aspect of the café premises occupying the ground floor of a three-storey building at the corner of Wellmeadow Street and Lady Lane. Ornate rounded windows decorate the top floor of the façade. In 1928 Wellmeadow Street was a busy area of the town. Contemporary photographs show tram tracks running down the centre of the cobble stone street. There is commercial activity in the surrounding properties and, in the 1900 photograph, to which I have referred, a tavern stands two doors along from the café.

The building in which the café was located was owned by the Reid family until, in 1959, it was purchased by the municipal authorities in Paisley and promptly demolished. In 1928 the proprietor of the Wellmeadow Café was Mr Francis Minghella (his name is misspelt as 'Minchella' in the *Donoghue v Stevenson* pleadings). He commenced trading at the café in around 1927 and probably ceased trading in 1931; '… it is probable that the case of *Donoghue v Stevenson* lasted longer than Minghella's business.'[1] Mr Minghella was 37 years of age at the time of Mrs Donoghue's visit. After he gave up the café Mr Minghella became a labourer in the highways department of the Paisley local authority and held this job until his retirement. He died on 20 March 1970.

A flavour of the atmosphere of the café and others like it, run by the Italian community in Scotland, is provided by the remarks of John F Leechman during the course of a conference which took place in Paisley in 1990. Mr Leechman was the son of Mrs Donoghue's solicitor and was a student when the case was making its way through the courts:

'You may think it unusual, too, that these ladies would go into an Italian ice cream shop. These Italian shops had been appearing all over Scotland since the end of World War I. Italian people migrating to Scotland at that time were almost all involved in operating cafes selling ice cream. People with small houses and large families had nowhere to go and talk, and cafes filled a vacuum in social life. They provided a place where young people, and older people too, could enjoy conversation with one another out of their houses, without the family listening in. ... In cold weather these cafes sold hot peas and vinegar.'[2]

The Claimant: May Donoghue

The *Donoghue v Stevenson* pleading introduces the parties in the most succinct terms, 'The pursuer is employed as a shop assistant, and resides at 49 Kent Street, off London Road, Glasgow. The defender is an aerated-water manufacturer, and carries on business at Glen Lane, Paisley.'[3]

A combination of the public record and the remainder of the pleading provides some additional detail.[4] May Donoghue's life was

1   McBryde, WM *'Donoghue v Stevenson*: the Story of the "Snail in the Bottle" Case' in Gamble, AJ (ed) *Obligations in Context* (W Green, 1990), p 17.
2   Leechman, JF 'Mrs Donoghue's Solicitor' in Burns QC, P T and Lyons, S J (eds) *Donoghue v Stevenson and the Modern Law of Negligence The Paisley Papers* (The Continuing Legal Education Society of British Columbia, 1991), p 276.
3   Condescendence I.
4   I am indebted to the original research of Professor William M McBryde, *'Donoghue v Stevenson*: the Story of the "Snail in the Bottle" Case' in Gamble, AJ (ed)

short (by today's standards) and unfortunate (by any standards). Apart from lending her married name to the most famous case in English and Scottish law, she lived a private, even obscure, life and has been dependent on later biographers with an interest in the litigation to rescue her from what the great historian EP Thompson once called, 'the enormous condescension of posterity.'[5] Her birth certificate, which can be viewed at the General Register Office in Edinburgh,[6] discloses that she was born May McAllister on 4 July 1898. Her father, James McAllister, was a steelworker and her mother, Mary Jane, a dyefield worker, and they lived, where their daughter was born, in the Cambuslang parish area in the County of Lanark to the east of Glasgow. On 19 February 1916 May McAllister married Henry Donoghue in Glasgow (who was eight years older than his 17-year-old wife). On 25 July 1916 Mrs Donoghue had a son: Henry. The couple's next three children were born prematurely and none lived longer than a fortnight. Mr and Mrs Donoghue had no more children. In 1928 the couple separated and, as at 26 August, they remained married, but were living apart (as indicated above, Mrs Donoghue lived with her brother at the 49 Kent Street address).

Mrs Donoghue was with a friend in the Wellmeadow Café. We do not know whether they travelled together from Glasgow to Paisley or whether they met on arrival in Paisley. We do not know whether they entered the café together. We do not even know the purpose of Mrs Donoghue's visit to Paisley. We do not know the identity or even the sex of Mrs Donoghue's friend; the pleaded case does not tell us, referring only to 'The said friend.' The only person to provide any detail with which to colour in the identity of the friend was Lord Macmillan whose speech contains the following passage, 'The appellant drank part of the mixture, and her friend then proceeded to pour the remaining contents of the bottle into the tumbler. As *she* was doing so a decomposed snail floated out with the ginger beer

---

Obligations in Context (W Green, 1990) and Alan Rodger QC, 'Mrs Donoghue and Alfenus Varus' (1988) 41 CLP 1 for much of the information which follows. Alan Rodger QC is now a law (Supreme Court Justice) lord: Lord Rodger of Earlsferry.
5   Thompson, EP *The Making of the English Working Class* (Victor Gollancz, 1963).
6   Birth certificate reference: 4052179 CE. Death certificate reference: 4052180 CE.

[emphasis added].'[7] We do not know the source for this biographical morsel, although it has been suggested that the sex and identity of the friend was referred to by counsel during the hearing of the appeal.[8] It is, however, clear that there is little, if any, foundation, for the rumour that Mrs Donoghue used the Wellmeadow Café as the location for an extra-marital affair. We can be reasonably confident from the little information provided by the contemporary record that the person who bought and served the famous drink was certainly Mrs Donoghue's friend, but we will never know whether this person was also her lover.[9] Mrs Donoghue's pleading in the Court of Session tells us that her friend ordered and was served a pear and ice;[10] as far as we know, this drink was untainted.

By February 1931 (if not before) Mrs Donoghue had moved out of her brother's flat in Kent Street to a new address around a mile away: 101 Maitland Street. This was another poor area of the city, but was located close to the commercial centre of Sauchiehall Street and, somewhat incongruously, Glasgow's Theatre Royal. In the same way that the municipal authorities demolished the building occupied by the Wellmeadow Café and Mrs Donoghue's 1928 address at 49 Kent Street, the 101 Maitland Street property has also gone. Maitland Street is a steep walk up Hope Street from the centre of the city and Glasgow's Central station. It is now dwarfed by large residential tower blocks (constructed, at a guess, in the 1960s or 70s); a large single-storey police station squats on the corner at the end of Maitland Street.

Mrs Donoghue continued to live at Maitland Street (with her son Henry who worked in the shipyards) until 1937 when Henry married. She then moved to the other side of the river Clyde: a Glasgow corporation flat at 156 Jamieson Street. She continued to work as a shop assistant. In 1945 she divorced the husband from whom she had by now been separated for many years and reverted to using

---

7   [1932] AC 562, 605.
8   Rodger, A 'Mrs Donoghue and Alfenus Varus' (1988) 41 CLP 1, 6, n 62.
9   See, in this context, Linden, AM 'The Good Neighbour on Trial: a Fountain of Sparkling Wit' (1983) UBC Law Review 67, 71: 'I doubt that Mrs Donoghue, if she had been living a secret life, would have sued and thereby risk exposing it for such a small claim.' While this is possible, it seems unlikely that Mrs Donoghue, who sued as a 'pauper', would have regarded her claim as 'small'.
10   Condescendence II.

her maiden name: May McAllister (the name recorded on her death certificate, 'Formerly married to Henry Donoghue against whom she obtained Decree of Divorce'). Her son Henry's marriage resulted in divorce and, in 1943, he returned to live with his mother at the Jamieson Street flat. Henry later remarried and had seven children.

Mrs Donoghue died (intestate) of a heart attack (on the death certificate, a 'myocardial infarct') at 4 pm on 19 March 1958. She died in the Gartloch Mental Hospital (it is assumed that she had suffered from mental illness at the end of her life). She was just 59 years of age. A photograph of Mrs Donoghue has recently been unearthed. It was taken in 1952, just a few years before she died, and shows her holding the twin baby daughters of her son on the day of their christening. Mrs Donoghue, wearing a bonnet at a jaunty angle, holds a child in each arm and smiles, somewhat tentatively, at the camera. The photograph (which can be viewed on the website of the Scottish Council of Law Reporting) was provided by her grand-daughter, Margaret Tomlin, who now lives in Dorset.[11] Another contact with May Donoghue is provided by her signature which survives on several documents (most notably on an affidavit of 16 February 1931 by which Mrs Donoghue sought to prosecute her appeal as a pauper unable to provide security for any adverse costs order).[12] Mrs Donoghue's signature is clear and well-formed; the decorated first 'M' and final 'E' suggest that she signed this declaration of her poverty with a flourish.

The Defendant: David Stevenson

Glen Lane, Paisley lies on the other side of the railway track from Wellmeadow Street, behind Gilmour Street station (less than a mile from the café).[13] At the time that Mrs Donoghue entered the Wellmeadow Café the Paisley business of David Stevenson (a firm)

---

11   It appears that a further photograph of May Donoghue, taken in 1945, was lodged in the course of her divorce proceedings, but it has not been found (see, Mc-Bryde, WM '*Donoghue v Stevenson*: the Story of the "Snail in the Bottle" Case' in Gamble, AJ (ed) *Obligations in Context* (W Green, 1990), p 18. The website entry records that, by the time of her death, Mrs Donoghue was using her mother's maiden name: Mabel Hannah.
12   The original is held by the House of Lords Records Office.
13   The ginger beer bought by Mrs Donoghue's friend had not travelled far from bottling plant to café.

manufactured lemonade and ginger beer (formally referred to in the law report as 'aerated water' products) at 11 Glen Lane. The drinks were bottled next door at 12 Glen Lane. In her pleading Mrs Donoghue's advisers could not resist a somewhat gratuitous allegation about the general cleanliness of the Glen Lane bottling plant (one wonders how she was planning to make good this allegation at trial):

> 'The pursuer believes and avers that the defender's system of working his business was defective, in respect that his ginger-beer bottles were washed and allowed to stand in places to which it was obvious that snails had freedom of access from outside the defender's premises, and in which, indeed, snails and the slimy trails of snails were frequently found.'[14]

David Stevenson, the defendant in the snail litigation, was born in Paisley on 13 March 1863. The business was founded by David Stevenson's father (also David Stevenson), an occasional cowfeeder and farmer, some time before the factory premises in Glen Lane were purchased in 1870. At the time of his death at the age of 69 years on 12 November 1932 (while the litigation was still being pursued) David Stevenson held shares in St Mirren football club: an indication of his extra curricular interests.

Following the death of David Stevenson his son (also David Stevenson) and his widow, Mary, took over the running of the business. On 1 July 1950 the firm became a limited company: David Stevenson (Beers and Minerals) Limited. In 1956 the Stevenson family sold their interest in the company. The Glen Lane premises are no longer there (having also been demolished during the 1960s).

Photographic examples of David Stevenson ginger beer bottles from the 1920s show dark (brown) opaque bottles bearing the following in white lettering, 'D. STEVENSON GLEN LANE PAISLEY.' The bottles are wholly lacking in the presentational or promotional embellishments which we associate with soft drink containers today. The bottle is extremely plain in appearance (it looks like it ought to contain a folk medicine of some kind). The colour of the glass reinforces the argument presented by Mrs Donoghue's counsel to the House of Lords: 'the conditions under which the ginger-beer was put

14   Condescendence III.

upon the market being such that it was impossible for the consumer to examine the contents of the bottle.'

Ginger beer is (typically) a carbonated soft drink which is flavoured with ginger, lemon and sugar. The basic ingredients are water, sugar, ginger and, to produce fermentation, yeast culture. Traditionally, a fungus – ginger beer plant – is used in the fermentation process for ginger beer, although brewers' yeast can also be used. The drink can be alcoholic (up to 11% by volume in some recipes), although dilution by the addition of carbonated water means that ginger beer is now generally regarded as a soft drink (the alcoholic content was very mild in most commercially produced ginger beer by the early decades of the twentieth century).[15] Ginger beer was first brewed in England in the early eighteenth century. By the turn of the twentieth century ginger beer had reached a peak of popularity and it has been estimated that, by the 1930s, there were as many as 3,000 breweries in the UK alone (with a large number of breweries in North America where the drink was also popular).

The refreshing natural effervescence of ginger beer is the product of carbon dioxide produced during the brewing process. Traditionally, it has a cloudy appearance and, after bottling when the liquid is allowed to be still, sediment collects. The cloudiness of the finished beverage and the collection of sediment strongly influenced the design of the bottles used to contain commercially produced ginger beer. For marketing and aesthetic reasons brewers sought to disguise the less appealing characteristics of their product: opaque bottles were used to ensure that the consumer could not see what he was buying (or, if he swigged direct from the bottle, drinking). From around 1790 onwards stoneware bottles were used. This was followed by opaque, dark-coloured glass of the sort used by David Stevenson's business.

Mullen v Barr[16] which is considered in greater detail below, concerned the consumption of ginger beer brewed in Glasgow by A G Barr & Company Limited. Barr's ginger beer was released to the consumer retail market in sediment-concealing dark bottles of

15 It has been said that the dilution of ginger beer's alcoholic content was, in the UK, the result of excise duties imposed by the Excise Act 1855: Yates, D 'Root Beer and Ginger Beer Heritage' (Spring 2003).
16 1929 SC 461.

opaque glass. It was alleged and, indeed, established that a bottle labelled 'Barr's Perfect Stone Ginger Beer', advertised as containing 'nothing but the finest ingredients', also contained the mortal remains of a small mouse (tucked into the sedimentary layers at the bottom of the bottle). In the course of litigation brought in the Scottish courts by the intended consumers of the tainted ginger beer, the Court of Session heard evidence of Barr's brewing and manufacturing processes. This included information about the brushes used to clean out the glass bottles returned to the manufacturer before they were refilled and returned to the market (there was speculation during the course of judgment that Barr's employee had not wielded the brush with sufficient care and efficiency so as to clear out the sediment, and all that it might contain, from the bottom of the bottle). There was additional evidence before the court from the manufacturer that their system of cleansing and inspection was the best known in the trade and that their annual output was between one and a half and two million bottles and that, in the course of 35 years, there had been no other case in which a dead mouse had been found in the bottle. In the course of his judgment Lord Hunter said this about the ability of retailers to inspect the contents of Barr's ginger beer bottles:

> '... one finds that the ginger beer is bottled by the defenders and labelled by them as of their manufacture. The tab over the cork of the bottles indicates the price at which the public are to be entitled to purchase the beer. The retailer dealer does not make any examination of the contents of the bottles before exposing them for sale. To open the bottles would be prejudicial to the beer, and the tabs on the corks are intended to give the consumer confidence that the bottles have not been tampered with after they have left the manufacturers' premises. The bottles are so dark in colour as to prevent the retail dealer or the consumer from detecting the presence of foreign or deleterious matter by any ordinarily careful examination of the bottle.'[17]

Today's consumers are only now re-learning the thriftiness of their parents and grandparents. During the course of my lifetime we have lost and are now (albeit slowly) regaining the practice of reusing or

---

17 *Ibid*, at p 477. At trial, a witness called by the claimants who had worked in a whisky distillery, gave evidence that it was the practice of his employer to hold dark bottles to a lamp in order to check the contents.

recycling the materials in which consumer goods are packaged. In the 1970s my father regularly saved and returned the glass bottles in which the teeth-rotting fizzy drinks myself and my sister loved were sold. By returning the empties, he was refunded a deposit on each bottle. This practice was, effectively, dead by the time I was an adult, but, by the 1970s, had been in place for the decades during which mass produced consumer food and drinks had been available. A deposit was charged for the bottle which was then returned (eventually to the manufacturers' factory) so that it could be reused. In addition to creating a risk of contamination (the recycling of bottles meant that foreign objects could enter the bottle while it was being prepared for reuse) the recycling process also meant that bottles could be returned to the wrong manufacturer. A 1954 article in the *Paisley & Renfrewshire Gazette* which featured David Stevenson's firm contained the following, 'A problem is caused by the large number of bottles returned which do not belong to the Paisley firm. There is a bottle exchange in Glasgow which handles these "interloupers" and returns them to their rightful owners. The Paisley bottlers also receive theirs in return.' In his detailed and scholarly article on *Donoghue v Stevenson* William McByde speculated that the bottle containing the ginger beer served to Mrs Donoghue did not actually emanate from David Stevenson's premises.[18] Support for this theory can be found in the fact that Mrs Donoghue's pleading averred that, 'the ginger-beer was manufactured by the respondent [David Stevenson] to be sold as a drink to the public ...; that it was bottled by the respondent and labelled by him with a label bearing his name; and that the bottles were thereafter sealed with a metal cap by the respondent.'[19] Stevenson's initial answer to this averment was that he had never issued bottles bearing pasted labels sealed with a metal cap. It seems possible (at least) that the ginger beer consumed by Mrs Donoghue did not come from the Glen Lane premises of the man she sued.

18   McBryde, WM 'Donoghue v Stevenson: the Story of the "Snail in the Bottle" Case' in Gamble, AJ (ed) *Obligations in Context* (W Green, 1990), pp 19 - 20.
19   [1932] AC 562, 563.

What happened in the café?

For all the nibbling at the margins of the story which legal writers have been doing (almost) since the case was decided, what most readers really want to know is what happened in the café. For the facts (as alleged) we are wholly reliant on the pleading filed with the Court of Session. It tells the following story:

> 'At or about 8:50 pm on or about 26th August 1928, the pursuer was in the shop occupied by Francis Minchella, and known as Wellmeadow Café, at Wellmeadow Street, Paisley, with a friend. The said friend ordered for the pursuer ice-cream, and ginger beer, suitable to be used with the ice-cream as an iced drink. Her friend, acting as aforesaid, was supplied by the said Mr Minchella with a bottle of ginger-beer manufactured by the defender for sale to members of the public. The said bottle was made of dark opaque glass, and the pursuer and her friend had no reason to suspect that the bottle contained anything else than the aerated water. The said Mr Minchella poured some of the said ginger-beer from the bottle into a tumbler containing ice-cream. The pursuer then drank some of the contents of the tumbler. Her friend then lifted the said ginger-beer bottle and was pouring out the remainder of the contents into the said tumbler when a snail, which had been, unknown to the pursuer, her friend, or the said Mr Minchella, in the bottle and was in a state of decomposition, floated out of the said bottle. In consequence of the nauseating sight of the snail in such circumstances, and of the noxious condition of the said snail-tainted ginger-beer consumed by her, the pursuer sustained … shock and illness … .'[20]

At a time when snail porridge famously appears on the menu of a Michelin starred restaurant, the reference to 'snail-tainted ginger beer' may sound more like an aperitif than something which would provoke nausea. However, Mrs Donoghue's reaction to the discovery of the snail is likely to have attracted attention. We know from the pleadings that, after Mrs Donoghue saw the decomposed snail, her mysterious friend identified the name and address of David Stevenson from the label pasted on the side of the bottle (the unidentified friend may justifiably be regarded as *the* key player in the litigation; the 'said friend's' quick thinking reaction to the plight of Mrs Donoghue

20 Condescendence II.

obtained the real evidence which made the proceedings possible). In the light of the pleading, we know the date and time that the ginger beer and ice cream were bought and from where. We know who bought it and for whom. We even know about the sickly drink that Mrs Donoghue was going to make using the ginger beer and ice cream. It seems likely that Mrs Donoghue's reaction to tipping and pouring out the remaining contents of the ginger beer bottle was a violent one and would have excited the attention of other patrons of the café and of Mr Minghella. However, was there ever a decomposed snail in the bottle? Was there any real foundation for Mrs Donoghue's nausea, shock and illness? Mr Stevenson's case was that nothing had happened and there was no foundation to Mrs Donoghue's claim. Mrs Donoghue was forced to go to court to establish what, if anything, had happened to her in the Wellmeadow café on that Sunday evening in August.

The facts of the case recorded in the 1930 volume of the Session Notes, where the decisions reached by the Scottish Court of Session are recorded, are also sparse. They record, for example, that Mrs Donoghue suffered only gastro-enteritis as a result of her experience; by contrast with the Appeal Cases report of the outcome in the House of Lords where it is noted that Mrs Donoghue suffered from 'shock and severe gastro-enteritis.'[21] The reason why the facts are not set out in detail in the headnote reports or in the judgments of the courts which heard the case at first instance and on appeal is that the hearings proceeded on the basis of assumed facts; that is, if Mrs Donoghue could prove her allegations (which were contested), did she have a cause of action in law? It was only if this question was answered in her favour that the case was to be remitted for trial of the factual issues. Lord Atkin put it like this at the start of his speech when the appeal reached the House of Lords, 'My Lords, the sole question for determination in this case is legal: Do the averments made by the pursuer in her pleading, if true, disclose a cause of action?'[22] The stance of Mr Stevenson was uncompromising, he maintained:

> '... that the [factual] averments of the pursuer were irrelevant, in respect that the defender, as manufacturer, owed no duty of diligence to a purchaser of goods which had been distributed by him to retail

21   [1932] AC 562, 563 (HL (Sc)).
22   *Ibid*, at p 578.

traders, unless such goods were of a character which could be classed as intrinsically dangerous, and that the goods manufactured by him were not of that class.'[23]

Mrs Donoghue's pleading alleged that she had been constrained to seek the attention of her general practitioner as a result of her exposure to the snail. It went on to allege that, 'Even while under medical attention she still became worse, and on 16th September 1928 had to receive emergency treatment at the Glasgow Royal Infirmary.' It is not easy to imagine what sort of medical treatment, whether emergency or otherwise, might be provided to someone who has consumed a couple of sips, even a mouthful, of snail-tainted ginger beer. In response to this allegation, Mr Stevenson made no admission and raised a causation defence: Mrs Donoghue's August 1928 illness, if any, was caused by the poor state of her own health, rather than by the consumption of a snail or Stevenson's ginger beer.

In a case decided in Canada in 1939 (by the Manitoba Court of King's Bench) the judge stated that he had carefully read the judgments in *Donoghue v Stevenson* and concluded that Mrs Donoghue had the opportunity to see and did see the contents of the bottle before she drank anything.[24] He believed that, 'In a certain degree there was lack of special precautions which might have been taken' – presumably, by looking carefully at the bottom of the glass to make sure that nothing nasty was floating there before drinking. It appears that this Canadian judge might have been prepared to make a finding of contributory negligence if Mrs Donoghue's case had come before him.

Of snails

As we have seen, Mrs Donoghue's pleading conjured an image of a snail infestation at Mr Stevenson's premises. Snails were said to have freedom of access from outside the premises and were alleged to be seen with their 'slimy trails' within the plant. It seems appropriate that the last word in this Chapter should go to the snail. Snails are 'soft-bodied, unsegmented gastropod molluscs ... moving on a large, slimy,

23   1930 SN 117 (Ct of Sess (OH)).
24   *Hammond & Hammond v Davidson & anor* [1939] 2 WWR 97.

muscular foot.'[25] Snails can be distinguished from their close cousin, the perhaps less appealing slug, by a conspicuous, external hard shell into which they are able to retract their body. History does not relate which of the several species of snail inhabiting the British Isles was the cause of Mrs Donoghue's fright, but the commonest variety found here is the garden snail (*Helix aspersa*). Adults of this species live for several years and, unlike slugs which may remain active when temperatures remain above freezing, hibernate in winter (in clusters in dry holes in walls or under plant pots). Snails are hermaphrodites, but 'cross-mating is usual and courtship and mating behaviour is often very elaborate.'[26] A young snail will feed for around twelve months before maturing and reaching adult size. Garden snails are the *petit-gris* which feature on French restaurant menus:

> 'All English snails are edible but there are two species of particular interest to the forager gourmet. Largest, and rarest, is the so-called Roman snail, *Helix pomatia*, which was indeed introduced by the Romans as a food. These are relatively rare, but occasionally locally prolific. … My only snail quarry … is the common (or garden) snail, *Helix aspersa* … . Most average-sized suburban gardens that are not mercilessly sprayed with pesticides probably have enough snails in them to make a nice starter for two. And if you take to the hedgerow, you can find enough for a feast.'[27]

If collected while hibernating the snail's gut will usually be empty and they need not usually be purged[28] before being boiled in salted water and served (shelled) in a garlic butter sauce. If snails are gathered while active they need to undergo a purge before they can safely be cooked and eaten (the purge consists of five days of being fed exclusively on a diet of lettuce leaves followed by a 48-hour fast before the saucepan).[29]

---

25   Buczacki, ST and Harris, KM *Pests, Diseases & Disorders of Garden Plants* (Harper Collins, 3rd ed, 2005), p 135.

26   *Ibid*, at p 137.

27   Fearnley-Whittingstall, H *The River Cottage Cookbook* (Harper Collins, 2001), p 378.

28   Although purging would still be sensible.

29   In Greece (particularly in Crete) snails are often served in a stew: *Salingaria Stifado*. Snails harvested in areas rich in thyme are particularly prized.

Any gardener will know about the damage that can be caused to young plants by snails and slugs. The humane and organic method by which to kill those snails which are surplus to the evening's dining requirements is by the use of a beer trap which, remaining effective for two or three nights, 'attracts ... [snails], intoxicates them and drowns them.'[30] Not a bad way to go. *Donoghue v Stevenson* suggests that, for those who don't have alcohol in the house, ginger beer – if you can find a supermarket which still sells it – works as well as the stronger stuff.

---

30   Buczacki, ST and Harris, KM *Pests, Diseases & Disorders of Garden Plants* (Harper Collins, 3rd ed, 2005), p 137.

2. INTO THE SCOTTISH COURTS

'Not for me to expound the implications of *Donoghue v Stevenson*. To
be quite candid, I detest that snail.'

Lord Justice MacKinnon (President of the Holdsworth Club of the
University of Birmingham, from an after-dinner talk prepared for the
Club in May 1942)

Cases involving foreign objects in ginger beer bottles were not
unknown to the Scottish courts in the 1920s[1]. Francis Mullen
was an ironworker in Coatbridge. His wife bought a bottle of
ginger beer for the couple's children: John and Francis. The ginger
beer was bought from a retailer. The manufacturer was A G Barr &
Company Limited of Glasgow. The bottle was very darkly coloured;
indeed, so dark that its contents could only be seen when the bottle
was held up to the strongest light. Mrs Mullen poured out some of
the ginger beer for her children and they drank it. They then noticed
a dead mouse lying with the dregs in the bottom of the bottle. The
children became ill as a result of drinking the contaminated ginger
beer. Mr Mullen brought an action against the manufacturer in the
Glasgow Sheriff Court. He sought £75 in damages for each child.
At around the same time that Mr Mullen's children were consuming
mouse-flavoured ginger beer in Coatbridge, Mrs Jeanie Oribine was
having a similar experience in Port Glasgow. Mrs Oribine's son bought
her a bottle of ginger beer manufactured by Barr & Company (a firm
which was, effectively, under the same management and control as the
defendant in the Mullen case). Again, the bottle was darkly coloured.
Again, Mrs Oribine drank some of the ginger beer before seeing a
dead mouse floating in the bottle. She also claimed to have suffered
personal injury as a result. Mrs Oribine, like the Mullens, brought
proceedings against the manufacturer; this time, in the Greenock
Sheriff Court. Her claim was for £500 in damages. The claim brought
by Mr Mullen's children was dismissed by the Sheriff. Mrs Oribine,
by contrast, was successful. Mr Mullen's children appealed to the
Court of Session, as did the manufacturer, Barr & Company, in Mrs
Oribine's case. The appeals were heard together on 16 and 17 May

---

1   *Mullen v AG Barr & Company Limited* 1929 SC 461.

1928 and a proof before answer was allowed. Accordingly, it was held that, as a matter of fact, there were dead mice in the two bottles, that ginger beer from the bottles had been consumed and that illness had resulted. It was further held by the court that the claimants had purchased ginger beer manufactured by the relevant company/firm. The court also determined, again as a matter of fact, that the mice were in the bottles (which were sealed) when they left the manufacturers' factories and that the system adopted by the manufacturers for cleaning the bottles before filling them with the drink was the best available in the trade. There was no direct evidence of any negligence on the part of any employee of the manufacturers.

On the basis of these proven factual allegations, the claimants argued, when the appeals were heard over three days in early March 1929, that negligence on the part of the manufacturers should be inferred. If the system was, in a general sense, efficient and appropriate *and* if the mice were in the bottle when they left the plant then there must have been negligence by the manufacturers' employees. In other words, the court should infer negligence from the proven facts because dead mice do not normally float in bottles of ginger beer in the absence of negligence by the person(s) responsible for filling the bottles. Lawyers refer to this evidential presumption of negligence (absent proof of the same) as *res ipsa loquitur*: the facts speak for themselves. By contrast to Mrs Donoghue, whose appeal was reserved by the House of Lords for nearly six months, the claimants did not have to wait very long for a decision: less than a fortnight passed (following the conclusion of the argument) before the Second Division of the Court of Session gave judgment (on 20 March 1929). The claimants in both appeals lost and lost decisively (on the facts and on the law).

The Court of Session first held that the appeals did not justify drawing an inference of negligence without proof of the same: while the mice might have found their way into the bottles and remained there by mischance, it could not be inferred that this was the result of negligence. A submission that the facts could speak for themselves in establishing liability was only available where the defendant failed to provide a non-negligent explanation for the occurrence which caused the claimant injury or loss. The majority judges of the Court of Session held that the manufacturer had, in each appeal, discharged the burden of providing a non-negligent explanation because, as a matter of fact, it had been determined: (a) that the manufacturers' cleaning system was the best in the business (the machinery was modern, efficient and well maintained and there was a sufficient number of employees); and, (b) the efficacy of the manufacturers' system was exemplified by the absence of any similar previous incident over several decades of operation (and the production of millions of opaque bottles containing fizzy pop).

For good measure, and more ominously for Mrs Donoghue, the majority in the Court of Session also held that even if the claimants had been able to prove negligence on the part of the manufacturer, no duty of care would have been owed by the manufacturer to the ultimate consumer and, in the absence of a duty of care, 'mere proof of negligence is unavailing, and the action will not lie.'[2] By reference to the authorities, it was held that, in the absence of a contract, a duty of care was not owed by a manufacturer putting a product on the market, except where: (a) the manufacturer knew that the product was dangerous and that fact was concealed from the purchaser (in which case the manufacturer would be guilty of negligence or, in appropriate cases, fraud); or where (b) the manufacturer was the producer of goods which were dangerous *per se* (the judgments give the example of explosives) and failed to warn the purchaser of this fact.[3] There was a dissenting voice in the Court of Session when the *Mullen v Barr* appeals were heard:[4] Lord Hunter. He reviewed the authorities in the course of his judgment, at rather greater length than the judges in the majority, and, emboldened (in particular) by the decision of the Privy Council in *Dominion Natural Gas Company*[5] and by the decision of the Court of Appeal in *Heaven v Pender*[6] held that because the bottles were sealed and were so dark as to prevent reasonable examination of the contents by retailer or consumer:

2   1929 SC 461, 469 *per* the Lord Justice-Clerk.
3   Junior counsel for the claimants had valiantly sought to persuade the court that the ginger beer manufacturer could be equated with a dealer in gelignite.
4   For the majority: Lord Ormidale and Lord Anderson. The Lord Justice-Clerk (Alness) reserved his opinion.
5   [1909] AC 640.
6   (1883) 11 QBD 503.

'... there is such a relationship between the manufacturer and consumer as to impose a duty upon the former to exercise care that the latter does not suffer injury. The duty may not be of the absolute character which rests upon one who deals in goods that are dangerous in themselves; but it is none the less a duty which will give the consumer a claim of damages if he can establish a case of negligence against the manufacturer.'[7]

Lord Hunter was quite satisfied that, on the question of mixed fact and law (*viz.* had the claimants proved negligence), there was negligence on the part of the manufacturers and/or their employees. The claimants were entitled to their inference that 'decaying animal matter in the shape of dead mice' found its way into the two bottles either because the system for cleaning the bottles was defective or because of carelessness on the part of an employee in failing to detect the presence of the mice and to remove the same. In other words, the proven facts justified drawing an inference of negligence. The unsuccessful claimants (the pursuers) in the *Mullen v Barr* appeals sought to take their cases to the House of Lords and petitions were served, but the appeals were ultimately abandoned; it seems likely that the threat of adverse costs orders acted as a deterrent.[8]

As I have indicated, judgment in the conjoined appeals in *Mullen v Barr* was delivered on 20 March 1929. Mrs Donoghue's Summons, filed in the Court of Session, was signed at Edinburgh on 9 April 1929. *Mullen v Barr* was not a happy omen and the lawyers in the case, if not Mrs Donoghue herself, would have been acutely aware of this. Mrs Donoghue's solicitor, Walter G Leechman of W G Leechman & Co, Glasgow, was the agent for the solicitors who acted for the claimants in *Mullen v Barr*. There was another ominous portent for Mrs Donoghue. A Mr Clyde acted as junior Advocate for both companies in the *Mullen v Barr* proceedings (led in the appeals by Mr Keith, KC). He was also retained as junior (this time to Mr Normand, KC) by Mr Stevenson when Mrs Donoghue's case reached the Outer House. Mrs Donoghue, a person of the most modest means, embarked on proceedings against a well established businessman in a

7   1929 SC 461, 477.
8   1929 SLT 412.

court which had just reached an unfavourable decision in a case with facts strikingly similar to those of her own.

Mrs Donoghue and the Court of Session: interlocutory skirmishes

The Court of Session is also known as Her Majesty's College of Justice in Scotland. Its judges are Senators of the College; the collegiate nature of the institution derives from the close connection between the Scottish legal traditions of the early/mid sixteenth century (when the Court was established) and those of continental Europe. Unlike its English equivalent the Court of Session is the offspring of a continental legal culture. The Court of Session sits in Edinburgh: in the Parliament House (set back off a cobble-stone courtyard from the Royal Mile which runs from the Castle to the Palace of Holyrood House). This grand location was the venue for Mrs Donoghue's proceedings, but it seems unlikely that she ever travelled there from her home in the poorer quarters of Glasgow.

Mrs Donoghue's claim spent a little over nineteen months in the Court of Session: from April 1929, when proceedings commenced, to November 1930 when the appeal of Mr Stevenson was allowed and it was necessary for Mrs Donoghue to take her claim from Edinburgh to London and the law lords. The procedural history of Mrs Donoghue's claim can be found in a single black, leather-bound volume of Appeal Papers which is held by the Parliamentary Archives.[9] The same volume contains other (less celebrated) Scottish appeals which came before the Appellate Committee of the House of Lords in 1932. The *Donoghue v Stevenson* appeal papers are not headlined or emblazoned on the front or spine of the anonymous volume which contains them. They contain the pleadings of the parties and a summary of the procedural (interlocutory) history as the case progressed through the Court of Session on its way to the House of Lords. There is a modest explanatory heading which simply reads, 'Negligence – Whether duty owed to person injured – Duty of manufacturer of article to ultimate consumer – Bottle of ginger beer bought from retailer – Bottle

---

9   Volume 873 ; File reference HL/PO/JU/4/3/873. Some of this material can now also be found on the excellent website of the Scottish Council of Law Reporting (www.scottishlawreports.org.uk).

containing dead snail – Consumer injured by drinking contents – Liability of manufacturer to consumer.'

The full decision of Lord Moncrieff (the Lord Ordinary), sitting at first instance in the Outer House of the Court of Session on 27 June 1930, appears in the Appeal Papers. Lord (Alexander) Moncrieff was a fully paid-up member of Edinburgh's legal aristocracy and came from a distinguished family of Scottish lawyers. The Scottish legal world was small and close-knit: Lord Moncrieff was a close friend of Lord Macmillan (who later presided over Mrs Donoghue's appeal in the House of Lords) and provided one of the necessary character references when Macmillan was called to the Scottish Bar.[10] There was, however, a less conventional side to Alexander Moncrieff's character. In his spare time he wrote poetry and was an Honorary Fellow of the Royal Society of Edinburgh. His daughter Margaret became a famous cellist and, later, a children's writer.[11] Lord Moncrieff was later promoted to become the Lord Justice-Clerk of the Court of Session and was also elevated to membership of the Privy Council.

The Appeal Papers in *Donoghue v Stevenson* also contain a complete record of the opinions of the judges of the second division of the Court of Session, on appeal from Lord Moncrieff, which were delivered on 13 November 1930 (before the case made its way to the House of Lords for a second appeal). It is a curiosity that the judgments at first instance and on appeal in the Court of Session in this most celebrated case have not been fully reported. One can only find a perfunctory summary of the judgments in the Session Notes and it is still necessary to dig out the Appeal Papers from their store in the Parliamentary Archive.[12] *Donoghue v Stevenson* does not give up its secrets easily.

Mrs Donoghue (erroneously referred to in the Session Notes report as *Mary*, rather than *May*, Donoghue)[13] commenced proceedings against Mr Stevenson. Her summons, signed at Edinburgh on 9 April 1929 (within three weeks of the decision on appeal in *Mullen*

10   Lord Macmillan, *A Man of Law's Tale* (Macmillan & Co Ltd, 1952), p 30.
11   See the obituary of Margaret Moncrieff: *The Times* (6 December 2008).
12   As indicated, some of the Appeal Papers can now be found on the internet, but the record is not yet complete.
13   1930 SN 117 and 1930 SN 138.

v Barr) claimed that Mr Stevenson, 'Ought and should be Decerned and Ordained, by decree of the Lords of our Council and Session, to make payment to the pursuer of the sum of £500 sterling, with interest thereon at the rate of £5 per centum per annum from the date of the decree to follow hereon.' Mrs Donoghue, like Mrs Oribine, sought £500 for the shock and gastro-enteritis which followed her encounter with the snail (it seems likely that her legal team would have had this sum in mind as appropriate quantum as a result of Mrs Oribine's earlier claim). She claimed a substantial sum: applying the retail prices index, Mrs Donoghue's claim for damages would now exceed £25,000 (the sum would be greater by reference to today's values, if a multiplier derived from average earnings were applied).[14] She also claimed £50 in expenses. Mr Stevenson's pleading in response, settled by Mr Clyde of counsel, was uncompromising. The claim was defended, first, on the basis that Mrs Donoghue had no claim in law. Second, it was denied that she could prove the facts on which she relied (even if these were relevant). Third, it was denied that Mrs Donoghue had suffered any injury. For good measure, it was alleged that the sum claimed by Mrs Donoghue (£500) was excessive.

Mrs Donoghue's allegations as claimant were set out in a series of condescendences (which were answered by Mr Stevenson). These crucial allegations contain the only narrative account of what happened in the Wellmeadow café during the evening of 26 August 1928. The identity and status of the parties is set out and Mrs Donoghue's lawyers plead her description of events. The factual allegations which underpinned Mrs Donoghue's case on breach of duty were pleaded as follows (followed by Mr Stevenson's terse answer to the same):

'**COND. III**. The shock and illness suffered by the pursuer were due to the fault of the defender. The said ginger-beer was manufactured by the defender and his servants to be sold as an article of drink, to members of the public (including the pursuer). It was, accordingly, the duty of the defender to exercise the greatest care in order that snails would not get into the said bottle, render the ginger-beer dangerous and harmful, and be sold with the said ginger-beer. Further, it was the duty of the defender to provide a system of working his business that was safe, and would not allow snails to get into his ginger-beer bottles

14   Applying an average earnings-based multiplier the damages would amount to a sum exceeding £99,000. See the entertaining website: www.measuringworth.com.

(including the said bottle). Such a system is usual and customary, and is necessary in the manufacture of a drink like ginger-beer to be used for human consumption. In these duties the defender culpably failed, and pursuer's illness and shock were the direct result of his said failure in duty. The pursuer believes and avers that the defender's system of working his business was defective, in respect that his ginger-beer bottles were washed and allowed to stand in places to which it was obvious that snails had freedom of access from outside the defender's premises, and in which, indeed, snails and the slimy trail of snails were frequently found.

Ans.3. Denied. Explained that the system employed at the defender's factory is the best known in the trade, and no bottle of ginger-beer ever passed out therefrom containing a snail.'

Mrs Donoghue's fourth and final condescendence dealt with the effects of her exposure to the snail:

'**COND.IV**. The pursuer suffered severe shock and a prolonged illness in consequence of the said fault of the defender and his servants. She suffered from sickness and nausea which persisted. Her condition became worse, and on 29th August 1928 she had to consult a doctor. She was then suffering from gastro-enteritis induced by the said snail-infected ginger-beer. Even while under medical attention she still became worse, and on 16th September 1928 had to receive emergency treatment at the Glasgow Royal Infirmary.

Ans. 4. Not known and not admitted. Explained that the alleged injuries are grossly exaggerated. Explained further that any illness suffered by the pursuer on or after 26th August 1928 was due to the bad condition of her own health at the time.'

Donoghue v Stevenson came before Lord Moncrieff (the Lord Ordinary) for the first time on 21 May 1929 (Mrs Donoghue was represented by Mr Gibson of counsel and Mr Stevenson by Mr Clyde). The case was adjourned to 5 June 1929 on which occasion Mr Gibson was granted permission to amend the pleading to add Mr Minghella, the proprietor of the Wellmeadow café, as a defendant to the action (alongside Mr Stevenson). On 24 June 1929 Mr Minghella served answers to Mrs Donoghue's allegations. From July onwards he was also represented by junior counsel (Mr Cameron) at interlocutory hearings before Lord Moncrieff. Mrs Donoghue's advisers evidently had doubts about the action against Mr Minghella (with whom Mrs Donoghue had no contract, who was not a manufacturer of ginger beer and who, like Mrs Donoghue, had no opportunity to examine or inspect the ginger beer bottle before it was served). At a hearing before Lord Moncrieff on 18 October 1929, the record states as follows, '... the Lord Ordinary, after hearing parties in discussion in the Procedure Roll, continued the cause in order that the pursuer might have an opportunity of reconsidering her position.' Within three weeks Mr Gibson, counsel for Mrs Donoghue, was back in front of Lord Moncrieff seeking the Court's permission (granted on 19 November 1929) to abandon the claim against Mr Minghella. It may be that the discussion in the Procedure Roll to which the record refers was prompted by Lord Moncrieff himself (an expression of judicial scepticism can do wonders for the narrowing of the issues between the parties). Indeed, there is a suggestion of this in the written skeleton argument drafted on Mr Stevenson's behalf (by Mr Normand KC and Mr Clyde) when the appeal reached the House of Lords:

> 'The Record was, thereafter, closed and a discussion took place in the Procedure Roll before Lord Moncrieff, Ordinary. At the end of this discussion the Appellant (Mrs Donoghue) asked for, and was granted, time to consider her position. As the result of that consideration the Appellant, after some wavering of opinion, finally decided to drop the action as against Mr Minchella [sic] and to proceed with it as against the Respondent, and the action now stands as an action against the Respondent alone. The averments of the Appellant, as they now are, retain, however, traces of the metamorphoses through which the action has passed.'[15]

While Mr Minghella lost his chance for legal immortality,[16] he was awarded costs (against Mrs Donoghue) for his brief involvement in the action: a sum of £66 1s 5d was, after an assessment (taxation), awarded on 12 December 1929. Mr Stevenson was also awarded his costs against Mrs Donoghue as a result of the abortive claim against Mr Minghella (after taxation, a sum of £42 4s 10d). On 20

---

15   See, Parliamentary Archives. Also reported and set out in greater detail in Taylor, M 'The Good Neighbour on Trial: a Message from Scotland' (1983) 17 UBC Law Review 59, 62 – 63.

16   He also suffered the indignity of having his name consistently misspelt in the Appeal Papers: *Minchella*, rather than *Minghella*.

December 1929 it was recorded that Mrs Donoghue had failed to pay Mr Minghella the costs which had been awarded to him.

There was a further amendment to Mrs Donoghue's case which was presented on 17 June 1930. Junior counsel (Mr Gibson) obtained permission to add the following allegation:

> 'The said ginger-beer bottle was fitted with a metal cap over its mouth. On the side of the bottle there was pasted a label containing, inter alia, the name and address of the defender, who was the manufacturer. It was from this label that the pursuer's said friend got the name and address of the defender.'

It was clearly thought by those advising Mrs Donoghue that they needed to be explicit about how they identified Mr Stevenson as the relevant manufacturer (one wonders whether this also followed a discussion in court between counsel and judge). As I have suggested above, it was Mrs Donoghue's quick-thinking friend, the mysterious companion in the café, who provided this identification evidence. Mr Stevenson's legal team swiftly provided the following answer to this allegation, '… the defender has never issued bottles answering the description given by the pursuer.'

Lord Moncrieff heard the case on 27 June 1930.

Mrs Donoghue and the Court of Session: first instance

Lord Moncrieff brought to an end the interlocutory overture by finding for Mrs Donoghue. His opinion is nearly twenty pages long. Much of it is devoted to consideration of the authorities and Lord Moncrieff clearly had to work hard to reach a finding favourable to Mrs Donoghue. He observed, somewhat caustically, that if the case could be decided on general principles and without reference to authority then the question of law which it involved would not have presented 'any exceptional difficulty.' Lord Moncrieff's opinion is not always the easiest of reads. The manner in which he deals with the case law is circumlocutory. His summary of the parties' rival contentions, while clearly informed by exchanges between Bench and Bar in the course of argument and couched in Scotland's legal language of 1929, does little to elucidate matters for the reader.

However, the Lord Ordinary's own views are clear enough. His opinion commences with a recital of the conditions required for a finding of liability. First, it was necessary that there be a general duty owed by the wrongdoer to the victim, of which the wrongdoer was in breach. Second, there should be a 'relation' between the wrongdoer and victim which brings the victim 'within the consideration of the discharge of the duty.' The commentary which follows this proposition makes it clear that this condition imports a requirement of what most common lawyers would now term foreseeability. That the wrongdoer foresee that the victim, 'within a reasonable anticipation, may be found to be within the outlook of a danger resulting from failure to discharge the duty.' Third, there should be a causal connection between the breach of duty and the resulting injury. Lord Moncrieff further directed himself, on the basis of this three point analysis, that, '… the duty … is dependent on the quality of the accompanying danger; while the relation is dependent only on the outlook or prospect of incidence of the danger, and is not dependent on its quality.'

According to Lord Moncrieff, the quality of the danger in a *Donoghue v Stevenson* scenario was the subtle potency of the risk presented by tainted food or drinks, which potency was increased by the distribution of these consumables in sealed bottles destined for the purchaser: the ultimate consumer. These factors led Lord Moncrieff to the conclusion, as a matter of general principle, that:

> 'I am unhesitatingly of the opinion that those who deal with the production of food or produce fluids for beverage purposes ought not to be heard to plead ignorance of the active danger which will be associated with their products, as a consequence of any imperfect observation of cleanliness at any stage in the course of the process of manufacture.'

This 'active danger' was, so Lord Moncrieff stated, 'highly relevant' to the inference of a duty of care and such duty was not an onerous one, '… being nothing more exacting than a duty of taking all reasonable precautions to ensure that an ostensible food be not replaced by a latent and actual poison.'

Having summarised the general direction of his thinking, Lord Moncrieff turned to the parties' arguments and the authorities. It was argued for Mr Stevenson, and accepted by Lord Moncrieff, that the

English case law established that, ' the foundation of any liability to exercise diligence in the preparation for purposes of sale of articles other than "dangerous articles" is in the law of contract only and not in the law of tort.' In other words, a person in Mrs Donoghue's position who was the ultimate consumer of an innocuous, rather than dangerous product, was required to pursue her action against the manufacturer in contract on the basis of a breach of warranty. If, like Mrs Donoghue, this unfortunate consumer had no contract with the manufacturer and, therefore, no action for breach of contract, then she could not sue in tort either. Lord Moncrieff did not bother to disguise his own antipathy to these English propositions and adopted criticisms made by the English law academic, Sir John Salmond, about the narrowness of the English approach and the injustice that it might cause.[17] Leading counsel for Mr Stevenson (Mr Normand KC) conceded in argument that there had been no decision by a court in Scotland which made the English approach part of the law of Scotland. Lord Moncrieff was not about to import the narrow English approach into Scottish law and evidently felt that this gave him the flexibility necessary to return to general principles (he had already made it clear that if a 'first principles approach' were taken then Mrs Donoghue won her case).

This left a final hurdle for Mrs Donoghue to overcome and it was a considerable one. What was to be done about the very recent decision of the Court of Session (on appeal) in *Mullen v Barr*? In this case only Lord Hunter had unequivocally affirmed the existence of a duty of care owed by the manufacturer to the ultimate consumer. Lord Moncrieff acknowledged that the facts of *Mullen v Barr* were 'almost identical' to the facts of *Donoghue v Stevenson*. He was able to discount the opinion of the Lord Justice-Clerk (Lord Alness) on the basis that he had reserved his opinion on the question whether a duty of care was owed (and the case proceeded on the footing that negligence had not been proved even if a duty of care did exist). Lord Ormidale, who relied primarily on the authorities in concluding that no duty of care was owed, was also discounted on the basis that his opinion was counter-balanced by the dissenting opinion of Lord Hunter. One commentator has additionally suggested that Lord Moncrieff was able

---

17   Lord Moncrieff quoted from the 7th edition of Sir John Salmond's textbook on the *Law of Torts*. A textbook later written by Professor RFV Heuston.

to bypass Lord Ormidale's opinion on the basis that the latter 'did not understand the authorities anyway.'[18] This left Lord Anderson who, like Lord Ormidale, had unequivocally concluded that no duty of care was owed. Lord Moncrieff observed that Lord Anderson's opinion in *Mullen v Barr* referred to a concession made by the claimants (pursuers). The relevant portion of Lord Anderson's opinion reads as follows:

> 'It was conceded by the pursuers that the general rule of law was against their contention that the defenders were liable to them for negligence. There was no privity of contract between the defenders and the pursuers. The contract of the defenders was with the retailers who sold the ginger-beer to the pursuers. In circumstances such as these the general rule would seem to be that breach of a manufacturer's contract with A to use care in the manufacture of an article does not of itself give a cause of action to B who is injured by reason of the article proving to be defective in breach of the contract.'[19]

Lord Moncrieff was clearly puzzled by this concession which bore little resemblance to the summary of the claimants' argument which appears in the *Mullen v Barr* law report (indeed, it is entirely contradicted by the law reporter's summary of the claimants' argument).[20] Lord Moncrieff implicitly suggests that Lord Anderson's opinion in *Mullen v Barr*, based on an erroneous concession by the claimants' lawyers, presented the wrong conclusion. This very close reading of the precedent opinions enabled the Lord Ordinary to side-step *Mullen v Barr*:

> 'I am of the opinion that there is no authority in Scotland for refusing to a party who has sustained injury as a direct result of the negligence of the manufacturer of goods designed to reach him through retail dealers, a right of action founded on a negligent omission to introduce proper safeguards, or to exercise due diligence to exclude infection of the articles in the course of manufacture. I am not satisfied that a

18   McBryde, WM '*Donoghue v Stevenson*: the Story of the "Snail in the Bottle" Case' in Gamble, AJ (ed) *Obligations in Context* (W Green, 1990), p 24. This is not, of course, what Lord Moncrieff himself states. One assumes that Professor McBryde bases this hypothesis on the fact that Lord Moncrieff had himself reviewed the (English) authorities and arrived at a different conclusion.

19   *Mullen v Barr* 1929 SC 461, 479.

20   *Ibid*, at p 465.

distinction is taken by the law of England upon this matter between goods which are or are not dangerous per se. If such a distinction be taken, I fail to find a warrant for it whether in logic or in expediency; and as the question appears to be entirely open, I decline to decide that any such distinction forms part of the law of Scotland.'

The record in the Appeal Papers states that Lord Moncrieff 'repelled' Mr Stevenson's argument that Mrs Donoghue's factual averments were irrelevant because she had no cause of action in any event (being unable to establish a duty of care). Lord Moncrieff awarded Mrs Donoghue her costs (save for the costs orders made against her when the action against Mr Minghella was abandoned) and ordered that her claim would proceed to a trial of the factual issues between the parties on a day to be fixed. Before Mrs Donoghue had a chance to prove the presence of the dead snail in her ice cream float and the illness which resulted, Mr Stevenson had launched an appeal against Lord Moncrieff's conclusions on the breach of duty issue.

Mrs Donoghue and the Court of Session: appeal to the Second Division

The four-man bench which heard Mr Stevenson's appeal was identical to the bench which had resolved *Mullen v Barr* in favour of the defendant manufacturers: the Lord Justice-Clerk (Lord Alness); Lord Ormidale; Lord Hunter; Lord Anderson. Unsurprisingly, the outcome for Mrs Donoghue was also identical. The Lord Justice-Clerk was somewhat coy about his reasons for reserving his opinion on the breach of duty point in *Mullen v Barr* (although he stated that he had made it clear that the authorities presented an insuperable obstacle to the *Mullen v Barr* claimants). He also observed, 'Now, the only difference – and, so far as I can see, it is not a material difference – between that case and this case is that there we were dealing with a mouse in a ginger-beer bottle, and here we are dealing with a snail in a ginger-beer bottle. *Quoad ultra* the circumstances appear to be identical.' Lord Ormidale and Lord Anderson sought to dispose of Mrs Donoghue's claim in a paragraph apiece. They simply referred back to their *Mullen v Barr* opinions; it was, stated Lord Ormidale, 'quite impossible' for him to resile from the opinion which he had expressed as to the law in *Mullen v Barr*. Lord Hunter, dissenting in Mrs Donoghue's favour, also restated his *Mullen v Barr* conclusion.

He also commented briefly on Lord Moncrieff's judgment at first instance (being the only judge in the second division to do so). He stated that he was far from satisfied that there was a difference between the English and Scottish jurisprudence on the duties of manufacturers and, as we shall see, this was the basis on which everyone proceeded when Mrs Donoghue appealed.

Conclusion

The curtain-raiser to the House of Lords appeal was disappointing, if predictable. The judges of the Second Division of the Court of Session simply contented themselves with a backward glance at their decisions in *Mullen v Barr*. Despite this unhappy precedent the son of Mrs Donoghue's solicitor (himself a Scottish solicitor who took over his father's firm) has been quoted by a Canadian judge (Mr Justice M R Taylor) in correspondence as follows:

> 'My father did not have such a high opinion of the Scottish judges of the time, even in the Appeal Court here. He felt that the judges in the House of Lords, being English and Scottish and using 'equity' as part of their base ... would be more equitable in their decision.'[21]

Mr Leechman's optimism about Mrs Donoghue's prospects was shared by a number of eminent lawyers north of the border. These included leading counsel representing Mr Stevenson (Mr Normand KC) who wrote to Lord Macmillan on 19 September 1942, 'I personally thought that the HL would decide as they did in fact decide, but that we had a very strong case on the facts. If the case had gone to proof I think it would have been fought and possibly on the issue whether there was a snail in the bottle ... .'[22] Mr Normand KC suggested that the Dean of the Faculty of Advocates also believed that Mr Stevenson would lose in the House of Lords. Normand was clearly keen to dissociate himself from the tactical decision to fight *Donoghue v Stevenson* on the law, rather than the facts.

---

21 Taylor, M 'The Good Neighbour on Trial: a Message from Scotland' (1983) 17 UBC Law Review 59, 64.
22 This letter appears in Lord Atkin's private papers which are held by Gray's Inn (File Reference AK1/JUD/1/1), but is also referred to in Lewis, G *Lord Atkin* (Hart Publishing, 1999).

By the time of the House of Lords appeal Mr Leechman may have lost more than his confidence in the capacity and inclinations of the Scottish judges in the Court of Session. Robert Gibson who had faithfully represented Mrs Donoghue through the interlocutory stages in the Court of Session and onto hearing and appeal was replaced as Mr Morton KC's junior when the case reached the House of Lords. A Mr Milligan, who had been second junior before the Second Division, took over as first and only junior counsel.[23]

23   This may, of course, be no reflection on Mr Leechman's confidence in Mr Gibson, but may, instead, relate to Mr Gibson's availability or may simply reflect Morton's preference.

3. IN THE HOUSE OF LORDS

'… we should be careful
Of each other, we should be kind
While there is still time.'

Philip Larkin, 'The Mower'

'Our almost-instinct almost true:
What will survive of us is love.'

Philip Larkin, 'An Arundel Tomb'

Mrs Donoghue launched her appeal by a petition filed on 25 February 1931 (three months or so after Mr Stevenson's decisive victory in the Court of Session). Her appeal occupied just two days in argument: 10 and 11 December 1931. The decision was reserved and the speeches were not delivered until 26 May 1932 (when, as the law report tells us, 'The House took time for consideration' it was for an unusually long time, exceeding six months).[1] The decision was reported in the official series: [1932] AC 562. The headnote is, depending on your taste, a model of clarity and brevity or, if you prefer, wholly fails to do justice to a decision which revolutionised (perhaps, even created) the modern law of negligence.[2] Asquith LJ took the latter view, commenting, two decades after the House of Lords' decision, that the case, '… may not decide quite so little as is contained in its somewhat conservative headnote.'[3] In its entirety, the headnote in the Appeal Cases reads as follows (leaving out the references to other cases):

---

1 The House of Lords Journal (164 *Journal of the House of Lords* 180) records that it was originally intended that the speeches would be delivered on 14 April 1932, but, for unknown reasons, this was postponed.

2 Lord Hope of Craighead, 'James McGhee – a Second Mrs Donoghue?' [2003] 62 CLJ 587, at p 587, 'The law of liability for negligence was revolutionised by the decision of the House of Lords in *Donoghue v Stevenson*. Indeed, one might even say that the modern law of negligence was created by it.'

3 *Candler v Crane, Christmas & Company* [1951] 2 KB 164, 189 (CA). He was not the only judge to comment on the brevity of the headnote. The Chief Justice of the New Zealand Court of Appeal made a similar criticism in a case decided in 1958: *Furniss v Fitchett* [1958] NZLR 396, 401 *per* Barrowclough CJ (NZCA).

'By Scots and English law alike the manufacturer of an article of food, medicine or the like, sold by him to a distributor in circumstances which prevent the distributor or the ultimate purchaser or consumer from discovering by inspection any defect, is under a legal duty to the ultimate purchaser or consumer to take reasonable care that the article is free from defect likely to cause injury to health: – So held, by Lord Atkin, Lord Thankerton and Lord Macmillan; Lord Buckmaster and Lord Tomlin dissenting.'

The decision is reported in the Appeal Cases as 'M'Alister (or Donoghue) (Pauper) v Stevenson.' The inclusion of Mrs Donoghue's married and maiden names created confusion (particularly among those south of the Scottish border) as to the proper citation of the case. In 1933 Lord Macmillan, a Scot, wrote to the Law Quarterly Review to clear up the problem, '... apt to arise ... in consequence of the practice in Scotland of naming a married woman in legal documents and proceedings by her maiden as well as by her married surname with the (infelicitous) disjunctive "or" interposed.'[4] Lord Macmillan's peevish note to the Law Quarterly Review is the work of a pedant, he directs that, 'It is very desirable that this source of confusion should be removed and that when a married woman is appellant or respondent in a Scottish appeal her married name alone should be used in the name of the case when reported, so that the identity of the case in the Scottish and the English Reports may be preserved and uniformity of citation preserved.'[5] While he was at it, Lord Macmillan took the opportunity in the same note to complain about the wholly unrelated tendency of English lawyers to refer erroneously to cases decided in the Scottish Court of Session as 'Sessions Cases', rather than 'Session Cases'. Mutual misunderstandings of this kind between those on each side of the Tweed run through the House of Lords judgments (as they had through Lord Moncrieff's opinion when the case was heard at first instance).

Mrs Donoghue sought and obtained permission to pursue her appeal before the House of Lords *in forma pauperis* (a status that

4   Lord Macmillan, 'The Citation of Scottish Cases' (1933) 49 LQR 1.

5   The legal historian Sir Frederick Pollock suggested an alternative citation which he believed would have been used by the pre-eighteenth law reporters. He advocated calling *Donoghue v Stevenson* 'the snail's Case': Pollock, F 'The Snail in the Bottle and Thereafter' (1933) 49 LQR 22.

she had not sought when her claim made its way through the Court of Session). Professor McBryde has questioned how Mrs Donoghue managed to fund her litigation in the Court of Session where she was the recipient of adverse costs orders and had been constrained to fight an appeal in which she had been unsuccessful. He points out that her Advocate in the Court of Session, Robert Gibson, was not one of the counsel allocated, under a Faculty of Advocates' scheme, to the cases of the poor.[6] As a pauper Mrs Donoghue was able to sue without providing security for the costs which would be due to Mr Stevenson if her appeal failed. The petition signed by Mrs Donoghue in February 1931 in support of her application to sue as a pauper indicates her reduced circumstances, 'That the Petitioner being very poor, as by the affidavit and certificate annexed appears, is by reason of such her poverty unable to prosecute her Appeal, unless admitted by your Lordships to do *in forma pauperis.*' Mrs Donoghue's Affidavit in support of the same petition somewhat pathetically deposes, 'I am very poor. I am not worth five pounds in all the world.' An accompanying certificate of poverty was signed by the Minister and two elders of Mrs Donoghue's Church.

We have already seen that Mrs Donoghue's life was short and its circumstances were, it seems, generally unhappy. It is hard to escape the conclusion that life had treated her badly from an early age. The litigation on which she embarked at the end of the 1920s had foundered in the Second Division of the Court of Session. She had decisively lost on appeal. She had been ordered to pay more than £100 in costs to Messrs Stevenson and Minghella. This had rendered her, effectively, bankrupt and she was prosecuting her claim as a pauper (presumably relying on the kindness, if that is the right word, and advice of her solicitors). By 1931 Mrs Donoghue was in need of a Good Samaritan and, in Lord Atkin, she found one.

Argument

An attractive practice of the House of Lords in its judicial capacity was the comparative absence of pomp and circumstance (by comparison, for example, with the United States Supreme Court). The argument in

---

6   See, McBryde, WM '*Donoghue v Stevenson*: the Story of the "Snail in the Bottle" Case' in Gamble, AJ (ed) *Obligations in Context* (W Green, 1990), p 17.

the House of Lords would have been presented in a fairly anonymous committee room (albeit within the very grand precinct of the Houses of Parliament). The law lords would have sat, in ordinary suits, alongside each other at a half-moon-shaped table and counsel would have addressed the court (at the same level as the judges) from tables. There is no transcript of the argument in the House of Lords. We will never know which points found favour and which fell flat. The interjections, comments, encouragements and, no doubt, occasional sarcasm (perhaps even, at times, scorn)[7] of the judges have all been lost. All that we have is what appears in the Appeal Papers and in the law report where there is a very short summary of what was argued by counsel on each side. The author of this summary was the law reporter, rather than counsel who argued the appeal, and we cannot assess the accuracy of the summary or the emphasis that was placed on various sections of the argument.

Counsel for Mrs Donoghue (George Morton KC and W R Milligan, both of the Scottish Bar) filed a supplemental statement when Mrs Donoghue's appeal came before the Appellate Committee. It is a document of modest length (just two pages) and does not indicate great industry (being, effectively, a recapitulation of Lord Moncrieff's opinion, finding for Mrs Donoghue, in the Outer House of the Court of Session). Mrs Donoghue's written argument, including this supplement, can be found in the Appeal Papers in the Parliamentary Archive.[8] The supplemental statement commences by stating that the Second Division had relied on *Mullen v Barr*[9] and the general principle, subject to exceptions, that a third party could not rely on the breach of a contract to which he was not a party and that, absent an action in contract, there was no other relevant liability. The supplemental statement goes on to present the argument for departing from *Mullen v Barr* in curiously self-effacing (almost apologetic) terms:

> 'The Appellant humbly maintains that the duty owed by a manufacturer to members of the public who purchase goods through a retailer is not capable of so strict a limitation. She contends that

---

7   Given the general tone of Lord Buckmaster's speech, it is hard to believe that he would have sat silently and courteously through the submissions of Mrs Donoghue's counsel.

8   Volume 873; File reference HL/PO/JU/4/3/873.

9   1929 SC 461 (Ct of Sess).

where anyone performs an operation, such as the manufacture of an article, a relationship of duty independent of contract may in certain circumstances arise, the extent of such duty in every case depending on the particular circumstances of the case.'

The 'particular circumstances' relied on for seeking to impose a duty on Mr Stevenson arose, counsel for Mrs Donoghue argued, from the fact that he 'manufactured, bottled, labelled and sealed, and invited her to buy' ginger beer. The extent of the duty was located in a requirement of reasonable care to ensure that the ginger beer did not contain substances likely to cause Mrs Donoghue, the ultimate consumer, injury. Counsel sought to underpin Mrs Donoghue's argument by reference to the fact that Mr Stevenson had so regulated his business that products were put on the market in conditions which made it impossible for the retailer to interfere with the bottles and equally impossible for the retailer or purchaser to see what was inside the sealed bottles.

The summary of Mrs Donoghue's argument which appears in the Appeal Cases law report bears a close resemblance to the written case found in the Parliamentary Archive (perhaps a copy of the written case was provided to the law reporter). It indicates that counsel commenced by recognising the problem that precedent and, in particular, English precedent created for the Appellant's case.[10] Counsel sought to circumvent this with the usual response of a lawyer faced with unhelpful precedent: an attempt to distinguish the earlier cases on their facts and so to suggest that they were decided on the basis of specific factual premises which differed from the instant case. This was followed by a bolder assertion, 'No case can be found where in circumstances similar to the present the Court has held that the manufacturer is under no liability to the consumer.' As in the written argument, counsel described how the Court of Session proceeded on the assumption that there were only two established exceptions to the general principle that a manufacturer bore no duty of care to a

10   Only seven cases are referred to in the written argument presented by Mrs Donoghue's counsel to the House of Lords: *Mullen v Barr*; *Parry v Smith*; *Langridge v Levy*; *George v Skivington*; *Thomas v Winchester*; *Heaven v Pender*; *Dominion Natural Gas Company v Collins*. These cases appear, by passing reference, in side notes (there is no commentary on them in the written argument).

person with whom he had no contract. The first exception was where the article which caused harm was dangerous. The second exception was where an article which was not dangerous in itself was, in fact, dangerous to the knowledge of the manufacturer as a result of some defect. As the written argument indicates, Mrs Donoghue's case in the House of Lords was that these two exceptions were too limited and were not justified by precedent or principle. Counsel suggested, instead, that the existence of a duty of care should depend on an examination of all the circumstances of the case and that a duty would be owed by the manufacturer where, as in *Donoghue v Stevenson*, he 'puts upon a market an article intended for human consumption in a form which precludes the possibility of an examination of the article by the retailer [Mr Minghella] or the consumer [Mrs Donoghue]'. In these circumstances, counsel argued, the manufacturer would be 'liable to the consumer for not taking reasonable care to see that the article is not injurious to health.'

Unsurprisingly, counsel for Mr Stevenson presented an argument which ran with the grain of the earlier case law, embracing the precedents instead of seeking to distinguish them. By contrast to the written argument presented on Mrs Donoghue's behalf, the written case for Mr Stevenson in the Parliamentary Archive is encrusted with the citation of authority and detailed commentary on the same. Counsel started with a bald proposition which was advanced as a summary of the law: 'In an ordinary case such as this the manufacturer owes no duty to the consumer apart from contract.' It is impossible to know whether the law reporter transcribed this *verbatim* from the oral or written argument presented on appeal or whether it is his own summary of what counsel argued. However, the unconscious irony of the reference to *Donoghue v Stevenson* as an 'ordinary case' is a nice touch. Counsel for Mr Stevenson, the respondent, went on to acknowledge the two exceptions to the general principle that the manufacturer owed no duty to consumers with whom he had no contract and criticised the argument of Mrs Donoghue's counsel in seeking to introduce a third exception: namely, 'the case of goods intended for human consumption sold to the public in a form in which investigation is impossible.' Counsel argued that an exception of this kind was not justified by anything said in any earlier reported case or, indeed, in the dissenting judgment of Lord Hunter when *Donoghue v Stevenson* was heard, at first-tier appeal, in the Court of Session. In the light of this the remainder of the summary of the respondent's argument simply refers to the earlier case law which the House of Lords was invited to follow. The law report informs the reader that George Morton KC – leading counsel for Mrs Donoghue – replied to the respondent's submissions, but the law reporter does not tell us the content of the reply.

A striking aspect of the argument presented to the House of Lords is the reliance placed by both sides on precedent. The practice of locating a legal argument in what the courts have previously decided is, of course, a uniform forensic technique in common law jurisdictions where judge-made law provides a large part – usually, the largest part – of the law. However, one might have expected to find more appeals to general principle and policy (perhaps, even, to morality) in the argument for Mrs Donoghue. Instead, what is advanced is the rather limp proposition that, 'The English authorities are not consistent, and the cases relied on by the Court of Session differed essentially in their facts from the present case.' This, together with the brevity of Mrs Donoghue's written argument, suggests that it was the judges in the majority – primarily Lords Atkin and Macmillan – who made the running on Mrs Donoghue's behalf. The judges had the self-confidence to set aside precedent where it was inconvenient and to advance the law by reference to more abstract notions of fairness and right conduct. Judicial thinking and research (in particular, the thought processes of Lord Atkin) enabled the neighbour principle to emerge.

Speeches

Most lawyers like hierarchy and the lawyers of the United Kingdom jurisdictions like it more than most. Barristers are listed on the white boards outside their Inns of Court addresses in order of seniority (from the date of their call to the Bar): QCs and the most senior at the top and the most junior tenant at the bottom. Hierarchy is one of the foundations of the doctrine of precedent. Courts are constrained to follow the decisions of the courts higher up the judicial food chain. In the English jurisdiction this means that the High Court follows the Court of Appeal and the Court of Appeal follows the House of Lords (now, the Supreme Court). Even in the House of Lords there was a hierarchy and this meant that the speeches (the law lords delivered their judgments as a speech on the floor of the House) were delivered in order of seniority. Lord Buckmaster went first because he was the first to be elevated to the Appellate Committee. However, when judgment was delivered in *Donoghue v Stevenson* Lord Buckmaster was not present to read his own speech and Lord Tomlin, the other dissenting voice, did so for him (history does not record what Lord Buckmaster was doing that day). The order of seniority required Lord Atkin to take the second place and then Lord Tomlin, then Lord Thankerton and finally the (comparative) new boy: Lord Macmillan.

There are five separate speeches in *Donoghue v Stevenson*. While this was not unusual in the 1930s, it would have been open to any law lord simply to record that he agreed with the speech and reasons of Lord X and to leave it at that. Lord Tomlin, who delivered the shortest speech, came closest to doing so, although even he could not resist saying 'only a few words' to explain his own thought process. The length and detail of the speeches in *Donoghue v Stevenson* is one indicator of the importance of what was decided. The two longest speeches were delivered by judges in the majority: Lord Atkin's speech being the longest, closely followed by Lord Macmillan. The minority's approach was grounded in precedent; it was clearly necessary for the majority to work rather harder to justify their departure from the same. The extra work was worth it. History has been kinder to the judges of the majority. Lord Justice Denning, sitting in the Court of Appeal in the early 1950s, referred to Lords Buckmaster and Tomlin as, 'timorous souls who were fearful of allowing a new cause of action', by contrast to Lords Atkin and Macmillan, 'the bold spirits who were ready to allow it if justice so required'[11] (one cannot help thinking that Denning LJ's use of 'bold spirit' was as much a reference to himself as to the *Donoghue v Stevenson* judges). As early as 1933 the legal historian Sir Frederick Pollock was writing in these terms about the minority speeches,

> 'We have to thank the Scots Lords of Appeal for overriding the scruples of English colleagues who could not emancipate themselves from the pressure of a supposed current of authority in English Courts. Lord Buckmaster and Lord Tomlin are the last men one would have suspected of timidity, but in this case they were less courageous than

---

11   *Candler v Crane, Christmas & Co* [1951] 2 KB 163, 178 (CA).

Lord Birkenhead would surely have been if he were still with us. Parts
of their opinions read as if they had forgotten that they were judging
in a Court of last resort.'[12]

Lord Atkin's speech

Lord Atkin's speech is justly celebrated for the formulation of what is
now known as the neighbour principle. The roots of this are explored
elsewhere in this book, but, in slightly abbreviated form, it requires
that:

> 'You must take reasonable care to avoid acts or omissions which you
> can reasonably foresee would be likely to injure your neighbour. Who,
> then, in law is my neighbour? The answer seems to be – persons who
> are so closely and directly affected by my act that I ought reasonably to
> have them in contemplation as being so affected when I am directing
> my mind to the acts or omissions which are called in question.'[13]

Lord Atkin knew, at the time he was drafting his speech, that
its effect would be explosive. He commenced by stating, in terms,
how important the case was. Indeed, he made it clear that he did not
believe that a more important problem had come before the House of
Lords, 'both because of its bearing on public health and because of
the practical test which it applies to the system under which it arises.'
He went on, like Lords Buckmaster and Macmillan, to record that
the case was to be determined according to Scots law, although he
had been told by counsel on both sides (and had satisfied himself
by his own researches) that English and Scots law were identical
on the issues to which the appeal gave rise. In fact, it appears that
the requirement of a duty of care as a condition for a finding of
liability in negligence was, by the late nineteenth century, at least as
well known to Scots law, as it was to English law. An 1892 Scots
law textbook on reparation recorded that, 'A duty must be set forth,
and a breach of duty proved.'[14] Indeed, it has been argued that Scots
and English law had, in the field of negligence, largely converged by
the time that *Donoghue v Stevenson* reached the House of Lords.[15]

---

12   Pollock, F 'The Snail in the Bottle and Thereafter' (1933) 49 LQR 22, at p 22.
13   *Donoghue v Stevenson* [1932] AC 562, 580 (HL(Sc)).
14   Glegg, AT *A Practical Treatise on the Law of Reparation* (1st ed, 1892), p 8.
15   Reid, K & Zimmermann, R (eds) *A History of Private Law in Scotland* (OUP,

This convergence has been variously ascribed over the years to the imperialistic tendencies of an English-dominated House of Lords and, perhaps, more prosaically, to commonalities of language and legal vocabulary, together with the independent and parallel development of Scots law duty of care concepts.

The road to the neighbour principle was, in Lord Atkin's speech, a short one. In the Appeal Cases report his speech starts on page 578 and his famous formulation of the neighbour principle is at page 580. Having set out his stall so early, the remainder of the judgment is devoted to justifying his advancement of the law. In spite of its later characterisation as a clean break with precedent, Lord Atkin went out of his way to seek support for the neighbour principle in the existing case law. First, by reference to the decision of the Court of Appeal in *Heaven v Pender*[16] and then through a succession of earlier authorities which, he believed, lent support to the proposition which he had identified. This was, however, only part of his task. The next stage was to consider and knock down the authorities, 'which have been referred to in the Courts below as laying down the proposition that no duty to take care is owed to the consumer in such a case as this.'[17] Lord Atkin's consideration of the inconvenient precedents was informed by the following example:

'A manufacturer puts up an article of food in a container which he knows will be opened by the actual consumer. There can be no inspection by any purchaser and no reasonable preliminary inspection by the consumer. Negligently, in the course of preparation, he allows the contents to be mixed with poison. It is said that the law of England and Scotland is that the poisoned consumer has no remedy against the negligent manufacturer. If this were the result of the authorities, I should consider the result a grave defect in the law, and so contrary to principle that I should hesitate long before following any decision to that effect which had not the authority of this House.'[18]

2000), pp 544 – 545. For a rather different view of developments in Scottish law since 1932, see: Brodie, F 'In Defence of Donoghue' [1997] JR 65.

16 (1883) 11 QBD 503 (CA).

17 [1932] AC 562, 584.

18 *Ibid*, at p 582.

In this sense, Lord Atkin's speech contains both abstract generality (the neighbour principle) and some incredulity at what was being advanced in argument: a sense that what was said by Mr Stevenson's counsel could not, when tested by a practical hypothetical, be right. Lord Atkin went on to make it clear that the law would be equally deficient if it failed to give a remedy to those injured by products other than food and drink: proprietary medicines, ointments, soaps, cleaning fluids and powders (to take the 'articles of common household use' listed in the speech). The facts of *Donoghue v Stevenson* conveniently pre-empted any argument by the defendant manufacturer that the intervention of some unidentified third party was the reason why the bottle of ginger beer was defective: the bottle was sealed and opaque and, therefore, if a snail had found its way into it this could only have been the result of the defendant's negligence. Again, Lord Atkin deploys rhetoric, a form of passionate advocacy, in aid of his argument, 'I do not think so ill of our jurisprudence as to suppose that its principles are so remote from the ordinary needs of civilized society and the ordinary claims it makes upon its members as to deny a legal remedy where there is so obviously a social wrong.'[19]

Following his case by case demolition of the authorities which, it was argued, did not support his view of the law, Lord Atkin concluded by referring to a US case, *MacPherson v Buick Motor Co*,[20] which was decided by the great American judge, Benjamin Cardozo.[21] Lord Atkin praised Cardozo J's 'illuminating judgment' and drew support for his own approach from the US authority.

The final words of the speech contain the following appeal:

'My Lords, if your Lordships accept the view that this pleading discloses a relevant cause of action you will be affirming the proposition that by Scots and English law alike a manufacturer of products, which he sells in such a form as to show that he intends them to reach the ultimate consumer in the form in which they left him with no reasonable possibility of intermediate examination,

19   *Ibid*, at p 583.
20   217 NY 382.
21   Cardozo sat on the US Supreme Court from 1932 until his death in 1938, but his best years as a judge are regarded as the eighteen years he spent on the bench of the New York Court of Appeals from where most of his famous judgments were delivered.

and with the knowledge that the absence of reasonable care in the preparation and putting up of the products will result in an injury to the consumer's life or property, owes a duty to the consumer to take that reasonable care.'

He went on to suggest that he regarded this proposition as so elementary – so based on 'sound common sense' – that only a lawyer could doubt its accuracy.

Lord Buckmaster's speech

Lord Buckmaster's concern was to ensure that his dissent was rooted in precedent:[22] an examination of the 'decided cases to see if they can be construed so as to support the appellant's case.' Lord Buckmaster stated that he was applying the judge-made common law of England.[23] While its principles could be adapted to meet new conditions which had not previously been contemplated, 'these principles cannot be changed nor can additions be made to them because any particular meritorious case seems outside their ambit.'[24] The general position was, he stated, that the breach of the defendant manufacturer's contract with A to exercise care and skill in the manufacture of the article in question does not provide B with a cause of action against the defendant when he is injured by the defective quality of the same article. To this general proposition, there were, Lord Buckmaster directed himself, only two exceptions recognised by the common law. First, where the article is dangerous in itself. Second, where the article is not dangerous in itself, but where the defect which makes it dangerous is known to the defendant manufacturer. What makes the difference in both of these cases is that the manufacturer knows that the article which he sells on is dangerous.

Following these opening remarks Lord Buckmaster went on to analyse the cases which he regarded as opposed to Mrs Donoghue's arguments. Among these, the most important, perhaps, was *Winterbottom v Wright*:[25] an 1842 decision. Buckmaster regarded this

22   Or, at least, in his reading of it.
23   Which in this regard was, as indicated above, the same (or so everyone agreed) as the law of Scotland.
24   [1932] AC 562, 567 (HL(Sc)).
25   (1842) 10 M & W 109.

decision as authority for the proposition that, 'the manufacturer of any article is not liable to a third party injured by negligent construction, for there can be nothing in the character of a coach to place it in a special category.' The *Winterbottom v Wright* claimant (C) was the driver of a mail coach. He had a contract of employment with a company (B) which had, in turn, contracted with the Postmaster-General to provide horses and men to drive the mail coach between Hartford and Holyhead. The Postmaster-General also had a contract with a further company (A) which was responsible for the supply, maintenance and repair of the mail coach used by C. As a result of latent defects in the coach it broke down while C was driving, he was thrown from the coach and sustained injuries which left him, as the law report states, 'lamed for life.' C sued A: a company with which he had no contract. His action was dismissed. In judgments which could scarcely be more distant from the present law of employers' liability and modern notions of health and safety, the judges in the Exchequer Division held that, absent previous case law to support the claimant's position and without a contract between him and the defendant, he had no cause of action. The judgments express, in extravagant terms, incredulity at the audacity of the claimant's argument. Lord Abinger CB, who delivered the leading judgment, stated, 'Unless we confine the operation of such contracts as this to the parties who entered into them, the most absurd and outrageous consequences, to which I can see no limit, would ensure.'[26] Alderson B, whose judgment in *Winterbottom v Wright* was cited with approval by Lord Buckmaster, had this to say, 'The only safe rule is to confine the right to recover to those who enter into the contract: if we go one step beyond that, there is no reason why we should not go fifty.' The judges who decided *Winterbottom v Wright* feared the floodgates: the provision of a cause of action to those with 'absurd and outrageous' claims where none had existed before. The same concern echoed through Lord Buckmaster's speech, but it was drowned out by those who wanted change.

It was when Lord Buckmaster reached the cases advanced in support of Mrs Donoghue's argument that he was able to deploy what Professor Heuston later described as his 'almost passionate

26   *Ibid*, at p 114.

sarcasm'.[27] He swatted aside *George v Skivington*,[28] which concerned the sale of some hair wash which had caused an injury to the claimant (who had not bought it), with the comment that 'few cases can have lived so dangerously and lived so long.'[29] He dealt with dicta of Brett MR in *Heaven v Pender*,[30] which concerned some collapsing staging and an action by an injured workman against the occupier, a case central to Lord Atkin's formulation of the neighbour principle, by commenting that this case was about occupier's liability and 'had nothing whatever to do with the question of manufacture and sale.'[31] Indeed, he went further and described *Heaven v Pender* as a '*tabula in naufragio*[32] for many litigants struggling in the seas of adverse authority': 'So far, therefore, as the case of *George v Skivington* and the dicta in *Heaven v Pender* are concerned, it is in my opinion better that they should be buried so securely that their perturbed spirits shall no longer vex the law.'[33] It is not easy to understand the violence of Lord Buckmaster's objection to the Appellant's argument in purely legal terms. He goes much further than a straightforward appeal to contrary precedent would ordinarily demand. One might conclude that there is an additional, even an extra-legal, concern or some other personal animus at play.

The conclusion of Lord Buckmaster's speech makes it clear that he finds against Mrs Donoghue because 'the authorities are against ... [her] contention, and, apart from authority, it is difficult to see how any common law proposition can be formulated to support her claim.'[34] Lord Buckmaster believed that if the principle for which Mrs Donoghue contended were known to Scottish or English law then there would be more than one case (*George v Skivington*) to support

---

27   Heuston, RFV *Lives of the Lord Chancellors 1885 – 1940* (Clarendon Press, 1964), Appendix.
28   LR 5 Ex 1.
29   By contrast, Asquith LJ later observed that the majority decision in *Donoghue v Stevenson* ensured that 'after a long and rough crossing ... [*George v Skivington* had] limped into port.' *Candler v Crane, Christmas & Co.* [1951] 2 KB 164, 190 (CA).
30   (1883) 11 QBD 503 (CA).
31   [1932] AC 562, 573 (HL (Sc)).
32   An example of the Latin now frowned on in the English courts: 'plank in a shipwreck.'
33   [1932] AC 562, 576 (HL (Sc)).
34   *Ibid*, at p 577.

it. Lord Buckmaster expressed, in emphatic terms, his support for the judgment of Lord Anderson in the Scottish case *Mullen v Barr & Co*:[35] 'where the goods of the defenders are widely distributed throughout Scotland, it would seem little short of outrageous to make them responsible to members of the public for the condition of the contents of every bottle which issues from their works.'

Lord Macmillan's speech

Lord Macmillan commenced with the facts of the case before moving on to one of the principal objections to the arguments advanced on behalf of Mrs Donoghue: namely, that she had no contract with the manufacturer. His response to this was, first, that the existence of a contractual relationship between parties, where such existed, did not preclude the existence of additional legal relationships (like, for example, a duty of care in tort). Accordingly, there was no reason in principle why the same set of facts should not give one litigant an action in contract and another an action in tort or delict. Second, Lord Macmillan stated, the fact that there was an 'incidental contract' between the manufacturer and retailer was irrelevant to the allegation of carelessness advanced by Mrs Donoghue: 'The appellant in the present instance asks that her case be approached as a case of delict[36], not as a case of breach of contract.'[37] Given that Mrs Donoghue was not suing in contract, Lord Macmillan was unable to see how an earlier contract, reached between manufacturer and retailer and to which she was not a party, should affect her legal rights. His judgment in this regard was influenced by the writings of Sir Frederick Pollock, the great legal historian, from whose textbook on the law of torts Lord Macmillan quoted a lengthy passage.

After his opening remarks Lord Macmillan also went on to review the English and American authorities. Macmillan arrived, via what he referred to as the 'inconclusive state of the authorities', at the following proposition:

35   1929 SC 461, 479.

36   'Delict' is the word used for 'tort' in Scottish law (and, when translated, in the legal systems of continental Europe).

37   [1932] AC 562, 611 (HL (Sc))

'The law takes no cognizance of carelessness in the abstract. It concerns itself with carelessness only where there is a duty to take care and where failure in that duty has caused damage. In such circumstances carelessness assumes the legal quality of negligence and entails the consequences in law of negligence. What, then, are the circumstances which give rise to this duty to take care?'

Lord Macmillan answered his own question by stating that the law used the standard of the reasonable man in determining whether a particular relationship gave rise to a duty of care. In other words, the judgment of the hypothetical reasonable man should be used to determine whether a duty of care was owed and whether the duty of care had been breached. His answer to Lord Buckmaster's proposition that additions could not be made to the common law principles found in existing case law was that, 'The criterion of judgment must adjust and adapt itself to the changing circumstances of life'. The next sentence of the judgment is his own famous and much-quoted aphorism: 'The categories of negligence are never closed.'[38] Applying his reasonable man test, Lord Macmillan was able to conclude, first, that if Mrs Donoghue were able to prove her factual allegations then Mr Stevenson had 'exhibited carelessness in the conduct of his business.' Second, Mr Stevenson, as 'a person who for gain engages in the business of manufacturing articles of food and drink intended for consumption by members of the public in the form in which he issues them', owed a duty of care to Mrs Donoghue. Third, it was reasonably foreseeable that if Mr Stevenson conducted his process of manufacture carelessly then he might injure those persons whom he expected and wanted to consume his products (which class included Mrs Donoghue). In the circumstances, there was no reason not to find that Mr Stevenson owed Mrs Donoghue a duty of care (a duty to take reasonable care) which provided her with a viable cause of action in law.

Lord Macmillan's speech is layered with references to the fact that counsel had agreed that the position was the same in Scottish and English law, as applied to the facts of Mrs Donoghue's claim:

38   *Ibid*, at p 619.

'My Lords, the recognition by counsel that the law of Scotland applicable to the case was the same as the law of England implied that there was no special doctrine of Scots law which either the appellant or the respondent could invoke to support her or his case; and your Lordships have thus been relieved of the necessity of a separate consideration of the law of Scotland. For myself, I am satisfied that there is no specialty of Scots law involved, and that the case may safely be decided on principles common to both systems.'[39]

In a scholarly article on Lord Macmillan's speech Alan Rodger QC (who later became a law lord – Lord Rodger of Earlsferry – and was, at the time of the article, Solicitor-General for Scotland), suggested that an earlier version of Lord Macmillan's speech dealt with the Scottish position and was recast, before being delivered in the House, so that it applied to English law as well. He speculates that the reason for the redrafting was the persuasive attention of Lord Atkin who induced Lord Macmillan to alter the first draft of his speech so as to avoid the result that the 'appeal would be decisive for the smaller Scottish jurisdiction, [while] it would leave the position unclear for English law and the systems based on it throughout the world.'[40] There may be some support for this contention in Lord Macmillan's extra-judicial comment (recorded in his autobiography) that, 'In almost every case, it would be possible to decide the issue either way with reasonable legal justification.'

Whatever the reasons for the redrafting of Lord Macmillan's speech, he was clearly pleased to record his view that there was no difference between the law of England and Scotland on the issues raised by Mrs Donoghue's appeal, 'I am happy to think that in their relation to the practical problem of everyday life which this Appeal presents the legal systems of the two countries are in no way at variance, and that the principles of both alike are sufficiently consonant with justice and common sense to admit of the claim which the appellant seeks to establish.'[41]

---

39   *Ibid*, at p 621.
40   Rodger, A 'Lord Macmillan's Speech in *Donoghue v Stevenson*' (1992) 108 LQR 236, 246. Lord Rodger's article is based on the prints of Lord Macmillan's speeches found in papers bequeathed to the Faculty of Advocates' library: *House of Lords Judgments 1930 – 1937*.
41   [1932] AC 562, 621 (HL(Sc)).

Unusually, Lord Macmillan left his own account of the reasoning which underpinned his speech in *Donoghue v Stevenson* in a rather self-congratulatory autobiography: *A Man of Law's Tale*.[42] This contains a general description of Lord Macmillan's practice when preparing judgments in Lords and Privy Council appeals. He never dictated his speeches, but, instead, prepared them in two stages: first, preparing a rough draft of the speech 'in which I made sure that all the points were included'; second, a perfected draft 'in which I arranged the sequence of the argument, cut out superfluities, and tried to improve the wording.'[43] Lord Macmillan introduces his brief account of *Donoghue v Stevenson* by commenting on his relatively junior status in the Lords when the case was heard. He notes that it was obvious, from an early stage in the proceedings, that there was going to be a division of judicial opinion. Lord Macmillan, who knew Lord Buckmaster well from their time as practising lawyers, was clearly surprised by the 'almost violent' tone of the more senior judge's speech:

> 'When we came to write our judgments Lord Buckmaster employed all his mastery of argument in a vigorous, almost violent, demolition of the appellant Mrs Donoghue's contention which he declared to be insupportable by any common-law proposition. Lord Tomlin agreed with him. Lord Atkin took the contrary view which he announced with no less confidence.'[44]

Characteristically, Lord Macmillan assigned himself the leading role in *Donoghue v Stevenson*, 'I had to make up my mind with which of my seniors I should agree; the decision would depend on my vote.'[45] He went on to make it clear that, from the outset, he took the view that Mrs Donoghue should win and was impervious to Lord Buckmaster's 'appeal to those who differed from him not to disturb with impious hands the settled law of the land.' Lord Macmillan's description of

---

42   Lord Macmillan *A Man of Law's Tale* (Macmillan & Co Ltd, 1952). This was published posthumously. Atkin also embarked on an autobiography, but never completed it. It would have been illuminating to read his own insights into *Donoghue v Stevenson*.

43   Lord Macmillan *A Man of Law's Tale* (Macmillan & Co Ltd, 1952), p 148.

44   *Ibid*, at p 151.

45   *Ibid*.

Donoghue v Stevenson concludes with a lengthy quotation from his own speech. Of the neighbour principle there is no mention.

Supporting speeches

The additional speeches of Lord Tomlin (who also dissented) and Lord Thankerton (who joined the majority) can be dealt with more briefly. Lord Tomlin delivered the shortest speech and did little more than confirm that he agreed with every particular of Lord Buckmaster's approach. Like Lord Atkin he could see no reason of logic or principle for distinguishing the duty of a manufacturer of food stuffs from the duty owed by any other manufacturer. Lord Tomlin did not believe that the fact the drink consumed by Mrs Donoghue was in a sealed container made any difference to whether or not a duty of care existed, although he conceded that if a duty of care did exist, the fact that the container was sealed might make it easier to establish liability against the manufacturer. Unlike Lord Atkin, Lord Tomlin was quite satisfied that there was no general duty of care. He was persuaded that *Winterbottom v Wright*, the only authority to which he made reference in his speech, was wholly against Mrs Donoghue.

Lord Thankerton's speech has a distinctively Scottish flavour. The summary of counsel's argument in the Appeal Cases suggests that the only Scottish case referred to by counsel was that involving the mouse in the ginger beer: *Mullen v Barr & Co Ltd*.[46] That no Scottish authority was cited by counsel would seem to be confirmed by Lord Macmillan's speech: 'At your Lordship's Bar counsel for both parties to the present appeal, accepting, as I do also, the view that there is no distinction between the law of Scotland and the law of England in the legal principles applicable to the case, confined their arguments to the English authorities.' Notwithstanding the absence of argument on the same Lord Thankerton's speech consists of commentary only on Scottish authorities: in addition to *Mullen v Barr & Co Ltd*, he also referred to *Kemp & Dougall v Darngavil Coal Co*,[47] *Clelland v Robb*[48] and *Gordon v M'Hardy*.[49] Given that these cases were not

46 1929 SC 461 (Ct of Sess).
47 1909 SC 1314.
48 1911 SC 253.
49 (1903) 6 F 210.

cited in argument and do not feature in the judgments of the other law lords, it seems likely that Lord Thankerton carried out his own research.[50] He was clearly keen to ensure that the Scottish roots of *Donoghue v Stevenson* were reflected in his own speech, even if not in the speeches of his fellow judges.

Lord Thankerton commenced by clearing the ground. First, Mrs Donoghue had no contract with the person that she sued and was not bringing a claim in contract. Second, in order to bring a claim in negligence, she had to establish that, in law, a duty of care was owed to her. Third, the claimant did not fall into the 'exceptions' identified by Lord Buckmaster; that is, the person injured by an article dangerous *per se* or by an article with a defect which, to the knowledge of the manufacturer, made it dangerous. Lord Thankerton's view was that the English case law, dealt with by Lord Atkin, made it clear that it was impossible to list, 'amid the ever varying types of human relationships, those relationships in which a duty to exercise care arises apart from contract ... .' For Lord Thankerton, as for Lord Macmillan, the categories of negligence were never closed. The inconsistent nature of the English authorities, as he and Lord Atkin read them, liberated Lord Thankerton to conclude that he could return to first principles:

> 'The special circumstances from which the appellant claims that such a relationship of duty should be inferred may, I think, be stated thus – namely, that the respondent, in placing his manufactured article of drink upon the market, has intentionally so excluded interference with, or examination of, the article by any intermediate handler of the goods between himself and the consumer that he has, of his own accord, brought himself into direct relationship with the consumer, with the result that the consumer is entitled to rely upon the exercise of diligence by the manufacturer to secure that the article shall not be harmful to the consumer.'[51]

Lord Thankerton supported this basis for his decision by reference to *Gordon v M'Hardy*[52] (a Scottish case). In *Gordon v M'Hardy*

---

50   Although Macmillan did make brief reference to *Gordon v M'Hardy* at the conclusion of his speech: [1932] AC 562, 622 (HL(Sc)).
51   *Ibid*, at p 603.
52   (1903) 6 F 210.

the claimant (pursuer) sought damages from a grocer who had sold tinned salmon to the deceased (the claimant's son). The salmon was contaminated with poison. The grocer escaped liability on the basis that he could not examine or see inside the tin to check whether the salmon was free of contaminants. Although the manufacturer was not a defendant (defender) in the action, Lord Thankerton thought it would reflect poorly on the law if the 'meticulous care of the manufacturer to exclude interference or inspection by the grocer ... should relieve the grocer of any responsibility to the consumer without any corresponding assumption by the manufacturer.'[53] In other words, Lord Thankerton's concern was that the claimant should not be left without a remedy against someone in circumstances where a wrong had been done. This stands in the starkest contrast to Lord Buckmaster's approach and his direction that, 'A man is entitled to be as negligent as he pleases towards the whole world if he owes no duty to them.'[54]

Conclusion

A legal academic may welcome having five separate speeches to read. The process of working out what was decided in any given case is complicated by differences of reasoning and result which are likely to be found where there is more than one speech (particularly, where there is more than one dissenting voice). In this jurisdiction lawyers are now discouraged from using legal Latin, but references to the *ratio decidendi* (in short, 'the *ratio*' – the reason for a decision) are still common. What then was the ratio of *Donoghue v Stevenson*? It has been suggested, somewhat facetiously, that a restrictive reading might confine the significance of the decision to the proposition that there is a duty not to sell opaque bottles of ginger beer containing dead snails to Scottish women.[55] Scarcely more expansive was the reaction of the Solicitor's Journal to the case in a 1932 report: 'There might be a distinction between draft and bottled beer, the former falling without and the latter within the present case.'[56] More ambitiously, the

---

53   [1932] AC 562, 604 (HL(Sc)).
54   *Ibid*, at pp 574 – 575.
55   Commentary by Professor Stone in *Province and Function of Law*, reported by RFV Heuston in '*Donoghue v Stevenson* in Retrospect' (1957) 20 MLR 1, 6.
56   (1932) 76 Sol J 387, 388.

decision could be stretched to accommodate the principle that there is a duty not to distribute defective objects (of any sort) capable of causing any kind of damage to any person.

Legal commentators have focused our attention on Lord Atkin's neighbour principle. It is this principle which has driven the development of the law of negligence and inspired books and articles. It is, however, questionable whether the neighbour principle even forms part of the ratio of *Donoghue v Stevenson*. Lord Atkin could not decide the case by himself. It was only the supportive assistance of two colleagues which secured Mrs Donoghue her victory. The ratio has, therefore, to be found in a reading of all three majority judgments. It is striking that neither Lord Macmillan nor Lord Thankerton make any reference to the neighbour principle or to anything which looks much like it. Lord Thankerton did state that he so entirely agreed with the judgment of Lord Atkin that he could not usefully add anything to it, but he was careful to make it clear that this was because of Lord Atkin's treatment of the English case law (rather than because he had been won over to the neighbour principle).[57] Indeed, Lord Thankerton's reasoning was couched in much more limited terms, as I have pointed out above. Lord Macmillan came a little closer to the neighbour principle in the closing passages of his speech, 'In the present case the respondent, when he manufactured his ginger-beer, had directly in contemplation that it would be consumed by members of the public. Can it be said that he could not be expected as a reasonable man to foresee that if he conducted his process of manufacture carelessly he might injure those whom he expected and desired to consume his ginger-beer?'[58] However, this is not the neighbour principle in the unexpurgated form apparently advocated by Lord Atkin and taken up in later cases. The principle that a duty of care will exist where a person reasonably foresees that his acts or omissions will be likely to result in damage to another is a more 'restricted' answer to 'the lawyer's question' than can be found in the Lucan Gospel, but it was not sufficiently restricted for even the majority-supporting judges in *Donoghue v Stevenson*.

57   [1932] AC 562, 604.
58   *Ibid*, at p 620.

Professor Heuston, writing in 1957, described the *ratio* in *Donoghue v Stevenson* in the following terms: (a) negligence is a separate and distinct tort; (b) a contractual relationship between the parties to the action is not a prerequisite for liability in tort; and, (c) manufacturers of products owe a duty of care to the person who ultimately consumes or uses the product. The neighbour principle pointedly does not appear in Professor Heuston's description:

> 'The ... [neighbour principle], although perhaps the most commonly cited and in many ways the most significant, cannot properly be regarded a part of the *ratio decidendi* of the decision. No amount of posthumous citation can of itself transfer with retrospective effect a proposition from the status of *obiter dictum* to that of *ratio decidendi*; no doubt it will serve to magnify greatly the interest and importance of the case, but that is another matter.'[59]

Perhaps the author of the Appeal Cases headnote should, after all, be excused for the conservative approach taken in reporting the decision.

---

59   Heuston, RFV '*Donoghue v Stevenson* in Retrospect' (1957) 20 MLR 1, 9.

4. A LEGAL CAST LIST:
JUDGES AND LAWYERS

'But here a very natural, and very material, question arises: how are
these customs or maxims to be known, and by whom is their validity
to be determined? The answer is, by the judges in the several courts
of justice. They are the depository of the laws; the living oracles, who
must decide in all cases of doubt, and who are bound by an oath to
decide according to the law of the land.'

William Blackstone, *Commentaries on the Laws of England* (1765)
Vol. I, p 69

Among the many curiosities of *Donoghue v Stevenson* is that
it was decided by a very junior bench. Of the five law lords
who formed the tribunal, only one had more than five years'
experience as a judge in the highest court: Lord Buckmaster, who had
served as Lord Chancellor in the short-lived Asquith Government of
1915 – 1916. Most of the *Donoghue v Stevenson* law lords shared
an active interest in political life and, for some of them, this was not
confined to a general involvement in public affairs; their involvement
was actively party political and they may accurately be described as
politician-judges. Reforms to the Appellate Committee of the House
of Lords[1] and the ancient office of Lord Chancellor have robbed
constitutional reformers of two of their campaign totems (pre-reform,
for example, the Lord Chancellor simultaneously exercised legislative,
executive and judicial functions). These reforms are very recent.[2] At
the time that *Donoghue v Stevenson* was decided the highest court in
the land counted among its members those who had aspired to and
held high political office. These men[3] might have offended those who
supported a separation of powers in our constitutional arrangements,

1   The Supreme Court as it now is.
2   Lord Macmillan was a very keen supporter of the House of Lords (and the role
of the Lord Chancellor) in the exercise of judicial function, seeing this as 'the product
of a long process of evolution, and however logically indefensible, it has the justification of working and working well.': Lord Macmillan *A Man of Law's Tale* (Macmillan & Co Ltd, 1952), p 143.
3   They were all men until the appointment of Baroness Hale of Richmond in 2004.

but their active interest in public and political affairs seems likely to have brought something to the bench; a readiness, perhaps, to see the policy implications of a decision. To see where the law had gone wrong and to seek to put it right (although, it has to be said, Lord Buckmaster, the most party political of them all, proved this proposition by contradicting it).[4]

Law lords: the majority

Lord Atkin

James Richard Atkin was born on 28 November 1867 to an Irish father and a Welsh mother. It is appropriate that a judge who was to have such a profound impact on the jurisprudence of the wider common law world was born in Brisbane, Australia where his father was a member of the legislative assembly of Queensland. Atkin's father originally came from Fernhill, County Cork. His mother's family were Welsh and claimed descent from the Welsh princes. Atkin's father died while he was still a boy and his mother returned with her two sons to live with her family in Merionethshire, North Wales. Atkin subsequently considered himself a Welshman. He was educated at Christ College, Brecon and then at Magdalen College, Oxford where he studied 'Greats';[5] he held scholarships to both institutions. Atkin's health was not robust and this affected his sporting and academic pursuits at University. A friend attributed his failure to achieve a better than second class degree ('a great mortification to him') to the effects of poor health while a student (influenza during his finals).[6]

---

4   Unlike their American counterparts, academics and other writers on legal topics in this jurisdiction have shown limited interest in the lives of judges. Apart from the excellent work of RFV Heuston, Geoffrey Lewis and a few others, the legal biography genre is not a crowded market: Heuston, RFV *Lives of the Lord Chancellors 1885 – 1940* (Clarendon Press, 1964); Lewis, G *Lord Atkin* (Hart Publishing, 1999); Paterson, A *The Law Lords* (Macmillan, 1982); Lee, S *Judging Judges* (Faber & Faber, 1988). For criticism of the quality of American-style 'psycho-biography' see, Deakin, S, Johnston, A & Markesinis *Markesinis and Deakin's Tort Law* (Clarendon Press, 6th ed), p 81.
5   The final honours school of classics and philosophy at Oxford University, conventionally regarded as providing a rounded, liberal education.
6   Gutteridge, HC 'Lord Atkin of Aberdovey' (1944) 60 LQR 334, 335.

Atkin married Lucy Hemmant when he was 26 years of age. She was the daughter of William Hemmant who had, at one time, been acting Premier of Queensland and was a friend of Atkin's father, but had later returned to England and settled in Sevenoaks, Kent (Atkin became a close friend of the Hemmant family). After Oxford Atkin joined Gray's Inn, the Inn of Court which is traditionally most closely connected with Wales and the Welsh, and was called to the Bar by Gray's in 1891. In some autobiographical fragments in Atkin's legal papers (held by Gray's Inn) he comments that, at the time that he was admitted to the Inn, it lacked the prestige that it later recovered, 'There were several old benchers whose connection with the law was shadowy: and there was no one in busy practice at the Bar.'[7] Atkin was, and always remained, a great supporter of both legal debates (moots) and of the tradition that student barristers dine formally in Hall before they can be called to the Bar. Atkin later wrote that dining at the Inn (and sharing two, 'sometimes three' bottles of wine) exposed him to students from around the common law world[8] and also 'encouraged comradeship' with his fellow aspiring barristers. Atkin was, however, critical of the education then offered by the Council of Legal Education which organised lectures and examinations for Bar students; the principal purpose of Atkin's attendance at the Council was, he wrote, to qualify as soon and as early as possible.[9]

Following call to the Bar, Atkin entered Chambers on the first floor of 3 Pump Court in the Inner Temple. His room was rented from and shared with a Mr Moncrieff whose father had been Scottish Lord Justice-Clerk (sitting in the Court of Session in Edinburgh).[10] His room mate earned his living from journalism and from the examination of witnesses in Scottish legal proceedings. Atkin wrote that this early exposure had acquainted him 'with Scots procedural

---

7   File reference: ATK1/BIOG/1/2.

8   *Ibid.* Atkin writes of dining in Hall with, '… a consular officer from Japan, a native of Barbados, an Irish nationalist.'

9   *Ibid.*

10   This Lord Moncrieff was James Wellwood Moncrieff (later, the 1st Baron Moncrieff of Tulliebole) who was born in 1811 and, after first serving as Lord Advocate, became the Lord Justice-Clerk from 1869 until 1888. Exemplifying the narrow circles in which lawyers of this period moved, this Lord Moncrieff was also a relative of the Lord Moncrieff who, as Lord Ordinary, presided over Mrs Donoghue's claim when it was heard at first instance in the Court of Session.

terms which therefore did not take me unawares when it became my duty to hear Scots appeals.'[11] Atkin, like many barristers, does not seem to have lacked confidence in his own ability, and would not have been intimidated when Mrs Donoghue's 'Scots appeal' reached him from the Court of Session.

Atkin's pupillage was spent in the Chambers of the common law master T E Scrutton who was later elevated to the Court of Appeal (only to be leap-frogged by his former pupils, Lords Wright and Atkin, who both went one level further up the judicial hierarchy and reached the House of Lords). Atkin later expressed his regard and gratitude for Scrutton ('my master and subsequent colleague') in a generous reference, 'Lord Justice Scrutton, to whom I personally owe what success I have reached. Everyone will not be as lucky.'[12] The fatherless Atkin lacked the means and connections to have a head start in his career at the Bar and, in the early years of practice, there was little work available for him; he was dependent on the financial support of his father-in-law. In the notes he wrote in preparation for his autobiography Atkin meticulously records the fee income that he generated during his early years in practice: in 1891 £35; in 1892 £37; in 1893 £59; in 1894 £100; and in 1895 £110.[13] Atkin's friend, Professor Gutteridge KC, recounted this anecdote in the generous obituary that he wrote:

> 'I well remember an occasion on which he and I were passing along a London Street when Atkin pointed to a building and said: "I can never see that without thinking how lucky I have been!" That building contained the office of a well- known scholastic agency, and Atkin told me how a few years before he had walked into that office with despair in his heart to make inquiries as to the possibility of obtaining a mastership at a public school.'[14]

11   File reference: ATK1/BIOG/1/2.
12   *Graya* (the Gray's Inn Journal), 'TRAINING FOR SUCCESS AT THE BAR.' In the Atkin archive at Gray's Inn. File reference: ATK1/PERS/3/2.
13   Atkin archive. File reference: ATK1/BIOG/1/2. The notes which Atkin wrote for his autobiography record the fee income for each calendar year between 1891 and 1898. Decades after achieving the greatest success that a lawyer can have in this jurisdiction, he was proudly recording that, after 1898, his fees 'kept increasing.'
14   Gutteridge, HC 'Lord Atkin of Aberdovey' (1944) 60 LQR 334, 335.

The turning point in Atkin's fortunes came when he met the Official Assignee of the Stock Exchange at the Sevenoaks home of his father-in-law. The speculation which followed the conclusion of the Boer War produced commercial litigation in the law of agency and, in particular, its application to the activities of stockbrokers. The interest which Atkin showed in this work led to his involvement in stock exchange proceedings. As often happens in practice at the Bar, success in one field opens doors to other areas of work and Atkin went on to develop an excellent reputation in commercial (in particular, marine insurance) and common law work. As a junior Atkin appeared regularly before the Masters of the King's Bench Division who dealt with most of the interlocutory or procedural business of the High Court and, then as now, occupied high-ceilinged rooms down long corridors in a tucked away corner of the Royal Courts of Justice on the Strand reached via an area known as the 'Bear Garden'. The conduct of litigation in the Bear Garden was, and still is, noted for its speed and the robustness of the approach taken by the Masters (some have more patience than others). Gutteridge comments that Atkin: '... had an almost uncanny instinct for the separation of the grain from the chaff: bad points were never taken, no matter what the client might say; but good points were driven home tersely and with characteristic vigour. He never allowed his temper to become ruffled ... .'[15]

Atkin's health suffered because of the volume of work that he undertook as a junior barrister, but his practice continued to thrive and, in 1906 (before he had reached the age of 40), he was promoted to the ranks of King's Counsel. Atkin's practice took on a more commercial flavour during his short career in silk before his next step: becoming, in 1913, a judge of the King's Bench Division. As well as presiding over proceedings concerning commercial and insurance matters, he acquired an excellent reputation in criminal proceedings (a curious anomaly of the English tradition of appointing judges which continues today is that those appointed can find themselves regularly presiding over trials in areas of law in which they never practised and of which they have little, if any, experience). An antique photograph album of this period which can be found in the Atkin archive at Gray's Inn shows the newly appointed judge arriving at

15   *Ibid*, at p 336.

a provincial court for the winter assizes of 1914.[16] In a succession of black and white photographs Atkin, in full-bottomed wig, is attended by liveried footmen wearing tricorn hats and is driven to court in a carriage drawn by four black horses. Atkin looks vulnerably young in the photographs and smiles shyly at the camera (perhaps embarrassed by the magnificent silliness of it all).

Atkin was promoted again to the Court of Appeal in 1919 where, as indicated above, he joined his former pupil master, Scrutton LJ. As a judge, Atkin was regarded as, 'Gentle, firm, patient, learned in the law, dignified ... .'[17] In 1928 Atkin was raised to the Barony and appointed to the Appellate Committee of the House of Lords. His friend and colleague in the Lords, Lord Wright, wrote after Atkin's death of his 'fervent and almost passionate devotion' to English law and described the literary style of Atkin's speeches as, 'chaste, composed, easy, accurate.'[18] Atkin's biographer, Geoffrey Lewis, has suggested that it is Atkin's literary ability – his capacity to take Biblical and philosophical themes and turn them into stirring legal rhetoric – that has contributed most to the influence of his judgments: in *Donoghue v Stevenson* giving English jurisprudence, 'its most quoted metaphor.'[19] Lord Wright was a great admirer of Atkin's speech in *Donoghue v Stevenson*. In the days which preceded judgment in the Lords, Atkin received the following note from Lord Wright: 'I have been reading with admiration your magnificent and convincing judgment in the snail case – also Macmillan's which is very good. I am glad this fundamental rule of law will now be finally established. ... I find Buckmaster on snails very disappointing. I have not seen Tomlin's efforts on the same subject.'[20]

It is perfectly clear that Atkin's devoted Christian faith provided a starting point for his development of the neighbour principle.[21]

---

16   File reference: ATK1/PERS/5/3.
17   *Dictionary of National Biography*.
18   Lord Wright 'Lord Atkin of Aberdovey' (1944) 60 LQR 334, 333.
19   Lewis, G *Lord Atkin* (Hart Publishing, 1999), p 61.
20   The letter is in the Atkin archive. File reference ATK1/JUD/1/1.
21   He shared this approach to the law with another great legal innovator, Lord Denning. See, Lord Denning *The Family Story* (Butterworths, 1981), p 181: 'In coming upon legal obstacles, it is not enough to keep your law books dry. It is as well to have a Bible ready to hand too. It is the most tattered book in my library. I have drawn

In October 1931, within three months of the start of argument in *Donoghue v Stevenson*, Atkin gave a lecture in which he revealed the direction of his thinking on the connections between law and morality:

'It is quite true that law and morality do not cover identical fields. No doubt morality extends beyond the more limited range in which you can lay down the definite prohibitions of law, but, apart from that, the British law has always necessarily ingrained in it moral teaching in this sense: that it lays down standards of honesty and plain dealing between man and man. The idea of law is that the obligations of a man are to keep his word. If he swears to his neighbour, he is not to disappoint him. In other words, he is to keep his contracts. He is not to injure his neighbour by word. That is to say, he is not to libel or slander him. He is not to commit perjury in respect of him, and he is not to defraud him into acting to his detriment by telling him lies. He is not to injure his neighbour by acts of negligence; and that certainly covers a very large field of the law. I doubt whether the whole of the law of tort could not be comprised in the golden maxim to do unto your neighbour as you would that he should do unto you.'[22]

The thoughts and rhetoric of this autumn lecture were echoed the following spring in Atkin's speech in *Donoghue v Stevenson*. It appears that, in later years, he was able to make use of 'the snail and the ginger beer bottle case' as an aid to the moral instruction of his family; his oldest grandson, later Lord Aldington, recalls it featuring in discussions during Sunday lunch.[23] His daughter Elizabeth Robson has written that her father asked his children 'whom we thought was our neighbour' and, after *Donoghue v Stevenson* was decided, told them 'that he was making law by that judgment.'[24]

Professor Gutteridge KC, writing after Atkin's death, expressed the view that judges and practitioners of law can be divided between those who, as a matter of base philosophy, believe that claimants or Plaintiffs who have established a *prima facie* case have

---

upon it constantly. So did Lord Atkin in the great case of *Donoghue v Stevenson* which transformed the law of negligence.'

22   Lord Atkin 'Law as an Educational Subject' [1932] JSPTL 27, 30.

23   As reported in Lewis, G *Lord Atkin* (Hart Publishing, 1999), p 57.

24   Atkin archive. Also reported in McBryde, WM '*Donoghue v Stevenson*: the Story of the "Snail in the Bottle" Case' in Gamble, AJ (ed) *Obligations in Context* (W Green, 1990), p 26.

demonstrated that they have been wronged and are entitled to remedy ('claimants' men') and those whose instinctive dislike of litigation and litigants causes them to view claims for damages with suspicion and to exhaust any possibility of a defence before determining that the defendant is liable ('defendants' men').[25] Professor Gutteridge was in no doubt that Atkin was a claimants' man and conscientiously sought to uphold the rights of the individual. An illustration of this can be found in *Liversidge v Anderson*[26] where Atkin's powerful dissenting speech also conveys something of his celebrated rhetorical style. This case, which reached the House of Lords in 1941, arose out of an action for false imprisonment brought by the claimant against the Home Secretary. The Secretary of State had made a detention order against the claimant in accordance with powers contained in emergency legislation. The claimant applied for particulars of the Secretary of State's Defence in the proceedings and the latter simply pointed to the emergency legislation and a recital in the order that he believed the claimant to be of 'hostile association'. The majority (which included Lord Macmillan) held that the legislation was properly construed as enabling detention by exercise of executive discretion and, accordingly, a court could not inquire whether, in fact, the Home Secretary had reasonable grounds for his belief. Atkin, the lone dissenting voice, did not accept this; the most celebrated passage in his speech commences with criticism of judges who, on a question of construction involving the liberty of the individual, 'show themselves more executive minded than the executive.' Atkin, like the majority, based his dissent on the construction of the contentious words in the legislation (he simply construed these words in a different way), but he also approached the construction exercise from a governing principle which he described with characteristic eloquence; his judgment is a satisfying read, informed by historical perspective and moral indignation:

> 'In this country, amid the clash of arms, the laws are not silent. They may be changed, but they speak the same language in war as in peace. It has always been one of the pillars of freedom, one of the principles of liberty for which on recent authority we are now fighting, that judges are no respecters of persons and stand between the subject and

25   Gutteridge, HC 'Lord Atkin of Aberdovey' (1944) 60 LQR 334, at p 340. Gutteridge recognised that this was a convenient simplification.
26   [1942] AC 206 (HL(E)).

any attempted encroachments on his liberty by the executive, alert to see that any coercive action is justified in law. In this case, I have listened to arguments which might have been addressed acceptably to the Court of King's Bench in the time of Charles I.'[27]

Lord Macmillan, who sided with the majority and was, one supposes, one of the object of Atkin's scorn, stated in his own speech that he yielded to no one in recognising the value of the courts' jealous scrutiny of decisions threatening the liberty of the individual. He based his decision on a rather limp comparison of the rules of pleading in Scotland and England (criticising the claimant, who litigated in the English courts, for having failed to plead his case with sufficient particularity) and, somewhat startlingly, on the proposition that, 'at a time of emergency when the life of the whole nation is at stake it may well be that a regulation for the defence of the realm may quite properly have a meaning which because of its drastic invasion of the liberty of the subject the courts would be slow to attribute to a peace time measure.' It is hard for any lawyer to escape the conclusion that Atkin emerged from *Liversidge* with more credit than Macmillan.

For his 1982 socio-legal work on the law lords Paterson spoke to some of those who had known Atkin. He was described as a judicial activist; someone who, in the account of Lord Radcliffe, would 'positively ... prefer that a case should go on for ever [in argument in the Lords] to the possibility of an argument of which they disapproved remaining on its legs.'[28] Atkin was a lobbyist: keenly aware that only three law lords are required to form a majority, he was generally prepared to lobby a colleague 'in his room (and elsewhere) in the hope of winning him round.'[29] Atkin's daughter described how, 'He continued to use his powers of persuasion when he was sitting as a Lord of Appeal and would come home and say that he thought he had won his brothers over to his side or "so and so is still not convinced but I think he may be tomorrow."'[30] Not everyone took a benign view of Atkin's persuasive techniques and the robustness of his own

27   *Ibid*, at p 244.
28   Paterson, A *The Law Lords* (Macmillan, 1982), p 69.
29   *Ibid*, at p 113.
30   *Ibid*, at p 117.

views, '... it irked his colleagues that he was not open to persuasion in return.'[31]

Towards the end of his life Atkin started writing his autobiography. He wrote in a spidery (at times illegible) hand on lined paper. There are many crossings out and blotting smudges. These autobiographical fragments are now tied together with pink legal tape and filed in the Gray's Inn archive.[32] Atkin's draft proceeded no further than the time of his marriage and it was not until Geoffrey Lewis' work, nearly four decades later, that Atkin got the biography that he deserved.

Where his judicial work allowed, Atkin was actively involved in the wider legal world, particularly in the field of legal education. Among other activities he was Chairman of the Council of Legal Education (improving the quality of the education which he had received from the Council), sat on the Governing Board of the University College of Wales, Aberystwyth and took an active interest in the teaching of law at the University of London and its constituent colleges. Atkin was President of the Medico-Legal Society and remained devoted to Gray's Inn of which he was, on two occasions, Treasurer and where he lived while in London. He is described in a history of Gray's Inn as having 'exercised a most potent influence on its affairs. His figure slight and erect, his manner modest and charming, his face firm and keenly intelligent, yet gentle and reposeful, its clear-cut outline emphasised by the dome of his bald head – everything about him suggested the quiet strength and immoveable integrity that was his being.'[33] This somewhat idealised sketch of Atkin during his time as a senior resident of Gray's Inn is reflected in the Inn's portrait of him. However, Atkin's likeness is not, like many others in the Inn's collection, a judicial swagger portrait. He wears a simple benchers' gown over a lounge suit and gazes benignly down from the side of the Hall (sandwiched between Sir John Holt and Lord Birkenhead). From this vantage point Atkin continues to enjoy the comradeship of the students dining below.

Lord Atkin died at Aberdovey on 25 June 1944.

---

31   *Ibid.*
32   Atkin archive. File reference ATK1/BIOG/1/2.
33   Cowper, F *A Prospect of Gray's Inn* (Graya, 2nd ed, 1985), p 128.

Lord Thankerton

William Watson was born in Edinburgh on 8 December 1873. The third son of a judge (also a Lord of Appeal in Ordinary: Lord Watson of Thankerton), he also achieved the highest judicial office. After an undistinguished academic career in England (achieving only a third in law at Cambridge), his capacity for work took him to the Faculty of Advocates (admitted in 1899), to the rank of King's Counsel (just fifteen years later) and to a post as Advocate Depute in 1919. The Scots evidently appreciated the talents of their countryman in a way that the English did not. Along the way Thankerton was appointed Procurator of the Church of Scotland in 1918 and served as the Unionist Member of Parliament for South Lanarkshire from 1913 to 1918. In 1922 Thankerton was appointed Solicitor-General for Scotland and, successively, Lord Advocate (becoming, at the same time, a member of the Privy Council). In October 1924 Thankerton returned to the House of Commons as the Conservative Party MP for Carlisle. Just five years later he was advanced to the House of Lords as a Lord of Appeal in Ordinary (passing, like his father, to the highest judicial office directly from the bar).

Thankerton's obituary in *The Times* recorded, with magnificent condescension, that his appointment to the Appellate Committee was 'not unexpected but was received with no great warmth'[34] and another biographer has speculated that Thankerton's manner in court might have contributed to his unpopularity, '... as he had a habit of arguing somewhat aggressively with counsel and this did not decrease with the years. It was also said that his habit of knitting while on the bench irritated some counsel.'[35]

Thankerton is regarded as a cautious and conservative judge. His approach to the law is illustrated by his decision in *Fender v Mildmay*[36] which, in the Lords, was decided on the basis of a 3:2 split where the majority included Thankerton and Lords Atkin and Wright. The case arose out of an archaic cause of action: breach of a promise of marriage (the Respondent having failed to honour a promise to marry

34   *The Times*, 14 June 1948.
35   Simpson, AWB (ed) *Biographical Dictionary of the Common Law* (Butterworths, 1984), p 525.
36   [1938] AC 23 (HL).

the Appellant after obtaining a divorce from his previous wife). The majority held that no rule of public policy prevented the contractual promise from being enforced. In the course of his clear and succinct speech Thankerton said this:

> 'In the first place, there can be little question as to the proper function of the courts in questions of public policy. Their duty is to expound, and not to expand, such policy. That does not mean that they are precluded from applying an existing principle of public policy to a new set of circumstances, where such circumstances are clearly within the scope of the policy ... ... the courts must be watchful not to be influenced by their view of what the principle of public policy, or its limits, should be.'

Despite this cautious warning to himself and fellow judges, history will, perhaps, remember Thankerton best as being on the reforming, majority, side in *Donoghue v Stevenson*. He chose in his short speech to praise the approach of Lord Atkin (at least in his treatment of the precedents), rather than his fellow Scot and member of the majority, Lord Macmillan, 'I have had the privilege of considering the discussion of ... [the] authorities by my noble and learned friend, Lord Atkin, in the judgment which he has just delivered and I so entirely agree with it that I cannot usefully add anything to it.'[37] As I indicate above, Thankerton's judgment in *Donoghue v Stevenson* is, perhaps, the most distinctively Scottish. The only authorities that he cites are Scottish and he does not refer to a single English decision, although, as we have seen, he adopts Atkin's treatment of the same.

Lord Thankerton died in London on 13 June 1948.

Lord Macmillan

Hugh Pattison Macmillan was born and educated in Scotland. He was the only son among the six children of a Church of Scotland Minister, the Reverend Hugh Macmillan (who later became Moderator of the General Assembly of the Free Church of Scotland). Macmillan never forgot his upbringing as a son of the Presbyterian manse and, as a young man, assisted in preparing an edition of John Knox's *History of the Reformation in Scotland*. Macmillan was born in Glasgow on 20

---

37   [1932] AC 562, 604.

February 1873 and was educated at the Collegiate School in Greenock and then at Edinburgh University (where he read Philosophy) and, subsequently, at Glasgow University (where he read Law). By contrast to some of those with whom he sat in the Lords on the *Donoghue v Stevenson* appeal Macmillan's academic career did not disappoint: he achieved a first class degree in Philosophy and was awarded a scholarship during his law studies in Glasgow.

Macmillan went on to become one of the great names of his generation at the Scottish Bar. He spent three years in the Glasgow office of a solicitors' firm before being admitted to the Faculty of Advocates in 1897.[38] Despite lacking connections and influence Macmillan was successful enough to take silk in 1912. His practice continued to grow and he became in great demand as leading counsel (developing a particular expertise in local authority matters).

Macmillan had no known leanings to the Labour Party or to Socialism (he had, in fact, previously been adopted as a Unionist candidate for political office), but this did not prevent him from being appointed Lord Advocate by Ramsay MacDonald's Labour Government in 1924 (a non-political appointment as Scotland's senior law officer which was necessitated by the absence of suitable candidates within the ranks of Labour's Scottish politicians). Macmillan's appointment as Lord Advocate was accompanied by his being sworn in as a member of the Privy Council (he was also made an honorary bencher of the Inner Temple).

Macmillan returned to the Bar when the Labour Government fell and, for this second phase of his career, established himself as a barrister in London Chambers where his many appearances before the highest tribunals led to his appointment as standing counsel to Canada and Australia (from where appeals, at that time, were still ultimately destined for the law lords sitting in the Privy Council).

Macmillan was appointed a Lord of Appeal in Ordinary (with the conventional peerage) in 1930, just a year before argument was heard in *Donoghue v Stevenson*. He loved being a member of the House of Lords (observing modestly, 'I had for some years known that this was

---

38   Macmillan spent an apprenticeship, reading or 'devilling' for the Scottish Bar, with Charles J Guthrie who later became a judge of the Court of Session.

to be my ultimate destination'), describing his time there as 'some of the best years of my life.' He later provided the following summation of his colleagues on the *Donoghue v Stevenson* bench, 'Who could complain of tedium in days spent in the company of ... Lord Akin, shrewd and acute; Lord Tomlin with his gifts of intellectual charm; ... and Lord Thankerton with whom I shared memories of many years of association in the Parliament House in Edinburgh?'[39]

Macmillan's abiding interest in public service outside the law led him to accept an appointment as Minister of Information in 1939 – 1940 before he returned to the Appellate Committee in 1941 (where he continued to serve until retirement in 1947). He collected a great string of public appointments: among them, chairmanship of the Treasury Committee on finance and industry (1929 – 1931), the chairmanship of the Royal Commission on Lunacy (1924 – 1926) and, less predictably perhaps, the chairmanship of the committee on the preservation of works of art in enemy hands (1944 – 1947). Macmillan was instrumental in efforts to make the Faculty of Advocates' library collections more widely available for public use (it became the National Library of Scotland in 1925); his own extensive library was evenly divided between the House of Lords and the Faculty of Advocates after his death. Macmillan received honorary degrees from no fewer than thirteen Universities and was appointed GCVO in 1937.

One obituarist has recorded the following, rather catty, verdict on Macmillan: '... immensely successful, yet he never fulfilled his expectations. ... On the bench Macmillan seemed to spread himself thinly. He not only served on a myriad of government commissions and committees, he used his position as a law lord to sit on literally hundreds of educational, cultural and political committees. ... He remained a prolific writer and, many claimed, a collector of the famous.'[40]

Unusually for a judge, but perhaps characteristically for a man whose interests lay in the public, as well as legal, realm, Macmillan wrote a

---

39   Lord Macmillan *A Man of Law's Tale* (Macmillan & Co Ltd, 1952), p 149.
40   Robert Stevens in Simpson, AWB (ed) *Biographical Dictionary of the Common Law* (Butterworths, 1984), p 336.

rather immodest autobiography which was published posthumously in 1952: *A Man of Law's Tale*. His autobiography claims, by contrast to what was later hinted by Lord Denning,[41] that he always intended to find for Mrs Donoghue.[42] Like Atkin's formulation of the neighbour principle, Macmillan's speech in *Donoghue v Stevenson* also contains an aphorism which has entered the textbooks and histories of the common law world: 'The categories of negligence are never closed.'[43]

Macmillan was involved in two cases of public interest and importance which reached the Lords during and just after the Second World War. In *Liversidge*, as we have seen, he sided with the majority. In *Joyce v DPP*,[44] which concerned the post-war prosecution of the Anglo-Irish traitor and broadcaster of Nazi propaganda, William Joyce ('Lord Haw-Haw') Macmillan found, again with the majority, that Joyce could be tried for high treason in England, although his crimes were committed overseas.

Lord Macmillan died in Surrey on 5 September 1952.

Law lords: the dissenters

Lord Buckmaster

For a Victorian, the career of Lord Buckmaster's father, John Buckmaster, is remarkable for its social mobility. He started work as an agricultural labourer in the village of Slapton, Buckinghamshire at 10 years of age. He later became a joiner, attended teacher training college and then involved himself in political activism as an agitator for the cause of free trade. John Buckmaster secured the patronage of Prince Albert whom he assisted with the 1851 Great Exhibition. By the time that his third son, Stanley Owen Buckmaster, was born on 9 January 1861 John Buckmaster was on the staff of Imperial College, London and the family lived in a house in Wandsworth.

---

41   See, Lord Denning *The Discipline of the Law* (Butterworths, 1979), pp 229 – 230 (Lord Denning appears to have believed that Atkin persuaded the Scottish members of the Lords to find for Mrs Donoghue).
42   Lord Macmillan *A Man of Law's Tale* (Macmillan & Co Ltd, 1952), p 151.
43   [1932] AC 562, 619.
44   [1946] AC 347 (HL(E)).

Stanley Buckmaster attended Aldenham School: a Grammar endowed during the reign of Elizabeth I for the education of poor boys. From there he obtained a scholarship in Mathematics to Christ Church, Oxford (the College committee which recommended him for a Junior Studentship included Charles Dodgson of *Alice Through the Looking Glass* fame). Like Atkin, Buckmaster was frustrated in his ambition of achieving a first class degree; the examiners awarded him a second in Mathematics (provoking a series of exculpatory correspondence from Buckmaster to his father whose two older sons had achieved first class degrees).[45] In June 1884 Buckmaster was called to the Bar by the Inner Temple and became the pupil of Edward Beaumont at 6 New Square, Lincoln's Inn.

It took time for Buckmaster to establish himself at the Bar and, like Atkin, he actively considered an alternative career. Indeed, he took this rather further than Atkin by applying (unsuccessfully) for the post of Chief Clerk at the City and Guilds Institute. Buckmaster supplemented such income as he had by lecturing, writing (on bills of sale) and examining. Over time he acquired a reputation in the County Courts of the Midlands Circuit and success on this circuit led to briefs in the County and Police Courts in and around London. Eventually, Buckmaster was briefed in a chancery case. He then practised in common law and chancery until opting to specialise in chancery (which led him to choose to join Lincoln's Inn which has traditionally provided a home to chancery practitioners). Buckmaster took silk in 1902 (eighteen years after call). During his years in silk Buckmaster was instructed by Macmillan (who, as a Scottish Advocate, required the assistance of English leading counsel in a case involving an allegation of fraud). In his autobiography Macmillan describes Buckmaster's industry while preparing the case for appeal to the House of Lords. Preparation commenced at Buckmaster's Chambers in Old Square, Lincoln's Inn on Friday, continued through dinner at Buckmaster's Club (the Garrick) until the early hours of Saturday morning before concluding at Buckmaster's Porchester Terrace home late on Saturday night. Despite the rigour of life as Buckmaster's junior (or, perhaps,

---

45   Some of the notes of commiseration at his degree result which were received by Buckmaster from his teachers and tutors have the tone of condolences following a bereavement.

because of it), Macmillan's assessment of Buckmaster was highly complimentary (even allowing for the generally polite tone of judicial autobiography), 'I thought then and have always thought that he possessed the most relevant and most cogent powers of exposition and argument that I have ever known.'[46]

In 1889 Buckmaster married Edith Lewin and the couple settled in West Hampstead. On hearing of the engagement his father wrote to him:

> 'I am very glad that you are not engaged to a frivolous, empty-headed woman, and there seems no reason why you should not live happily together in a moderate kind of way. You must bear in mind that your income will be liable to fluctuations, but if you have your health and concentrate your mind on your profession I think … you have a fair prospect. You may not be Lord Chancellor but you may in your own home be equal to him in happiness, which does not consist in the abundance of our possessions, but the fewness of our necessities.'[47]

Politically, Buckmaster was a Liberal. In the 1880s he had been to hear Gladstone speak and had spoken in support of the Liberal candidate for Evesham in Worcestershire (close to the city of Worcester in whose County Court Buckmaster had first achieved success at the Bar). In 1903 Buckmaster was adopted as the Liberal party candidate for the borough of Cambridge and he was returned as Member of Parliament at the 1906 general election.[48] In his maiden speech he bravely chose to set party advantage and political convention aside by defending a judge suspected (by the Liberal Party) of having shown bias (to the Conservative Party) in his judgment in two election petitions. Buckmaster later explained his actions by asserting that he sought to defend the 'great system' of justice embodied by the judge, rather than the judge himself. Buckmaster lost his seat in the second general election in 1910, but was adopted for the Yorkshire seat of Keighley and subsequently returned to the Commons.

Buckmaster acquired a great reputation as an orator in the rather florid rhetorical style of his time. A first hand account of his speaking

---

46   Lord Macmillan *A Man of Law's Tale* (Macmillan & Co Ltd, 1952), p 119.
47   As reported in Heuston, RFV *Lives of the Lord Chancellors 1885 – 1940* (Clarendon Press, 1964), p 255.
48   With a majority of 308 on a turnout of 94%.

ability, published by one devoted fan in 1925, records the impression that he made on those listening:

> 'He is a man of medium height; and lean. He has a lean face; high cheek bones, hollow cheeks, an aquiline nose, deep set blue eyes, and an earnestness of manner that reaches the quality of solemnity. As he begins to speak he twists a gold ring on his left hand, he twists it rapidly, eagerly; it is the sole indication of nervousness he displays. He speaks with admirable, clear and easily heard voice, which never falters, which speaks admirable, choicely arranged, finely inflected language ... .'[49]

In October 1913 Buckmaster was appointed Solicitor-General (replacing Sir John Simon, twelve years younger than Buckmaster, who was promoted to become senior Law Officer).[50] In May 1915 Buckmaster, exceeding his father's expectations, became Lord Chancellor in succession to Lord Haldane (after Sir John Simon, then Attorney-General, declined to accept the post). While most commentators were generous about the appointment, *The Times* sourly described Buckmaster's appointment as, 'the reward for tolerable success at the Bar, and diligent but commonplace party services.'[51] After just eighteen months as Lord Chancellor, the Government which Buckmaster served lost office. Buckmaster devoted the remainder of his career to his judicial work (primarily in the House of Lords and Privy Council). Further honours were awarded to Buckmaster. In 1930 he was appointed GCVO and, three years later, was promoted within the peerage when he was made a Viscount.

One of the ironies of Buckmaster's role as leader of the dissenting voices in *Donoghue v Stevenson*, seeking to maintain the status quo, is that his reputation as politician and judge is that of a liberal reformer. His reforming interests led him to advocate, among other causes, liberalising the divorce laws (so as to recognise desertion as a ground for a decree), the abolition of capital punishment, female suffrage, birth control and improving the quality of housing for the poor. His judicial pronouncements also contain evidence of his reforming zeal.

---

49   (1925) 3 Canadian Bar Review 495.
50   Attorney-General.
51   *The Times*, 25 May, 1915.

In *Bourne v Keane*,[52] decided by the Lords in 1918, Buckmaster, setting precedent aside, spoke strongly in defence of the freedom of a Roman Catholic testator to make bequests (the case concerned the legality of a bequest funding Masses for the repose of the testator's soul and the judgments contain wonderfully detailed treatments of the Elizabethan Church settlement and the Roman Catholic emancipation statutes of the late eighteenth century). In the common law field, shortly before *Donoghue v Stevenson* reached the Lords, Buckmaster was unconcerned by the niceties of whether a child injured by a machine was technically characterised as licensee or trespasser. He was simply satisfied, on the facts, that there was negligence and that the occupier was liable (Buckmaster's speech in this case, *Excelsior Wire Rope Company Limited v Callan*,[53] demonstrates an engaging familiarity with the games that children played in the 1920s and contains a detailed description of one such game: 'Prisoner's Base'). Buckmaster's reforming instincts were such that he was rumoured to have been considered for a return to the woolsack in 1924[54] – so becoming a member of Ramsay MacDonald's Labour Government – although the appointment famously went to Lord Haldane.[55]

In his summary assessment of Buckmaster's contribution to the law of torts Heuston describes his speech in *Donoghue v Stevenson* in the following terms, 'Buckmaster dissented in a speech of almost passionate sarcasm: he thought the majority had passed the permissible limits of judicial law-making. Time has vindicated the majority rather than Buckmaster: *Donoghue v Stevenson* has been applied in scores of subsequent cases. But his dissent is still of value to the jurist because it makes plain the extent of the change effected by the majority.'[56] An alternative verdict might emphasise Buckmaster's position as politician, as well as judge. Might it be that, in *Donoghue v Stevenson*, his passionate advocacy of limits to the law-making power of (unelected) judges was informed by his own experience as an

---

52   [1919] AC 815 (HL(E)).
53   [1930] AC 404 (HL(E)).
54   Heuston, RFV *Lives of the Lord Chancellors 1885 – 1940* (Clarendon Press, 1964), p 299.
55   Who gave his name to the Haldane Society of Labour Lawyers.
56   Heuston, RFV *Lives of the Lord Chancellors 1885 – 1940* (Clarendon Press, 1964), Appendix.

(elected) politician and a belief that those who change the law should account for their views and actions to the electorate.[57] Buckmaster's entry in the *Dictionary of National Biography* records the following, refreshingly unsanitised, assessment by a distinguished fellow judge,

> '... when Lord Dunedin was asked: "Whom do you regard as the greatest colleague you have had?", he answered: "You will be surprised when I tell you – Buckmaster; I have not and I never have had any sympathy with Buckmaster's political ideas and performances and I think him to be a sentimentalist – unless he is sitting on his arse on the bench; there he is one of the most learned, one of the most acute, and the fairest judge I ever sat with; and he will leave much in the books.'[58]

At least one advocate who appeared before Buckmaster took a rather different view. In his autobiography DN Pritt QC described an occasion when Buckmaster tried, in a series of hostile interventions, to 'smash' the appeal that he was arguing, 'The warfare went on for a day or two, and then Lord Buckmaster said: "Mr Pritt, their Lordships ... would like to know how long this nonsense is going to continue." [Pritt] replied: "About ten days, if interruptions continue on their present scale, and a few days less if they diminish."' Like most of the courtroom anecdotes told by barristers, the story concludes with a triumph: having eventually lost his temper to shout at the law lords, 'Your Lordships are going to hear this case!', Pritt duly won his appeal.[59]

Lord Buckmaster died at his Hyde Park home on 5 December 1934.

57   Russell, G *Dictionary of National Biography 1931 – 1940*, Entry on Buckmaster, p 120, 'Any temptation to find a construction of the law which would "right a wrong" in the particular case or would mitigate a hardship caused by the law itself was resolutely resisted. No one ever saw more clearly that hard cases make bad law, and that the cure in such cases was for parliament.'
58   Russell, G *Dictionary of National Biography 1931 – 1940*, Entry on Buckmaster, p 120.
59   Reported in Paterson, A *The Law Lords* (Macmillan, 1982), p 68.

Lord Tomlin

Thomas James Cheshyre Tomlin was born in Canterbury, Kent on 6 May 1867. His education, following a conventional path, took him from Harrow to New College where he graduated in 1889 with a first in Jurisprudence to which, two years later, he added a second in the BCL. Tomlin and Atkin completed their undergraduate studies at Oxford in the same year: Tomlin with a first in Jurisprudence; Atkin with a second in Greats. Tomlin was called to the Bar at the Middle Temple in 1891 and his practice at the Chancery Bar later led him to join Lincoln's Inn (he subsequently became a Bencher at Lincoln's). Tomlin's Pupil Master was RJ Parker (later to become Lord Parker of Waddington) and, after the completion of pupillage, he continued to devil for Parker until the latter's elevation to the Bench in 1906 (after six years as junior equity counsel to the Treasury).

Parker's appointment to the Bench coincided with an increase in the volume and quality of work available for his former pupil and Tomlin was appointed junior equity counsel to the Inland Revenue and other government departments (although he did not succeed his Pupil Master as junior equity counsel to the Treasury). Tomlin took silk in 1913 (in common with the conventions of the Chancery Bar of the time Tomlin was first attached to the court of a specific judge before, in 1919, he 'went special' which gave him the right to appear in the court of any judge). In silk, Tomlin's practice expanded beyond the Chancery Division and he regularly appeared in the House of Lords and Privy Council.

Tomlin was appointed as a judge of the Chancery Division in 1923 and, from there, in 1929 he became a Lord of Appeal in Ordinary (without an intermediate appointment serving time in the Court of Appeal). Tomlin's professional career did not, by contrast to some of those with whom he presided in *Donoghue v Stevenson*, include any time as a serving politician. While he served as Chairman of certain Committees and Royal Commissions (including the Royal Commission on the Civil Service, the University of London Commissioners and the Home Office Advisory Committee on the Cruelty to Animals Act) his career was not a public one. The appointment of Tomlin to the bench was not politically influenced. He was appointed and served as a lawyer. One biographer commented, 'Tomlin espoused a highly formalistic approach to law. He sought a balanced approach and his speeches, for instance, in workmen's compensation cases, are a model of fairness. Yet he is remembered most for his cautious decisions.'[60] Tomlin's brief speech in *Donoghue v Stevenson* may be regarded as exemplifying such caution. He largely confines himself to commenting that the reasoning and conclusions of Buckmaster 'accord in every respect with my own views',[61] but also observes that the majority decision would have 'alarming consequences';[62] it may be that those two words express most accurately what Tomlin really felt about the extension to the law which the majority proposed.

Lord Simonds spoke warmly two decades after Tomlin's death, 'It is not seemly to weigh the pronouncements of living judges, but it is, I think, permissible to say that the opinion of few, if any, judges of the past command greater respect than those of Lord Tomlin.'[63] Unlike some of his more celebrated contemporaries, Tomlin has been immortalised. In a 1927 Practice Note,[64] before he reached the House of Lords, he described a procedural order for the compromise of proceedings by which a stay was achieved upon terms which were scheduled to the order, but did not otherwise form part of the order. This somewhat obscure technical innovation has guaranteed lasting fame: lawyers today routinely draft and refer to 'Tomlin orders'.

Lord Tomlin died at Canterbury on 13 August 1935.

Lawyers

Mrs Donoghue was represented in the House of Lords by George Morton KC who led W R Milligan (both of the Scottish Bar). Mr Stevenson's counsel were W G Normand (then Solicitor-General for Scotland) who led J L Clyde (of the Scottish Bar) and T Elder Jones (of the English Bar).

Normand was born in Fife in 1884 and successively educated at Fettes College, Oriel College and the Universities of Paris and

---

60   Robert Stevens in Simpson, AWB (ed) *Biographical Dictionary of the Common Law* (Butterworths, 1984), p 509.
61   [1932] AC 562, 599.
62   *Ibid*, at p 600.
63   *Government of India v Taylor* [1955] AC 491, 50 (HL).
64   [1927] WN 290.

Edinburgh. He was admitted to the Faculty of Advocates in 1910. His career was interrupted by service in the First World War (as an officer in the Royal Engineers) between 1915 and 1918. On his return to practice his ascent in the legal and political arenas was rapid: he was appointed King's Counsel in 1925; in 1929 he became Solicitor-General for Scotland; in 1931 he was elected Unionist Member of Parliament for West Edinburgh. He occupied the post of Solicitor-General at the time of the *Donoghue v Stevenson* appeal. In 1933 Normand became Lord Advocate and two years later he vacated his seat in Parliament in order to become a judge: Lord Justice-General and Lord President of the Court of Session. In 1947 Normand himself reached the House of Lords when he was appointed a Lord of Appeal in Ordinary. He continued to sit intermittently in the Lords after his retirement in 1953. He died in Edinburgh on 5 October 1962.

Normand's first junior, James Latham McDiarmid Clyde, was born in Edinburgh into a distinguished Scottish legal family in 1898. His father was James Avon Clyde: Lord Justice-General and Lord President of the Court of Session between 1920 and 1935. After attending the Universities of Oxford and Edinburgh Clyde followed his father to the Faculty of Advocates (to which he was admitted in 1924). He took silk four years after judgment in *Donoghue v Stevenson*. Between 1950 and 1954 he was Conservative MP for North Edinburgh and served as Lord Advocate from 1951. In 1954 he again followed his father by becoming Lord Justice-General and Lord President of the Court of Session. Clyde died in 1975.

Leading for Mrs Donoghue was George Morton KC. Morton was 62 years of age when he appeared in the House of Lords (having been in silk since 1918). By 1932 he had served as Advocate-Depute between 1911 and 1917 and had also sat on the bench as Sheriff of Dumfries and Galloway between 1917 and 1924. *Donoghue v Stevenson* was his swansong at the bar. He was appointed to the bench as Sheriff of Aberdeen, Kincardine and Banff in 1932 and died on 17 July 1953 (by which time he had been knighted). Morton's junior, Milligan, had already achieved fame before he became entangled in *Donoghue v Stevenson*. As a student he raced Lord Birkenhead around a College quadrangle (a race which was later immortalised in the film *Chariots of Fire*).[65] He also became a politician and was later appointed Lord Advocate. The official web site of the Oxford University Athletics Club continues to honour W R Milligan as a member of the 1920 world record-holding team for the 4 by 880-yard relay.[66] Milligan apparently never met Mrs Donoghue. Her case proceeded on the law, rather than the facts, and so it is unlikely that she attended any consultation with counsel in Edinburgh or the hearing in the Court of Session.[67]

Walter Leechman, Mrs Donoghue's solicitor, was also politically inclined: a councillor who sat on the Glasgow City Council. He specialised in reparation cases and founded a legal dynasty. One son took over the family law firm in 1950 and another became a judge of the Court of Session: Lord Leechman. Mr Leechman's solicitor son recorded his father's support for compulsory education, his dislike of inequality and his concern for the less fortunate. One can see how Mrs Donoghue would have excited his sympathy and Mr Leechman's son is convinced that his father, by apparent contrast to counsel, would have met Mrs Donoghue and her friend, and satisfied himself that both were telling the truth and would make credible witnesses. Mr Leechman did not permit his family to read the Sunday newspapers or to go to the cinema, although he did make an exception for Charlie Chaplin films. There was clearly a gentle side to him, 'He loved nature. He was always gathering wild flowers and comparing them with the ones in books he had in his bookcase. He kept bees and would not harm a bee, although they did not have the same love for him – sometimes he would go into the office with his eyes practically closed as a result of bee stings, although he always used a net.'[68]

---

65   Taylor, MR 'Mrs Donoghue's Journey' SCLR Internet site.

66   Completed in 7:50:4.

67   This information was passed by Milligan to Lord Rodger and is recorded in Rodger, A 'Mrs Donoghue and Alfenus Varus' (1988) 41 CLP 1, 8, n 94. It should, however, be noted that Gibson, not Milligan, represented Mrs Donoghue when her case was before the Outer House at first instance in the Court of Session.

68   Leechman, JF 'Mrs Donoghue's Solicitor' in Burns QC, P T and Lyons, S J (eds) *Donoghue v Stevenson and the Modern Law of Negligence The Paisley Papers* (The Continuing Legal Education Society of British Columbia, 1991), p 275.

5. ROOTS OF THE NEIGHBOUR PRINCIPLE

'Our hope as Christians is not fundamentally in man's naked goodwill and rationality. We believe that he can overcome the deadly selfishness of class or sect or race by discovering himself as a child of the universal God of love. When a man realises that he is a beloved child of the Creator of all, then he is ready to see his neighbours as brothers and sisters.'

Runcie, R 'Our Neighbours are indeed like us' (from the sermon preached at the service of Thanksgiving which followed the Falklands Conflict: St Paul's Cathedral, 26 July 1982)

Darwin's theory of evolution provides a convenient metaphor for the development of the tort of negligence as a cause of action. Causes of action which developed during the common law's formative period adapted over time to new social conditions. With the benefit of hindsight, a family tree can be drawn to chart the evolutionary processes which connect the action on the case to the tort that we know today. There has been the discovery of occasional 'missing links' along the way; only the fittest causes of action have survived.

The law of product liability, as it was in the early years of the twentieth century, neatly illustrates how far we had come before *Donoghue v Stevenson* was decided. A consumer's options in tort were, at this time, very limited (he may well, of course, have a straightforward cause of action in contract if he was the purchaser of the relevant goods). If the goods purchased proved to be dangerous in circumstances where the claimant had relied on a fraudulent misrepresentation that they were safe then a cause of action in tort would be available. Equally, if the goods were within a category of articles acknowledged as dangerous *per se* then a cause of action would usually be available to the consumer injured by the same and this cause of action could be pursued against the supplier of the goods. An adjunct to this cause of action existed where the supplier had knowledge of some defect in the goods which made them dangerous (and, again, in these circumstances, there is case law, prior to 1932, which acknowledges a cause of action). It was outside these existing categories that the injured consumer would run into difficulties which *Donoghue v Stevenson* eventually swept away. However, the formulaic approach to product liability which existed prior to *Donoghue v Stevenson*, and which may appear primitive to those used to the modern tort of negligence, had evolved over many centuries.

Negligent acts and omissions have always been with us and these have formed the subject matter of legal disputes since the earliest case notes were written down. The tort of negligence, however, was young when *Donoghue v Stevenson* was decided. It would probably surprise the present generation of undergraduate law students to learn that the standard practitioner textbook, *Clerk & Lindsell on Torts* (supposed by some to be as old as the law itself), did not contain a separate chapter dedicated to the law of negligence until its 1947 edition. Against this background *Donoghue v Stevenson* represents a pivotal moment: confirmation that negligence is a distinct tort and the identification of the duty of care as the means by which to move the law forwards and, at the same time, to identify its boundaries.

The evolution of negligence: a succinct chronology

The opinions of those law lords who dissented in *Donoghue v Stevenson* were driven by precedent: the concern that the law should not advance beyond the limits established by previous decisions. The discussion in the House of Lords was concerned with the substantive law. That is, with the established rules and principles which should properly be applied to the facts of Mrs Donoghue's case; it was in this context that the doctrine of precedent became relevant. At a much earlier stage in its evolution English law was even more formalistically bound up with questions of precedent. Until the nineteenth century, the common law was principally concerned with precedent as it governed *procedural* formalities, rather than substantive rules and principles. A remedy would only be provided by the courts where there was an existing procedure, a precedent, to provide a means to redress. In other words, the development of the law and its substantive rules was inextricably linked to the law of procedure and, specifically, to the Writ: the document used to commence proceedings in the King's courts.

From around the twelfth century onwards it was necessary for the prospective claimant to purchase a writ for issue in the Court of Common Pleas and, in many instances, the King's Bench. Writs for this purpose were purchased from the King's Chancery. At first, these writs simply acted like a passport: providing access to the courts for those who had paid for the privilege. Accordingly, the Chancellor and his clerks were able to draw up writs for use by litigants in the form most appropriate to the right being asserted or the remedy sought. Whilst precedent played a part in this process (providing forms of words and standard phrases and texts) the system was sufficiently adaptable to meet the needs of the individual claimant and the particular circumstances of his case. However, over time the accretions of past practice hardened into something less malleable. As the distinguished legal historian Professor Baker has described it, 'Once a writ had been issued it became a precedent for the future, and there was a reluctance to change the formula if it was found serviceable.'[1] Precedent promoted fairness and consistency and also proved convenient (it was, no doubt, easier to adopt a previous precedent than to draft a new one from scratch). By the middle of the thirteenth century, the reluctance to change serviceable formulae, to which Baker refers, had produced a register of precedents. In 1258 the Provisions of Oxford required that the Chancellor, who presided over the Chancery (responsible for the issuing of writs), be sworn to issue no writs lacking precedent without the consent of the King's Council. The system of precedent was of fundamental importance where it governed the procedure, the writ, used to commence proceedings in the courts of Common Pleas and King's Bench. First, without the use of the appropriate writ (the correct writ from the register of precedents) no remedy could be provided by the King's courts. Second, and of no less importance, the selection of writ drove the litigation from start to finish and directed the procedure and modes of trial that would be used to determine the outcome. As a consequence of this, the substantive law (the abstract rules and principles which form the curriculum of today's undergraduate law student) was, for most purposes, synonymous with the forms of originating process, the writs, used to commence legal proceedings. In the Law French of his day Stonor J, a fourteenth-century judge, was able to say, '*bref*

---

1   Baker, J H *An Introduction to English Legal History* (Butterworths, 4th ed, 2002), p 55.

original est fondement de ley' (as translated by Professor Baker, 'The original writ ... [is] the basis of the law.')[2]

There were a variety of original writs and their taxonomy was a major concern of the earliest legal textbook writers. The writ of trespass was of considerable importance in the development of the law of negligence. In the precedent-heavy procedures of the thirteenth century courts a writ of trespass was available to commence one's action where the commission of the wrong was accompanied by force and arms ('*vi et armis*') or where the wrong was against the King's peace ('*contra pacem regis*'). Only wrongs concerned with the use of force or with the breach of the King's peace were sufficiently serious to infringe the King's interest and so to justify access to his courts. However, the requirement of force and arms became inconvenient for those who required access to royal justice for more prosaic disputes (including disputes alleging what we would now recognise as negligence; self-evidently, a defendant who performed a task for the claimant in a negligent or careless manner could not be said to have performed it with force). Litigants began to side step the formalities and proceedings alleging the use of force were commenced where this was little more than a legal fiction (some judges were prepared to overlook this manipulative use of court procedures). In time, the fiction was abandoned altogether and, from around the middle of the fourteenth century, writs can be found which omitted the words, *vi et armis*. The new writs started to reflect the particular circumstances, the special facts, of the individual claimant's case. The special facts were introduced with the use of the latin '*cum*': 'Whereas ...' (a usage which was still being utilised in the pleadings in Mrs Donoghue's case). Those forms of action where force and arms was not alleged – what Professor Baker refers to as the 'non-forcible trespass' cases – came to be known as trespass on the case.

At this stage in its development an action in breach of contract was often described as a tort or trespass. Indeed, it was common to allege negligence in the performance of a contract and throughout the sixteenth and seventeenth centuries the case reports disclose a number of cases in which negligence was alleged where the parties were in privity of contract with each other. In 1600, for example, the Countess

---

2   *Ibid*, at p 56.

of Shrewsbury brought a claim in the Court of Queen's Bench against Richard Crompton, a Master of the Bench of the Middle Temple. It was alleged that the Countess had let a house to Master Crompton and he had negligently burnt down the house by failing to keep an eye on the fire. The parties to this action had a contract, the lease, with each other. However, the basis for the action lay in the negligence of the defendant. The claimant lost; the court was not persuaded that the tenant of the property, who took the house only to occupy and use it and undertook no charge of looking after it, was liable ('No one would say that if a tenant ... suffered the house to fall down for want of repair, without giving notice to the lessor that it was in decay, an action would lie. ... Likewise here.')[3]

Eventually, contract emerged as a distinct cause of action (an action of *'assumpsit'*) founded on a promise supported by consideration (the price of the promise). It came to be seen as wholly distinct from actions in tort to the extent that, by the mid-1600s, there was objection to the pursuit of an action in contract and an action in tort in the same proceedings. While contract was establishing itself as a distinct cause of action, allegations of negligence continued to require something more than the negligent act or omission itself in order for the defendant's wrongdoing to be actionable. There were cases where the defendant had undertaken to provide a service or a particular task for the claimant (see, for example, the Countess of Shrewsbury's case referred to above where the action foundered because no such undertaking could be found when the court examined the parties' relationship). The presence of an undertaking could convert a non-actionable careless act into a cause of action which could be pursued in the courts. Equally, in the absence of an undertaking, claimants took to alleging a negligent failure to comply with the customs of the realm as a means by which a non-actionable wrongdoing could become a tortious act. Categories of case can be found where a breach of the custom of the realm was utilised.

While actions for what we would now refer to as negligence continued to develop in this rather piecemeal fashion, trespass cases

---

3   *Countess of Shrewsbury v Crompton* (1600) *per* Gawdy J. Reported in: Baker, JH and Milson, SFC *Sources of English Legal History Private Law to 1750* (Butterworth, 1986), p 565.

which did not involve the use of force continued to be categorised by distinct procedural forms. Ultimately, trespass became detached from the action on the case and these forms were later distinguished by an eighteenth-century judge (Fortescue J) in the following way: if a man threw a log onto the highway and struck a person passing by then an action would lie in trespass; if, conversely, a log was left on a right of way so that a passer by might trip over it then an action on the case would be available.[4] In other words, if the defendant *directly* caused injury then he was liable to be sued in trespass and if he was the *indirect* cause of such injury then case would be used. In his influential 1926 article on the history of negligence Winfield refers to this phenomenon as the distinction between a commission and an omission and charts the development of negligence as the emergence of liability for omissions:[5]

> '[Referring to Coke's judgment in the *Earl of Shrewsbury's case*[6]] We may pause here to note the identification of nonfeasance with negligence, and to stress the inference that action upon the case for omission in general must have crossed Coke's mind as a possibility, even if not much use was made of it in practice.'[7]

The distinction between the direct and indirect commission of injury found expression in *Blackstone's Commentaries on the Laws of England* which was first published in 1765: '... whenever the act

---

4   *Reynolds v Clarke* (1725).
5   The nonfeasance/misfeasance distinction survives in a number of present day causes of action; for example, in highway claims, save for the statutory cause of action for nonfeasance in the form of a failure to maintain the highway (s 41 of the Highways Act 1980), there is no cause of action at common law against the highway authority for nonfeasance. It has been argued that the real utility of *Donoghue v Stevenson* was in eradicating an erroneous failure to distinguish nonfeasance and misfeasance: the misuse of *Winterbottom v Wright* as authority for denying a remedy to those injured by negligent misfeasance: see, Smith, JC & Burns, P '*Donoghue v Stevenson* – the Not so Golden Anniversary' (1983) 46 MLR 147, 159. However, Smith & Burns believed that *Donoghue v Stevenson* was overused and extended the limits of liability much further than Lord Atkin ever contemplated – at pp 162 – 163: 'Fifty years after the decision ... the pendulum has now swung from over-particularisation to the other extreme of over-generalisation and in spite of all warnings of even Lord Atkin himself, nearly all negligence cases are being forced onto the Procrustean bed for his "neighbour principle."'
6   9 Rep 46.
7   Winfield, PH 'History of Negligence in Torts' (1926) 42 LQR 184, 193.

itself is directly and immediately injurious to the person or property of another, and therefore necessarily accompanied with some force, an action of trespass *vi et armis* will lie; but, if the injury is only consequential, a special action of trespass on the case may be brought.'[8] However, a looser approach to the treatment of actions in negligence can also be found from the seventeenth century onwards. In *Boulton v Banks*,[9] for example, decided in the reign of Charles I, an action upon the case was brought against the owner of a mastiff which killed a farrowing sow. Objection was taken to the form of proceedings used by the claimant (case, rather than trespass), but the court held that, 'the action well lies: for it is not lawful to keep dogs to bite and kill swine.' Similarly, in *Star v Rookesby*,[10] a case from the reign of Queen Anne, the claimant and defendant occupied adjoining land separated by a fence that was in disrepair. The defendant's cattle escaped through the fence onto the claimant's land where they caused damage. The court considered, among other things, whether the action lay in case (for nonfeasance in the negligent failure to keep the fence in good repair) or in trespass for the damage (directly) caused by the cattle while on the claimant's land. The answer was, 'Either trespass or case lies; trespass, because it was the plaintiff's ground and not the defendant's; and case, because the first wrong was a nonfeasance and neglect to repair, and that omission is the gist of the action; and the trespass is only consequential damage.'

From the eighteenth century onwards an improvement in road surfaces made carriage driving faster and resulted in more running down actions:[11] the birth of accident litigation and with it, perhaps, the compensation culture beloved of today's middle market press drove the development of the law.[12] Disasters and transport related

---

8   Morrison, W (ed) *Blackstone's Commentaries on the Laws of England* (Cavendish Publishing Limited, 2001), vol III, p 163.

9   7 Car. 1. Roll 276; 79 ER 822.

10   1 Salk. 335; 91 ER 295.

11   See, for example, *Aston v Heaven* (1797) 2 Esp. 533; 170 ER 445. The case proceeded in the Court of Common Pleas, and comprised an action brought against coach owners by passengers injured as a result, so they alleged, of the negligent driving of a coach: *per* Eyre CJ, 'This action stands on the ground of negligence alone.' The passengers' action was dismissed.

12   Professor Baker suggests that entrepreneurs with capital (for the development, for example, of roads and other infrastructure) and the ability to pass the overheads

fatalities were not confined to the roads during the eighteenth and nineteenth centuries. The development of railways and industrial shipping also supplied what Cornish and Clark have referred to as the 'morbid glamour' which is nowadays reserved for aviation disasters.[13] Throughout the eighteenth and nineteenth centuries the growth in industrial mass transportation, the accidents associated with this and the easier availability of defendants with assets who could be sued all contributed to an increase in personal injury litigation and, with this, the development of the law. Between 1875 and 1899 12,870 railway employees were killed at work and 68,575 were injured.[14] Death and injury on such an industrial scale resulted in litigation.

By the middle of the eighteenth century, the neighbour principle itself (or, at least, something very close to it) found recognition in a well-known text on the *Law Relative to Trials at Nisi Prius* (printed in 1768 from a mid-eighteenth-century manuscript; it later became a standard text):

> '**Of injuries arising from negligence or folly**. Every man ought to take reasonable care that he does not injure his neighbour. Therefore, whenever a man receives any hurt through the default of another, though the same were not wilful, yet if it be occasioned by negligence or folly the law gives him an action to recover damages for the injury so sustained. ... where the defendant, by uncocking his gun, accidentally wounded the plaintiff who was standing by to see him do it. If a man ride an unruly horse in any place much frequented (such as Lincoln's Inn Fields) to break and tame him, if the horse hurt another, he will be liable to an action; and it may be brought against the master as well as the servant, for it will be intended that he sent the servant to train the horse there; or it may be brought against the master alone.[15]

---

associated with litigation to their customers also supported the development of the law: Baker, JH *An Introduction to English Legal History* (Butterworths, 4th ed, 2002), p 412.

13   Cornish, WR and Clark, G de N *Law and Society in England 1750 – 1950* (Sweet & Maxwell, 1989), p 484.

14   *Ibid*, at p 485 citing the 1900 Royal Commission on Accidents to Railway Servants.

15   The case to which the author refers is *Mitchell v Allestry* (1676). This running down action concerned a woman knocked over by a carriage drawn by two 'wild and untamed mares' being broken to carriage driving in a crowded and, therefore, highly unsuitable place (Lincoln's Inn Fields). The action did not comfortably fit into any of the existing categories. There was judgment for the injured claimant. The Court

The servants of a carman ran over a boy in the streets and maimed him by negligence; an action was brought against the master, and the plaintiff recovered. ... However it is proper in such cases to prove that the injury was such as would probably follow from the act done: as, that many people were assembled together near the place at the time of his whipping the horse, or that the person run over was standing near and within sight.'[16]

A person ought to take reasonable care not to injure his neighbour. One's neighbour is the person who (it can be foreseen) will probably be injured as a result of one's failure to act with reasonable care. The author of this treatise, containing its 'precocious generalisation',[17] identified the neighbour principle (or something very close to it) more than 180 years before Lord Atkin did. It seems likely that this author was influenced as much by the New Testament as he was by the case law to which he refers. The identity of the author of the *Law Relative to Trials at Nisi Prius* is not wholly clear, although Professor Baker believes that it might have been Lord Bathurst (1714 – 1794) (successively, Solicitor-General, Attorney-General, Lord Chancellor from 1771 to 1778 and a contemporary of Lord Mansfield and Sir William Blackstone).[18] If Lord Bathurst was, indeed, the author of the treatise then his prescience must deserve greater celebration than the damning verdict of one biographer that, 'By a universal consensus of opinion Earl Bathurst is pronounced to have been the least efficient Lord Chancellor of the ... [eighteenth] century.'[19]

From the nineteenth century onwards there was comparatively rapid progress towards what we now know as negligence. Winfield (inviting 'instant criticism') places the arrival of an independent tort

---

accepted the claimant's plea that, 'It was the defendant's fault to bring a wild horse into such a place where mischief might probably be done by reason of the concourse of people.' *Mitchell v Allestry* (1676) can be found in Baker, JH and Milson, SFC *Sources of English Legal History Private Law to 1750* (Butterworth, 1986), p 572.

16   Baker, JH and Milson, SFC *Sources of English Legal History Private Law to 1750* (Butterworth, 1986), p 578.

17   Cornish, WR and Clark, G de N *Law and Society in England 1750 – 1950* (Sweet & Maxwell, 1989), p 505.

18   Baker and Milsom record that the treatise was formerly attributed to Sir Francis Buller: Baker, J H and Milson, S F C *Sources of English Legal History Private Law to 1750* (Butterworth, 1986), p 578, n 6.

19   *Dictionary of National Biography.*

of negligence in the period from 1825 onwards, 'Perhaps one of the chief agencies in the growth of the idea is industrial machinery. Early railway trains, in particular, were notable neither for speed nor for safety. They killed any object from a Minister of State to a wandering cow, and this naturally reacted on the law.'[20] The general utility of Lord Bathurst's neighbour principle, while regarded as a statement of useful jurisprudential principle, was not deployed as the means by which to advance the law of negligence until it was picked up by Brett MR at the end of the nineteenth century and, ultimately, by Lord Atkin in the first half of the twentieth century. By the end of the nineteenth century a cause of action in negligence was acknowledged to lie in a series of categories (whether closed or otherwise): carelessness in the exercise of a trade or profession; failure to keep the roads in reasonable repair; road traffic accidents and colliding vehicles. However, there was no overarching body of principle. The concept of the duty of care, capable of general application, was far from fully formed.

A tort of negligence

By the later nineteenth century, negligence was coming of age. The case law at the turn of the century provides an interesting lesson in social history. Its subject matter comprises defective, horse-drawn carriages, negligent surveyors, coal wagons without brakes, farm boys kicked in the head by ill-tempered horses and, perhaps, most strikingly, a bottle of ginger beer which, instead of poisoning its consumer, exploded in his face. In *Bates v Batey & Company*[21] the claimant, a 12-year-old boy, bought a bottle of ginger beer from a shopkeeper in Barnes in south west London. The shopkeeper had, in turn, bought the bottle from the defendants: manufacturers of ginger beer and mineral water. The manufacturers had filled the bottle with ginger beer, but had purchased the bottle from a third party. The claimant took the bottle home and tried, without success, to open it. In the course of doing so, the bottle exploded in the claimant's face and he lost his right eye as a result. The claimant brought proceedings against the defendant for his injuries. The claimant's case at trial was that they ought to have seen the defect in the bottle which caused it

---

20   Winfield, PH 'History of Negligence in Torts' (1926) 42 LQR 184, 195.
21   [1913] 3 KB 351 (KB).

to explode and that if they had exercised reasonable care and skill in their examination of the bottle then they would have discovered that it was defective (in other words the defect was patent, rather than latent, and could have been discovered by the exercise of reasonable care). The case was tried by a jury and, on these factual issues, the claimant succeeded. Horridge J, who heard the case, also concluded that the defective bottle of ginger beer was dangerous. However, the claimant's claim was dismissed. Horridge J held, following an 1851 decision in another product liability case called *Longmeid v Holliday* (which concerned an exploding lamp),[22] that the defendant could not, in the absence of a contract between the parties, be held liable unless he had actual knowledge of the relevant defect (the fact that the defect could be discovered by the exercise of reasonable care and skill did not assist the claimant). Bates' case reached the courts two decades too early for him to enjoy the fame that is now reserved for Mrs Donoghue.

The pre-*Donoghue v Stevenson* case law is remarkable for its caution. The case law is quite rigidly formulaic. If the facts of one's case did not fit comfortably within one of the factual categories in which a duty of care had been held to exist then no remedy was available. An 1889 textbook listed no fewer than fifty six different duties of care[23] and in 1951 Asquith LJ was able to describe the pre-*Donoghue v Stevenson* case law in the following terms:

> 'These categories attracting the duty had been added to and subtracted from time to time. But no attempt had been made in the past to rationalise them; to find a common denominator between road users, bailees, surgeons, occupiers, and so on, which would explain why they should be bound to a duty of care and some other classes who might be expected equally to be so bound should be exempt ... .'[24]

Judgments in the nineteenth century are replete with warnings about the opening of floodgates. *Langridge v Levy*,[25] an 1837 decision of the Exchequer of Pleas, concerned what we would now recognise

---

22   (1851) 6 Ex 761.
23   Beven, T *Principles of the Law of Negligence,* London: Stevens and Haynes, 1889.
24   *Candler v Crane, Christmas & Co.* [1951] 2 KB 164, 188 (CA).
25   2 M & W 519.

as product liability. A purchaser bought a gun from the defendant. The defendant had fraudulently represented to the purchaser that the gun had been manufactured by a certain manufacturer and, furthermore, that it was safe for use. In fact, the gun had been made by a different, inferior manufacturer, and was unsafe for use. The purchaser's son, the claimant, used the gun which exploded and caused injury. The claimant had no contract with the defendant; the gun had been purchased by his father. Equally, the claimant was not the recipient of the representations made by the defendant about the quality of the gun. In spite of this, the claimant's claim succeeded. It was held that if the claimant had purchased the gun in reliance on the fraudulent misrepresentations of the defendant then he would have had an action. Equally, so the court held, the defendant knew that the claimant would use the gun and the claimant relied on the defendant's representations in making use of the gun. In these circumstances, the defendant was liable for the consequences of his fraud. The court declined, however, to accept the proposition (advanced by the claimant in argument) that whenever a duty of care was owed and a claimant injured in breach of that duty liability would follow regardless of the existence of a contract. The judge, Parke B, felt that acceptance of this principle would lead 'to that indefinite extent of liability' and he was not prepared to set a precedent to that effect.

During the century that followed *Langridge v Levy* was scrapped over by both sides in the duty of care debate. It was regularly cited in argument and referred to in judgments throughout the nineteenth century. Even in *Donoghue v Stevenson* Lord Buckmaster acidly commented that it was clearly based on fraudulent misrepresentation and, therefore, it was 'rather surprising that it has so often been cited for a proposition [a more general duty of care] it cannot support.'[26] Lord Atkin agreed and believed that *Langridge v Levy* added nothing positively or negatively to questions about the duty of care in negligence.[27] In 1883 the Master of the Rolls questioned the basis on which *Langridge v Levy* had been decided.[28] The immediate purpose of the fraudulent defendant must have been to induce the claimant's

26 [1932] AC 562, 567 (HL(Sc)).
27 *Ibid*, at p 588.
28 *Heaven v Pender* (1883) 11 QBD 503, 511 *per* Brett MR (CA).

father to purchase the gun and, after he had been paid, it would have been 'wholly indifferent' to him whether or not it was used by the claimant. The real issue, so Brett MR held, was whether the claimant's action could have been sustained on grounds of negligence 'without proof of actual fraud.'

Concerns about the extension of liability can be found in many other cases decided in the Victorian and Edwardian periods. On the one hand, as noted above, the courts were concerned that liberalising the law would lead to a multiplicity of claims (whether just or unjust), but there was a more principled reason for keeping a tight hold on the list of those who were owed duties of care. Most members of the Victorian establishment were enthusiastic exponents of classical contract theory: liability in law should be based on contract and the court should not interfere with the parties' freedom to contract by recognising rights where there was no contract. This was not a good time to be an employee (particularly in the dockyard or railway trades) and the decisions of the courts in this period appear bizarre to a modern personal injury lawyer. In 1891 Lord Bramwell suggested that the acceptance of wages was the *quid pro quo* for running the risk of being injured in the course of one's work.[29] *Winterbottom v Wright*,[30] decided in 1842, is a high water mark of the conservative approach to the duty of care. The claimant was a coach driver injured, in the course of his employment, as a result of latent defects in the construction of a mail coach. The claimant's employer contracted with the owner of the mail coach to provide horses and drivers. The claimant brought his action against the owner of the coach. It was held that he could not maintain an action against the owner. The judges could not have been more emphatic in their rejection of the claimant's action: 'We ought not to permit a doubt to rest upon this subject, for our doing so might be the means of letting in upon us an infinity of actions';[31] 'Unless we confine the operation of such contracts as this to the parties who entered into them, the most absurd and outrageous consequences, to which I can see no limit, would ensue';[32] 'If we were

29 *Smith v Charles Baker & Sons* [1891] AC 325 (HL(E)).
30 10 M & W 109.
31 *Ibid*, at p 114 *per* Lord Abinger CB.
32 *Ibid*.

to hold that the plaintiff could sue in such a case, there is no point at which such actions would stop. The only safe rule is to confine the right to recover to those who enter into the contract: if we go one step beyond that, there is no reason why we should not go fifty.'[33] In the course of his speech in *Donoghue v Stevenson*, Lord Atkin, fastidiously distinguishing *Winterbottom v Wright*, pointed out that the claimant in that case had alleged no negligence by the defendant apart from breach of contract.[34] There was, as Lord Atkin pointed out, no duty of care alleged by the *Winterbottom v Wright* claimant to have been owed to him save for the contractual duty. Given that the claimant had no contract with the defendant it was not surprising that the court had dismissed the claimant's claim. On this basis, Lord Atkin concluded that *Winterbottom v Wright* was no obstacle to Mrs Donoghue's claim (another example of the care taken by Lord Atkin to ensure that the neighbour principle was seen to emerge from the existing case law, rather than arriving fully formed).

Occasionally, there was a glimpse of a more generous approach to the law. In *George v Skivington*,[35] decided in 1869, the claimant was injured after using a hair wash which had been sold to her husband for her use. There was no fraud and there was no contract between the claimant and the defendant, but there was negligence. It was difficult to say with any conviction that the hair wash was dangerous in itself. Nevertheless, the Court of Exchequer held that the claimant had a good cause of action: '[an action on the case based on] ... unskilfulness and negligence in the manufacture of ... [the hair wash] whereby the person who used it was injured.'[36] In the decades which followed most courts regarded *George v Skivington* as an anomalous decision which it was difficult to justify. It was felt that *Winterbottom v Wright*, a more persuasive expression of orthodoxy, accurately stated the law.

---

33   *Ibid*, at p 115 *per* Alderson B. The same observation was made, without attribution, by Lord Buckmaster in *Donoghue v Stevenson*: [1932] AC 562, 577.
34   [1932] AC 562, 589. Cf. Lord Buckmaster's more cursory treatment of the same authority at p 568.
35   (1869) LR 5 Ex 1.
36   *Per* Kelly CB. In *Donoghue v Stevenson* Lord Buckmaster reserved particular venom for the fact that *Langridge v Levy*, a case which he regarded as being concerned with fraud, had been relied on by the Court of Exchequer in *George v Skivington* to justify a claim based on negligence: [1932] AC 562, 570.

We have clearly come a long way since *Winterbottom v Wright* was decided. That a proposition (the injured employee should have a remedy against the negligent company) which seemed an outrage in the mid-nineteenth century is now a common place is due in large part to *Donoghue v Stevenson*.

The final decades of the nineteenth century are book-ended by two important Court of Appeal decisions: *Heaven v Pender*,[37] decided in 1883, and *Le Lievre & another v Gould*,[38] in 1893. The subject matter was very different. *Heaven v Pender* was an action arising out of an accident at work. *Le Lievre*, by contrast, concerned the negligence of a surveyor and the consequential losses of mortgagees. In modern legal practice we are accustomed to very narrow specialisms. It would be unusual for a Court of Appeal considering a professional negligence case to have much, if any, regard to the authorities for accidents at work and employers' liability. Legal practice was very different at the time that the tort of negligence emerged. No one seems to have regarded it as odd or unusual that the Court of Appeal in *Heaven v Pender* and *Le Lievre* should, in spite of the dissimilarity in subject matter, consider the same principles and refer to the same authorities. At a time when the development of an independent tort of negligence was itself controversial the courts did not have the luxury of worrying about the minutiae.

In *Heaven v Pender*, the claimant was employed by a ship painter. His employer had a contract with the ship owner. The ship owner had a contract with the defendant dock owner for the provision of premises and scaffolding to enable the painting work to take place. The claimant was injured in the course of his employment when a defective scaffold rope snapped. He sued the defendant dock proprietor. The claimant's claim was dismissed at first instance and he appealed. The leading judgment was delivered by Brett MR. He had no doubt as to the basis of the claimant's action: 'The action is in form and substance an action for negligence.'[39] The following paragraph of the judgment identifies the ingredients of the tort in a recognisably modern form: '... want of attention amounting to a want of ordinary care is not a good cause

37   (1883) 11 QBD 503 (CA).
38   [1893] 1 QB 491 (CA).
39   (1883) 11 QBD 503, 506.

of action, although injury ensue from such want, unless the person charged with such want of ordinary care had a duty to the person complaining to use ordinary care in respect of the matter called in question.'[40] Accordingly, a duty to exercise ordinary (reasonable) care was the precondition for the commission of the tort. If breach was established and damage caused as a result then a finding of liability would follow. 'The question in this case', said Brett MR, 'is whether the defendant owed such a duty to the plaintiff.' Brett MR went on to refer to some of the established categories of cases where it had been accepted that, in the absence of a contractual relationship between the parties or any fraud, a duty of care did exist: those in control of vehicles on the public highway; railway companies which contracted with one person to carry another; occupiers permitting persons to come onto their land. The difficulty that he faced was that the circumstances of Mr Heaven's case did not fall into any established category. Brett MR solved this conundrum by returning to first principles. The reason that two drivers approaching each other owed a duty of care was because, if reasonable care and skill were not exercised, there would be an 'injurious collision' between them. Furthermore, 'every one ought by the universally recognised rules of right and wrong, to think so much with regard to the safety of others who may be jeopardised by his conduct' and, if reasonable care was not exercised and injury resulted then, 'the law, which takes cognisance of and enforces the rules of right and wrong, will force him to give an indemnity for the injury.'[41] It was, therefore, appeal to a universal principle, a natural law of right and wrong, that justified the rule which Brett MR applied to the case (Brett MR's biographer in the *Dictionary of National Biography* observed that, when sitting in court, a 'characteristic utterance' from him was that 'law was not a science but rather the application of right and wrong'. This was intended as a criticism). Brett MR's formula lacks the specifically Christian underpinning of Lord Atkin's neighbour principle, its incorporation of the words of Scripture, but it is clearly drawn from the same well. From this starting point Brett MR formulated the following 'larger proposition':

40   *Ibid*, at p 507.
41   *Ibid*, at p 508.

'... whenever one person is by circumstances placed in such a position with regard to another that every one of ordinary sense who did think would at once recognise that if he did not use ordinary care and skill in his own conduct with regard to those circumstances he would cause danger of injury to the person or property of another, a duty arises to use ordinary care and skill to avoid such danger.'[42]

Brett MR was apparently so convinced of the generality of this principle that he made clear that it included, 'all the recognised cases of liability.' In other words, the piecemeal development of the tort of negligence – identifying categories of case (factual situations) in which a duty of care was owed – was to be no more. Instead, the Brett MR formula could be deployed. Thus, a duty of care would be owed and an action in negligence might be available where a person supplied goods or machinery to another knowing that, unless reasonable care and skill were exercised in the supply of the goods or machinery, a danger of injury might result. Clearly, in *Heaven v Pender* the claimant's case satisfied the Brett MR formula. A duty of care had been owed by the defendant to the claimant and liability was established.

Brett MR's formula was a direct descendant of the principle expressed in Lord Bathurst's treatise. Equally, it is the secular ancestor of Lord Atkin's neighbour principle. It could comfortably have been applied to Mrs Donoghue's case half a century later. However, the roots set down by *Heaven v Pender* proved to be shallow. The reaction to the expansive approach of Brett MR began immediately. Indeed, it began in the same case. Cotton and Bowen LJJ agreed with the Master of the Rolls that the claimant should win his appeal. However, they based their decision on much narrower grounds. Their Lordships believed that the claimant was entitled to succeed in his action because he was present at the dock for the purposes of his work and, being 'engaged in work in the performance of which the defendant was interested', he fell within one of the existing categories of (occupiers' liability) case in which a duty of care had been held to exist. Cotton LJ went out of his way to make it clear that he did not espouse the same principle identified by his senior colleague, the Master of the Rolls, 'I am unwilling to concur with the Master of

---

42   *Ibid*, at p 509.

the Rolls in laying down unnecessarily the larger principle which he entertains, inasmuch as there are many cases in which the principle was impliedly negatived.'[43] The 'many cases' which Cotton LJ had in mind included *Langridge v Levy* and *Longmeid v Holliday*. In case there was any doubt about their disagreement with Brett MR's approach, Cotton and Bowen LJJ concluded their joint judgment by saying again, with a degree of magnificent judicial understatement, that they did not, 'entirely concur with the reasoning of the Master of the Rolls.'[44] By the time that *Donoghue v Stevenson* was decided Brett MR's apparently universal formula was so out of favour with judicial conservatives that Lord Buckmaster offered the prayer that it be, 'buried so securely that ... [its] perturbed spirit shall no longer vex the law.'[45] Even Lord Atkin had doubts about the potential expansiveness of Brett MR's formula; he felt it necessary, in a product liability context like *Donoghue v Stevenson*, to qualify the formula so that it applied only where goods were to be used immediately and where the ultimate consumer would have no possibility of examining them prior to consumption (an approach which he felt was consistent with what Brett MR intended).[46] Sir Frederick Pollock was rude about Brett MR's formula in one of the earliest academic writings about *Donoghue v Stevenson*: 'The precision of a neat draftsman', wrote Pollock, 'has never been counted among ... [Brett MR's] accomplishments.'[47]

Le Lievre & another v Gould[48] concerned professional negligence. A surveyor provided certificates to confirm the progress of building works. Mortgagees advanced loans to the builder on the strength of the certificates. The surveyor had not been appointed by the mortgagees and there was no contract between them. As a result of the surveyor's negligence, without any fraud on his part, the certificates were inaccurate and, unsurprisingly, the mortgagees lost money as a result. They sued the surveyor. The claimants failed at first instance (before the Official Referee) and in the Divisional Court. They appealed. The Court of Appeal contained two of the judges involved in *Heaven v*

43 *Ibid*, at p 516.
44 *Ibid*, at p 517.
45 [1932] AC 562, 576.
46 *Ibid*, at pp 581 – 582.
47 Pollock, F 'The Snail in the Bottle and Thereafter' (1933) 49 LQR 22, 25.
48 [1893] 1 QB 491.

Pender. By this time Brett MR had been raised to the peerage as Lord Esher MR and he was joined by Bowen LJ. The third member of the Court of Appeal was AL Smith LJ. The judgment of the Master of the Rolls is constructed in a similar fashion to his judgment in *Heaven v Pender.* He starts by considering the duty of care and whether the defendant owed a duty to the claimants: ' A man is entitled to be as negligent as he pleases towards the whole world if he owes no duty to them.' He was quite satisfied that *Heaven v Pender* which, unsurprisingly, the claimants sought to rely upon, had no application: 'That case established that, under certain circumstances, one man may owe a duty to another, even though there is no contract between them. If one man is near to another, or is near to the property of another, a duty lies upon him not to do that which may cause a personal injury to that other, or may injure his property.' In other words, *Heaven v Pender* was explained as a case where the foreseeability of harm which justified the imposition of a duty of care resulted from the physical proximity of the parties or their property.[49] Indeed, cases where there was such proximity were just another category of factual situation where a duty of care was recognised. Clearly, the apparent universality of Brett MR's formula had some limits after all. Bowen LJ who had declined to follow the lead of the Master of the Rolls in *Heaven v Pender*, had little difficulty in deciding the appeal against the claimants. AL Smith LJ described the principle in *Heaven v Pender*, '... a duty to take due care ... when the person or property of one was in such proximity to the person or property of another that, if due care was not taken, damage might be done by the one to the other.'[50] He felt that *Heaven v Pender* went no further than this (which was still further than Cotton and Bowen LJJ were prepared to go) and noted archly that, nevertheless, '... it is often cited to support all kinds of untenable propositions.' It is interesting to note that even in those cases decided in the decade between *Heaven v Pender* and *Le Lievre* claimants won in spite of Brett MR's formula, rather than because

49　In *Donoghue v Stevenson* Lord Atkin expressed the view that Brett MR had not intended that physical proximity was the only basis for a duty of care. Proximity should, he stated, 'extend to such close and direct relations that the act complained of directly affects a person whom the person alleged to be bound to take care would know would be directly affected by his careless act.' [1932] AC 562, 581.
50　[1893] 1 QB 491, 504.

of it. In *Elliott v Hall*,[51] for example, an 1885 decision, a claimant was injured at work while he was unloading a defective coal wagon (an accident which features in several of the negligence claims in the decades before *Donoghue v Stevenson* was decided). His claim was brought against the defendant colliery owner (whose employees had allowed the defective truck to leave the coal yard), rather than against his employer (the purchaser of the coal). Grove J had no doubt that a duty of care was owed: the claimant had a duty to unload the coal and the defendant had a contract with the claimant's employer and knew that the latter's employees would be unloading the coal. The web of contractual relationships and the knowledge of the defendant justified the conclusion that a duty of care was owed. Grove J made it clear, however, that that claimant was, 'entitled to recover quite independently of the decision of the Court of Appeal in *Heaven v Pender*.'[52]

Heaven v Pender continued to be marginalised as the nineteenth century came to an end. In 1897 the House of Lords treated it as an eccentric adjunct to the established category of cases involving occupiers[53] and those supplying apparatus for use in the course of employment (where a duty of care had already been held to exist).[54]

---

51   (1885) 15 QBD 315.

52   *Ibid*, at p 319.

53   See also, the Scottish case *Kemp v Dougall v Darngavil Coal Co. Ltd.* 1909 SC 1314, 1319 *per* Lord Kinnear (Ct of Sess): 'Now, I think the principle upon which it may be found in cases of this kind that there is a duty owed by one party to the other is established by ... *Heaven v Pender*, and the rule which results ... appears to me to be this, that there is an obligation on the part of the occupier of property, whether it is fixed or moveable, to those who come upon that property on business which concerns the occupier, and come at his invitation express or implied, to take reasonable care by himself or by others that a person so coming shall not be exposed to unnecessary hazard.' A year later the Court of Session reiterated that in order to bring a claim in negligence a duty of care must exist: *Clelland v Robb* 1911 SC 253. The implication was that the claim must fit within one of the existing categories in which a duty of care had been held to exist.

54   *Caledonian Railway Co. v Mulholland or Warwick* [1898] AC 216 (HL(Sc): yet another case involving a defective coal wagon; this time, a fatal accident claim. See also, *Dominion Natural Gas Company Ltd v Collins & another* [1909] AC 640 (PC) where it was held, without any reference to *Heaven v Pender*, that a duty of care was owed in the case of a person performing an operation or setting up and installing a machine.

The same approach was taken by the Court of Appeal in *Earl v Lubbock*[55] decided in 1904: a case which involved a man injured at work when the wheel of a van that he was driving fell off. The Master of the Rolls (by this time, Collins MR) pointed out that in *Le Lievre* Brett MR (Lord Esher MR as he had, by then, become) had publicly recanted the heresy expressed by him in *Heaven v Pender* (sloughing off his radicalism as he put on ermine robes).[56] There was no universal formula by which the courts could test whether a duty of care existed. By the time that the House of Lords decided *Cavalier v Pope*[57] in 1906 not a single reference to *Heaven v Pender* was made in their Lordships' speeches. In this case the tenant's wife was injured by the dilapidated state of premises. The owner of the property had contracted with the tenant to carry out repairs, but had negligently failed to do so. The wife's claim failed because: (i) she had no contract with the owner; (ii) there was no fraud by the owner (sufficient to bring the claimant within the *Langridge v Levy* rule); and, (iii) the claimant knew of the danger posed by the dilapidated house, but chose to run the risk anyway (an absolute impediment, so Lord Atkinson held, to a successful claim).

Chapman or Oliver v Saddler & Company[58] was decided, by a Scottish House of Lords, just three years before *Donoghue v Stevenson*. Lords Buckmaster and Atkin were both sitting as members of the House. The defendant's case was presented before the House of Lords by W G Normand KC who, as we have seen, appeared for Mr Stevenson in *Donoghue v Stevenson*. *Oliver v Saddler & Company* was another accident at work claim. The claimants were the dependants of a porter. The defendant stevedore company had unloaded a cargo of maize from a ship moored at the port of Leith near Edinburgh. The defendant provided rope slings to remove the

---

55   [1905] 1 KB 253.
56   Lord Esher MR shares the fate of a number of other judges referred to in this book in that his *Dictionary of National Biography* biographer damns him with the faintest praise: 'He was by no means incapable of handling technical issues, but had little patience for them.'; 'His brusque and direct manner ... was regarded by some as the epitome of good sense, and by others as alarmingly simplistic.'
57   [1906] AC 428 (HL(E)). See also, *Bottomley v Bannister* [1932] 1 KB 458 (CA) where *Cavalier v Pope* was followed.
58   [1929] AC 584.

bags from the ship to the quayside and, once on the quayside, the defendant's responsibilities came to an end. The defendant allowed a porterage company to use the rope slings which were, conveniently, already tied around the bags of maize. No charge was made for this and the defendant company employed a person to inspect the rope slings to make sure that they were in a serviceable condition. A rope sling broke while the cargo was being moved and, as a result of this, the porter was killed. His dependants sued the stevedore company whose employee's failure to inspect had caused the accident. The House of Lords was unanimously satisfied that a duty of care was owed and that liability was established. Lord Buckmaster fastidiously declined to utilise the formula of Brett MR in *Heaven v Pender* and Lord Atkin, who had been a member of the House of Lords for less than a year, did not make reference to it in the course of his short speech. Both judges were satisfied that the deceased had been owed a duty of care. While Lord Atkin's conclusion that a duty was owed was based on a number of grounds, he believed that it was significant that the rope sling was provided by the stevedore company defendant in 'conditions of danger' knowing that the porters 'would have no reasonable opportunity of examining the sling.'[59] He returned to this theme and applied it in a product liability context in the course of his speech in *Donoghue v Stevenson* where he posited the situation where a manufacturer placed food in a container knowing that this would be opened by the eventual consumer in circumstances where the latter would have no reasonable opportunity to examine the contents of the container before consuming them. If, said Lord Atkin, the manufacturer had negligently mixed the contents of the container with poison before sealing it and this caused injury to the consumer it would be a 'grave defect in the law' if the latter was left without a remedy against the manufacturer.[60] The final speech in *Oliver v Saddler & Company* was delivered by Viscount Dunedin. He too agreed that the deceased's dependants had a valid claim against the defendant and he based this on the fact that the use to which the rope sling was being put was an obviously dangerous one in circumstances where the defendant knew that the sling was to be used in this way and had acquiesced to the same. Viscount Dunedin was wary that the

59   *Ibid*, at p 596.
60   [1932] AC 562, 582.

decision of the House and, in particular the speech of Lord Atkin, might be used as a precedent to widen the scope of the law:

'I also had the advantage of reading the judgment just delivered by Lord Atkin; but I do wish to express emphatically the very narrow limits within which my concurrence is confined, for I cannot help feeling that this decision might be drawn into a precedent for what it does not warrant.'[61]

The lid which conservative occupants of the bench had kept on *Heaven v Pender* in the half century since it was decided was about to be blown off.

The magnificent rhetorical language, the use of New Testament allusion and the vehemence of its critics might prompt the conclusion that Lord Atkin's neighbour principle emerged in a spontaneous act of creation: a jurisprudential big bang. It was, of course, nothing of the sort. It owed as much to the writings of Lord Bathurst and the judicial work of Lord Esher MR as it did to the fertile mind of Lord Atkin. The greatness of the neighbour principle lies in the fact that it captured the imagination; it excited people. While others had chipped away at the legal edifice (the sterile taxonomy of those to whom duties of care were owed), it took the excitement generated by Lord Atkin's great principle to move the law forwards in a more coherent direction.

US authorities

At around the time that the English courts were struggling with the tort of negligence as it emerged from the shadow of contract and fraud, courts in the United States of America were engaged in a similar exercise. The evolution of a distinct law of negligence seems, however, to have followed as circuitous a path in the US as it did in England and Wales. Indeed, it was not just the law of negligence, but the law of torts as a whole that took time to emerge. The first US treatise on torts did not appear until 1859; the first case book was not published until 1874 and American law schools did not teach

---

61   In *Donoghue v Stevenson*, Lord Atkin commented that the decision in *Oliver v Saddler & Company* was based on the direct relationship, albeit not based on contract, of the deceased and the defendant and on 'the circumstance that the injured porter had no opportunity of independent examination of the defective rope sling.' *Ibid*, at p 586.

torts as a separate subject until 1870.[62] As in the United Kingdom, it was the suitability of the law of negligence as the means by which to regulate the private obligations of citizens during a period of rapid industrialisation that saw this tort develop during the later nineteenth century.

It is tempting to regard the history of the tort of negligence during this period as the history of great men: the development of the law on the American side of the Atlantic owes much to a famous judge, Benjamin Cardozo (Associate and then Chief Justice of the New York Court of Appeals until 1932 when he became an Associate Justice of the US Supreme Court) and his opinion in *MacPherson v Buick Motor Company*.[63] One American commentator has observed that Cardozo J's *MacPherson* judgment 'imposed liability [on a defendant] who would almost certainly ... not have been liable if anyone but Cardozo had been stating and analyzing the prior case law.'[64] A similar observation can surely be made of Lord Atkin in *Donoghue v Stevenson*. In the course of his speech in *Donoghue v Stevenson* Lord Atkin commented on the satisfaction that he had derived from testing his own formulation of the law by reference to the judgments of the American courts and repaid the debt that he owed to the same, 'The mouse had emerged from the ginger-beer bottle in the United States before it appeared in Scotland [in *Mullen v Barr*], but there it brought a liability upon the manufacturer.'[65]

Two US cases are referred to in the course of the judgments in *Donoghue v Stevenson*: *Thomas v Winchester*[66] and *MacPherson v Buick Motor Company*. They were both decided in the New York State jurisdiction. The first in time is *Thomas v Winchester* (decided in 1852), later described by Cardozo J as a 'landmark of the law'. It seems likely that this came to the attention of the House of Lords as a result of the detailed attention devoted to it in the opinion of Cardozo J in *MacPherson* (there is little evidence of any independent research into US law in the *Donoghue v Stevenson* speeches). *Thomas*

62   White, GE *Tort Law in America: An Intellectual History* (OUP, 1980), p 3.
63   (1916) 217 NY 382 .
64   Gilmore, G *The Ages of American Law* (1977), p 75.
65   [1932] AC 562, 598 (HL(Sc)).
66   (1852) 6 NY 397.

v Winchester was a product liability case in which the unfortunate claimant was poisoned. Mr Winchester was a dealer in drugs intended for the medical market. He carelessly mislabelled a solution containing extract of belladonna, a dangerous poison ('deadly nightshade') as every schoolboy knows, by indicating that the bottle contained (harmless) extract of dandelion. The drug passed through several hands before reaching a dispensing chemist who prescribed extract of dandelion for Mary Thomas' ailment. The drug was purchased by Mrs Thomas' husband for her use. She used the drug and became very ill as a result. Winchester relied on *Winterbottom v Wright*: absent privity of contract between himself and the ultimate consumer of the drug, there was no duty of care and, therefore, no liability in tort. The New York Court of Appeals disagreed. It was held that Winchester was liable to Mrs Thomas, the ultimate consumer of the drug, because, although she was unknown to him, his negligence had created an imminent danger. The imminence of the danger justified the imposition of a duty of care. The rule expounded by the New York Court of Appeals in *Thomas v Winchester* was sufficiently robust to be applied in the 1908 decision: *Torgeson v Schultz*[67] where the claimant was injured when a bottle of aerated water manufactured by the defendant exploded. The court held that, in spite of the absence of a contract between the claimant (who was an employee of the purchaser) and the defendant the latter was liable, 'under the doctrine of *Thomas v Winchester*, and similar cases based upon the duty of the vendor of an article dangerous in its nature, or likely to become so in the course of the ordinary usage to be contemplated by the vendor, either to exercise due care to warn users of the danger or to take reasonable care to prevent the article sold from proving dangerous when subjected only to customary usage.'[68] Most observers would regard it as stretching a point to regard a bottle of fizzy pop as presenting an imminent danger. As Cardozo J observed in *MacPherson*, almost any object can be used in a manner that will make it dangerous. The challenge in applying the imminence of danger test lies in knowing how to draw the line and how to formulate a test that will assist in knowing how to draw the

---

67   192 NY 156.
68   *Ibid*, at p 159.

line. Perhaps, the *Bates* litigant would have been more successful if his case had been tried in New York.[69]

Benjamin Nathan Cardozo was born in New York into a family of Sephardic Jews in 1870. His family was widely supposed to have originated in Portugal, but had reached the United States before the American Revolution. Cardozo pursued undergraduate studies at Columbia University and later entered the law school at the same college. His eminence as a judge erased the shadow cast over his early life by the charges of judicial corruption levelled at his father who was also a judge and who was constrained to resign his office in the face of a threat of impeachment. By all accounts Cardozo led an austere life which was devoted to his siblings and to hard work. He never married; his biographer states that he 'lived for the law, and the law made him famous'[70] and his greatest work as a judge was in the private law of obligations, torts. In addition to the intellectual qualities which Cardozo brought to the Bench, the literary quality of the judgments that he delivered helped to earn him fame. There is an ease and fluency to his judgments (a readability) that makes them a pleasure to read. In this Cardozo shares much with an English judge with whom he has often been compared (Lord Denning MR), although Benjamin Cardozo's judgments lack the rather abbreviated prose style that identifies a Denning classic.

MacPherson came before the New York Court of Appeals in 1916, within a couple of years of Cardozo J's promotion to the court (in 1914). In common with Lord Atkin, Cardozo did not waste time in making a name for himself on the Appellate Bench and *MacPherson* is now regarded as one of his most important judgments. The case raised issues with which any English (Scottish or Commonwealth) common lawyer of the period would have been intimately familiar. Indeed, the opinion of Cardozo and the dissenting opinion of the then Chief Justice of the Court, Willard Bartlett, are informed by detailed consideration of the English cases discussed above. *MacPherson* concerned a defective motor vehicle. The defendant company took the case very seriously. It sent a lawyer from Detroit to Saratoga Springs, New York where the case was tried and ensured that expert

---

69   *Bates v Batey & Company* [1913] 3 KB 351 (KB).
70   Kaufman, AL *Cardozo* (Harvard University Press, 1998), p 3.

witnesses gave evidence on its behalf. However, the jury found for the claimant and this decision was affirmed by the Appellate Division. The defendant appealed. The facts are elegantly summarised in the opening passage of Cardozo J's opinion (for the majority of the court) which also provides an example of the distinctive clarity of his prose:

> 'The defendant is a manufacturer of automobiles. It sold an automobile to a retail dealer. The retail dealer resold to the plaintiff. While the plaintiff was in the car, it suddenly collapsed. He was thrown out and injured. One of the wheels was made of defective wood, and its spokes crumbled into fragments. The wheel was not made by the defendant; it was bought from another manufacturer. There is evidence, however, that its defects could have been discovered by reasonable inspection, and that inspection was omitted. There is no claim that the defendant knew of the defect and wilfully concealed it. ... The charge is one, not of fraud, but of negligence.'[71]

This set of facts will be familiar from the discussion above. A case of product liability where there is no contract between the negligent actor and the injured party and where there is no evidence of fraud (of the kind that would provide the claimant with a straightforward cause of action). In headline terms, the issue in *MacPherson* was whether the doctrine of *Thomas v Winchester* could be stretched sufficiently wide to encompass the less propitious facts of the later case. Cardozo was satisfied that, by 1916, even if *Thomas v Winchester* had, which he clearly doubted, originally been limited in application to objects imminently dangerous to life (poisons, explosives, deadly weapons) it was no longer so confined. The *Thomas v Winchester* rule was capable, it was held, of wider application to objects which while not imminently dangerous in themselves became so because of their defective construction (*Torgeson v Schultz* was cited as an example of a case in which such a conclusion had been reached). Cardozo went on to consider Brett MR's formula in *Heaven v Pender* from which he quoted in full. He noted that the judges sitting with Brett MR in that case did not agree with him and he also observed that the problem with attempts to formulate rules capable of general application is that they

---

71   (1916) 217 NY 382, 384. In fact, Cardozo's recital of the facts achieves a studied neutrality. He failed to mention that the claimant was driving a sick neighbour to hospital at the time that he was injured.

'may involve errors of inclusion and of exclusion.'[72] Nevertheless, Cardozo recognised Brett MR's formula as the concise expression of the 'tests and standards' of US law (at least in New York State) which he had found in the cases following *Thomas v Winchester*. The boldness of Cardozo J's approach to Brett MR's formula, resuscitating it as a statement of general principle capable of practical application, stands in marked contrast to the manner in which this judgment was treated on the British side of the Atlantic.

Cardozo J stated that the application of what he called the 'principle of *Thomas v Winchester*' would be justified where: (1) the nature of an article or object would, if negligently made, be reasonably certain to endanger life or limb; (2) such danger was accompanied by knowledge that the article would be used by persons other than the immediate purchaser; (3) the manufacturer of the finished article or object, placed on the market, must fail in his duty of inspection; and, (4) the ultimate user of the article must have no opportunity of examination or inspection of the finished article before using it (and the manufacturer should know that the article will be used 'without new tests' by the ultimate consumer). If these conditions were satisfied then 'the manufacturer of this thing of danger is under a duty to make it carefully.'[73] The factual difficulty in the application of this test which was expressly acknowledged by Cardozo related to the probability of danger and whether this condition was present in any given case. He dealt with this in the following way:

> 'There must be knowledge of a danger, not merely possible, but probable. It is possible to use almost anything in a way that will make it dangerous if defective. That is not enough to charge the manufacturer with a duty independent of his contract. Whether a given thing is dangerous may be sometimes a question for the court and sometimes a question for the jury.'[74]

In other words, it was a question of fact to be determined on a case by case basis. Cardozo went on to refer to a number of the English cases (*Winterbottom v Wright, Elliott v Hall* and *Dominion Natural Gas Company v Collins* among them), commenting that, in England,

72   *Ibid*, at p 389.
73   *Ibid*.
74   *Ibid*, at p 390.

the limits of the *Thomas v Winchester* approach in negligence, were 'still unsettled'. He was quite satisfied, however, that in America there was 'nothing anomalous' in a rule ' which imposes upon A, who has contracted with B, a duty to C and D and others according as he knows or does not know that the subject-matter of the contract is intended for their use.'[75] Cardozo J, providing the opinion of the court, was able to persuade three of his seven colleagues to agree with his approach. One colleague (Pound J) did not vote. Another (Hogan J) agreed with the result in the case, if not (expressly at least) with Cardozo J's reasoning. The Chief Justice, Willard Bartlett CJ, did not agree with Cardozo and delivered a detailed dissenting opinion. Like the dissenting law lords in *Donoghue v Stevenson*, the Chief Justice's concern was that the decision extended the liability of the manufacturer 'further than any case which has yet received the sanction of this court'.[76] Willard Bartlett also referred to *Winterbottom v Wright* and to *Thomas v Winchester* as an exception to the principle established in the English authority. However, his reading of the *Thomas v Winchester* rule was far less expansive than that of Cardozo. He believed that the judgment of the *Thomas v Winchester* Court of Appeals drew a clear distinction between 'an act of negligence imminently dangerous to the lives of others and one that is not so.'[77] He had no doubt that the facts of *MacPherson* placed it very firmly outside the category of cases previously held to fall within the *Thomas v Winchester* rule:

'In the case at bar the defective wheel on an automobile moving only eight miles an hour was not any more dangerous to the occupants of the car than a similarly defective wheel would be to the occupants of a carriage drawn by a horse at the same speed; and yet unless the courts have been all wrong on this question up to the present time there would be no liability to strangers to the original sale in the case of the horse-drawn carriage.'[78]

Cardozo, by contrast, had no time for those who argued that case law concerning the danger, or otherwise, of horse-drawn carriages could be applied to the brave new world of the motor car: 'Precedents

75   *Ibid*, at p 393.
76   *Ibid*, at p 396.
77   *Ibid*, at p 398.
78   *Ibid*, at p 400.

drawn from the days of travel by stage coach do not fit the conditions of travel to-day.'[79] The people of New York had new, and faster, modes of transport and, by implication, they must have new legal principles to apply to the accidents which they caused as well.

An Australian judge took the view that Lord Atkin's speech in *Donoghue v Stevenson* did no more and no less than to align English/ Scottish (and, therefore, British Empire) law with Cardozo's statement of principle in *MacPherson*. In a letter in the Atkin archive, dated 6 March 1933, Evatt J of the High Court of Australia, wrote to Lord Atkin from Sydney:

> 'The snail case has been the subject of the keenest interest and debate at the Bar and in the Sydney and Melbourne law schools; on all sides there is profound satisfaction that, in substance, your judgments and the opinion of Cardozo J of the USA coincide, and that the common law is again shown to be capable of meeting modern conditions of industrialisation.'[80]

Lord Atkin's reply is not in the archive, although one suspects that he would have been more ambitious for his own statement of principle than to view it simply as an expression, for the courts of the wider Empire, of the new American orthodoxy. There are important points of difference between Lord Atkin's neighbour principle and Cardozo's approach in *MacPherson*. While both judges sought to cast their statements of the law against the background of the precedents (and, where possible, sought to reconcile the same) there is little doubt that Lord Atkin appreciated that he was shaping the law and pointing it in a different direction. Cardozo's opinion in *MacPherson* is, by contrast, much more modest in scope and intention. For the most part it consists of the consideration of established principle. There is no attempt to describe the approach as a radical break with the past. On the contrary, there is little attempt to suggest that any important issue of principle is being determined. A number of American writers have regarded the modesty of the opinion as being characteristic of the Cardozo style, '... articulated in modes of analysis that deemphasized activism, minimized innovativeness, and suggested that judicial

79   *Ibid*, at p 391.
80   Atkin archive. File reference ATK1/JUD/1/1.

wisdom lay in tentative, measured, incremental decision-making'.[81] It should, however, be remembered that the defendant company in *MacPherson* had argued that the duty that it owed to others was limited to those with whom it had a contract and that no duty of care was owed to 'all the world'. This argument was emphatically rejected by Cardozo: the duty of care owed to others was unfettered by contract or any previous course of dealings. Within the conditions that he had carefully set Cardozo's statement of the duty of care had, like Lord Atkin's more expansive neighbour principle, potential for general application.

In *Donoghue v Stevenson* itself, Lord Buckmaster, perhaps unsurprisingly, dealt dismissively with the American case law. Indeed, the impression that one forms from reading his speech is that he considered *Thomas v Winchester* and *MacPherson* only in deference to the argument of counsel (having first reminded himself that such cases had neither close application nor authority in a Scottish court, '... for though the source of the law in the two countries may be the same, its current may well flow in different channels.')[82] Lord Buckmaster's view was that *Thomas v Winchester* was based on the fact that the drug sold was dangerous in itself and that the vendor had been asked to sell a different article altogether. *MacPherson*, which was not closely analysed, was explained as having something to do with Cardozo's view that a motor vehicle might reasonably be regarded as a dangerous article (a view which Lord Buckmaster evidently did not share).[83] Lord Atkin described Cardozo's opinion in *MacPherson* as 'illuminating' and stated that the American judge had stated the principles of law in a manner consistent with his own views. Lord Atkin stated that he had no doubt that if Cardozo J's formulation of the law were to be applied to Mrs Donoghue's case then she would succeed in her appeal. Lord Macmillan also lavished praise on Cardozo (who, by the time that *Donoghue v Stevenson* was decided, had become an Associate Justice of the US Supreme Court). In the course of his speech he quoted extensively from Cardozo's

81   White, GE *Tort Law in America: An Intellectual History* (OUP, 1980), p 123.
82   [1932] AC 562, 576.
83   *Ibid*, at p 577.

Opinion in *MacPherson*,[84] but did not otherwise embark on detailed consideration of this authority. It appears that Cardozo J and Lord Macmillan first met at a lunch party given by Professor Goodhart in New York: later editor of the Law Quarterly Review. Both Lords Atkin and Macmillan are likely to have been familiar with the *MacPherson* case as a result of an article written by Professor Francis Bohlen which appeared in the Law Quarterly Review in 1929.[85] It is surely possible that *MacPherson* was also the subject of a discussion at lunch when Lord Macmillan met Justice Cardozo.[86]

MacPherson was decided by a native New Yorker judge sitting in a New York court directing himself by reference to New York (and some English) precedents. However, Cardozo's biographer records that Cardozo's statement of the law was applied across the US State jurisdictions and had, within a remarkably short period of time, become 'all but universal law in the United States.'[87] American commentators have questioned whether the ready acceptance of *MacPherson* meant that, sooner or later, a rule expressed in the same terms would have been established even without Cardozo J's helping hand. This incremental process of law-making, extending the law by travelling the shortest possible distance from established precedent, had already been identified by Cardozo J: he referred to it as the 'method of sociology'. In *MacPherson* it was, 'Analogy powered by public policy considerations – his perception that the exceptions to the original rule were more generally applicable than the rule itself – [which] convinced him to reformulate and improve the governing doctrine.'[88]

Lord Atkin and Holy Scripture

On the evening of 9 May 1930 Lord Atkin, in his capacity as an Honorary Doctor of Laws of the University of Birmingham, gave the

---

84　　*Ibid*, at pp 617 – 618.

85　　Bohlen, F 'Liability of Manufacturers to Persons other than their Immediate Vendees' (1929) 45 LQR 343.

86　　See, the interesting thoughts on this subject of John D Gordon III: 'The American Authorities in *Donoghue v Stevenson*: a Resolution' (1999) 115 LQR 183.

87　　Kaufman, AL *Cardozo* (Harvard University Press, 1998), p 274 recording the view expressed by Professor Prosser in the 1950s.

88　　*Ibid*, at p 275.

after dinner speech to the University's Holdsworth Club of student lawyers. While he publicly disavowed any intention to deliver a sermon, there is a religious tone to certain passages of the speech:

> '[The Law] maintains and publicly maintains and enforces a very high standard of integrity. Law and morality are, of course, not synonymous, and the demands of morality and the moral code no doubt extend into spheres where the Law does not set its foot. But in dealings as between man and man the English Law does set up a high, but not too high, attainable standard of honesty and fair dealing which, to my mind, is of the very greatest value to the whole community and especially to the commercial community. ... The man who swears unto his neighbour and disappointeth him not is a person commended by the law of morality, and the Law enforces that by an action for breach of contract. There is the high standard which is set up as between agent and principal, as between trustee and beneficiary, and, indeed, the whole of the English Law, supplemented by rules of equity relating to fraud, appears to me to constitute in the principles of the Law a most valuable guide to the public at large.'

Lord Atkin returned to similar themes the following year when, in another lecture, this time in the Great Hall of King's College, London in the Strand he spoke on 'Law as an Educational Subject'. Again, he referred to the fact that law was not identical to morality and deployed the example of the honest contract maker as a person whom both morality and the law would recognise as possessing virtue. However, at the time that the King's College lecture was delivered in late October 1931, Lord Atkin added another example to his list of the situations in which morality could be said to justify the law. In addition to entering honest contracts, the moral actor was 'not to injure his neighbour by acts of negligence; and that certainly covers a very large field of the law.' Indeed, Lord Atkin went on, 'I doubt whether the whole law of tort could not be comprised in the golden maxim to do unto your neighbour as you would that he should do unto you.'

As indicated above, it was as much the language used by Lord Atkin in *Donoghue v Stevenson* and his use of New Testament allusion that captured the imagination of his audience and helped to ensure that the neighbour principle became the instrument by which the boundaries of the tort of negligence were expanded. In the King's College lecture Lord Atkin deployed Christ's central teaching which finds expression in the Gospels of St Matthew and St Luke. St Matthew has Christ give the following teaching during the Sermon on the Mount, 'Therefore all things whatsoever ye would that men should do to you, do ye even so to them; for this is the law and the prophets.'[89] This teaching is not, as Christ indicates, confined to the New Testament. Leviticus contains the following injunction, 'Thou shalt not avenge, nor bear any grudge against the children of thy people, but thou shalt love thy neighbour as thyself.'[90] St Luke records Christ offering this teaching after he had called his disciples, '... as ye would that men should do to you, do ye also to them likewise.'[91]

By the time that *Donoghue v Stevenson* came before the House of Lords Lord Atkin had moved on from the use that he made of Christ's central teaching, 'the Golden Rule' as it is sometimes called, to the Parable of the Good Samaritan. This appears in St Luke's Gospel and is introduced as follows:

> 'And, behold, a certain lawyer stood up, and tempted him, saying, Master, what shall I do to inherit eternal life? He said unto him, What is written in the law? how readest thou? And he answering said, Thou shalt love the Lord thy God with all thy heart, and with all thy soul, and with all thy strength, and with all thy mind; and thy neighbour as thyself. And he said unto him, Thou hast answered right: this do, and thou shalt live. But he, willing to justify himself, said unto Jesus, And who is my neighbour?'[92]

The lawyer's question was, as lawyers' questions often are, a trap. His intention was that Christ, who lacked the formal Biblical training which he had enjoyed, would fail to answer the question in a manner which was consistent with Scripture. In fact, Christ gets the lawyer to give the answer himself and he does so by displaying his knowledge of Leviticus. This does not, however, provide a reliable guide to how the Scriptural rule is to be applied in practice. Leviticus was a source of the New Testament Golden Rule that one should love one's neighbour, but did not explain how this was to be done. Christ used the Parable of the Good Samaritan to explain the rule. The Parable answered the

89   Matthew 7:12.
90   Leviticus 19:18.
91   Luke 6:31.
92   Luke 10:25 – 29.

lawyer's question. As we have seen, Lord Atkin, exemplifying his extra-judicial pronouncement that the law and (Christian) morality are not synonymous, was constrained to give a more 'restricted reply' to the same question. The Lucan Gospel is widely supposed to have been based on the Gospel of St Mark and, therefore, is regarded as being of later date. The *Oxford Companion to the Bible* dates it between AD 80 – 85 and suggests that the intended readership were predominantly Gentile Christians in a Greek-speaking setting.[93] The Samaritan who was the subject of Christ's Parable was a member of a group which was distinct from the wider Jewish community. They were a conservative community observing the Sabbath and the religious dietary laws with particular strictness. It is in this context that the Parable – the answer to the question, 'Who is my Neighbour?' – makes sense. Conventionally, one's neighbour might, in Roman Judea, have been regarded as a fellow member of one's own religious community or people. A Samaritan, regarded as a member of a heretical sect of Judaism, conveniently stood as the foreigner; as the person whom an observant Jew would not have viewed as his neighbour. However, it was the Samaritan, the foreigner, who came to the aid of the man fallen among thieves. That the Samaritan was chosen, in distinction to the Priest and the Levite (the leaders of the community), as the hero of the Parable neatly illustrated the universality of Christ's Golden Rule:

'If the question had been "Is the Samaritan my neighbour, too?" the answer would have been a pretty clear-cut no given the situation at the time. But Jesus now turns the whole matter on its head: The Samaritan ... makes himself the neighbour and shows me that I have to learn to be a neighbour deep within and that I already have the answer in myself. I have to become like someone in love, someone whose heart is open to being shaken up by another's need. Then I find my neighbour, or – better – then I am found by him.'[94]

In their work *On Kindness*[95] Adam Phillips and Barbara Taylor describe how the early Christian thinkers argued over kindness of the sort exhibited by the Good Samaritan: whether it was innate in

93   Metzger, BM & Coogan, MD (eds) *The Oxford Companion to the Bible* (OUP, 1993).

94   Ratzinger, J (Pope Benedict XVI) *Jesus of Nazareth* (Bloomsbury), p 195.

95   Phillips, A & Taylor, B *On Kindness* (Hamish Hamilton, 2009), Chapter I.

human nature or whether it was obtained by the grace of God alone (mankind lacking innate virtue). By the eighteenth century the Scottish philosopher Adam Smith believed that the free operation of the market – its beneficent 'hidden hand' – would ensure that individual endeavour (for greater profits or for new consumer goods) would ensure that all benefited. The harnessing of the market as the means by which to ensure that one could afford to be kind found one of its keenest advocates in Margaret Thatcher who, while Prime Minister, famously answered a question from a political interviewer about inequality by observing that, 'No-one would remember the good Samaritan if he'd only had good intentions; he had money as well.'[96] In an eccentric reading of the Parable she apparently believed that, by the creation of wealth, the Good Samaritan had been able to bind the Israelite's wounds and ensure that accommodation was provided for him at the Inn. It is hard to escape the conclusion that Mrs Thatcher was more beguiled by the (surely incidental) economic detail of the Parable ('he took out two pence, and gave them to the host, and said unto him, Take care of him; and whatsoever thou spendest more ... I will repay thee')[97] than by its message of compassion towards strangers.

Lord Atkin was not the first lawyer to reach for his Bible when formulating a legal rule. Another famous lawyer, Lord Denning, once wrote, 'In coming upon legal obstacles, it is not enough to keep your law books dry. It is as well to have a Bible to hand too. It is the most tattered book in my library. I have drawn upon it constantly.'[98] Given the Scriptural lineage of the neighbour principle it does not come as a surprise that it was used by Lord Bathurst to explain tortious liability in the middle of the eighteenth century (it is perhaps surprising that it was not being used much earlier than this). Indeed, Scripture has more

96   London Weekend Television, *Weekend World* 6 January 1980 (Full transcript available at the Thatcher Foundation website). Some years later, Mrs Thatcher provided the following, rather more considered, commentary during an interview with David Frost, '... the Good Samaritan was a man of substance, saw someone who needed help and therefore gave of what he had. Someone else might not have been a man of substance, that might have walked across the road and just given all the kindness and loving care and attention. But both of them would have given what they got. There's a widow's mite, as well as the gift from the much more wealthy man.' (TV-AM interview, 7 June 1987).
97   Luke 10:35.
98   Lord Denning *The Family Story* (Butterworths, 1981), p 181.

Baron Atkin of Aberdovey (1867 – 1944)
'Who then, in law, is my neighbour?'

Portrait in oils by Sir Oswald Birley (1926).
By permission of the Treasurer and the Masters of the Bench of the
Honourable Society of Gray's Inn.

Viscount Buckmaster (1861 – 1934) '... apart from authority, it is difficult to see how any common law proposition can be formulated to support ... [Mrs Donoghue's] claim.'

Bromide print by Walter Stoneman (1915).
By permission of the National Portrait Gallery.

Baron Macmillan of Aberfeldy (1873 – 1952) 'The categories of negligence are never closed.'

Whole-plate glass negative (13 June 1924).
By permission of the National Portrait Gallery.

Wellmeadow Street, Paisley in the early 1900s.

By permission of the Paisley Museum and Art Gallery.

Mrs May Donoghue holding her twin granddaughters in June 1952.

By permission of Margaret (Maggie) Tomlin (Mrs Donoghue's granddaughter).

And all because of a drink!

Shock that lurked in a ginger beer bottle

THE famous case began innocently enough with two friends having an ice cream in a cafe.

But trouble loomed when Mrs May Donoghue and a friend decided to have a ginger beer with their ices.

For the bottle was made of dark glass, so Mrs Donoghue could not see what she was about to drink.

And when the drink was poured out the decomposing remains of a snail fell out.

Mrs Donoghue became ill and was taken to hospital suffering from shock and what appeared to be a severe case of gastro-enteritis.

When she got better, she consulted a lawyer and sued David Stevenson, a Paisley aerated water manufacturer, for £500.

Her argument basically was that people who manufactured goods for public consumption owed a duty of care to their customers.

Her lawyer claimed the snail must have crawled in where the bottles were being stored before being filled.

The case was taken all the way to the House of Lords, where Lord Atkin summed up the crucial question in the case in

this way: "The rule that you are to love your neighbour becomes, in law, you must not injure your neighbour.

"You must take reasonable care to avoid acts or omissions which you can reasonably foresee would be likely to injure your neighbour."

The case went back to the Court of Session, but no evidence was led and the case was settled out of court in December 1934. Mrs Donoghue is believed to have received about £200.

If the case came up today Mrs Donoghue would seek compensation under the Consumer Protection Act, but the Atkin dictum is used in a variety of legal cases.

One recent example was the case brought against the Chief Constable of West Yorkshire alleging that he and his officers were negligent in the murder hunt for the Yorkshire Ripper and, as a result of this, other victims died unnecessarily.

This case was thrown out on the basis that the relationship between the two sides — as defined in Donoghue versus Stevenson — was not a close enough one on which to base a negligence case.

By WILMA RILEY

TWO legal experts travelled thousands of miles to Paisley to celebrate the 60th anniversary of a world-famous legal action.

Justice Martin Taylor, a supreme court judge in Vancouver, Canada, and retired lawyer John Leechman, who is now living in Perth, Australia, made a special pilgrimage to the site of the snail in the bottle case.

In 1928, May Donoghue ordered a bottle of ginger beer in the Wellmeadow Cafe in Paisley. She drank some of the contents and when her friend poured out the remains of the drink, the decomposing body of a snail oozed out.

This started what is probably the world's most famous legal action.

Special

And both men are fascinated by the case — and its implications.

Justice Taylor has made a special study of the case and regularly lectures on it to Canadian law students.

And Mr Leechman, who travelled 12,000 miles to be here, has a

close personal link with the case for his father was the acting solicitor for Mrs Donoghue.

To commemorate the anniversary of the famous drink, both men visited the site of the Wellmeadow cafe and of the Stevenson's soft drinks factory, which have both since been demolished.

And at the site of the cafe, Justice Taylor revealed that plans were afoot for the Canadian Bar Association to mark the site, which is now waste ground, with a special commemorative plaque.

MR Leechman celebrates the anniversary of the case by drinking some ginger beer as Justice Taylor pours it out. But there is no danger of anything lurking in this bottle of ginger beer ... the bottle is see-through!

He said: "The Canadian Bar Association is holding a meeting in England in 1990 and this will probably be one of the subjects under discussion.

"I am hoping it will be possible for the Bar Association to agree to put up something to commemorate the site.

"After all, the ruling in the case is one of the most important in legal circles and even today there is continuing controversy about how it should be applied in the courts. It is a fascinating case."

Mr Leechman said: "Although my father was involved in the case,

he never really spoke about it at home.

"It was not until I went to university that I heard about it — and became fascinated by it."

Both men were aided in their bid to retrace history by members of the Old Paisley Society, who researched the history of the case.

They became involved through Justice Taylor who joined the society as a overseas member many years ago.

And with their help the two men were taken to the site of the Wellmeadow cafe and then to where the ginger beer was produced.

They were also treated

to an evening of fun organised by the Society in the Sma' Shot cottages.

Trouble

And just to make the trip complete, the Society members went to the trouble of organising a mock-up of the interior of the cafe as a special treat for the two men.

Society President, Mrs Ellen Farmer, said: "We did a lot of research to make the interior as authentic as possible.

"We were also able to show the men a ginger beer bottle similar to the one that started the legal action."

Paisley Daily Express 31 August 1988.

By permission of the Paisley Daily Express.

Donoghue v Stevenson Memorial Park and Garden: August 2008.

Taken by the author.

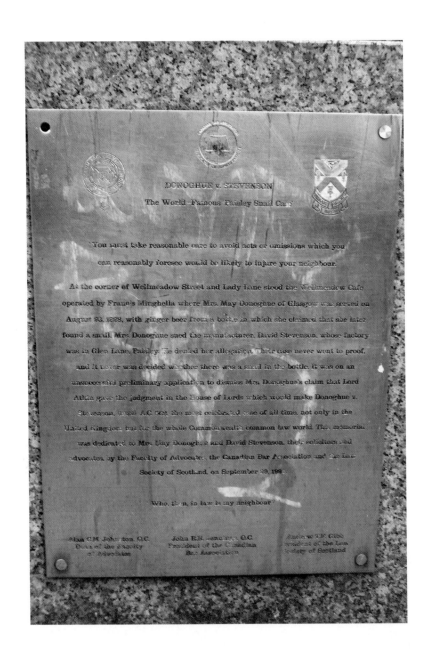

Memorial Tablet in August 2008

Taken by the author.

recently been used as a reference point for considering the Scottish law of dual vicarious liability.[99] What was novel about Lord Atkin's use of the same source material was his insistence upon the universality of the formula which he developed by using Scripture. His approach developed from his extra-judicial lecturing on the New Testament's Golden Rule to an identification of the Parable of the Good Samaritan, the universal compassion story, as (suitably modified) the means by which to advance the tort of negligence. Even from the secular perspective of our own age we can see that it was this feature of the judgment that helped to capture the imagination of the common law world and ensured that it was Lord Atkin's neighbour principle, rather than one of its many variants, that achieved lasting fame.[100]

---

99   Stewart, WJ 'A Note on Matthew 6, 24: the theology of dual vicarious liability' [2007] SLT 99.

100   The use of Lord Atkin's neighbour principle has been the subject of trenchant criticism by those who regard its presence in the *Donoghue v Stevenson* speech as merely rhetorical window-dressing or literary device: 'the final formulation of the "neighbour principle" alters the grounds of legal liability by transforming the Christian precept of loving one's neighbour into a legal responsibility for one's fellow man. Thus, the separation between law and morality, which is essential for the autonomy of law as a social institution, is being seriously eroded in this area.': see, Smith, JC & Burns, P *'Donoghue v Stevenson* – the Not so Golden Anniversary' (1983) 46 MLR 147, 148.

6. HOME REACTION

'Since *Anns v Merton London Borough Council* ... put the floodgates on the jar, a fashionable plaintiff alleges negligence. The pleading assumes that we are all neighbours now, Pharisees and Samaritans alike, that foreseeability is a reflection of hindsight and that for every mischance in an accident-prone world someone solvent must be liable in damages.'

CBS Songs Ltd v Amstrad Plc [1988] 1 AC 1013, 1059F-G *per* Lord Templeman (HL(E))

The jurisdictions of the common law world are not short of academic law journals. If a case as important as *Donoghue v Stevenson* were decided today, it would be reported on the online subscription services within moments and its importance and implications would be picked over in every academic journal from the UK to Papua New Guinea. In the early 1930s things were different. It took some time before academic lawyers, or anyone else for that matter, started to discuss the case. Sir Frederick Pollock was probably first out of the traps. In January 1933 Pollock hailed *Donoghue v Stevenson* in the pages of the Law Quarterly Review.[1] He had no doubt of its importance as a 'leading case' and described it as a 'notable step ... in enlarging and clarifying our conception of a citizen's duty before the law ... not to turn dangerous or noxious things loose on the world.' Pollock was equally gratified to note that, as a result of the courage shown by 'the Scots Lords of Appeal', the law in England had been 'brought into line with the prevailing opinion, as it appears to be, of our American learned friends, and certainly that of the learned judge, Cardozo J, who has succeeded Justice Holmes on the bench of the Supreme Court at Washington.' In the same volume of the journal there appeared a note from Lord Macmillan correcting Pollock's solecism in referring to the case by the 'cumbrous title' *M'Allister (or Donoghue) v Stevenson*. As we have seen, Lord Macmillan was keen to ensure that Mrs Donoghue's case was referenced by its shorter title: *Donoghue v Stevenson* it was and has remained. Pollock's alternative

---

1   Pollock, F 'The Snail in the Bottle and Thereafter' (1933) 49 LQR 22.

suggestion, that the case be known as 'the Snail's Case', never caught on.

A year after Pollock and Lord Macmillan's short commentaries, another succinct note appeared in the Law Quarterly Review.[2] The purpose of this was to alert readers to cases which, so the anonymous author suggested, had been decided differently as a result of *Donoghue v Stevenson*. The author wrote, perhaps with a degree of understatement, that *Donoghue v Stevenson* 'seems to have put new life into the law of tort.' In 1935 the author of yet another article in the Law Quarterly Review viewed *Donoghue v Stevenson* as a useful attempt, through judicial law-making, to limit the importance of what he described as 'an unnecessary fifth wheel on the coach' – the duty of care: a concept which the writer believed was 'incapable of sound analysis and possibly productive of injustice.'[3]

Apart from the attentions shown to it by Sir Frederick Pollock and the Law Quarterly Review, *Donoghue v Stevenson* slipped quietly into public consciousness. Lord Atkin's biographer has suggested that the legal profession did not fully comprehend the importance of *Donoghue v Stevenson* and its implications for the law of negligence until *Hedley Byrne v Heller* was decided in 1963 (although others might even claim that this did not happen until *Home Office v Dorset Yacht* in 1970). In 1935 Professor Winfield, who had surveyed the emergence of a tort of negligence in his seminal 1926 article,[4] wrote that, 'it cannot be doubted that the decision meets the needs of the community'.[5] The Solicitors' Journal noted the importance of the decision for 'millions of small transactions every day in the whole of the United Kingdom', but also pointed out that *Donoghue v Stevenson* had not attracted the public attention that it deserved.[6]

---

2   (1934) 50 LQR 459. It may be that Sir Frederick Pollock was the author of this Note.

3   Buckland, WW 'The Duty to take Care' (1935) 51 LQR 637. Buckland, writing from a Roman law perspective, suggested that contributory negligence, remoteness and even foreseeability might be used to limit the defendant's liability (as an alternative to considering whether a duty of care was owed).

4   Winfield, PH 'History of Negligence in Torts' (1926) 42 LQR 184.

5   (1935) 51 LQR 249.

6   (1932) 76 Sol J 387.

The early case law

The earliest references to *Donoghue v Stevenson* can be found in a personal injury action decided in 1932. *Farr v Butters Brothers & Company*[7] reached the Court of Appeal in June 1932 within a month of the judgment in *Donoghue v Stevenson* (McCardie J, hearing *Farr v Butters* at first instance, did not have the advantage of the House of Lords' decision). Like many of the nineteenth-century tort cases it concerned a fatal accident which had occurred while the deceased was at work. The deceased worker was an experienced crane erector employed by builders to whom the defendant, a crane manufacturer, sold a crane. The crane was sold in separate parts and it was the job of the deceased to assemble the parts of the crane so that it could be used. During the course of the assembly operation the deceased discovered a fault with certain cog-wheels; they moved stiffly and did not fit together. He dealt with this by marking in chalk the places where the wheels did not fit and said that he would report the fault to his principals. However, the deceased did not stop working on the crane and, before the faults had been repaired, he was standing under the crane when a section of it fell and struck him; killing him in the process. The accident happened as a result of the defects that the deceased had discovered while he was assembling the crane. The claim failed at first instance. Indeed, McCardie J held, after the claimant's evidence had been given, that there was no case to answer: there was no evidence that the defendant manufacturer knew that the crane was dangerous or defective and there was no concealed defect in the crane. Furthermore, the judge held, the causative negligence was that of the deceased who, as an experienced employee, had discovered the relevant defect and yet had continued to work on the crane before the defect was repaired. The claimant appealed and, as I have indicated, by the time that the appeal was heard, what Scrutton LJ described as the 'very important judgment' of the House of Lords in *Donoghue v Stevenson*[8] was available. The Court of Appeal rejected the argument that *Donoghue v Stevenson* provided the claimant with a cause of action that she would not otherwise have had. Counsel for

---

7   [1932] 2 KB 606 (CA).
8   Or *M'Alister v Stevenson*/*M'Alister's case* as he and the other judges in the Court of Appeal termed it.

the claimant implicitly accepted that the neighbour principle applied only to latent and undiscoverable defects; it was argued on her behalf that a visible and identifiable defect could still be a latent danger: an argument which Sir Frederick Pollock described shortly afterwards, somewhat contemptuously, as 'desperately ingenious'.[9] The Court of Appeal felt so confident in dismissing the *Farr v Butters* appeal that it did not call on counsel for the defendant to respond to the submissions advanced by the claimant.

Scrutton LJ gave the leading judgment in *Farr v Butters*. He commenced his commentary on *Donoghue v Stevenson* by reminding himself that, 'English judges have been slow in stating principles going far beyond the facts they are considering.'[10] This may be regarded as indicating some suspicion of the potential reach of his former pupil's neighbour principle. Indeed, taken literally, it may suggest that Scrutton LJ believed that the neighbour principle was not altogether English (perhaps because it featured in a decision made by Professor Heuston's 'celtic majority'). At a later point in his judgment Scrutton LJ observed that Lord Atkin's 'general proposition' (being the neighbour principle) went 'wider than is necessary.'[11] It certainly went considerably further than Scrutton LJ and his two colleagues in the Court of Appeal were prepared to go in entertaining the arguments of the claimant. For Scrutton LJ the fatal flaw in the claimant's argument centred on the fact that the deceased, by contrast to Mrs Donoghue, had an opportunity of 'independent examination' of the product which caused him injury. It was only where the ultimate consumer lacked the opportunity of independent examination that the 'proximate relationship' between the manufacturer and consumer could come into being and create the manufacturer's liability in tort. In other words, the proximate relationship was the condition for the existence of a duty of care and, in the absence of such duty, there was no liability.[12] Given this reading of *Donoghue v Stevenson*, it is not surprising that the *Farr v Butters* appeal was dismissed. Scrutton LJ

9   Pollock, F 'The Snail in the Bottle and Thereafter' (1933) 49 LQR 22, 26.

10   [1932] 2 KB 606, 612.

11   *Ibid*, at p 614.

12   '... if the manufacturer had left a reasonable possibility of examination, either through an intermediate person or by its use, there would be no liability, because there would be no duty.' *Ibid*, at p 620 *per* Greer LJ.

went out of his way to restrict the application of the neighbour principle and appears to have taken a dim view of the fact that, in the most celebrated passage of his speech, Lord Atkin had gone further than he needed to in order to find for Mrs Donoghue:

'Throughout ... [Lord Atkin's] judgment, in passage after passage, he makes the liability turn upon the question of the proximate relationship, and rests the proximate relationship on the fact that there could be no intervention between the manufacturer and the consumer, because the way in which the ginger-beer was put up prevented examination, so that there was no intermediate person who could or would examine.'[13]

The less than enthusiastic welcome that *Donoghue v Stevenson* received in *Farr v Butters* and the anxious concern that its application should be limited was replicated by other commentators both judicial and academic. Sir Frederick Pollock, commenting on *Farr v Butters*, regarded that decision as a salutary lesson for 'adventurous counsel and over-ingenious teachers of law ... . [Notwithstanding the 'untenable exaggeration of the rule in the Snail's Case'] We still have to take notice that there are such things as inevitable accidents which are nobody's fault, and accidents which are the sufferer's own fault because he had warning and failed to use reasonable caution.'[14]

Nearly a decade was to pass before the Court of Appeal had another opportunity to grapple with *Donoghue v Stevenson*. *Haseldine v C A Daw & Son Limited*[15] was another personal injury case; this time the subject matter concerned a defective lift in a block of flats. The lift was thirty five years old and, to the knowledge of the landlord of the block of flats in which it was installed, had never been overhauled. The landlord had a contract with a firm of engineers who were responsible for adjusting, cleaning and lubricating the lift machinery on a monthly basis. Some of the lift components needed to be replaced and the engineers informed the landlord. However, the engineers were not of the opinion (and did not tell the landlord) that they considered the lift to be dangerous. During the course of a routine maintenance visit an employee of the engineers adjusted a component within the lift, but negligently failed to replace it properly.

13   *Ibid*, at p 616.
14   Pollock, F 'The Snail in the Bottle and Thereafter' (1933) 49 LQR 22, 26.
15   [1941] 2 KB 343 (CA).

This caused the component to fracture when the lift was next used by the claimant (a seamstress). The effect of the malfunction was that the lift plummeted to the bottom of the shaft and the claimant suffered personal injury as a result. The claimant brought proceedings against the landlord and the engineers. Her case reached the Court of Appeal and, in its consideration of the case against the engineers, the Court revisited *Donoghue v Stevenson* and *Farr v Butters*. The case for the engineers was based on two grounds: first, that the law of negligence continued to be based on a 'catalogue of particular duties' and that '*Donoghue v Stevenson* did but add one more to the list'; second, that *Donoghue v Stevenson* did not, in its decision as to the duty owed by manufacturers, reflect any general principle capable of extending also to repairers (a class of defendant within which, so counsel argued, the engineers fell). Scott LJ described the task faced by counsel for the engineers as an 'arduous' one. The first argument was dismissed on the basis that it represented an erroneous reading of the history of the tort of negligence: '... although the English theory of torts had grown up first through forms of action and then through particular decisions, an analysis of our year books and generally of our case law down to 1881 discloses the gradual emergence of legal principles as its basis, and, perhaps, one may say especially so with regard to the law of negligence.'[16] The second argument advanced for the engineers was so self-evidently incorrect (on any fair reading of the majority speeches in *Donoghue v Stevenson*) that it was easily dismissed by Scott LJ.

Scott LJ attributed much of the credit for the majority decision in *Donoghue v Stevenson* to the judgment of Lord Esher MR in *Heaven v Pender*[17] and felt that this early attempt at formulating a general principle had been treated in a manner which was unjust by Cotton and Bowen LJJ (being the Lords Justices who sat alongside Lord Esher in *Heaven v Pender*). Scott LJ's view of the neighbour principle was that it represented a successful attempt by Lord Atkin to rescue

16   *Ibid*, at p 359. Scott LJ derived considerable assistance from Oliver Wendell Holmes' work on the development of the common law: 'By his book he made as great a contribution to the elucidation of principle as any one man had ever made up to then, and I believe his work greatly helped the free and natural development of English common law.'
17   (1883) 11 QBD 503.

Lord Esher from 'undeserved obloquy'. He went on to note that, in a 'curious repetition of history', Lord Atkin's efforts to state the law in terms of general principle had, like Lord Esher's efforts before him, been the subject of 'unfair criticism' and Scott LJ made it clear that, in this regard, he had in mind Scrutton LJ's judgment in *Farr v Butters*:

> 'Does not such criticism miss the real value of attempts to get at legal principle? The common law of England has throughout its long history developed as an organic growth, at first slowly under the hampering restrictions of legal forms of process, more quickly in Lord Mansfield's time, and in the last one hundred years at an ever increasing rate of progress as new cases, arising under new conditions of society, of applied science and of public opinion, have presented themselves for solution by the courts.'[18]

Inevitably, Scott LJ's conclusion was that the lift engineers clearly did owe a duty of care to any person using the lift in the ordinary way in circumstances where there was no reasonable opportunity for examination of the lift before use was made of it and when the use of the lift by another person must be expected or contemplated by the engineers. Goddard LJ agreed. Clauson LJ dissented on the grounds that there was no proximate relationship between the engineers and the claimant sufficient for her to be owed a duty of care (it was his view that the duty of care would be too widely cast to apply to engineers who simply carried out repairs to a lift for a landlord who then, in turn, permitted third parties to make use of it).

This summary of what I have described as the early case law concludes with two cases which do not concern personal injury: *Deyong v Shenburn* and *Candler v Crane, Christmas & Company*. It was in this context that the apparent universality of Lord Atkin's neighbour principle was most robustly tested. In *Deyong v Shenburn*[19] the clothing of a pantomime dame was stolen from his theatre dressing room during the Christmas season at the Palace Theatre, Camberwell. He brought proceedings in the County Court against his employer and succeeded in establishing that the employer was negligent in failing, despite the claimant's request, to ensure that a lock was placed on the dressing room door. It was also found by the judge that the

18   [1941] 2 KB 343, 362 – 363.
19   [1946] 1 KB 227 (CA).

dressing room attendant was absent through ill health on the day of the theft and, as a result of the defendant's negligence, had not been replaced until after the theft had taken place. These victories proved to be pyrrhic. The claimant's action failed at first instance and in the Court of Appeal. In the absence of a relationship of bailment or any contractual obligation with respect to the clothing, there was no duty of care. The leading judgment in the Court of Appeal was delivered by du Parcq LJ and bristles with warnings not to widen the application of *Donoghue v Stevenson*:

> 'There has to be a breach of a duty which the law recognizes, and to ascertain what the law recognizes regard must be had to the decisions of the courts. There has never been a decision that a master must, merely because of the relationship which exists between master and servant, take reasonable care for the safety of his servant's belongings in the sense that he must take steps to ensure, so far as he can, that no wicked person shall have an opportunity of stealing the servant's goods. That is the duty contended for here, and there is not a shred of authority to suggest that any such duty exists or has ever existed.'[20]

This passage represents a curious throwback to the days when one had first to find a category of case in which a duty of care had been found to be owed before the claimant had any sustainable cause of action in tort; it is obviously difficult to reconcile with the neighbour principle and with Lord Macmillan's pronouncement that the 'categories of negligence are never closed.' An interesting feature of *Deyong v Shenburn* (in addition to its rather exotic subject matter) is that junior counsel for the claimant was one T Elder Jones who was second junior counsel for Mr Stevenson when *Donoghue v Stevenson* reached the House of Lords: the man with the singular distinction of being the sole representative of the English Bar before the Appellate Committee (there is a pleasing symmetry in the fact that in *Deyong v Shenburn* he would have been arguing the opposite of what he and his leader had argued in *Donoghue v Stevenson*).

Candler v Crane, Christmas & Company[21] was a professional negligence action brought against a firm of accountants. The claimant considered investing £2,000 in a limited liability company, but sensibly

---

20 *Ibid*, at p 233.
21 [1951] 2 KB 164 (CA).

wished to see the company's accounts before committing himself. The company's managing director, keen to see the claimant's investment, directed the defendant accountants, who were in the process of completing the company's accounts, to get on and finish the same so that they could be shown to the claimant. A clerk employed by the defendant knew that they were to be shown to the claimant and also knew that he was proposing to invest in the company. The claimant was shown the company's accounts when they were completed and, having seen them and discussed them with both the defendant's clerk and with his own accountant, invested his money in the company. In fact, the accounts had been negligently prepared and were littered with errors and inaccuracies. They provided a wholly inaccurate picture of the state of the company which was wound up within a year with the result that the claimant lost the whole of his investment. The claimant brought an action in negligence against the defendant accountants. At first instance it was held that no duty of care was owed by the defendant to the claimant and the action was dismissed. The claimant appealed. The appeal failed in the Court of Appeal. The majority (Cohen and Asquith LJJ) held that the principle that, absent a contractual or fiduciary relationship between the parties, no duty of care was owed in tort with respect to negligent misrepresentations had not been abrogated by *Donoghue v Stevenson*. Asquith LJ relied on the famous decisions in *Derry v Peek*[22] and *Le Lievre v Gould*[23] in support of his conclusions. He was quite satisfied that, even on the widest reading of the judgments, *Donoghue v Stevenson* was not intended to overrule this case law.

Asquith LJ then went further. First, he thought it significant that *Donoghue v Stevenson* had not been applied, in the two decades or so since it was decided, to any case that did not involve physical damage or injury. Second, he directed himself (probably correctly) that the other majority judges in the *Donoghue v Stevenson* House of Lords (Lords Thankerton and Macmillan) had not endorsed Lord Atkin's neighbour principle and had not themselves intended to formulate any overarching general principle. Third, he said (perhaps incorrectly) that Lord Atkin had not himself intended to lay down any

22   (1889) 37 Ch D 541 (HL(E)).
23   [1895] 1 KB 491 (CA).

principle of general application. Fourth, he doubted the argument that had been advanced by the claimant on appeal that *Le Lievre v Gould* could be distinguished on the grounds that in that case there was insufficient proximity between the parties to support the existence of a duty of care. It will be recalled that even Lord Atkin's neighbour principle is qualified as owed to those 'persons who are so closely and directly affected by my act that *I ought reasonably to have them in contemplation as being so affected when I am directing my mind to the acts or omissions which are called in question.* [emphasis added]' It was suggested by counsel for the claimant that this requirement was not satisfied in *Le Lievre v Gould*, but was satisfied in *Candler v Crane, Christmas & Company*. In that way, the claimant sought to sidestep the logic of *Le Lievre v Gould* (being, that his claim should also fail). Asquith LJ rejected this attempt to avoid the application of *Le Lievre v Gould* and dismissed the appeal. Cohen LJ agreed with Asquith LJ.

The third Judge in the Court of Appeal was Denning LJ who went on to achieve lasting fame when he was 'demoted' from the House of Lords to occupy, as he did for decades in the last half of the twentieth century, the position of Master of the Rolls. Denning LJ did not agree with the approach taken by the majority. His consideration of the key issue in the case – whether a duty of care was owed – commenced by identifying what he believed to be 'two cardinal errors' which had, at the time that *Le Lievre v Gould* was decided, acted as a brake on the development of the law. The first error was the belief that only those who were parties to a contract could sue on the contract or on any subject matter arising out of the contract. The second was that no cause of action was available for negligent misrepresentation, even in circumstances where the representation was intended to be acted upon by the representee and where, in fact, he did rely on the representation and sustained losses as a result. Denning LJ made it clear that it was his intention to 'destroy' the submissions based on these errors and the instrument of destruction that he chose to deploy was *Donoghue v Stevenson* (and, in particular, the neighbour principle of Lord Atkin).[24] Denning LJ rejected in emphatic (and, so far as his own judicial career

---

24 'Let me first be destructive and destroy the submissions put forward by Mr Foster [for the accountants]' [1951] 2 KB 164, 178.

was concerned, prophetic) terms the argument that the law should not advance because there had been no earlier cases which supported the contentions of the claimant, 'If you read the great cases ... you will find that in each of them the judges were divided in opinion. On the one side there were the timorous souls who were fearful of allowing a new cause of action. On the other side there were the bold spirits who were ready to allow it if justice so required. It was fortunate for the common law that the progressive view prevailed.'[25] Denning LJ was equally dismissive of the contention that the character of the loss or damage sustained as a result of the tortious act – whether the damage was physical or financial – should determine whether a duty of care was owed. It was his view that the logic of recovery according to the principles laid down in *Donoghue v Stevenson* was as capable of application to cases of financial loss, as to physical damage, although he conceded that in the former case it may be difficult to establish the requisite proximity between tortfeasor and victim. Denning LJ held that those exercising a professional calling, like 'accountants, surveyors, valuers and analysts', owed a duty of care not only with respect to the contents of their reports, but also in their conduct of the work which resulted in their reports. Such persons owed a duty to exercise skill and care to those closely and directly affected by their work whether or not there was a contractual relationship between the parties. In the circumstances, Denning LJ concluded that a duty of care was owed by the defendant accountants and, therefore, that liability was established. He acknowledged a proximity test to limit the application of his approach: 'did the accountants know that the accounts were required for submission to the plaintiff and use by him?'[26] Provided this qualification was satisfied and there was, as a result, sufficient proximity between the parties, Denning LJ was in no doubt that a duty of care was owed. A further twelve years were to pass before the House of Lords concluded that he was right. By this time, *Donoghue v Stevenson* had been sitting on the library shelves for more than three decades.

---

25   *Ibid.*
26   *Ibid*, at p 181.

Hedley Byrne v Heller

This 1963 decision of the House of Lords may be regarded as exemplifying the rapid progress made by the English common law from the 1930s onwards. Professor Fleming regards *Hedley Byrne & Company Limited v Heller & Partners Limited*[27] as having 'opened the door to negligent economic loss, almost reaching into the borderland of contract.'[28] The claimants were advertising agents who had placed a substantial forward order for a company on such terms that the claimants would be personally liable for the orders. The claimants asked their bankers to enquire into the credit worthiness of the company's financial stability and the bankers made enquiries in turn of the defendants who were the company's bankers. The defendants' references for the company were favourable, but they stated that their references were 'without responsibility'. The claimants relied on the representations that they had received and placed orders. They sustained losses of £17,000 when the representations turned out to be false. The claimants brought proceedings against the defendants for negligent misrepresentation. Their claim failed at first instance, on appeal to the Court of Appeal and, ultimately, in the House of Lords. The interest of the decision in the Appellate Committee lies in its consideration whether a cause of action was available to the claimants in principle (and, for the purposes of this book, the manner in which the House dealt with the effect of *Donoghue v Stevenson*). The House of Lords took the view that a duty of care could arise in circumstances where, 'someone possessed of a special skill undertakes, quite irrespective of contract, to apply that skill for the assistance of another person who relies upon such skill ... .'[29] The recognition of a potential duty of care in these circumstances demonstrates the distance that had been travelled in the law of negligence in the period since cases like *Le Lievre v Gould* were being decided. Given the House of Lords' conclusions on this issue, 'it must follow that *Candler, Crane, Christmas & Co* was wrongly decided.'[30] In fact, the *Hedley Byrne v Heller* claimants failed in their appeal because the defendants had expressly and effectively disclaimed responsibility which, it was held,

---

27   [1964] AC 465 (HL(E)).
28   Fleming, P *The Law of Torts* (Sweet & Maxwell, 9th ed, 1998), p 154.
29   [1964] AC 465, 502 *per* Lord Morris of Borth-y-Gest.
30   *Ibid*, at p 487 *per* Lord Reid.

precluded the existence of a duty of care; their victory on the point of principle was a hollow one.

In the course of his speech in *Hedley Byrne v Heller* Lord Devlin explained Lord Atkin's neighbour principle, which he preferred to describe as a 'proximity principle', as having a general and a specific character. The general conception was based on the existence of a duty of care in circumstances where the requirement of proximity between the parties was satisfied because A regarded B as 'so closely and directly affected by ... [A's] act that ... [A] ought reasonably to have him in contemplation as being so affected when ... [A was] directing ... [his] mind to the acts or omissions which are called in question.'[31] The specific proposition arising out of the general conception concerned the liability of Mr Stevenson, the manufacturer; in other words, the application of the general conception in a product liability context:

> 'Now, it is not, in my opinion, a sensible application of what Lord Atkin was saying for a judge to be invited on the facts of any particular case to say whether or not there was "proximity" between the plaintiff and the defendant. That would be a misuse of a general conception and it is not the way in which English law develops. What Lord Atkin did was to open up a category of cases giving rise to a special duty. It was already clear that the law recognised the existence of such a duty in the category of articles that were dangerous in themselves. What *Donoghue v Stevenson* did may be described either as the widening of an old category or as the creation of a new and similar one. The general conception can be used to produce other categories in the same way. An existing category grows as instances of its application multiply until the time comes when the cell divides.'[32]

It was by this incremental method, moving from the general to the particular, that English law evolved and, for Lord Devlin, this was the key to the advances achieved with the assistance of *Donoghue v Stevenson*. However, like the other law lords in *Hedley Byrne v Heller* he took the view that the claimants had 'tried to press *Donoghue v Stevenson* too hard', believing that while Lord Atkin's general conception might be of assistance, the specific proposition which

31   *Ibid*, at p 524.
32   *Ibid*, at pp 524 – 525.

flowed from it could not easily be applied to the facts of *Hedley Byrne v Heller*.[33]

Home Office v Dorset Yacht

The 1970 decision of the House of Lords in *Home Office v Dorset Yacht Company Limited*[34] is commonly bracketed with *Donoghue v Stevenson* and *Hedley Byrne v Heller* as the third and final entry in a competition for the greatest tort decisions of the twentieth century. Like *Hedley Byrne v Heller* it owes much to *Donoghue v Stevenson* and the law lords' speeches contain detailed commentary on Lord Atkin's neighbour principle.

Home Office v Dorset Yacht arose out of what appears to have been a nostalgic attempt to recreate Lord Baden-Powell's expeditionary trip to Brownsea Island, Poole Harbour (which resulted in his seminal work, *Scouting for Boys*). The Home Office also took a group of boys to Brownsea Island. The boys were occupants of a borstal and, between them, had convictions for breaking and entering, theft and taking vehicles without consent. Most of the boys had records of absconding from borstal institutions. Under cover of darkness one night, the boys escaped from the supervision of the borstal officers who were with them and, while at liberty, boarded and cast adrift a motor yacht which belonged to the claimants and which was moored in Poole Harbour, just off Brownsea Island. For good measure the borstal boys had, before boarding the claimants' motor yacht, sailed another yacht into collision with her. The claimants' motor yacht was severely damaged and they brought an action in negligence against the Prison Commissioners (later amended to the Home Office). A preliminary issue was identified for trial: namely, 'whether on the facts pleaded in the statement of claim the defendants their servants or agents owed any duty of care to the plaintiffs capable of giving rise to a liability in damages ... .' The claimants succeeded at first instance

---

33 '... they take the specific proposition laid down by *Donoghue v Stevenson* and try to apply it literally to a certificate or a banker's reference. That will not do, for a general conception cannot be applied to pieces of paper in the same way as to articles of commerce or to writers in the same way as manufacturers.' *Ibid*, at p 525.
34 [1970] AC 1004 (HL(E)).

and on appeal (in a Court of Appeal presided over by Lord Denning – by now, Master of the Rolls). The defendant appealed.

The House of Lords concluded (on a 4:1 split, Viscount Dilhorne dissenting) that a duty of care was owed by the Home Office to the owners of the damaged motor yacht and the preliminary issue was, therefore, determined in the claimants' favour. Lord Diplock's speech contains the most careful analysis of Lord Atkin's neighbour principle that has yet been seen. He had no doubt of the importance of the task that had fallen to the House of Lords in *Home Office v Dorset Yacht* which he regarded as being on a par with that undertaken in *Donoghue v Stevenson* and *Hedley Byrne v Heller*: namely, deciding to extend the English law of negligence to recognise a right to recover damages where no such right had previously been recognised. Lord Diplock's tentative view was that this task was, essentially, and by contrast to what most judges do in most cases, 'law-making' and concerned the resolution of competing issues of public policy. For Lord Diplock, it was for this reason, rather than because of its rhetorical brilliance, much less its use of Biblical allusion, that Lord Atkin's neighbour principle had a seminal effect upon the law of negligence.[35] After all, Lord Diplock pointed out, the Parable of the Good Samaritan concerned, in the conduct of the Priest and the Levite who passed by on the other side, '... an omission which was likely to have as its reasonable and probable consequence damage to the health of the victim ... , but for which the Priest and Levite would have incurred no liability in English law.'[36] It is this kind of close-up analysis of Scripture, when applied to legal principles, that has been satirised by some commentators as 'hard theology makes bad law.'[37]

Having boldly recognised the policy role played by judges in recognising duties of care where none had previously existed, Lord Diplock was keen to explain and to limit the judicial role in these circumstances. While his intention appears to have been to highlight the constraints placed upon judicial 'law-making', the fact that he recognised that this was the task undertaken by the judiciary in hard

35   *Ibid*, at p 1058D.
36   *Ibid*, at p 1060F.
37   See, Smith, JC and Burns, P '*Donoghue v Stevenson* – the Not so Golden Anniversary' (1983) 46 MLR 147, 148.

cases and his willingness to attempt an explanation of how judges went about this task was radical so far as English law was concerned. Lord Diplock's approach to the identification of a (new) duty of care had two stages: an inductive and then a deductive or analytical stage. During the first stage the 'analyst' or judge considered previous decisions where a duty of care had been held to exist and identified relationships between the parties and conduct which possessed characteristics A, B, C and D (and decisions where no duty of care had been found to exist where such characteristics were missing). In the second stage, the inductive proposition[38] was converted to the following affirmative: 'In all cases where the conduct and relationship possess each of the characteristics A, B, C and D ... a duty of care arises.'[39] Lord Diplock accepted that there was a practical limitation to his two-stage approach: namely, the 'sheer volume of reported cases' and the fact that selecting previous decisions to be analysed, and eliminating certain cases (to make the task of the analyst more manageable), might skew the process of identifying the characteristics present when a duty of care had been held to exist. Lord Diplock acknowledged that, in hard cases, one or more of the identifying characteristics, A, B, C or D, would be missing and it was in these cases that a policy decision, or the exercise of judicial law-making, was called for. However, even when resolving a policy issue, when the judge's task would necessarily be less constrained by previous decisions, Lord Diplock believed that precedent retained a role:

'The policy decision will be influenced by the same general conception of what ought to give rise to a duty of care as was used in approaching the analysis. The choice to extend is given effect to by redefining the characteristics [ie. A, B, C, D etc.] in more general terms so as to exclude the necessity to conform to limitations imposed by the former definition which are considered to be inessential.'[40]

Lord Diplock tested his two-stage approach by applying it to Lord Atkin's neighbour principle against the background of the submissions made by the claimants in *Home Office v Dorset Yacht*. He

---

38   That is, in these cases a duty of care was found to exist and factors A, B, C and D were present in each of them.

39   [1970] AC 1004 , 1059B.

40   *Ibid*, at p 1059D-E.

had no doubt that what he described as Lord Atkin's aphorism, used as a guide to the characteristics (Lord Diplock's A, B, C, D etc.) found to exist in the relationships and conduct giving rise to a duty of care, represented a 'milestone in the modern development of the law of negligence.'[41] However, like Lord Devlin in *Hedley Byrne v Heller*, he took the view that the Dorset Yacht claimants had sought to press Lord Atkin's neighbour principle too far. Lord Diplock's view was that the neighbour principle, 'misused as a universal ... is manifestly false.'[42] If, so Lord Diplock asserted, Lord Atkin's aphorism had 'universal' application, rather than being merely a handy guide to the identifying characteristics which might enable a judge to test whether a duty of care existed in a given situation, it would have provided the Good Samaritan with a cause of action against the Levite and would also, without more (and, save for the express disclaimer of responsibility), have been directly applicable in *Hedley Byrne v Heller*. This was not, as Lord Diplock explained, the case.

Having disposed of any notion that the neighbour principle had universal application, Lord Diplock made it clear that he regarded *Home Office v Dorset Yacht* as differing from *Donoghue v Stevenson* in two important respects: both as to conduct and as to the relationship between the parties. First, the damage sustained by Dorset Yacht was the direct consequence of a tort consciously committed by third parties responsible in law for their own acts and this conduct was interposed between the alleged negligence of the defendant and the damage sustained by the claimants. Second, the defendant had two neighbour relationships: one with the claimants and another with the third parties. These might give rise to competing and conflicting duties of care. Accordingly, 'This appeal, therefore, also raises the lawyer's question: "Am I my brother's keeper?" A question which may also receive a restricted reply.'[43]

The other judges forming the majority in *Home Office v Dorset Yacht* adopted a more prosaic method to dismiss the defendant's arguments. Lord Reid was quite satisfied that the damage sustained by the claimants was foreseeable and this was a necessary, if not

41   *Ibid*, at p 1060E.
42   *Ibid*.
43   *Ibid*, at p 1061D *per* Lord Diplock.

sufficient, condition for a finding of liability. Lord Reid's commentary on the neighbour principle perhaps comes close to according it the 'universal' status that Lord Diplock described as a 'misuse':

'*Donoghue v Stevenson* ... may be regarded as a milestone, and the well known passage in Lord Atkin's speech should I think be regarded as a statement of principle. It is not to be treated as if it were a statutory definition. It will require qualification in new circumstances. But I think that the time has come when we can and should say that it ought to apply unless there is some justification or valid explanation for its exclusion.'[44]

For his part, Lord Reid was quite content to make use of the neighbour principle and the process of its evolution, to shoot down the defendant's argument, expressed by Sir Elwyn Jones QC (then Attorney-General), that the absence of authority for imposing a duty on the Home Office should preclude the House of Lords finding that a duty of care was owed. Such arguments, thought Lord Reid, belonged to the turn of the twentieth century (even when presented by the Attorney-General) and had no place in a post-*Donoghue v Stevenson* age.

Even Viscount Dilhorne, who dissented from the view of the majority, acknowledged that his dissent needed to be justified in the context of *Donoghue v Stevenson* and Lord Atkin's neighbour principle. Like Lord Diplock he was unpersuaded that Lord Atkin intended his famous aphorism to have universal application and did not believe that limiting the same by requiring that the consequences of an actor's acts or omissions be reasonably foreseeable provided any meaningful method by which to identify when a duty of care was and was not owed. Instead, Viscount Dilhorne believed that the neighbour principle, while useful in identifying those to whom a duty of care was owed, could not be used to determine whether a duty of care existed in the first place. Viscount Dilhorne found support for his conclusion in the judgment of du Parcq LJ in *Deyong v Shenburn* and

---

44   *Ibid*, at p 1027A-B. Lord Morris of Borth-y-Gest similarly regarded Lord Atkin's neighbour principle as an important and generally recognised 'statement of principle', although, like Lord Reid, he accepted that it could not be applied 'as though ... [the] words were contained in a positive and precise legislative enactment.' *Ibid*, at p 1034F.

concluded – as Lord Buckmaster did in *Donoghue v Stevenson* itself – '... we are concerned not with what the law should be but with what it is. The absence of authority shows that no such duty now exists. If there should be one, that is, in my view, a matter for the legislature and not for the courts.'[45] That this conclusion appeared, at least to the law lords forming the majority in *Home Office v Dorset Yacht*, distinctly quaint, old-fashioned and even untenable in the light of *Donoghue v Stevenson*, shows how far the law had moved in the four decades which separated the two House of Lords decisions.

Setting boundaries: proximity, foreseeability and policy

One reading of the developments that have taken place since 1932 might emphasise the limitations that judges, including those who are otherwise enthusiastic about Lord Atkin's approach, have sought to place on the application of the neighbour principle. Such efforts underline the potential universality of Lord Atkin's principle and its attractiveness to Lord Denning's 'bold spirits' who have sought to establish duties of care when none have previously existed. Efforts to set boundaries have, as we have seen, been focussed on the requirement of foresight: Lord Atkin's identification of one's neighbour as the person 'so closely and directly affected by my act that I ought reasonably to have them in contemplation as being so affected when I am directing my mind to the acts or omissions which are called in question.' The elegant simplicity of this test has, however, perplexed judicial conservatives and radicals alike. Does it simply import a test of reasonable foreseeability, perhaps more suitable for dealing with issues of causation and remoteness of loss, as a means of identifying when a duty of care is owed? Does the neighbour principle permit a court to have regard to other factors in determining whether or not a duty of care is owed (for example, past decisions of the courts, considerations of public policy or even more abstract concepts of fairness)? In a wider sense, why should the common law use the concept of a duty of care to limit the wider boundaries of liability in any event – isn't that the task of the standard of care and causation or remoteness of damage? The last four decades[46] have seen the courts

---

45   *Ibid*, at p 1045G-H.
46   That is, the years that have passed since *Home Office v Dorset Yacht* was before

of the United Kingdom and of the wider common law world grapple with these issues on a regular basis. While something of an uneasy truce has, in recent years, been achieved, the battle over these issues was raging fiercely when Professor Heuston addressed my class of undergraduates at the beginning of the 1990s.[47]

Anns v Merton London Borough Council[48] reached the House of Lords in 1977. It concerned a block of flats which had been constructed on ground that was subject to subsidence. The subsidence ultimately resulted in damage to the flats and those tenants who held long leases brought proceedings against the defendant local authority (and others) for negligently failing to inspect the foundations of the premises before approving the building works on the basis of plans that were submitted by the builders (it was argued that a careful inspection would have disclosed the need to build the flats with deeper foundations). The key issue in the case was whether a duty of care was owed by the local authority to the tenants at all. There were other considerations which made it differ from those cases which had already been considered in the duty of care context. First, the defendant local authority was not responsible for the defect which had caused structural damage in the form of sloping floors and cracked walls. Instead, the local authority had simply failed, in its supervisory function, to protect the tenants from the consequences of the builder's negligence. Second, the local authority exercised a statutory function in its supervision of building works and, so the argument went, this should be the subject of scrutiny by the legislature, rather than by the courts. Third, there was no accident causing damage in the form of injury to person or to other property; the tenant's loss was a purely financial or pecuniary one measured by the impact of the subsidence on the value of their property interest or, alternatively, the cost of repairs.

In answering the question whether a duty of care existed at all Lord Wilberforce acknowledged his debt to what he termed the 'trilogy of cases in this House': *Donoghue v Stevenson*, *Hedley Byrne v Heller* and *Home Office v Dorset Yacht*. He also advocated a two-stage test for the question whether a duty of care existed and the two

---

the House of Lords.

47   See Prologue.

48   [1978] AC 728 (HL(E)).

components were foreseeability (Lord Atkin's neighbour principle) and policy:

> 'First one has to ask whether, as between the alleged wrongdoer and the person who has suffered damage there is a sufficient relationship of proximity or neighbourhood such that, in the reasonable contemplation of the former, carelessness on his part may be likely to cause damage to the latter – in which case a prima facie duty of care arises. Secondly, if the first question is answered affirmatively, it is necessary to consider whether there are any considerations which ought to negative, or to reduce or limit the scope of the duty or the class of person to whom it is owed or the damages to which a breach of it may give rise.'[49]

The policy considerations which extended beyond considerations of proximity or neighbourhood (the second stage in Lord Wilberforce's test) might include anxieties about the class of persons to whom a duty of care would be owed (as, for example, in *Hedley Byrne v Heller* where concern was expressed about the number of persons who might rely on the tortfeasor's misrepresentation) or about the nature of the loss suffered (whether purely economic or otherwise) or, indeed, about whether a private law duty of care should be acknowledged in a case where the parties' relationship was governed in the public sphere by statute (as in *Anns v Merton* itself). Ultimately, Lord Wilberforce and all of his colleagues in the House of Lords concluded that a duty of care was owed by the local authority to the tenants. He made clear his belief that the logical outcome of *Donoghue v Stevenson* (and, in particular, the neighbour principle) was the existence of a private law duty of care which extended, in cases of sufficient proximity, even into the statutory functions of public bodies. However, he also acknowledged that the full implications of this (the full reach and radicalism of the neighbour principle) had not been realised until the decision of the House of Lords in *Home Office v Dorset Yacht*.

Lord Wilberforce's bold attempt at a refinement of the neighbour principle which would enable it to be universally applied to ever new and more far reaching factual contexts was first doubted and then definitively overruled. Old tensions and anxieties about the potential reach of the *Anns v Merton* test quickly surfaced (reflecting a current

49   *Ibid*, at pp 751H-752A.

in common law thinking about the importance of precedent and an unwillingness to recognise a duty of care where none had existed before that, as we have seen, can be traced back to the early nineteenth century and beyond).[50]

In 1985 the High Court of Australia declined to apply Lord Wilberforce's two-stage test in a case called *Sutherland Shire Council v Heyman*.[51] Brennan J criticised the possibilities for a 'massive extension of a prima facie duty of care' which *Anns v Merton* appeared to create. Instead, Brennan J's preference was for an incrementalist approach to novel categories of negligence which were developed 'by analogy with established categories'. In *Yuen Kun Yeu v Attorney-General of Hong Kong*[52] the Privy Council, hearing an appeal from the Court of Appeal, directed that, in future, the two-stage test in *Anns v Merton* should not be regarded as in all circumstances a suitable guide in determining whether or not a duty of care was owed. Instead, it was necessary to have regard to whether a close and direct relationship between the parties existed and this involved consideration of all the circumstances, including the reasonable contemplation of harm being caused to the claimant by the defendant's failure to exercise reasonable care and any considerations of public policy which might militate against the existence of a duty of care.

The rapid retreat from Lord Wilberforce's approach in *Anns v Merton* culminated in *Murphy v Brentwood District Council*[53] in which the House of Lords decided that Lord Wilberforce was simply wrong. This case, like *Anns v Merton*, concerned a local authority's approval of the plans for the construction of a property. The local authority had relied on the advice of a consulting engineer which had not properly taken account of miscalculations in the design of

---

50   The reaction to *Anns v Merton* was given impetus by the decision of the House of Lords in *Junior Books Ltd v Veitchi Co Ltd* [1983] AC 520 (HL(Sc)) in which, following Lord Wilberforce's two-stage test, a duty of care had been recognised by a majority in the House of Lords in the context of a case involving pure economic loss. The horror with which this extension of the boundaries of liability in tort was, at least in some quarters, greeted swiftly resulted in a questioning of the underlying principle and, therefore, further questions about the reliability of *Anns v Merton*.

51   (1985) 60 ALR 1, 43.

52   [1988] AC 175 (PC).

53   [1991] 1 AC 398 (HL(E)).

the foundations. As a result of the defective foundations there was extensive damage to the walls and pipework of the house. The claimant owner of the property did not carry out repairs, but sold the property at an undervaluation. The purchaser moved into the house and did not carry out repairs. The claimant's claim was for pure economic loss, represented by the difference between the market value and the value that the house had realised when sold. The House of Lords held that *Donoghue v Stevenson*, Lord Atkin's neighbour principle, applied to impose on the builder of a property a duty to exercise reasonable care and skill to avoid injury or damage through defects in its construction to those whom he might reasonably contemplate would be affected by his acts or omissions. However, this duty only extended to latent defects. Accordingly, where a defect was discovered before any injury to person or damage to property, other than the defective house itself, had occurred, the loss suffered by the claimant was pure economic loss and, accordingly, was irrecoverable because no duty of care was owed in respect of it. The House of Lords went further and held that the local authority's duties were regulated by public law duties in the form of supervising compliance with building regulations and so forth. The extension of the local authority's duties by the imposition, alongside public regulation, of a private law duty of care was contrary to public policy and should not be permitted; such extension was a matter for Parliament. The Lord Chancellor stated as follows: 'For this House in its judicial capacity to create a large new area of responsibility on local authorities in respect of defective buildings would in my opinion not be a proper exercise of judicial power.'[54] *Murphy v Brentwood* may be said to represent the most successful attempt to cram the genie (or perhaps, for present purposes, the snail) back in the bottle.

During the early 1990s further attempts to formulate a general principle by which to test the existence of a duty of care have been made. In *Smith v Eric S Bush*,[55] for example, Lord Griffiths posited a test based on (i) foreseeability; (ii) proximity; and (iii) (as a final catch all) justice and reasonableness. This was the test that was in vogue at the time of my undergraduate tort studies. In *Caparo Industries Plc*

---

54   *Ibid*, at p 457C-D *per* Lord Mackay of Clashfern LC.
55   [1990] 1 AC 831 (HL(E)).

v Dickman & Others[56] the House of Lords returned to these issues again (this case concerned, among other things, reliance on a report by auditors which was alleged to have been negligently prepared). Lord Bridge of Harwich summarised the stage that he believed that the common law had reached in its search for a test by which to identify whether a duty was owed:

> 'What emerges is that, in addition to the foreseeability of damage, necessary ingredients in any situation giving rise to a duty of care are that there should exist between the party owing the duty and the party to whom it is owed a relationship characterised by the law as one of 'proximity' or 'neighbourhood' and that the situation should be one in which the court considers it fair, just and reasonable that the law should impose a duty of a given scope upon the one party for the benefit of the other.'[57]

Lord Oliver of Aylmerton agreed that the three criteria identified by Lord Bridge should be used, but was not wholly persuaded that, in reality, the three criteria were conceptually different, '... in some cases the degree of foreseeability is such that it is from that alone the requisite proximity can be deduced, whilst in others the absence of the essential relationship can most rationally be attributed to the court's view that it would not be fair and reasonable to hold the defendant responsible.'[58]

Professor Fleming, writing from an Australian perspective, regards the criteria identified by the English courts in the last two decades as, essentially, meaningless (or, at least, as synonymous and incapable of separation). He believes that Lord Atkin's 'restricted reply' and what he views as its encouragement of a concentration on foresight or 'proximity' has 'cast a baleful shadow over judicial ruminations on duty':

> 'The judicial tendency to take refuge in seemingly bland, neutral concepts, like foreseeability and proximity, under the pretence that they represent "principle" has its roots in the embarrassment with

---

56   [1990] 2 AC 605 (HL(E)).
57   *Ibid*, at pp 617-618.
58   *Ibid*, at p 633.

which British conservative tradition has generally treated the role of policy in judicial decision-making.'[59]

Professor Fleming has welcomed the intrusion of policy – the use of the criterion of justice, fairness and reasonableness in determining whether a duty of care is owed – as a realistic recognition of what has been happening all the time: judges have been considering the implications of a decision for society at large and looking beyond the dispute involving a particular claimant and defendant.[60] Judges have, as Lord Diplock acknowledged in *Home Office v Dorset Yacht*, been making law and have been doing so in a manner which is of fundamental importance to the way in which we conduct our relationships and regulate our conduct. In a House of Lords decision reported in 2001, Lord Browne-Wilkinson said this:

> 'In English law the decision as to whether it is fair, just and reasonable to impose a liability in negligence on a particular class of would-be defendants depends on weighing in the balance the total detriment to the public interest in all cases from holding such class liable in negligence as against the total loss to all would-be plaintiffs if they are not to have a cause of action in respect of the loss they have individually suffered.'[61]

The judicial discretion which is necessarily involved in this exercise may mean that we have moved, in the decades since *Donoghue v Stevenson* was decided, from consideration of what is, essentially, a legal question – is a duty of care owed? – towards a merits-based, factual enquiry – is this a case where a finding of liability should be made?[62] As a late addition to the criteria by which the courts test whether a duty of care is owed, the policy-based approach (whether

---

59   Fleming, P *The Law of Torts* (Sweet & Maxwell, 9th ed, 1998), p 153.

60   Other academic commentators would agree: see, for example, Conaghan, J & Mansell, W *The Wrongs of Tort* (Pluto Press, 2nd ed, 1999), pp 13 – 21. See also, Beever, A *Rediscovering the Law of Negligence* (Hart Publishing, 2007), p 3.

61   *Barrett v Enfield London Borough Council* [2001] 2 AC 550 (HL(E)).

62   See, Smith, JC and Burns, P '*Donoghue v Stevenson* – the Not so Golden Anniversary' (1983) 46 MLR 147, 162: 'It is much easier from a judicial standpoint to admit the duty (unless negated by statute or precedent) and go to the factual merits.'

it is fair, just and reasonable to recognise a duty of care) has, perhaps, emerged as the pre-eminent consideration.[63]

---

63   See also, Lord Denning MR in *Spartan Steel v Martin & Co* [1973] QB 27, 37D (CA): 'The more I think about these cases, the more difficult I find it to put each into its proper pigeon-hole. Sometimes I say: "There was no duty." In others I say: "The damage was too remote." So much so that I think the time has come to discard those tests which have proved so elusive. It seems to me better to consider the particular relationship in hand, and see whether or not, as a matter of policy, economic loss should be recoverable, or not.'

7. INTO THE COMMON LAW WORLD

'... it is of the utmost importance that in all parts of the Empire where English law prevails, the interpretation of that law by the courts should be as nearly as possible the same.'

Trimble v Hill (1879) 5 App Cas 342, 345 *per* Sir Montague E Smith (PC)

'We have inherited a body of law ... . We take its method and its spirit as well as its particular rules. ... Here, as it is in England, the common law is a body of principles capable of application to new situations, and in some degree of change by development.'

Skelton v Collins (1966) 115 CLR 95, 135 *per* Windeyer J (High Ct Aust)

The reception given to English law and, specifically, the English common law by the commonwealth jurisdictions of the world has long been a source of study and, for a certain breed of English judge, a source of considerable pride as well.[1] In a characteristically misty-eyed observation Denning LJ adopted the metaphor of the transplanted tree to describe the migration of the common law from the fertile soils of home to the more demanding terrain of the 'African continent'.[2] Denning's tree was, predictably enough, 'an English oak.' In the light of the United Kingdom's colonial history it is hardly surprising that English law was carried around the world by the same tides that carried our language and political system. However, the export of the English common law and the precedential importance accorded to decisions of the higher courts – in particular, the House of Lords and its alter ego, the Privy Council – continued for centuries after the first colonists reached the shores of Canada, Australia and New Zealand. In 1879 the Privy Council held, in the context of an appeal from New South Wales, that colonial courts should even consider themselves bound by the decisions of

---

1   For an excellent survey of the subject, see McPherson, BC *The Reception of English Law Abroad* (Sup Ct of Qld Lib, 2007).
2   *Nyali Ltd v Attorney-General* [1956] 1 QB 1, 16 (CA).

the English Court of Appeal.[3] While this rule was later modified by a 1927 Privy Council decision (this time in an appeal from Ontario) to the effect that only decisions by the House of Lords and Privy Council should be regarded as binding,[4] as recently as 1943 the Australian High Court was directing the Australian courts to follow a decision of the House of Lords in preference to a decision on the same subject by the High Court.[5] The system of Privy Council appeals from the commonwealth jurisdictions to the Judicial Committee, sitting at the heart of Government in Downing Street, continued to ensure that decisions by judges predominantly drawn from the United Kingdom jurisdictions were accorded precedential status over large swathes of the globe. Appeals from their courts to the Privy Council were only abolished by Canada in 1949 and by South Africa in 1950. The termination of such appeals from the Australian courts took place in stages: first, in matters of federal law; second, in matters of state law which had been the subject of a determination by the Australian High Court; and, ultimately, in matters which had been the subject of determination by the state Supreme Courts.[6] After July 1987 no further appeals reached Downing Street from Australia, but even in 1989 an academic treatise on Australian tort law could, without irony, be entitled 'Throwing Off the Chains: English Precedent and the Law of Torts in Australia'.[7] This may be a late example of what an Australian Commonwealth Prime Minister[8] memorably described as the 'cultural cringe', but seems a little self-conscious to anyone familiar with the vast corpus of indigenous Australian law of the last few decades.

It was against this background, close to what may be regarded as the high water mark of the English common law's reach, that *Donoghue v Stevenson* was decided by the House of Lords. It is fitting that one of the earliest and most enthusiastic readers of the

---

3   *Trimble v Hill* (1879) 5 App Cas 342.
4   *Robins v National Trust Co* [1927] AC 515, 519 (PC).
5   *Piro v W Foster & Co Ltd* (1943) 68 CLR 313 (HC).
6   Privy Council (Limitation of Appeals) Act 1968 (Cth); Privy Council (Appeals from the High Court) Act 1975 (Cth); Australia Act 1986 (Cth).
7   Luntz, H in Ellinghaus, MP, Bradbrook, AJ and Duggan, AJ (Eds) *The Emergence of Australian Law* (Butterworths, 1989), p 70.
8   Paul Keating.

decision – and, in particular, of Lord Atkin's neighbour principle – was Evatt J, a judge of the Australian High Court (appointed to that court at the astonishingly precocious age of 36), who wrote to Lord Atkin in March 1933 to inform him of the keen debate and interest that *Donoghue v Stevenson* had aroused at the Australian Bar and in the University law schools.[9] A focus for Evatt J's satisfaction with the decision was what he believed to be the coincidence in the thinking of Lord Atkin and Cardozo J. It seems clear, therefore, that some of the earliest commentators were keen to see *Donoghue v Stevenson*, and the apparently universal neighbour principle, used as the means by which to encourage a uniformity of approach in the tort principles applied in the common law jurisdictions of the world. Indeed, decisions by the courts of what is now the Commonwealth, both before and after 1932, exhibit an outward-looking confidence in the treatment of the jurisprudence of the United States and the wider common law world that is not always reflected in the judgments of the English courts during the same period. These days the vocabulary of the neighbour principle and its successors - the duty of care and its constituents, foreseeability, proximity and so forth – forms part of the common language of the law used in courts from Aberdeen to Cape Town and from London to Vancouver. The fact that tort lawyers around the world can speak to each other in a language that all can understand owes much to *Donoghue v Stevenson*. Lord Atkin's neighbour principle captured far more than the imagination of the London and Edinburgh Bars.

Canada

Canada's political and cultural ties to the United Kingdom and the supervisory role played (well into the twentieth century) by the Privy Council, together with its geographical proximity to the United States of America, mean that it occupies a unique position in the common law world. Shifts and currents in judicial thinking south of the US/ Canadian border appear to have prompted a bolder approach by Canadian judges to issues of negligence liability than could be found in the United Kingdom jurisdictions in the early years of the twentieth century.

---

9   Atkin archive. File reference ATK1/JUD/1/1.

These factors provide an explanation for the otherwise obscure decision of Drysdale J, sitting in the Novia Scotia Supreme Court, in *Buckley v Mott*:[10] a case which pre-dates *Donoghue v Stevenson* by more than twelve years. This was also a product liability claim. The claimant purchased a chocolate bar which had been manufactured by a Halifax-based manufacturer and released to the market through a retail dealer. The claimant's case was that negligence in the defendant's manufacturing processes meant that the ingredients of the chocolate bar included powdered glass. The claimant consumed the tainted chocolate bar with the result that the powdered glass entered his alimentary canal 'with very injurious results.' The claimant sued the defendant. The defendant's argument was the familiar one that the claimant, having no contract with the manufacturer, was owed no duty of care in tort or in contract. Drysdale J agreed that the claimant was a stranger to the contract and could not sue on it. However, he was satisfied, by a succinct review of the English and US authorities, that a tortious duty of care had long been 'engrafted' on to the contractual framework. The judge was satisfied that the defendant manufacturer did owe a duty to the public at large. The judgment is brief; it runs to barely a page and a half of the law report. It contains reference to just four cases: *Dominion Natural Gas Company v Collins*[11] and then three cases from the United States, *Thomas v Winchester*,[12] *Salmon v Libby*[13] and *Tomlinson v Armour*.[14] While Drysdale J stated that he had made an examination of the 'numerous cases on the subject, both English and American' there is little evidence of this in the judgment. It is, however, possible to state with some confidence that it was the US authorities that did more to influence the bold decision reached by the judge than anything decided on the other side of the Atlantic. Drysdale J made it clear that he based his decision on a principle developed by the American courts to the effect that where a person manufactured and put into circulation a dangerously faulty article then they are both negligent and liable in negligence to any person injured by it, 'it being the proximate cause of injury to the plaintiff

10   (1919) 50 DLR 408.
11   [1909] AC 640 (HL).
12   (1852) 6 NY 397.
13   (1906) 219 Ill 421.
14   (1908) 75 NJLR 748.

without any reference to contract relation existing ... .'[15] It will be recalled that in *Donoghue v Stevenson* Lord Buckmaster, leading the charge for the minority, identified only two exceptions to what he regarded as the general rule that, in the absence of a contract, no cause of action would be available to the injured consumer against the manufacturer:[16] the first was where the relevant article was dangerous in itself (as self-evidently inapplicable to a chocolate bar as to a bottle of ginger beer); the second was where the article was not itself dangerous, but had become dangerous as a result of some defect and this was known to the manufacturer (again, there was no evidence of this in *Donoghue v Stevenson* or in *Buckley v Mott*). The decision in *Buckley v Mott* is impossible to reconcile with Lord Buckmaster's exceptions to his suggested general rule. To this extent, the sum of $700 awarded by Drysdale J to the injured claimant represents a very considerable extension to the law as it was generally understood in England at the time. It is difficult to discern from the judgment itself any recognition that new law was being created (or, indeed, any recognition that something of significance had been decided). However, the anonymous law reporter, annotating the decision in the 1919 volume of the *Dominion Law Reports*, fully understood its importance. In a review of a number of English, US and Canadian authorities it is observed that, 'The interest in this case lies in the fact that it is the first of its kind to be tried in a Canadian Court. A careful search has disclosed very few cases either in the English or American Courts on the specific branch of this general question of the liability of a packer or manufacturer of food to the ultimate consumer, who purchased the same from a middleman.' Neither Drysdale J nor the law reporter made any reference at all to *MacPherson v Buick Motor Company*,[17] decided by the New York Court of Appeals just three years earlier: a curious omission given the importance which Drysdale J attached to the US case law.

Buckley v Mott was not the only occasion on which the Canadian courts grappled with issues of product liability in tort and resolved them in the claimant consumer's favour in the decades immediately

---

15   (1919) 50 DLR 408, 409.
16   [1932] AC 562, 569 (HL(Sc)).
17   (1916) 217 NY 382.

preceding *Donoghue v Stevenson*. *Ross v Dunstall*[18] was an appeal from Quebec which reached the Canadian Supreme Court. It concerned the manufacture of bolt-action rifles which, when reassembled by the purchaser after cleaning, became dangerously defective. The evidence was that the rifles were in excellent condition and good working order when placed on the market. However, they required cleaning and this necessitated the removal of the bolt. After cleaning, the rifle had to be reassembled and the defendant manufacturer provided no instructions on how this should be done. The claimant purchasers of the rifles were injured when the bolt of the rifle was driven back through the breach while being fired. Quebec has a continental-style Civil Code regime (as distinct from a common law system) for the determination of liability in tort and *Ross v Dunstall* was litigated and decided by reference to article 1053 of the Civil Code.[19] However, the Supreme Court's consideration of the Code provisions was very closely influenced by the English and US jurisprudence and, in particular, by *George v Skivington*, *Heaven v Pender* and *MacPherson v Buick Motor Company*. The Supreme Court treated the rifles as having a latent defect (arising out of the necessity of reassembly after cleaning) and regarded the manufacturer as liable whether or not he knew of the defect and the danger created as a result. In a passage of his judgment which follows discussion of English and American authority, and anticipates what would be said by the majority in *Donoghue v Stevenson* over a decade later, Anglin J stated as follows:

> 'The law cannot be so impotent as to allow ... a manufacturer to escape liability for injuries – possibly fatal – to a person of a class who he contemplated would use his product in the way in which it was used caused by a latent source of danger which reasonable care on his part should have discovered and to give warning of which no steps have been taken.'[20]

It is tempting to conclude that the judges in Canada (and, for that matter, the United States) had, without the passionate disagreements

18   (1921) 62 SCR 393.
19   See, Mignault J: 'In the absence of any contractual relations between two persons, the one is liable to the other if, being *doli capax*, he has caused him damage by his fault, whether by positive act, imprudence, neglect or want of skill.' *Ibid*, at p 419.
20   *Ibid*, at p 403.

which split the House of Lords and without Lord Atkin's deployment of Christian metaphor, quietly resolved the *Donoghue v Stevenson* conundrum many years before the English/Scottish courts managed to do the same.

The familiarity of Canadian lawyers and judges with these issues may explain why some of the earliest references to *Donoghue v Stevenson* can be found in the courts of that jurisdiction.[21] In a case decided early in 1933 which was brought in contract, rather than tort, and which concerned some bread containing broken glass (which injured the claimant as he was eating it) Middleton JA, in the Ontario Court of Appeal, commented on the 'now somewhat extended list of cases based upon the fondness of mice and snails to seek a last resting places in ginger beer bottles where they remain undiscovered until they reveal themselves in a ripened condition to a dissatisfied customer.'[22] By 1939 Adamson J, sitting in the Manitoba Court of King's Bench was able to say, 'The facts and the principle of the *Donoghue* ... [case] are now so well known that it is unnecessary to recite them.'[23] In one of the earliest applications of these principles, in 1933, Donovan J, sitting in the Manitoba Court of King's Bench, applied *Donoghue v Stevenson* to find for a defendant landlord in an action against a tenant who had, through his negligence, caused an explosion and then a fire at the let premises. The decision was reached independently of any covenants in the lease and Donovan J quoted from and applied Lord Macmillan's observations as to remoteness of damage in finding that, 'the defendant must be held to have definitely foreseen the danger of explosion, and as aforementioned, he took no precautions to minimize the risk.' There is, however, very little in the judgment to indicate that the judge was considering whether a duty of care was owed (indeed, this seems to have been assumed), rather than simply considering whether the damage sustained was too remote.

---

21   Accompanied by some of the earliest academic and practitioner commentary as well: see, for example, MacDonald, VC 'Torts – The Liability of Manufacturer to the Ultimate Consumer' (1932) 10 Can B Rev 478 and DeRoche, WEP 'Torts – Negligence – Duty of Care – Liability of Contractor to Third Person' (1935) 13 Can B Rev 112.
22   *Negro v Pietro's Bread Co Ltd* [1933] OR 112.
23   *Johnson v Summers* [1939] 1 WWR 362, 365.

O'Fallon v Inecto Rapid (Canada) Limited,[24] decided by the Supreme Court of British Columbia in 1938, concerned, like *George v Skivington*, a consumer who used a hair product and suffered personal injury as a result. The claimant sent her son to a local shop to purchase a hair dye which was manufactured by the defendant. The claimant used the dye and, as a result of an unusual reaction to its chemical properties, developed a skin condition. It appears from the report – although this is not wholly clear – that the potentially harmful properties of the dye might have been known to the defendant manufacturer and that the product packaging contained some form of warning to this effect. Donovan J concluded that not enough had been done to bring the warning to the claimant's attention and the defendant was found liable. The judgment refers, albeit in the briefest terms, to *Donoghue v Stevenson* and to the Australian case, *Grant v Australian Knitting Mills*,[25] but it may be possible to reconcile this decision with English law prior to 1932 (at least, as described by Lord Buckmaster) in the sense that the defendant manufacturer had some knowledge of the latent dangers presented by his product. The same volume of the *Western Weekly Reports* contains *Johnson v Summers*,[26] also decided in 1939 (this time by Adamson J sitting in the Manitoba Court of King's Bench). The claimant in that case, injured when a radiator fell on her foot, failed because she could not establish a case on the facts. However, the judge was quite satisfied that *Donoghue v Stevenson*, which was binding on him, was intended to be of general application and that the 'old error that where there is a contract there is no duty to persons not privy to it and consequently no action for negligence' had been comprehensively corrected by the House of Lords. Indeed, Adamson J reminded himself that this 'error' had been corrected in Canada by the Supreme Court decision in *Ross v Dunstall* in 1921.

Donoghue v Stevenson repeatedly crops up in the Canadian law reports of the 1940s, but this section ends in 1952 when *Guay v Sun Publishing Company Limited*[27] was decided by the British Columbian Court of Appeal. The judgment of the Court of Appeal in this case

---

24 [1939] 1 WWR 264.
25 [1936] AC 85 (PC).
26 [1939] 1 WWR 362.
27 (1952) 5 WWR 97.

contains references to *Donoghue v Stevenson, Candler v Crane, Christmas & Company*[28] and *Wilkinson v Downton*.[29] The *Guay* case arose out of the negligent (rather than defamatory or malicious) publication of a false report in a newspaper: the *Vancouver Sun*. The claimant lived in Vancouver and was separated, at the relevant time, from her husband. She read in the *Vancouver Sun* that her estranged husband and their three young children had all died in a collision between a car and a train on the other side of the country in northern Ontario. In fact, the report was false: Mr Guay and the children were neither killed, nor injured. The negligence of the reporter(s) caused the false report. Mrs Guay alleged that she had sustained physical and mental injury as a result of reading the false report and brought an action against the publisher of the newspaper.[30] There was obviously no contract between her and the defendant. She relied instead on a cause of action in negligence. She succeeded at first instance and the judgment was appealed to the British Columbia Court of Appeal. By a 2:1 split, the Court of Appeal allowed the appeal and Mrs Guay's claim was dismissed. Sidney Smith JA, for the majority, delivered a short judgment with which Robertson JA concurred. While he was prepared to accept that *Donoghue v Stevenson* had changed 'legal ideas', he did not accept the submission for Mrs Guay that it had any application to words, as distinct from physical acts. The majority held that there was clear authority which directed that the principle in *Donoghue v Stevenson* did not extend that far,[31] quite apart from the decision of the English Court of Appeal in *Candler v Crane, Christmas & Company*.[32] The dissenting voice in the *Guay* case belonged to O'Halloran JA. His judgment is considerably longer than that of Sidney Smith JA and also devotes much more attention to the authorities. O'Halloran JA's judgment, like that of Lord Atkin before him, places considerable weight on the perceived injustice of denying a remedy to Mrs Guay. While the majority concluded that a finding of liability would place an impractical burden on 'a large newspaper office', O'Halloran JA

---

28   [1951] 2 KB 163 (CA).
29   [1897] 2 QB 57. See also, *Janvier v Sweeney* [1919] 2 KB 316.
30   Cf. *McLoughlin v O'Brian* [1983] 1 AC 410 (HL) and *Alcock v Chief Constable of South Yorkshire* [1992] 1 AC 310 (HL).
31   See, for example, *Balden v Shorter* [1933] 1 Ch 427.
32   [1951] 2 KB 163 (CA).

was concerned that the contrary conclusion would 'place defenceless law-abiding citizens at the mercy of conscienceless vendors of sensationalism.'[33] Quite apart from these considerations of policy, O'Halloran JA was satisfied that *Donoghue v Stevenson* was intended to have a universal application:

> 'It is hard to conceive that a court, speaking with the authority and responsibility of the House of Lords, would have expressed itself in Donoghue's case in such embracing and unconfined terms regarding fundamental principles of English law, if it had not then intended to state principles of general application in the law of negligence as a distinct, independent and substantive tort. If the House had not so intended, limitations or qualifications would surely have been introduced ... or at least some broad hint would have been given by such masters in expression of the English language as Lords Atkin, Thankerton and Macmillan ... .'[34]

O'Halloran JA went on to characterise any attempt to restrict what he regarded as the principle in *Donoghue v Stevenson* as a throwback to the nineteenth century with its 'fixed number of classes of remedies caged in artificial categories.' By contrast to Cardozo J and Lord Atkin, who were both keen to emphasise that the principles they identified could be located in the existing case law, O'Halloran JA was unembarrassed in his embrace of modernity. For him, *Donoghue v Stevenson* represented a brave new world populated, one supposes, by brave new judges like himself and Denning LJ (who, as we have seen, dissented in *Candler v Crane, Christmas & Company*).[35] However, a more dispassionate reading of his judgment reveals a degree of overstatement. It is quite clear that what O'Halloran JA referred to as the '*Donoghue* concept of the tort of negligence' is really Lord Atkin's neighbour principle. As I have pointed out elsewhere, it is questionable whether the neighbour principle – in unqualified form –

---

33   (1952) 5 WWR 97, 104.
34   *Ibid*, at pp 108 – 109.
35   It is worth pointing out that while O'Halloran JA had no doubt that *Donoghue v Stevenson* could be applied to claims for damages arising out of loss of money, he also believed that Mrs Guay had suffered an injury to her physical health and that she was, therefore, entitled to a finding of liability even on the narrowest application of *Donoghue v Stevenson*. Cf. the New Zealand decision – *Furniss v Fitchett* [1958] NZLR 396 (Sup Ct NZ) – which is discussed below.

is really part of the ratio of *Donoghue v Stevenson*. In addition, while O'Halloran JA was keen to enlist Lords Macmillan and Thankerton in his efforts to extend the law, these law lords studiously avoided using the same metaphor as Lord Atkin and may be said to have found for Mrs Donoghue for reasons that had little to do with the formulation of any new or universal principle. The dissenting judgment in *Guay v Sun Publishing Company Limited* may be regarded as a fine example of what Sir Frederick Pollock had predicted in 1933: the 'untenable exaggeration of the rule in the Snail's Case' by 'adventurous counsel and over-ingenious teachers of law.'[36] *Guay v Sun Publishing* was taken, on a further appeal, to the Canadian Supreme Court.[37] Mrs Guay lost again. Kerwin J stated that he regarded her case as falling within the authorities which dealt with negligent words (of which *Derry v Peek*, *Le Lievre v Gould* and *Candler v Crane, Christmas & Company* were conspicuous examples). Cases of this kind, so the Canadian Supreme Court stated, should not be dealt with by reference to the principles established in *Donoghue v Stevenson*.

Australia

Evatt J wrote to Lord Atkin to congratulate him for *Donoghue v Stevenson* in March 1933. He had a very early opportunity to apply the decision he so admired. In June the same year the Australian High Court, sitting in Melbourne, heard an appeal which concerned the tortious liability of a manufacturer. The outcome would influence the future direction of the common law both in Australia and elsewhere: *Australian Knitting Mills Limited & another v Grant*.[38]

Richard Grant was a 38-year-old medical practitioner living in Adelaide. He bought some woollen underwear, marketed under the name 'Golden Fleece', from a retailer. The retailer had purchased the clothing from a manufacturer which had, after manufacture of the material, design and assembly, wrapped and tied the garments and attached a label bearing the manufacturer's details, a description ('pure woollen underwear') and detailed instructions as to washing.[39]

---

36 Pollock, F 'The Snail in the Bottle and Thereafter' (1933) 49 LQR 22, 26.
37 [1953] 2 SCR 216.
38 (1933) 50 CLR 387.
39 Together with a guarantee that the articles would be replaced if they shrank after

The manufacturer sold the underwear directly to the retailer and the retailer sold it to Dr Grant. On 28 June 1931 Dr Grant put on a vest and a pair of long-legged underpants. Nine hours later he felt an itching on the front of both shins. He wore the pants and vest again the following day. The itching continued and red patches appeared on his shins. The claimant continued to wear the clothing for a rather unhygienic seven days (they remained unwashed during this time). He then changed into the other pants and vest that he had purchased from the retailer. By this time the areas of redness had grown and 'papules' had developed 'some of which showed a tendency to weep'. Dr Grant had scratched at the itchy patches on his legs and caused them to bleed. He consulted a dermatologist. The condition spread to other areas of the claimant's body and he was forced to take to his bed and then to travel to New Zealand in order to escape the heat of the South Australian summer. Ultimately, he was admitted to hospital where he underwent what sounds like a peculiarly South Australian form of treatment: the injection of a preparation containing gold in an attempt to stimulate the skin cells. The claimant and his legal team concluded, after scientific analysis (although, by this time, the clothing had been washed), that the webbing at the end of the pants had been treated with sodium sulphite and that this chemical irritant had caused the injury. This issue of fact – whether there was a harmful chemical in the product – remained in issue throughout the litigation both at first instance and on appeal. The claimant brought proceedings in Adelaide against the retailer and against the manufacturer. His cause of action against the retailer was in contract and he relied on an implied term of reasonable fitness for purpose in the South Australian Sale of Goods Act (a transcription of the English statute of the same title). Dr Grant's action against the manufacturer was in tort. The claim was tried by the Chief Justice of the Supreme Court of South Australia (Murray CJ). It occupied twenty days of court time. Dr Grant succeeded both against the retailer and manufacturer and was awarded £2,450 against the defendants (together with the costs). Both defendants, represented by the same legal team, appealed to the High Court. So far as the action against the manufacturer was concerned, the defendant's argument was based on the narrowest reading of *Donoghue v Stevenson*. Namely,

---

washing in accordance with the manufacturer's instructions.

that unless the product was dangerous *per se* or was known by the manufacturer to be dangerous as a result of some defect,[40] an action in negligence would only be available where a 'special relation' existed between manufacturer and consumer because the product was released to the market in a form which precluded any reasonable opportunity of examination and also because any likelihood of interference by any intermediary party was removed. In other words, it was only because the ginger beer bottle was (1) opaque and (2) sealed that Mrs Donoghue succeeded in establishing a cause of action in tort. The contrary case against the manufacturer was, unsurprisingly, located in a wider reading of the House of Lords' decision and submissions based on the manufacturer's knowledge that the product would reach the consumer in exactly the same form that it left the factory.

The majority in the High Court ducked the issues of law raised by the action against the manufacturer. While Dixon J summarised the argument of the parties with respect to the duty of care, he overturned the finding of fact at first instance that the underwear contained a sulphur compound of sufficient strength or quantity as to create a real likelihood of injury for the wearer. Dixon J carefully set out the chronology of the appearance of the claimant's symptoms and summarised the expert evidence of the dermatologists and chemists called on each side of the court. He concluded that the claimant had not proved his case on causation. This conclusion as to the factual evidence and the burden of establishing causation disposed of both causes of action (Starke and McTiernan JJ agreed). However, Starke J concluded that the claimant's claim against the retailer also failed because the evidence was such that he could not prove reliance on the skill or judgment of the retailer sufficient to provide him with a viable cause of action under the sale of goods legislation.

Unsurprisingly, in the light of his letter to Lord Atkin, Evatt J dissented. Herbert Vere Evatt, appointed a High Court Justice at the age of 36 after a stellar career at the Sydney bar, has been described as having a 'pro-union and pro-worker stance' and, in his judicial career, as having 'used sociological jurisprudence and conceptions of legal

---

40   As we have seen, this was as far as Lord Buckmaster was prepared to go in recognising an exception to the principle that no action would lie in tort to a person who was not a party to the contract with the manufacturer.

and moral rights to achieve what he thought were socially desirable results.'[41] Evatt J was satisfied that the judgment of Sir George Murray as to the facts and causation was correct and should not be overturned. Dr Grant had normal skin and had not previously suffered from dermatitis despite the fact that he had always worn pants and vests made of wool. The skin irritation had manifested itself in the same place on each shin and within a short period of Dr Grant putting on the underwear. There was no evidence of any other potential external cause for the skin irritation, save for the woollen underwear. Equally, there was evidence that, after washing, the clothing still contained a quantity of sodium sulphite. Against this summary of the evidence, and assisted by the expert evidence called by Dr Grant at trial, Evatt J concluded that failures in the defendant's manufacturing processes caused the skin condition. The next issue was whether a duty of care was owed by the defendant manufacturer to Dr Grant. Perhaps in deference to the submissions of counsel for the manufacturer, Evatt J referred first to the *Donoghue v Stevenson* judgments of Lords Macmillan and Thankerton. He acknowledged, without accepting, the argument that these judgments rested on narrower foundations than that of Lord Atkin. However, he was satisfied that the facts of Dr Grant's case justified a finding that a duty of care existed between him and the manufacturer, however widely or narrowly the speeches of Lords Atkin, Macmillan and Thankerton were read. In particular, the fact that the ginger beer bottle was sealed did not provide any basis for distinguishing *Donoghue v Stevenson* from *Grant v Australian Knitting Mills Limited.* First, the manufacturer of the Golden Fleece underwear 'clearly intended that his products should not, one by one, be inspected and examined by the retailer' and, second, the label attached by the manufacturer to the underwear provided directions as to washing and guaranteed replacement of the items if they shrank after being washed in accordance with the manufacturer's instructions. This was, so Evatt J held, conclusive evidence that the manufacturer intended to create a direct relationship between itself and the consumer. However futile the manufacturer's guarantee may be in contract to the non-contracting consumer, it was Evatt J's judgment that the manufacturer's label provided evidence of a deliberate intention to create a 'close',

---

41   Bayne, P in Blackshield, T, Coper, M & Williams, G (eds) *The Oxford Companion to the High Court of Australia* (OUP, 2001), p 252.

'special' and 'direct' relationship with the consumer. In this sense, Lord Atkin's requirement of foresight or, as it has also been described, proximity – 'persons who are so closely and directly affected by my act that I ought reasonably to have them in contemplation as being so affected when I am directing my mind to the acts or omissions which are called in question' – was present. The manufacturer owed a duty of care and, having been negligent in its manufacturing processes and having caused injury as a result, was liable to Dr Grant.[42] Evatt J was, as we have seen, particularly pleased that *Donoghue v Stevenson* had, as he saw it, aligned the law of England and, therefore, Australia with the decision of the New York Court of Appeals in *MacPherson v Buick Motor Company*.[43] He concluded his consideration of the duty of care question by expressing the view that the principle recognised in *Donoghue v Stevenson*, generally applicable to products other than food and drink and to relationships other than that of manufacturer and consumer – 'has been applied even more generally in the United States',[44] referring specifically to *MacPherson*. Evatt J also concluded that the claimant had made known to the retailer the particular purpose for which the underwear was required and so had relied on the retailer's skill and judgment sufficient for him to establish an implied condition that the underwear be reasonably fit for purpose. Emboldened by the dissenting judgment of Evatt J, Dr Grant took his case to London by appeal to the Privy Council.[45]

Five judges sat in the Privy Council (including the then Lord Chancellor, Lord Hailsham). The only member of the *Donoghue v Stevenson* House of Lords who was present when *Grant v Australian Knitting Mills Limited* reached the Judicial Committee in 1935 was Lord Macmillan. However, the single opinion of their Lordships was delivered by Lord Wright. For what were, essentially, the same

---

42   The less contentious issue of the standard of care was expressed by Evatt J, borrowing from a formula developed by Sir Frederick Pollock, as the requirement of 'reasonable diligence to ensure freedom from possible non-apparent defects which would be likely to make the product noxious or dangerous in use'. See, (1933) 50 CLR 387, 441 citing, Pollock, F 'The Snail in the Bottle and Thereafter' (1933) 49 LQR 22, 23.

43   (1916) 217 NY 382.

44   (1933) 50 CLR 387, 441.

45   *Grant v Australian Knitting Mills Ltd & anor* [1936] AC 85 (PC).

reasons as Evatt J the Privy Council concluded that the decision of Sir George Murray as to the facts and causation should be reinstated. The fact that Dr Grant's disease was external in origin and coincidences of time and place, together with the presence of sodium sulphite in the washed garments, meant that he had proved his case as to causation. Equally, there was fault in the manufacturing processes of the defendant manufacturer; the process was intended to be foolproof and, if harmful chemicals were left in the garments when they left the factory, then that could only be consistent with fault. However, as Lord Wright stated, these matters did not establish a case in law. In order for the manufacturer to be liable, a duty of care had to be owed. Again, this brought *Donoghue v Stevenson* into play. The Privy Council quoted part of Lord Atkin's speech, but they did not refer to the neighbour principle. Instead, it was held that the views of the majority in *Donoghue v Stevenson* were accurately expressed in the following passage:

> 'A manufacturer of products, which he sells in such a form as to show that he intends them to reach the ultimate consumer in the form in which they left him with no reasonable possibility of intermediate examination, and with the knowledge that the absence of reasonable care in the preparation or putting up of the products will result in an injury to the consumer's life or property, owes a duty to the consumer to take that reasonable care.'[46]

In other words, it was this proximity, whether physical or otherwise, between the manufacturer and the ultimate consumer which supplied a duty of care in tort where there was no contractual relationship. The Privy Council, including Lord Macmillan, neither referred to the neighbour principle nor approved any universal test based on the same. The 'essential factor' was that, 'the consumer must use the article exactly as it left the maker, that is in all material features, and use it as it was intended to be used.'[47] It was this factor that supplied the proximity or control that was necessary for a duty of care to be owed. Where there was a duty of care then negligence constituted a 'specific tort in itself, and not simply as an element in some more

---

46   *Donoghue v Stevenson* [1932] AC 562, 599 *per* Lord Atkin.
47   [1936] AC 85, 104 *per* Lord Wright (PC).

complex relationship or in some specialized breach of duty.'[48] Lord Wright was keenly aware of the difficulty involved in defining this duty of care in hard cases. At the time of manufacture there may be no specific person to whom the duty could be owed: the manufactured item might be destroyed before it reached the consumer or be scrapped or, for some other reason, be used in a manner inconsistent with what was intended by the manufacturer after passing through several hands on its way to the ultimate consumer. The Privy Council suggested that the duty of care might remain inchoate and only 'become vested by the fact of actual use by a particular person.'[49] However, these factors, while giving rise to potential evidential problems, did not, in principle, prevent a duty of care from being owed. In Dr Grant's case, the presence of the chemical in the pants, as a result of negligence in the manufacturing process, was a latent defect which could not be detected by any examination that might reasonably be made. The pants and vest were worn, without first being washed, in exactly the manner contemplated by the manufacturer and it was immaterial to the duty of care that came into being as a result that Dr Grant had a parallel cause of action in contract against the retailer. Lord Wright prophetically foresaw the difficult issues which *Donoghue v Stevenson* would raise – '... many difficult problems will arise before the precise limits of the principle are defined: many qualifying conditions and many complications of fact may in the future come before the Courts for decision';[50] however, he was satisfied that, on any fair reading of the House of Lords' decision, Dr Grant should succeed. It was also concluded by their Lordships that Dr Grant's claim in contract against the retailer should also succeed.

It was, perhaps, Dr Grant's good fortune that the High Court of Australia contained the dissenting voice of one ardent fan of Lord Atkin's judgment. Equally, the appeal from this Court reached another judge, Lord Wright, who had taken the trouble to write to Lord Atkin to offer congratulations on the decision in *Donoghue v Stevenson*.[51]

---

48   *Ibid*, at p 103.
49   *Ibid*, at pp 104 – 105.
50   *Ibid*, at p 107.
51   File reference ATK1/JUD/1/1. Letter from Lord Wright to Lord Atkin: 'I have been reading with admiration your magnificent and convincing judgment in the snail case – also Macmillan's which is very good. I am glad this fundamental rule of law

Grant v Australian Knitting Mills Limited was not only an early application of *Donoghue v Stevenson*, Lord Wright's judgment is a particularly thoughtful rumination on the meaning and limits of the new tort of negligence (even if he was not prepared to offer much substantive guidance on these matters himself). While it is striking that, in its consideration of the action against the manufacturer, the *Grant* case contains no references to any Australian case law, it is apt that both Evatt J and Lord Wright applied principles identified by a law lord born in Brisbane.

In Dr Grant's case *Donoghue v Stevenson* had an early, but rather tentative, introduction to the Australian courts. However, it was applied with increasing confidence in the decades which followed: in 1939 to a worker injured when he spilt sulphuric acid over himself (albeit that the trial judge believed that this case would have fallen within the pre-1932 category of case in which a duty of care was owed because the causal agent was dangerous *per se*);[52] in 1947 to a worker killed when a wooden tray negligently manufactured by the defendant shed its load;[53] and, in 1962, to a man injured when a stage negligently designed by an architect collapsed beneath him.[54] In *Voli v Inglewood Shire Council*, which reached the High Court of Australia in 1962, Windeyer J's judgment provides an indication of the distance travelled by the common law in Australia in the period since *Australian Knitting Mills Limited & another v Grant* in the mid-1930s:

'Whatever might have been thought to be the position before the broad principles of the law of negligence were stated in modern form in *Donoghue v Stevenson* ..., it is now beyond doubt that, for the reasonably foreseeable consequences of careless or unskilful conduct, an architect is liable to anyone whom it could reasonably have been expected might be injured as a result of his negligence. To such a

---

will now be finally established.'

52   *Carlyle v Adelaide Chemical & Fertiliser Co Ltd* [1939] SASR 458 (Sup Ct of SA).

53   *Whelan v Asbestos Cement Pty Ltd* [1947] SASR 86 (Sup Ct of SA).

54   *Voli v Inglewood Shire Council & anor* (1962-63) 110 CLR 74. (High Ct of Aust).

person he owes a duty of care quite independently of his contract of employment.'[55]

His Honour went on to state that, while attempts had been made to argue that no duty was owed, save where the manufacturer sold products in such a form that they were intended to reach the consumer in the same condition as when they left the factory and with no reasonable possibility of intermediate examination (being the basis on which Dr Grant's case was resolved), 'later cases have established that what is significant is not whether an intermediate examination of the article was possible. It is whether it was contemplated that, in the ordinary course, the article would be examined or tested, or in some way treated before it was taken into consumption or use.'[56] This refinement was much closer to the neighbour principle in its unexpurgated form than what Lords Wright, Macmillan and the rest of the Privy Council had in mind in the *Grant* case. By the end of the 1960s judges in the State Supreme Courts of Australia were openly referring to the 'neighbour duty' of Lord Atkin.[57]

In more recent years, the reaction to an expansive approach to duties of care in tort, of the kind contemplated by *Anns v Merton*, was given impetus by the judgment of Brennan J in the Australian High Court in *Sutherland Shire Council v Heyman*.[58] However, it has been pointed out, in an Australian context, that *Donoghue v Stevenson* has been the basis for expansion of the law in all sorts of directions:[59] among them, to 'nervous shock' injuries; to injury sustained by unborn children; to the constraints placed on the law of occupiers' liability by the status of the injured visitor. In the 'imperial march of negligence'[60] across the Australian legal landscape, *Donoghue v Stevenson* has usually been in the first column.

---

55   *Ibid*, at p 84.

56   *Ibid*, at p 86.

57   See, for example, D'Arcy J in the Western Australia Supreme Court in *Bossie v M & D Bossie Pty Ltd* [1968] WAR 97.

58   (1985) 60 ALR 1.

59   Underwood, P 'Is Mrs Donoghue's Snail in Mortal Peril?' (2004) 12 Torts Law Journal 39.

60   A phrase coined by Spigelman CJ: Spigelman, JJ 'Negligence: the Last Outpost of the Welfare State' (2002) 76 ALJ 432.

New Zealand

Applications of *Donoghue v Stevenson* can be found in the courts of New Zealand at around the same time that this case was first being cited on a regular basis in Australia and Canada. Whatever the limitations of the communication methods used by the lawyers of the 1930s, it did not take long for the voice of the House of Lords on such an important issue of principle to be heard by the judges of the wider common law world. In 1934 Blair J delivered a cautious judgment in which, on the basis of *Farr v Butters*,[61] he distinguished *Donoghue v Stevenson*.[62] By 1958 the Chief Justice of the New Zealand Court of Appeal, boldly extending what he referred to as 'the principle of *Donoghue v Stevenson*' to a case where nervous shock resulted from the reading of a certificate, stated as follows: 'Lord Atkin's statement of that concept [the neighbour principle] is known to every lawyer and is much wider than is indicated by the headnote to the report of the case in the Law Reports. It has been applied, with some amplification of what he said, by the highest authority.'[63]

Maindonald v Marlborough Aero Club & New Zealand Airways Limited[64] reached the Supreme Court in 1934. It concerned a fatal air accident. The deceased travelled as a passenger in an aircraft which was operated by the Marlborough Aero Club. The aircraft had been repaired by New Zealand Airways Company following an earlier accident. The contract between the company and the club provided that the relevant aircraft was to be repaired to a standard consistent with the grant of a certificate of air worthiness. Following the repair the aircraft was inspected by the aviation authorities and the requisite certificate was issued. There was a loose cotter pin in the internal machinery of the aircraft which caused a bolt to become detached. This caused the crash. The deceased's widow brought proceedings against the club and against the company. The claimant's case against the club was dismissed on the ground that she could not establish causation. Her case was that there was a breach of statutory duty in that the

---

61   [1932] 2 KB 606 (CA).
62   *Maindonald v Marlborough Aero Club & New Zealand Airways Ltd* [1935] NZLR 371 (Sup Ct NZ).
63   *Furniss v Fitchett* [1958] NZLR 396, 401 *per* Barrowclough CJ (NZCA).
64   [1935] NZLR 371 (Sup Ct NZ).

club had failed to conduct a ground inspection of the kind required by aviation regulations. However, the evidence was that the inspection required by the regulations would not, in any event, cover the defective section of the aircraft's machinery. In the circumstances, it made no difference whether or not the inspection was conducted in accordance with the regulations. In addition, it was held that the contract between the deceased and the club contained a clause excluding liability for an accident of the kind which killed the deceased.

The claimant's claim against the company which had conducted the repairs to the aircraft was brought in common law negligence and relied on the application of *Donoghue v Stevenson*. The claim required a finding of fact that the aircraft had been defective when it left the defendant company's premises. The judge was not prepared to find that the cotter pin was loose when it left the repairer; he directed himself that the claimant had failed to discharge the burden of proof which she bore in this regard. In the circumstances, the claim failed and it was unnecessary for the judge to go on to consider the legal argument. However, in deference to the arguments of counsel, Blair J also went on to consider the duty of care issues. The judge was not persuaded that *Donoghue v Stevenson* was distinguishable because it concerned the repair of an object (the aircraft), rather than its manufacture: 'In principle there does not seem to be any difference in the two cases, and I shall so assume'.[65] The argument that *Donoghue v Stevenson* should be confined to manufacture (and so not apply to repairs) was, as we have seen, demolished by the English Court of Appeal some twelve years later in *Haseldine v C A Daw & Son Limited*.[66] However, by the time that Mrs Maindonald's case reached the Supreme Court, *Farr v Butters*[67] had been decided by the English Court of Appeal. Blair J quoted at length from the judgment

---

65   *Ibid*, at p 382 *per* Blair J.
66   [1941] 2 KB 343 (CA). The fact that a claim was pursued against a repairer, rather than a manufacturer might have made it more difficult for a claimant to establish proximity on the basis that the article had not been interfered with or altered on its journey from the repair yard. From an evidential perspective, it would usually be easier to establish such proximity when an article left a manufacturer's premises brand new and in pristine condition than where an older article was entrusted to a person for repairs to be carried out.
67   [1932] 2 KB 606 (CA).

of Scutton LJ in *Farr v Butters* which, as he explained, 'went to great pains to show the precise limitations of the doctrine of liability laid down by the House of Lords in [*Donoghue v Stevenson*].'[68] On the facts of *Maindonald v Marlborough* it was held that the defect in the machinery of the aircraft which was created by the loose cotter pin was readily examinable prior to Mr Maindonald's fatal crash. In the circumstances, the requisite proximity was missing between the claimant and the defendant repairers. Mrs Maindonald's claim was, therefore, dismissed in this regard as well. This decision seems astonishing to a personal injury lawyer of the present day; that Mrs Maindonald's action should fail on highly technical grounds against both the club which had carried her husband in an obviously defective aircraft and against the company which had carried out the repairs. The New Zealand jurisdiction later provided an enthusiastic home for the more expansive definitions of a duty of care which can be found in cases like *Anns v Merton*.[69] It is curious, therefore, that its earliest consideration of *Donoghue v Stevenson* resulted in an application of *Farr v Butters* and the narrowest reading of the House of Lords' decision. Blair J stated, in the course of his judgment, 'My duty is only to administer the law, not to make law for hard cases. If a Judge allowed himself to be swayed by sad cases there would be a lot of bad law that would set up a crop of harder cases and cause untold mischief.'[70]

A rather bolder approach is evident in *Grant v Cooper, McDougall and Robertson Limited* which reached the New Zealand Supreme Court in 1939.[71] The claimant in this action was a sheep farmer. His rams were dipped in a substance manufactured by the defendant company. The sheep dip had been purchased by the claimant from a vendor who was not a party to the action; the claimant had no contract with the defendant. The dip solution was diluted with water before the rams were exposed to it, but the rams were injured when exposed

---

68   [1935] NZLR 371, 383.
69   See, Todd, S (General Ed) *The Law of Torts in New Zealand* (Thomson, 4th ed, 2005), p 120: 'The *Anns* approach at first commanded widespread support. It was quickly accepted on a number of occasions in the New Zealand Court of Appeal ... .' Citing *Scott Group Ltd v McFarlane* [1978] 1 NZLR 553 (NZCA).
70   [1935] NZLR 371, 381.
71   [1940] NZLR 947.

to the poisons contained in the dip. The claimant commenced an action based on the defendant's negligence in failing, by appropriate labelling, to warn him of the poisonous constituents of the dip and the risk that livestock exposed to it might be poisoned. The defendant argued, first, that the claimant's action could not be maintained because the opportunity to inspect the sheep dip before use was made of it broke the continuity of the defendant's control such that there was insufficient proximity to satisfy the conditions for a *Donoghue v Stevenson* duty of care. Northcroft J appears to have accepted the principle, but held on the facts that the claimant had no reasonable opportunity (by simply opening the containers holding the dip and pouring the same into a bath) to apprehend the danger which the sheep dip posed before his rams were immersed. The second argument for the defendant was also rejected; namely, that *Donoghue v Stevenson* was distinguishable because the substance manufactured by the defendant had been altered or interfered with (by dilution with water) before any damage was sustained (the dilution had, it was argued, removed the proximity between manufacturer and consumer). Northcroft J said that accepting the defendant's argument would rob consumers of the protection which *Donoghue v Stevenson* would otherwise provide and would also remove much of the practical effect of the House of Lords' decision:

> 'These goods were manufactured and distributed in contemplation of their being mixed with water before use. This is equally true of many commodities manufactured and distributed, and which might be expected to come within the rule of ... [*Donoghue v Stevenson*]. I do not consider that I am entitled to narrow the application of that case so as to make it not available in respect of all goods sold for use and of which use cannot be made without interfering by mixing with some other substance.'[72]

By the 1950s Lord Atkin's threshold test for finding a duty of care – 'You must take reasonable care to avoid acts or omissions which you can reasonably foresee would be likely to injure your neighbour' – was being applied by the New Zealand Court of Appeal on a routine

---

72   *Ibid*, at p 949.

basis.[73] However, in *Perkowski v Wellington City Corporation*[74] the Court of Appeal was required to consider the extent to which a general cause of action in negligence, arising from an expansive approach to the duty of care based on *Donoghue v Stevenson*, could sit alongside the common law rules on occupiers' liability. This was a fatal accident case where the claimant's husband dived into shallow seawater at low tide from a springboard erected by the defendant local authority. The claimant's case was based on the alleged fault of the local authority in failing to warn the deceased about the depth of the water into which he had dived. It was conclusively determined by the New Zealand Court of Appeal that, while it was theoretically possible for a general duty of care of the kind described by the House of Lords in *Donoghue v Stevenson* to sit alongside the duty of an occupier, any injuries resulting from the dangerous condition of the premises could only be actionable as a result of the occupier's duty and liability would vary depending on the status of the visitor: whether invitee, licensee or trespasser.[75] In the course of his judgment Barrowclough CJ considered whether the local authority's act in erecting the springboard and its omission to warn of the risks of diving from it into shallow water were the kinds of 'acts or omissions' which Lord Atkin had in mind when describing the neighbour principle. He answered his own question in the following way:

> 'Clearly not. No question of occupier of premises or structures could possibly have arisen in *Donoghue v Stevenson*. If acts or omissions such as those which the evidence shows the Corporation to have performed or made are acts or omissions to which Lord Atkin referred, then his judgment would have had the effect of overruling the long line of cases which have defined an occupier's duty by declaring an occupier to be under an altogether new and different duty in respect of the condition of his premises. There is not a word in his speech, or in the speeches of any other member of the House, to suggest that he or they had any such intention.'[76]

---

73 *Baynes v Union Steam Ship Co of New Zealand Ltd* [1953] NZLR 616, 631 *per* O'Leary CJ (NZCA). This case concerned an accident at work.
74 [1957] NZLR 39 (NZCA).
75 Categories largely swept away in England by the Occupiers' Liability Act 1957.
76 [1957] NZLR 39, 60. It has been pointed out that in Australia in the 1950s and 1960s *Donoghue v Stevenson* was relied on by the Australian High Court 'to free the law relating to occupiers' liability from its historical shackles so as to ameliorate the

The end of the 1950s was marked by three cases which cast light on the principles developed in *Donoghue v Stevenson* in a variety of applications. First, the extension of the principle to a case where a woman suffered nervous shock as a result of reading a certificate written by her general practitioner.[77] Second, a case in which an occupier was exonerated from liability for personal injury which resulted from the careless work of an apparently competent and reputable contractor to whom he had entrusted the work.[78] Third, a refusal by the New Zealand Supreme Court to award damages to the personal representative of a fireman who had attended a fire at a premises which had earlier been negligently assessed by a Government inspector of factories.[79]

Of these three cases, *Furniss v Fitchett*,[80] decided at first instance in the Supreme Court by Sir Harold Barrowclough (Chief Justice of the New Zealand Court of Appeal), represents the widest reading of *Donoghue v Stevenson* and Lord Atkin's neighbour principle. Mr and Mrs Furniss were longstanding patients of Dr Fitchett, a general practitioner. Their marriage became strained and, in a suprising departure from patient/doctor confidentiality, Dr Fitchett provided Mr Furniss with a certificate which expressed the view that Mrs Furniss exhibited 'symptoms of paranoia' and should be examined by a psychiatrist as a result. Mrs Furniss subsequently separated from her husband and commenced proceedings to obtain maintenance payments from him. In the course of cross-examination at a hearing in the maintenance proceedings, Mr Furniss' solicitor produced Dr Fitchett's

---

lot of trespassers who were injured while on another's land. The decision was also the basis of the Court's subsequent successful move to rationalise and simplify the principles relating generally to occupiers' liability.' Davis, J in Blackshield, T, Coper, M & Williams, G (eds) *The Oxford Companion to the High Court of Australia* (OUP, 2001), p 226.

77   *Furniss v Fitchett* [1958] NZLR 396 (Sup Ct NZ).
78   *Lyons v Nicholls* [1958] NZLR 409 (NZCA).
79   *The Queen v Bell* [1958] NZLR 449 (NZCA). In this case, the Court of Appeal held, distinguishing *Donoghue v Stevenson* and applying dicta of Lord Wright in *Grant v Australian Knitting Mills*, that a fireman attending an emergency had a reasonable opportunity of inspection or examination of the affected premises. Accordingly, the requisite proximity between the Government inspector (who might reasonably expect the fireman to carry out his own inspection) and the deceased fireman was missing.
80   [1958] NZLR 396 (Sup Ct NZ).

certificate. Mrs Furniss alleged that she suffered nervous shock as a result and brought proceedings against the general practitioner. The case against Dr Fitchett was not based on negligence in the production of the certificate (it simply reflected his professional opinion as to Mrs Furniss' condition). Instead, the claimant's case was that the doctor was negligent because of the manner in which he released the certificate and in not foreseeing that, at some stage, Mrs Furniss might be confronted with it in circumstances which might cause her injury. The judge directed himself that it did not matter that the contents of the certificate were both true and accurate (as an expression of Dr Fitchett's professional opinion). He was satisfied that the doctor was negligent because he ought to have foreseen that 'his patient would be likely to be injured as the result of his action in giving to her husband such a certificate as he did give, and in giving it to him without placing any restriction on its use.'[81] Equally, Barrowclough CJ was satisfied that these factors also supported the proposition that a duty of care was owed by the general practitioner to Mrs Furniss. There was no reason to exclude cases of nervous shock from those in which a duty of care was owed; while Barrowclough CJ accepted the principle that Lord Atkin's principle was limited to cases of physical injury to person or property, he stated that he regarded nervous shock as 'physical injury in the presently relevant sense.'[82] However, the introductory remarks of Barrowclough CJ in the passage of his judgment which deals with the duty of care make it clear how expansively he was prepared to read Lord Atkin's neighbour principle:

'The well-known torts do not have their origin in any all-embracing principle of tortuous liability. There are many references in the books to the difficulty of laying down such a principle. Nevertheless, in *Donoghue v Stevenson* ... Lord Atkin said: "... in English law there must be, and is, some general conception of relations giving rise to a duty of care, of which the particular cases found in the books are but instances." ... Lord Atkin's statement of that concept is known to every lawyer and is much wider than is indicated by the headnote to the report of the case in the Law Reports. It has been applied with some amplification of what he said, by the highest authority.'[83]

81   *Ibid*, at p 403.
82   *Ibid*, at p 402. A conclusion that might be regarded as contentious.
83   *Ibid*, at p 401.

While the Chief Justice went on to acknowledge some limitations to the universality of Lord Atkin's neighbour principle, the only one that he expressly referred to was the need for physical injury to person or property. He was satisfied that Mrs Furniss was owed a duty by Dr Fitchett and was entitled to recover damages for the nervous shock caused by his negligence.

Conclusion

The discussion in this Chapter has been selective. This is not an exhaustive, much less an academic, commentary on developments in the law of negligence in the common law jurisdictions which I have selected. I have described the cases which interest me and which may represent the first drafts as the emergent tort of negligence developed in the decades which followed *Donoghue v Stevenson*. Some tentative conclusions can be drawn. First, that the influence of the case law in America (and in the New York State jurisdiction in particular) influenced the law of tort in jurisdictions other than those of the United Kingdom. By the time that the majority in *Donoghue v Stevenson* sought support from Cardozo J for their decision, the courts of Canada had already adopted a bold and explicitly US-flavoured approach to the law of tort. Second, it took very little time before the courts of the wider common law world came to regard *Donoghue v Stevenson* as representative of the orthodox position. This seems to have had less to do with the precedential weight accorded, at that time, to the decisions of the House of Lords and Privy Council and more to do with the fact that the common law judges swiftly came to regard Mrs Donoghue's case as both intuitively and legally correct. One feels – from reading the correspondence of Evatt J and, with some exceptions, the decisions reached by courts of the 1930s in Canada, Australia and New Zealand – that *Donoghue v Stevenson* and the neighbour principle were released to a world which was ready for them. The potency of the House of Lords' decision is vividly demonstrated by the infiltration of an essentially alien duty of care concept into the Roman-Dutch law of delict found in South Africa[84]

---

84 See, Neethling, J, Potgieter, JM & Visser, PJ (eds) *Law of Delict* (4th ed), pp 148 – 149: 'Negligence is, as stated above, generally determined according to the test of the reasonable man. On occasion, our courts have not applied this test and have followed English law in applying the so-called "duty of care" doctrine.' Citing *Cape*

and by the application of Lord Atkin's neighbour principle[85] by the courts of the Republic of Ireland in the 1960s which, by that time, did not accord binding weight to the decisions of the House of Lords.[86] Third, the wider common law world, the sheer volume of tort cases and the bewildering variety of factual applications available in Canada, Australia and New Zealand, provided an ideal seed bed for the development of negligence. The courts of these jurisdictions were heavily influenced, indeed directed, by the decisions of the House of Lords and Privy Council, but decisions emanating from these courts came to influence the law of the United Kingdom jurisdictions in their turn (*Grant v Australian Knitting Mills Limited* and *Sutherland Shire Council v Heyman* provide obvious examples of this). Indeed, advances in the law, justified by *Donoghue v Stevenson*, were in several areas achieved by courts in the common law jurisdictions long before such advances took place in the United Kingdom. Finally, one sees that the protean quality of the majority speeches in *Donoghue v Stevenson* make them attractive to judges of all persuasions – not just to 'bold spirits' like Lord Atkin, Lord Denning, O'Halloran JA and Barrowclough CJ – but also to those of a more conservative mindset. The neighbour principle provides a means by which to advance the law into all sorts of new areas, but the limitations acknowledged by the majority in the course of their speeches can also be used to justify refinements and exceptions. There is always something in *Donoghue v Stevenson* for the lawyers and the judges to argue about. We are still arguing about it now and we are, as I have indicated, using a common language – the language of Lords Atkin, Macmillan and Buckmaster – to do so.

Town Municipality v Paine 1923 AD 207.

85   Together with commentaries on the same by later English courts.

86   See, McMahon, B and Binchy, W *Irish Law of Torts* (Butterworths (Ireland), 2nd ed, 1990), p 90. See also, *Healy v Bray Urban District Council* [1962-63] Ir Jur Rep 9, 17 *per* Kingsmill Moore J (Sup Ct of Ireland): 'Neither the decision nor the opinions expressed are binding on us, but the opinions of such eminent authorities as to the application of the principle laid down by Lord Atkin in *Donoghue v Stevenson* must carry weight.'

8. CONCLUSION

'That weavers in particular, together with scholars and writers with whom they had much in common, tended to suffer from melancholy ... is understandable given the nature of their work, which forced them to sit bent over, day after day, straining to keep their eyes on the complex patterns they created. It is difficult to imagine the depths of despair into which those can be driven who, even after the end of the working day are engrossed in their intricate designs and who are pursued, into their dreams, by the feeling that they have got hold of the wrong thread.'

Sebald, WG *The Rings of Saturn*

As a result of the decision of the House of Lords the judgment of Lord Moncrieff, sitting at first instance in the Court of Session, was restored. Mrs Donoghue had established her case in law. The *Paisley and Renfrewshire Gazette*, describing Mrs Donoghue as Mrs Macalister (which would have incurred the wrath of Lord Macmillan), succinctly reported the outcome of proceedings in the House of Lords as 'Appeal allowed: Snail in Ginger Beer Case'. This did not, of course, mean that May Donoghue was entitled to an award of damages. She would now need to prove her factual case: the presence of the snail in the bottle; the negligence of Mr Stevenson; the illness that she had suffered by consuming the snail-flavoured ginger beer. It will be recalled that Mr Stevenson vigorously denied that any bottle manufactured by his factory contained a snail. It was equally denied that Mr Stevenson's business had ever issued a bottle of ginger beer of the description given by Mrs Donoghue. A trial in the Court of Session would determine whose version of events was correct. This was scheduled to take place in January 1933.[1]

Nearly a decade later, in wartime, Lord Justice MacKinnon was invited to give an after dinner speech to the law students at the University of Birmingham (he was the President of their Holdsworth Club). The speech was originally scheduled for May 1942, but was apparently postponed for reasons related to the war effort. A copy of

---

1   Interlocutor of 4 November 1932, as reported in McBryde, WM '*Donoghue v Stevenson*: the Story of the "Snail in the Bottle" Case' in Gamble, AJ (ed) *Obligations in Context* (W Green, 1990), p 26, n 23.

the speech appears in Lord Atkin's papers at Gray's Inn.[2] The speech was, perhaps, prepared for a well-oiled audience (in need of cheering up) as the attempt at levity in the following passage suggests:

'Not for me to expound the implications of *Donoghue v Stevenson*. To be quite candid, I detest that snail. I think that my friend, Lord President Normand, explained to you that the problem in the case arose on a plea of relevancy – the Scots equivalent of a demurrer. I think that he did not reveal to you that when the law had been settled by the House of Lords, the case went back to Edinburgh to be tried on the facts. And at that trial it was found that there never was a snail in the bottle at all. That intruding gastropod was as much a legal fiction as the Casual Ejector.'

Lord President Normand was, of course, the former Solicitor-General for Scotland who had appeared as leading counsel for Mr Stevenson before the House of Lords. Lord Justice MacKinnon's jokey revelation probably went down well with his audience of law students. However, it was also noticed by Lord Atkin who was obviously diverting himself with some recreational reading during the long vacation of 1942 and so had a copy of the speech. He sent the speech to Lord Macmillan (who was selflessly spending the holiday period with his wife in Brockenhurst in the New Forest, '... more in order to give our staff a bit of relaxation than for our own sakes.')[3] Lord Macmillan turned detective and, following the thread back to the man who was there at the time, wrote to Normand (enclosing a copy of MacKinnon's speech). He received the following reply dated 19 September 1942:

'My dear Macmillan, I have not yet seen MacKinnon's address to the Holdsworth Club. His account, as you report it, of *Donoghue v Stevenson* is not accurate. The case never went to trial. I speak from recollection, but I think it can be trusted, and what I remember is that the defender died soon after the HL decided the point of relevancy. The pursuer did not move to have the defender's executors sisted as a party and there were no further proceedings. So much for the sake of history.'[4]

2   File reference ATK1/JUD/1/1.
3   *Ibid.* See letter from Lord Macmillan to Lord Atkin dated 21 September 1942.
4   *Ibid.*

Normand's recollection of the chronology was correct. On 12 November 1932, by which time the case was back in the Court of Session awaiting trial (proof), David Stevenson died. In his meticulously researched 1990 article Professor McBryde states that, 'A year elapsed and David Stevenson's executors were sisted as parties to the case which then settled.'[5] Lord Macmillan sent Normand's letter on to Lord Atkin and added the following note in his cover letter of 21 September 1942:

> 'My dear Atkin, I, too, was struck by that statement in MacKinnon's Holdsworth Club address. I was sure it was wrong. Before answering your letter, however, I wrote to Normand in order to verify my impression, and this morning I have a letter from him of which I enclose a copy. You may take it as quite certain that the case never went to trial. Whether there was or was not a snail in the bottle must remain one of history's unsolved problems.'[6]

An article published in October 1955 in the Law Quarterly Review suggests that a myth had grown up that there was no snail in the bottle.[7] Indeed, in a 1954 decision of the Court of Appeal (in the form of a Practice Note) Jenkins LJ, ignorant of the private correspondence referred to above, stated confidently, '... the House of Lords heard the preliminary issue in *Donoghue v Stevenson* ... and when the trial was heard there was no snail in the bottle at all.'[8] D Ashton-Cross, the author of the Law Quarterly Review article, was keen to set the record straight and corresponded with the solicitors for Mr Stevenson who informed him of the death of the defendant and the subsequent settlement by his executors.

The answer, therefore, to the question – what really happened in the café – is that we will never know. There was no trial. No witnesses gave evidence. No decision on the alleged facts was ever reached. The legacy of *Donoghue v Stevenson* is a purely legal one, unencumbered by inconvenient and messy factual evidence with its truths and untruths. The eccentric curiosity of the facts attracts the attention, but

5   McBryde, WM '*Donoghue v Stevenson*: the Story of the "Snail in the Bottle" Case' in Gamble, AJ (ed) *Obligations in Context* (W Green, 1990), p 26.
6   Atkin archive. File reference ATK1/JUD/1/1.
7   Ashton-Cross, D '*Donoghue v Stevenson* [1932] AC 562' (1955) 71 LQR 472.
8   *Adler v Dickson & anor* [1954] 1 WLR 1482, 1483 (CA).

it will never be known whether the offending snail was or was not the 'legal fiction' of MacKinnon's imagination. Rather like its somewhat shadowy protagonists, the absence of a factual determination – the void – which lies at the heart of the proceedings has only added to the mythic value of the 'Snail's case'.

It does, at least, seem clear that there was a settlement. Professor McBryde records that the settlement sum was £100, although he acknowledges that it is difficult to be accurate about this.[9] McBryde's source for the settlement sum was Professor Heuston and he, in turn, heard about it from Lord Macmillan[10] who, one presumes, would have been told by Lord Normand. Lord Rodger was told by Mrs Donoghue's grandson that it was believed that the settlement sum was £500 (the sum claimed in the proceedings),[11] although this seems likely to be an exaggeration within the Donoghue family. In fact, a more accurate account of the settlement might have been provided by the son of Mrs Donoghue's solicitor who, for the purposes of an article published by the Canadian Judge, Mr Justice Taylor, in 1983, stated that he believed the sum paid by the executors of the estate to have been £200.[12] While, by contrast to her lawyers, Mrs Donoghue never had her day in court, she achieved what would at the time have been a significant sum (particularly to someone suing *in pauperis*). How the money was spent (if, indeed, it was spent) will remain another mystery.[13]

The idea of pilgrimage is no longer confined to those of religious conviction. Increasingly, pilgrimages involve visits to sites of sporting or literary significance. Jane Austen's house at Chawton and Dove Cottage in the Lakeland fells receive thousands of visitors each year.

---

9   McBryde, WM *'Donoghue v Stevenson*: the Story of the "Snail in the Bottle" Case' in Gamble, AJ (ed) *Obligations in Context* (W Green, 1990), p 26, n 26 citing Heuston, RFV *'Donoghue v Stevenson* in Retrospect' (1957) 20 MLR 1, 2.

10   Heuston, RFV *'Donoghue v Stevenson* in Retrospect' (1957) 20 MLR 1, 2, n 5.

11   Rodger, A 'Mrs Donoghue and Alfenus Varus' (1988) 41 CLP 1, 9, n 98 referring to a letter of 24 July 1973 which he had received from Thomas Donoghue.

12   Taylor, M 'The Good Neighbour on Trial: a Message from Scotland' (1983) 17 UBC Law Review 59, 65.

13   In his 1988 article Alan (now Lord) Rodger records that, at her death, Mrs Donoghue's total estate was a little more than £364: Rodger, A 'Mrs Donoghue and Alfenus Varus' (1988) 41 CLP 1, 9, n 1.

This comparatively recent phenomenon has not yet extended to sites of legal significance. However, the site of the Wellmeadow Café in Paisley is an exception. Prior to 1990 the site of the cafe was waste ground:[14] a metaphor, perhaps, for the factual void which lies at the heart of the case. Between 28 and 30 September 1990 a conference on the law of negligence was organised in Paisley by the Canadian Bar Association, the Faculty of Advocates, the Law Society of Scotland and the Old Paisley Society. The conference was entitled, 'The Pilgrimage to Paisley: a Salute to *Donoghue v Stevenson*.' Delegates received presentations from, among others, Professor McBryde, Alan Rodger QC and Justices Brennan and Taylor (of the High Court of Australia and the British Columbia Court of Appeal respectively – Taylor J was a prime organiser of the conference weekend). The papers presented at the conference were collected in a book published in 1991 by the Continuing Legal Education Society of British Columbia which can be found in the Paisley Public Library: *Donoghue v Stevenson and the Modern Law of Negligence The Paisley Papers*. The conference programme records that, between 4.05 pm and 4.30 pm, the conference delegates paraded, with the accompaniment of pipers, to Wellmeadow Street. There are photographs in the Paisley library archive of them doing so (well wrapped up for Paisley's late September weather). At the site of the Café a memorial park and garden was formally dedicated. The afternoon's events concluded with a tea at 5 pm: 'With Ice Cream and Ginger Beer.'

In August 2008, some eighty years (nearly to the day) after Mrs Donoghue's journey, I made my own pilgrimage to Paisley, taking the train there from Glasgow on a damp afternoon. The memorial park is still at the corner of Lady Lane and Wellmeadow Street and is overlooked, from the other side of the road, by the austere Thomas Coats Memorial Church. The memorial stands alongside a busy road – Wellmeadow Street – between two derelict buildings: an abandoned bingo hall and what was once a chapel. The somewhat melancholy scene and weather was completed by a funeral which was taking place at the adjacent co-operative society. In the small park itself, there is a wooden bench, donated by the Canadian Bar and constructed of

14   See report in *The Paisley Express* for 31 August 1988, 'And all because of a drink!'

Canadian cedar wood, with decorative, snail-shaped roundels. The simple dignity of a rectangular marble stone is complemented by a metal plate on each side. On one side it is recorded that the Park was created by the Renfrew District Council on land dedicated to the public for fifty years by the Co-operative Wholesale Society and was opened by Lord Mackay of Clashfern PC, Lord Chancellor of Great Britain. Lord Mackay was assisted by, among others, the Lord President (Lord Hope), Justice Bertha Wilson of the Supreme Court of Canada and Sir Gerald Brennan of the High Court of Australia. The reverse side of the memorial stone records the following (after quoting the neighbour principle from the speech of Lord Atkin):

'At the corner of Wellmeadow Street and Lady Lane stood the Wellmeadow Café operated by Francis Minghella where Mrs May Donoghue of Glasgow was served on August 26, 1928, with ginger beer from a bottle in which she claimed that she later found a snail. Mrs Donoghue sued the manufacturer, David Stevenson, whose factory was in Glen Lane, Paisley. He denied her allegation. The case never went to proof and it never was decided whether there was a snail in the bottle. It was on an unsuccessful preliminary application to dismiss Mrs Donoghue's claim that Lord Atkin gave the judgment in the House of Lords which would make Donoghue v Stevenson ... the most celebrated case of all time, not only in the United Kingdom but for the whole commonwealth common law world. This memorial was dedicated to Mrs May Donoghue and David Stevenson, their solicitors and advocates by the Faculty of Advocates, the Canadian Bar Association and the Law Society of Scotland, on September 29, 1990.'

The memorial inscription avoids, with lawyerly precision, any assertions of facts which remained unproven. The oddity that, in 1990, the leaders of the common law world were making the location of an otherwise undistinguished and long-demolished cafe where something of factual significance may or may not have happened will, no doubt, have occurred to many of those who were present. The point, however, is that something significant did emerge from Wellmeadow Street and Mrs Donoghue had to travel there from Glasgow in order for this to happen.

The issues raised by *Donoghue v Stevenson* aroused strong passions at the time that it was decided. It is only necessary to read the speech of Lord Buckmaster to realise this. As we have seen, the drive to limit the potential universality of Lord Atkin's neighbour principle began almost immediately. Even those who expressed a grudging admiration for what the majority had decided in *Donoghue v Stevenson* were keen to make it clear that there had to be limits: 'The decision in the Donoghue case was one of good sense and social necessity, but social necessity and good sense require some limits.'[15] More recently, discussions about the proper reach of the law of negligence have resulted in Parliamentary debate and the passing of legislation seeking to influence the standard of care applied by the courts in certain areas of social activity.[16] However, the neighbour principle, whether or not it forms part of the ratio of the majority decision in *Donoghue v Stevenson*, has proved stubbornly resistant to constraint and restriction. In the decades which have now passed since 1932 it has inspired many efforts to extend the reach of the law of negligence to areas previously untouched by it. Not all of the advances made have proved to be permanent, but *Donoghue v Stevenson* continues to be taught to law students and continues to be cited in important cases.

Donoghue v Stevenson in the House of Lords is a case of speeches, metaphors and aphorisms. While Lord Macmillan and Lord Buckmaster's speeches have attracted interest, criticism and scholarship, it is Lord Atkin's speech that captures the hearts and minds of most lawyers. The singular ambition of his opinion, the energy with which it was expressed and the eloquent use of metaphor and Biblical allusion all helped to ensure that it was Lord Atkin's neighbour principle that emerged as the greatest gift given by English/Scots law to the wider common law world. The neighbour principle was the thread which enabled the tort of negligence to escape the labyrinthine complexity of the law prior to 1932 and also provided patterns for the development of negligence over the decades that followed. More than that, however, Lord Atkin's neighbour principle reminds us why the

---

15   DeRoche, WEP 'Torts – Negligence – Duty of Care – Liability of Contractor to Third Person' (1935) 13 Can B Rev 112, 114.
16   Compensation Act 2006 which received the Royal Assent on 25 July 2006. For an article by one of those who advised on the draft legislation, see: Parker, A 'Changing the Claims Culture' (2006) 156 NLJ 702.

law of negligence is important. Indeed, it reminds some of us why we chose to become lawyers in the first place.

SELECT BIBLIOGRAPHY

The list which follows is not wholly comprehensive, but may provide suggestions for further reading for those who are interested in the substantial academic literature. I have not provided page references for the specific passages in any textbook or article listed below where *Donoghue v Stevenson* (or any matter relevant to the same) is discussed. However, the footnotes in each chapter should provide a specific page reference where this is appropriate. Books and articles are listed together (in alphabetical order by reference to the surname of the author).

Holy Bible (King James version)

Ashton-Cross, D '*Donoghue v Stevenson* [1932] AC 562' (1955) 71 LQR 472

Atkin, Lord 'Appeal in English Law' (1927) 3 CLJ 1

Atkin, Lord 'Law as an Educational Subject' [1932] JSPTL 27

Baker, JH *An Introduction to English Legal History* (Butterworths, 4th ed, 2002)

Baker, JH and Milson, SFC *Sources of English Legal History Private Law to 1750* (Butterworth, 1986)

Bayne, P in Blackshield, T, Coper, M & Williams, G (eds) *The Oxford Companion to the High Court of Australia* (OUP, 2001)

Beever, A *Rediscovering the Law of Negligence* (Hart Publishing, 2007)

Bohlen, F 'Liability of Manufacturers to Persons other than their Immediate Vendees' (1929) 45 LQR 343

Brodie, F 'In Defence of Donoghue' [1997] JR 65

Buckland, WW 'The Duty to take Care' (1935) 51 LQR 637

Buczacki, ST & Harris, KM *Pests, Diseases & Disorders of Garden Plants* (Harper Collins, 3rd ed, 2005)

Cane, P *The Anatomy of Tort Law* (Hart Publishing, 1997)

Castle, R 'Lord Atkin and the Neighbour Test: Origins of the Principles of Negligence in *Donoghue v Stevenson*' (2003) 7 Ecc LJ 210

Charlesworth & Percy on Negligence (Sweet & Maxwell, 11th ed, 2006)

Conaghan, J & Mansell, W *The Wrongs of Tort* (Pluto Press, 2nd ed, 1999)

Cornish, WR & Clark, G de N *Law and Society in England 1750 – 1950* (Sweet & Maxwell, 1989)

Cowper, F *A Prospect of Gray's Inn* (Graya, 2nd ed, 1985)

Deakin, S, Johnston, A & Markesinis *Markesinis and Deakin's Tort Law* (Clarendon Press, 6th ed)

Denning, Lord *The Discipline of the Law* (Butterworths, 1979)

Denning, Lord *The Family Story* (Butterworths, 1981)

DeRoche, WEP 'Torts – Negligence – Duty of Care – Liability of Contractor to Third Person' (1935) 13 Can B Rev 112

Dictionary of National Biography

Dugdale, AM & Stanton, KM *Professional Negligence* (Butterworths, 3rd ed, 1998)

Farmer, E *A Century of Paisley* (Sutton Publishing Limited, 2002)

Fearnley-Whittingstall, H *The River Cottage Cookbook* (Harper Collins, 2001)

Fleming, P *The Law of Torts* (Sweet & Maxwell, 9th ed, 1998)

Gilmore, G *The Ages of American Law* (1977)

Glegg, AT *A Practical Treatise on the Law of Reparation* (1st ed, 1892)

Gordon, JD 'The American Authorities in *Donoghue v Stevenson*: a Resolution' (1999) 115 LQR 183

Gutteridge, HC 'Lord Atkin of Aberdovey' (1944) 60 LQR 334

Heuston, RFV *Salmond on the Law of Torts* (Sweet & Maxwell, 11th ed, 1953)

Heuston, RFV '*Donoghue v Stevenson* in Retrospect' (1957) 20 MLR 1

Heuston, RFV *The Law of Torts in 1960* (Lecture Notes from 1960 Conference of British, Canadian and American Law Teachers)

Heuston, RFV *Lives of the Lord Chancellors 1885 – 1940* (Clarendon Press, 1964)

Heuston, RFV & Buckley, RA *Salmond & Heuston on the Law of Torts* (Sweet & Maxwell, 21st ed, 1996)

Holloway, R *Introduction to the Gospel According to Luke* (Canongate Pocket Canons, 1998)

Hope, Lord 'James McGhee – a Second Mrs Donoghue?' [2003] 62 CLJ 587

Howarth, DR & O'Sullivan, JA *Hepple, Howarth & Matthews' Tort: Cases and Materials* (Butterworths, 5th ed, 2000)

Kaufman, AL *Cardozo* (Harvard University Press, 1998)

Klar, LN *Tort Law* (Thomson, 3rd ed)

Lee, S *Judging Judges* (Faber & Faber, 1988)

Leechman, JF 'Mrs Donoghue's Solicitor' in Burns QC, P T and Lyons, S J (eds) *Donoghue v Stevenson and the Modern Law of Negligence The Paisley Papers* (The Continuing Legal Education Society of British Columbia, 1991)

Lewis, G *Lord Atkin* (Hart Publishing, 1999)

Linden, AM 'The Good Neighbour on Trial: a Fountain of Sparkling Wit' (1983) UBC Law Review 67

Linden, AM & Feldthusen, B *Canadian Tort Law* (Butterworths, 8th ed, 2006)

Luntz, H in Ellinghaus, MP, Bradbrook, AJ & Duggan, AJ (Eds) *The Emergence of Australian Law* (Butterworths, 1989)

Lunney, M & Oliphant, K *Tort Law: Text and Materials* (OUP, 3rd ed)

MacDonald, VC 'Torts – The Liability of Manufacturer to the Ultimate Consumer' (1932) 10 Can B Rev 478

Macmillan, Lord 'The Citation of Scottish Cases' (1933) 49 LQR 1

Macmillan, Lord *A Man of Law's Tale* (Macmillan & Co Ltd, 1952)

McBryde, WM '*Donoghue v Stevenson*: the Story of the "Snail in the Bottle" Case' in Gamble, AJ (ed) *Obligations in Context* (W Green, 1990)

McMahon, B & Binchy, W *Irish Law of Torts* (Butterworths (Ireland), 2nd ed, 1990)

McPherson, BC *The Reception of English Law Abroad* (Sup Ct of Qld Lib, 2007)

Metzger, BM & Coogan, MD (eds) *The Oxford Companion to the Bible* (OUP, 1993)

Morrison, W (ed) *Blackstone's Commentaries on the Laws of England* (Cavendish Publishing Limited, 2001)

Neethling, J, Potgieter, JM & Visser, PJ *Law of Delict* (4th ed)

Parker, A 'Changing the Claims Culture' (2006) 156 NLJ 702

Paterson, A *The Law Lords* (Macmillan, 1982)

Phillips, A & Taylor, B *On Kindness* (Hamish Hamilton, 2009)

Polenberg, R The *World of Benjamin Cardozo: Personal Values and the Judicial Process* (Harvard University Press, 1997)

Pollock, F 'The Snail in the Bottle and Thereafter' (1933) 49 LQR 22

Ratzinger, J (Pope Benedict XVI) *Jesus of Nazareth* (Bloomsbury)

Reid, K & Zimmermann, R (eds), *A History of Private Law in Scotland* (OUP, 2000)

Rodger, A 'Mrs Donoghue and Alfenus Varus' (1988) 41 CLP 1

Rogers, WVH *Winfield & Jolowicz on Tort* (Sweet & Maxwell, 16th ed, 2002)

Simpson, AWB (ed) *Biographical Dictionary of the Common Law* (Butterworths, 1984)

Smith, JC & Burns, P '*Donoghue v Stevenson* – the Not so Golden Anniversary' (1983) 46 MLR 147

Spigelman, JJ 'Negligence: the Last Outpost of the Welfare State' (2002) 76 ALJ 432

Stewart, WJ 'A Note on Matthew 6, 24: the theology of dual vicarious liability' [2007] SLT 99

Stewart, P & Stuhmcke, A *Australian Principles of Tort Law* (Cavendish Publishing Limited, 2005)

Taylor, M 'The Good Neighbour on Trial: a Message from Scotland' (1983) 17 UBC Law Review 59

Thompson, EP *The Making of the English Working Class* (Victor Gollancz, 1963)

Todd, S (General Ed) *The Law of Torts in New Zealand* (Thomson, 4th ed, 2005)

Trindade, F & Cane, P *The Law of Torts in Australia* (OUP, 3rd ed, 1999)

Underwood, P 'Is Mrs Donoghue's Snail in Mortal Peril?' (2004) 12 Torts Law Journal 39

White, GE *Tort Law in America: An Intellectual History* (OUP, 1980)

Winfield, PH 'History of Negligence in Torts' (1926) 42 LQR 184

Wright, Lord 'Lord Atkin of Aberdovey' (1944) 60 LQR 334

Yates, D 'Root Beer and Ginger Beer Heritage' (Spring 2003)

INDEX

MEMORIES CAN'T WAIT

RORY O'ROURKE

Memories Can't Wait © 2024 Rory O'Rourke

ISBN 978-1-7385350-0-2
Published by Rory O'Rourke

Designed by The Book Refinery Ltd
www.thebookrefinery.com

The right of Rory O'Rourke to be identified as the author of this work has
been asserted in accordance with the Copyright,
Designs and Patents Act, 1988.

A CIP catalogue record for this book is available from the
British Library.

Dedicated to:
My wife, Tammie, and daughter, Scarlett

And in memory of:
Sheila O'Rourke, the Queen of Sheba

PREFACE

I've always liked a feelgood story. It's what I set out to create, and I'd like to think I've achieved that.

My writing has allowed me to put into words aspects of life that I think are the most important – love, kindness, humour and reconciliation.

We're here for a good time, not a long time, right?! Nevertheless, that shouldn't preclude us from working hard and contributing positively to the lives of others, as well as our own, to put a smile on people's faces and warmth in one's soul.

The characters that form the core of my debut novel are far from biographical, or even relate that closely to anyone I know, bar one or two exceptions. Problem is, no matter how hard you try to make things up, the chances are your idea for a plot has happened to someone somewhere before. It's what makes this story so relatable. So, I've borrowed one or two events and relocated them in places I know, and no doubt they will resonate with you.

The struggles we all have in life are real, so the victories need celebrating, as often as possible in my opinion. Perhaps some of us have it easier than others – it's all relative, right? – and it depends on your perspective to some extent. Most of us will never be shot at, but if you're in the armed forces, it could happen a lot. Many of us haven't starved ourselves for days on end, but try being a single mum with bills to pay. And only a small percentage of us have been imprisoned. Having your freedom taken away could have a very profound effect on the rest of your life, or you may simply shrug and put it down to experience.

We are all different, and that's what makes us human, and utterly wonderful in our own way.

The trials my characters endure were chosen to exemplify this. They hopefully inform the reader that there is always someone worse off than you, and they are closer than you think. Not exactly helpful when you're presented with dire circumstances, but true nevertheless. It's not what we do, or how we act, when everything is going well. It's what we do when disaster strikes. Have we the strength to make things right?

Mikey, Jake and Rob know what life is about. Their adventures are meant to show us how the smallest actions and inconsequential words can have a dramatic effect on others. Just being in the room, opening a door, smiling at a stranger, whistling a jolly tune or releasing a wasp from the confines of a double-glazed window, *it's nice to be nice*. Try it.

On the flipside to all this optimism, there are those who are out to destroy. People who want to covet, to inflict pain and misery, just because they can. Unfortunately, there are too many of them out there. These people are often hard to avoid, so sometimes, we have to run straight at them, swinging punches.

I've always thought one good deed deserves another and that karma is a bitch. If you think the same, this is the book for you.

Thank you for buying *Memories Can't Wait.* I really hope you like it.

Ror

1

FACE THE MUSIC

Fulwood Crown Court, London: 13 December 2021

"All rise!"

Jake Webster stood in the dock as the wiry, stern-faced judge walked solemnly into a court background of shuffling and murmuring. The clerk begged those attending to be seated and began organising his notes and tapping on a laptop.

Panic congealed in Jake's stomach. How had he let this happen? He felt more alone than ever before – even more than as a seven year old sitting in a dark kitchen, his stomach grumbling, wondering when, or if, his mother would return.

He shook his head slowly in disbelief. He was no better than the men his mother had known – the druggies and booze-riddled arseholes she called boyfriends. Violent and abusive men he had learnt to avoid.

"Will the defendant please rise?"

Jake rose, looking every inch the professional. The irony hadn't escaped him that only weeks prior, he had sat in judgement for children to be taken from their neglectful parents, and now he was facing removal from society for *its* protection from *him*.

He had a look of sadness in his eyes. It wasn't put on for the sake of the judge. It was simply how he looked. Throughout his life, looking small and weak had got him bullied and beaten – a target.

"Are you Jake Webster, born 12 August 1994, currently residing at 15 Wick Road, Homerton, London?" the clerk asked.

"I am."

"Mr Webster, you stand before the court having been charged with grievous bodily harm with intent, contrary to Section 18 of the Offences Against the Person Act 1861, on the night of 27 August 2021, at Fandango's Nightclub, Kentish Town Road, London. How do you plead?"

As the charge was read, Jake twitched a wry smile at Tamara Norazu, his solicitor, who gave him the slightest of reassuring nods from behind her desk.

He glanced at the empty gallery and wished to God Mikey and Rob were there – not that they were in a position to help; the judge had acceded to the prosecution's request that the gallery be closed to avoid any undue distress to the victim. This had suited Jake, until this very moment, when he felt like the ground was opening beneath his feet, plunging him into the abyss with no one to stop his descent.

He hadn't blamed Mikey for what happened. It wasn't his fault. In fact, Jake held himself responsible entirely. He had crossed the line, and although he hadn't meant to injure anyone, he had. Even so, if he were to ask himself 'Would I do it again?', his answer would be an emphatic yes. Jake had to protect Mikey, and himself of course – which was going to be his barrister's first line of defence.

Now, alone in his oak-veneered cubicle, which reminded him of an upright coffin, Jake wasn't so sure self-defence was going to be a successful approach. How could he be confident? He was at risk of being sent to jail – literally a university for the bullies he had spent a lifetime swerving, where he could.

John Devlin had disagreed. He was full of confidence. Optimism personified. In the last six months, their friendship had grown as strong as anything he had with Mikey and Rob. He said the right things at the right time, but where was he now?

Friendships. Jake mocked himself. What would they mean when he was locked up in a prison cell with some career criminal? What use would banter be then?

Despite his sense of foreboding, Jake was willing to accept his punishment and leave his life of relative luxury behind, happy to have been there to protect his friend from a far worse outcome. The beautiful irony being he had likely protected many more people long into the future, by putting Ben Stockton, and the other two bastards, out of service for a long time.

Admittedly, Stockton had got his comeuppance a little harder than most. As had quite a few others recently. They just kept coming, walking into pain with a wide, arrogant grimace. They had all deserved what they got; John was right about that.

And that was Jake's problem: his actions alone were the reason he was standing in the dock in Fulwood Crown

Court, facing up to ten years in prison, while paraplegic Ben Stockton was in a wheelchair, half blind and unable to walk.

"Not guilty, Your Honour."

2

PAYDAY FRIDAY

*The Swann & Key, Kentish Town, London: 27 August 2021
(4 months earlier)*

Jake was sat cross-legged, his arms folded, bouncing his foot in time to Elton John, as he waited patiently for his two friends to arrive. He knew Mikey would be on time, and Rob at least thirty minutes late.

He loved the taproom, so called because it was a part of a public house where the working class of the 1800s would meet and draw their tankards of beer direct from barrels propped on oak trestles. They'd stand shoulder to shoulder in the dank candlelit room to drink the frothy, flat stew of hops and barley until they ran out of money or friends – or until the barrel ran dry; a tradition maintained for decades by generation after generation of modern-day porters, navvies, street vendors and scroungers. Jake was happy to play his part in history.

Deep green-glazed tiles, topped by a rope-textured dado rail, snaked around the perimeter of the room. Light-green marble mullions framed sash windows with stained glass inserts and bullseyes. The high ceiling was constructed of vaulted red brick arches and riveted steel beams to support yet another brewing room on the first floor, which was now the landlord's apartment.

The taproom floor was covered with yellow, red and black mosaic tiles with a fleur-de-lis patterned outer edge. A white swan with a key in its mouth was the centrepiece. A Latin inscription beneath read *Bibendum hodie cras moriemur* – 'Drink today, tomorrow we will die.' Jake tipped his glass of gin and tonic to the prophetic advice.

Even after one hundred and fifty years of steady drinking, the room was effectively unchanged, save for some rewiring and central heating, which reassured Jake, perhaps because nothing could change it, no matter how hard people tried. He mused how life used to be and wondered if he would have made it back then. He loved tradition, history and customs. He was fascinated and amused by superstition and the irrational beliefs people had.

The relevance of the word Swann, spelt with two ns, was a mystery. The extra letter may have been an abbreviated 'and', the sign writer possibly mistaking its relevance. Either way, it had stuck and been written that way ever since, and Jake loved that – as if the pub had lived with a disability and grown stronger because of it.

The narrow room had a significant slope to one end, where there was evidence of an old doorway long since bricked up. According to George, the landlord, the old brewers used to empty the spent malt husks directly onto the floor, then brush them out onto the street, where they'd be fed to livestock at the market.

Jake liked the idea of the waste being used sustainably and made a mental note to tell Jasmin about it when she returned from her retreat in India. He hadn't spoken to her in over two weeks, which wasn't strange – at least not for them. When Jake had suggested they communicate more, she'd huffed that she didn't like wasting time with idle chit-chat. In truth, he was happy with the arrangement.

He loved the eclectic mix of patrons, especially at this time on a Friday night when those leaving work after a long week would punctuate their journey home with a cheeky beer or two. He grinned at Mikey's referring to this end-of-work stopover as 'having a black 'un' – an expression used in the North East by miners, when they would walk from the pit – their faces black with coal dust – straight into the pub to get drunk.

Jake imagined the hard times the working class had endured and the sheer brutality of life back then. They worked to live. It was that, or starve. Their community spirit was unbreakable, even in war, when so many lost their lives.

He didn't decry the present-day workers in their suits and uniforms, with their straight white teeth and electric bicycles. The trials of life were anything but simple these days. He knew the hardship some folk had, dealing with the silent, violent husband, mounting debt and the stress of maintaining a peaceful co-existence.

Over the last seven years at Fulwood Borough Social Services, he had witnessed unspeakable cruelty and deprivation. Unsurprisingly, it was the women and children who took the brunt of the abuse. He knew families suffered in silence for years. It was his job to protect the vulnerable, and it wasn't easy.

Jake's patch of East London was often described as a rich cultural mix, usually by those who hadn't been there, but there was nothing sophisticated about it, or culturally uplifting, in his opinion. Knife crime and robbery were currently at epidemic levels. He was glad he didn't live there any more or have to risk walking the streets at the wrong time.

He'd learnt to deal with threats and confrontation from a young age, growing up in a one-parent family a lot of the time. His mother, Denise, rarely spoke of his birth father and actively changed the subject if it arose. Stewart McAlister was the only father figure he had ever known, a blessed relief from the parade of failed relationships his mother had had.

At eight years old, his life became 'normal'. There were no drugs or house parties, no screaming and shouting, no black eyes or fat lips; there were no strange men walking naked into the bathroom and using the toilet while he was brushing his teeth. It was Stewart who introduced Jake to martial arts. It was Stewart who accompanied him to classes and trained with him every day. It was Stewart who encouraged Jake at school and celebrated when Jake got straight As.

He'd saved Jake; there was no doubt about that. He showed up at the right time and played his part bringing together the family unit, at least for a little while. His influence on the shy little boy was absolute, more so than Jake could ever thank him for. Taking him to martial arts classes was Stewart's attempt to bring him out of his shell and enjoy the company of other kids. As it turned out, Jake was ideally suited to it. His composure, awareness and agility saw him rise through the ranks and become one of the most capable proponents of kung fu, taekwondo and clinch fighting the school had ever turned out.

At 5ft 6in and weighing 70kg, he hardly had a rugby player's physique, but he was an athlete in every sense of the word. His arms and legs were like steel rope, and his stomach and chest were dense with muscle. He could take on any opponent in any circumstance and strike a deadly punch in the confines of a telephone kiosk with one hand tied to his foot – if he wanted to that is. Which he never did. Unless he had to.

Jake was a quintessential passivist from head to toe, who used his wits and disarming countenance to take the upper hand – or walk away; and when he couldn't walk away, it was because people had made the same mistake. They'd assumed he was weak because he was small. He knew them better than they knew themselves – unintelligent, selfish, tyrannical and aggressive, throwing their weight around and getting nowhere. It never ended well for them.

***

Jake blinked away negative thoughts of his upbringing, when – as if landing in a parallel universe – he heard Mikey's deep Geordie voice herald his arrival to no one and everyone at the same time.

"The fun has arrived!" Mikey announced at the top of his voice while holding his arms out like a messiah.

From his position in the taproom, Jake watched with amusement as Mikey shook hands with a bunch of dirt-covered construction workers in hi-vis vests and hobnail boots, patting them on the back, creating small dust clouds, which he wafted away as he spluttered.

"How's the week gone, lads? You're not working the weekend, I hope?" He gave them all his winning smile and told them to stay safe.

"Who the fuck was that?" one of the workers enquired of his bemused mates as Mikey meandered towards the bar.

On the table to the right of the ornately carved oak bar, a group of exhausted hospital workers sat in silence. At the head of the table a burly, blonde-haired nurse in a dark-green two-piece uniform, complete with a watch hanging under her Alexa Taylor name badge, jumped to her feet. She ran to Mikey and wrapped her not inconsiderable arms around his neck like she hadn't seen him in years and began bouncing from one foot to the other in a kind of robotic smooch. Mikey had no choice but to reciprocate the hug with his mechanical dance partner, just to avoid dislocating one of his vertebrae.

"Mikey, where have you been? I've not seen you in ages! Tell me you're out tonight. Course you are. You gonna buy me a drink? Who you in with?" Alexa's barrage of rhetorical questions came like a machine gun.

Releasing her vice-like grip, Mikey edged her back to her stool, where he crouched down to her level. "I've been here and there, sweetheart, but I'm happy I'm here now," he said warmly.

Her face lit up and she swung around to face her friends. "This is Geordie Mike I was telling you about."

Her excited introduction was met by three disengaged male faces. Mikey threw out his hand to a tall thin guy called Colin, who had a hooked nose and long, cold fingers.

Nametag-less male number two showed similar enthusiasm, with a welcome grip you might expect from a cadaver. Alexa's third friend, Welsh Ian, gave a curt nod and kept his arms crossed. None of them introduced himself.

"You guys on a black 'un, or what?" Mikey asked, receiving confused expressions in return.

"I don't know what you're talking about, mate. Speak English, will ya." The terse response came from Ian, the balding, tubby hospital porter in a pale-blue uniform, clearly not overjoyed by the attention Alexa was giving to Mikey.

"Fucking shut it, Taff!" Alexa snapped at him angrily with narrow eyes, her stubby finger pointing at the rotund Welshman, who laughed nervously.

"I was only joking, Al. Just having a laugh with your pal, innit," he said, sounding scolded.

Alexa's scowl turned into a swoon as she pivoted all her attention back to Mikey. "Will I see you later, or have you got plans? You're probably out at some swanky party, eh? Or at the casino or summat?" Her second volley of questions came as casually as a ten-pound sledgehammer, not sparing the feelings of the sullen-faced Ian, who obviously had designs on her himself.

"It's Fruit's birthday, darling. We'll be getting hammered and finishing up in Fandango's, all being well." Mikey didn't have the heart to lie to her – she was always so sweet to him.

Alexa didn't realise 'Fruit' was Rob's nickname (on account of his surname being De Freitus and sounding like 'fruit', according to Mikey at any rate). And she didn't care. She only had eyes and ears for Mikey.

Mikey slithered out of her grip, gently holding her down by kissing her on the head.

"I'll see you all later then," he said, shooting the guys with his finger gun and winking.

He jinked his way through to the taproom, shaking hands and waving at people like a US congressman rallying the voters. He didn't miss anyone out, especially not the old boys, who flashed their gravestone grins and rocked backwards and forwards, thrilled to be spoken to by such a thoroughly nice chap.

Jake sprang up out of his seat in one fluid movement holding his arms out as Mikey strode into the taproom, only to be left hanging with his mouth wide open mid-sentence, like some discarded blow-up sex doll.

Mikey did an about turn, and while hanging on the jamb of the doorless opening, he whistled at George, who was busily pulling pints. Those stood close by winced and ducked at the screech of Mikey's E sharp. In the noise of the crowd, Mikey shouted his order towards the bar, then lurched back towards his friend.

"Jakey-boy! How are you doing, mucker?" he asked, flinging himself into Jake's embrace.

"I'm aces, Mikey, what's the score with you, man? It's like watching Donald Trump walk into the room when you turn up." Jake's eyes lit up at the sight of Mikey's faux modesty.

"Hey, I had a lucky escape there with Alexa. She's got a touch like a baby elephant." Mikey's turn of phrase was often tactless, but rarely misunderstood.

Before they could get started on their recap of the last few weeks, George barrelled over, agitated and sweaty.

"It's not feckin' table service, you know," he huffed as he bounced his way towards them, arms raised carrying empty glasses.

"Why don't you queue up at the bar like everyone else?" George's voice was half an octave higher than normal in slight irritation.

"We just wanted to see you in the flesh, George, and have the gas, didn't we, Jake?" Not waiting for back-up, Mikey thumbed in the direction of the bar. "Besides, if one of them dopes were to spill blackcurrant juice on my new white shirt, I'd have to borrow one of yours!"

George chuckled at Mikey's chiding, took their drinks order and headed back to the bar.

"Pull one for Fruit, will ya, George! He'll be here shortly!" Mikey shouted at George's flabby back.

"Righto," he said.

"You don't half push your luck," Jake said, shaking his head in disbelief. "I can't believe he doesn't tell you to piss off."

"It's nice to be nice, Jake. You ought to try it one time."

Mikey's sideways insult got him a beermat flung from Jake's side of the table. A moment of panic hit his face as it struck his gleaming white shirt.

It is nice to be nice, Jake thought, and Mikey was the epitome of niceness, even to those who didn't deserve it.

"We can't all be like Mikey Stott. The world would implode, mate." Mikey nodded in agreement to Jake's conclusion, and they laughed in unison.

"This is the last Friday of the month, and that only means one thing – lock up your daughters." Mikey scanned the room for targets as George waddled back with Mikey's pint, Jake's G&T and a Guinness for Rob.

"Now," George breathed as he placed the drinks on the table, "there you go, Jack."

"It's Jake," Jake corrected.

"Same difference, isn't it?"

Jake faked a smile and decided silence was called for.

The 150kg, fifty-four-year-old landlord plonked himself down on a stool next to Mikey and took a much-deserved breather. His lungs wheezed in effort and beads of sweat burst from his heavily wrinkled forehead. George Horgan was the antithesis of Mikey and Jake in every way possible. He sat legs apart, with his fleshy hands propping himself up, his gut spilling over his belt in all directions. The thin strap of worn black leather struggled dutifully to contain the tensile load through the prong snagged into the very last hole available. His forearms, which were the size of loaves of crusty bread, had been used to throw dozens of leary pissheads into the street over the years, and those long nights had taken their toll on him. His eyes had fatty folds of skin beneath that looked like mini croissants dotted with a sprinkling of skin tags.

He was a *regular walking boulangerie*, Jake thought to himself, wondering how he had let himself get into this state.

George swiped a damp, heavily stained tea towel off his shoulder and mopped his brow, flinging it back with a thwack. "Feck, it's hot, lads."

Mikey and Jake nodded out of courtesy. George's body odour was ripe, evidenced by light-brown concentric rings on his faded blue shirt, which reminded Jake of a chromatography experiment he used to do at school.

"Where's Hooray Henry?" George asked, nodding at Rob's untouched pint of Guinness.

"He's always late, he'll be here shortly. It's his birthday today, so we'll let him off this time," Jake said.

"Is he bringing Lauren with him? I fucking hope not." Mikey directed his question at Jake, while answering it himself.

Jake shrugged. "I've no idea, mate. He ignores the 'no girlfriends on Friday nights' rule. She doesn't even like it here. She never stops whining about it being a dump and having no Prosecco!" He laughed at his own quip and caught the look of annoyance on George's face.

"Hey, no offence, George." Jake raised his two hands in apology.

"None taken, Jack." George snorted.

Taking the veiled insult as a cue to leave and get back to the bar, George heaved his body upright, untangled his scrotum from the creases of his trousers and left.

Averting his eyes, Mikey blindly handed over a twenty-pound note and reminded him to get one for himself. Stuffing it in his front pocket, George shuffled off, taking with him any forlorn hopes Mikey may have had of getting any change.

"She's a gorgeous lass, Jake, but fuck me, she's a snobby cow. I've no idea how Fruit puts up with her."

"Love is blind, mate," Jake said shrugging.

He rarely said a harsh word about anyone, especially not Rob's girlfriends. He knew how much of a hard time he had had with his ex, Maddie Parker, and recent events hadn't helped when she'd returned from Africa only to start up a relationship with some other guy.

"She'd have to be blind – I've seen him in the showers. She's only after him for his money, trust me." Mikey waggled his little finger while taking a slurp from his pint.

The ritual they had of meeting on the last Friday of the month was regular if not routine. There were no fixed rules as to how long they would stay out, who would attend or even the venue itself. The only thing that never changed was that they met for the craic and had a good time. It was a personal commitment of sorts, and as much as they chided and ridiculed each other, they cherished what they had, and Payday Friday was a celebration of it.

They had grown up in entirely different worlds. Jake came from a one-child, single-parent family from the East End of London, Mikey from a working-class family in Tyne and Wear, and then there was Rob, the heir to the De Freitus estate, and a lineage that went back hundreds of years.

Rob wasn't embarrassed by his family wealth or history, but he was hardly effusive about it either. All said and done, he was doing very well for himself; and in recent years, backing his own advice, he had made a small fortune on top of the sizeable stipend he received.

That was a head shaker for Mikey, learning that Rob got money from his 'estate'. He'd failed to comprehend the staggering level of wealth Rob's family had. It was one of the few things that made him angry – knowing as many deprived families from the North East as he did, where a small fraction of the interest in one day would have a life-changing effect.

Despite his misgivings, Mikey's resentment of the north—south divide temporarily disappeared when Rob quadrupled his modest £10,000 investment in a couple of short-term venture capital trust schemes. It was easily enough money to pay for the deposit on his one-bedroom studio, and he wired his parents £5,000 of bunce, to make himself feel better.

Jake had done well too, but feared his mother was using her windfall for more nefarious reasons.

Rob, on the other hand, was operating on a completely different level and had been quietly amassing his wealth. His pad in Primrose Hill cost over £1.8m, and without doubt was the most luxurious apartment Mikey and Jake had ever set foot in.

They were all out there to live their best lives, and yet, there was something missing. Each of them felt it – they had for a while – perhaps it was something they had lost and were looking for, with no hope of knowing what it was. A twenty-eight-year itch that had become more irksome as time passed; the spiritual and emotional reliance they had on each other now seemed redundant and an embarrassing memory of being immature juveniles at university.

Despite Jake's insistence that 'a problem shared is a problem halved', he was far from open about his own emotional wellbeing or hang-ups. The self-denial in seeking help to come to terms with his own anxieties was in sharp contrast to the skills and insight he offered others in his day job. Truth was, he had seen sights few people could stomach, and he wondered himself where he put the images and how he slept at night. Still, that was his problem, not theirs.

***

Robin De Freitus sauntered into the pub wearing Ray-Bans® that sat wonkily on the bridge of his nose, armed with his tall, wide-eyed girlfriend, Lauren Preston. She couldn't have looked any more out of place among the hoi polloi of Kentish Town, as she failed to hide the thinly veiled look of horror pulling at the edges of her mouth. She sashayed through the bar in harmony with the bounce of her glossy, wavy, shoulder-length brown hair. Mikey's dusty, hi-vis-clad comrades in construction made no attempt to disguise their appreciation. With gaping mouths like goldfish, they tracked Lauren as she passed by, showering them in a vapour trail of expensive perfume.

An enormous, grimy, ginger-haired guy said something obscene behind his pint glass, which got raucous laughter from his equally grubby drinking partners.

"Ignore the sexist fat pigs."

"Ignore who, darling?" Rob replied, disinterestedly.

"Those guys in the yellow jackets – they said something disgusting." Lauren wrinkled her nose.

"Ahh right, will do. Take no notice, darling, they're only jealous of your beauty and my luck."

Rob rolled out the compliment almost without thinking. Oblivious of everyone around him, he focussed only on getting to the taproom. He skipped onwards, weaving through the crowded bar at a speed a little quick for Lauren in her heels, who was making way too much bodily contact with strangers for her liking.

"I don't know why you come in here," she muttered to the back of his floppy brown hair. "It's a dive and full of scummy men and gross women."

"Where the fuck is my pint of Guinness?" Rob demanded of his two friends from the taproom entrance.

"Fruit, my old boy!" Mikey exclaimed, trying to sound posh and ending up sounding West Country. He bounded over and threw his arms around Rob, mimicking Alexa's welcome technique. "Happy birthday, you old fuck-stick."

Mikey's welcome went on for at least thirty seconds before he turned his attention to Lauren. He angled towards her for a welcome hug, which she tried gallantly to fend off. As he embraced her, he breathed her in, rubbing his designer stubble against her cheek. The prickly texture made her go rigid. He leant back, with a crimson-red lipstick battle scar up the side of his face.

"Hello, darlin', how are you?" He tried to sound heartfelt.

"Hello, Mikey, I'm fine thank you. Nice to see you all again." Lauren flashed a strained smile in their direction.

"A little early to have lipstick all over his face but entirely predictable," Jake mumbled.

Mikey released his hold on Lauren, causing her to fall back a step. Jake eased forward, taking hold of her hands to steady her and air-kissed both sides of her head in a display of total restraint.

"Hello, Lauren. Let me get you a drink," he offered.

Ever the gentleman, Jake steered Lauren towards his seat and headed off to get her 'an ice-cold Prosecco with a slice of strawberry in a tall, *clean* flute'. Lauren emphasised the hygiene requirements of her chosen beverage, as if handing out dirty glassware was an option people might choose. She had dispensed with manners several years ago, so Jake did as he was told, not waiting for a please or thank you.

While Mikey and Rob caught up and gulped down their beers, Lauren reapplied her make-up and lipstick using a small foldaway mirror that she extracted from her handbag. She thought about using the ladies room but decided against it.

Jake returned quickly but empty handed, much to the irritation of Lauren's questioning eyes glaring just above her pink compact.

"It's on its way. Thea just had to nip down to the cellar for a fresh bottle."

Lauren returned wordlessly to the reapplication of her lipstick.

Jake turned to Rob, who was honing in on him with arms wide. "How's Jackie Chan been doing?" Rob asked.

"Doing great thanks, pal. How's the world of high finance? You get that account you were looking for? French art dealer in Paris, wasn't it? He sounds like a top geezer."

"With any luck, mate." Rob waved his crossed fingers in front of his friend. "We've got that drinks party at the Vaults in Aldgate on Thursday, don't forget. I want you and Mikey to come along and meet some of the characters I've had to deal with. They're totally bonkers, but a good bunch. Pierre

Montreaux will be there. I want you to meet him and give me your take."

"No can do, I'm afraid," Lauren interjected. "There's limited space, and I'm sure they wouldn't like it anyway, with all the boring high-finance types in attendance." She mocked Jake's earlier reference and flicked a patronising smile.

"Don't worry about it, precious." Mikey smiled easily in response. "Me and Jakey will find something to amuse ourselves, won't we, mate?" He was keen not to make his friend backtrack out of the invite.

Rob was having none of it. "Hang on a minute – where does it say Lauren Preston Wealth Management? The last time I looked, it was my name in flashing lights outside the building, so if I want to invite my friends, or any Tom, Dick or Harry come to think of it, I will. That OK with you?" His voice dripped in sarcasm. He clearly felt emboldened by the presence of his friends, neither of whom felt comfortable listening to his curt response.

"Well, there's no need to be like that, I was just saying what Roger told me earlier."

Lauren, flushed with anger, decided she'd risk a visit to the ladies after all, just to avoid the uncomfortable looks she was getting.

Mikey stared as she left, swallowed, and licked his lips. Eventually, he returned his gaze from Lauren's arse back to Rob.

"Mikey, you couldn't afford it, mate, and besides, you wouldn't last five seconds with her, even if you got that far."

Rob elbowed Jake and they both bent double, laughing at Mikey's indignant expression.

"Howay, lads, gimme a break, I'm not that bad." Mikey protested at the implication that his sexual performance was below par.

At that moment Thea Horgan, daughter of the repugnant George, stepped into the taproom and headed straight for Mikey's table. Once she'd offloaded Lauren's Prosecco, Mikey jumped off his stool and threw his arms around her.

"Hey baby, how are you doing?" he asked, staring into her dark-green eyes and kissing her on the lips.

She lapped up the attention and breathed in the manly aroma of Mikey's freshly ironed shirt and aftershave. She unravelled herself, but her hands lingered on his abdominal muscles and slid up to his chest. She pouted and took a deep breath as the memory of his naked body took a hold of her.

"I'll be glad to get out of here," she said eventually. "I need a few vodkas down me. Are you buying, Mikey?" Thea knew he wouldn't say no.

"Sure, no problem. Maybe see you in the club later, yeah?" Mikey was racking up the tête-à-têtes by the minute.

With her arm still wrapped around Mikey's waist, Thea faced Rob and Jake.

"You are looking lovely, as always," Rob said, before blowing a kiss across the table.

Lauren returned from powdering her nose and killed the mood instantly. She slid deftly onto the bench seat next to Rob and picked up her drink, inspected the glass rim for any residue, and took a sip.

"Is this Prosecco?" she asked abruptly.

"Yep," came Thea's monosyllabic reply.

"Apparently, you've run out of strawberries," Lauren sniffed haughtily.

Thea broke the awkward silence. "So, how's Maddie getting on, Rob? Is she still in Africa?"

"No, she's back now. I haven't seen her in a while, though," Rob said, shuffling uncomfortably on his seat.

Thea knew her work was done by the sight of steam coming out of Lauren's ears.

Rob leant forward and beeped his phone over the credit card reader hanging off her waist, desperately hoping the conversation was over.

"Well, see yas later then, and happy birthday, Rob." She sang the words, brushing her hand through Mikey's hair as she returned to the bar.

"Bitch," Lauren seethed, tucking her arms and clenched fists under her gravity-defying bosom.

Just mentioning Rob's ex-girlfriend was enough to make her teeth grind. Rob sensed his birthday night out was descending into an argument.

"Happy birthday, Fruit. Hope you got some nice presents." Jake tried his best to move the conversation on and raised his glass in a mirthless toast. He needn't have worried – Lauren had snatched her phone from her bag and begun texting at lightning speed and taking selfies.

"I was at work all day, but now I'm here, and it's time to get wrecked," Rob said, raising his glass once more.

"So, let's talk about next Thursday. As I was saying, I've got this works do on and you have to come. It'll be a great laugh." Rob was almost pleading with them.

"Only if there's room, Fruit. We don't want to be a ballache. Maybe get Lauren to double-check, eh?" Jake said in good faith.

"No, of course there is! No need for that!" He waved half-heartedly at Lauren, who was smirking at something she'd received in response to her digital self-portrait.

"It's not a posh do, just come as you are. The booze is free and there'll be a buffet."

Jake grinned and nodded his agreement, as did Mikey.

"We'll be there, mate," he reassured him.

Jake briefly imagined having a party with the misfits he worked alongside. The thought of it amused him and frightened him in equal measure.

"Well, it's gonna be a busy week then," Mikey chipped in. "It's the Highfield Cabbage Club Show next Saturday, remember, and you both said you would come to that. My ol' man is looking forward to seein' yas." Mikey held up his palms and hoped they weren't about to gyp on him.

Highfield was a pit village on the outskirts of Newcastle upon Tyne, which held its annual flower and vegetable growing competition in the late summer. Mikey hadn't been in years, for one reason and another, but this year Brian, his father, was entering his leeks and marrows and Jackie, her dahlias and alliums. Mikey had done the big sell on the day and was desperate to take his mates home to meet his family again and show some faith. As much as Brian and Jackie were proud of the life Mikey was living in London, they desperately missed him. FaceTime and telephone calls just didn't cut it sometimes; they needed to be close to him, to rekindle the fire in their broken hearts.

"Mikey ... chill, mate," Rob said calmly. "I've already booked us first-class tickets from King's Cross. We wouldn't miss it for the world, would we, Jake?" Jake nodded with gusto and Mikey beamed with pride.

"What we owe you, mate?" Jake got his phone out ready to transfer Rob the cost of the train tickets.

"Don't panic, it's been a good month." Rob winked again and gave Jake the thumbs up.

"I've also booked us in at the Malmaison on the Quayside. I guess we might end up 'doon the toon'."

Rob's Geordie accent needs work, Mikey thought to himself, and he made a mental note to ask him not to take the piss out of the wrong people, to avoid any 'disagreement'. An image of Fozza, the local headcase, popped into his head and he began to wonder whether taking two southerners into the parochial capital of the world was a good idea after all.

Rob continued. "While we have our diaries out, we've got Royal Ascot on 25 September. Tarquin Pendlebury has a runner. It's a great day out."

"Sounds great that, Fruit," Jake joined in enthusiastically.

"Aye, sound," Mikey said, albeit a little deflated. He'd suddenly realised that he was offering a cabbage growing competition with the great unwashed gardeners of Highfield, and Rob was lining up an afternoon on the piss with the Queen.

Jake wasn't the least bit concerned he was bringing zero to the table. There was nothing in his locker room they'd be remotely interested in.

"Rob, you can't just invite whoever you like, you know." Lauren's words stuck in her throat. "You'd better check with Roger is what I mean, to make sure there's enough space." She smiled at the boys without an ounce of warmth.

"I've already arranged it, so wind your neck in." Rob's impatient response was the straw that broke the camel's back, or more likely, the excuse Lauren was waiting for to make an exit. Her bottom lip trembled as she snatched up her handbag and coat.

"You've been mean to me all night and I'm fed up with it. I'm not sitting in this dump being abused by you and your mates a moment longer." Lauren waved her arm angrily towards Mikey and Jake.

"Lauren, I'm sure Rob didn't mean to be short with you," Jake pleaded.

"Fuck off, all of you! I'm going to Alicia's."

Rob followed her out in a flood of crocodile tears. They could hear Lauren shouting at him on the street through the open window. To their surprise, she threw her arms around him and buried her head in his neck. She then got into a black cab and left, alone. It appeared there was a limit as to how far she was prepared to scream and shout at her multi-millionaire boyfriend.

Rob returned and slumped onto the bench seat vacated by Lauren and let out a long sigh. Mikey glanced across at Jake with a 'what to do next' expression. With his chin resting on his chest, Rob wrinkled his forehead and looked up at them.

His straight white teeth bore a devilish grin. "I'd call that a result, wouldn't you?"

They let out a huge cheer, followed by another one of Mikey's ear-splitting whistles towards the bar.

"More beer, Georgie Boy!"

3

SEEDS IN THE WIND

The Collingwood Arms, Kentish Town Road, London:
27 August 2021

Hansie Van Heerden leant on the bar, head bowed, staring at his size twelve suede brogues. His white and green checked shirt strained around his massive back, and his sleeves rolled up over his bulbous forearms.

"Thank the Lord that week is over," he mumbled to himself, blowing out a long sigh of relief. His huge frame heaved then sagged under the weight of his shoulders.

Another week of tedium endured and, for once, his weekend wouldn't be hijacked by a last-minute sicknote from his lazy-arsed staff. He daydreamed of being back in the veld.

"Huh," he said out loud, shaking his head. The irony of it all. The boys on the farm would do literally everything he told them. They'd work fourteen hours a day and be grateful. *These fuckers won't lift a bat*, he thought, making a mental note of the ones he would love to slap, to frighten them into working harder, or clear the fuck out.

As North London Estates Manager for the Environment Agency, it was down to Hansie to ensure on-call staff were in place and prepared for any eventuality. Despite his continual requests for more staff and resources, they weren't coming anytime soon, which meant Hansie was working twice as hard.

His home on the Eastern Transvaal was sparsely populated. He could go weeks without seeing anyone – just the way he liked it. Not here, not in London: there were millions of people dumping rubbish, fly-tipping, polluting, thieving and generally making his job of managing parks, trails and nature reserves way more difficult than it needed to be. Worse still, he wasn't allowed a gun, or even a decent hunting knife.

The Du Toit estate was a fraction bigger than the area of North London and the home counties. It had four times as many rivers, innumerable rare species of fauna and flora, poisonous snakes, scorpions, and bugs that would burrow into you and eat you from the inside out. There were two mammoth copper mines that spewed pollution into the air and rivers, causing issues for wildlife and farm animals. The daily temperatures ranged from 0 to 40 degrees, and heat exhaustion could kill you if you didn't keep well hydrated. Yet, he managed that with a quarter of the people he had at his disposal in London, *and it was a damn sight easier to control than this hellhole.*

He missed home, the harsh beauty of the veld. He missed the influence he once had, the man he used to be. The droughts were relentless and cruel, but when the rains came, it was almost apocalyptic. The clouds over the Steenkampsberg would build for weeks, as if they were taking a run-up to gain as much momentum as possible, to right a wrong, to turn the desert to meadow. A deep, constant rumbling thunder giving fair warning of the frontal assault destined to overwhelm the land. He grinned at the memory of hailstones the size of golf balls bouncing off the back of his sheep. The smell of the rain on the dry soil, pre-empting the shoots of fresh vegetation which seemed to appear within hours, and the scent of the flowers that took their opportunity to bloom no matter how fleeting it may have been.

"Not in this godforsaken country! Weather for rats and slugs," Hansie mumbled to himself, curling his top lip in disgust.

The lush-green rolling hills of the Epsom Downs and the Chiltern Hills had been forgotten – or blanked out more like. Nothing could compare to home, but he knew he could never go back. Not now, not ever.

He waved his empty glass at the barman.

"One minute, big man!" Ben shouted.

If Hansie felt at home anywhere outside South Africa, it was here in The Collingwood Arms. He saw it as an extension of his other haven: the rugby pitch. Playing rugby, he could truly be himself. He could speak directly and with authority. No one questioned him, and if necessary, as it often was, he could give people a slap without being arrested or sacked. Ten minutes in the sinbin was an acceptable punishment to him. The thought of it cheered him up, just like the prospect of his dinner.

He'd already been into the kitchen and chosen a tomahawk steak the size of a tennis racket from Ebbo the Nigerian chef and fellow African, although he was clearly from the wrong hemisphere, which Hansie reminded him often. He'd given strict instructions on how it was to be prepared and seasoned and how he wanted his mushroom sauce.

Ebbo had given Hansie his biggest smile, his shiny jet-black skin intensifying the whiteness of his teeth. "Yes, boss Hansie, only the best."

Neither Ebbo nor Hansie found their dialogue the least bit improper, although the other kitchen staff cringed under their toque blanches. But Ebbo was no fool. Hansie and his friends were good customers, and pandering to his old-fashioned colonial attitude wasn't difficult for him. And besides, Duane had asked him not to be offended, and, in truth, he wasn't.

The Colly, as it was affectionately referred to, had been renovated two years before, when an Australian businessman, Duane Long, bought the place and renamed it from the uninspiring Red Lion to The Collingwood Arms. He had remodelled it into a sports-themed bar and restaurant, which had become extremely popular with expats of many nationalities, as well as locals. Large wooden double doors hung on stainless steel pivot hinges that bounced backwards and forwards like in a Wild West saloon, making an audible whoomph as they met in the middle. The doors, and much of the bar furniture itself, had been flown in from an old tavern in New South Wales which had gone out of business.

Even though a sign had been erected saying 'Beware, Swinging Doors', there were at least half a dozen incidents a night where people walked into them, head down entranced by their mobile phones. Duane could have locked the doors to operate one way, but the outback was a dangerous place. He liked the idea of importing a little danger. Besides, black widow spiders and spitting cobras were impractical.

Beneath Hansie's brogues, there was a sea of black and white chequered tiles, like the type you see on a floor detergent advertisement, where some energetic housewife is leaning on her mop admiring her work, then laughing playfully at the family dog leaving muddy footprints all over the place. The Colly was only a third full, but by ten o'clock the pied floor would be invisible, and Mrs Mop would have to start all over again the next morning.

The interior walls were bare yellow brick set in grey lime mortar, covered with dozens of signed and framed black and white, armless sports shirts from Duane's favourite Aussie rules football club in Melbourne. Wrought iron columns supported the vaulted brick arched ceilings, which were covered with vintage tennis rackets, cricket bats, fishing rods and a myriad of other sporting paraphernalia.

The highchairs and booths were upholstered in a rich red leather with press stud backs and brass rivetted edges. Brass and copper lampshades hung from ceiling chains and wall mounts, splashing light and shade onto the high-top tables and columns.

Access to the Outback Restaurant to the right of the entrance was through a wood-panelled square passageway adorned with didgeridoos, plastic eucalyptus bushes and a stuffed kangaroo called Keith. The chessboard-tiled floor had given way to rough-sawn nine-inch solid walnut floorboards that produced a resounding clunk under foot.

"Have you got a hole in the back of your neck, Hansie?" the stick-thin barman asked in a friendly tone, as he placed another beer in front of him.

"Huh? Nee man, the first always goes down easy, Bru. It's lekker."

Hansie tried his best to sound chipper. Ben was a nice enough guy and a very efficient barman. He didn't want him thinking he was hard work – he'd struggle to get served later when it filled up.

"Where's that beautiful bride of yours?" Ben asked as casually as he could, hoping she would make an appearance.

"She's on her way. Out with the girls, I think," Hansie replied.

He couldn't go anywhere, or meet anyone, without them asking about his wife, Trixie. He wasn't complaining – it was a first-world problem he had dealt with for years, and a side effect of having an attractive wife. It didn't bother him if guys came on to her. If it did, he'd be even more angry with life. Besides, she liked the attention, for the most part, and he knew where her loyalties lay.

Trixie loved London and had acclimatised to the metropolitan lifestyle; it was like she'd lived there all her life, not hundreds of kilometres from civilisation in the dusty plains of Mpumalanga. Hansie, on the other hand, hadn't settled one bit. His tirades about his new life, although amusing to friends, left many stunned into silence and laughing nervously at the angry behemoth growling and gesticulating.

Hansie wished his friends would get a move on. All this stewing and self-pity was only making him worse. He had to straighten his face before Trixie arrived. She was part of the New World Order now and wouldn't listen to him complaining.

How Trixie had dealt so clinically with the past, with what had happened to her and her family, Hansie could not understand. The flashbacks still haunted him – the nightmares and the bouts of anger had mostly subsided, but when they did come, it was awful, for everyone. How could she be so strong, and he so weak? She was the warrior now, leading the way; he was meek, following like a lamb to the slaughter. At this rate, if he didn't sort his shit out, he could end up a stay-at-home dad. He laughed inwardly at his self-deprecation and unlikely ending in domestic hell.

"Hey, Slim!" A huge hand came crashing down on his back with a loud slap, causing Hansie to jump out of his skin. Danie always referred to Hansie as Slim, after a character from an old Afrikaans folk song called Hansie Slim, who wanted to explore and climb mountains, while his mother decried his ambition, wanting him to stay at home.

"Fok, Doos!" Hansie growled.

"Hoe gaan dit, Bru?" Danie Schoeman held out his hand and hugged his countryman.

"Lekker, man, howzit?" The warmth of Hansie's welcome for his friend was barely above freezing.

"Lekker? You need to speak to your face. You look like you've just shot your dog." Danie never shied away from speaking his mind.

Danie's wrinkle-free, bright-blue eyes showed not one ounce of worry or stress, in sharp contrast to Hansie's, which were sunken and dull, with a ridge of bone running across his eyebrows like a rubber bumper from a 1980s saloon car.

"Hey, where's Varkie? Is he waiting outside 'till we get the beers in'?" Danie laughed.

"Who knows, Bru – he'll be arguing with someone somewhere. Or stuffing his face." Danie's playfulness lifted Hansie's mood.

"Hey, Bru." Danie's voice softened. "Seriously, are you OK? You don't look too pleased with life?"

Hansie drew in a deep breath. "We've got this citizenship hearing in a couple of weeks. I'm not confident. They'll send us home if we're rejected … I'm trying not to think about what happens then."

"For God's sake, have you seen the number of asylum seekers paddling here on boats from France? It's a fucking joke, Bru. You and Trixie should be sorted by now."

Danie's soft and deliberate tones were supportive and consoling. He could see a chink of improvement in his giant friend, whose shoulders seemed to lift at his response.

"You're right, Bru." Hansie's face cracked into a reluctant smile. "I'm sure it'll work out, I'll just grin and—"

The words stuck in his mouth as he saw Varkie scurry into the bar, his eyes pinballing in search of his friends.

Stephane Koetze, aka Varkie, which translated as piglet in English, scurried over to the wall of South African beef standing at the bar. Varkie was the serious type – fidgety and squirrelly, never completely relaxed, no matter where he was. He shook hands rather than embracing his enormous friends. At 5ft 5in, he was the runt of the group in terms of size and strength. His untucked shirt failed to hide the spread of one too many braais.

"The girls will be here in about half an hour." His expression was full of concern. "I think I'll order some nibbles. What do you think – will we have time?"

"How do you keep so skinny, Varkie?" Danie teased his diminutive friend.

Varkie looked up to see his two friends chomping on a handful of Parma ham they had taken off a platter on the bar, ordered by Hansie ten minutes beforehand.

"I know you by now, Bru." Hansie grinned and washed his snack down with a swig of beer, failing to stifle a loud belch. "Help yourself, it's lekker."

Varkie needed no encouragement and reached in.

"Moenie waag nie, Stephane Koetze!" A shriek like broken glass came from his six o'clock, followed by a thwack of his wrist. Varkie spun around and was shocked to see Grethe, his wife, scowling at him, flanked by Mariette Schoemann and Trixie Van Heerden, smirking, and wagging their fingers.

The remnants of Hansie's dour mood evaporated instantly at the sight of Trixie flashing her huge blue eyes in his direction. He reminded himself for the hundredth time it didn't matter where he lived so long as this beautiful woman was by his side. He wrapped one of his bulbous arms around her and buried his head in her immaculate dark-blonde hair, which sent a shudder of electricity through his bones.

He towered over her and asked, "Hey, pumpkin, do you want a drink?"

"No, I want to hug the most handsome man in the pub," Trixie purred, hooking her thumbs into Hansie's shirt and pulling him towards her.

"Let's go eat." Varkie ruined their moment and received yet another whack across the shoulder from Grethe.

"Fok, Varkie, kan jy aan niks anders dink nie?" Grethe said, poking his stomach.

"I'm hungry, eh! Let's go!" he retaliated, and, in a moment of rare decisiveness, he led the way.

***

Mikey careened through the Colly's swing doors, which rebounded off their stoppers into the path of Jake and Rob, who had to lurch backwards to avoid faceplanting. After two hours in The Swann, necking beer and taking the piss out of George Horgan, Jake made the call, with uncharacteristic assertiveness, that it was time to move on.

Jimmy Jones and His Deputies had the place bouncing with their version of American Pie, which Mikey sang along to as he followed Jake to the bar, hugging and kissing people he barely knew, or didn't know at all.

"A large G&T – no slice, lots of ice – a Guinness and a San Miguel, right?" Ben shouted towards Rob, anticipating their order from the last time they were in – his sure-fire way of getting a decent tip.

Three minutes later, and devoid of twenty quid, Rob spun around, tucked his elbows in like a downhill skier and shimmied his way back to the boys.

"Jake!" he shouted, though he got no response over the noise emanating from the Don McLean wannabe on the mic. It didn't help that Jake seemed to be distracted.

"Jake! For fuck's sake!" he shouted again, unheard. His grip on the three drinks loosened.

In the nick of time, Mikey returned and unpicked his beer from Rob's fingertips.

"Are you expecting someone, Jakey?" Mikey asked the back of his head.

"Huh? Me? Noooo, no, I was just looking around to see if I knew anyone, that's all," Jake said without conviction.

"Jasmin making an appearance tonight, mate?" Rob asked, mischievously.

"Who? Jazz? Hell no, could you imagine?" Jake panicked for a moment that she might pitch up and ruin his night, like Lauren had tried and failed to do.

"Maybe he's got some secret bird on the go, Mikey – keeping it quiet. You know what a dark horse he is. A closed book is Jake." Rob elbowed Mikey, hoping he would continue with the piss-take.

Ignoring him, Mikey returned the elbow to Rob's drinking arm, causing him to spill Guinness down the back of his hand.

"There's Trixie over there. She's sat in a booth with some mates. Haway, let's bob over and have a chat. She's fuckin' gorgeous. She'd make a bulldog break its chain." Mikey's vernacular hadn't diminished one iota in the seven years he'd spent in North London.

Wringing the black-brown creamy liquid off his hand and shirt sleeve, Rob said, "Mikey, have you seen the size of her boyfriend, Henry – he's bigger than my garage door?"

"It's Hansie, numbnuts, and he's South African. Plays rugby for the Boks. He's a mate of mine, don't worry. Besides, he's not here." Mikey flashed a dangerous grin at his friend.

"I don't want his fucking life story, mate. If he turns up and sees you trying to get off with her, he'll tear you a new arsehole." Rob's warning was offered in all seriousness but utterly ignored as Mikey strode off to gatecrash Trixie's party.

"Nice one, Jake," Rob complained. "Thanks for the assistance. There's a good chance Mikey'll get murdered over there. Jake?! Are you tripping out or something?" Rob's words met deaf ears.

"Sorry, mate, I've seen a pal of mine … I'll be back in a minute." With that, Jake ducked away, handing Rob his now empty glass to go with his own.

Rob's patience was beginning to wear thin. Lauren had marched off in a huff, Mikey was destined for the emergency ward and Jake was uncharacteristically evasive.

"Some birthday night out this is," he griped to himself dejectedly.

"Happy birthday, darling!" Rob's gloom was suddenly lifted by the most beautiful woman he had ever met.

***

"Well, well, fancy meeting you here, John." Jake ambled up to his friend with his hand out.

John Devlin was a clean-cut, fit-looking thirty-something with tanned skin, brown eyes, perfectly manicured designer stubble and short brown hair. His tailored, royal-blue suit and light-blue cotton shirt gave him a relaxed but sophisticated appearance. His build was far from bulky. In fact, he made Jake look big in comparison. At 5ft 5in and a smidgen over

60kg, he was built more like a long-distance runner or a jockey.

"Hey, Jake! How are you?" John held his hand out. "Sit down, I'll buy you a drink."

"I'll get it, Jonny, it's my round." A camp-sounding, plump man with a cheery face shuffled to his feet and rested his chubby hand on John's sleeve. Turning to Jake he said, "I assume you'd like a large one?" After wiggling his eyebrows, he minced his way to the bar laughing to himself.

"Take no notice of Patrick, he's always like that. It's like working with Julian Clary most days." John held his hand on Jake's back and beckoned him to slide back into their booth.

Three sets of eyes bore down on him like a bench of magistrates.

"Let me introduce you to my team. Everyone, this is a very good friend of mine, Jake Webster. Jake, this is Molly, Derek and Justin." John nodded and gestured left to right at his co-workers sat on the opposite side of the booth.

"Very pleased to meet you all. John tells me you are the best in the business."

Jake's unfounded compliment was the truth, although he didn't know it himself – not yet at least. John Devlin Public Relations & Media Management was one of the most sought-after agencies in North London and the city. At thirty-five years old, John had grown his company to forty staff and recently opened a satellite office at Media City in Manchester. There was no doubt he was the poster boy at JDPR and revered as one of the best PR men in the business, having salvaged several high-profile reputations in recent years and charged significant fees to compensate for his efforts. Like Jake, he was calm and passive, and used his charm and soothing tones to pacify his overbearing, panicky clients.

Like every good employer, John knew he had nothing if he didn't have hardworking, engaged and talented staff. There were few boundaries at JDPR, and even fewer rules or regulations. It often seemed like chaos reigned – outsiders were confused as to who made the decisions, or who was in charge. John forbade anyone from using their position as a reason to be unhelpful. He wanted *them* to make the big decisions, not him, and be loud about it. He insisted on affirmation and celebrated open displays of confidence. The engagement between what appeared to be a bunch of misfits and cranks was incredibly productive – lucrative too, with each employee receiving a share of the profits and regular bonuses.

"The best in the business?" Molly asked from the corner of the booth. "Does that mean we get a pay rise, John?" She grinned into the bottom of her empty glass to avoid eye contact.

Molly was in her mid-twenties. She wore a grey suit and a gaudy purple silk blouse. Her bleached blonde hair was tied in a ponytail, with a matching purple bobble.

Before John could back-heel her request, Justin interrupted. "Good luck with that one, Molly – you know he's as tight as cramp." He winked at Jake and tipped a nod at John, as if expecting an immediate rebuttal.

Justin was in his mid-forties but looked like he was in his late fifties. He had a permanent stench of stale cigarettes on his breath, and his body looked flaccid and underemployed. If it wasn't for his spectacularly alert blue eyes and impish sense of humour, he would have given George Horgan a run for his money as being the least presentable person Jake knew.

"Humph!" Derek chimed in, looking over his laptop, while typing furiously. The sixty-year-old, grey-haired computer geek, with eyebrow hair so long it had grown over the front of his horn-rimmed glasses, wasn't the most communicative person in the office – but on the matter of pay, he was all ears.

Jake wondered what he could be typing so urgently in a crowded pub.

John's sixty-second character assassination had come to its natural end. His team smirked and giggled at his apparent discomfort at being laid bare in front of his friend. The no holds barred approach to working at JDPR extended to him – there was no hiding place. Whatever he could have said in response would have encouraged the trio to continue to berate him, so he stonewalled them with a smile.

"And you've met Patrick, our resident Finbarr Saunders."

Patrick returned with the drinks on a black and white chequered tray. He set them down and handed them out.

"I like to play mother." He batted his eyelids at Jake and sniggered at his own quip.

"Give it a rest, Patsy, for fuck's sake," Justin huffed, rolling his eyes. He slid off the bench. "I'm nipping out for a fag."

Patrick thought about following up his crudity but decided against it. Instead, he jumped into Justin's seat, propped himself on his elbows and leant towards Jake.

"So, Jake, what's your story?" Patrick only had one setting, and that was being downright nosey.

Jake hesitated to answer, but in the spirit of openness and friendliness, he acquiesced. "What do you want to know?"

"Where did you and John meet?" Patrick hid his face using his glass.

"Where did we meet?" Jake repeated, pretending he'd missed the inference Patrick was making and wishing he hadn't encouraged this invasion of his privacy.

"He means, how do we know each other?" John clarified in a deadpan tone.

"Oh, right. We attend the same martial arts club in Camden – Matsumoto Mixed Martial Arts Centre. Do you know it?"

"Ha! Kung fu – are you kidding me? I couldn't punch my way out of a wet paper bag." Patrick laughed at himself again and looked around to see if others were laughing. They weren't.

"I didn't know you did all that martial arts stuff, John." Patrick was on a roll, directing back-up questions at his boss.

"Yeah," John said casually. "I've been going there for a few months now. It's a bit late in the day to be learning to fight, but it's good for my fitness, and you never know, I might become a fourth dan black belt, like Jake."

"A black belt?!" Patrick drew out the words, impressed. John instantly regretted giving him more ammunition. "You don't look very tough, Jake."

He eyed Jake up and down, revelling in his obvious discomfort.

"Martial arts are used more for defence than attack, but sometimes being on the front foot helps, if you don't want people to take advantage of you."

"Ooh, I don't mind." Patrick laughed alone once more. "So, what do you do for a living?"

Patrick persisted with his interrogation. John was wondering if all this freedom of speech thing he'd encouraged at work wasn't coming back to bite him.

Patrick flung his arms to stop Jake answering. "No! Don't tell me – I'll guess, I'm good at this." He eyed Jake up and down again, holding his chubby pink chin in his hand.

"You don't work as a tradesman – no one has hands like that and uses a screwdriver – and I don't think you're a policeman or a fireman either. You seem too nice for that."

"Err, excuse me," Molly butted in. "My brother's a copper and he's a lovely bloke."

Patrick closed his eyes, ignoring her rebuke, and pressed his fingertips into his temples, as if he was telepathic. "You're an actor!" he exclaimed, pointing into Jake's face.

"Close," Jake said dryly, tipping his drink at his inquisitor. "I'm a social worker."

"You're not very good at this game, are you, Sherlock?"

Derek's sardonic sense of humour put an end to Patrick's twenty questions, and Jake took it as his cue to leave. He'd grown tired of Patrick's snooping.

"Listen, it's been great meeting you all – I need to get back to my mates." Jake turned to John. "Probably see you on Tuesday at the club, eh?"

"Yeah, deffo, if I don't see you sooner."

John's expression gave Jake the sense he was missing something. He didn't know what, or wait to find out.

***

Maddie Parker stood with her ankles crossed, as she stirred her mojito with a straw and bit her bottom lip. Her balletic, lithe body twisted slightly to the sound of Slim Whitman on the mic. She blinked a few times, as she waited patiently for the open-mouthed statue opposite to say something. Her brown eyes, like huge pools of crude oil, dominated the features on her pixie-like face, which was framed by her short black choppy hair. Her lips glistened in the lamplight as her jaw rotated an ice cube around in her mouth.

Rob remembered how he used to trace her cheekbones with his fingers, encircling a small mole under her right eye, the only blemish on an otherwise flawless face. She wore tight-fitting white three-quarter length hipster jeans and a gold sleeveless crop top that accentuated her slim torso and pushed up her small but perfectly proportioned breasts. In his eyes, she was perfect in almost every way. Moving to Malawi for two years to save the starving population was the only thing Rob could say she ever did wrong.

After the first few seconds of suspended animation, his face lit up like a Christmas tree. He dumped the empty glasses on a nearby table and edged closer to his petite ex-girlfriend. His hands latched onto her tiny waist, and his thumbs brushed the skin of her exposed midriff. He pulled himself in and she angled her head upwards.

"Thank you, princess. You remembered," he said, and kissed her gently on the side of her mouth. She turned her head into him, pressing her ice-cold lips against his cheek.

He pulled back and Maddie filled the void by shaking her empty glass. "Buy you a birthday drink?" She stirred her straw, making the ice cubes chatter.

"That would be lovely."

Rob breathed in deeply and thought, *my night has just got a whole lot better.*

***

"Hey Trixie, how are you darling?"

Mikey stood at the end of the high-backed booth facing Trixie and her friends. From a distance, and with the back-up of his two friends, his confidence knew no limits. Now, standing opposite the Amazonian beauty queen and her two ladies in waiting, it had evaporated completely.

"Hey, Mikey!" Trixie slid off the booth and flung her arms around his shoulders and kissed him on the cheek, leaving yet another lipstick battle scar.

Mikey made zero attempt to hide his appreciation of every curve and line of Trixie's long slender body, which was clad in tight stonewashed jeans and a black leather, strapless basque. He clung onto her with his eyes closed, blanking out the surroundings and breathing in the sweet aroma of yet another stunning woman.

Trixie turned him around and hooked her arm around his waist. Her shiny pink talons bit into his hip. The skin on the inside of his left arm was in contact with her bare back, soaking in the warmth of her body. Volcanoes of goose pimples burst from his skin. He shuddered and prayed her friends weren't crotch watching.

"Girls, this is Mikey," Trixie announced, with Alexa levels of enthusiasm.

"He's from Newcastle, in the North East, so he speaks a little strange," Trixie whispered past the back of her hand.

Her friends looked bemused as to who could have turned her into a giggling teenager. Trixie had to endure a lot of male attention wherever they went, and although she secretly enjoyed it, she had never responded to anyone, no matter how many drinks they bought her or how good-looking they were.

"Hello, girls. Are you having a nice night?" Mikey's normal charm offensive disappeared momentarily, making way for boyish awkwardness. He fixed them both with his hazel eyes and a smile that could penetrate the most resolute of defences.

"We are much better now, aren't we, Mariette?" Grethe pursed her lips at him.

He blushed, swallowing bashfully, which made him look even more endearing. Trixie slid back into the booth, holding his hand, and pulled him in behind her.

"Waar het jy hierdie ou weggesteek, hy is pragtig?" Grethe reverted to Afrikaans to ask Trixie where she'd been hiding Mikey.

"He plays rugby with Hansie, don't you, Mikey?" Trixie had Mikey's hand sandwiched between hers on her lap.

The booth was designed to sit six people, but right then it was feeling considerably smaller.

"Well, I don't play with him exactly – I play against him. He plays for the Boks. I play for Camley. We are up against them in a couple of weeks or so. You'll have to come and watch."

Mikey was looking forward to the game, but not the pain he'd be in straight after.

"You look very fit, Mikey. Are you a builder or something?" Mariette gave Mikey a wide-eyed look he'd seen a thousand times before.

"No, I'm assistant manager at Fulwood Sports. It's how I know Trixie. She comes to PT sessions, don't you, darling?" Mikey turned and smiled proudly at his student.

"I'm not surprised." Mariette teased her friend and winked.

Mikey laughed and joked, talking about his home in Newcastle and his absent friends. In turn, the girls taught Mikey swear words in Afrikaans and laughed raucously when he repeated them in his Geordie accent so he could use them against the Boks in their up and coming match.

***

Mikey stood up to top up the girls' glasses and gave the empty bottle of Prosecco a shake.

"You girls need another bottle of plonk?" He was just about to slide away when Varkie stepped over to the table.

"Hey, Piglet, what are you doing here?" Mikey hadn't reasoned that Grethe was Varkie's wife, and his mockery went down like a cup of cold vomit.

Varkie glared at Mikey silently for a few seconds and turned his attention to Grethe. "Hoekom praat jy met hom?" Varkie gritted his teeth aggressively as he pointed in Mikey's direction.

"I'll talk to who I want, when I want!" Grethe said, not in the habit of taking criticism or responding to his jealousy.

Mikey watched the uncomfortable spectacle with a huge smirk on his face.

Hansie loomed over and patted Varkie on the head like a dog, breaking the tense atmosphere. "Calm down, Bru, it's only Mikey."

There was no love lost from where Varkie stood. He had played inside centre for the Boks in opposition to Mikey for the last three years, and there was no doubt who was the better player. In fairness to him, there were few players in that position in the entire league who could match Mikey's ability and speed, but he didn't see it that way.

Ignoring Varkie, Mikey said, "Hansie! Howzit? Lekker, Bru?" Mikey used his new vocabulary and winked in Mariette's direction, who spat out her drink and snorted into her glass, struggling to contain her amusement.

"You been getting lessons in Afrikaans, eh, Bru?" Hansie's amused tone was accompanied by his idea of a friendly face.

"It's good to talk, mate." Mikey was on his feet now and facing Hansie, the bones in his fingers cracking under the weight of his handshake.

Mikey shuddered at the thought of rucking with this man mountain in a couple of weeks, making a mental note to stay the hell out of his way.

It is good to talk, Hansie thought silently to himself, though not a skill he had in his armoury.

Mikey turned his attention to Danie standing next to him. "By process of elimination, you must be Doctor Mariette's husband?"

"Danie. Doctor Danie, in fact." Danie's face was kind and smiling.

He had heard Hansie and Varkie speak about Mikey before – their opinions at opposite ends of the scale. On shaking hands with the handsome, tall Englishman, and having heard the fits of laughter emanating from the girls' booth for the last fifteen minutes, he concluded Hansie's take was accurate.

"Why is every South African you meet a doctor or a dentist?" Mikey's sweeping generalisation had an element of truth to it.

Many countries' immigration policies, or at least immigration through legal channels, required those applying to have a means of support and an established trade, or occupation. This didn't include plumbers and joiners – far from it. The red-carpet treatment was rolled out for medics, nurses and scientists.

"I'm an electrical engineer," Varkie announced. His sarcastic attention-seeking made Grethe cringe.

"Nice one, Piglet." Mikey antagonised him further. "Why don't you engineer us up some beers from the bar, there's a good chap?"

Danie hid his face in embarrassment for his friend and Hansie sniggered, which only made Varkie angrier. Varkie put his drink down on the table and clenched his fists. He stepped into Mikey's face and puffed out his chest. He had had enough. The banter had gotten to him. It always did. "You wanna make me, Doos?"

"Sit nou, Stephane!" Grethe had taken all she could and yanked him by the arm, pulling him onto the bench seat beside her.

"Come on, Piglet, I was only joking, mate." Mikey's olive branch was ignored.

Returning to Mikey's point, Danie said, "There's a fair few South African doctors here in the UK, Mikey, that's for sure."

"Do you work in the same place as Mariette?" Mikey was genuinely interested in the couple, who seemed extremely well matched.

"I work at St Bart's. I'm a consultant paediatric oncologist."

Those three words hit Mikey harder than any punch Varkie was lining up for him, and he would have taken the hit without complaint. His expressive, happy face collapsed on its axis, and for a few seconds, he struggled to breathe. His sister Kaitlyn's doctor in Newcastle had the exact same title. Unknowingly, Danie had triggered the trauma Mikey had endured watching his sister's heavily anaesthetised body wither and die in front of him. Those three innocent yet incendiary words rekindled the horrific memories buried in his mind.

Mikey seemed to shrink by inches as he battled to keep control of his emotions. His jaw dropped open and he felt himself falling into an abyss. He trembled as if winter had come early. Tears began to well up in the corners of his eyes, which he scrunched away angrily.

"You OK, Bru?" Hansie asked, confused as to why Danie had caused such a reaction.

Danie wasn't confused. In those fleeting moments, he saw in Mikey what he had seen in the faces of dozens of bereaved parents: a haunted expression of impotence and loss.

"Sorry, yes, I'm fine, Hansie. Thanks," he lied.

Mikey's voice trembled as he reluctantly explained himself. He took a shaky gulp of his beer to calm his nerves. Hansie and Danie remained silent, sensing that it was the only thing they could do to help – giving him the space to choke back the grief and blink away the images in his head.

Eventually he spoke. "Even when you don't want to be reminded about it, sometimes it takes you by surprise. She was so lovely, you know. I miss her every day."

Danie's eye twitched a half-smile, feeling a palpable sense of loss, as he always did.

"Memories can't wait, Bru."

Mikey took a deep breath and held it. Biting down hard on the inside of his cheek to divert his emotion into physical pain, he tasted blood in his mouth. The trauma had all but subsided.

"No, Danie, they can't," he conceded.

Hansie looked on, feeling strangely envious. His own grief and anger he held deep down inside for no one to see. Any avenue for its release was blocked at the pass, every time. Would he ever be able to feel the rush of pain build and then evaporate like Mikey did, rather than it congealing and festering in his soul?

"Come on, Bru," Hansie said, ruffling Mikey's hair. "I'll buy us a lekker beer. We'll wait all day for Varkie to put his hand in his pocket."

***

Rob sipped his Guinness and kept his eyes locked on Maddie's. They stood in silence staring, waiting for the other to say something.

"Are you going to the club later?" Now he had her attention, Rob was anxious not to let her out of his sight for too long.

"I was planning to, yes. The girls will want to go, I guess," Maddie answered without much enthusiasm. "Unless you have any better ideas?"

"Mikey and Jake will want me to go to the club," he stalled. "But I reckon I can shake them off. If you fancy coming back to mine, I think I have a bottle or two in the fridge."

Maddie heard his voice tremor as her hand slipped around his hip.

His posturing was futile. With the charade over, Maddie said, "OK, let me just tell the girls I'm heading home, and I'll meet you at the front door."

Jake returned as she made to leave. "Hey, Maddie, what a nice surprise."

"Jake, I've missed you guys so much. I was just saying to Rob it's been years, wasn't I, Rob?"

Rob agreed nervously, wondering where the conversation was going.

"Are you coming to Fandango's, Maddie? We better get a move on, or we won't get in. The queue will be horrendous."

Jake was in organisation mode. His hatred of being late and hanging around queuing was kicking in.

"I'll just finish drinking this pint with Maddie and I'll catch you up, mate," Rob said on the fly. "Save me a place in the queue, will you."

"OK. Lovely to see you again, Maddie. You look the picture of health by the way." As much as he wanted to give Rob a slap to rouse him from her spell, Jake knew it would be pointless – that was the last they'd see of him that night.

4

WRONG PLACE. WRONG TIME

Fandango's Nightclub, Camden, London: 27 August 2021

"Mr Bell, is that you?"

"I've told you never to ring me unless it's an absolute emergency." Morris Bell cupped his phone in his hand and shrugged an apology to those around him as he meandered his way past a group of criminal injury lawyers smoking expensive cigars and drinking from huge brandy glasses.

"I think it's a bad time and the wrong place, Mr Bell. There are too many cameras, and the guys I spoke to last week don't want to know me. There are four new bouncers on shift tonight that I've never even met before."

Ben Stockton's face was a subtle shade of panicking pink. His eyes bulged, and beads of sweat raced from his temples down the side of his face, pooling onto his cheap pay-as-you-go mobile phone he had pressed against his chubby jowl.

"You've done it a dozen times before, for God's sake! What's the matter with you, man?" Morris Bell raged through gritted teeth.

He had no time for the nonsense he was hearing from his overweight stooge. He had to prepare for his acceptance speech as a Life Treasurer of the Legal Circle Guild, an honour bestowed to only seven members in the last thirty years, all of whom were now dead.

"I've just got a bad feeling about this one, that's all. It's not easy, you know. This club is too busy, Mr Bell. You should visit it and see for yourself. The padded jacket you got me is a nightmare. I'm sweating cobs every night. Delroy thinks I'm a fucking idiot wearing it in this heat."

Bell's patience was at an end. He paused to calm his voice before speaking. "You're right, you're totally right. I'm going to get someone else to do it. I'll just use you in a support role. I'll send Doda over to you now – you can explain it in person that you've had enough."

Bell had no time to listen to the idiot any more. He would dispose of Stockton and find someone else.

Stockton's face drained of blood and his heart leapt in his chest. "No!" he screeched into the phone. "It's fine, I'll do it, I'll find a mark. No problem, Mr Bell, leave it with me."

"Make it tonight. Do not disappoint me." Bell hung up and returned to his erstwhile colleagues.

***

"I can't believe you didn't tell her to fuck off."

Mikey was livid with how their night had been torpedoed by the prodigal daughter.

"For fuck's sake, she's just toying with him. I thought she had a boyfriend anyway. He's playing with fire. And what if Lauren turns up at his place?"

Mikey knew Lauren wouldn't turn up. She'd be in some swanky West End wine bar by now with all her posh mates.

"Don't worry, mate, I'm here and all's good. We'll have a laugh. Let's check out the band and see who's in there." Jake tried his best to rescue the mood, in a very rare instance of role reversal. "How'd it go with Trixie anyway? Did Harry turn up and piss on your chips?" Jake now resorted to using Mikey's own vernacular to get his attention.

"His name is Hansie, ya loon," Mikey said half laughing. "He's not a bad lad to be honest. I like him and his mate Danie. Great lads."

Mikey hadn't admitted that out loud before, but he'd come to realise he liked Hansie Van Heerden. The guilt at paying so much attention to Trixie gnawed at his conscience. They showed genuine sensitivity during his panic attack, wrapping their arms around his shoulders like a non-contested scrum, not letting go until his composure had returned. It was a brotherly thing to do, and it took him by surprise that they should care so much. His burden was shared and the pain expunged, at least for a little while.

"Well, better luck next time, eh Mikey?" Jake's words couldn't have been further from the mark this time around.

Besides, he couldn't take Trixie off Hansie, even if he wanted to. The look she gave him was one of unquestionable love and adoration. Whatever had gone before, they had created an unbreakable bond that he could only dream of having with a girl. What they had was what he wanted dearly, what he knew he was looking for, and what he was certain he wouldn't find in the arms of some random girl in a nightclub.

***

After queuing for twenty minutes, they eventually made it to the front and walked up the three steps off the street towards a set of double doors. Two bouncers in black nylon bomber jackets with blue plastic ID armlets, black trousers and heavy steel toe cap shoes flanked the entrance door to the left. They eyed everyone with suspicion.

"All right, lads," Mikey said in a friendly tone. "Here's hoping it's a quiet night, eh?"

Bouncer number one standing to the left thrusted out an unwelcoming hand, which landed on Mikey's chest, pushing him back sharply.

"You can't come in, you've had too much to drink. Stand aside," he said.

"What?! You're joking, aren't ya?" Mikey asked in disbelief.

"Listen, arsehole, if I say you're not coming in, you're not coming in. Now take your boyfriend and fuck off, before I give you a slap."

His pink fleshy face and neck began reddening and one of his eyes bulged, while he pointed angrily at Mikey and Jake, who returned bemused expressions.

"What's your problem? I only asked if you were OK, and you won't even let us in. You on your period or something?"

Mikey's wind-up did not go down well with the guy, nor with bouncer number two, a huge overweight, black guy with a shiny bald head, bad teeth and yellowing eyes, clearly suffering from some iron or vitamin deficiency.

"You better move on, sweetheart, before you get hurt," he growled. There was no mistaking the malevolence in his voice.

"What seems to be the matter, Ben?" A slightly built Asian man appeared from behind them in a smart suit and tie and directed his question at his angry pink-headed doorman.

"These gentlemen were being aggressive, Mr Aziz. I've refused them entry. Now, they are determined to get themselves into trouble."

"Are they friends of yours, John?" Mr Aziz pointed his question past Mikey and Jake, who immediately spun round when a response came from over their shoulders.

"Indeed they are, Jamal. I think there's been a misunderstanding here. Are we OK to come in? I hope you have my booth reserved?"

John Devlin stepped forward and grabbed Jake's and Mikey's elbows in one fluid motion.

"Of course," he said with warmth. "Delroy! Ben! Get out of the way for God's sake."

Jamal wafted at them to move aside. The nylon strip security tape was unhooked, and Mikey gave Ben and Delroy a sideways smirk as he passed, pushing his luck, as he ever did.

"Hope you guys have a quiet night now."

***

Rob's flat, Fitzroy Road, Primrose Hill, London

Rob and Maddie sat next to each other in the cab as they headed to his apartment in Primrose Hill. She had her arm through his, yawning and snuggling into him. The pain she had put him through now a distant memory.

His reverie stopped dead in its tracks when it occurred to him that Lauren may have made her way back to his place instead of going to meet Alicia in Richmond. He quickly texted her to ask if she was having fun. She replied 'Yes, see you tomorrow, maybe.' He rolled his eyes at her attempt to play hard ball with him.

The cab squealed to a halt and Rob paid with his phone. He walked to the foyer with Maddie hanging on his arm.

On the fourth floor they exited the lift and turned left towards his apartment. He swiped the key across the scanner, which beeped as it unlocked his door and disarmed his alarm.

"Oh, Rob, I love it. Look at the view, it's so nice. How many bedrooms does it have?" Maddie wasted no time snooping around.

Rob's heart skipped another beat. *What if Lauren was waiting to surprise him in bed?* Unlikely, he told himself.

"Three – go take a look if you like," Rob mumbled sarcastically as she strode away.

The modern open-plan living area was clean and expensively furnished. He could see Maddie's bare footprints on the solid oak floors as she padded noisily from room to room, silenced by the occasional Persian rug and a zebra skin. Rob's box room, where he stored his unused Peloton and drawing materials, received most of her attention.

"You into Peloton these days?" Rob yelled at her from behind the kitchen counter.

She reappeared and sauntered into the living area. "What? Peloton? What's that?" she asked, confused. "I'll have a green tea, if you have it?" She yawned and stretched – the party girl was just about wiped out, she conceded to herself, and it wasn't even midnight.

He brought her tea over in a tall glass cup and saucer with the tea bag floating in the steaming hot water. He took a swig of his wine and placed his glass on the table. They sat facing each other as Maddie sipped on her tea, her dainty shoeless feet tucked under her bottom. Neither was a big talker, and they both hoped the other would break the silence.

Rob yielded, again. "You look lovely."

"Thanks," Maddie said dismissively. She wasn't one for compliments – giving or receiving them. "You've done well for yourself. This place must have set you back a few quid."

Rob shrugged in response. After yet another long awkward silence, he asked the burning question.

"Why did you leave?"

"You know why, darling," she said, seething inwardly at having to explain herself. "Let's not go over old ground, eh? I want to know what you guys have been up to. How's Mikey? Was he out tonight? I didn't see him." Her eyes flicked away from Rob as the lie came out of her mouth.

She had waited for Rob and his friends to arrive for over an hour. She knew he'd stop by The Collingwood, and she knew he'd be with Jake and Mikey on his birthday. As soon as Mikey had sloped away to ingratiate himself on someone, she had made her move.

"Yeah, he was out. You know what he's like – a social butterfly, can't sit still. He'll be gutted he missed you."

They both knew that wasn't true. Maddie and Mikey had had a blazing row in the run-up to her departure for Africa. He had told her she was selfish and cruel. She had given as good as she got, telling Mikey to mind his own business. The ill feeling remained. Mikey had known their long-distance relationship wouldn't last. The lack of contact would eat away at their love, and that's how it played out.

***

They chatted their way through three quarters of a bottle of wine and two more cups of green tea, before Maddie said she had better be going. Rob had no clue what move to make next, so he got up and walked over to the kitchen counter to get his phone.

"OK," he said reluctantly. "I'll call you a cab."

He hesitated. "I don't know your address."

Maddie got to her feet and walked over to him, took the phone out of his hand and dropped it in a fruit bowl stacked with kiwis and grapes. She put her hands on the back of his neck and pulled him towards her. She kissed him on the lips, her tongue flicking across his teeth.

She released him. "I can stay if you want me to?"

Her eyes locked onto his, and he flew straight into the flames.

***

Fandango's Nightclub, Camden, London: 27 August 2021

A surly waitress huffed with one hand on her hip as John repeated his order over the music blaring from the dance floor.

"Mikey, can I introduce you to John. John, this is Mikey Stott."

"Thanks for what you did out there, John – that bouncer is a total wanker." There was no argument from anyone around the table.

"No worries, Mikey," he said modestly. "Jake's told me a lot about you and Rob. You've been friends a long time – he said you went to Loughborough Uni together."

Mikey was a little taken aback. He and Rob had heard nothing of Jake's friend, not even one conversation to say he even existed. He looked in Jake's direction, as he replied to John. "Yeah, been mates for years. Share everything with each other, don't we, Jake?"

"Ha, yeah, pretty much." Jake's discomfort was hidden in part by the dimly lit alcove they were seated in.

"John's a student at Shin's place. He comes to my beginners' classes on a Tuesday and Thursday night."

"It's tough, let me tell you," John joined in, trying to sound upbeat.

The conversation was hard work, mostly down to Mikey's lack of participation, which he thought he could be forgiven for, having had an anxiety attack, Rob bailing out on him, two bouncers taking an instant disliking to him, and now some random recalling his fucking life story.

What next? he mumbled to himself.

"Cheers!" John toasted the other two, who lamely clinked their glasses.

Mikey necked half of his double Jack Daniels and Coke and brought the glass down onto the tabletop in front of a wall of green and yellow cotton flowers. His 'what next?' question was answered sooner than he expected.

"Get your cute butt on that dance floor – you owe me a boogie!" Alexa Taylor stood with her hands resting on her spacious hips, her ginger-blonde hair hanging loosely on her heaving chest and a huge smile on her pudgy face.

Before Mikey could answer, she clamped his wrist in her sweaty hand and lifted him from the booth like a naughty child. A wide grin spread across Jake's face, seeing Mikey tripping over his own feet as he was hauled away.

As they approached the dance floor, Alexa shouted at the top of her voice, "The fun has arrived!"

Mikey couldn't help smiling in her direction. *It certainly had.*

***

"Your mate seemed a little nonplussed. Did I say something to offend him?"

"No, of course not. He gets a little rowdy when he's had a few beers, that's all. Dancing with Alexa is the best thing for him right now. Trust me."

"She's all woman," John joked, thumbing at Alexa, who was twerking on the dance floor.

Jake was right. He knew Mikey better than anyone, although he should have mentioned John before now. He'd been a lot less open in recent months, whereas once he'd tell his mates everything. Something had been stopping him of late, as if he needed headspace, to hold back, to make up his own mind about things.

They refilled their glasses a few times more, before Mikey ambled over towards them, his face moist with exertion.

"Rack 'em up, Jakey-boy, my mouth's drier than a nomad's flip-flop. I need a hit and miss. Back in a minute."

As Mikey headed off to the toilets, he bumped into an ominous black figure blocking his way.

"Oops, sorry, my mistake," Mikey apologised, before he even knew who it was he had collided with.

Ben the bouncer grabbed him by his damp shirt collar. "You're leaving, pretty boy," he said through gritted teeth.

"Hang on a minute, I haven't done anything. Fucking geroff!"

Mikey began to struggle to break free of Ben's hold on him, only for another pair of arms to clamp around his upper body from behind. He felt a punch to his ribs, which knocked the wind out of him. His feet were lifted off the ground by Delroy, who was responsible for the reverse bear hug. Ben loosened the hold he had on Mikey's neck and pinched down hard on his top lip and nose with his thumb and index finger, causing excruciating pain to fly up into Mikey's sinuses and through his gum line.

The two bouncers dragged Mikey to the landing. Through watery eyes he could see what was coming – he had to act fast.

He contorted his torso and wrapped his legs around one of theirs, as if collapsing a maul. The manoeuvre was effective. Ben and Delroy lost their balance and tumbled forward on top of him, crashing into a large plastic pot plant.

Ben jumped to his feet and straddled Mikey's back, lifting him a foot or so off the ground. He then swung him like a battering ram into the wall, with a bone-shaking thud.

Mikey's world went black.

***

"Jesus, Jake, they've got Mikey!"

From his position in the VIP booth, John had a perfect view of the corridor leading to the exit and toilet block. Jake sprung to his feet and held out an arm to John. "Stay here – do not get involved!"

He dodged the onlookers and sprinted over towards his prone friend, whose head was pressed awkwardly against the wall with a Mikey-shaped dent in it. Ben was crouched over him, raining punches down on the back of his head. When he stood to catch his breath, Delroy decided it was his turn to stick the boot in and stepped forward to kick the side of Mikey's exposed head and face. The ramifications of a kick with such weight raced through Jake's mind in an instant. As Delroy lifted his right boot back, ready to swing down his tree trunk of a leg, Jake ankle tapped him, diverting the pendulous trajectory towards Delroy's standing foot. The sickening crack of Delroy's Achilles tendon snapping could be heard over the music. He crumpled to the floor, and writhed in agony.

A third bouncer, called Calum, came running over growling and swearing at anyone in his way. Jake backed up against the door frame of the ladies toilets. There was no doubt about Calum's motivations, especially having just witnessed what Jake had done to his hapless colleague. He looked at Jake's sad face and small features with menacing eyes.

With eleven inches of height advantage, and at nearly double Jake's weight, Calum was in no doubt as to who was going to win this contest. *I'm bigger, so I'm better.*

Bullies always thought like that, and Jake knew it, which was *his* advantage. Calum balled his huge fist and pulled it back, like a Saxon catapult about to sling rocks over a castle wall. He launched the tattooed knuckles of his right hand straight at Jake's face with unstoppable momentum.

After twenty years of mixed martial arts training, and even with a belly full of G&T, Jake had an eternity to avoid it, telling himself to wait as long as he dared for its arrival – he needed maximum impact. His stance was perfectly balanced: knees flexed to about ten degrees, one foot slightly in front of the other, posture relaxed yet coiled like sprung steel.

Calum's fist missed Jake's skull by a couple of millimetres, striking the corner of the door jamb with immense force, accompanied by yet another bone-splintering ending.

Although the chances of Calum using that hand again for the next couple of months were reasonably slim, the threat to Jake was far from over, and in the same fluid movement he used to swerve the haymaker, he arched a lightning-fast uppercut into Calum's groin, causing his initial scream of intense pain to suddenly pitch down into an audible guttural groan.

Jake looked down at Delroy and Calum spooning each other, like a pair of oversized unborn twins. He headed over to Mikey, who was spitting blood onto the carpet and stirring into consciousness. In the corner of his eye, he could see Ben approaching. Fast.

"We're leaving, mate, OK." Jake surrendered to him with his palms out in front.

Ben wasn't listening. He was about to make the exact same mistake as Calum had – the opportunity to inflict pain was just too good to miss. He lunged and swung a punch. Jake dropped his right shoulder, pivoted his hips and gripped onto Ben's overreaching right arm. He stepped inside using Ben's forward movement to slam his back onto the floor.

It was at that moment that Jake's life was to change irrevocably. The crimson-faced thug hit the landing with a dull thump and slid across the lino cresting the top stair. He fell in stages, bouncing off the banister, pulling picture frames from their housings. His descent ended with him propped awkwardly against the wall at the foot of the stairs. It seemed to take forever.

And then the screaming started.

"My back! Ahhh, my back!"

✳✳✳

Mikey's head swam; muffled sounds and indiscernible shapes added to his confusion. When his vision cleared slightly, he could see Jake, encircled, with his hands in the air.

"Police! Police! Everybody, stand still! You – on your knees!" A tall, stick-thin policeman pointed his baton at Jake from the bottom of the foyer, conflicted as to whether to make chase or assist the injured party. Jake made the decision an easy one and put his hands up and faced the wall.

In the corner of the landing, behind an upturned plastic aspidistra, a pair of strong, fleshy, camouflaged arms picked Mikey up from under his armpits and steered him away from the scene of immobilised nylon and polyester.

"Come on, Mikey, sort your shit out – the feds are here, you need to get gone."

Alexa had turned up in full emergency recovery mode, barking out the orders. She barged past several onlookers, with Mikey hanging off her shoulder, and headed for the emergency exit, which had been opened by people mistaking the arrival of the police for a drug bust.

Outside, the warm night air did nothing to stop the lights spinning and Mikey's stomach churning.

"I'm gonna blow," Mikey said, giving fair warning to Alexa, who, in return, gave him a sharp slap across his face.

His nausea disappeared and he straightened up a little. The NHS didn't use that technique universally, but it had always worked for her.

***

Stumbling down a side street, Alexa stopped for a breather and propped Mikey against a garden wall, holding his arm with one hand while she unstrapped her heels. She picked him up, threw his arm around her shoulder and began hobbling towards her flat, like they were rolling in last in a drunken three-legged race.

She leant Mikey against the door to her apartment block. A neighbour's dog yapped as she dug her keys out of her purse. Inside, she caught sight of the narrow staircase and lamented her decision to rent a third-floor flat.

"There is only one way to do this," she said, taking a deep breath. And like an Olympic powerlifter, she bent at the knees, allowing Mikey to topple forward, and hoisted him onto her shoulder.

She discarded her heels at the front door and chose to leave her left hand free to stabilise their ascent. Mikey let out a deep groan of complaint, and she prayed to God he wouldn't barf down her back, over her new dress. With one arm wrapped around his backside and one holding onto the banister, she planted her right foot on step one.

After two landings and several bumps of Mikey's semi-conscious head against the wall, she made it to her flat, without dropping her fragile cargo once. Having had the foresight to hold onto her keys, she found the lock quickly and let herself inside.

Her bedroom was immediately to the right, and she was in no mind to pick Mikey up again, so she kicked the door with her foot, shuffled straight in and dropped his listless body onto her unmade bed. The springs and headboard creaked at the load it was having to bear.

Alexa arched her back and let out a huge sigh of relief before switching on the light. She smiled at her prize, more out of pity than anything else.

He's such a lovely goofball. They could've killed him. She made a note to give Jake a hug when she saw him next.

She swung Mikey's legs round and rolled him over onto his back. She checked his airways and the bump on his head. It wasn't bleeding, and it didn't look like there was any serious damage.

Sitting him up, she half unbuttoned his shirt, pulled it over his head and let it drop onto the chair under her dressing table. She pulled off his socks and shoes with two quick flicks of the wrist, then whipped off his trousers with his boxer shorts glued to the insides.

A small gasp escaped her lips when she saw his penis rolling around on his leg. *Ha, I've seen a thousand dicks in my life as a nurse, and none of them has made me do that.*

Rolling him into the recovery position, she propped his right arm under a sequined pillow. She left his face hanging off the side of the bed and his left arm trailing on the floor. His right leg she straightened, with his left bent at the knee for stability; he was in the recovery position and unlikely to choke on his own vomit from there. She congratulated herself and went to the kitchen.

She noisily emptied the unwashed pots and pans out of a faded orange plastic bowl that was buried in the sink. She gave it a quick swill, returned to her bedroom and positioned it on the floor directly in line with Mikey's face.

Sitting on the edge of the bed, she stroked his bruised back and admired his naked body bubbling with strength. She wished he was lying there in different circumstances. She imagined what it would be like to be his girlfriend, meeting him after one of his rugby matches, holding his hand in the bar while he got ribbed by his mates. He would look down at her and wink with the promise of what lay ahead.

She would make his meals and clean his boots, and he'd make her laugh and get her fit down the gym. She would be known as Mikey's Girl and not Big Al, a nickname she loathed and which made her cry when no one was looking. She wanted to be demure and cherished. She wanted to be teased and tickled. To have someone make love to her and cuddle her to sleep. Was that too much to ask?

Her nose tingled as the tears welled in her eyes. *Maybe it was the alcohol – I always get a bit teary after a few cocktails*, she told herself, wiping her cheeks. No, that wasn't it. She knew what it was – Mikey would never be hers. He'd never settle for someone like her. Why would he?

She turned to leave the room and blew him a kiss. Only then did it occur to her to ask herself where she was going to sleep.

The couch was too small. She considered knocking on her neighbour's door, but how would she explain to Doreen that she had a gorgeous hunk in her bed and that, if it was OK, could she sleep in her spare room.

The answer presented itself in the worst possible way, when Mikey threw up into the bowl. She stood over him, with no option open to her.

"I'll have to sleep here next to him, or he could choke on his own vomit," she whispered. Justification enough in her mind.

She stripped off and put on a two-piece woolly pyjama set and climbed in next to him. She patted his buttcheek, kissed him on the back of his head and went to sleep.

5

A FRIEND IN NEED

Fulwood Police Station, London: 28 August 2021

Jake felt the cold from the concrete wall of cell No. 7 seep into his back. The constant barrage of drunken abuse spewing from the neighbouring cells meant there was no chance of sleeping, even if he wanted to.

His windowless abode was as spartan as you could imagine a room to be. He'd swerved the blue rubber mattress stretched across the steel bench, preferring the tiled floor, which smelt like it had recently been bleached and rinsed, evidenced by small damp areas that hadn't yet evaporated. The toilet was a stainless-steel bowl cantilevered from the wall, surrounded by a collage of unspeakable smears and bodily residue.

He shook his head in disbelief. He'd always thought of himself as a law-abiding citizen with respect for the police, who had an incredibly difficult job. The arresting officer had done his best to change his opinion on that score. PC Will Jones, a name he'd remember for a good while to come, was six feet of skin and bone, with thinning blonde hair and a complexion resembling a practice dartboard.

Jake had offered no resistance during his arrest, yet the overzealous bastard had insisted on cuffing him and manhandling him into the waiting police van. The custody sergeant, on the other hand, a friendly fellow called Nick Lynch, had done his very best to put Jake at ease. He was a fit-looking man in his early fifties, with a totally bald head, kind green eyes and a caring disposition, which he showed to everyone, even to a foul-smelling vagrant called Derek.

During the sixty-minute journey to the police station, the tiny square cage in the back of the Ford Transit van had provided zero protection against the rancid-smelling unfortunate arrested for defecating in the street. Jake thanked God for small mercies that he hadn't taken his ablutions in his trousers.

PC Jones yanked Jake out of the van with his wrists still cuffed and hauled him to the custody desk.

"Thank you, Will," Sergeant Lynch said pointedly. "Please uncuff the gentleman."

"Sergeant, this individual is responsible for seriously assaulting three security staff at Fandango's. They have all required medical attention at hospital, and one has serious back injuries. I respectfully suggest we leave him restrained until he is put in his cell." PC Jones was taking no chances. His officious, jobsworth attitude was well practised.

"Noted," Sergeant Lynch said disinterestedly without looking up from his desk. "Uncuff him all the same."

He had seen every shape and size of criminal in his twenty-nine years as a police officer, and he knew a bad person from a good one.

"Thank you." Jake nodded respectfully in his direction and avoided eye contact with Jones.

"You're welcome, Mr…?"

"Webster. Jake Webster." Jake finished his introduction while rubbing his lacerated wrists.

"I'm guessing you've never been here before, Jake?" Sergeant Lynch's voice was easy and measured, but serious enough to hold Jake's attention, despite the cacophony coming through the walls from behind his desk.

"No, sir," Jake replied.

"OK, so what's going to happen now is, I will read you your rights and PC Jones will explain to me the reasons why you have been arrested. If they are valid, you will be detained subject to interview." He spoke slowly and concisely. "I will itemise your valuables and put them into safe keeping. You will be searched for anything that may harm you or others. Have you any weapons, drugs or sharps in your pockets?"

"No, sir."

"OK, we'll then take a few photographs and fingerprints, and a DNA sample. I will ask you a series of questions. Once we have finished, you will likely be escorted to a holding cell, in preparation for interview. Do you understand?"

"Yes, sir."

"I will call your solicitor, or one will be provided. Would you like us to call a relative or a friend to let them know you are here?"

"No, thank you. My friend has already called my solicitor."

"What is the name of your solicitor, Jake, please?"

"Tamara Norazu. I'm sorry, I don't know who she works for."

"Well, when she arrives, we'll show her to the interview room." Lynch smiled reassuringly at Jake.

"Don't worry, Jake. Tamara will have you out of there in no time. When she does, I'll be there to pick you up. You can come back to mine for a little while, don't worry." John's last words to him from outside the van doors.

"OK, if we can get down to it … I have a feeling tonight is going to be a busy night," Sergeant Lynch said wearily.

***

Tamara Norazu was buzzed into the station at 3:30am. She walked straight to the front desk and presented her identification.

"I'm representing Mr Jake Webster. My name is Tamara Norazu, of Bates and Chandler," she said, while she signed into the visitors' book.

Her jet-black hair was pulled into a tight ponytail, which accentuated the lines of her cheekbones.

"Good morning, Miss Norazu," Sergeant Lynch said politely. "Please take a seat."

"I'll check which interview room is booked for you and call in the OIC. May I offer you a cup of coffee?" Lynch was almost apologetic. It wasn't his fault she'd been called out, but he couldn't turn off his protective fatherly demeanour.

"That's very kind of you, Sergeant, but no thank you."

She sat down opposite the custody desk and stifled a yawn. Jones arrived a few minutes later and asked her to follow him to interview room four. The windowless room was furnished with a simple metal-framed desk bolted to the floor and four moulded, armless chairs. Jones dropped a manila file on the table containing the arrest notes. Tamara opened the file without invitation and began reading studiously.

"I'll bring your client, shall I?"

Tamara looked up without speaking to him, and he left the room.

Moments later Jones returned with Jake. "Miss Norazu, may I bring to your attention that Mr Webster has hospitalised three individuals this evening and—"

"No, you may not, constable," Tamara interrupted. "I'm well aware of my client's temperament and do not need any advice from you. Now if you don't mind, I wish to consult with him privately. I will call you when we are finished."

Jones left, slamming the door behind him.

Jake sat opposite Tamara and waited patiently, as the sound of the door reverberated on its hinges. The compact room was carpeted and painted battleship grey with white skirting and architraves. It was like a palace in comparison to the cell he had just vacated.

"Hello Jake, I'm Tamara. John called me to act for you. Firstly, are you OK?" Tamara held her hand out and shook Jake's warmly. She was surprised he hadn't as much as a scratch on him, apart from the laceration from the handcuffs.

"I'm fine, thank you. How's Mikey, is he hurt badly?" Jake didn't want to ask the police in case they put out a search for him and locked him up as well.

"John said Mikey was being helped to his feet by a girl he'd been dancing with called Alexa. Do you know her? She may be a witness to what happened."

"Alexa? Yes, I know of her. She's just a friend. She's a nurse I think." Jake was lifted by this news. If he was with Alexa, he couldn't be in better hands.

"Please, tell me what happened, and let's see if we can't sort this mess out. I'll make some enquiries about Mikey. I'm sure he's OK, don't worry."

***

After thirty minutes and several replays of events, she had all the information she needed for the time being and put her pen down.

"He was lucky you were there, Jake, otherwise he would be in hospital right now, with injuries I can only imagine," Tamara said in a hushed tone.

She continued: "I suppose I ought to tell you that all the bouncers were taken to hospital, one with a suspected broken back and a serious eye injury. The other two have a shattered hand, broken wrist, snapped Achilles tendon and severely swollen testicles."

Jake shrugged. "I'd do it again in a heartbeat. I hate bullies."

"Glad to hear it. Me too. I'll call the OIC back in. Let's get this over with."

***

Jones sat facing Tamara and Jake. He tried to appear forceful but came across as petulant and aggressive. He took a pair of recording discs out of their wrappers and slid them into the machine on the table, pressed record and spoke into the microphone.

"The time is 05:15hrs on Saturday, 28 August 2021. In attendance are me, PC Will Jones badge number 1-9-7-4; Miss Tamara Norazu, solicitor for the accused; and Mr Jake Webster, the accused," Jones sneered.

"Please introduce yourself for the sake of the tape, giving your name, age and address."

Jake spoke, as did Tamara.

Jones shuffled his notes and stared at Jake, before pressing his fingers together in a steeple on the tabletop.

"OK, Mr Webster, for the sake of the tape, I must caution you that you do not have to say anything, but it may harm your defence if you do not mention when questioned something that you later rely on in court. Anything you do say may be given in evidence. Do you understand?"

"Yes, sir," Jake replied.

"So, in your own words, do you want to tell me what happened?" His attempt at camaraderie fell way short of the mark.

"No comment," Jake said, under instruction from Tamara.

Jones sighed and looked up from his blank pad of paper. "I've got three severely injured doormen in hospital that say you put them there. One of them may never walk again, while the others won't play sport for a while." Jones sniffed at his glib comment.

"Constable Jones," Tamara interrupted, "in your notes, you have made no mention of any interviews conducted with any of the injured parties, apart from a Mr Stockton, who you had a brief discussion with. Have you in fact interviewed them and this is part of their statements?"

Tamara could read the guy like a book. She had told Jake: 'He'll start mild and friendly. Failing that, he'll try to be a little more persuasive. He'll talk about their families and lengthy spells in prison if you fail to cooperate.'

"You are correct, Miss Norazu – interviews haven't taken place yet. We will conduct them in due course once they are able to participate. We will also be taking a look at the CCTV evidence, which will likely show your client inflicting these injuries on the security staff in the course of their duties while ejecting Mr Webster and his friend from the building."

Tamara returned her well-practised non-committal stare.

"So, I'm giving Mr Webster the opportunity to put across his side of the story now, then we can all go home." His false smile failed to reach his eyes.

"Constable Jones, the evidence you have presented to me has conflicting witness statements from people at the scene, even after you and your colleagues had arrived. Two of the three injured parties have yet to provide any statement whatsoever, and Mr Stockton alleges my client assaulted him and threw him down the stairs. The man is nearly twice the size of my client, as are the other two. How do you suppose that happened?"

"Well, that's what I'm trying to establish, but you keep interrupting, and your client seems unwilling to help my investigation," Jones snapped, his voice getting louder and his face reddening.

"My client has no obligation whatsoever to help you in your investigation. It is you who must find the burden of proof against him, and you have nothing. The conclusions you have reached are fanciful and erroneous. You have detained my client on hearsay and on the account of a doorman who had a vendetta against my client and his friend, for reasons only he knows. Furthermore, you have subjected my client to harassment and abuse, holding him in your police van for over an hour, in handcuffs. The skin on his wrists is lacerated and bruised as a result." She held up Jake's wrists in physical evidence.

"If you resist arrest, the cuffs can bite into your skin. You know that."

His lame response was ill-thought-out – and music to Tamara's ears.

"From the evidence you have provided, my client was the first person you saw, so he was the one you arrested – in fact, the only one. Did it not occur to you that the doormen themselves may have been complicit in their own injuries, that they may have precipitated the aggressive behaviour? In your disclosure notes, you have made no reference of any kind to resistance offered by my client. In fact, you noted that 'he complied willingly with my requests'. Are you now saying he resisted arrest?"

"No, not exactly, I haven't completed writing my notes—"

"If you have no further evidence to present or questions to ask, I insist you release my client without charge – immediately. I insist the record reflects that my client has received injuries to his wrists from your restraints, which I have photographed and will present in due course."

"We are allowed to hold your client for a period of—"

"Spare me, constable," she said, holding her hand in front of his face. "I know the law, and trust me, I know about police brutality and harassment. Now do you intend to charge my client or not?"

"If you will permit me to ask my questions, you will get the answer to yours." His tone was quieter this time, and Tamara allowed him to proceed.

"Mr Webster, you entered Fandango's Nightclub at approximately 23:30hrs, did you not?"

"No comment."

"And you and your friends drank until 00:45hrs, correct?"

"No comment."

"At that time, you were asked to leave by Mr Stockton, and you refused. Then you assaulted Mr Stockton and two other doormen, resulting in their admission into Fulwood General Hospital with serious injuries. Isn't that the case?"

Jake was a little surprised at how wrong Jones' information was, and he was tempted to correct him, when, out of his peripheral vision, he saw Tamara wave her finger over her notes.

"No comment."

Jones continued to ask questions and proffer accusations, to which he received the same response. After twenty minutes he was totally exasperated, and quietly seethed to himself. He slowly got to his feet.

"I need to consult with the custody sergeant. Interview paused at 05:52hrs. PC Jones leaving the room."

He returned a couple of minutes later and sat down, looking a good deal less sure of himself. He restarted the tape, announced the time and repeated the caution he had given Jake earlier.

Looking at Jake with unfathomable hatred in his eyes, he said, "Mr Webster, without further evidence, you will not be charged. However, you will be released under investigation. In the event further evidence comes to light – and I'll do my best to make sure it does – you will be recalled for further interview, and possibly charged. Do you understand?"

"Yes," Jake replied, dispensing with the polite approach.

"You are free to go. Collect your belongings from the custody sergeant."

Jones switched off the tape and Jake and Tamara got to their feet. "I'm sure when you see the CCTV footage you will change your statement. Those bouncers might have something to say too. Nasty bunch, they are – I wouldn't want to make enemies of those guys."

Jake could have wiped the smile off his face with one slap, but he'd caused enough damage for one night. Tamara sensed it too and steered him out of the room.

By the time they had signed out, John had arrived and was pacing up and down outside in the early morning sunlight. He threw his arms around Jake. "Are you OK, mate?"

"I'm fine, John, thanks to Tamara."

Jake looked over at his solicitor and nodded in gratitude. "I can't thank you enough. You were amazing in there."

"All in a day's work, Jake."

Tamara knew a good client when she met one. She decided Jake was honest the moment they met.

"Just be aware this is far from over. From what you told me, and what I understand of the reports coming from the hospital, you may be back here sooner than you think. This is a serious matter. PC Jones has taken a dislike to you, and I wouldn't be surprised if his investigation isn't extremely thorough."

John Devlin's Flat, The Docklands, London: 28 August 2021

They made the journey back to John's place in silence. John sensed Jake didn't want to talk, so gave him space to think.

His apartment was on the top floor of a new dockside complex called The Harbour, surrounded by coffee shops, eateries, beauty salons and expensive haute couture outlets. John offered Jake one of the guestrooms to freshen up and suggested he get some sleep.

"I'll put us some breakfast on, shall I? I'm starving," John asked, though he didn't wait for an answer, as was his habit, Jake had noticed.

Jake made straight for the bathroom, which was well equipped with soap, toothbrushes and other essentials. He tried burning the skin off his back to rid himself of the memory of the previous night, and the filth of the cell.

He returned to the bedroom and found an array of designer shirts, trousers, jeans and jumpers laid on the bed. A small laundry bag had been left next to his old clothes.

"I've left some of my baggier fitting clothes out for you, Jake, if you don't want to put your old gear back on. Help yourself, OK?" John's muffled voice came through the door.

"OK, thanks." Jake didn't really know what to say or do. The clothes looked brand new but without tags, and there were a few pairs of socks and boxer shorts still in their packaging. He made his selection and got changed. It felt a little strange wearing someone else's clothes, but they fitted well enough. He felt like a new man.

His stomach growled at the smell of fried bacon filtering through from the kitchen. Before satiating his hunger, he took one last look at the room and its stunning view across The Docklands – at the old cranes, capstans and cobbled quaysides; the contrast between the ultra-modern skyscrapers used by banks and corporations was extreme, but perversely quite fitting, like a regenerated or repurposed place of industry.

Jake allowed himself a wry smile. An hour ago, he'd been sitting in a filthy police cell; now, he'd been teleported into expensive luxury, as if in another world, another time. He made his way through to the kitchen, taking in the stylish elegance of John's apartment. He couldn't begin to estimate how much this place cost, but it was up there with Rob's flat in Primrose Hill, if not more.

How do people amass such wealth? he asked himself.

"Take a seat, we're almost ready," John said, busily flipping eggs on a griddle.

Jake slid onto an orange leather high stool and tucked his legs under the counter, which was topped by a smoked-glass shelf.

John had prewarmed two plates and set them out with napkins and cutlery, which he positioned with geometric accuracy. He had poured out orange juice into tumblers, and coffee from a percolator. Jake could see no sign of mess. John's cooking organisation was on another scale. Mikey would be impressed.

The pair wolfed down eggs, bacon, fried tomatoes and mushrooms, while Jake brought John up to speed with what went on in interview room four.

After tidying up, John joined him on the couch and patted him on the back. He wasn't a touchy-feely guy, but he felt his friend needed some reassurance.

Jake sat forward and propped his elbows on his knees. "John, I'd like to say how grateful I am for everything you did for me last night. I barely know you, and you've gone the extra mile for me. I really appreciate it." Jake spoke in hesitant clumps, like he'd forgotten how to speak English.

"That's what friends are for."

John's bashful response was a little open ended, and Jake found it hard to disagree. But it was true – he hardly knew the bloke, and here he was sitting in his clothes, having been fed like a king and rescued from a police cell. Perhaps Rob could have arranged his release all the same, and no doubt if he'd known about his predicament he would have, but John was literally a stranger – he owed Jake nothing. He decided to park his uncertainty for the time being and thank his lucky stars he did what he did.

After a long silence, Jake spoke again. "Apparently, one doorman has a serious back injury. He may never walk again."

A cloud of despair enveloped him at the thought of inflicting such long-lasting injury, even on someone as malicious as Ben Stockton.

"Fair play to you, Jake. They were intent on killing you and Mikey, and *you* are worried about *them*?" John shook his head in bewilderment. "I think they got what they deserved. Besides, you only tapped the black guy's ankle – he kicked himself and broke his own leg. And what about the tall guy? He proper fucked himself up. I bet it hurt when he punched that door frame."

John couldn't help sniggering.

"And what about that right hook you gave him to his wedding tackle? Ouch! That had to hurt – and I mean a lot. And if I'm not mistaken, you used a tai otoshi body drop to throw the fat, pink-headed guy, right?" John sounded impressed.

"You are correct. Go to the top of the class." Jake gave John a small ripple of applause. "He made it a bit easy for me to be honest. He literally sent me a postcard telling me what he intended to do. I hadn't expected him to fly so easily through the air, then he seemed to roll down the stairs in slow motion."

John sensed a dark cloud descending again. "Listen, Jake, if you weren't there, what do you think they would have done to Mikey? You know what. They would have kicked the shit out of him, and they would have gotten away scot-free. Trust me, you did good. And when you next see Mikey, he'll say the same. And besides, there was something about that Ben guy I didn't like. He had a look on his face, like he'd done it before. He had his eye on you and Mikey, long before you got to the front of the queue. I saw him eyeing you both and pointing at you, then saying something to the black guy."

"To be fair, that happens a lot to Mikey." Jake rolled his eyes in unison to the chirping noise of his phone bursting into life.

"Speak of the devil," Jake said.

6

WAKE UP. MIKEY

Flat 7, 212 Holmes Road, Kentish Town, London: 28 August 2021

"Come on, Mikey, I'll race you to the swings!" Kaitlyn sprinted off giggling excitedly, with Mikey hot on her heels.

As she ran, her body seemed to turn translucent, ethereal almost, fading in front of his eyes. She pumped her arms and legs frantically. The movement caused her limbs to disintegrate, consumed by the ground beneath her feet, until she collapsed with exhaustion. Mikey picked her up to cradle her in his arms. She held his face and kissed the salty tears from his eyes, and pressed her fingers on his trembling lips. Her hands turned to dust and ran like sand down his cheeks. He didn't scream or shout out. He'd stopped crying for help and praying to God many years ago.

The joy of seeing her was inevitably short-lived, as he knew it would be. He was prepared for the tidal wave of grief – it never disappointed. Everything was so clear, predictable. He had to smile for her. He had to put on a brave face and shoulder the burden of her pain. The hurt seared through him like acid in his blood. He needed to feel the suffocating pain; that way, Kaitlyn wouldn't.

He cursed his tears. He didn't want to sadden her, so he laughed, hollow and strained, pretending to enjoy the fleeting moment that was about to end his nightmare.

***

As Kaitlyn's memory retreated in readiness for the next night of torment, Mikey's consciousness began flickering into life, although his attempt to rejoin the real world was not going particularly well.

He woke like an old computer from the 1990s booting itself up one function at a time; screeching and groaning sounds bouncing around his head. His eyes seemed to be glued shut, despite the tears that lubricated them.

His body was racked with sharp stabbing pains, as if he were lying on a mattress of garden tools. He swallowed, and his epiglottis closed and opened like a rusty gate, making him wince. He sensed a slight tightening around the right side of his mouth and attempted to lick some moisture into his lips. It made no contribution other than to alert him to the unmistakable metallic taste of dried blood.

His right eye was sore and swollen and would remain out of order for the time being. His good eye scanned the surroundings of the dark room and took in a blurry yellow frame of sunlight around a curtain wafting in the cool breeze of what appeared to be a very promising autumnal day.

Well, that explains something, he concluded silently to himself. *I don't have curtains, so I'm not at the flat.*

The banging in his head began to subside, although his erratic breathing caused his torso to tremble and tense. He heard a choked snore and felt the duvet being yanked off his legs, leaving his 6ft 3in muscular frame naked and exposed.

With his arse pointing upwards and his body laid in what could only be described as the recovery position, he felt the fresh morning air blow over him, leaving huge goose pimples on his legs, buttocks and back. He certainly didn't feel like he was in a position of recovery. He felt like he'd been trampled by a buffalo.

The lumpy mattress had a frayed, piped edge, which had left a pirate-like pink line across his face. His contorted jaw gaped open, drawing in dry air, which stung his throat. A frilly pink pillow adorned with prickly sequins was trapped between his right arm and ear.

Whose bed am I in? he asked silently of himself, in a tone reminiscent of Loyd Grossman.

His mother flashed into his head, wagging her finger and giving him one of her disapproving looks. He shook her image out of his head. The imperceptibly small movement of ridding his mind of his mother's admonishment sent shock waves through his neck, ribs and back, causing him to gasp. He made a mental note not to do that again.

What the fuck, lads? Why the fuck didn't you get me home safe? He questioned his absent friends despite having no recollection of the events leading up to now.

Although blinded by brain fog, he realised he hadn't ended up at either of their flats, as he wasn't on Jake's couch and Rob had Egyptian white cotton sheets and satin pillowcases – only the best for Rob. This place looked two-star at best.

It must be a bird's room, no bloke would settle for frills and sequins on the bedclothes.

Mikey failed to acquiesce to political correctness, as he was reminded incessantly by Jake's terminally absent girlfriend, Jasmin. Unlike Mikey's current mystery bed partner, Jasmin hated men, especially those who invaded her personal space. Mikey's total lack of awareness and casual attitude about massively important issues like climate change and globalism made her rigid with anger. It was ironic that her unequivocal, left-wing, socialist views were poles apart from those of a guy from Tyne and Wear with such staunch working-class roots.

Mikey allowed himself a small, if not temporary, smirk of victory, following his deduction. Ever the optimist, he mused over who it might be.

The quarter-full bowl of vomit on the floor beneath his head led him to the conclusion it must have been a very heavy night. It also explained the tightness around the right side of his face. An off-yellow concretion of sputum, which hadn't quite made it into the bowl, had dried out like some half-buried, ancient subsea artefact.

There's a thing, he thought, ignoring the putrid deposits. *Who would be so caring as to put me in the recovery position in their own bed and give me a bowl to blow my chunks into?*

Mikey knew the importance of first aid and life-saving measures, having attended any and every first aid course available at work. *Bride material right there,* he concluded.

He gave the mystery woman a motionless pain-free nod of thanks and wondered if there was a bacon butty on the go. In literally sixty seconds, he saw himself married to a girl who merely sought to protect her own carpet and not wake up next to a corpse.

Shit me, my mam would have beaten the crap out of me if I'd have come home like this, he thought, grimacing as the pain returned to his ribs.

He laughed inwardly, as he remembered the time when he and a school pal had spent a summer's afternoon at the Highfield Cabbage Club, stealing half-drunk bottles of Newcastle Brown Ale from the beer tent. As he staggered through the front door, his mum, Jackie, grabbed him by the scruff of the neck for vomiting in the garden over her prized dahlias. Wielding a two-foot, wooden toilet brush like a hatchet, she beat him as he scrambled to his bedroom under a barrage of bleach-flavoured blows, the stiff brown bristles leaving him looking like a plucked chicken. Good times.

Holy fuck, where am I? he pleaded with himself once more.

Beneath the swaying curtain he could see his bedfellow's dressing table, laden with perfume bottles, make-up, nail varnish, creams, brushes, a spilled packet of wipes, scrunches of toilet tissue and a variety of hairdryers, straighteners, charging cables and other electrical equipment. The wires tumbled off the edge like a nest of mating garter snakes. The sweet funk of stale perfume and make-up told him his swollen nose wasn't fully out of commission.

It would take an hour to sort that lot out, he thought.

Mikey caught sight of the mirror, or rather the reflection of the wardrobe opposite, and a yellow and green patterned dress hanging on the part-opened door that looked vaguely familiar. His overworked left eye noticed his clothes dumped haphazardly on the floor.

How am I supposed to put those back on – unfolded and creased? I'll look like I've been dragged through a hedge.

The penny dropped, as Mikey came to an unavoidable conclusion.

She must have taken my clothes off.

He would never have dumped them like some miser at a jumble sale – and he always slept in his boxers. For a few seconds Mikey felt violated, like he'd been date raped or something.

He seethed at the sight of his new shirt in a crumpled heap. His patience with this one-time Florence Nightingale was now wearing thin. Even accounting for her hospitality and care, he couldn't countenance walking up the aisle with such a disorderly girl with no regard for other people's property. Mikey hated mess, especially dust, and this place hadn't seen Mr Sheen flying around in a good while.

He noticed his shoes under the dresser, laces still tied, like someone had yanked them off his feet and thrown them on the floor. His desire to be somewhere else was growing exponentially by the minute, as was his need to take a piss.

He used his free arm to survey the damage to his face. His top lip was swollen and tender, and he had two puzzling vertical scratches parallel to his philtrum. He drew his pinkie down the stubbly groove under his nose to his upper lip and removed the regurgitated residue of yesterday's meals. He peeled the morsels of part-digested food from his nostrils, right eyelid, and from around his mouth and flicked them into the orange reservoir of unpleasantness.

Aside from his bruised eye and cheek, a few scratches and a fat lip, he wasn't overly worried about his looks, although a large egg-like bruise on his left temple was a bit unsightly.

If he was back home in Tyneside, his mother would have suggested rubbing butter on it – a practice she and his gran both swore by to reduce swelling and prevent discolouration. Rather than turn himself into a human crumpet, Mikey would settle for a little Olbas Oil when he got back to his flat.

At this point he was certain he'd been in a fight. He hoped it wasn't with the mystery woman who'd been lying next to him. What worried Mikey the most was that he had no clue whose bed he was in and what had happened to leave him prostrate in the land that vacuum cleaners forgot. He closed his eyes and tried to remember.

It was Friday at The Swann, and it was Rob's birthday. He let out a sigh of relief as the fog started to lift. He closed his now fully operational set of eyes, and the tumultuous events of the previous night began flooding back into view. A feeling of deep dread swept over him.

***

How the fuck did I end up in bed with Alexa Taylor? Even with the evidence staring him in the face, Mikey had more questions than answers.

"Wakey-wakey, Mikey," Alexa said cheerily.

"Hey, Alexa. Heavy night, eh?"

"You could say that. My back is fucking killing me." Alexa stood arched next to the bed, pushing her huge bosom in Mikey's direction.

Mikey wondered for a moment if he had crossed the Rubicon. He swung his legs out of bed and flipped up into a sitting position. Pain shot up his back and neck, and he gasped. His head was swimming, and he could feel bile rising in his stomach.

"Are you OK?" she asked with some concern. "You took a bit of a beating."

"I feel like I've been run over by a buffalo." His swollen lip affected his speech.

"It was three buffalos actually," Alexa mocked. "Your friend rounded them up. They won't be running over anyone else for a while. He's a tough little cookie, that one. You owe Jake a pint or two for saving you from a lot worse than you got." Alexa was intent on levelling up the credit where it was due.

Mikey stood up and turned to face her. "Can I use your toilet please, darling?"

Alexa stared wide-eyed at Mikey's morning glory, the sunlight casting a resplendent yellow stripe across the shaft.

"I think that's for the best. You're pointing in the right direction – it's through that door." She nodded towards the corner of the room.

Mikey remembered too late that he was naked, and piss hard. He snatched his clothes off the floor to hide his embarrassment and scurried towards the bathroom. Alexa gave him some privacy and headed off giggling to herself to make a cup of tea.

Once Mikey was dressed, he slinked out of her room into the kitchen towards the sound of the kettle whistling impatiently on the gas stove. His nostrils were disappointed at detecting no aroma of fried bacon. He sat at the kitchen table and smiled awkwardly at Alexa, as he tried to take stock of the situation.

"So, I guess I owe you for getting me out of there in one piece? Thanks, darling, I don't know what to say."

"Listen, Mikey, it wasn't your fault. Those arsehole bouncers had it in for you. They want locking up."

He smiled at the depth of concern in her voice. "I can't even remember leaving the club or how I got here," he said, looking at Alexa for answers.

"I carried you up the stairs and put you to bed, didn't I?! You were totally out of it. I had to bunk up with you as I had nowhere else to sleep, and I was worried about you choking on your vomit."

Mikey's Florence Nightingale theory was confirmed. She skipped the explanation about undressing him while he was comatose. She didn't think bringing it up was necessary.

"I don't know how to thank you, Alexa. I owe you big time – you are literally my lifesaver. Welsh Ian is a lucky guy. I'll tell him the next time I see him."

"If it's all the same, can we keep this to ourselves? He might not understand."

Mikey readily agreed to her proposal. They sat opposite each other drinking their mugs of tea and laughing about the previous night's events, oblivious of the nightmare scenario Mikey had created for his friend.

Alexa cooed at Mikey and enjoyed every minute of her first, and likely last, breakfast meeting with him. Mikey beamed back at her and realised how lucky he was to be rescued by such an amazingly capable girl.

When he stood to leave, Alexa's face visibly saddened. "I'll not forget what you did for me, darling, I really won't. You are a beautiful person," he said earnestly.

It was the truth, and although there was little or no comparison to be made with his sister in a physical sense, the depth of affection in Alexa's eyes he'd seen in Kaitlyn's. It made him swallow the emotion clotting in his throat.

"Anytime, Mikey," she whispered into his chest, as he hugged her goodbye.

7

ONE DOOR OPENS

Fulwood Sports Centre, Kentish Town, London: 29 August 2021

Mikey's walk to work gave him time to stew further about the events over the weekend. He'd met Jake in Renoir's Café the previous day after his recovery run around Primrose Hill, which usually cleared his mind and helped reset his positivity – not this time.

"Why you not like my food, Mikey?" Mustafa, the Turkish owner of Renoir's, was attentive, if not abrupt.

"It's great, Mustafa, I'm just feeling a bit queasy that's all. Too many beers last night." Mikey patted his stomach, hoping he would buy his lame response. He didn't.

"Wait here. I have something for stomach." Mustafa walked towards his counter, waving his arm impatiently and talking in Turkish at full volume to his assistant.

Jake rolled his eyes and returned to Mikey. "Listen to me, mate, there's no need to apologise or feel bad. If it had happened anywhere to anyone, I would've done the same. Those guys were going to kill you, man, and that's a fact." He leant over the table and squeezed his shoulder.

"Tamara was amazing. She said nothing would come of it, in spite of the guy's injuries. It was just an unfortunate accident. He's likely to make a full recovery." Jake wanted to believe the story he'd created as much as anyone.

Mustafa slammed a pair of shot glasses filled with three fingers of milky-looking fluid on the table.

"Raki!" he announced with pride. "In Turkey we call this 'Lion's Milk'. Good for digestion. Drink!"

They took a deep breath and necked the aniseed liquid, which burned their throats and warmed their stomachs.

"Thanks, Mustafa," they said in unison, suppressing a cough.

"You want more?" Mustafa loomed over their table with a huge grin and his hands propped on his hips.

"No!" the lads exclaimed.

Mustafa left grinning; his work was done.

The raki did nothing for either of them. Mikey still felt ropey, and Jake still had his awful feeling of foreboding.

***

Mikey slunk into Fulwood Sports Centre hoping not to engage with anyone, especially not Euan McArdle. He looked like he'd been in a car crash – the least said, the better.

His attempt to remain incognito lasted no longer than sixty seconds.

"Mikey, hey, how are you?" Joy Wong appeared from behind a column in the entrance way in front of the turnstile barriers. "Oh my God, what happened to your face?" She switched off her rotating mechanical mop and rushed over to him.

Joy Wong was one of Mikey's go-to people at work. It was safe to say she was in his inner circle of friends. At 5ft 1in and no heavier than 55kg, she was the epitome of petite, but she was incredibly strong and an athlete in every sense of the word. A 'pocket rocket', as Mikey would refer to her.

At twenty-seven, she had built up her cleaning company from nothing. Joy Wong was another force of nature, and it was easy to see why she and Mikey were good friends.

"Hey, sweetheart." Mikey reached down to peck her on the cheek. "I got into a bit of trouble at Fandango's on Friday night. Don't say anything though, please, I'm trying to keep it quiet. I'm gonna pretend I got injured playing rugby."

She reached out and held his hand. "I leave you alone for five minutes, then you get all beat up. What happened?" Her voice was soft and caring. She caressed his face and brushed her fingers past both sides of his jaw, as if carrying out a medical examination. Mikey got temporarily lost in her face, recognising not for the first time how beautiful she was.

"Let's have a coffee later and I'll tell you all about it. Don't worry, OK." Her little hand squeezed his in agreement.

An image of Kaitlyn flashed into his mind for no reason at all, triggering a surge of emotion that caught his breath. Joy saw it and hugged him. Pain from his ribs shot through his torso. She could sense something wasn't right – other than the pain coursing through his body – his eyes had lost a little of their spark and looked glassy. He was upset, and that upset her.

"I finish at noon. I'll see you in Bannister's. Let's do lunch, OK?" she said, her dark-brown eyes boring into his.

He agreed, dodged her gaze and left as quickly as he could.

***

Mikey got to his office without any further inquisition. He dropped into his chair and buried his head in his hands. He gave himself a mental slap, rubbed the moisture from his eyes and straightened his back.

Come on, Mikey, sort your shit out, man. His father's no-nonsense encouragement echoed around his head.

He began organising his impeccably neat desk, when his heart sank at remembering it was the 4M – the Monthly Monday Morning Meeting. If he thought he could avoid the glare of his co-workers for the day, his hopes ended there and then.

***

He entered the meeting room to find it empty – unsurprisingly, considering it was still only 8am. He turned on the lights and did a quick tidy-up, straightening the chairs, cleaning the whiteboard, and connecting his laptop to the wireless overhead projector. He turned on the air conditioning and gave the place a quick blast of heat before Euan came in and switched it off.

One of the fluorescent tubes blinked intermittently. Rather than give Euan reason to chastise old Albert the caretaker for not checking the lights routinely, he ran to the basement for a replacement.

On his return, he found Gordon Watson, aka Big G, was the first through the door. He sidled over to Mikey to shake his hand, took the tube off him, and swapped it out without using the stepladder. At 6ft 8in, there was nowhere Big G could go without some wag asking him, *How's the weather up there?* His facial features and angular jawline gave him a Balkan mobster appearance, whereas in reality, he was as meek as a lamb and the best PT instructor Mikey had.

His enormous frame was wrapped in a thick blanket of dense muscle that had been squeezed into a white T-shirt. Mikey had asked him to come and play rugby for Camley, but he had seen the damage done to Mikey most weekends, and the state of his face left him in no doubt he'd made the right decision not to bother.

"Hard game was it, Mikey?" Big G's voice was quiet despite his size.

"Huh? Yeah, you should see the other guy." Mikey rolled his eyes as he slid Big G the meeting agenda.

Lisa Asquith and Carla Umwhezi arrived together and headed straight to the coffee machine. Lisa was the safeguarding officer and managed most of the special needs classes. Mikey shuddered to think of life without her. He appointed her based on necessity rather than any long-term recruitment plan.

Three years previously Euan McArdle dangled the opportunity for Mikey to attend a residential course for 'specialist management'. Mikey jumped at the chance of a week in Aberdeen. He was stunned to find out the true nature of the assignment: 'Sports training for physically and mentally handicapped adults' – the exact opposite end of where Mikey saw his career development.

He had made no secret to his colleagues that he aspired to be an elite sports psychologist and training coach, and he saw the Shinewell Group as the perfect opportunity to get there. Until then. Euan poured scorn over his ambitions, and when the local council approached Fulwood with a lucrative proposal to set up classes, he saw it as the perfect opportunity to scupper his career path and earn the club income.

The unintended consequences were that Mikey did not hesitate to make good on his commitment, setting up the mobility and training classes. His never-ending supply of energy and enthusiasm created what fast became an over-subscribed success story. The fees Fulwood were paid by the council to develop their services were substantial and Lisa was recruited to meet the sudden demand.

Lisa was taking her first swig of coffee when she caught sight of Mikey's battered face. "Oh my goodness, Mikey, what happened to you?"

"Ah, it's just a scratch, nothing to worry about. Thanks for asking." Mikey shrugged his response and waved a hand at her casually.

"Morning, Carla, can I pour you a coffee?" Mikey changed the subject again to avoid the glare of attention.

The tall Ghanaian mirrored Lisa's concern. She took her coffee and flicked him a concerned smile. If there was ever a man who Carla thought she could be truly open with, it was Mikey Stott. She owed him that much at least.

Carla Umwhezi was Head of Swimming and Leisure, which included maintaining the pools, saunas, steam rooms, hydrotherapy suites and wellbeing studios. It was safe to say she was one of the most confident and impressive people Mikey had ever met.

Two years earlier, when Carla was a paying member, they had become good friends. One morning Mikey had arrived for a swim before his shift and he'd begun bragging about his athletic prowess to Carla, who then challenged him to a swimming contest.

"Whatever distance you want, Mikey – you choose." She threw down the gauntlet and Mikey picked it up. If he had had any sense, he'd have slapped himself around the face with it.

"There's one condition, Mikey – if I win, you need to make sure my application for the Head of Swimming and Leisure is approved for interview."

Mikey accepted the challenge, not even asking for a forfeit. In truth, if he'd known she was applying, he would have recommended her anyway.

Early the following morning, before the pool filled up with members, they met for a twenty-length race. Mikey's unease was palpable, when he caught sight of Carla's long, athletic body stepping out of the changing rooms. Seeing Lisa, Joanne Fulton from Catering and Beverly Lancing from Admin looking down on them from the gallery only compounded things.

"Did you invite the audience?" Mikey asked, thumbing upwards.

"Apparently the word's got out, Mikey," Carla said nonchalantly.

She flicked her legs, and rinsed her arms, flopping her head left and right, accompanied by loud cracks.

"Who will say go?" Mikey asked nervously.

"I'll go when you go." Her response did nothing to allay his fear.

Mikey launched himself into the pool and began to swim a rapid and regular stroke. At the first turn, he lifted his head and saw Carla about a quarter of the way behind him, swimming a slow and deliberate breaststroke with her head tilted backwards, as if she was avoiding getting her face wet.

He pushed off and began swimming the return leg, his confidence returning. At the second turn, he saw her at the far end, maintaining her slow and steady pace. As they passed each other, he glanced in her direction and gave her a pitiful and patronising grin. At the next couple of turns, he took the time to wave at the three girls in the gallery, whose curious expressions hadn't changed. They waved back and laughed inaudibly behind the plate glass screen. At the eighth turn, he estimated he was just over four lengths clear and at that point he was about to suggest no contest. He was thinking how best to explain to Carla that she was at a huge disadvantage, as he'd been swimming for years and had completed two Ironman competitions.

He waited as she plodded towards him, her progress inexorable and a whimsical look on her face, like she was enjoying every minute. In an instant she dived beneath the surface, flipped and rolled her body and launched off the end wall, while barely causing a ripple in the water. Seconds later, she surfaced and freestyled to the opposite end of the pool. She turned with an ease of movement he had never seen before, and she pivoted and corkscrewed back towards him.

Mikey pushed himself off the side of the pool. His never-say-die optimism that he could still win assisted in his climb to what would be a new level of sporting humiliation. At the twenty-metre point he saw Carla glide past him doing backstroke, as if he was floating still on the water. At the turn, he could see her flopping in and out of the water swimming butterfly stroke and eating up the distance between them. After fourteen lengths he calculated they were about neck and neck, which was when the exhibition took a turn for the worse – at least for Mikey.

Carla began swimming from lane 3 to 5 to beneath him in lane 4. She popped up out of the water and waved at her friends, sending them into fits of laughter. On his penultimate length of the pool, Mikey decided to put everything into a fast finish. He swam as hard as he ever had – his focus was absolute, and his shoulders burned with the effort. As Carla swam beneath him for the last time, she tucked her thumbs into the waist band of his trunks and yanked them clean off his legs, assisted nobly by his own forward momentum.

Any vestige of pride remaining was stripped away from him with a flick of her wrists. He swam with his butt cheeks on show to the end of the pool, where Carla stood twirling her prize around her index finger.

"So, Mr Ironman, do I get that job?"

As it turned out, Carla was a bronze medallist for Ghana in the 2015 swimming world championships. It also turned out she was amazing at her job.

***

Euan McArdle waddled into the meeting room fifteen minutes late, with the wiry Elaine McIlroy, his ever-present head of finance, close behind. Elaine and Euan had a lot in common: they both hailed from Glasgow, and they were both obnoxious, self-serving and universally loathed by everyone attending the 4M meeting.

"Morning, everyone."

Euan shimmied along one side of the meeting room, his huge gut rubbing against the back of people's chairs. He held a paper bag containing his breakfast in one hand and his laptop bag in the other, which he dropped clumsily at the head of the table. Elaine made him a cup of coffee, which she set down next to his food, turning the handle to face his right hand. Apparently, he liked it that way.

He took off his suit jacket with what appeared to be considerable effort and handed it blindly to Elaine to hang up on the coat rack. The display of subservience grated the other women present, who despised her for allowing the sexist fat pig to treat her in such a way.

The smell of the fried food permeated the room, and Mikey's appetite came flooding back. His mind flitted back to Saturday morning and he grinned at the thought of Alexa and the care she had shown him.

Euan gave him a puzzled look. "What happened to you?"

"Huh? Rugby." Mikey's explanations were becoming more condensed.

Beverly Lancing and Joanne Fulton sat at the opposite end of the table as far away from Euan as they could possibly get. As manager of the restaurant and catering, Joanne told herself that she ought to bear some of the responsibility for this obese man chomping his way through a footlong all-day breakfast sandwich, as it was her kitchen that had made it for him.

She mouthed, "Are you OK?" while circling her own face with her pointed finger.

Sitting next to Big G was Will Halperson, who was responsible for events and special projects for the Shinewell Group and only attended Fulwood on an ad hoc basis. Will was a small, suntanned and smartly dressed man, with his phone glued to his ear. His ability to make things happen in the face of a hundred impassable hurdles was legendary. He was Mr Fixit, a name he had borrowed from Jimmy Savile, and one he insisted on keeping, despite the unfortunate connotations.

"Would you mind giving me a little room, Will? You're crowding me."

Elaine McIlroy was tall, stick-thin and hated being in close contact with people. The windowless room did nothing to alleviate her feeling of claustrophobia.

"No problem, Elaine," Will responded, shuffling his chair away from hers and towards Big G's. "Is this far enough?" He waved his arm through the two feet of space between them, his comment dripping with sarcasm.

"Thank you, that's fine." She crossed her legs and pushed her circular horn-rimmed glasses up onto the bridge of her bony nose.

"Shall I start, Mr McArdle?" Mikey asked, as everyone waited in silence for Euan to finish his mouthful of food.

Euan insisted on his staff using his surname. The pathetic show of authority only served to alienate him further from his team.

"What do you want – a red carpet? Get on with it," Euan said, food flying from his mouth and landing on the table in front of him.

He leaned forward to pick up the errant morsel of bacon and followed up with another noisy bite from his sandwich. He slurped at egg yolk dripping through his chubby fingers and wiped his sleeve across his bulbous chin. Beverly Lancing couldn't look at him. She sat arms folded, with one hand holding a tissue over her nose and mouth.

"Thanks everyone for coming in a little earlier than normal." Mikey glanced at Euan, who was oblivious to his sarcasm. "We all have the agenda, and I'd like to get through it in good time so that Will can tell us about the event we have in December that will impact on us all and be a massive coup for Fulwood."

Will gave a muted thumbs-up to the group, who raised their eyebrows and shuffled forward in their seats with interest.

"Ooh, tell us more," Joanne chirped with genuine enthusiasm.

"Will has secured a £50,000 Professional Squash Association World Gold Event to be played on a glass court specially built for the competition, in the main hall. Players will be competing from all around the world. We've beaten Hammersmith and Chiswick Leisure to this, and, apparently, BBC Sport intend to televise it and stream it online. I know Will has worked hard on this himself and has potential sponsorship deals lined up."

"Aren't we getting a little ahead of ourselves here?" Euan interrupted the mood like the fun sponge he was. "This hasn't been approved by HQ yet."

"It has actually, Euan. The email was sent out last Thursday. I've already been on to the PSA World Tour and BBC Sport. Legal are on it with the Ts & Cs," Will explained.

"It's Mr McArdle to you, Sonny Jim, and I've not heard anything about it." Euan stared aggressively at Will as the remnants of his sandwich prolapsed out of his grip and dropped onto his copy of the agenda.

"Well, you were copied in on the email from Amanda congratulating everyone, and I've emailed you confirmation myself. If you don't read your emails or meeting notes, it's hardly my fault."

Carla, Lisa and Joanne smirked listening to Euan's bluster and revelled in Will's uncompromising stance.

"Well, I've not seen it, have I?! I'm busy running this sports centre in case you haven't noticed." Euan's blood pressure was rising, ably assisted by the six thousand calories he'd just consumed.

"OK, we'll come back to that." Mikey moved on before Will could answer Euan's rhetorical statements, mindful that he had swimming lessons to supervise in an hour.

"Beverly has kindly sent her admissions and membership numbers to me in advance, which I've included in the meeting notes. You can see we've had yet another 150-plus head increase this quarter, taking membership to over 2,000, which is an all-time high for Fulwood. It's been a team effort, but a very special thanks must go to Carla and Lisa for the swimming classes, especially those for the special needs and the elderly, which are booked up for months to come. Our TripAdvisor count has gone through the roof."

Mikey began the applause and winked in the direction of Carla and Lisa, which made him wince in pain. Carla chuckled at his discomfort and nudged Lisa, who beamed with pride.

"Humph! Get a room, for goodness sake." Euan mocked their achievement as he balled up his spent sandwich wrapper.

"Perhaps now is a good time for Elaine to present the accounts for the quarter, to show the impact we are having on the P&L?"

Mikey's segue was well timed – he could see Euan's glib comment had riled Lisa.

Elaine's face was consumed with panic. She turned to Euan for help, who laced his fingers across his engorged, grease-speckled pot belly and offered none.

"I – I – I don't think it's your place to advertise the financial position of the company to everybody, Michael. Mr McArdle will present this himself if he sees fit."

Her evasiveness was matched by her pomposity and embarrassment, which made little sense to those present, as they had financial responsibility for generating income in their own departments.

The meeting went reasonably quickly after that. Will presented his project plan for the squash competition, which everyone except Euan and Elaine seemed excited about.

With two minutes to spare, Mikey brought the meeting to a close, asking, "So, if we can go around the room for any other business, Elaine?"

She shook her head, as if saying words was just too much effort. Everyone else had nothing to add and thanked Mikey for organising the meeting, relieved to be leaving Euan's presence relatively unscathed.

At that point, Euan burst into life. "As a matter of fact, I have an announcement to make." He stood up and let out a part-muffled belch, which he blew down the length of the table while failing to excuse himself.

"I regret to say that I must warn all of you there may be a few changes to staffing levels in the next few months. HQ have asked me to investigate cost-cutting measures. I know this may come as a surprise to you, but we must face facts – which are that we are not profitable enough. No amount of swimming classes, membership uptake and sporting events is going to change that."

"What?!" Mikey exclaimed, speaking for everyone in the room. "Where has this come from? I don't believe it! Is this a joke? Surely extra classes, more members and sporting events are *exactly* what make profit?"

All pretence at tiptoeing around the man went out of the window.

"You need to calm down, sonny, or you may find yourself at the front of the redundancy queue." Euan jabbed his greasy finger in Mikey's direction.

Mikey's body stiffened. He clenched his jaw and tried to regulate his breathing. The pain in his ribs, neck and face was anaesthetised by a sudden surge of adrenaline.

Mikey had worked hard to build this team. Their attitude was exemplary. Despite Euan, they gave 100% to Fulwood. This didn't make sense. Only Elaine seemed free from anxiety, or from any trace of surprise; she sat with a supercilious sneer on her weaselly face.

How could they do any more for these greedy bastards? What did these faceless bureaucrats expect from them? Mikey raged inwardly.

"Thank you," Euan said to quell the mumblings around the table. He paused for effect and leaned on the table, which gave a slight squeak under his weight.

"This is a feasibility study at present. Do not complain to HR or Amanda – it will only draw attention to yourself. Let's all of us work together to find a solution to the problem. You guys mean so much to me, I'd hate to lose any of you. We are like a family here." Euan's patronising tone was excruciating.

"A word of warning to you all"—his clipped Scots brogue deepened as he attempted to be serious—"I suggest you all keep your noses clean and your heads down."

Euan's warning had barely hit home, when Luke from the front reception desk knocked on the door and craned his head in through the gap.

"Sorry to interrupt. Mikey, the police are in reception. They need to speak with you. Privately."

***

"Thank you for agreeing to talk to us, Mr Stott." PC Will Jones smiled as warmly as he could to put Mikey at ease. It didn't work. His pockmarked pasty skin and his small, insipid eyes made it hard for Mikey to hold his gaze.

"This is DS Cantly, who is leading our investigation into an alleged assault at Fandango's Nightclub on Friday night."

Mikey gave the two men a polite nod and said, "I assumed you'd want to talk to me. I just wasn't expecting you to turn up at my place of work. Could you not have given me a call or something?"

Mikey's discomfort was palpable. Being interviewed by the police was nerve-wracking enough, without the entire building knowing about it.

"If you like, we can do this down the station at a time that suits you," Jones sneered.

Mikey thought the less time spent in their presence the better.

"No, it's fine, you're here now, let's get it over with."

Even though the room had just housed nine people, including Big G and Euan, who each filled two places on their own, Mikey was feeling decidedly claustrophobic.

"What can you tell us about what happened, Mr Stott?" Jones thought correctly that a direct approach would bring results.

"What can I say – those bouncers want locking up. They could have killed me. I only bumped into him on the way to the toilets, then him and his arsehole mates decided to fill me in."

"Are you referring to a Mr Stockton, Mr Bance and Mr Wittingham – the security staff?" Cantly looked at his notes as he read out the names of the three bouncers.

Mikey shrugged in response. "Sorry … yes … I remember one was called Ben and the other Delboy, or something. I never saw a third fella." Jones scribbled hurriedly as Mikey spoke.

"Delroy Bance," Cantly corrected. "You didn't see Calum Wittingham?"

"There were lots of them, but only two grabbed me. Look at my face, for God's sake – they did this. He pinched my lip, punched me in the ribs and threw me against a wall, where I got this." Mikey pointed at a lump on the side of his head. "They were going to throw me down the stairs before I tripped them up and we all fell into a pile on the floor. If it wasn't for Jake, I'd be dead, I reckon."

"Is that right? Shocking! What did Jake do, Mike? May I call you Mike?" Cantly's bedside manner was well practised.

"Sure. And it's Mikey. I don't know exactly, I was unconscious. I know they didn't get the chance to finish the job as Jake stepped in and stopped them."

"After Jake stopped them, what happened next?"

"I've no idea. Jake said he had to go to the police station to speak to you guys about the fight. It wasn't his fault, he was just protecting me from those lunatics."

"So, Jake beat up the bouncers, to protect you?" Jones chipped in, earning himself a subtle kick to the shins from Cantly.

"No, he didn't hit them or anything. I think he tripped one up and the other punched a door and broke his hand. The guy who fell down the stairs was an idiot. He ran at Jake and when he ducked out of his way, he took a nosedive."

Mikey was feeling good about putting the record straight. They needed to hear what happened and how Jake had saved his life.

"Anyway, they picked on the wrong guy with Jake. He might be small, but he's lightning fast with his hands. You don't become a fourth dan in mixed martial arts for nothing."

"Is that right? I do mixed martial arts fighting myself," Cantly lied. "Where does Jake train? I'm interested to know."

"Matsumoto's Mixed Martial Arts Centre in Camden. He teaches there too. You should go in," Mikey told him proudly.

"After the scuffle in the corridor where you got the bump on your head, what happened then, where did you go?" Cantly's friendly tone had Mikey singing like a canary.

"I don't remember anything else until I woke up the next morning in Alexa's house." Mikey regretted saying her name the second it came out of his mouth.

"Alexa? Who's that, your girlfriend?" Jones wrote frantically without lifting his head.

"No, just a friend." Mikey prayed they wouldn't ask for her address.

"We'll need her contact details, Mr Stott. She could be a witness." Jones held his pen at the ready while Mikey reluctantly dug the information out of his phone.

Cantly read back Mikey's account. He spun the witness statement around and handed it to Mikey to sign on each page, which he did.

"Well, that's about it for now, Mr Stott. Thank you for your co-operation." Cantly's formality returned even before the ink had dried on the paper. "We may have a few more follow-up questions."

"OK. Call me on my mobile and I'll come to the station. I don't want you coming here again – my boss is a pain in the arse." The officers said nothing in reply, offering no sympathy.

"Are you going to make an arrest then? Will I need to attend court or something?" Mikey suddenly wanted the whole thing to go away.

Cantly looked at Mikey with cold intent. "It's a serious matter. We have an obligation to protect people against violent individuals. Are you aware that Mr Stockton may never walk again? That Mr Bance's leg is in plaster up to his knee and he will spend twelve weeks out of work? And Mr Wittingham is this afternoon booked in for reconstructive surgery on his shattered hand and wrist? He also has inflamed testicles. Jake Webster was solely responsible for those injuries and must account for his actions. We will apply the full force of the law to see that justice is served. You yourself witnessed Mr Webster tripping one of the men and throwing another down the stairs. Mr Webster will likely face criminal charges, yes."

"Wait, what do you mean you're gonna charge Jake? You can't! What about the bouncers? They were the ones who started it. I told you he was trying to protect *me* from *them* – he's done nothing wrong. You can't do that." The panic was rising in Mikey's voice. He realised all too late he'd been played.

"We'll be in touch," Jones said, walking out of the door.

***

Lisa was stood at the side of the pool pulling her arms in a front crawl motion and encouraging her gaggle of pensioners to wade through the hip-deep water.

Over the sound system, *The Proclaimers* were doing their best to motivate the group of octogenarians, some of whom looked like they'd actually walked five hundred miles that morning.

"Mikey, tell her to stop! We need a beer!" yelled Alfred, one of the fitter gentlemen swimmers – and a total charmer.

"I'll see you in the bar, Alf. Your round," Mikey replied, and the other swimmers all cheered as Alfred's swagger disappeared.

Mikey turned to Lisa. "How'd the Thunderbirds class go? Did you manage on your own?"

The Thunderbirds were a class of Down's syndrome adults, aged eighteen to thirty-five, and more than a handful for one supervisor. Mikey had named each class after a superhero and given the swimmers a nickname of their choice, which many went so far as to have embroidered onto their swimsuits and caps.

"They were fine. Susan cried when she found out you weren't here. Jules gave her a hug and she was OK after that. Arthur was sick in the changing rooms, again. I thought he was going to keel over at one point. It's not the first time he's done that." Genuine worry etched on her face.

"I'll have a chat with him."

"Big G supervised the men getting changed and cleaned up the puke. Arthur said he put too much sugar on his Weetabix. I called his grandma, and she came to pick him up."

Lisa smiled gently at Mikey. "Are you OK, sweetie? Do you want to talk about the meeting?"

"I'm fine, darling, and don't worry about that fat bastard, I'm sure he's just flexing his muscles. He's a complete wanker – there's no way we aren't making money. It's packed in here morning, noon and night."

Mikey was certain Euan was pulling their chain about staff redundancies, but he couldn't fathom why, other than because he was a total power-hungry arsehole.

"Do you want to do lunch with me and Carla? We can chat about it. I'll be finished here soon." Lisa wrapped her arm around his waist and pulled him against her.

Before Mikey could let her down, Alfred trundled by. "Hello, hello, what's all this?"

"Mind your own business, you nosey old sod." Lisa directed her insult in Alf's direction, who grinned his graveyard smile in return.

"I'm meeting Joy. You're welcome to join us, if you like."

"Thanks, Mikey, but three's a crowd, eh?" she said with a warm smile.

Bell and Sandringham Legal, Farringdon, London: 29 August 2021

"Report." Bell snapped his one-word welcome.

"Stockton's at Lexington Health, and out of sight."

"Did he make it convincing? Did he use the pig's eye like I asked?"

"He did. He was wailing like a banshee apparently. The ambulance took him to A&E and Choudary had him turned around at the door."

"Good. Get him to the safe house as quickly as possible and make sure he stays put. Get Doda to remind him. We can't have the idiot wandering about."

"There were some slight complications – the mark wasn't the target in the end. His friend stepped in. Made a mess of two of the bouncers – they were badly injured. Stockton's covered in bruises too."

"Who cares? Bruises are good. Make sure Choudary takes plenty of photos. Let's see if we can't get this turned around nice and quick, shall we? The sooner the guy's convicted, the faster the insurers will pay out. We need the other two bouncers out of the picture. It'll only complicate matters. Send Doda to shut them up."

He hung up and lit another cigar.

Fulwood Sports Centre, Kentish Town, London: 29 August 2021

The Fulwood Sports complex occupied a sprawling but imposing red-brick building on the Camden Road. Originally a public swimming baths, it had been modernised and extended. Its four swimming pools, basketball arena, tennis and squash courts and spa surrounded a central core housing the gymnasium, meeting rooms and restaurant.

Bannister's was a trendy, well-appointed restaurant located on the top floor. It had become the epicentre of the complex, with viewing galleries, a roof garden, breakout areas, an award-winning internet café and a coffee shop that sold the best pastries in London, according to Joanne.

Mikey launched himself up the narrow staircase three steps at a time; he didn't want to be late for Joy. Bannister's reminded Mikey of The Collingwood Arms, with its vaulted brick ceilings, tiled floors and bare walls adorned with pictures of British athletes from bygone days.

He reached the entrance and held the door open for a couple of elderly ladies.

"Thank you, ladies. See you both soon," he said with a smile.

"Ooh, you remind me of a young Errol Flynn," one of them said with a glint in her eye.

"That's very kind of you," Mikey responded, having no clue who they were referring to.

Joy was sitting alone in the back corner out of the way of prying eyes. He diverted to the serving area and leaned over the counter. "Hey, Jo, please may I have an egg, couscous and quinoa salad with no dressing, and a dark roast Colombian with hot milk?"

"Your date has already ordered for you both. I'll bring it over in a minute." Joanne gave him a sly grin and nodded in Joy's direction. "You can't hide in this place, Mikey," she said grinning.

Mikey was left speechless. He turned on his heels and made his way over to Joy.

"Hey, sweetheart. Did you order my lunch?"

"I did," she replied with a nod.

"How did you know what I was going to have?" He bent down and kissed her on her cheek. The slight aroma of cleaning fluid remained, but she had applied vanilla-flavoured lip gloss, which he approved of.

"Hmm, let me think." Joy placed her finger against her chin in faux thought. "You often go vegetarian on a Monday, after a heavy weekend. The couscous usually gets sold out quickly, so I knew you'd want that if it was available. Right?"

"Go on," Mikey said suspiciously.

"You have egg with everything. I thought I'd put quinoa on it as I've seen you eat that before. You never eat salad dressing. I ordered the same." She winked and shot him with her finger gun, mimicking his own cheesy signature.

There was a very short list of people who genuinely intrigued Mikey, to the point where he thought about them when they weren't there, wondered what they were doing and wished they were with him. Joy Wong was in that illustrious company, and he'd been thinking about her a lot. The irony was, even after knowing her for over two years, he knew very little about her, which just added to the mystery.

He'd often wondered why he hadn't asked her out, telling himself when the time was right, he would. But he knew why – he didn't want her to say no. So, if he never asked, she never would. It puzzled him why his charm and confidence evaporated in her presence and were replaced by a genuine warmth and appreciation – a respect perhaps – which held him back from what he'd craved the day he'd met her.

"Hmm, you can read me like a book. I may need to vary my eating habits in future … keep you on your toes."

Joy giggled in return. "Not really. I asked Jo what you'd have – I just made the rest up."

He was clearly being double teamed and didn't mind one bit.

Joy looked at his battered face, still handsome beneath the abrasions and swelling, but there was more, something deep down inside, that gave him a look of vulnerability. She had studied him a lot, pleading silently with him, asking what he was thinking when he thought no one was watching. Such sadness – as if he was lost.

A slither of fury cut through her at the thought of the men who had harmed him. Her anger pivoted into fear and dread, like how she worried about Jules. Her face hollowed out thinking of what could have happened to Mikey, or what might happen to Jules.

"I worry for you, Mikey. I hate the thought of you being hurt." She looked away, betraying her true feelings for him, which she hadn't yet accepted herself. She took a well-disguised deep breath while clenching her jaw. Her bottom lip quivered for a fraction of a second.

"Hey, hey, don't be silly, we'll have none of that. I'm OK, just a few scratches and a bump on the head, that's all. It's no big deal. Don't be upset – you'll set me off. I'll be crying like a baby in a minute."

He reached across and held her hand. He didn't care who saw him. Her strong fingers laced through his. He glanced down at their hands entwined and felt a twinge in his stomach.

"I'm glad I've got you and Jules on my team, though. With your telepathic powers of deduction and Jules's ability to stop people crying with one cuddle, I can't go wrong." His gentle touch and his goofy humour hit the mark, and Joy's smile returned.

Joanne broke the tension by walking over with their meals. Mikey held onto Joy's hand as she set the plates of food on the table, not willing to let go – a defiant statement of intent. He was pleased she hadn't pulled away.

"I hope you are hungry, the pair of you," Joanne said cheerily.

"Thanks, Jo," they both said in harmony, shaking out their napkins like synchronised magicians.

Despite having no appetite, Mikey emptied the plate of food into his stomach, while he replayed the events of Friday night, the 4M and the interview with the police. Joy barely made a dent in hers.

"So, what did your friend say? Is he OK with what you said to the police?" Joy's question confirmed Mikey's own fear that he had inadvertently made things worse.

"He had his solicitor call me and she said I'd done the right thing and not to worry. The police would have found out about Jake being a black belt anyway, so better they find out now than later. She suspected they'd charge him based on the severity of the injuries to the bouncers."

"You know it's not your fault, Mikey. Those guys were clearly out to get you. Your friend Jake sounds like he can handle himself." Joy imagined a huge, burly bodyguard, like Big G, standing next to Mikey wherever they went, making sure no harm came to him.

Mikey shrugged his shoulders and shook his head. He had played out the ending to this nightmare many times, and each time he saw Jake in jail, dealing with a whole new world of nasty bastards.

"I don't understand why they didn't arrest you as well?" Joy continued with her on point questions. She didn't miss a trick.

"Alexa, a girl I know, saw what had happened and pulled me out of there." He tried to sound as casual as he could, hoping her line of questioning would stop. Fat chance of that.

"She took you home? That was nice of her to look after you."

Mikey heard the disappointment in her voice. "She's not my girlfriend or anything, we're just friends. I know her from the pub. She carried me up three flights of stairs on her back and put me to bed with a bucket beside me. I wasn't a pretty sight. I owe her a lot. I'm not sure I would've made it on my own." Mikey looked at Joy, who had a puzzled expression.

"She carried you up the stairs? She must be a strong girl." Joy had done the math.

"She is," Mikey said, puffing out his cheeks.

After a minute of awkward silence, Joy spoke up. "I want you to promise me you will look after yourself, Mikey. Try and stay away from these people who want to hurt you." She looked earnestly at Mikey, cutting through his bravado. "You could have been killed by those thugs. Don't go there again. Please tell me you'll stay away from there?"

"I will, darling, don't worry." His response was not dismissive or casual – he spoke softly and meant it. He didn't like being the source of worry for her; she had enough on her plate.

"Listen, Mikey, I'm away for a week from this weekend. I need you to look after Jules for me when he's here. Will you do that? He misses me and can be a bit of a handful at home for my mum. Just chat with him and ask him questions, will you? He worships the ground you walk on. He thinks you're a superhero. Please don't tell him about those guys who hit you, though – he'll have nightmares. Huh, I'm going to have nightmares myself."

"Of course I will, sweetheart. I'll check which days he's at the gym or taking swim lessons and we can go for a Coke or something. Don't worry about it, I'll look after him and Arthur. Tell you what, send me his number and I'll keep in touch with him – how about that? I'll send him texts to keep him company. Tell your mam I'm here if she needs anything – shopping, errands, whatever, OK? I run past your house anyway. It wouldn't take me five minutes to nip to the shops." Mikey's banged-up face shone through all the bruises.

"Thanks, Mikey, I appreciate that. You have no idea how busy things get for me."

Her happy eyes vanished as a familiar but unwelcome figure appeared behind Mikey.

"Well, well, this looks all cosy, doesn't it?"

Euan looked down on them, a large polystyrene takeout box propped on top of his belly. Neither Joy nor Mikey felt the need to answer him.

"You need to come to my office and explain your outburst in the 4M, young man. And while you're at it, you can fill me in on why the police are swarming all over my sports centre. It's not good for business. You should know better than to bring your personal life into work."

Euan's stomach heaved up and down, his shirt buttonholes dilating under the cyclical load.

"No problem, Mr McArdle. Is 2pm OK? I've a class at 1pm." Mikey wanted to tell the man to go fuck himself, but swearing's for the ignorant, according to his grandma Beryl, so he put on his happy face and agreed to his demand.

"Don't be late," Euan replied, curling his lip. He leered at Joy, who held his gaze, then he turned and left.

"I hate that man. He's a vile, disgusting pig. He makes me want to be sick."

"Welcome to the club," Mikey agreed. "I'd better get back to work, Joy. Send me Jules's number, will you, and thanks for my lunch." Mikey's phone pinged and buzzed in his tracksuit bottoms as he got to his feet.

"You're welcome," she said, standing up. "Don't run past my house next time. Come in and I'll make you some Thai green tea. You'll love it."

She placed her hand on Mikey's hip and reached up on her tiptoes to kiss him gently on the side of the mouth, where his lip was swollen. She held it for half a second longer than was necessary, leaving a translucent salve of vanilla in her wake.

That's a keeper, Mikey thought, as a shiver ran down his spine and into his trousers.

As she walked away, he realised they had sat together for an hour, and he still knew nothing of her life. *Where was she going next week?* He hadn't asked, and she hadn't said. She had picked up on everything he'd said, asked questions and given feedback, but he'd asked her nothing about herself. Her concern for his welfare had touched him. Why hadn't he asked her about her problems, especially Jules. *What an ignorant bastard!* He'd squeezed her hand, and she'd held on in full view of everyone. *What did that mean? Why was he such a putz around her?* He felt like a self-absorbed twat.

One thing he did notice was her abhorrence of Euan. Understandable, he thought, although it seemed more than that. Horrible visions swam through his mind. *Had the odious fucker done or said something?* He expelled the thoughts quickly before anger overwhelmed him.

He walked down the stairs slowly, deep in thought. He checked his phone and saw two texts from Joy: Jules's contact information and another message.

> Thank you again for a lovely lunch, pls look after yourself, I worry so much for you. Don't let that pig Euan bully you. I really appreciate you keeping an eye on Jules, he means the world to me. Here's a picture to remind you of me. See u in a couple of weeks. J. xx

Mikey opened the attachment to see a headshot of Joy laughing, holding a champagne flute. He stared at the image. *Man-o-man, she's pretty. I wonder what she was laughing at. I hope I get the chance to make her laugh like that one day.*

> Enjoy your trip. I'll look after Jules, and myself. See u soon. M. xx

8

LARRY THE PEN

De Freitus Wealth Management, The City of London: 2 September 2021

Rob leaned back in his office chair and groaned out a stretch. His watch beeped to tell him to get ready for the Vaults.

The news of Jake's arrest and Mikey being beaten up had left him kicking himself that he hadn't been around to help. He knew Mikey could be a handful when he got drunk and part of him was unsurprised to hear he had got into a fight with a bouncer.

He knew he wasn't to blame – Jake had told him that much – but trouble seemed to follow Mikey around sometimes. He hoped he would be on good behaviour tonight. He didn't want to give his father or Lauren any more ammunition; they made no secret of their disapproval of his friends. Lauren had only just started speaking again since storming off. The silence had been blissful.

Friday night had been some night, when all was said and done, and when Maddie eventually left, he felt on top of the world, like he could breathe again. He hadn't felt this level of excitement in a long time. He'd begun making plans, telling himself to keep calm and not jump the gun. *It's only one night, it doesn't mean anything.* But it did.

Maddie hadn't changed a bit – in the physical sense at least. It was like they had never been apart. She had slept with her face tucked into the crook of his neck while he'd spent hours kissing her head, stroking her back and breathing in her scent.

When she stirred, they had sex again without a word being spoken. While she dressed, he made her some toasted bagels with cream cheese and green tea to wash it down. She sat at his breakfast bar and demolished the food like she hadn't eaten in a week.

Their conversation had been neutral and unchallenging – no mention of her boyfriend, Jacob, or Lauren – no plans for meeting again – no commentary on what had just passed between them. They knew each other well enough by now. Don't ask questions that can't or won't be answered. He knew their night wasn't a one-off. She seemed to have a sense of purpose and longing. Her angst and aggression had gone; she now had a focus and an air of confidence about her, perhaps even a vulnerability that she was somehow shielding. He loved it, whatever it was.

'Speak soon,' she had said, and left.

Since that morning, he had checked his phone what felt like several hundred times, hoping she would text or call. She hadn't.

It's no big deal. She's busy, doing her own thing. He kidded himself he wasn't bothered.

He thought about spilling the beans to Jake and Mikey. He wondered what he would tell them when they asked – and they were bound to ask. He'd cross that bridge when he got to it – when he and Maddie got back together, because surely that was going to happen.

What will my father say? He laughed out loud questioning himself as to why he would give a fuck. After years of trying to please him, there was nothing he could do to meet his expectations – so much so, he quite enjoyed annoying the man, up to a point.

Rob had made his career choice solely because his father demanded he follow in his footsteps as the heir to the De Freitus estate, and not waste his time working in art and design. Maddie had loved his creative side and how bright he was, his ability to speak several languages, his modesty and above all his talent.

He'd sketched her portrait a hundred times. Each time, he'd captured her spirit to perfection. He knew her better than anyone. It was telling that never once had he drawn his father, or Lauren for that matter, and neither had asked him to.

As much as Maddie loved him back then, she despised him for kowtowing to Roger's demands. 'If you had an ounce of integrity, you'd tell him to go fuck himself.' She'd raged that he'd sold his soul for the sake of money.

It hadn't escaped him that Maddie now appeared enthralled by the opulence of his penthouse apartment and how well he had done for himself. Her interest in his creative side seemed to have waned. He knew working for De Freitus Wealth Management was a sell-out, but there was no going back. What choice did he have? Besides, he was quite good at it, and if Maddie liked it now, then all the better.

In the last eighteen months he'd secured dozens of lucrative accounts with some incredibly wealthy people. 'Money talks' one client had told him, and it did. His clients' recommendations had brought in even more eager, greedy millionaires to gorge in the trough. No one was more surprised by Rob's success than Roger himself.

Some may have mistaken his father's lack of acknowledgement for reluctant parental pride, or not allowing Rob to get 'too big for his boots'. Not Rob. He had seen his father's reaction to his achievements all his life. He knew it for what it was: utter resentment. When Rob had joined the company Roger had assigned his fresh-faced graduate prodigy to Lawrence Smalling, also known as Larry the Pen, on account of his habit of twizzling his biro between his index finger and thumb like a mini baton in a marching band. Larry led the Europe business unit responsible for venture capital trusts and investments. He didn't have high hopes for his apprentice at the beginning, having heard Roger's character assassination, which at first glance was reasonably accurate. Larry quickly realised Rob had only one way of operating – his way.

Larry had a wicked sense of humour and was not averse to a practical joke or two. He'd once asked an Icelandic friend of his to call in and ask about investment plans, suggesting to Rob that he should learn Icelandic to make the guy 'feel more at home'. He'd asked his friend to introduce himself as Antti Hystaamen.

Much to Larry's annoyance, causing the joke to fall flat, Rob held a basic conversation with him in Icelandic, having studied at home online for a couple of weeks.

"It's just the same as German really, with more inflections," Rob had said at the time.

Rob's first serious appointment was on the currency exchange desk, then he spent a furlough in Paris for six months working an exchange for a competitor business. On his return, he went into mergers and acquisitions and in recent years he'd joined the private wealth management team, which Larry ran himself. Throughout his time, Larry had guided and nurtured 'the boy', who had now become 'the man', and it was safe to say they had become great friends. He dreaded the day when Rob would eventually decide that he'd had enough. Perversely, he hoped he would, for his own sake.

Rob changed into his freshly laundered, navy blue Armani suit and began looking forward to the evening ahead. It was rare he spent time with his mother, and to have Larry, Jake and Mikey in the same room was going to be fun.

His phone vibrated into life in his pocket. Rob's face lit up as he read the message.

> Hey, not heard from you. Hope everything is OK. Maddie. X

"What are you smirking at? You on a promise?" Larry marched into his office without knocking and interrupted Rob's delight.

"Come on, or we're going to be late, and I need a couple of Guinnesses before we start. I hate these dos," Larry said.

Rob tucked his phone away. He'd respond later. He jumped to his feet and threw his arm around his boss. "Come on, Larry, it's my round."

Vaults Bistro Bar, Aldgate, London: 2 September 2021

Mikey stood at the bar, glad to get through what had been a tough week. Only one day to go before they could seriously wind down for the weekend and enjoy real north-eastern hospitality at the Highfield Cabbage Club.

"How's the face, mate?" Jake scanned Mikey's head and jaw for damage. His bruises were at the late stages of yellowing and the swelling around his eyes had all but gone. The scratches below his nose had scabbed up and peeled off, leaving two faint pink strips.

"I'll be fine. I've had far worse from rugby," Mikey said, clinking his pint of lager against Jake's G&T.

"Where's Fruit? He told me to be here at 7pm. He'll be late for his own funeral."

"The party's in the roof garden upstairs. He might be already up there." Jake tried to sound upbeat. "What's up, Mikey, you don't seem yourself? Is work all right?"

"That fat fuck, Euan, reckons we need to cut back on staff. I can't believe it. We're understaffed as it is. I do all the rotas and I'm covering shifts left, right and centre. If we had anybody go sick, we'd be screwed, now he's talking about cuts," Mikey blurted in a thirty second rant.

"Thing is, Mikey, if I were to listen to anyone at your place, it wouldn't be him – it would be you. You are the true driving force there. You are the one responsible for its success, and everyone at Head Office knows it."

"I hope you're right, mate. Anyway, less about my shit, what about you? I hope I didn't say anything wrong to the police the other day?" Mikey asked.

Jake had worked hard all week to banish negative thoughts and get on with his routine. Shin Matsumoto had been interviewed by the same officers and given them a similar backstory; he knew he was in trouble.

Jake gave a wistful smile. "Don't worry, mate. I've heard nothing yet. Come on, let's see if we can find our host."

They jogged up the modern checker-plated, metal staircase to the roof garden, where they were met by Lauren, who failed miserably in her role at offering a warm welcome.

"Hey, Lauren. You look lovely as always. Is Fruit here?" Mikey angled forward to peck her on the cheek.

"Don't!" she snapped impatiently, holding a manicured hand up to Mikey's puckered face. "You'll smudge my make-up again. And no, he's not here yet. He'll be with Larry somewhere getting pissed."

She was determined not to accept their olive branch, not that they needed to feel contrite – she was the one who flounced off. Neither was in the mood to beg for forgiveness, so they shrugged and walked past her.

The rooftop garden bar was perched at the rear of the four-storey Georgian terrace pub in a glorious suntrap surrounded by high-rise office blocks. It was spacious and well appointed with wicker sofas covered with sheepskin throws to help warm the bones of those less hardy to the summer breeze. Broadleaf yucca plants, hanging baskets and vines of honeysuckle bordered the perimeter, producing a sweet aroma that disguised the acrid smell of exhaust fumes from the never-ending pulse of traffic below.

Mikey strode onto the patio and began welcoming strangers, shaking hands, and introducing himself as if they were expected to know who he and Jake were. He saw Linda De Freitus, Rob's mother, standing sipping her drink, looking amused by a flamboyant-looking fifty-something couple wearing an all-white linen suit and matching dress.

"Hey Linda, how ya doin', pet?"

Linda loved Mikey's northern twang and he didn't disappoint by hamming it up. She excused herself from her company briefly and threw her arms around the boys. "Aww, hello my beautiful boys, I've missed you guys so much. How long has it been since I saw you both?" Linda's shoulder-length, blonde bob caught the wind and covered their faces as she hugged them.

"Where's Robin? That boy is such a sloth, isn't he?" As much as she loved her son dearly, Linda did not spare the rod for him. His lack of punctuality grated on her, as it did Roger, who, irritatingly, was even worse at keeping time.

Mikey uncovered his face from her sweet-smelling hair that had stuck to his stubbly jaw. "You know what he's like. He'd be late for his own funeral."

"Let me introduce you to some of our guests. You'll like these people – he's French and she's Italian. Watch she doesn't take a bite out of you." Linda slid between them and hooked her arms through theirs.

"Pierre, Marcella, this is Mikey and Jake. They are good friends of Robin." Linda stepped back and stole two glasses of champagne from a passing waitress, while they all shook hands.

"Bonjour. You can call me Monty. Everyone does," Pierre said.

"Monty and Marcella are close friends with Larry. They own art galleries in Paris and Rome and are looking to invest with DWM."

"Well, I don't blame you both. We've done very well, haven't we, Jake?" Mikey didn't give Jake a chance to join in the conversation, allowing him only a brief nod of agreement.

"Rob has worked miracles for us," Mikey said, nodding emphatically.

Marcella, who could easily have been mistaken for Sophia Loren's long-lost twin sister, listened attentively with her eyes half closed, struggling gamely to understand his Geordie accent.

She blew thick, cherry-flavoured smoke into the air, which trailed into Jake's face, unconcerned by the pollution she was creating around her. She then dropped the butt into an empty glass, having made no attempt to find an ashtray. Her mastery in the art of not giving a toss was in abundance.

The laid-back laissez-faire French way of life would suit Rob down to the ground, Jake thought absentmindedly, while breathing in the fruity secondary effects of Marcella's cigarillo.

Once Monty and Mikey's conversation had ebbed, Marcella turned to Jake. "How long have you guys been together?"

She'd made an erroneous inference from Mikey's comments and Jake's body language, much to Jake's amusement and Mikey's horror.

"We're just good friends, Marcella. We aren't gay, are we, Mikey?" Jake explained, grinning at Mikey spluttering, while receiving a confused and far from apologetic look from the tall Italian aesthete, who was unaccustomed to reading situations wrong.

"Hell no!" Mikey exclaimed.

She sniffed at Monty holding her two fingers in his direction, prompting him to reach into his jacket pocket to flip open a battered old pewter cigarette case. Marcella slipped another cigarillo out from behind the elastic strap that held them in place. She swished her thick, black hair away from her face and inhaled the flame ready and waiting in Monty's hand. It was a rehearsed action, not one of a subservient husband – Monty was far from henpecked. Their simple nonverbal cooperation was a display of mutual trust and faith.

Mikey stared at Marcella in fascination, like he was looking at someone famous and out of place. He grinned like an idiot. He was a sucker for a beautiful woman, and Marcella was certainly that. She flicked her eyebrows in reply to him glowering at her – perhaps a warning, as if at any point she would maul him to death.

"Where do you guys live? In Paris? I'd love to go there," Mikey said.

"Ah oui, Paris – Montmartre. Do you know it?" Monty's reply was warm and enthusiastic, if not a little rhetorical. He had a feeling the young handsome Englishman openly admiring his wife hadn't travelled too far from home.

"Isn't that where they have street artists and a huge church – Le Sacré-Coeur, isn't it?"

An image of Joy leapt into Mikey's head, of her dancing and laughing with her glass of champagne, skipping and blowing him a kiss against the backdrop of the Eiffel Tower, her huge brown eyes full of excitement.

"Bravo, Mikey," Marcella said. It was rare for an Englishman to impress her, but this one had. They were in for an interesting evening. "You must visit us. We will show you the heart of Paris, hein?! And now you aren't gay, you must bring your girlfriend with you."

Marcella's deadpan humour made both Jake and Mikey burst into laughter. "You're a knockout, Marcella," Mikey said, grinning from ear to ear. "I don't have a girlfriend, by the way." Mikey gave her a wide-eyed look and winked in Monty's direction, to reassure him he was just playing along.

"No, no, no!" She waved her hand in protest in front of his face, leaving a meandering trail of smoke behind. "I think there is someone special in your life, hein – I see love in your eyes. I think there is a very lucky girl out there, Monty, n'est-ce pas?"

Monty slowly nodded in agreement.

"You think about her a lot, I think so, hein?" Marcella's tone hardened a little and she tried to fix her eyes on Mikey, who looked sheepish and embarrassed. "Yes, you are very much in love. Perhaps she doesn't know it yet, hein? You have not been so brave." Marcella turned to look in Linda's direction; a curious look on her face confirmed she was right.

"Well, well … this is a turn-up for the books. Is there anything we should know, Mikey?" Jake's contribution to the conversation only worsened his discomfort.

"What's this, the Italian Inquisition?" Mikey scowled playfully at Marcella in a plea to spare him any further interrogation.

Monty laughed out loud and wrapped an arm around him. "Love happens to us all one day. Don't fight it, my handsome

English friend, or it will fly away. And you never know, you may find yourself a wife like mine." He nodded in Marcella's direction.

Marcella leaned forward, kissed Mikey on the cheek and whispered into his ear, "Si sei fortunato."

"If you're lucky," Monty said, by way of translation.

***

Larry and Rob arrived, accompanied by Lauren draped over Rob's elbow.

"Hello Linda, so lovely to see you," Lauren said without sincerity. Her parental loyalty lay strictly with Roger.

Larry made the introductions. "I see you have met Rob's friends. This is Robin De Freitus, the finest wealth manager at DWM. Monty and Marcella Montreaux."

"Bonjour Monty et Marcella, c'est un plaisir de vous rencontrer tous les deux. J'ai tellement entendu parler de vos galeries. J'aimerais savoir quelles expositions vous avez en ce moment." Rob's welcome and small talk about their art exhibitions had the effect he'd hoped for.

Monty struggled to hide his pleasure hearing an Englishman speak so fluently. Marcella inhaled her cigarillo while eyeing Rob with suspicion..

"Sì, lo sappiamo, e sarai il benvenuto quando verrai a Parigi. Conosci molti artisti francesi specializzati in arte moderna?" Marcella spoke quickly in Italian, asking him if he knew many French modern artists. She held his gaze, wondering how he would respond.

After a few seconds, Rob blinked and said, "Amo il lavoro di Laurence Perratzi. Infatti l'ho incontrato alla London Art Fair due anni fa. Ho due dei suoi pezzi a casa mia." Rob told her he loved Laurence Perratzi's artwork and that he had two of his pieces. He added that they met at the London Art Fair two years ago.

Marcella gave Rob the slightest of nods. He'd passed her test, she raised her glass. "Touché."

Larry unhooked Lauren a little more forcibly than she appreciated and led her back towards Roger De Freitus, who was talking to some old, austere-looking gentlemen near the entrance. She would cramp Rob's style, so he wanted her out of the way.

"Thanks for coming over to visit us, Monty. I hope you like what you see." Rob turned to English to avoid looking like a smartass.

"You have some very interesting friends, Rob. You can learn a lot about a man from the company he keeps. Mikey and Jake are very amusing, no?" Marcella bulldozed her way into the conversation, while curling a lip in Lauren's direction as she was shuffled away by Larry.

Rob concentrated on the positive and gave the pair the shortened version of their back story. "I bring them along so that there's at least two normal people in the room. Present company excepted, of course."

"Lauren is a pretty girl. How long have you been together?" Marcella saw Rob's features flatten, just as she had anticipated. She knew love, and there was none between them – she was sure of that.

"Six months or so. She works for my father." Rob's tone deepened slightly as he said his name out loud.

Marcella had met the loathsome Roger De Freitus thirty minutes earlier when he was strolling around shaking hands and waving like he was royalty. He had his arm wrapped around his PA's back just above her backside. She saw the way he leant into every woman he met to kiss them, touching them with his soft fleshy hands.

"Oh, hello Pierre. Larry has told me so much about you. So pleased you could make it. Is this your lovely wife?" Roger had drawled.

Marcella had backed away from him, blowing smoke between them as a kind of forcefield against his lurid advances.

"Very pleased to meet you, Mariella," Roger had said, barely noticing her after his rebuttal and turning his head as if to move on.

Marcella had seethed over being introduced as a wife – and then the oaf couldn't even remember her name.

"Le tue mani vaganti mi fanno ammalare. Sei un porco sudicio." Marcella had told him his wandering hands made her feel sick and he was a filthy pig. She had no way of knowing whether Roger spoke Italian, but she couldn't care less.

"Ahh, Italian, how nice. Please enjoy yourselves." Roger then strolled off oblivious.

Changing the subject from Lauren, Rob said, "I worked in Paris for nine months. I loved it – I would move there in an instant if I could. There are so many galleries and so much to see. I love art and art history. I wanted to study it at university, until my father suggested I 'follow in his footsteps'." Rob curled his lip involuntarily.

"You can do whatever you want, Rob. You are a young man with the world at his feet, hein?" Monty was showing genuine interest in Larry's protégé and got the feeling they would know each other for a very long time to come.

"Thanks, Monty. I'm committed to DWM now – besides, I get to meet interesting people like you guys." Rob smiled amiably and clinked glasses.

The conversation continued and they talked at length about emerging artists, contemporary impressionism and old school avant-garde. The more they spoke, the more the Montreaux knew they had made the right decision listening to Larry, despite Marcella's ambivalence towards Roger De Freitus.

Rob scabbed a smoke from Monty, and they began to look at their diaries to arrange a visit to Paris. His mind raced. A fact-finding mission was on the cards for sure. He'd have to fend Larry off if he was to take Maddie with him. She could visit her headquarters for the weekend. *This could work*, he told himself. Rob's concentration drifted he was so consumed by the prospect of it all, when, as if by magic, the reason for his dreamlike state reappeared.

"Fancy meeting you here!" Maddie said, stirring the ice in her empty glass. "Aren't you going to introduce us to your friends?"

Rob stood transfixed for the second time in a week. "Hey, wow, erm," he stuttered. "I didn't know you were coming tonight." Rob threw his arms around her and kissed her on the cheek.

"This is Monty and Marcella Montreaux from Paris. Kim and Maddie Parker from … London." Rob tagged on the geographical reference with a nervous laugh. "Kim works for DWM as an analyst and Maddie is a medic working for Doctors in Africa."

She wasn't a doctor as such, but Rob found it easier to describe her that way rather than disclose what she was utterly unqualified to do but did anyway.

"Enchanté." Monty bowed slightly and shook hands with them both. Marcella gave a slight nod while smoke drizzled from her nostrils. "Let me get you a drink, ladies." Monty decided he would be host for a change and walked off to find some champagne.

"Not for me, thank you," Maddie called out to Monty as he turned to leave.

"So, Maddie, I assume you and Rob know each other well, hein?" Marcella didn't miss a thing. Rob was on high alert, wondering what his face was giving away and praying Lauren wouldn't walk over.

"Yes, we went out together for a few years. When I went to Africa, we decided to give each other some room. We were only young, and well, you know how it is. We'll always be close friends, though, won't we, Rob?" Maddie spoke confidently in contrast to Rob's stammering.

"Oh, yes, absolutely." He didn't like the sound of being just friends and felt a little deflated, then reminded himself it was her way of being neutral. His blushes were spared when he heard Larry shout his name from a large booth where he was sitting with Antti Hystaamen.

"I'll just be a moment." Rob left the group, happy to be cut some slack.

Linda had also left to mingle, and Kim was looking around taking in the atmosphere.

Marcella spoke in French to Maddie, assuming she could speak the language on account of her working for a French-based NGO. "So, when is the baby due, Maddie?"

Maddie's healthy glow deepened into a full-on crimson blush. Her blood ran cold, and her eyes widened in panic. She averted Marcella's gaze, flicking her eyes at her mother momentarily to see if she understood what Marcella had just said. She didn't. She stood planted to the spot, rigid with indecision.

"I was twenty-one when I had my first child. I stopped smoking and drinking as well. I had a beautiful rosy complexion, just like yours. I'd hold my stomach for comfort just like you are doing now. I felt ill all the time, a little lost and very frightened – just like you are, no?" Marcella paused for a response that didn't come.

Maddie's huge brown eyes burrowed into Marcella's, imploring her to stop talking.

Marcella reached out and held her hand. "It is a wonderful time of your life. You must enjoy every minute," she said softly and with compassion.

"I was just asking Maddie if she works in Paris sometimes." Marcella returned to English once Rob returned.

"Yes, er, I, I do." Maddie finally found her voice. She seemed weak and confused for a moment before smiling broadly.

"Well, you must come and visit us too. Perhaps come with Rob – I'm sure he wouldn't mind." Marcella raised her eyebrows in his direction. From his reaction, she concluded he didn't know of Maddie's condition. And she was not going to be the one to tell him.

"Well, er, yes, that would be … nice." A dentist would have pulled his teeth out quicker.

When Maddie finally decided to go to the ladies room, Rob followed her as tactfully as he could. He hung around the toilet door for a few minutes, talking to a few people at random, and then intercepted her as she made her way back towards the group.

"Hey, darling, are you OK? I was worried about you there." He fought the urge to cuddle her and looked around furtively.

"Yeah, I'm fine," she lied.

"That trip to Paris sounds like fun, eh?" Rob put in a tentative bid to see what Maddie's reaction would be.

Maddie smiled up at him. "It does. Would you take me if I asked you? Wouldn't Lauren mind?" Maddie knew the answer to her first question and immediately wished she hadn't asked the follow-on.

"I guess we'd both have to keep it to ourselves, wouldn't we?" Rob looked down at his shoes awkwardly.

After a long moment of silence, Maddie reached out to take Rob's hand. "Let's meet for a coffee next week and chat about it. I'm in the city for meetings on Thursday." The confidence was back in her voice.

"Sounds great," Rob said.

"We're going shortly as I don't feel so well. Let's say 1pm – maybe do lunch? Text me the details OK?"

She leaned forward and kissed him on the lips, holding it for a couple of seconds before making her way back to her mother. He had no time to object. Not that he ever did.

9

ODD BEDFELLOWS

Renoir's Café, Camden Road, London: 4 September 2021

Jake swiped through the turnstile at Camden overground station, took a left under the rusted blue railway bridge and headed to Mustafa's place.

George Horgan's 'belly-buster' breakfast was enough to stop an elephant. Rob voted against it this time, so Renoir's it was. No one argued.

They'd been to Mikey's home in Highfield twice before, both times for stag parties; the first in Sunderland and the last time in Newcastle. On both occasions, the night ended with Mikey vomiting over a random girl – one at a bus stop; the other in a nightclub.

Ironic, Jake thought. *The only time he was wholly innocent of any wrongdoing was at Fandango's and he nearly gets himself killed.*

Jake loved this part of London, especially in the morning when everyone was still finding their feet. The traffic noise was relentless, accompanied on percussion by a piling hammer from a nearby construction site.

He passed groups of men speaking loudly in a foreign language, their guttural accents unfamiliar to him – Sub-Saharan African or Middle Eastern perhaps; either way, they seemed happy to be alive.

He stopped at an isolated vegetable stall. He recognised only half of the oddly shaped food on display, most of which he wouldn't know how to cook. After asking a few questions about the produce, Jake thanked the vendor and swivelled to leave, not before seeing the crestfallen look on the young man's face, who had taken it as a good omen that he was making a sale even before he had laid out his wares. Jake retreated a step and bought half a dozen apples for the journey. Fair's fair.

A young Asian guy about twenty years old stretched his arms skywards and yawned out loud as he leaned against his stall of mobile phone accessories. He wore a creased beige thobe and white kufi skullcap. Morning prayers came a little early for this budding entrepreneur.

A short overweight girl of African descent, with impossibly long hair, had a similar set-up, selling hair products and offering braiding and weaving at £50 a head. *What else would you braid*? Jake wondered to himself. She smiled pleasantly at Jake as he strolled past, and he did the same. *It's nice to be nice.* Mikey's idiom had stuck in Jake's head. *That guy gets under your skin*, he thought, grinning to himself.

Jake's empty stomach complained at the neglect he had put it through, triggered by the smells emanating from numerous shops selling sweet pastries, bread, and even kebabs, cooked to recipes from Syria, Morocco, Lebanon and Egypt. The world map had been rewritten by restaurateurs and café owners from across the world now existing side by side, together in culinary harmony.

The country of choice for breakfast was not France, as the name Renoir's might infer, but Turkey. Mustafa Sharif had bought the place from a Pakistani guy called Abdul, who had changed it from Emilio's to Pandora's Palace. Mustafa had changed it to Renoir's – he'd never heard of a restaurant named after a woman before and thought it was odd. Equality had a little way to go before finding that corner of the Ottoman Empire.

He arrived ten minutes early to find Mustafa had placed a reserved sign on their regular table. He made himself comfortable, with his back to the wall. Several wasps crashed and buzzed angrily against the front window next to him, searching for a way through the impenetrable, invisible barrier imprisoning them. Jake took a menu and gently wafted them out. The doorbell pinged repeatedly each time an insect made a successful bid for freedom. He smiled inwardly as they zigzagged into the sky, never to be seen again.

"OK, OK, Jakey, give me one minute, my friend, I'll be with you," Mustafa yelled from behind the counter, mistaking Jake's insect altruism and the sound of his doorbell for his impatience to be served.

"No problem," Jake responded guiltily.

Mustafa returned hurriedly, balancing on his hairy forearm a tall glass teacup and saucer, a copper-clad cafetière of dark-brown tea, and a chunk of honeycomb leaking on a small plate.

"This is the best tea in Turkey," Mustafa confirmed as he poured. "You try!" Jake thanked him and reached for the cup.

"No, no, no – you must take the honey and drizzle it into the tea first. This will give you a lot of energy, huh?!" He bent his arm upwards at the elbow and winked lewdly.

To Jake's relief, Mikey burst through the door at the stroke of eight, with a rucksack over his shoulder.

"As-salamu alaykum!" Mikey threw out his arms to greet his host, who could easily be described as the furthest thing from a practising Muslim you could wish to find. Even though he was here only one week ago, Mikey embraced Mustafa, then held him at arm's length, as if he was his long-lost brother.

"Alaykumu s-salām, my friend. Take a seat and I'll bring you some coffee."

Mustafa walked away talking. His deep booming voice could be heard three streets away.

"Fruit text and said he'd be ten minutes late. He told me to order him his usual with a green tea."

Rob liked to dole out the orders and felt no sense of ever overreaching his authority. A life of luxury meant there were always people to run around after you. Neither Mikey nor Jake minded one bit – they were a team. Rob had arranged the train fares, a car at the station and the hotel on the Quayside. Or at least his secretary had.

Jake and Mikey ordered the food, keeping one eye on the clock to get to King's Cross in time for their train.

"Did you see who turned up for the party on Thursday?" Mikey's voice was edged with the irritation he only had when talking about Maddie Parker.

"Yeah, I saw her. She left early with her mother," Jake answered without interest.

"Aye, not before necking on with Fruit in the middle of the bar. If Lauren had seen them, she would've had his nuts for new earrings."

Jake sniggered. "It's his business, mate. If he wants to tell us about her, I'm sure he will. We have a three-hour train ride ahead of us – it's his perfect opportunity."

Their food arrived and they decided not to wait for Rob, having learned years ago that his degree of tardiness could swing into hours rather than minutes. Five minutes later he arrived, as if proving the exception to the rule. He flung the door open and marched in with Lauren in tow.

Explains why he didn't want to go to The Swann, Jake thought to himself.

Mikey watched them sit down in a mixture of shock and disbelief. His heaped fork halted halfway on its journey to his mouth.

"Hey guys, sorry I'm late – it was Lauren's fault, she takes ages getting ready." Rob's excuse came without a scintilla of sincerity, and Lauren couldn't care less either.

"She said she'd give us a lift to the station – save us getting a cab."

The relief on Mikey's side of the table was palpable. He did not want any uninvited guests tagging along, and definitely not her.

Lauren began to soak in her surroundings before brushing invisible crumbs off the spotlessly clean table. It would've been clear to a blind man she was unimpressed. Her face was expressionless and remained so even when she met Mikey's and Rob's gaze. A simple 'hello' or 'hi' was too much to ask from her, so a non-verbal stalemate prevailed.

After a few awkward moments, Jake couldn't bear it any longer. "That's very kind of you, Lauren. Can I order you a coffee or some breakfast?"

"I'll have a skinny latte. I'm not hungry." Please and thank you still hadn't found their way into her vocabulary.

Mikey and Jake continued to devour their fry-ups, munching noisily through a side of buttered sourdough toast.

Mustafa barrelled over to the group, positioning his eggs Benedict in front of him.

"Hey Fruity! I have your favourite green tea on its way," he said while leering in Lauren's direction. "And who is the pretty lady? Would you like something to eat, my dear? Let me get you some of my finest Turkish coffee." His warm welcome was completely wasted on her.

"This is Lauren, Rob's girlfriend," Jake interrupted. "She'd like a skinny latte, if that's OK?"

"Ahh, you are back from Africa. Fruit has told me all about you." Mustafa's mistaken identity and his attempt at friendly banter hit the buffers, big time. Lauren stiffened and her face turned to stone. The smirk on Mikey's face only made her fury rise even faster.

"Oh, he has, has he? Well, maybe Maddie will drive you to the station." Lauren spat her name through gritted teeth as her temper got the better of her. She snatched her arm out of Rob's grip.

"Don't touch me!" she snapped, then marched out without saying goodbye, or hello.

A feeling of déjà vu swept over everyone. As Rob scurried off after her, Mustafa held his palms up with a bemused look on his face.

"What did I say?"

***

Rob didn't return to Renoir's for cold eggs and gloopy hollandaise sauce, choosing instead to get a lift from his irate girlfriend, to give him time to placate her.

Mikey and Jake grabbed their bags and paid the bill, reassuring a nervous Mustafa that it wasn't his fault. They stepped out onto the busy pavement, laughing at the comedic foot-in-mouth timing that sparked the fireworks. Their laughter, or at least Mikey's laughter, came to an abrupt halt when they walked straight into the path of Joy Wong.

"Hey Mikey!" Joy's face lit up.

She, and the guy she was with, were wearing two-piece red tracksuits with a blue trim and a flag stitched onto the lapel and towing huge red racket-shaped sports bags on wheels. The flag on their lapels was likely the Thailand flag, Mikey thought to himself later, as it was emblazoned on the back of their tracksuit tops in big white capital letters. *Very patriotic*, he thought.

"Hey, I thought you were going away?" he asked hesitantly, while looking at the man standing rigidly at her side, void of warmth and glaring with open hostility.

"Yes, I am. Today actually. Lee and I are catching a flight to Paris at one." Joy noticed Lee stand half a step closer to her at the same moment Mikey's eyes dropped to his feet dejectedly.

"Ah, right, that's nice. Well, you'd better get going. Safe journey, OK." Mikey nodded and flicked the briefest of smiles, though it failed to reach his eyes.

The contrast from when they had met at the start of the week in Bannister's could not have been starker. He turned and left, leaving Jake in his wake.

"Nice to meet you both," Jake said as he skipped into a run to catch up with Mikey, who had used his long legs to put distance between them.

LNER, King's Cross, London: 4 September 2021

The boys sat in an obdurate silence, broken only by the cushioned thumps of the train's suspension over joints in the track, each waiting on the other to begin their inescapable line of questioning.

Chris, the train steward, announced his presence over the scratchy intercom and made the £12 soup and a sandwich offer sound like nouvelle cuisine - information only Rob was interested to hear, having foregone breakfast to embark on his peacekeeping mission.

Jake glanced at Mikey, his forehead pressed against the window, oblivious to the bright sunshine, his mind somewhere else completely – and if he had to guess, he'd say it was somewhere between Paris and Bangkok. He knew his friend better than anyone. He wore his heart on his sleeve and kept his brain in his pants. In truth, though, he was pleased to see that someone had piqued his interest enough to leave him looking almost forlorn, saddened even.

Joy, it appeared, was the mystery girl Marcella had alluded to. She had made an impression on him like few he could remember in recent years, and neither he nor Rob had heard mention of her existence until then.

Jake thought about calling him out but didn't. What would *he* want from the others? Impertinent questions about *his* love life? No. They'd never intruded before, so why now? They'd wait, incommunicado. A game of rock, paper, scissors with no hand movements.

Rob sat arms crossed, with his head lolloping left and right, while he pretended to doze off to avoid the inevitable questions he knew would be coming. The subject of Maddie would arise sooner or later. He hadn't quite worked out what he was going to say, or how much of his depth of feeling towards her he'd divulge. Who was he kidding? They both knew fine well what she meant to him.

She'd rolled up in the pub, fluttered her eyelashes at him and he'd turned to mush, dumping his pals like hot potatoes. It was having to explain himself that he was finding difficult to come to terms with, after everything that went on the last time, and the effort they'd made bringing him around.

The break in their relationship had given them time to realise they were meant to be together, he told himself. He was different now – more confident, more worldly – and if he wasn't mistaken, she was different too.

Mikey squeaked against the window, from a small patch of condensation emanating from his temple. He had had a fitful night's sleep, with the prospect of going home and being reminded of all the good things in his life – and all the bad things too. His trauma intensified when he visited his family, as evidenced by his tear-stained pillow that morning. When he looked into his parents' eyes, he would have to use every ounce of resolve not to break down. *Obfuscation was the trick*, he concluded to himself. He had an oven-ready subject to talk about that would distract him and his mother. Jackie would be overjoyed to hear he'd met someone who she could have girly conversations with, although Mikey wasn't sure Joy was the girly type. What he did know, was that he was jumping the gun, big time. He couldn't help himself.

In the short term, he had other crosses to bear. He'd have to explain his uncharacteristically charmless display in front of Jake outside Renoir's. It hadn't gone unnoticed.

It was clear to them all that the team dynamic was strangled and uncommunicative. It had been for a while, but today it had been ruined by a spoilt princess, a mystery woman, and the sword of Damocles.

Jake broke the silence. He always did. The guy who said the least always spoke up first.

"So, the feds have been busy dredging up dirt on me this week. It's going to take a minor miracle for me to swerve this one." Jake delivered his opening gambit with a game attempt to put a positive spin on his dire circumstances.

"Jake, let me tell you something, mate – you're innocent. Those arseholes have got fuck all to do other than try and lever arm you into submission. It isn't going to happen, is it, Fruit?"

"No fucking way," Rob said, having been roused from his pseudo slumber by an elbow to the ribs. "I know the best law firms in town. I'll make sure you get the best brief there is. They won't know what's hit them. They haven't re-arrested you yet either – chances are it will all blow over."

Jake's spirits were bolstered by Mikey and Rob's baseless conviction of his innocence, so he decided having a positive mental attitude was the best way forward.

"Thanks, fellas, it is appreciated. I'm sure it'll work out. I've got you guys in my corner, right? I can't fail."

He was becoming an expert at hiding his true feelings of late, and for the sake of Mikey and his vegetable extravaganza, he would maintain the facade.

"Damn right, mucker," Mikey asserted, leaning over to fist-bump Jake. A few minutes of reflection passed, all three deep in thought. The topic of Jake's uncertain future had brought perspective exactly where it was needed.

Mikey cleared his throat. "She's a nice lass, you know. Joy, I mean."

Jake and Rob said nothing and listened.

"She's in charge of the cleaning at Shinewell. I have a lot of time for her. Smashing girl. Her brother's called Jules, he's a good friend of mine. He has Down's syndrome. Helps me and Lisa with swim classes. Top bloke."

Rob met his random one-sided bullet list with a look of total confusion, as if he'd missed something.

"He's referring to his work colleague, Joy – we met her outside the café earlier," Jake explained on Mikey's behalf, giving Rob the subtlest of winks.

"I think she plays squash, or tennis. Not sure about the guy she was with. She hasn't mentioned a boyfriend or anything. Yeah, smashing lass."

Mikey trailed off into deep thought, resuming his 1,000-yard stare out of the window. He kicked himself at running off down the street like some petulant, weak-willed teenager, just because he thought – wrongly, as it turned out – she had a boyfriend.

Shortly before the train left the station, he received a text:

> Hey Mikey, that was a pleasant surprise seeing you. Please forgive Lee, he's an idiot sometimes. I hate travelling with him, but we play in the same team, so I have to. I've missed you this week. Jules told me you've been swimming with him. I'm so grateful. He loves you so much. Let's have dinner when I come back. J. xx

Having thought about it a little longer, he could have worked it out for himself. She wouldn't have sent him a picture of her laughing and smiling or kissed him on the side of the mouth like that if she had a boyfriend. And she wouldn't have held his hand at lunch and worried so much about his wellbeing. He'd been stupid and presumptuous. He hoped she wouldn't care.

> It was lovely to see you. Sorry we had to rush, we were late for our train. Jules is ace. I'm teaching him lifesaving techniques, he wants to be a lifeguard. ☺ Dinner sounds great, I'm buying. I can't wait. See you soon, safe flight. M. xxx

"I don't speak Thai, but I'll eat my hat if that's her boyfriend. She gave him a right bollocking after you left. I don't think she was impressed with the way he was staring at you." Jake confirmed Mikey's unspoken conclusion. "Tell you what though, mate, she's gorgeous. Why don't you ask her out?" Jake always knew how to bring a smile to his face.

Mikey shuffled in his seat. "Nah, she's just a mate."

No one was fooled.

"What the fuck are you talking about, Mikey? It's written all over your face that you like the girl. Even Marcella Montreaux saw it the other night, and she's never met you before. What are you worried about anyway, ya big wuss – she can only say no, right?" Rob regretted his taunts immediately, as the spotlight then shone down on him.

"I'll take no advice off The Scarlet Pimpernel over there." Mikey's riposte was all that Rob deserved and got a loud snort of laughter out of him. "What's the score with you and Maddie then? Is it back on the cards or what? Is that why Lauren has the hump with you all the time?"

Rob grinned at his hands clasped around his half-empty paper cup of cold green tea. "It's complicated."

"No shit, Sherlock." Mikey wasn't letting him off the hook. "We know what she means to you, mate, but we saw the aftermath the last time she fucked you around. I'm not her biggest fan, but..." Mikey struggled to find the right thing to say.

"Listen, if she's the one for you, then so be it, we'll welcome her back with open arms. Won't we, Jake?" He smiled warmly and locked hands with his reluctant friend, like they were about to have an arm wrestle.

"Of course," Jake said earnestly.

"Cheers, lads." Rob nodded at them both, appreciative that they hadn't hung him out to dry too badly.

None of them mentioned Lauren. It seemed unnecessary. They were utterly unsuited to each other, and Rob knew it more than anyone. He had to do something, and soon.

Chris the train steward ended the three-way period of introspection with a crackly, well-timed declaration: "Ladies and gentlemen, the onboard bar in coach G is now open for the purchase of refreshments."

Mikey put two fingers in his mouth and let out his loudest whistle yet. "Three beers, Georgie Boy!"

Newcastle upon Tyne: 4 September 2021

Adam Kowalski held aloft his whiteboard with the name Dafretuss scrawled on it in red ink. *Close enough*, Mikey thought when he spotted it. They threw their bags into the boot of the E-Class Mercedes.

Rob took charge of the logistics, instructing Adam, rather abruptly it seemed to Jake and Mikey, to go to the Malmaison Hotel on the Quayside, wait while they checked in, then drive to Benwell, where they'd be a couple of hours or so. He was to return at 4pm and take them to Highfield Working Men's Club.

"Fruit, for fuck's sake, give the guy a chance, man. I don't even think he speaks English." Mikey came to the rescue of the panic-stricken driver.

Rob made no apology. "OK, just take us to the Malmaison." He turned around to see his two pals on the back seat rolling their eyes. "Please," he added, posthumously.

"And do me a favour, Fruit, try not to be too posh, or southern, when we get to the club later. The locals can get a bit tasty if they think you're taking the piss."

"Well, I've heard it all now! Did you hear what Mr Diplomacy just said, Jake? Apparently, *I* need to watch *my* ps and qs so as not to offend the fine people of Highfield." Jake grinned broadly, deciding not to take sides.

As they passed beneath the famous green and blue Victorian landmark bridges crossing the Tyne, Jake was reminded of the nights he spent nursing a 100kg, vomit-covered, blonde pain in the arse. They were great times.

Was this to be the last time he came here?

If he was prosecuted and found guilty, could their friendship endure the years he'd spend in prison? They'd forget about him, surely. Out of sight, out of mind. They'd find new friends and partners, start a family, move on. He wouldn't return here for years, if ever. He swallowed back the tidal wave of melancholy sweeping over him and took a deep breath to steady himself.

***

They checked into their hotel, dumped their bags and were back on the road in less than ten minutes. Adam had enjoyed a decent smoke, if the smell coming off his clothes was anything to go by. He'd also been successful at organising a bunch of flowers for Mikey's gran after Rob had slipped him some cash when they arrived.

"Thanks for coming to see my gran, lads. She'd go nuts if she knew I was in town and hadn't gone to visit her."

"No worries, we can't wait to see her." It wasn't often Rob said or did anything nice for people he barely knew, so Mikey was pleased he'd reserved one of his rare moments of pleasantness for Beryl.

It took no longer than fifteen minutes to drive to Beryl's house in Benwell. Mikey made the executive decision that having a chauffeur would be too embarrassing in Highfield, despite being quite useful, so he gave Adam the rest of the day off.

They jogged up the garden steps to Beryl's bungalow and Mikey knocked on the door.

"What the hell are ya standing out there for, ya pillock! Come in, for the love of God!"

The *all-seeing eye* – as Mikey's father Brian referred to Beryl – had seen the lads arrive and walk up the path from her chair. Her dubious welcome came through the partially open bay window.

A loud pinger sounded as they opened the door. The compact hallway was filled with a curious odour of freshly baked cake and a sharp piney smell of disinfectant. Mikey turned and cracked his head on a low-hanging light fitting, sending it swinging. He steadied himself on a semi-circular, glass occasional table that was bolted to the wall, with a small mirror set so low it cut off Mikey's reflection at his sternum.

Noticing the plastic thread protector along the hallway, Mikey asked, "Should we take our shoes off, Gran?"

"Don't be soft, bonny lad, I'm not the Queen of fecking Sheba." The lads pursed their lips to suppress their laughter.

In the dimly lit hallway Mikey caught sight of a picture of himself and Kaitlyn sitting on the causeway at Holy Island, their feet dangling in the water. He reached up to touch it and grinned as he brought the memory back to life.

They turned into the living room, where the eponymous Beryl Stott stood with her thin arms outstretched, awaiting her only grandson, whom she loved more than anything in the world.

Beryl was eighty-three years old and, mentally, as sharp as a knife. Physically, her body had succumbed to the ravages of old age. Osteoporosis had given rise to a noticeable curvature of her back that was more inconvenient than painful. Her face was lined with years of happiness and laughter, clearly where Mikey's positivity gene originated from. Sadness was etched deep into her soul, but she wouldn't show it. She absorbed negative feelings and locked them up safe 'ready for the devil', she would say.

"Howay, give your gran a cuddle." Beryl teetered over to Mikey, who filled a significant percentage of the space in the living room.

"You look more and more like your mother every day."

He towered above her like a protective giant and gently wrapped his arms around her, feeling her fragility. She reached up and held his face in her hands, her shrunken pale-blue eyes burrowing into his, trying to read what was going on inside his head. Satisfied with what she saw, she allowed her slender hands to squeeze his biceps and shoulders, sizing him up.

"Look at the size of you. Your grandad had arms like that. He could pick me up above his head and spin me round, ya knaa, like I was a ragdoll." Mikey's bulk brought the memory of her late husband swimming back in all its glory.

"Gran, you remember Rob and Jake, don't you?"

"Of course, I bloody do, I've not gone doolally yet, ya knaa." Beryl shuffled over to them both, kissed them on the cheek and stroked their faces. She paused at Jake a second longer.

"Such sad eyes you have, bonny lad. I worry about you." She squeezed his hand with her cold bony fingers. Jake felt them tremble against his palm.

"Sit down while I put the kettle on. I don't have coffee or any of that green tea shite, so don't ask." Rob bit his bottom lip to stop himself from laughing again.

Beryl returned with a tray holding four porcelain cups and saucers, a jug of milk, a bowl of sugar and a silver tea pot, covered in a black and white striped tea cosy, with a delicious-looking Victoria sponge cake centre stage.

"Pull that table out, Robert, there's a good lad." Rob jumped to his feet to drag a table out of a nest of three, then he reached up to take the tray from her.

"Do you take sugar, Jack?"

"No, thank you, Mrs Stott." Neither Jake nor Rob found it necessary to correct Beryl. Like Adam, she was close enough.

Beryl poured the tea and sliced up the cake. The lads munched away in silence, nodding their approval.

"Come on then," she said eventually, looking in Mikey's direction. "What's her name? I haven't seen that look in your eye for a long while, and don't give me your usual flim-flam. By the clip on yer, you're smitten with someone – who is it? I want to know." Both Jake and Rob twisted to face Mikey with mischievous grins on their faces.

"Howay, Gran, gimme a break," Mikey responded nervously.

"Don't you 'howay Gran' me, Michael Stott Junior. Tell me." Beryl sipped her milky tea then set the cup down on the table. She was all ears, and so were his friends – they'd both plated up another chunk of cake and were enjoying the spectacle.

"I barely know the girl. We've just had our lunches together, that's all. It's not serious, Gran. There's nowt to tell yer, really."

"Not serious, my foot. You've gone the colour of beetroot, man! Look at him!" She motioned at his two friends, who did as she asked and saw Mikey's otherwise olive complexion turn crimson in embarrassment.

"So, have you asked her out? And don't lie, as I'll know." Beryl twisted the knife a little more.

Mikey looked down at his shoes momentarily and, giving up any pretence, nodded. "I have, yeah. When she comes back from Paris, we're heading out for a bite to eat. Satisfied?" Mikey folded his arms defensively.

"Fast work that, Mikey," Rob chipped in with surprise.

"Her name is Joy," he said, ignoring the smirking double act sitting next to him. Just saying her name out loud, and alluding to what might be, was like a weight off his chest.

"Let me tell you, Mrs Stott, she is absolutely gorgeous. I met her this morning. She was on her way to Paris. I'm sure you would love her." Jake lightened the conversation and gave Joy his most enthusiastic vote of approval.

"Ooh, she's French, eh? I've never met anyone from France before. Does she have joie de vivre?" Beryl teased Mikey, winking at Jake and Rob, who burst into hysterics.

Mikey paused while he waited for Rob and Jake to finish high-fiving his gran.

"She's not French, she's Thai. Her name is Joy Wong. She does the cleaning where I work."

Rob had expected Beryl to blanch at the idea of her only grandson going out with an *Oriental*, hoping for someone who had a career and a means to support herself, not menial work like cleaning.

Beryl's perspective on life was the opposite of Rob's. She had worked hard cleaning office blocks in the centre of Newcastle for over thirty years, earning a living to raise her two boys. She was full of pride and relief, having seen them both serve their country in the army. Nothing came easy for Beryl, nor did she expect it to. You make your own luck, she always told them.

Seeing Mikey in front of her now, it was like history repeating itself. She had had a wonderful life with her husband and remembered every moment with fondness. Their motto was to work hard, live life and be happy whatever you do. Even when she'd watched his body eaten from the inside out by cancer – an inevitability she'd accepted from him working in the coal mines – she hadn't considered life unfair or blamed the government. She never would. She felt blessed.

When she met Michael senior, he was covered from head to foot in coal dust. Even so, she saw in his eyes the same warmth and love she could see in Mikey's clean-cut, well-groomed exterior.

If she was honest with herself, she would have preferred the more hygienic version – far less cleaning and washing – but despite the soot, she was powerless to ignore his charm and good looks. And now, for a man like Michael junior lost in love so deep he could barely put it into words, she didn't doubt that this Joy was the luckiest girl alive.

"Well, I couldn't care less if she's from Timbuktu – if she makes you happy, that's all that matters."

Jake couldn't have put it better himself. "Your gran's right, mate. Grab the opportunity with both hands. You'll regret it if you don't."

***

Their Uber arrived and they got up to leave. One by one they embraced Beryl tenderly, and reluctantly left to meet the next generation of the Stott family and mingle with the hoi polloi of Highfield.

"You're the best, Mrs Stott. We'll be back soon to visit," Jake said, feeling a clot of emotion catch his throat as he realised this was probably the last time he would see this amazing, funny and astute lady. His body sagged under the sudden weight of sadness, grieving her passing even as she stood in front of him.

Beryl stroked his face with her cold leathery palm. "Chin up, bonny lad, everything will be OK."

She couldn't have known about his situation, but she could see the turmoil bubbling inside of him. As confident and capable as Jake was, it took this old lady to strengthen his inner resolve. After everything she had gone through, she still had more to give.

Highfield Working Men's Club, Newcastle: 4 September 2021

They arrived at Highfield Working Men's Club twenty minutes later, debussing into bright sunshine, with seagulls screeching and swooping overhead. They made their way to a small blue and white pagoda with a modest entrance sign swinging in the wind, which Mikey had to duck to avoid cracking his head a second time.

Rob whispered, "Why are we paying when you can just walk straight in through the car park?"

"There are probably some tight bastards out there, Fruit, who think all of this is laid on for their benefit and they don't have to pay the £1.50 admission. We're not like that, are we? So, we'll stump up like everyone else." Mikey rolled his eyes at his friend in disbelief.

Highfield Park was located on six acres of common land between Lowervale Rugby Club to the east and Highfield Working Men's Club to the west. Benwell Road formed the northern perimeter and to the south hundreds of garden allotments quilted the patch of land that led down to the north bank of the River Tyne. Wooden shacks were scattered about the allotments, with smoke trailing skywards from compost heaps. Mikey remembered his grandad cooking a fry-up on his pot belly stove, a reward for weeding his vegetable patch.

The area of rich alluvial soil had been dedicated in trust for communal use by the 18th century temperance industrialists who owned it. It was an attempt to encourage their mill workers and miners to grow their own food and sustain a God-fearing way of life, rather than drink and frequent public houses and places of ill repute.

In truth, starvation was the driving force behind its success. The people grew food, grazed livestock and fished the river – or they went hungry. So they created a flourishing community on an area known as 'the high field'.

The people lived an austere lifestyle far from the ostentatiousness exhibited by their wealthy, pious overlords, who built stone plaques into churches and schools to celebrate their philanthropy. Some might say little had changed in the intervening years.

Nowadays, there was no need to grow vegetables – supermarkets were stacked high in produce – yet for nearly three centuries, the Highfield community had nurtured their land and continued the tradition of growing food, as if their lives depended on it.

The August fete was by far the most celebrated in their calendar, marking the end of the summer growing season, which, by the size and quantity of specimens on show, was a successful one. Most of Highfield's population of 2,100 had turned up in style. Children screamed excitedly on the funfair rides, and a group of lads were playing football using piles of clothing for goalposts.

As Mikey, Rob and Jake strolled into the park, a classic Gavioli & Cie fairground organ piped out 'Entry of the Gladiators' at full volume, heralding their arrival.

Jake was mesmerised by the place, by the purity of people around him. He imagined a time when the public's thirst for excitement was quenched by a strongman lifting weights or a bearded lady or a flame thrower – frivolous curiosities that enchanted them for the rest of their lives.

They visited the hook-a-duck stall and chanced their arm throwing wooden balls at the coconut shy, where Jake hit the same one three times without it budging an inch.

"Have you got those things glued down, mate?" he asked light-heartedly.

"Bring your sister next time, bonny lad." The old man in charge waved him away with a toothless smile.

Empty-handed, they made their way to the beer tent, which backed onto the club house. The heat of the sun had taken its toll, and without a single word of debate they filed in. The tent was furnished with dozens of picnic benches lined up in front of a long bar made of old pallets, straw bales and scraps of timber and decorated with bunting and streamers. Rob purchased £60 of beer tokens, which bought them each a commemorative pint glass and a lapel badge, as well as eight pints each.

Rob did the math: *how do they make any money at £2.50 per pint and a free glass?*

Mikey scratched his head, deliberating which of the forty-plus beers he was going to drink. He chose a session IPA called *Cobbler's Thumb*, on the basis it looked red and wasn't too hoppy. Jake asked if they had any gin and was directed towards the bar with an affronted grunt from the barman. Ignoring his directions, Jake selected a pale ale called *In Good Time*, and was pleasantly surprised by how much he liked it. Rob chose a porter named *Sump Oil*, as it was the closest thing to a pint of Guinness.

Mikey was looking around the tent in search of his parents, when a familiar voice bellowed out from behind him.

"Aalreet, young Stotty! Where have ye bin hidin', man?"

A shaven-headed giant strode forward as people cleared a path to avoid being trampled underfoot. His bulbous arms were covered in blurry and undecipherable tattoos, which he wrapped around Mikey's shoulders to give him what any self-respecting grizzly bear would describe as a welcome hug. His sand-coloured desert boots and khaki shorts gave him an off-duty soldier appearance, complemented perfectly by an army-green cotton vest that strained to contain his enormous torso.

"Fozza! How ya doin', man?" Mikey said and unravelled himself from his grip.

"Hey mate, I was gutted to hear about Malcolm. How's Barbara managing? You're looking after her, aren't you?" Mikey knew that Fozza, otherwise known as Jason Foster, had lost his father, Malcolm, to cancer recently. It had affected him badly, leaving him prone to being aggressive and to bouts of depression.

Malcolm had been Lowervale RFC's Life President, a Highfield WMC trustee and a pillar of the community. He was diagnosed over the Christmas period and dead within a month. A blissfully short illness in Mikey's expert opinion.

As a Highfield trustee, Malcolm's reputation for honesty and transparency was known throughout the community. At 6ft 5in and weighing 150kg, few would question his integrity. He had taken to heart the club's motto, 'Share ye the Wealth', and at every opportunity ensured those who needed help the most received it.

Myth had it, that at one committee meeting, when the treasurer declared the accounts were showing a deficit of £350.48, Malcolm responded in all seriousness, "I vote we give it to the poor people." Several members seconded the motion.

"Cheers, bonny lad," Fozza replied solemnly. "We all miss him. He turned out for the veteran's team last season, ya knaa." Fozza's face was full of happiness talking about his father – his idol, and a hero to many, including Mikey.

"Fozza, this is Rob and Jake, my muckers from London." Mikey pointed towards his friends in turn. Fozza looked down at them with disinterest.

"Your father sounds like a perfect gentleman, Jason. Mikey's told us all about him. You must be proud of what he achieved in his life."

Rob's rhetorical question caused Mikey to hold his breath – literally anything could set Fozza off when it came to the subject of Malcolm. How he'd react nobody knew.

"Appreciated." Fozza nodded in acknowledgement. "Shame you boys didn't get to meet him."

After a few minutes of catching up and two swigs to empty his pint glass, Fozza made a move for the bar. Mikey took his opportunity to put some distance between them.

"Fruit, are you fucking mad or something? There's no stopping that bloke if he gets one on him." Mikey went a little pale in remembering the last time he'd gone berserk.

"He seemed OK to me, what's all the fuss?" Rob's walk on the wild side didn't impress Mikey one bit, and Jake wasn't relishing the prospect of coming to the rescue either.

Mikey led his friends into the main marquee, which was crammed with fold-up tables and market stalls selling everything from pot pourri to Land Rover parts. Half of the tent was partitioned off, reserved for competitors to display their produce, and it was filled with the scent of sweet-smelling flowers and freshly picked vegetables. Parsnips that were four feet long trailed off the show tables, and leeks the size of Fozza's bicep were having their roots combed by growers as young as eight years old.

The city dwellers looked on in amazement. This was Jake's second trip to a real market stall in one day and Rob's first visit since he was a student. Mikey had grown up in this environment and hoped one day he would live in a place like Highfield again.

His mind wandered to Joy, not for the first time. He was certain she would love Cabbage Club Day. He snapped a few photos and sent them to Jules and Arthur. Just then, he caught sight of his mother making a beeline for him. He stepped into her embrace, barging past Jake and nearly knocking him over.

"You were supposed to call me the minute you got here!" Her rebuke was accompanied by a friendly but audible slap on his bare T-shirted arm.

"I was about to, Mam, and then Fozza came over, and you can't ignore that fella." Mikey's face beamed brighter than it ever had, as he leaned in for a second and more sustained hug.

"How are my handsome boys doing? Holy hell! You three look like a boyband or summat. I bet you have to beat the girls off with a cricket bat!"

Rob and Jake bashfully hugged and kissed Jackie as she deposited her expensive-smelling perfume over their shirt collars.

"Lovely to see you again, Jackie. Looks like you've been doing those floor exercises I sent you – you're in great shape."

Mikey cocked his head at Rob, in response to Jake's smooth talk. He was rubbing off on him. It had only taken ten years.

"Thank you for noticing, Jake," she said and slapped Mikey again on the same arm. "He's just like his father."

"Well, that's fine by me," Mikey said, his eyes fixed on Brian, who appeared at Jackie's shoulder.

"Bring it in, big lad."

Mikey buried his head in his father's shoulder, and they embraced like they'd just returned from the front line. There was zero pretence. They loved each other more than life itself, and neither let go or gave way to propriety.

"It's good to see you, Son," Brian said, glowing with pride.

Rob and Jake looked on. Their experience of familial love and affection was not the same – far from it. Jake's was literally non-existent, and Rob's was dysfunctional, to say the least. Neither were envious; in a way, they felt the love by proxy, such was the depth of affection the Stotts had for one another and those around them. It seemed to overspill.

"Let me get you lads a pint. You must be dying of thirst in this heat, eh?" Brian nodded and leaned towards the beer tent, in a bid for freedom.

"Not so fast, soldier." A hawk-like grip with bright-red talons wrapped itself around his forearm. "You said you'd help me shift those straw bales into the sheep pens!"

"Leave it to us, Jackie." Jake stepped into the fray. "We'll give him a lift and have it done in minutes." Twenty minutes later they were standing at the makeshift bar drinking ale, covered in chaff and sheep shit.

***

The afternoon raced by. The heat of the sun had created an unquenchable thirst. The stout Rob had been drinking had had a liberative effect on his usual stuffy demeanour. So much so, he'd begun talking in Italian to the owner of Giuseppe's pizza house, who was born and bred in Stockton-on-Tees and whose Italian vocabulary was limited to calzone, pepperoni and margherita. He'd also shared a few racing tips with some guys at the bar, who'd begun frittering away their hard-earned wages using online betting apps.

"I'm gunna head in and find your mother soon, Son. I'd do the same if I were you – the tables will go quick in the main hall," Brian said.

After another few beers Mikey decided to take his father's advice and headed off to round up Rob.

"Hello, Mikey, haven't seen you in a long while."

Nicola Smith was blocking his path, nursing an empty bottle of Corona. The 5ft petite blonde wore a floaty pink summer dress covered in red flowers; her canvas wedges helped out with the height imbalance. Her slim waist accentuated her bust, which was considerably bigger than when Mikey had last fumbled with it in Bentley's nightclub. On her wrist, she wore what, to Mikey at the time, was a very expensive coral bracelet, which he'd presented to her on Valentine's Day as a gesture of his teenage devotion, only to be dumped a few weeks after for some older guy called Scott: "I don't want to invest any more emotional attachment in you."

"Oh, hello Nic, you OK?" Mikey said, as pleasantly as he could muster.

"I'm well, thank you. Nothing changes much round here," she said, dismissing three hundred years of tradition. "I hear you're in London these days. I see your mother in Asda from time to time."

"Aye … yeah … well, listen, I've got to get back to my mates. I'll see you around." Mikey started to leave when she held his hand to stop him.

"If you fancy meeting up some time – you know, when you're home – give us a ring. It'll be nice to catch up. Properly, I mean." She whipped off her sunglasses and fixed her slate-blue eyes on him, which widened suggestively as he looked down on her.

"What the fuck's going on here?" snarled a tall man with crooked teeth.

Mikey snatched his hand back and began to plead his innocence, recognising the guy who had usurped him over eleven years ago. Before he could say a word, Nicola cut him off.

"Oh, shut up, Scott. He only came over to say hello, didn't you, Mikey?" Nicola lied with ease.

"Yeah, well, nice to meet you again," Mikey stuttered in reply and left.

***

Mikey found Rob holding court with a group of girls asking him to speak Russian.

"Are you having a good time, Fruit?" he said sarcastically.

"Ya otlichno provozhu vremya." Rob replied that he was having a great time, his sixth pint of Sump Oil giving his Muscovite accent an authentic drawl. Shrieks of approval came from Rob's newly formed fan club, and he winked conspiratorially at Mikey and shot him with his finger gun.

Mikey rolled his eyes. "Listen, we're going inside to grab a table before it gets full. See you in there, OK?" He had to shout above the noise of a group of guys bellowing into a phone, cheering and shouting.

"Net problem, ya naydu tebya." Rob said no problem and that he would find him.

Mikey shook his head in exasperation, not understanding a word. He turned and walked back to Jake.

"Vladimir Fruitenko seems to have the situation under control over there," Mikey reported to Jake over chants of "Rob! Rob! Rob! Rob!"

They passed through a glass atrium and walked along a narrow corridor which led to the toilets and into the main entrance of the club, where a sign on the outside said 'Members only'.

To the left, they could see a huddle of middle-aged women playing bingo in a high-ceiling annex that had been repurposed from a men-only taproom to a bingo room, in an attempt to bring everyone together. The unintended consequence being, most of the women stayed there, separated from their husbands, who sat in the lounge, where the women used to sit.

The corridor that led to the 'Main Room', named to maintain the club's reputation for austerity, was lined with long oak boards listing the club presidents back to the early 1800s, with a row of framed photographs above. Malcolm Foster's image was unmistakable; he was an older, more refined version of his son, with the same military bearing. On the opposite wall, Lowervale RFC Club Captains were recorded in an identical roll call. Michael Stott's name was listed in gold leaf in 2010 and 2011.

Jake turned to his friend and patted him on the back. "Captain at eighteen years old. Says it all." Mikey shrugged modestly and pointed to one of several blue and white striped shirts encased in frames accompanied by action shots of games where they had won the league.

"Fozza was an awesome second row, you know, and I've heard stories that Malcolm was even better, back in the day. Imagine trying to stop those guys. It took the whole team to bring Fozza to the ground sometimes. He was a gentleman, though. Whenever he stood on anyone, he always said sorry."

Although Mikey was keen to avoid the guy, he had the utmost respect for him. He was a man who'd seen unspeakable scenes of death and destruction in his short life – it was hardly surprising he suffered with anger management.

"Mikey, you have some amazing friends up here, and it's a privilege to know them, it really is."

Rob had crept up behind them and begun belching and hiccupping, giving Euan McArdle a run for his money. Mikey and Jake frogmarched him to the lounge and made him drink pints of water and have some food. The night was young and having Rob blow his chunks on the dancefloor was not good form.

***

By 9pm the hall was packed to the rafters. A Neil Diamond tribute act, who doubled as a magician by the name of Magic Marty, had completed his first set and was visiting tables, mesmerising people with his sleight of hand.

Mikey's table had expanded in number due to Rob's unlikely popularity. Several of his new friends had joined them and were celebrating their luck at having backed a 25-1 winner at Chepstow Racecourse, thanks to Rob.

Four of Mikey's old school pals had also materialised: Bunhead, so called on account of a hairstyle he once had; Cheesey, because that was his actual name; Lurch, because the guy was quite tall; and Haj, named on the basis he was a builder known for doing half a job.

Looking at his friends, Mikey couldn't help conceding he'd lost some of the connection to his roots. In truth, he'd wanted it – he'd pushed them away and run for the hills like a coward. Kaitlyn's death had left him angry and hateful. By leaving Tyneside, he was leaving behind the hurt and the pain. He regretted it deeply. He'd have to live with the shame, and the selfishness of leaving his parents alone when they needed him the most. And the irony was, it had done him no good. The memory of Kaitlyn's death haunted him, even after all this time, and as much as he wanted the pain to leave him, he clung to it. It was the only thing that assuaged his guilt.

He looked at the faces he'd seen growing up as a kid – a bit older, fatter, balder and a little worn out, even in their late twenties. He didn't think he was being judgemental. What he saw in them he craved for himself. It was contentment and reconciliation.

It didn't matter what happened, these people would always be here. He could return at any time and he'd be welcomed, and when he left again, he'd be missed. It wasn't that his Highfield pals lacked ambition, it just didn't really mean anything to them. Their aspirations were much simpler and easier to understand. They just needed enough to get by and enjoy life, look after their loved ones, and make them proud.

Fozza loomed into view and slumped into his seat that he insisted Brian reserve for him. He slammed his pint down in front of him. The chanting from the posse stopped as though a stylus had been dragged from a record. Even Magic Marty got the message and made himself disappear.

"What's up, bonny lad?" Brian asked.

"Nowt, just fed up that's all." Fozza's whole countenance was rigid with menace, and everyone could see it, apart from Rob. Or maybe he was the only one who could see it for what it was – a cry for help.

"Fozza, old boy, I've got just the thing to cheer you up!" Rob said at the top of his voice. He wobbled to his feet and ambled off towards the exit. Fozza looked up snarling. His wafer-thin patience was running out fast.

Jake took the hint from Mikey and followed Rob to the foyer to find him rummaging around under a desk outside the treasurer's office. He decided it was nothing too sinister, so headed to the toilets.

***

Jake pushed through the toilet door and into a 24ft x 16ft open space, flanked on the left by a row of stainless-steel basins and cubicles, and on the right by a 1930s communal urinal, with ornate pillared separators and a grooved standing plate.

Armitage Shanks had gone to some considerable effort to design a urinal fit to collect millions of gallons of recycled ale, but it was clearly too much for the drainage system, which needed immediate attention due to the eight-inch-deep bath of yellowy-brown piss that had collected in the trough.

Jake chose a cubicle for the sake of his shoes and trousers, which had already taken a battering from a small flock of sheep. When he exited the cubicle, fastening his belt, he was abruptly grabbed around the neck and lifted off the balls of his feet.

"I've got a message for your mate. If he goes near my Nic again, I'll fucking kill him."

Scott Rawlinson, the guy who'd usurped Mikey's throne over ten years earlier, released his chokehold on Jake and punched him in the kidneys, sending him staggering towards the basins.

He turned around slowly, letting the pain in his back ebb. "Why don't you tell him yourself? He's out there in the main hall. I'll get him for you, if you want?" Jake pointed to the door as if to give him directions and noticed what was obviously one of Scott's friends blocking it.

"Well, after I've given you the good news, maybe I will," Scott said, brimming with confidence.

"I really don't want any trouble. I'm just here for a good time," Jake pleaded, while circling between Scott and the urinal.

Scott didn't want to hear reason, or submissiveness. It didn't matter to him – he was going to inflict pain and misery, and that was that. He lunged with both arms outstretched to push Jake back towards the urinal. It was a predictable move and one which Jake hoped he'd make.

He clasped Scott's exposed left wrist, twisting and arcing it further upwards, which sent a bolt of pain up Scott's arm into his elbow. Jake crouched inside him, pulled him forward and used his momentum to slam his back into the piss-filled porcelain trough. The impact and Scott's weight combined to dislocate his left shoulder and cause more agony to course up through his neck. He screamed in pain, so Jake pressed his boot against his good shoulder to partially submerse his head in the murky fluid.

Like a primary school teacher getting control of a class of rowdy infants, Jake put his finger to his lips to silence Scott. "Shh."

He sensed movement and looked sideways. "Stay where you are, my friend, if you don't want an early bath like your friend here."

Jake's advice caused the underling to freeze mid-stride. "Clever fellow that. I like him," Jake said to Scott.

"I guess you had it in your little head you'd beat me up, to get at Mikey, hmm? Because he spoke to your girlfriend? You didn't like that, did you?" Jake waited for an answer, which didn't come, so he pushed his head a little further into the putrid yellow liquid that was gradually soaking into Scott's clothing, proving to him that once urine leaves the body, it doesn't stay warm for very long.

"Yeah, OK." Scott begged him to stop.

"How's that worked out for you, hmm? I'd say not very well."

Scott shook his head in agreement.

Jake nodded towards Scott's right arm, trapped beneath his prone body. "I hope your flashy watch is waterproof."

Fear began to fill Scott's face the more he heard the chilling undertone in Jake's voice.

"I've met people like you before – people who are bigger and tougher than me. You think because I'm small and don't want any trouble – and I didn't, I told you that – you can beat me up. I dare say Nicola's had a few hidings from you over the years, hmm? Put her straight about a few things, have you?"

Jake waited for a few seconds for his words to sink in, then decided to bring the conversation to an end. The smell of human waste was getting up his nostrils, and he didn't want anyone else involved in his toilet trouble. Certainly not the police.

"I'm going to let go of your arm and take my foot off your shoulder, then I'm going to walk back to the Main Room. *You* are going home to get a bath. Put some ice on that shoulder – get your pal here to pop it back in for you."

Scott nodded vigorously, after Jake encouraged him with a tweak to his wrist. Jake stepped back, safe in the knowledge Scott was going nowhere without the help of his friend. He washed his hands and wiped the piss stains from his shoes, maintaining eye contact, just in case Scott got all brave again.

As he turned into the foyer, he saw no sign of Rob – just an old boy asleep behind a desk. He made for the bar. *This calls for a gin and tonic*, he thought to himself. *Thirsty work drowning bullies.*

***

On entering the foyer, Rob noticed a reception table with several spent flyers folded and stacked beneath, the type used to advertise who was performing that night, or what guest beers were on offer. The A1 banners were blank on the reverse side and perfect for his purposes.

He'd overheard Mikey reminiscing about Fozza's and Malcolm's playing careers for Lowervale, and how they'd both served their country and the community, when a seed of an idea germinated in his mind.

A felt-covered noticeboard lay propped up against the wall behind the reception desk, manned by old Joe Gallagher, who was snoring through his handlebar moustache, with his hands folded over his waistcoated beer belly. A cash box sat wide open in front of him, with what looked like several hundred pounds in it, weighted down by a shiny lump of anthracite coal.

Rob lifted the noticeboard onto the sideboard behind Joe, angling it away from people walking past. He used some crocodile clips that were attached to the edge of the reception desk to fix the paper sheet to the board. To Rob's delight, it was a perfect size. He rummaged through the drawers and found an assortment of coloured Sharpies, then set to work.

Over the next twenty minutes his hand swept over his impromptu canvas. He became lost in his effort to capture a moment in history, a memory of a moment in time long past. As he drew, he explained his thought process for his work of fiction to his dozing assistant and thanked him for his invaluable feedback.

He visited the foyer several times to reacquaint himself with the finer nuances of the photographs and the expressions of both subjects, but he was missing something, and he couldn't quite pinpoint what.

After another ten minutes, he bade farewell to sleepy Joe, picked up the wooden board and lumbered back into the Main Room, staggering past crowded tables and apologising to a few people who'd felt the sting of impact as he shuffled past.

"Where's everyone gone?" Rob's question received no answer, just a panic-stricken look from Mikey and others.

He thumped the board down on the beer table, positioning it with its back facing Mikey, Brian and Fozza. "I just need to make a few minor adjustments and I'll be done. Jason, if you don't mind, could you look straight at me, please?"

Rob was oblivious to the rage building in his subject, exemplified by the veins bulging in Fozza's neck and forehead and his fists bunched on his lap.

"Perfect – stay exactly like that. Oh my God, that is fucking it, don't move a muscle."

Rob held the board in his left hand to stabilise it and busily sketched with his right, the risk to his life and the flow of his creativity in ignorant harmony.

"Fruit, I don't think this was a good idea, mate," Mikey whispered through gritted teeth. Rob was too engrossed to hear his warning.

In a short time, while Rob applied the finishing touches, a group had gathered behind him, much to the annoyance of Magic Marty, whose audience was wholly uninterested in a four of hearts playing card stuck to his forehead.

The onlookers stared at the portrait, dumbstruck. One or two of the girls from Rob's inaugural Slavic language class covered their mouths in amazement. A few began laughing nervously and pointing over at Fozza.

"Eeee, isn't that Mal there in the middle? Look at his face – aww man, it's amazing!" one girl screeched in excitement.

"I'm gunna fuckin' kill this bastad, Brian. No one disrespects my fatha." Fozza got to his feet quickly, sending his chair tumbling behind him with the backs of his legs. Fists and teeth clenched, he was ready to tear Rob, limb from limb.

"All done," Rob announced, and without a care in the world, he spun the board around to face the inferno of hatred.

The Main Room fell eerily silent as Fozza's eyes locked on Rob's magnum opus. At the centre was Malcolm driving forward in a blue and white hooped Lowervale rugby shirt, tethered by six Meadowfield players hanging from his ankles, legs and hips. Fozza was depicted with his arm wrapped around his father's back gripping a handful of shirt, his right shoulder tucked under Malcolm's left armpit. Opponents were being thrown to one side and trampled underfoot. Together, they were an unstoppable force, surging towards the try line – Malcolm's right arm was outstretched; the ball held fast.

Rob had captured the pride in Malcolm's face better than any photograph could, and he'd directed it towards his son. Their bodies were pummelled by the impact, but they hadn't registered the pain being inflicted by the opposition. It didn't matter – they were soldiers in arms, which was the title Rob had given his work.

His caricature style wasn't intended to be oversized or comical – far from it. He wanted it to touch the hulk of a man who stood before him. He wanted to show him what other people could see – the love he had for his father, and his father's love in return. A love he so dearly missed. Rob wanted to show him that he mustn't feel sad, he should be happy – happy to have had a father like Malcolm and not one like Roger, who didn't know of love or sacrifice.

It warmed and inspired Rob as he sketched, knowing what true parental love meant to Fozza. *This is how it'll be for me one day*, Rob thought. He'd play sports, show his child how to ride and paint, go fishing. He'd be the proudest dad, just like Malcolm was.

Fozza's arms hung loose under his sagging shoulders. His eyes bored down into the detail: he saw himself, the reciprocated love they had for each other, the pride and stoicism his dad had shown as his last breath passed his lips.

Anger flared suddenly, imagining the bodies of his enemies beneath his boot. He cursed them silently. He'd never played with his father on the same pitch, or fought with him in the same war, but he'd imagined it many times, only for this floppy-haired southerner to bring it to life.

"That's my dad," he whispered imperceptibly, biting his quivering bottom lip. Long overdue tears dripped off his cheeks onto his barrel chest, leaving dark pear-shaped splashes of grief on his faded green vest.

Mikey dispersed the crowd, who'd become as fascinated by the portrait as by the giant in floods of tears. Several girls wrapped their arms around him and brushed the tears from his face, their tiny bodies accentuating his gargantuan physique. Rob whispered to Jake, who went to the bar and returned with a bottle of brandy and a dozen glasses. He quietly handed a shot to everyone around the table.

"May I propose a toast?" When there was no objection he continued, raising his glass.

"To Malcolm Foster – a gentleman."

Once Fozza had collected himself, he sat with Rob and they chatted openly – about what was anyone's guess. They were incongruously suited to each other. Both had a gentle and considerate streak few had witnessed, until that night.

They were the oddest of bedfellows.

Fozza stood up to leave, and Rob handed him his drawing rolled up and tied off with some string.

"I really appreciate that, bonny lad. You've no idea what it means to me."

He held out his enormous hand and shook Rob's. His bleary eyes bore a sadness that would never completely leave him, but maybe now he'd live with it a little easier.

"You're welcome, Jason."

10

THE INTERVIEW

Fulwood Sports Centre, Kentish Town, London: 7 September 2021

"He said to meet at 12 noon, Arthur – it's now 11:50." Jules tapped on his oversized digital watch.

"Mikey's never late – it's rude to be late," he lectured his bored friend, who'd been looking forward to a large vanilla milkshake all day and could not understand why they'd been waiting so long.

Jules Wong and Arthur Soames were inseparable. Three years previously, they'd stood next to each other as strangers at the inaugural class, shivering with a mixture of trepidation and cold. They'd been assigned the names *Thunderball* and *Barracuda* by Mikey, who insisted everyone had a pool nickname or superpower title.

In the beginning, many of the class were so withdrawn they wouldn't even enter the pool and needed several visits of splashing around in ankle-deep water just to get used to the enormity of the change they were being subjected to.

One to one therapy sessions with staff, and latterly club members like Jules, helped newcomers pluck up the courage to join in. Mikey and his team had witnessed huge changes in their outlook on life – they'd become confident, independent and considerably fitter. When the time came that the older pupils were ineligible for junior classes, Mikey set up adult classes. And so it continued.

To the boys, Mikey, aka *Aquaman*, was their hero, and Lisa, or *Odessa*, as she was known in class, was his faithful sidekick. She ran most of the classes now, with help from Carla. Mikey only made an appearance if numbers, and physical impairment, required it.

"I don't see why we should wait. It gets so busy in here. What if they run out of milkshake, or it gets too late? My grandad will be here soon."

6ft 4in and 160kg Arthur loomed over his friend and fidgeted anxiously as people streamed in to buy food and drink that he was being made to wait for. Jules was happy to wait – he knew Mikey wouldn't be late. At least he hoped not, otherwise he'd have to pay for the milkshakes with the money he earned working for Joy, which he'd become extremely attached to, bordering on being miserly, even to his mother, who insisted he contribute to the household expenses. "Mummy, does Joy pay broad and lods like I have to?" he asked one day when she wasn't around.

Jules's phone pinged a message in his pocket.

I've ordered the milkshakes with Jo. She'll bring them over shortly. I'll be two minutes. Aquaman. ☺

By the time Jules had read out his message to his relieved friend, Joanne was walking over to their table with three milkshakes and three glasses of Coke.

"Who wants raspberry sauce in theirs?" Jo asked, just as Mikey arrived and bounced onto his seat.

"Yes please, Auntie Jo," came the reply from Arthur, who nodded vigorously.

"Can I have caramel please, Jo?" Jules's equally well-mannered request was granted. Jo swirled the creamy brown elixir onto the top of his shake until he shouted stop.

"Thanks, Jo, you're my favourite person in this café." Mikey pecked Jo's cheek and reached for his shake.

After they'd fist-bumped each other half a dozen times with both hands, the next five minutes was taken up with loud slurping sounds as they demolished their shakes in double quick time, ignoring the brain freeze pounding in their foreheads.

"So how did swimming go today?" Mikey quizzed the lads earnestly, burping his way through his question.

"Arthur felt poorly halfway through and had to get out of the pool. Lisa didn't want him to be sick in the water again." Jules rolled his eyes at his friend without a grain of sympathy.

"Well, I'm sorry to hear that, Barracuda. Are you feeling better now?" Mikey asked.

"My eyes are still a bit fuzzy. I'd feel better if I could have another milkshake…" Arthur looked furtively at Mikey, who wasn't falling for it.

"Pull the other one, big lad. I think one gallon of shake a day is enough. Besides, we have a weigh-in next week. I've been looking at the charts … it appears you are heading in the wrong direction."

Mikey raised his eyebrows playfully in Arthur's direction, hiding his concern about his dizziness.

"My grandad says 'an army talks on its stomach', and I should 'eat and be Mary'." Arthur folded his arms defiantly at Mikey, refuting his argument to deprive him of another shake.

In the face of such logic Mikey had no answer. "Fair enough, mate, but if you can't fit in your trunks, you'll have to come to swim lessons naked. Everyone will see your tallywacker."

Mikey wagged his index finger at Arthur, and the two boys burst into fits of laughter. When they finally stopped giggling, Mikey concentrated on the real reason he'd convened the meeting of the Superheroes Swim Class Committee.

"Hey Jules, when is Joy back from Paris?" He didn't need to sound so casual – Jules only ever heard the words and completely missed nuance.

"She said she'd be back on Monday. How many sleeps is that, Mikey?" Jules asked, trying to count on his sticky fingers.

"Three," Mikey said. "Has she had a good time playing squash with her friend … Lee, I think his name is? Have you met him before?"

Jules pursed his lips and furrowed his brow. "He's not a nice man. I hear him shouting at Joy on the phone sometimes. He uses the F-word."

Mikey twitched and felt his knuckles crack as he balled his fists under the tabletop.

"I'm sure he didn't mean anything by it … people get cross sometimes, like Mr McArdle does with me, but I don't pay any attention." He didn't want to get Jules upset. He could see just mentioning Lee's name had shut him down.

"Mr McArdle said I was a big dummy, but I know I'm not, because my gran said I was really bright," Arthur said with genuine sadness.

Euan's cruelty froze Mikey's heart. He made a mental note to deal with the horrible bastard in due course. For now, he had to get the conversation back on track – he was in jeopardy of losing his audience.

"I don't talk to people who say bad words," Arthur said to Jules. His sage-like advice soothed his friend, who nodded in agreement.

"Thanks, Arthur," Jules responded, smiling with eyes full of brotherly love. "You're my best friend. And you are Mikey. And Joy. And my mum." Jules had everyone covered in love.

"Hey, I'm going on a date with Joy … what do you think?" Mikey asked in a whisper.

Of all the people Mikey had met in the last few weeks he decided the most insight would come from someone who knew her most. In the absence of her mother, Jules was in the hot seat. He often produced mind-blowing wisdom that Mikey could only dream of emulating. If anyone knew he stood a chance with Joy in the long term, it was him.

"Can I come?" Jules asked immediately, confounding Mikey's theory, while swerving his question.

"If Jules is going, then I want to go too," Arthur pitched in. "Can we go to McDonald's?"

"Can I not go anywhere without you guys coming along? We've been to the cinema this week, pizza yesterday and milkshakes today. I've done three swim classes and we worked out with Big G, remember? Anyway it'll be at night-time – you'll be in bed by then."

The two boys looked crestfallen.

"I'll tell you what, guys … I've got a big game of rugby coming up soon, why don't you both come along and cheer me on? There's usually a barbecue afterwards – all you can eat."

The last part of the negotiation won the deal – at least for Arthur it did, who went into a huddle with his co-conspirator.

"OK, Mikey, it's a deal. How many sleeps until then?" Jules was a stickler for his diary, and Mikey only had himself to blame for that.

"Not many. I'll let you know." Mikey nodded, feeling like he'd won.

"Staff announcement: Michael Stott to the manager's office, please. Michael Stott to the manager's office. Thank you," Luke sang from the tannoy.

"Listen, fellas, I have to go. I'll text you both, OK? Make sure Arthur doesn't have any more shakes, Jules."

Arthur's shoulders slumped. Mikey stood up to leave, fist-bumping his homies one last time.

"Hey Mikey," Jules shouted as Mikey reached the exit. "Don't be showing your tallywacker to Joy on your date."

Mikey turned to see the two of them standing, waggling their fingers in the air.

***

Mikey knocked on Euan's door and waited, playing along with his power trip. After twenty seconds or so, Euan called out, "Enter."

Euan was sat with his back to a large bay window covered by a beige Venetian blind that hadn't seen a duster in its entire life. The 20ft x 18ft space was by far the biggest single occupancy office in the building. A power grab to hide his inadequacy, Mikey concluded.

Mikey watched red London buses creep past the street below in a constant daily commute, strobing sunlight off their upper deck windows, which bounced off Euan's sweaty, bald head.

An antique glass-panelled oak bookshelf covered most of the right-side wall, heaped full of dog-eared back copies of motoring monthly, monster truck and bikers' magazines.

Wrappers, crisp packets, cartons and paper cups littered the carpet around his feet. Ironically, his bin was empty, apparently too far away to be of any practical use.

Mikey remembered Euan refused cleaners entry to his office. He kept it under lock and key when he wasn't there.

Just as well, Mikey thought to himself. *The smell of unwashed groin would make Joy puke.*

Piles of paperwork and reports lay on his desk, spilling out of his in-tray. Despite his demands that everything be printed out and delivered by hand, none looked to have been read.

An old bicycle leant against a disused coat stand in the corner. The rear tyre was flat, and the chain hung loose, crying out for oil. Mikey estimated he was still in primary school the last time Euan rode it.

"You have your interview with Amanda soon, is that right?" he asked, while tapping on his laptop and not making eye contact.

Mikey wanted to tell him it was none of his fucking business. "That's right."

He leaned back in his swivel chair, which creaked under the load. "I think it's a good move for you to be honest. I can't nursemaid you forever, it's time for you to stand on your own two feet."

His clipped Glaswegian accent made his words even more unbearable to take for some reason, or perhaps he'd just come to hate every utterance from his mouth.

"I'm quite busy, Mr McArdle. Is there a reason why you've called me here?" Mikey looked at his watchless wrist, as if to labour the point.

"I suppose you and your cronies have been bleating about the comments I made at the 4M last week? About staffing levels and profitability?" Euan raised one of his bushy eyebrows and rolled his tongue under his bottom lip.

Nope, we all think it's bollocks is what Mikey wished he'd said in reply. Instead, he just shrugged and rolled his eyes. He refused to pander to him.

Mikey had spent the week visiting each department head discussing revenues and cost budgets. They, like him, were puzzled as to Euan's assertion that Fulwood was losing money, especially given the profits they had made the previous year and the increased headcount of people in through the door since then.

"Well, for your information, big man," – Euan's temper flared at Mikey's indifference – "I've completed my evaluation and I'm making my recommendations to Head Office in the coming weeks." More silence followed.

"Are you going to let me know what they are, or am I to wait like everyone else?" Mikey was becoming tired of his posturing.

"Put it this way, getting that job at Belgravia may come in very handy for you … if you catch my drift?" he sneered. His plaque-encrusted yellow teeth still harboured the remnants of his breakfast.

Mikey remained silent.

"And if you don't get the job, maybe you could have a chat with one or two of your homeless mates you have in on a Thursday – they'll sort you out a bunk to sleep in at the YMCA." He laughed at his pathetic, cruel joke.

Mikey stood rooted to the spot. He knew who ran the place, and it wasn't Jabba the Hutt sitting in front of him.

If I got the job, my salary would come off Fulwood's wage bill and make the budget look a lot better. But why taunt me? Why is he being so vindictive to the one person making Fulwood so successful? It's self-destructive. Is this tub of lard jealous of my achievement and popularity, even with the homeless? I don't get it – the bloke hardly leaves his office, other than to fetch more food. In fact, the less involvement he has, the better. There's something else going on here.

"Well, I'll have to do my best then, won't I? If I'm the one to go, so be it. You'll have to do my job as well as your own. Shouldn't be too difficult – you're twice the man I am." Mikey looked him up and down and wrinkled his nose.

Euan slowly propelled himself forward in his chair and pointed his fat index finger in Mikey's direction. "Don't mess with me, boy. You may be able to find a new job easily enough, but the rest of them won't. Maybe I'll have a rethink. Cut back on the swim classes instead. Those spastics shouldn't be in the place anyway. They're a safety risk."

Euan could see by the reaction on Mikey's face that he'd hit a nerve and decided to press home his advantage.

"Be good to look at the cleaning contract as well, eh? Just look at this place – it's a fucking disgrace!" He waved his arm at the mess on his floor.

"That little Chinky lass might have a cute arse, but she's hopeless at cleaning. She should go back home. There's plenty of British folk could do what she does."

Mikey thought he was going to explode. His eyes flicked across Euan's desk looking for something heavy enough to beat him to death with. He drew in a deep breath and gritted his teeth. He could hear his gran in the back of his mind: 'Resist the devil and he will flee.' She was right. He just wanted to provoke Euan into saying or doing something he'd regret.

Euan's high-pitched laugh hit Mikey's back as he walked out of his office without saying a word

Fulwood Police Station, London: 8 September 2021

"For the benefit of the tape, the time is 16:05hrs, on Wednesday, 8 September 2021. Present are PC Jones; Mr Jake Webster, the suspect; Miss Norazu, the suspect's solicitor; and DS Cantly. Mr Webster has been reminded of his rights, and a caution read out explaining he does not have to say anything, but what he does say may be used in court."

Tamara's call on Sunday to tell him they were likely to press charges was a predictable, if not unwelcome, close to an amazing weekend in Tyneside – one that ended his faint hopes that the problem was going to disappear.

"Mr Webster, thank you for attending for interview." Cantly's tone sounded ominously confident. "During the last interview you were reluctant to provide my colleague, PC Jones, with any responses to our questions." He waited for a response and received none.

"It would be in your interests to answer our questions fully and truthfully, as it will help us determine whether we have enough evidence to prosecute. Or, if there is no case to answer, then we'll all go home." He tried to sound conciliatory and failed miserably.

"You haven't asked my client any questions yet, or presented any additional evidence – what do you expect him to say? Let me repeat what I told your colleague: we are not here to help you or obliged to say anything. Pressurising my client into speaking is coercive."

Cantly glared at Miss Norazu and reached for a TV remote control.

"Mr Webster, I'm going to show you some video footage of the incident that occurred on 27 August 2021 at Fandango's Nightclub." Cantly locked his eyes on Jake, then pressed play.

A grainy, coloured image flicked into life. The camera angle looked down towards the stairway leading to the front entrance. After ten seconds of no movement Jake stepped into the frame, holding his arms out in front of him and saying something. The footage had no audio. Ben Stockton came into view, lunging at Jake and swinging a punch. Jake could be seen gripping his arm, ducking underneath and throwing him over his shoulder, in a well-executed move. Jake then straightened, glanced to his right, and eventually raised his hands and leant against the wall. PC Jones then came into view and cuffed him.

The whole clip took forty-eight seconds from beginning to end. PC Jones reset the clip and played it again, as Tamara requested.

"Do you recognise the events recorded in the clip we have just shown you?"

"Yes, sir." Jake nodded.

It was the first thing Jones had heard other than 'No comment'. He scribbled some notes, relieved to be getting somewhere.

"We visited Matsumoto's Mixed Martial Arts Centre in Camden, which we understand you attend, is that correct?" Cantly asked.

"Yes, that's correct."

"In fact, having spoken with Mr Matsumoto, it's safe to say you are more than an attendee, Mr Webster. You are in fact a third dan mixed martial arts instructor, are you not?"

"I'm a fourth dan actually, but, yes, I give classes there on a Tuesday and Thursday."

"When we showed Mr Matsumoto the video, he confirmed to us that the move you employed on Mr Stockton was in fact a 'tai otoshi body drop'. Is that the case?"

"He ran at me swinging a punch – I had to protect myself. If I'd just stood there, he would have pushed me down the stairs."

Cantly sensed Jake's frustration growing.

"So instead of obeying Mr Stockton's demand for you and Mr Stott to leave the club, you refused and used practised lethal force to inflict life-threatening injuries on someone who was there to safeguard your wellbeing."

"Are you fucking serious? He rammed Mikey's head against the wall – he could've broken his neck. And while he lay unconscious on the floor, him and the black guy were punching him in the back of the head. *He* then came after *me*." Jake pointed at his chest.

"Mr Webster, if you don't remain calm, I will be forced to ask PC Jones to apply handcuffs."

"You'll do no such thing, DS Cantly. My client is rightly upset by your insinuation that he was the aggressor, and that Mr Stockton was the innocent party. Nothing could be further from the truth. It's pure supposition. Forty-eight seconds of selective video isn't going to cut it."

Ignoring Tamara's rebuttal, he continued. "In his account, Mr Bance states: 'Mr Stott was intoxicated and staggered into my colleague in the corridor. He became abusive, and when asked to leave, he refused. He threatened me with physical violence. My colleague Mr Stockton and I were left with no option other than to restrain him for the safety of other patrons. Mr Stott tripped over a potted plant and bumped his head.'" Cantly looked at Jake with a neutral expression.

"That's total bollocks and you know it."

Tamara put a calming hand on his and took over the questioning.

"DS Cantly, there's more than one camera in that corridor. I assume you have the footage from them?"

Cantly looked down at his notes and flicked his eyes sideways towards Jones. "It is with regret that we do not have any recordings from the other cameras in the corridor. They had malfunctioned and failed to record on the night in question."

"Well, that's convenient, isn't it?" Jake's frustration was turning into despair.

"It's not a matter of convenience, Mr Webster, it's statement of fact. It also means we do not have any footage of you assaulting Mr Whittingham and Mr Bance," Cantly added.

"May I see their statements?" Tamara held her hand out and Jones passed her a bundle of paperwork. Several minutes passed while Tamara read through their statements, shaking her head in disbelief.

"Neither Mr Bance nor Mr Whittingham witnessed the alleged assault on Mr Stockton, yet they were within six feet of it?"

"You have their statements, Miss Norazu," Cantly stated.

"So, they are unable to corroborate Mr Stockton's account?" Tamara asked with some surprise.

"That is correct. Furthermore, neither have commented in their statements about how they sustained their own injuries. Both gentlemen do not wish to press charges against Mr Webster."

Tamara's second surprise of the day was clouded with a whiff of suspicion, although she wasn't going to look a gift horse in the mouth.

"However, Mr Stockton has been very co-operative and wishes the full force of the law to be applied against Mr Webster."

"It's his word against my client's. You are wasting our time. No court is going to convict on that basis," Tamara said.

Silence filled the room.

"The injuries sustained by Mr Stockton are extremely serious. You have the doctor's reports and initial scans of his lower spine showing several crushed vertebrae. There are physiotherapist evaluations, an occupational therapist report, medical support recommendations and more. He will never walk again. Mr Stockton will be required to undergo hours of surgery and months of rehabilitation. Your client had the opportunity to walk away from the incident when asked to do so by Mr Stockton. He refused, choosing instead to use lethal force to exact revenge for his friend, who lay drunk on the floor. The CCTV footage shows Mr Stockton being thrown down the stairs at the hands of Mr Webster. He alone is responsible for what happened and needs to account for his actions."

Looking directly at Jake, Cantly paused and delivered his coup de grâce: "It is our intention to charge you, Mr Webster, for assault with intent, in contravention of Section 18 of the Offences against the Person Act 1861. We will also seek to deny Mr Webster bail to prevent any risk of recrimination to Mr Stockton or any of the witnesses."

***

"Mr Webster, do you understand the charges for the offences that have been put before you?" Custody Sergeant Lynch spoke to Jake in the same calm and reassuring tone.

"Yes, sir." Jake's throat was so dry, he could barely answer.

"Your solicitor has presented evidence to me of your good character and co-operation in this matter. I agree with her that you present negligible risk of flight or reoffending. However, as part of your bail conditions, between now and the date of your court appearance, you must not contact Mr Stockton or visit Fandango's Nightclub. Is that understood?"

"Yes, sir."

"If you are arrested again, or contravene your bail conditions, a warrant for your arrest will be issued and you will be detained and likely remanded in custody until the trial is over."

An image of Scott the usurper flashed through Jake's head.

"You will be required to attend your first court hearing at Fulwood Magistrates' Court on 29 September 2021. The precise details will be sent to your solicitor. You are free to go. Keep out of trouble, OK!" Custody Sergeant Lynch gave him a solemn but reassuring nod of his head.

Jake nodded meekly in response. "I will, thank you."

"Cut and dried. See you in court, Jake," Jones said from behind him, then walked away.

Bell and Sandringham Legal, Farringdon, London: 8 September 2021

"Hello, Mr Bell, are you there?"

"Report. I don't have much time."

"It's done, he's been charged. First court hearing on 29 September."

"Excellent. What about the medical evidence?" Bell asked. "Did Choudary sort all that out?"

"He did. To be honest, I'd have held some of it back. It hasn't even been two weeks and the guy looks like he's had more scans than Michael Palin's suitcase."

"Did Webster give any indication how he would plead?" Bell was in no mood for humour. He never was.

"No. If I were a betting man, he'll plead guilty and hope to avoid a custodial sentence. He looked as weak as a lamb. I don't care how much kung fu he's done, he won't last five minutes inside."

"Let's hope he does. Even if he pleads guilty, this will go to Crown for sentencing as the injuries are too serious," Bell said. "And what about Stockton, where's he?" he continued.

"I had him transferred in a private ambulance and taken to the house. No one saw him. He had plans to go to Scotland in his campervan with his girlfriend. Doda put him straight about that."

"The wretched man called me on the night it happened, trying to back out. You need to keep Doda updated in case Stockton goes AWOL or does something stupid. Get him to make a visit to the house. Speaking of which, has Doda spoken to the other two bouncers like I asked him to? We don't need complications. And what about the video evidence?"

"Yes, they're in no doubt what will happen if they don't follow his instructions. The footage has been wiped, apart from camera one. Don't worry, it's all sorted."

"Don't be complacent. There's a long way to go before we get to the claim. The sooner Webster's convicted, the quicker the insurance will settle. It's important we stay focussed. Paraplegia and loss of vision in one eye is an easy half a million pay-out, probably more. Make sure Stockton doesn't cock it up. If he does, you know what to do."

Fulwood Magistrates' Court, Kentish Town, London: 8 September 2021

Jake dragged his feet along Kentish Town Road, for once oblivious to the world, its industry, harmony, and parade of colour. The magistrates' court he'd be attending in a matter of weeks loomed up on his left. He shivered when he saw it. His life as he knew it was about to change. He'd have to adapt. What use was there in fighting? It seemed the law had him by the throat and there was nothing he could do about it.

As the scenarios ran through his head, Hansie and Trixie skipped down the steps to the street. The looks on their faces were as dire as his own.

"Hey," Jake said lamely.

"Howzit, Jake?" Trixie stopped, and Hansie kept walking.

"Are you guys OK? What's happened?" Jake's own problems disappeared momentarily.

"Ah, it's a long story. We're trying to confirm our citizenship, but we've hit a brick wall. Now we have to attend court and apply for 'leniency' and 'special dispensation' to remain here." Trixie provided the detail – Hansie clearly wasn't in the mood for small talk.

"That's awful," Jake said. "After all this time?"

Trixie was already shaking her head, defeated. "It's the Foreign Office. They aren't very proactive. We have three months left on our current visas and then we have to go back to South Africa." Trixie trembled involuntarily.

"Let me know if you think there's anything I can do, OK?" Jake knew he couldn't help, and with what the legal system had lined up for him, he'd need all the help he could get to save his own skin.

"You're very kind, Jake. Say a prayer for us."

She kissed his cheek and walked away.

Swann and Key, Kentish Town, London: 8 September 2021

John Devlin had hoped the charges were being dropped, but one look at Jake walking into the Swann and Key reminded him why he rarely relied on optimism.

"This is bullshit. The cops have one scratchy video and a few dodgy witness statements. It's got no chance in court, trust me," John said.

"Yet here I am."

"It's not going to happen," John confirmed emphatically.

"You seem to have forgotten the paraplegic, half-blind bouncer who now needs a wheelchair and round-the-clock assistance for the rest of his life. I did that to him. This is payback, pure and simple."

"The hell it is! I'm no mug, Jake. I know bullshit when I smell it – it's my job – and this stinks of it. How do we know the guy didn't have some pre-existing medical condition, or weakness in his vertebrae? If he did, he shouldn't have been in that job, right? He could've fallen down those steps at any time."

"You're reaching a bit now." Jake shook his head, unconvinced.

"Why were the other two bouncers so reluctant to say anything? It's not like you've nobbled them or anything. You'd think they'd be queuing up to see you prosecuted. Get some compensation."

Jake shrugged. His head hurt just thinking about it.

"OK, let me ask you this … when you visit a client – the Khans, for example. You were talking about them the other day, where the two kids are being abused, right? – what goes through your head every time you walk through the door? The very first thought. And don't give me that bullshit about unconscious bias or reflective practice."

"I know what you're trying to say, John, but it's not the same."

"Sure it is. You're immediately suspicious of one or more family members. You look at the home, the look in their eyes, the interactions they're having, their physical appearance, how they speak, what they say, what they said – everything. Well, so do I. This fucker Stockton is bent, I'm telling you. Better than that, I'll prove it to you."

"John, my bail conditions do not allow you to speak to the guy. Just leave it to Tamara, she has my back. I don't need you getting involved – I'll end up in jail for sure." Jake had had enough. He stood up to leave. "I'm tired, I'm going home."

"Just give me a few weeks and I'll prove it to you," John pleaded, though it was no use. He'd pushed him too far.

"Just stay the fuck out of it, John!" Jake snapped, and left.

Shinewell Headquarters, Swiss Cottage, London:
7 September 2021

"Michael, please come in. Take a seat. It's lovely to see you again."

Amanda Knowles shook Mikey's hand warmly then jogged back to her seat, moving with purpose that bordered on urgency. She was organised, efficient and perceptive. At forty-three, she could easily have been mistaken for someone in her early thirties, if not for the wrinkles around her eyes and her penchant for hot beach holidays. Her blonde, bobbed hair was cut high at the back and accentuated the line of her neck.

Mikey told himself to quit staring. He sat down, feeling the latent heat left by the previous interviewee seep through the seat of his pants, like a 19th century shift worker taking to his bed. He'd sat in the same chair twice before to receive awards for something or other.

The room dripped with opulence: oak-panelled walls, crushed velvet curtains and a state-of-the-art wireless video and sound system that disappeared into the ceiling space.

Looks like Shinewell Group is doing very well, Mikey thought to himself. *Hammering us workers for all they can.*

"Michael, thanks for attending interview. May I introduce Jim Bigsley, our Non-Executive Director, and Cheryl Neaves, our Head of HR, who I think you may have met before."

Mikey smiled in their direction.

"OK, let's get started, shall we. Jim would you like to begin?" Amanda offered casually.

Jim Bigsley was a small, balding man in his mid-fifties. Mikey estimated 5ft 6in by the cut of his dark-grey pinstriped suit. He couldn't see any discernible strength or condition in his body that would indicate any level of fitness – quite the opposite. His facial features looked soft and slightly flushed, like he had high blood pressure. His hands looked weak and his wrists thin. His fingernails were unnecessarily long. He doubted whether this pencil-neck had done a hard day's graft in his life.

Bigsley neither thanked nor registered Amanda's invitation and began his questioning without delay and without a welcome.

"Michael, you've been at Fulwood for seven years now, is that right?"

"Yes, it is. I joined as an Assistant PT in September 2014."

"Seven years in one place … it strikes me you aren't particularly ambitious. Why would you think you are the best person to manage Shinewell's flagship health club in Belgravia, when you're still coaching junior swim classes and swapping out lightbulbs?"

Mikey caught himself slightly, as he tried to work out which insult to respond to first without sounding irritated.

"*You* might say unambitious. *I* prefer loyal and dedicated. I've been promoted three times in that space of time, twice by your colleague Amanda as a matter of fact." He nodded in her direction.

"The last time, I also received an award for Shinewell Group Employee of the Year, for developing the largest cohort of junior swimmers in the North London swimming championships, in which we secured gold," he said, hesitating for affect, "for the third time in five years."

An unimpressed blank stare came in return, with no attempt to make a note of the point he'd made.

Mikey continued. "I'm a keen swimmer and like to participate where I can. I believe leading from the front and being visible is vitally important. I change lightbulbs instead of sitting in the dark."

Mikey smiled easily at Amanda and Cheryl, who pursed their lips to suppress a grin.

"Do you like to swim, Mr Bigsley? It's great exercise. You must come down and I'll show you around our facilities. We have a world champion swim instructor as part of our team."

"I'll ask the questions if it's all the same. We have other candidates to see and are limited for time."

His curt answer told Mikey all he needed to know – there was no chance he was getting this job. He knew he was the last one in, as Debbie on reception had told him. They were going through the motions, and the curious discomfort on Amanda's face confirmed it.

"Fulwood and Belgravia are completely different propositions, do you not think? What management skills have you learnt that you think will be effective in such a high-end establishment? For instance, do you think getting drunk and turning up for work on a Monday all black and blue is appropriate?"

The penny dropped. That fat bastard had put the boot in.

"I assume you are referring to the injuries I received after I was assaulted a few weeks ago?"

"From the information I have read in your file, black eyes, fat lips and bruises are a regular thing with you. I wonder, if you were successful in interview, would the same presentation style be suited to Belgravia?" Being supercilious came naturally to Bigsley.

"I'm not sure my 2,200 customers notice that much to be honest. If anything, they're enthralled by my sporting achievements – and failures – as I am by theirs. I'm twenty-eight years old, I play rugby for fun and to keep fit. It won't be long before I hang up my boots and take up sports that have less impact on my body. I have never taken one day of sick leave in seven years, so my injuries have never been that bad that I couldn't do my job."

Amanda winked at Mikey's answer as if to congratulate him.

Bigsley scribbled in his notes and turned the page to start again. "What personality traits do you think are your strongest and weakest?"

Now he asks for a SWOT analysis. How much are they paying this idiot? Mikey asked himself.

"I'd like to think I'm well thought of, a nice person – at least that's what I hear from members. I'm generous and supportive of everyone I know. I quite enjoy learning new skills and encouraging others to do the same, to develop themselves."

"And on the negative side?"

"I can be a little impatient, perhaps a little cocky, but I haven't been criticised too badly for that."

"You haven't? People spare you home truths, do they? Worried you may get upset?"

Mikey sensed he was being lined up.

"Would you say you were mentally tough, or prone to emotional outbursts?" Bigsley held Mikey's gaze.

"Emotional outbursts? No, I don't think so." Mikey looked confused but guessed his regular stand-up rows with Euan may be what he was referring to.

"Your personnel record has noted that in 2017 you were found by your boss, Mr McArdle, crying in your office. When he offered to help you, you became 'extremely unhinged and aggressive'."

Mikey remembered the incident well. It was the anniversary of Kaitlyn's death, a day he normally took as annual leave. He dearly wished he had that day. Euan had barged into his office at precisely the wrong time, to find him holding her photograph in his hand, tears running down his face.

"Why are you skulking? She's dead. Let it go."

Euan's cruel advice tipped Mikey over the edge. He grabbed Euan's jacket lapel, ready to punch him in the mouth.

"Mind your own business, you fat fuck." He pushed past the quivering man, and nothing more was ever mentioned, until now.

"I have no problems with my mental health, thank you."

Mikey's confident tone had now developed a sharp edge to it, brought about by his partially clenched jaw. Bigsley heard it as clear as day. He wanted him to lose his cool, and he had. Game over. He closed his notebook, took off his reading glasses and folded his arms.

"I've asked all my questions, Amanda - he's all yours."

His words were clouded by a sexist overtone, which the two women, whose remaining questions were discernibly less combative, ignored.

Mikey thanked them for their time and walked out of the room. Where his future lay, he didn't know, and at that point, he didn't care.

11

CUT THE BULL

Fulwood Borough Social Services, London: 9 September 2021

Jake's phone buzzed on his desk, making him jump. "Hello," he answered with zero enthusiasm.

"Jakey-boy, it's Mikey. How'd it go? What did the cops say? I rang but you didn't pick up." Despite Mikey's own disappointment, he had woken with renewed vigour.

"Not good, mate – I'm up before the magistrates on 29 September." Jake let out a big sigh.

"Tell me what that means, mate. I'm sorry, I don't get it – are they going to slap you with a fine, or what?"

"I need to decide on a plea first. The cops have charged me with assault with intent. It can carry a ten-year prison sentence. Either way, looks likely they're going to send me to jail. I'm fucked."

Mikey was dumbstruck. His stomach churned with guilt. He swallowed hard.

"What does your solicitor say? I can't believe she'd let you go down without a fight. And John? He was there – he'll know what to do, right?"

Jake told himself he owed John a call to apologise for shouting at him. He knew he was only trying to help.

"He reckons that Ben guy's dodgy. I've a meeting with my solicitor later this week. She may be able to negotiate with the police for a lesser charge, if I plead guilty."

"Guilty?!" Mikey shouted down the phone. "No way, man. I'd be listening to John. He knows his stuff. He's a PR expert, right? At least give him some time to explain what he thinks. Tamara might benefit from his insight too." Mikey's encouragement gave Jake the lift he desperately needed.

"I've nothing to lose, I suppose. Listen, Mikey, thanks for calling, I need to dash."

He hung up and left for his last ever meeting with his boss, Bernard Bradshaw.

***

"Front and centre!"

Bernard Bradshaw's military commands normally put a smile on Jake's face, but not today. He opened the door of his pristine, spartan office and walked over to shake his hand.

"What can I do for you, Jake?"

Bernard was sat with a straight back busily writing notes on a pile of reports he had stacked to his right, which were balanced out by a huge mug of tea to his left with an inscription on it that read, *'Wit nowt tek'n owt'*.

Bernard Bradshaw was totally bald apart from a thin strap of closely cropped salt and pepper hair that wrapped around the back of his head. Everything about him had purpose and direction. His clothes were pressed and co-ordinated and fitted his surprisingly fit frame to perfection. At sixty-three, he was coming to the end of his career, with the prospect of tending to his wife, who was suffering with the late stages of motor neurone disease and required round-the-clock help.

His piercing blue eyes peeped over the top of his frameless reading glasses to finally look at his young protégé. The desperation etched on his face was unmistakable.

Jake slid a white envelope across his desk. "I've got into trouble. I'm resigning from the department. I'm sorry." Jake had learned long ago that direct communication gets the message across the quickest. He knew Bernard would appreciate it.

Bernard put down his pen, swept his glasses off his face and muted his phone.

"Come on, son, let's have it. What's happened? I want a full debrief – from the beginning."

***

"If I stay, I'll bring the department into disrepute," Jake said, after explaining everything.

Bernard steepled his hands under his nose. "You'll plead not guilty, of course," he concluded, as if there were no other option for Jake to consider. "We meet these wasters every day of our lives, Jake. We cannot let them defeat us. I don't give a fig what video evidence they have, it proves nothing." Bernard had entered a war-footing and he wasn't for retreating.

"I don't think you understand—" Jake started.

"I understand all too well, lad." Bernard's words silenced him.

After a few moments Bernard changed tack. "I had a son – did you know that?"

Jake shook his head and raised his eyebrows in surprise. Truth was, he knew very little about Bernard. Something he regretted deeply.

"Lance Corporal Niall Bradshaw of the 1st Royal Fusiliers."

Bernard took a deep breath and raised his clenched jaw. Despite his no-nonsense approach to everything he did, he couldn't prevent his burning grief from surfacing when he talked about his son.

"It's a terrible thing to outlive your children." Bernard stopped what he was about to say, stifling the pain of the memory.

"The Taliban set fire to a school building, leaving twenty young girls inside to burn to death. Niall's platoon was on patrol and first to respond. They were pinned down by enemy fire. Several of his mates were hit. A few didn't make it home. He rushed into the building with no concern for his own safety, ignoring orders from his commanding officer. Niall knew he had little time and concentrated on getting the children to safety first. He coaxed them to follow him out of a side door, creating a silly Mexican wave game to keep them all connected in a string so they wouldn't get lost in the smoke. He was clever like that – always keen for everyone to join in at parties so no one was left out." Bernard smiled broadly.

"When Niall went back in for the teacher – Safia was her name – the building was ready to collapse. He found her buried under debris, and her hair and clothes were smouldering it was that hot. He doused his flak jacket with water from his canteen and wrapped her in it. He gave Safia his EBA, lifted her onto his back and made a run for the door."

Bernard swallowed hard, as if preparing himself.

"He missed the tripwire hooked onto a landmine on the way out of the building, the first time. 'Pure luck,' they said. The second time, he wasn't so lucky. As he passed through a narrow entrance way, he tripped the IED and it blew off both his legs, instantly. Shrapnel punctured his lungs and ruptured his liver. He lost the sight in both eyes and suffered third degree burns to 50% of his body. The teacher survived with some burns, but she lost her left arm."

Bernard sawed at his arm, and Jake imagined the poor girl writhing in agony.

"The explosion somehow catapulted Safia away from the fire. Her beautiful face was unmarked because she was wearing Niall's mask. She made a full recovery and returned to teaching."

Bernard nodded and smiled doggedly. "Niall held on long enough to come home, where he died in a military hospital on 14 February 2009, aged twenty-four." He announced the date like he was reading an epitaph.

Bernard grieved for a long time after losing the most precious thing in his life. He'd cried rivers of tears for Niall, but not anymore. He was proud of his actions – of him ignoring danger to save others in the face of certain death.

"I got to speak to him one last time, in hospital. His last words were, 'I did good, didn't I, Dad?' I told him he did, then he passed, holding my hand." Bernard took a deep breath to reset his train of thought.

"Sounds to me like you and Niall have a lot in common, Jake." He lifted his head to look into Jake's eyes. "You should ask yourself whether you'd do the same again, knowing now what might happen to you." He didn't wait for an answer.

"I know you would. It's why you're a social worker – you care. Probably too much for your own good. You remind me a lot of my boy. He had a kind heart and a giving nature, which he got from his mother, but he was tough, like you, with the same quiet, steely determination. He was a similar height and build to you and fit as a flea. He had the same sad eyes, like he was permanently lost or looking for something and he didn't know what. I suggested he join the army. He resisted at first and told me he wasn't cut out for that sort of thing. How wrong he was. When he signed on, he realised there and then he'd done the right thing. He found what he was looking for: a sense of purpose, the chance to make a difference. He died a happy man."

There was no emotion in Bernard's voice, just a longing to preserve Niall's memory. It was rare for him to feel comfortable talking about what happened, but today his story seemed to mean more, as if after twelve years, his absolute sacrifice continued to count for something.

"I've promoted you twice in seven years, Niall. Not because I needed to give you a pay rise or pander to your ambitions, but because I didn't want to lose you. I've come to rely on you. You are too important to me."

He didn't notice he'd confused Jake's name with that of his son, and Jake didn't correct him.

"I never give up on anyone, lad, don't you forget it. So cut the bull and let's get back to work, eh? I'll let Sandra know about your situation, and she'll do nothing, because she's one of us. You keep your resignation letter. If the worst happens, I'll accept it then, not a moment sooner."

He was right about Sandra Cummins, the Director of Social Services. She was tough as old boots, and her hearing of Jake's predicament would likely elevate his standing with her – not get him fired.

Jake put his letter in his pocket and stood to leave. "I'm sorry to hear about Niall, Bernard. He was so brave to do what he did. I wish I could've met him."

"He was. As were you. So let's say nothing more about it, lad. We've got the case meeting this afternoon – let's put our efforts into that. And besides, worse things happen at sea. That's why I joined the army."

Jake smiled ruefully at his gallows humour. He knew Bernard was right – there was too much at stake. He had a life to live and the lives of young children to protect, just like Niall had. He turned and walked back into battle.

Rubio's Restaurant, Aldgate, London: 9 September 2021

Rob picked Rubio's because it was closest to Maddie's workplace and no one knew him there. He looked at his watch and smiled meekly at the waiters, who suspected he'd been stood up.

After thirty minutes, he was beginning to think they were right, when Maddie pulled open the glass door into the restaurant, using all her weight to overcome the vacuum caused by the balmy summer breeze outside.

Rob jumped to his feet and waved in her direction. "Hey, Princess."

He kissed her damp rosy cheek. A curl of hair had glued itself to her clammy temple, which she unhooked with her finger. Her loose-fitting yellow summer dress clung stubbornly to her body as she sat down.

"It's great just to get out of the sun. It's roasting out there." Maddie's small talk replaced any welcome or apology Rob might have expected for her tardiness.

She shrugged her cropped cashmere cardigan onto the back of her seat and waved at a waiter, who took her drink order.

"Have you ordered food yet? I'm not hungry to be honest," she lied. She could have eaten a scabby horse.

"No, I was waiting for you. They do a great tofu and beetroot salad." He lied too – that was the last thing on the menu he wanted.

After they ordered, an awkward silence cloaked them for a few minutes.

"So, do you like the sound of a trip to Paris?" He went straight for the jugular.

Maddie grinned. She'd expected Rob to prevaricate. Perhaps he'd changed. She sized him up across the table. His floppy, mousy blonde hair was now styled and glossy. His skin glowed from his recent holiday, where he may have crawled out from under a parasol for more than five minutes. He sported an expensive-looking watch that peeped out from under his cufflinked sleeves.

Lauren had clearly given him a makeover. Money-grabbing bitch, she seethed to herself. *Well, I'm back, so it's time he moved on.*

"That sounds lovely, darling, but we've got a few other people to consider, don't you think?" She averted her eyes behind her glass of mineral water and failed to hide the irritation in her voice.

"I suppose," Rob replied dryly.

Humph! he thought to himself. *There was a time when she'd grab hold of my shirt and force me to look at her in the middle of an argument. Now, she can barely look at me for more than a few seconds. What had Jacob done to her? Time he was gone.*

She reached out and laced her fingers in his. "I want this, Rob, but we must tread carefully. I don't want people to be hurt."

Rob did all he could to not laugh in her face. The anguish she had put him through, and now she was worried about dumping a guy she'd only known for six months.

"We've grown up a lot since I left. I've had time to think, to find myself." She paused for effect. "I regret going to Africa, I really do. I should've stayed here with you."

Rob's face contorted at her admission. "Really?!"

"Yeah, but I think the separation is what we needed. It's given us a chance to make something of ourselves. Seeing you again has opened my eyes."

There were kernels of truth in everything she was saying, and by the look on his face, he was lapping it up.

"Let's go to Paris then. We can get to know each other all over again. What better place – we love it there." Rob squeezed her hand and smiled his lopsided grin.

"What about Lauren? What are you going to say to her?"

"Something similar to the conversation you'll be having with your boyfriend, I guess."

Rob's salty response stung her. "It was never going to last between me and Lauren. She's only after one thing. She hasn't done badly either. And when I spent the night with you, well, let's say it made my mind up."

Maddie jabbed angrily at the food on her plate, trying to control her annoyance at his casual attitude. He was nothing like Jacob and knew nothing about him. He likely never would; they lived in different worlds. *She* knew him, though. Jacob was gentle and strong, patient and loving. He'd grown up in a tight working-class family, who'd welcomed her with open arms. She was his princess now, an unfortunate and coincidental crown he'd bestowed upon her. He was utterly devoted to her in a way Rob never was. It was Jacob's lack of ambition and drive that was the major stumbling block for her. She'd tasted the high life and wanted it again – desperately – and unless they won the lottery anytime soon, that was to remain a thing of the past. She couldn't deny the hold Rob had on her. He was confident, intelligent, good-looking and successful.

The prospect of a future living off a bricklayer's wage filled her with dread. There'd be no impromptu first-class trips to Paris or Miami. She'd be counting the pennies from now until the day she died if she stayed with Jacob. So now was the time to cut free. She had to do it, before it was too late. For her own sake, and the sake of her unborn child.

Fulwood Borough Social Services, London:
9 September 2021

Jake collected his laptop and case files and made his way to the department meeting ten minutes early. He bumped into Bernard as he rounded the corner.

"Get us a brew, lad, I'm spitting feathers here. Don't drown it in milk, there's a good chap."

Bernard, ever the team player, grabbed Jake's belongings and nodded towards the kitchen before marching away whistling 'The Great Escape'.

Jake turned on his heels and did as he was asked. He didn't consider making a cup of tea a subservient task. *'The Chinese have been doing it for thousands of years, making a big song and dance about it,'* Bernard advised him on his first day.

Despite having drunk a pint of tea only minutes earlier, he knew, without a refill, Bernard wouldn't make the end of the meeting without being grouchy. He found his monogrammed mug sitting on the counter with a Yorkshire teabag inside and a mound of sugar heaped on top. The mug was caked in a brown stain that Bernard insisted wasn't to be cleaned – apparently it made the tea taste better. Jake filled it up from the hot tap, splashed some milk in it, stirred it until it resembled liquid rust, then made his way to the meeting.

All eight members of the Safeguarding and Child Protection Team were in attendance, each with a stack of case reports and a laptop.

"Thanks, everyone. Let's get started, shall we," Jake said.

The story of Niall's heroics had hardened Jake's resolve. How could he allow his life to be derailed by someone like

Ben Stockton, when Niall had run into a burning building – twice – under fire from the Taliban?

After two hours of rapid-fire case management, Jake summarised their actions and called for any other business to bring the meeting to a close. Irene Onocha, a large Nigerian woman in her late thirties, raised her hand.

"Yes! Jake, we haven't gone through your caseload. I'm involved in at least 25 of your urgent cases. We need to speak about Razzaq Khan. The referral team have raised at least ten issues in the last six weeks. The Intervention Officer has been pulling her hair out." Irene's wooden and metallic bangles clattered on her wrist, like an out-of-tune xylophone, as she waved her arms above her head in a fluster.

"Irene," Jake said submissively, "I've not forgotten. Let's grab some fresh coffee and go through them in Bernard's office, OK?"

***

"There have been ten separate reports filed on this case in the last six months. I've no doubt in my mind these children, and likely Ebrah Khan, are at serious risk." Irene summarised her concerns and presented them to Jake and Bernard, who couldn't argue with her conclusions.

"What did the school say? Did you speak directly with the head?" Jake knew what the answer would be.

"What can they say, Jake? Muhammed Khan refuses to send them to school, says he's homeschooling them. They're not legally obliged to inform the local DfE of their intentions. He knows how to play the system, how to create delay. God knows why, he's hardly ever there, and you'd think he'd want the kids out of his way if he hates them that much. The police have attended on four separate instances, due to reports from neighbours of screaming and loud thumps against the wall in the middle of the night."

"Do you think his wife is complicit?" Bernard didn't believe it, but every avenue had to be explored.

"No. She loves her kids. She's frightened to death of the man. Kelly, the IO, has been there many times and has reported tell-tale behaviour in little Razzaq that indicates significant signs of prolonged abuse. Haniya too. On one visit, she found them alone in the house with the front door wide open, hiding in the cupboard under the stairs eating a box of stale Sugar Puffs."

Jake allowed Irene to vent.

"We have oversight of all health visits, local education authority assessments and police reports. Razzaq has suffered a broken collar bone, bruises to his ribs, a dislocated elbow and he's deaf in one ear. Poor Haniya has had it worse. The last admission to A&E was to treat cigarette burns. During a medical inspection they saw traces of vaginal bleeding. She's eight years old, Jake."

"Let's get the home visit out of the way and take it from there. I'll attend myself," Jake said, seeing relief flood across Irene's face.

Irene took a deep breath. "I know bad people. Muhammed Khan is an abuser. If we leave this any longer, we know what will happen."

12

SOUNDS LIKE A PLAN

Bates & Chandler, Gray's Inn, London: 14 September 2021

Jake hadn't been in an office as plush as this in his entire life. Even the butler who brought the coffee and biscuits on a polished sterling silver tray wore solid-gold cufflinks and impossibly shiny Oxfords.

He often wondered who worked or lived in places like this. He knew there were rich people, of course, but what did they do to warrant working in such opulence? Law. An obvious answer, he concluded to himself.

Jake closed his eyes and shuddered at the cost he would have had to incur for this level of legal representation, if it weren't for John, who insisted he pay Tamara's fees, and Rob, who had already lined up the barrister.

"How have you been, Jake?" Tamara asked. "I hope all this hasn't been too upsetting for you. I can imagine you must be under a significant amount of stress."

Jake grinned inwardly. Stress? He didn't want to judge her, but what the fuck did she know about stress? Try growing up with a drug-addled mother and watching her abusive boyfriends beat her up. Did she ever have police battering the door down in the middle of the night, looking for drugs? And then, when a decent guy finally turns up and steers you on the right path, your mother sends him packing and he gets killed in a road accident? Yeah, he knew stress all right.

"I'm fine. I've been busy, which has helped take my mind off it." There was no point making life difficult for her. She was trying her best; that was all he could ask.

"OK, well, let's get down to it."

Tamara had Jake take her through the events of the night once more, insisting he include every single detail, no matter how inconsequential.

"Why are the CPS doing this, Tamara? The guy was going to kill me, as were the other two. I had to do something."

"Their justification is the video and the severity of the injuries. They're going to use your expert knowledge of lethal force as motivation."

It was simple for Tamara to understand. Inescapable almost. The video, the medical reports showing graphic images of bruising and lacerations, the experts' prognosis and the 4D X-rays of his fractured spine and eye socket looked every inch as bad as it sounded.

She sensed his anguish and changed her approach, explaining the law, timeframes, the legal process, plea bargaining and how determined she was to defend his position and rebut the evidence presented to the court.

Every report, document and witness statement she had asked from the CPS she had received, surprisingly quickly. On the one hand, this was good, as there would be no surprises later and plenty of time to prepare, but on the other, their case was strong.

"So, what are you saying? If I plead guilty, I can negotiate a lesser sentence, but either way it's going to Crown Court and I'm likely going to prison?"

She deliberated before replying. "We'll cross that bridge when we get to it, Jake. As your legal counsel, I'm making you aware of the facts. You're an intelligent guy – I want you to be fully engaged, OK?"

Jake closed his eyes and nodded. She was right. He wasn't a child; he understood what she was saying more than most. His job was literally the same as the CPS, laying down the consequences, managing expectations, meting out punishment.

"As I said, when the CPS assess their chances of a successful prosecution they do so based on the strength of the evidence, whereas we will refute it and vehemently defend your innocence."

Jake's mood darkened. He took little solace from what she was saying, which, if he was honest, sounded defeatist. Or was it realistic? Was he actually guilty of causing GBH? He couldn't honestly admit to doing what he did accidentally – it was a perfectly executed move. Shin Matsumoto would have been impressed, more so by the body throw than Delroy's ankle tap, or the punch to the tall guy's groin, but he hadn't wanted any of it. They came at him.

"Our position is that you acted in self-defence," Tamara said earnestly, as if reading his mind. "My job is to prove that, right?"

Jake nodded again. He felt adrift on the ocean, with no paddle, a prisoner to the winds of fate.

Optimism or pessimism didn't come into the equation. It was an assimilation of the facts. A judgement. He'd made hundreds of them and he hoped he'd made them in good faith.

"Don't be downhearted, Jake. We're far from giving up on this. The CPS need to prove intent beyond reasonable doubt, and from where we stand, there's a lot of doubt."

As if to back up her assertion, she played her trump card. "I had John Devlin on the phone this morning, asking about your case. He wants to help. I'm not at liberty to release details without your permission, but I'd take what John says seriously." She cocked her head as she passed the baton.

"He's convinced Stockton's dodgy. I don't see it. Why would he target me – I've never met him before? Even if he is a crook, it doesn't unbreak his back, or replace his eye, does it?" Jake regretted his morose comment the moment he saw Tamara's reproachful gaze.

"Listen to me, Jake. I'm here to prove your innocence. I don't fuck around. I'm 100% all of the time and I will leave no stone unturned, do you understand?"

Jake started to apologise for any offence he may have given, but she raised her hand and stopped him in his tracks.

"Let me tell you this. Having John Devlin and all his resources in your corner is a massive benefit to you, believe me. I would trust that man with my life. I've seen his work first-hand, and you should consider yourself fortunate he's giving this his highest priority."

Tamara's eyes had narrowed. The time for pussyfooting around was gone. Her patience was spent.

Jake was chastened. He should have returned John's calls and texts. Instead, he was drowning in self-pity. Now was not the time to manage on his own, as he always had. He needed help and support, much more than banter and camaraderie.

"He called to ask me to persuade you to let him help you. My advice is to accept his offer. If Ben Stockton's bent, trust me, John Devlin will find out."

John Devlin Public Relations, London: 16 September 2021

John trudged into his glass-walled boardroom and sat down heavily at the head of the table. He opened his iPad and looked over his notes, without reading them. The last couple of weeks had been tough. If he'd stopped thinking of Jake for more than ten minutes, it was because he was asleep, and he hadn't done much sleeping. His last call was short, but at least he'd got his agreement to help. His friend was suffering mentally, of that he had no doubt. Tamara confirmed what John already knew and implored him to keep a close eye on Jake.

Trouble was, Jake wasn't his number one fan right now, if their latest interactions at Matsumoto's were anything to go by. So, when he called Mikey to share his concerns, he felt he had no choice, though it was still underhand.

The call turned out to be helpful. Mikey promised to do his best to keep Jake's spirits up, although with the unintended consequence of reigniting his own guilt. He'd taken his team to The Colly that night knowing Jake would turn up with every intention of hanging out with him. He'd seen the look on the faces of the bouncers who'd taken a disliking to Jake and Mikey even before they'd got to the door. If he hadn't showboated with Jamal, getting them into Fandango's, none of this would've happened.

Still, what Jake had done and the risks he'd taken in protecting Mikey was nothing short of heroic. Those guys were huge, violent men, yet Jake ran straight in without a moment's hesitation. To have a friend like that was special. Now it was his turn to step up to the plate.

***

"Where's Justin?" John ground out, his lips thin with impatience.

Derek looked up from his laptop and gave a quizzical shrug in Patrick's direction, bemused by the uncharacteristic display of temper.

"He was on the blower to someone. He said he'd be right with us," Molly said, brushing crumbs off her Arsenal football shirt before taking another large bite of her blueberry muffin and adding to the mess. Her eyes rolled back in pleasure, as if nodding a vote of approval in the direction of her cake.

The sugar rush had barely taken hold in Molly's stomach before Justin hurtled through the door out of breath, bringing the stench of stale cigarettes with him in an invisible cancerous cloud.

"Sorry, John," he apologised, flattening his wayward thinning hair over his crown. "Just had to take that call. Very interesting actually," he said, to no one in particular.

John looked up from his paperwork, his face serious and lacking his usual warmth.

"This project remains off the books. If anyone has a problem with that, now's the time to say something," John said impatiently.

One of the few rules at JDPR was that you weren't allowed to be moody. A nervous silence hung in the air before Patrick spoke up.

"John? What's up, darling? You don't seem to be yourself today." Patrick's ever-present sarcasm had disappeared. "You're among friends here, right?" Patrick continued, directing his comment to his three colleagues, who nodded.

John let out a long sigh. He knew better than to railroad them.

"Sorry. It's been a difficult time," he said, unclenching his teeth. "This Stockton fellow I asked you to research a few days ago, he tried to assault my friend, who you met in The Colly. The guy ended up in hospital with a broken back, and now Jake's in the frame for it with the police. They intend to prosecute." John paused to collect his thoughts.

"I feel partly to blame. I got Jamal Aziz to get us access to the club when the bouncers had originally turned Jake and his pal away." He shook his head and scrubbed his face in his hands.

Molly walked over to give him a one-armed hug, holding her blueberry muffin to one side.

Derek lifted his head and spoke. "John, we're a team here, a family even. If you say jump, we say how high, right?" His display of unity had the rest of the group nodding in agreement again.

"Thanks," John muttered. He cleared his throat and shook himself into action, giving the team the heads-up on everything that had happened.

***

"Justin, you're on point with this. I need daily reports from now on, OK?"

"No problem," he said.

"Molly, set this up as Project Fandango on the system. As much as it's off the books, we still need to keep the records and evidence in good order, if it's to be used in court." His focus was returning. The group knew to prick up their ears and listen.

"Derek, I sent you all the information I had on Stockton – what have you been able to find?"

Derek's enormous eyebrows arched as he looked over the top of his glasses.

"It's what I've not been able to find out, more to the point."

John gestured for him to continue.

"This guy's a ghost. As of eighteen months ago, the person known as Benjamin Stockton, NHS number 7865/103/2741, simply doesn't exist. He's not registered at the address you gave me, he's never voted, he doesn't own any property, doesn't have any legal convictions and has no credit history of any description."

"Mikey spoke to him at the club. He had a northern accent. He may have moved here from up north. Have you spoken to Gill in the Manchester office?" John asked.

"With you saying it's off the books I've kept this to within the team."

"I'll get her up to speed. What about a passport or driving licence?"

"Neither, at least not in the last eighteen months. He has a National Insurance number and a tax record. They're genuine, it seems. That's all I can find."

"Has he changed his name by deed poll?" John offered.

Justin intervened. "The thing is, John, you don't need to go through the Deed Poll Office to change your name. You can do it any time you like, then contact the tax office or wherever and just inform them. With your newly named tax record, you can apply for all sorts of documents, utilities, etc. All it takes is someone who knows the systems to create the identities and then hand them over to someone else to use. You only need to go through the DPO if you want a driver's licence, which he doesn't have, at least not in the name of Ben Stockton."

"He's a security guard. Don't you need vetting to make sure you're trustworthy? Surely they look back further than eighteen months? How long's he been at the club? Give them a call, Derek, and ask about him. If you get nowhere, hack them and find out that way."

Derek nodded and began typing furiously.

"Do a bit of digging around on Jamal Aziz as well. I've known him years. Something tells me he's not involved, but he is a nightclub owner – he could be into all sorts."

He knew not to tell Derek how to suck eggs. He'd come up with some inventive means of extracting the information without giving away he'd even asked for it.

Justin smiled. "There's more from my end."

"Go on," John said, imploring him to get to the point.

"I got a friend of mine at HMRC to do a check on Mr Stockton's tax affairs. They're in perfect order – and when I say perfect, I mean pristine. He declared income of £56,000 exactly last year and paid his tax in full and on time."

"Wow, I think I might become a bouncer," Patrick chipped in. "That's good money for standing with your arms crossed all night." Although his comment was made in jest, he raised a good point.

"Agreed, Patrick. Was your pal able to give you the bank account it was paid from?" John asked, turning back to Justin.

"He did, which brings me to my interesting point … it's a nameless account based in the Cayman Islands. We've no chance of tracing it."

"Try anyway," he said, scribbling on his notepad. "Molly? What have you got?" John fixed his dark eyes on her intently.

"Well, it makes sense now," she said, the wheels whirring in her head. "I rang the hospital to enquire about Mr Stockton's welfare, and the nurse said he was discharged early on Saturday."

Molly was met by confused stares.

"I thought he had a broken back?" Patrick said on everyone's behalf. "Are you sure you have the right guy, Moll?"

"Hang on, hang on, I haven't finished." She drew a breath. "A private ambulance arrived and took him to a clinic in Putney, called Lexington Health. It specialises in rehabilitation from sports injuries and RTAs. A 'Dr Choudary' signed off the transfer documents."

John's mind was doing backflips. Who the hell is this guy?

"So," he started, counting the points on his fingers, "he's self-employed, pays his taxes on time, doesn't have a credit history, can't drive or travel abroad, yet he has private healthcare paid for by persons unknown." He paced the room, not quite believing what he'd heard.

"Molly, can you find out if he's still at the clinic and if not, where he's gone? Check out his home address – does he live with anyone? He'll have called home and kept them informed, is my guess."

Molly wrote frantically.

"How do you know he didn't pay for it?" Justin asked.

John spun around to face him. "£56,000 exactly, you said. That tells me he's claimed nothing by way of taxable expenses, pension contributions or health insurance. When I submit my return it's never an exact thousands of pounds. I'm claiming all sorts of expenses, so why wouldn't he? My guess is he knows nothing about that account in the Cayman Islands. He's a podgy doorman from Yorkshire for God's sake. I'm guessing he isn't paying for private medical care either."

"With no credit rating, he'll be living hand to mouth, no doubt being paid cash in hand. I doubt he's even got a bank account. If he has, it's not in the name of Ben Stockton," Derek said.

"Who's paying for everything then, John? And why?" Molly asked, bemused.

"Good questions, Molly," John said. "Right, heads up – here's what we're going to do."

Fulwood Sports Centre, Kentish Town, London:

20 September 2021

Mikey pounded along his circuitous route through Primrose Hill Park and back up Camden Road. He knew he was going to be seeing Joy later in the day, but still felt the urge to run past her house just on the off chance she'd walk out of her front door.

He usually ran to work on a Monday. It was like a therapy for him, an injection of endorphins to prepare him for the week ahead. Today's run was also an attempt to run off the beer from a particularly boozy after-match party, having thrashed Finchley 50-5. He got man of the match for three tries and mercifully finished without a single mark on his face or injury to his battered body.

The alcohol was relentless and the intake continued into Sunday when he coached the Colts to victory. For eighteen year olds, he admired their ability to drink copious amounts without throwing up. He grinned remembering the dozens of £1 fines he'd handed out for using mobiles in the clubhouse. One rich kid kept handing him pound coins, accepting the surcharge in good humour, such was his need to text his girlfriend.

Mikey yanked open the door, skipped over the defective turnstiles and made his way towards the showers. As much as he wanted the day to be over, there were conversations he needed to have and he'd enacted the plan in his head.

Euan was intent on destroying his career prospects. Why he had such a vendetta against him was baffling. Mikey had been polishing that turd for years, making him look good. He vowed to himself he wouldn't be beaten by a wanker like him. No chance. He'd fight tooth and nail to protect everything he'd built at Fulwood.

"Hey, stranger."

Mikey stopped dead in his tracks, his heart skipping a beat. Did I imagine that?

He turned to see Joy in her all-blue cleaning togs, leaning on her electric mop with her hand propped on her hip.

"Joy! What are you doing in so early?" Mikey knew her flight was due at midnight and was delayed by ninety minutes. He'd checked the moment he woke.

"Well, that's not much of a welcome," Joy said, feigning disappointment.

Mikey dropped his rucksack off his shoulder onto her clean floor, lunged forward and swept her off her feet, burying his head in her neck as he swung her around.

"I've missed you so much," he muffled through her thick black hair, as she squealed with delight in returning his embrace.

"Me too," she said, breathing the words into his ear, more than a little relieved he was just as excited as she was.

When she made terra firma, he cupped her face and kissed her on the lips gently, his favourite flavour of lip gloss making its mark on him once more. As he pulled away, she grabbed his shirt front, pulled him back and started the process all over again, this time with her mouth slightly open. His body stiffened.

The solid minute of 'welcome-back' kissing was punctuated with a synchronised inhale and exhale.

The mayhem of the last two weeks flitted through her mind; she'd taken twelve flights and played nine matches against some of the best squash players in the world, before being knocked out in the semi-finals of the Asian Cup by an Egyptian player who didn't know the meaning of good sportsmanship.

She'd worked her butt off, training for four hours a day, and had had to fend off the unwanted advances of her doubles partner, Lee Ng, who simply refused to get the message – until she kneed him in the groin. Then he understood.

She'd given six TV interviews in three different languages, met countless VIPs and dignitaries and had eaten enough hotel and airplane food to last her a lifetime.

Going home to sleep with jet lag was futile, so she grabbed her work clothes and dropped by the office to check in on her workforce, who, like her, were used to early mornings and were busy mobilising for work. Jules had left a drawing taped to her computer screen of the two of them eating ice cream at the beach with Arthur and Mikey.

"Welcome home," said Newcastle's answer to Barry White.

Their brown eyes locked. If they'd been reluctant to show how attracted they were to each other, they weren't now. They now knew what the whole of Fulwood Sports had been gossiping about for months, including Arthur and Jules, who'd been goading Mikey relentlessly for days about his tallywhacker.

"Are we still on for tonight? It's OK if you're too tired. You should spend some time with Jules and your mam." Mikey couldn't help touching her. He stroked the hair from her face and squeezed her hand, convincing himself she wasn't just a figment of his imagination.

"No way am I missing out on our date," Joy said emphatically. "It's all I've thought about for a fortnight."

Mikey took a deep breath to calm himself down.

"Can we go to Renoir's please?" Joy pleaded, wide-eyed. She wanted to be part of Mikey's life, to go where he went, meet the people he knew. Renoir's seemed to be a good start.

Oh my God, she is off the scale, he told himself. Look at those eyes and that smile, and she's been looking forward to tonight as much as me! He swallowed hard.

"If you like. It suits me if it suits you, darlin'?"

She giggled at his voice, as it reverberated through his chest and into hers. "You make me laugh how you say things. It's so funny."

"Well, you're going to have to get used to it."

"I'd like that," she purred. "I'd like that a lot."

**

"Michael Stott to the manager's office. Michael Stott to the manager's office." Luke's singsong voice came over the tannoy like he was announcing the departure of the next train to Clapham Junction.

Mikey pressed the speed dial for Euan's office, never more certain he'd be sitting behind his desk grappling with his crotch and eating some artery-clogging fast food. Euan picked up the phone after four rings and mumbled something Mikey couldn't decipher.

"Hello, Mr McArdle," Mikey said leaning into the speaker. "I'm just finishing a meeting with Lisa and Carla … I'll be with you in ten minutes, if that's OK?"

"A meeting? What about?" he snapped.

Mikey wondered why he even asked. He couldn't remember the last time he attended any meeting other than a 4M. Why would he even care? Nevertheless, he didn't want to tell him the real reason.

"It's a safeguarding meeting. You were invited, but you failed to respond. We'll include you in the minutes, if you like?" Mikey took every opportunity to poke the pig.

"Don't bother – I'm too busy to be concerned with matters like that. Get up here once you're done. And hurry up." He hung up.

"God, I hate that man," Lisa said, echoing what Carla was thinking.

"We all do, Lisa, so let's see what we can do to get rid of him, eh?" Mikey blinked his image out of his mind and returned to the matter in hand.

"I've had meetings with Jo, Beverly, Big G and Will. They've all told me their departments are operating at maximum capacity. Jo has had to take on an agency cook, just to give Dorothy a day off. She's burned out apparently," he said with a worried expression, imagining his gran having to work full time into old age. Mikey shook his head in homage to Dorothy's energy.

"When I asked Big G about gaps in his diary, he said, 'See you in the new year.'" Mikey rubbed his temples. "I increased his fees by 10% at the beginning of June, and he's still blocked out. The wellbeing clinic's the same."

"I don't understand it either, Mikey," Carla chimed in, as if reading his mind. "I've looked at Q1 to Q3, and we're 26% up on footfall, yet Elaine McIlroy's told me, without cutting costs – to the tune of at least £75,000 – we won't meet target. But when I check the sales budget, we're smoking it."

Mikey had checked the overhead recovery rate on costs and CAPEX and nothing had changed significantly from last year. He regretted not speaking with Amanda when he'd had the chance.

"Do you think the special projects are having any impact?" Lisa put in, not sounding confident she knew what she was asking.

Mikey shook his head. "I spoke with Will Halperson and he has it all fully costed. He estimated a net cash position no worse than £30,000, with a net projected profit of £40,000. That's not to mention the spin-offs and new memberships we'll get from the TV exposure."

Normally upbeat and positive, Lisa and Carla looked despondent.

"Hey, turn those frowns upside down. I'll get to the bottom of this – trust me," Mikey said, jumping to his feet.

***

As directed by a point of Euan's pen, Mikey sat down while Euan finished typing on his computer. The rusty bike hadn't moved in the last week and the mound of food wrappers had reached the empty wastepaper basket but not managed to find its way in.

Seconds passed before Euan spoke. "I'm sorry to be the bearer of bad news. You were unsuccessful in your job application for Belgravia."

Mikey could see the faintest of smirks pulling at the corner of Euan's mouth, schadenfreude getting the better of him.

Mikey flicked his eyebrows up in faux surprise. "You are well informed – I've not been told myself yet. It's a little unprofessional of HR to tell you before me, don't you think? Or did you give your mate Jim Bigsley a call?"

Since his interview, he'd had time to think. He knew he'd blown it – Jim Bigsley had made that abundantly clear – but there was something in the way Amanda Knowles had spoken to him that told him he was out of contention. She was almost overenthusiastic, not because she wanted him to get the job, more because she wanted him to think he'd had a chance.

'I can't wait to hear what you've planned for next year. Your influence in the Fulwood community is so important.'

'I'm not sure your success could be reproduced.'

'The Board of Directors has an incredibly high opinion of you.'

She'd let him down lightly so he wouldn't think he was nothing more than an also-ran, someone who'd gone as far as they could within the organisation.

"Well, erm," Euan spluttered into a nervous laugh, "truth is, I was keen to find out if I was losing my assistant. I'd need to think about reorganising the team, wouldn't I?"

Mikey eyed him suspiciously. He didn't believe a word he was saying. The last time he was in his office he suggested he buy a cardboard box and live under a railway bridge.

"Are we finished? I've got work to do." Mikey wanted the conversation to end but remembered too late that he had questions of his own.

Euan hated being directed by anyone, especially Mikey. He snatched his pen off his desk to somehow quell his anger.

"Yes, I have," he snapped. "It has been drawn to my attention you have been questioning department heads about productivity and profitability."

Interesting, Mikey told himself. "And? What of it?"

"I specifically told you not to do that at the 4M." Euan's voice rose in volume and pitch.

"No, you didn't," Mikey said, reaching into his file wallet and taking out a copy of the minutes, turning to the page on any other business.

"Here it is. 'Mr McArdle informed the team that he was undertaking a feasibility study into the prospect of redundancies to address the matter of low profitability. He asked us all to work together to find a solution to the problem.'" He slid the document over Euan's litter-strewn desk.

"So, I spoke to the guys to 'find a solution' – what was I supposed to do, wait around for you?"

Euan grabbed the document to read it for himself. "Have you distributed this? Have you? You had no right to note my comments in the minutes!"

His ludicrous statement put a confused grin on Mikey's face. "I had no right to note your comments? It's what happens in meetings. I asked if you had any other business and you stood up and said those very words. I've sent you the minutes in draft, and as per usual you haven't bothered to read them, have you?"

"So, you haven't sent them out yet?" Euan said, relief washing over his chubby face.

"No, of course not – you haven't signed them off. But if you sign them now, I'll get them distributed." Mikey poked the pig again.

"The study is confidential, you idiot," Euan spat as he leaned across his desk.

"Everyone on the distribution list was in the room, apart from Amanda, and she was the one who asked you to look into redundancies, you said, so what difference does it make?" Mikey was curious as to why he was so wound up.

"I'll edit them and send you them back. Now get out!" Euan shakily mopped his brow with his soiled handkerchief. "You are forbidden to ask staff any more questions about profitability! Do you understand?!" he bellowed.

Mikey had no intention of obeying his nonsense request.

2 Windermere Gardens, Haringey, London: 21 September 2021

The first rain in weeks hammered onto Tracey Ingham's kitchen window and dripped down in rivulets from her blocked gutters, splashing noisily on the plastic windowsill below. She hated the hot weather – she wasn't built for it – it just made the air dank and muggy.

A tear coursed down her chubby cheek and landed on the edge of the iron, evaporating into a hiss of despair.

That useless fucker was supposed to have cleaned the gutter out. I've only been asking for six months. What fucking use will he be now with a broken back? If he thinks I'm pushing his fat arse around in a wheelchair, he has another thing coming.

Ben had been the best thing to happen to her in years. She'd never been as flush with money, and apart from the odd slap when he'd had too much to drink, he'd been the perfect gentleman. He'd even tried bonding with her two-year-old son, to a fashion.

She looked up at the wonky cupboard door where she kept the Jammie Dodgers biscuit tin, normally crammed with cash. She'd often wake up in the morning to give her boy his feed, take a sneaky peek and find it topped up after one of his night shifts on the door. There was no better feeling.

Not now. Funds were on the low side, as was her stash of weed. It was time to seriously think about cutting back. Their campervan holiday to Scotland was the first thing to hit the skids, especially as he couldn't walk or drive.

She stood hunched over her ironing board in her creased jogging pants, having never jogged in her life. Why bother getting changed? She had nowhere to go and no one to impress.

A phone call! Was that too much to ask? A text even, to let her know he was OK and recovering, or that he'd decided to move on?

"Fucking arsehole!" she shouted, then cringed, hoping she hadn't woken her boy.

She'd called the hospital, who'd told her Ben had been admitted to a specialist private clinic in London, though they couldn't tell her which one because that would be 'in contravention of the Data Protection Act'.

"I'm his girlfriend, you stupid bitch! Tell me where he is, right now!" Her repeated calls to the hospital became more frustrated and abusive, until eventually they blocked her number.

She missed him. It was as simple as that. She missed the company, having a man around the house, having a father figure for Ross, and above all else, the money.

She lit another cigarette and inhaled the smoke, willing it to calm her nerves.

What now? she asked herself for the hundredth time. *He's gone, you stupid cow. He's found someone else. There's nothing wrong with him – he's left you, you idiot,* her inner voice of reason ridiculed.

Her daily mental torment was interrupted by the doorbell. She flip-flopped irritably to the front door.

"Who is it?!" she yelled through the letterbox.

Safe House, Bermondsey, London: 21 September 2021

Ben Stockton unlatched the white uPVC door and poked his nose out just enough to see who was standing on the other side. His eyes bulged in panicked recognition before the door barged open and knocked him on his backside.

Doda slammed it shut behind him and slid the deadbolt into place. He leant down and picked Ben up by his ear and his cheek. Ben yelped and grabbed the Albanian's thick, hairy wrist in a futile attempt to soften his grip.

Doda marched him into the kitchen and dumped him on a chair at the kitchen table. The place was littered with takeaway wrappers and containers. He leant over the sink and twisted the Venetian blind closed. Slits of fresh sunlight projected stark lines across Ben's bloated stomach, turning him into a fat, pink zebra.

At 6ft 5in and weighing 160kg, Doda Kelemendi looked like he'd been formed in a foundry out of wrought iron. His pockmarked, angular face and his dark sunken eyes and yellow teeth gave him a permanently sinister appearance. It was hard to imagine him smiling. Despite his murderous façade, he somehow looked younger than his forty-nine years. Perhaps his athletic frame confused people – though not Ben. He was just trying his best not to soil himself.

Doda's honed physique wasn't from working out in the gym, or playing team sports. He'd grown up working on his father's sheep and goat farm in Kukës, northern Albania, which explained why his hands and arms were so large.

At the age of fifty-five, in the late 1990s, his father enlisted to help the Albanian Kosovans in their war of independence from Yugoslavia. It was the last time Doda would see his father alive. Just three months in, he stood on a landmine and got blown to pieces. A similar fate would also see the end of his two brothers.

Doda was no coward, but he was no fool either. The demise of his family he accepted as serendipity. Rearing sheep and goats on the edge of a conflict zone proved to be very tiresome. He spent a lot of time fighting with poachers and disposing of their bodies. The war, on the other hand, offered many opportunities for a man of his skills. There were always legs to break and beatings to mete out for whatever transgressions the warlords saw fit to punish people for, and he had no problem accepting the spoils of war, so he sold the farm and moved on.

One such warlord, Agron Krasniqi, made his way to the UK to ply his trade in London, and took Doda with him. Even though Krasniqi's counterparts in Serbia were homicidal maniacs, sometimes it's better the devil you know, than the devil you don't. After only two years, Krasniqi annoyed a bigger fish, which put an end to his entrepreneurial activities – and his life. Doda became a free agent, and his services were in demand.

"Mr Bell has sent me. Do you know why?" Doda randomly fingered through the food to see if anything took his fancy. He settled for a chicken nugget.

Ben shook in fear.

"He asked me to check if you understand that you have a broken back and an eye missing, and that you are in bed, unseen by anyone?"

He walked over to Ben, whose pink head had turned a lot paler since his arrival. He slapped him hard across the face, causing his glass eye to shoot out of its socket and skitter across the linoleum floor. Doda sauntered over and crushed it under his heel, like a cockroach.

"I'm sorry – it won't happen again, please forgive me," Ben said, cowering under Doda's shadow. "I was hungry. Please tell Mr Bell I'll do as he says, it's no problem. I'll stay in my room, I swear."

Doda's fist came crashing down on the bridge of his nose. Ben's world went into darkness.

Morris Bell's request to not leave any visible marks on him since he'd have to give testimony in court went unheeded.

"Oh dear," Doda said, stamping on one of Ben's bare feet and crushing two of his toes. Trickles of blood from where he'd removed his toenails pooled beneath Ben's foot.

"You can't walk to the door now, fat boy," he sniggered.

On the kitchen worktop, Doda noticed the discarded bandage. He unravelled it and wrapped it tightly around Ben's head, covering his drooping eyelid, then stuck the edges of the bandage to his scalp with surgical tape. Finally, he poked his finger up into one of Ben's flattened nostrils, where he collected a globule of congealed blood and mucus and dabbed it on the bandage, to give the effect that his eye socket was weeping in blood – rather than missing, after falling out of a tree when he was ten and living in Rotherham.

"Mr Bell insists on keeping up appearances – you never know who might turn up," Doda said to his unconscious stooge.

He waited until Ben regained consciousness, then welcomed him back to his new reality with a manic grin on his face. Ben began acknowledging the injuries one by one, in sharp, dull waves of agony.

"Please, Mr Doda, I swear I'll be good. It was just a misunderstanding," he begged, tears streaming down his face and blood spraying off his lips.

"The next time you leave the bedroom, I cut your balls off with a knife and ram them down your throat. Do you understand?"

Ben's usable eye bulged in horror as he nodded in agreement to Doda's ultimatum.

"Where are your house keys? Give them to me – Mr Bell wants your laptop!" Doda yelled. When Ben hesitated, he raised his hand to slap him again.

"Please, no! They're on the hook at the front door. Don't hurt Tracey, she knows nothing about this. Please, I'm begging you."

"Tracey – she's your girlfriend, huh?" He licked his lips, and a hungry grin crept onto his face. "Maybe I fuck her for you. English women love Doda."

His cruel laughter echoed around the hallway as he snatched the keys from the hook and left.

2 Windermere Gardens, Haringey, London: 21 September 2021

"Who is it?" Tracey yelled, over the sound of the rain hammering on the porch.

"Hello, my name's Annabelle. I'm from Hammersmith and Fulham Legal." Molly was sure if anyone was going to answer, it wasn't going to be Ben Stockton himself, more like a girlfriend or his mother.

She had discussed her ploy with Justin in detail, who had told her not to enter the property under any circumstances if there were men inside, and always have her panic button and mace close to hand.

"Who? I've paid my council tax. Fuck off." Tracey was not about to let some slippery bailiff into her house.

"No, I'm sorry, Mrs Stockton, I've not explained myself very well. My name is Annabelle Wise – I'm here about your husband, Ben. I understand he's had a serious accident. We're personal injury specialists … I wanted to talk to you about his compensation award."

Molly always picked a girl's name from her senior school netball team. Annabelle was tall and bad tempered, a perfect combination for a goal attack.

Tracey opened the door furtively and eyed Molly huddled under her umbrella to keep out of the lashing rain.

"What do you know about Ben? Where is he?" Tracey demanded.

"I assume he's in hospital, Mrs Stockton. I understand he sustained severe spinal injuries due to an assault."

Molly wanted the flow of information to come in the opposite direction, but for now she was prepared to help her out. What she had learnt in the short period it took for her hair to frizz up, was that the woman was not his mother, or his wife. She was too young and she wasn't wearing a wedding ring. She assumed she was his girlfriend. Add to all that, she wasn't very happy.

"You mentioned compensation … how much?"

"Well, that's what I'm here to find out." Molly smiled.

***

Molly sipped at a mug of weak tea. "Thank you so much. Where's all the sunshine gone, eh?"

Her friendly conversational tone had begun to disarm Tracey, who appeared happy to have someone to talk to. While her host was in the kitchen Molly had scanned the room for family photographs and evidence that Stockton had recently been there. There was none. No sign of any man having lived there at all, only kids' toys and piles of ironing, none of which belonged to Stockton. She'd noticed a few letters stuffed behind an ornament on the fireplace addressed to a Lee Grassington, whom she took to be the last guy to ditch her.

"Sorry for earlier … I get all sorts of people knocking on the door."

Tracey looped a strand of greasy hair behind her ear, conscious of how frumpy and unkempt she looked, in comparison to her guest.

"And it's Tracey, Tracey Ingham. I'm not his wife." Her disgruntled tone told Molly that Stockton's future with Tracey was in serious jeopardy.

"Hey, no problem. It's nice to meet you, Tracey."

"So, what do you know about Ben? Is he OK?" Tracey's voice was tinged with an odd mixture of worry and ambivalence, as if she cared, but only to a point. Her grey pallor made it difficult for Molly to work out her exact age – mid-thirties she guessed. Her eyes were insipid and bloodshot. A yellow stain around her index and middle fingers was not the only clue to her nicotine addiction – the room reeked of smoke and in the ashtray next to her iron was a mound of butt ends.

"I have limited information, only what we've learned from the hospital, but apparently he's no longer there. Shortly after he was admitted, he was moved to a specialist clinic in London for tests and surgery. It seems like he took a bit of a battering. I understand the police have had someone in custody."

Molly did her best to get on team.

"Have you spoken to him?" Tracey's eyes widened.

"No, I haven't, I'm afraid. It's often the case that patients are under sedation for quite some time. I'm sure he'll make contact soon."

Molly didn't believe that for a minute. She doubted Tracey would ever see him again.

"Well, I wish he fucking would," Tracey murmured under her breath.

"Would it be OK if I took a few details, Tracey, to get things rolling? We can't really do too much without Ben's agreement. The sooner we get that, the quicker the insurance will pay out."

Tracey was all ears. "What do you want to know?"

***

Molly snapped shut her laptop and ended the meeting. "Well, it's been lovely to meet you, Tracey, and I hope to have news for you soon about how Ben's doing, OK?"

"Thanks, Annabelle. You don't know what this means to me, and Ben of course."

Tracey sounded almost excited at the prospect of receiving what could be hundreds of thousands of pounds in compensation. Maybe a few stints pushing him around in a wheelchair wouldn't be so painful.

She opened the door and Molly stepped out into the damp summer air. After they said their goodbyes, Molly retreated through the weed-covered garden, trying to keep her balance on the wobbly paving stones. As she reached the gate, an angry-looking hulk turned in off the street and walked towards the house.

"Hello," Molly said genially.

Doda stopped dead in his tracks and twisted his neck and shoulders. Molly quickened her pace and headed in the opposite direction, her heart pounding in her chest.

Joy's House, Primrose Hill, London: 21 September 2021

Mikey walked up Lilliput Terrace in Primrose Hill, kicking and crunching early dead leaves. He clutched onto a colourful bunch of dahlias and giant daisies he'd bought for Mrs Wong, as an introductory present.

The lady from the flower shop said she'd want them if her daughter's boyfriend came to visit. "Fat chance," she'd added forlornly.

Mikey wondered if it was a good move buying flowers, or whether Mrs Wong would think he was a charmer, which he was. There was no denying that.

"Beware of strange men bearing gifts," Beryl Stott had said to Rob while rummaging in a cupboard for a vase.

On balance he concluded it was a good idea, as he thought Joy would appreciate the sentiment.

He hadn't been on a proper date for months, and that had been a disaster, resulting in an early bath when the girl took exception to him dancing on a table with Thea Horgan. She threw her drink over him and left in a huff. Not the New Year's Eve he'd hoped for, but not all bad as it happened. He'd spent the night with Thea, covering old ground.

He liked Thea. She had a confidence about her that bordered on arrogance, which excited him. So much so, he didn't know whether to stick or twist sometimes. But it wasn't to be. Their relationship hit the rocks after only a short time, and without a single word of animosity. They liked each other way too much for that.

Mikey's anxiety in the bedroom department did not impress her one bit. Nor did his night terrors. He tried to explain things to her, but she didn't want complication in her life, and he understood that. In fact, quite a few girls had said the same thing to him. He hoped to God Joy wouldn't turn out that way.

He reached No. 17 at 7pm exactly and rapped on the door. A porcelain image of a buddha in prayer was fixed to the lintel of the door, which he assumed was a traditional Thai welcome. His heart pounded with excitement.

He'd called the restaurant to reserve the quietest booth and put a bottle of his favourite wine on ice. Mustafa was just as excited and promised Mikey he wouldn't say anything stupid. For the twentieth time that day, Mikey began to relive his earlier encounter with Joy. He swore he could smell her vanilla lip gloss permeating through the door.

The door swung open. Joy stood there, resplendent in baggy blue jogging bottoms, sliders and a white vest top.

"Hey!" Mikey said, faking it.

"I'm sorry, Mikey, I'm having a nightmare with Jules." He could see tears weren't far away.

"Thunderball? What's up, is he OK?" Mikey's humour quickly turned to concern.

"No, he's not OK, he's a little shit. He says I'm ignoring him, and he wouldn't eat his dinner."

Mikey tried to conceal his grin at how cross Joy was, which just added to her allure.

"I threw it in the bin and now he's crying because he's hungry. My mother is kicking off too. She says I should rest up," she said.

"Why don't I come in and have a word with him, man to man? I'm dying for a cuppa. You go and put the kettle on, and I'll sort him out." He smiled warmly.

"Oh, and these are for you," he lied.

Mikey's version of 'I told you so' hit the spot. Joy beamed temporarily and then a tear streaked down her cheek, which Mikey wiped away with his thumb without a fuss.

She guided Mikey into their expansive open-plan kitchen and living space. His stomach growled loudly at the smell of home cooking. A central marble-topped island, which looked like the place where everything happened, was surrounded floor to ceiling with glossy cupboards and built-in appliances. A huge Belfast sink was part filled with pans and a plate bearing the residue of an uneaten meal.

"Jules!" Joy shouted up the stairwell that he had a visitor.

Jules trudged down the stairs, wiping his face with his Newcastle United shirt sleeve. When he saw Mikey, his face lit up, and he ran over to embrace him, nearly knocking him over.

"Aquaman!" he yelled. "What are you doing here?" Jules buried his head on Mikey's chest, knocking the wind out of him again.

"Well, I was taking Joy out for our date, until Alan Shearer torpedoed that idea." Mikey wrinkled his forehead questioningly.

Jules didn't understand Mikey's reference to Newcastle United's past captain, but he understood he had done wrong and looked over at Joy.

"I'm sorry, sis." He began sniffling again, fearing he was in trouble with her, which he was. He hung onto Mikey like he was a safe haven.

"Tell you what, mate," Mikey began, releasing Jules's vice-like grip. "Why don't we get some pizzas in and play some games instead? You can show me your room and … where's your mam? I want to meet her."

Mikey looked over at Joy, who turned away to hide her face. He could tell she was exhausted in every sense of the word – and a little angry her night had been hijacked. Jules, on the other hand, was ecstatic at the new arrangement and bounded off looking for his mother.

Mikey gently wrapped his arms around her, suddenly aware of how petite she was. She heaved as she sobbed onto his shirt, letting the stress of the last three weeks pour out of her.

"I wanted tonight to be special, Mikey. It's all I've thought about for weeks."

Mikey got the impression tears didn't flow easily for Joy, but they did tonight. He didn't want to stop them. He saw them as a good sign. Despite Jules tearing his plans to shreds, Mikey felt a pang of guilt at adding to the pressure she was under. She'd travelled across the world, run her business, looked after the welfare of her family, and was now having to choose between him and Jules. He didn't want that – ever – and he'd make sure she knew.

"Special?! This is as special as it gets for me. Do you know how many times I've run past your door wondering what was on the other side? This is a dream come true."

Joy giggled at his humour, which stemmed the flow of tears.

"I think Jules and your mam are right, though. You look tired… And beautiful," Mikey tagged on, just in time.

"We can have our night at Renoir's any time, eh?" She nodded reluctantly.

He kissed the tears out of her eyes and inhaled her scent. He'd never get tired of that smell. She leant into him for shelter, harbouring in the hold he had on her.

There was no Father Wong. She'd never mentioned him, and there appeared to be no sign of him. No photos or male influence in the house at all, aside from Jules. She didn't need one, but it registered with Mikey at that very moment she needed him.

"Right, you go and sit down in the lounge. I'll pour you a glass of white and put your flowers in a vase, then Jules and I will order some pizzas."

With his arm wrapped around her, he guided her to the couch. She didn't have the strength to argue with him. Mikey shrugged off his jacket and placed his shoes on the doormat. He skipped into the kitchen and began opening and closing doors looking for the fridge and the wine glasses, talking to himself as he went. He found it eventually and ferried a large glass of ice-cold pinot grigio over to her.

With one hand tucked behind his back, waiter-style, he bent down to hand her the glass. The breeze from his body swept his aftershave down on top of her, like an invisible fog of testosterone. "Would Madam require anything else?"

Despite her fatigue, a surge of desire flooded through her. She combed her fingers through his hair and pulled his head towards her, wishing selfishly that she lived alone. She kissed him and let out a subdued groan, as she pinched her knees together.

"No, Madam, that's not on the menu tonight," Mikey quipped, as she let her grip loosen.

"I should think not!" Mrs Wong interrupted.

Mikey shot to attention and turned bright red. "Oh, hello Mrs Wong, I was just … erm ... bringing Joy a glass of wine."

"Ah, is that what you were doing?" Mrs Wong teased, and winked in Jules's direction, who doubled up laughing.

"Pleased to meet you, Michael."

He slithered around the couch to shake her hand. "Pleased to meet you too, Mrs Wong."

Her small hand was cold, yet her grip was strong. She backed off slightly to evaluate Joy's non-date more fully.

"Mummy, this is my friend Mikey. We're having pizza and playing games," Jules said, hopping excitedly, having taken possession of him.

Joy tucked her feet under her bottom and sipped her wine, captivated by their interaction. Mikey needed no introduction as Jules had not stopped talking about him since the moment they met at swim class. If the look on his mother's face was anything to go by, she was mildly impressed.

It was clear who Joy had inherited her looks from. Her mum was an identical aged copy of her, but there was more – she had the air of experience that parents have, cautiousness even, and from what Joy had told Mikey, it had served them very well. Mrs Wong was an impressive lady, and it was clear the apple didn't fall far from the tree.

Joy wasn't surprised Mikey's nervousness didn't last long. He launched himself into easy small talk with her mother while arranging Joy's flowers. He asked about her day, said how much he loved the house and talked about how well Jules was doing. There was no hint of brashness or showmanship. Joy noticed he'd turned down his accent and volume so that her mother could understand him, his deep voice taking on the softer cadence he used when they first became friends. She saw genuine amusement and fascination in her mother's face for the first time in a long time.

Lawan, as she insisted Mikey refer to her, was quiet and reserved. She had little opportunity to engage with people, her COPD restricting her movements. The London air was just too much to take in the summer months.

As the wine kicked in and soothed her nerves, Joy enjoyed the rarest of moments where she had no responsibility and nothing to do but watch and observe.

He is so handsome, she told herself, chewing on the side of her mouth.

She'd never dated a guy that tall before, with blonde hair and such kind eyes. Mikey was literally the heart and soul at Fulwood. His limitless energy and generosity astounded her, so much so, she had hesitated for a long time before talking to him. Perhaps she was like her mother more than she cared to admit, saddled with such hatred for her wretched and spiteful father.

Joy hadn't wanted anyone in her life, not just yet. Her experience of guys was that they inevitably let her down, or lost interest, just like her father had. They were possessive and one dimensional. And there was Jules. The thinly veiled abhorrence and discomfort on guys' faces when Jules welcomed them into his life with his rib-cracking bear hugs was all she needed to see, and unfortunately, she saw it all too often.

So, she'd given up. Until Mikey had arrived.

Mikey had already proven his loyalty and affection for Jules, doing so without hesitation, before she even knew him. It was unfettered and unabashed. He had shown Jules more love and dedication than their father, or any of the other guys, ever had. That's what had stopped her heart beating one day and slackened her jaw – she was in awe of how he had won her brother over so completely.

"I can see your breakfast from here," Mikey had shouted in Joy's direction from the poolside, her mouth gaping at seeing Jules swim like an eel up and down the pool for the first time.

Now he was in her house, with her family. It was like a dream. The irony was, it took the nightmare of him being beaten up for her to break down the final barrier. To begin the healing process for herself. To trust and be loved. Because surely that's what it was – she was head over heels in love with him.

***

A grandfather clock chimed eleven times in the corner of the hallway, heralding the end to what had been a wonderful evening. Jules had gone to bed on the instruction of his mother and Joy had fallen asleep almost immediately, snuggled into Mikey's arm on the sofa. It was time to go.

He picked up her surprisingly dense body and climbed up the stairs to her bedroom, which Jules had insisted on showing him during their tour of the house.

How Alexa had carried him up three flights of stairs was a miracle.

He shouldered the door open and hooked the pinkie of his lower hand around the edge of the duvet and pulled it back. He placed his precious sleeping cargo on the bed and wrapped the cover back over her.

"Sweet dreams," he whispered and kissed her forehead.

13

TARQUIN HAS A RUNNER

The Swann & Key, Kentish Town, London: 25 September 2021

"I think I'm gonna burst," Mikey groaned, leaning against the back of his chair, cradling his unborn food baby.

"I don't know why you order the belly-buster – you never finish it. I doubt even George could," Rob said, grimacing at George, who was clearing plates from an adjacent table, minesweeping a half-eaten pork sausage.

"Seems rude not to give it a try," Mikey said, looking to Jake for back-up.

"We can rely on you for that, Mikey." Jake smiled openly at his friend's refreshingly cavalier attitude to life.

"You don't make friends with salad, although chances are Fruit's going to have to, if it's all back on the cards with Vegan Maddie?"

They both turned to face Rob.

"It's complicated," Rob said amiably. There was no point denying it – it's what he wanted.

They'd met many times in the month since the night of Jake's arrest and things were moving in the right direction. The tickets for Paris were booked, they'd even talked about her moving in with him – once 'everything was settled', which Rob took to mean they'd ditched their respective partners and got together for real.

Mikey sensed the topic was making Rob feel uncomfortable, so he lay off. They never judged each other, they just did what they could to not let each other make a dick of themselves, which wasn't easy sometimes.

"Well, we're here if you want to talk about it, mate. If not, then we'll hear about it on the news, when Lauren has had you whacked."

Rob noticed Jake smirking.

"I don't know what you're laughing at. I reckon you bumped Jasmin off a long time ago and buried her under your patio."

It had been over six weeks since Jake had communicated with Jasmin. She'd told him she was leaving for Nepal to attend a spiritual retreat – 'to discover the ultimate ground of existence'.

'Jake, do you even know what I'm talking about? It's the primordial ground. We will transcend, achieve completion, purity and luminous clarity. Do not ring or text me under any circumstances – we need total silence and darkness to achieve dzogchen.'

He had no clue what she was papping on about, but he was happy to oblige her.

After what Jake thought was a safe seven weeks of incommunicado, he had explained in a brief text message his run-in with the police and had asked her to call him when she returned home, which hadn't happened, although she did send a return text.

> I have returned from the primordial ground. My mind stream is now purified and I am on the path of accumulation, in a prolonged state of effortless and instantaneous meditation, creating emptiness and calm, a horizon of pure joy and self-awareness. At least I was until I read your awful message.
> Only my heightened state of purity has enabled me to deal with this. I have discovered my own true condition, which does not include you.
> (Please can you post any of my things to my mum's house.)

"I had a text from her only yesterday. She's decided to move away to 'new ground' apparently. I think it's for the best." He nodded solemnly.

She had shown Jake kindness in the beginning and tried hard to involve him in her life, which he had appreciated, but closing the curtain on her quietly was the best way.

"Aww, mate, sorry to hear that. I liked Jazz. We had a good laugh together."

Mikey's utopian recollection of their friendship warmed Jake's heart, as there wasn't a single ounce of reciprocation from her. He merely took her ambivalence towards him as a joke. He simply didn't believe he could cause such revulsion.

"What the fuck is 'new ground', Jake?" Rob asked.

Jake shook his head. "Don't ask. She was hard work to be honest," Jake confessed. "I'll not be losing any sleep over her."

Thea came over to clear away their plates and put her arm around Mikey's shoulders as he rubbed his gut.

"Have you eaten too much? You'll end up like my dad!" She kissed the top of his head tenderly and reached down to massage his shoulders and chest.

Thea looked at the three of them, race day ready. Jake's light-grey tailored two-piece hugged his slender body. His magenta silk shirt glistened in the sunlight pouring through the window. Rob's outfit looked expensive – handmade worsted yarn – the matching yellow tweed jacket and trousers shortened to show off his Gucci loafers. To Thea, he still looked scruffy. Even the sunglasses he insisted on wearing indoors looked oversized and sat at an odd angle on his nose.

Mikey's royal-blue cotton suit and pristine white shirt accentuated his athleticism. He was built to wear clothes like that. If he had spent more than £200 on the entire outfit, she'd have been surprised. His waistcoat hugged his midriff like a second skin, and even after cramming a huge fry-up into it, he looked ripped.

Thea sighed, remembering him in her bed. She combed her fingers through the hair on the back of his head and bounced her hip against him.

"You boys are all dressed up nice. Where are you off to, the races?" Her hands brushed across the nape of Mikey's neck as she pinched his shoulder.

"Ascot," came Rob's abrupt response from behind the pages of his Racing Post.

"Oooh, I love the races." She pawed at the material on Mikey's waistcoat, as if willing it to fall on the ground.

"Will you take me one day, Mikey? To the races I mean."

"Sure." He swallowed to dry his throat and looked up at her green eyes bearing down on him. He didn't need to be a telepath to know what she was thinking. He'd seen that look before.

Her fingers went to work in his hair again, her nails scraping on his scalp and ears. She turned slightly and rubbed her pubis bone on his tricep, which made him flinch. He jumped to his feet.

"Right! I'm gonna pinch a loaf. What time's the driver here, Rob?"

He turned on his heels and headed for the toilets without waiting for an answer.

***

A Mercedes minivan with blacked out windows was waiting outside with the side door open. Once they were in, Grenville the Driver pressed the close button and the door slowly blocked out the light from what the forecast said was to be a warm and breezy September day.

"Think Thea's got the hots for you again, Mikey," Rob nodded encouragingly.

"Tell me about it," Mikey said, as if he'd had a lucky escape.

"Only one girl for you these days," Rob said, angling to Jake. "How'd your date go? Come on, spill the beans."

How did the date go? Mikey asked himself. *It was awesome, that's what.*

Unfortunately for Mikey, it was literally the last time he'd seen Joy, bar a few lunch dates. He had a midweek game and training with the Colts and the first team, and next week would be no better – Joy was covering her staff in offices in Central London and she was planning a trip to France to play squash. He had told himself a hundred times not to jump the gun, but it was hard, he couldn't stop thinking about her. And when Thea had laid it on a plate, he'd realised his appetite for fry-ups had disappeared.

"We just chilled at her house, then played games with Jules and her mother."

"Sounds like fun," Jake replied enviously. There was nothing he'd like more than that – a family night in with loved ones.

Loved ones? Ha! When was that likely to happen? Certainly not before all his legal shit was over – and that could be years. Who would want to snuggle up on the settee with an ex-con?

His chest tightened like it was wrapped in wire. He took a deep breath and gripped the door handle to neutralise the panic rising in him. The rush dissipated as quickly as it arrived.

"It was nice. Her mother is a lovely, intelligent lady. Speaks five languages like you, Fruit."

"I'm sure she's a better linguist than me. Thai and Mandarin are way harder to master." Rob's vote of approval made Mikey gush with pride.

"I can't wait for you all to meet her. Christmas is going to be awesome this year."

Mikey didn't mean to be insensitive, but his excitement about the future put a stop to the conversation quicker than a fire alarm.

Jake dropped his head in exasperation. "Listen, lads, don't let my shit get in the way of us having a good time, OK? I'm not in jail yet. With any luck, I might get off with a suspended sentence."

He knew that wasn't true, but it helped to be optimistic.

"Sorry, mate, we're just so worried for you, that's all. Aren't we, Fruit?"

Rob nodded solemnly.

"Well, don't. That bastard tried to kill you, Mikey. I'm not taking the wrap for him injuring himself in the process."

The lads heard a quiver in his voice that sounded out of place. It was fear, fear of the unknown.

"I've my hearing on Thursday at Fulwood Magistrates'. I'm pleading not guilty, so it'll go to Crown. I'm in for the long haul, but I know I've got you guys, Tamara and John to support me. Besides, I've a lot of work to do between now and then. And there's fun to be had, especially now I'm single again."

Jake flashed a lesser spotted toothy grin at his friends, who cheered in unison. Mikey whistled to an absent George Horgan for beer.

Just then, an interior compartment buzzed open between their chairs, and a bucket of iced beer presented itself.

Grenville the Driver was one of them.

***

Ascot Races: 25 September 2021

Linda De Freitus could hardly have wished for a more perfect day at the races. She relished them. At £2,000 per head, it was a day fit for the landed gentry, the rich and famous.

Who would have thought Linda Chesterton from Lichfield would make it to the big time. She knew why of course. She had swept Roger De Freitus off his feet and wrapped him around her finger more than thirty years previous. He was like a moth to a flame. Stupid man – he'd always allowed his dick to rule his brain. He always would. He was the only fly in the ointment of what promised to be a wonderful day.

She wondered to herself how best to avoid his clumsy hands later in the evening, when he'd finished mauling everyone else's wives. Her lip curled in disgust as she watched another unsuspecting female guest flinch in response to his grubby arm and nervously laugh and draw herself away. She sniffed and turned, making her thousandth empty promise to leave him before it was too late.

The sound of champagne corks popping and glasses chinking filled the room with party atmosphere. From her position, she could just about make out Princess Anne's bouffant two balconies away. She was surrounded by even richer guests, several of whom were wearing traditional Arab bisht robes and headdresses. New money in comparison to the De Freitus family.

Linda always found Arab men a little sinister – their need to wear dark sunglasses all the time, and how they stared unnerved her. They never seemed to eat or drink, or literally do anything. They just stood and stared, waiting to be seen. She was relieved not to see any Arabs on DWM's guest list.

It was bad enough dealing with Russian and Ukrainian oligarchs.

All her guests had arrived apart from Rob and his friends. She wasn't the least surprised by that. He was a free spirit like her – here for a good time, not a long time. Evie, on the other hand, was here for both. She could foresee her living at home her entire life, so accustomed was she to the finer things in life. There was no doubt she was her father's daughter. She looked and acted like him, and when Linda said no, he said yes. She could hear her squealing somewhere in the crowd with her rubber-lipped friends, whom she couldn't abide.

Why would they fill their faces with chemicals? They should get more exercise, ride horses, or play tennis. Their clothes don't fit with their huge bottoms and overspilling busts.

"Maybe I'm getting old," she murmured to herself.

"Hell no. It's about time you dumped Roger and ran off with your toyboy."

She spun round, startled. "You are a naughty boy, Michael Stott."

Linda slid into Mikey's outstretched arms, and he dodged her modest but stylish pink feather-strewn fascinator.

"Linda, you look gorgeous." Jake had to almost prise her away from Mikey just to be noticed.

"Oh decisions, decisions! Who to run away with?" Linda began to eeny, meeny, miny moe, before her twin sister, Lesley, appeared and grabbed Jake by the arm.

"Hands off! This one is mine," she said, planting her pink glossy lips onto Jake's impeccably manicured designer stubble.

"Lesley! I didn't know you'd be here!" Jake's face lit up and they embraced each other.

Lesley was Linda's not-so identical twin, who still lived in Staffordshire and held onto her Midlands accent like her life depended on it. Her close-cropped blonde hair sparkled with glitter. She wore bug-eyed sunglasses, and her bright teeth made her look like a retired catwalk model.

"I loathe these events, but I had a call from Robin, who said you were going to be here, and that's all the encouragement I needed. Apparently, I'm the only one clever enough to hold a conversation with you." She nudged him conspiratorially.

Everything she said was the truth. When Mikey had spoken with Rob about how to keep Jake's spirits up, he knew exactly who to invite.

"What am I, a bowl of tripe?" Mikey interjected, pretending to be offended.

Ignoring Mikey, Lesley yanked Jake towards the exit, her pink feather boa snaking around his neck. She grabbed two flutes of Veuve Clicquot and thrust one in his hand.

"Come on, let's explore. I want to go to the saddling enclosure," Lesley said, and left.

"He's a wily bugger, that son of yours. I often wonder if he cares about anything, then he pulls a master stroke like that," Mikey said.

"Robin told me Jake was suffering a bit. Is he going to be OK? Is there anything we can do?"

Linda had known the boys since they were eighteen, when they had visited over the Christmas period. Mikey and Jake were Rob's first real friends. She was genuinely relieved he'd had the sense to surround himself with people who were honest and trustworthy.

During one visit, Lesley had taken a shine to teenage Jake, who looked like a fish out of water, amongst the wealth and privilege. She had never had children, never married, and had established herself as a surrogate aunt from the word go.

"He's a strong guy, Linda, but I'm worried sick what might happen to him if he goes to jail. We're trying not to think about it. Rob's been great. He's sorted him a top barrister and has even resorted to ringing and texting."

"It's more than I get," Linda scoffed.

"Jake has a pal called John Devlin, who's in PR. He's helping Jake's lawyer with their defence case. He was there that night too." Mikey's mood was slipping just talking about it.

"Well, let's all pull together and get him through it, shall we?" Linda said.

***

"Bonjour, Monty, ça va?" Rob said.

"Ça va bien, Rob, merci et toi?" Monty was elated and relieved he'd shown up.

"I'm fine, thank you. Are you both enjoying the day?" Rob resorted to English so as not to make Marcella and Monty any less approachable than they already looked. Marcella's resting bitch face could carve granite.

"It's perfect," Marcella lied, blowing smoke directly in the ear of someone standing next to her. "Are your friends here today?" she asked hopefully.

"Yes, they are. They are looking forward to seeing you both again. Be careful with Mikey, he is very persuasive. He'll be visiting you in Paris if he thinks you'll put him up."

"Sure," Monty said in all sincerity. "He would be very welcome, perhaps with his new girlfriend, hein?" He winked in the direction of Marcella, who smirked knowingly.

"And should we invite you and Maddie also?"

Rob winced at Marcella's suggestion, then looked over his shoulder to see if Lauren was in earshot. Despite Rob telling her it was a boys' day out she had scabbed an invite with his sister, Evie, and was determined to cramp his style.

"Erm, yes, maybe." Rob's discomfort was obvious.

Marcella shrugged mischievously. She was nobody's fool and had worked out what was going on the first time she saw him and Maddie together.

"Talking of Paris, I've booked flights in October. I'm interested in seeing the galleries. Is that OK with you?"

"Sure," Monty said, raising his eyebrows in surprise. "We would love to see you there."

"I'll bring all the documentation for your wealth management plan and go through the next stages. I want to meet Paul also. I'll travel to Rome, if necessary. He sounds like my type of guy."

"You are interested in joining us, Rob?" Marcella ignored his soft soaping.

"It's complicated, but yes. I think I need a new direction in my life, and…" he hesitated, trying to find the right thing to say, "…your company ticks all the boxes for me."

"Let's talk soon then, hein? I think you will love it in Paris."

"Your 'complication'? Does it involve Lauren or Maddie?" Marcella was relentless and didn't care one jot.

Rob grinned and scratched his head. "There's no hiding place with you around." Marcella deadpanned him, waiting for an answer.

"That situation will be resolved in the coming weeks, Marcella, trust me." Rob turned serious for a minute.

"I do trust you, Rob, but you need to open your eyes."

She turned to Monty, who spoke quietly and quickly in her ear. She nodded in submission.

"We're going to take a stroll around. See you later," Monty said, as if it marked the end to their surreptitious conversation, leaving Rob to ruminate over Marcella's warning.

***

Having been bounced from the weighing room for not having the correct pass, Jake made his way to the Gin Room and left Lesley to it. The Gin Room had once been an old steward's office and was now filled with racing paraphernalia as well as a very impressive wall of gin, brandy and whisky. He found himself a vantage point on the balcony from where he could enjoy his overdue G&T, crammed with ice and a slice of orange.

The first slug hit the mark and he felt his nerves tingle. He opened his eyes and began his favourite pastime of people-watching, only to be interrupted by a man in his mid-fifties wearing a light-grey tailored suit, not dissimilar to his own, complemented by dark-tan Oxfords, polished to within an inch of their lives.

"This is a great spot to people-watch, don't you think?" the man said, sipping from his own G&T.

Jake turned to respond and hesitated. The man had a wistful and disarming demeanour, and there was something about the guy he couldn't quite place. His salt and pepper hair was styled perfectly, and so short the wind barely moved it. His slight but strong physique, honed from running many thousands of miles, Jake guessed, was covered in a healthy tan of someone who spent a lot of time abroad. He wasn't flashy and he didn't seem like he belonged there, but he was composed, something Jake recognised in himself – until recently at least.

He turned slowly to look in Jake's direction, his soulful, sad brown eyes mirroring Jake's.

"Yes, it is," Jake conceded. "I always wonder what people do, don't you, to be able to live such lavish lifestyles? Where do they all come from? Where are they going? What motivates them?"

They scanned the faces of people milling around beneath their balcony. The man took a deep breath after several minutes considering Jake's existentialism.

"I suspect many of them haven't done a hard day's work in their lives. They certainly don't know how to go without, or know what hardship means. They've never regretted a bad decision or rued a missed opportunity. What chance have the wretched souls got in life?"

The man wasn't judging them, merely stating a fact as he saw it, as if, paradoxically, they'd missed out by having everything they'd ever wanted.

Jake wondered which category the man would put himself into.

"I've always hoped never to regret. If you hide away frightened of doing something, perhaps worse things happen as a result. And then what? You're filled with guilt for being a coward," Jake said.

An image of Mikey's lifeless body flashed into his mind, kicked to death while he looked on. The panic of what might have been rose in him like lava in a caldera. He breathed it down, the effort causing his body to shake slightly in response.

"Jake. Jake Webster. Pleased to meet you."

The fellow thinker shook his hand firmly. "Alan Willoughby. Pleased to meet you, sir," he said smiling. "I'm just about to reload. It's my round, I think. G&T?"

Jake grinned at his joke and said, "You're too kind, Alan." And they walked to the now-empty free gin bar to fill up their glasses.

Jake learned that Alan was a widower, worked for the Foreign Office and had spent a lot of time in the Far East. He had no children and lived in Surrey, amongst other places. Although Alan was happy to talk about himself, his answers were non-committal and without specifics. Jake had no intention of prying any further – he enjoyed privacy as much as anyone – so was happy to talk about more open-ended subjects he knew little about, like horse racing.

"Who do you think will win the Cup, Alan? Do you think Bagshot Flyer stands a chance?" Jake assumed, wrongly, he would have the inside line.

"I have no idea. That's the man who owns it – you should ask him."

He turned to look at the huge TV screen behind the bar.

Jake's jaw went slack. "Jeeezus, that's Mikey!"

***

"I worry about him, Michael, I really do," Linda opened up, taking Mikey by surprise. "He's hooked up with that wretched girl Lauren, who is attracted to nothing but money. She's bad news, I tell you."

"Don't worry, Linda, I don't think she'll be on the scene for much longer. He's walking the tightrope with Maddie at the moment. I don't know who I prefer least."

Mikey was spilling the beans and he didn't care. He didn't agree with what Rob was doing and he hoped he'd sort his shit out. And quick.

"Oh, tell me that's not true, Michael!" Linda hardly cared for either of the girls and was more worried that her beloved son had inherited some of Roger's ways.

"Rob is gonna be great, trust me. He's hard as nails, Linda."

She snapped out of her gloom when she heard Tarquin Pendlebury call out her name from the parade ring and saw him waving like he was parking a jetliner.

"Linda, darling! I'm so glad you could come. Where's Lesley? She said she'd be here. Baggy is just itching to get out there and make Daddy proud of him."

Mikey stared incredulously at his gangly, camp host, who was straight out of a Jeeves and Wooster novel. Tarquin was clad in a bright off-white linen suit and green suede brogues.

For a sixty-four-year-old man, his teeth were ridiculously straight and white. His ponytailed grey hair was gathered in pink ribbons, leaving Mikey to wonder if the bloke was colourblind or had no mirrors at home.

"And who have we here, Linda darling? He is utterly divine! Tell me you're divorcing that odious husband of yours." Tarquin held out a limp hand for Mikey to shake.

"Mikey Stott. Thank you for your kind invitation into the parade ring, Mr Pendlebury."

Mikey was brought up to respect his elders and not be overfamiliar when in company.

"Dear boy, you will be coming to every race meeting in future. And call me Tarq – everybody does." His fluttering eyes left Mikey uneasy.

Tarq's wet fish of a handshake transformed itself into an octopus, and Mikey had to literally break the suction to yank his hand free of his clutch.

"So, do you think your horse has got a chance, Tarq?" Mikey tagged on his nickname awkwardly while drying his hand in his trouser pocket.

"I should bloody well say so, dear boy," Tarq protested, surprised he would even ask such a question. "I'd put my mortgage on him getting a place at least … if I had a mortgage." He snorted at his own vulgarity.

Jayne Chamley, Tarq's trainer, completed tacking the horse up ready for the race and bounded over to Tarq. She held him by his shoulders and kissed him roughly on both cheeks. Tarq made the introduction and Jayne wrenched everyone's arm in welcome, before going back into full feedback mode.

"Baggy is bred for a six-furlong trip and has a great engine and finishing speed. I've thought about putting cheek pieces on him, but the race is too important to experiment. He's drawn well in four. Charlie Bishop rides – he'll tuck him in upsides and open him up two out. If he doesn't hit traffic, he has a good chance." Linda and Mikey looked on in fascination.

"If he wins this, we'll have him out at Meydan in the winter. Tell me you'll both come?" Tarq implored.

"Aye, we'll be there, won't we, Linda?" Mikey gave Linda his widest eyes and squeezed her hand.

Her fingers intertwined in his and her arm possessively hooked into the crook of his elbow. The prospect of being in Dubai with Mikey filled her head with lurid thoughts. She gave herself a telling off but held onto his bicep all the same.

Inside the ring there were several groups of people all wearing huge hats, expensive-looking blazers and striped waistcoats. A gang of young men guffawed and laughed loudly, slapping one another on the back.

They'd be turfed out of Highfield going on like that! Mikey thought to himself.

A cameraman and a tall, blonde-haired woman in her early thirties sauntered over to Tarq. She was wearing an elegant pair of tan-coloured riding pants, long black boots, a white silk ruffled blouse and a black velvet jacket. Her make-up, nails and hair were flawless. She had a riding crop tucked under her arm and a microphone in her gloved hand. Mikey wondered if she'd ever sat on a horse in her life.

"Tarq, darling, have you anything for me on Baggy?"

Christina Lopez was keen to get the lowdown for her report back to the studio but didn't take her eyes off Mikey and flashed him a long easy smile.

Mikey couldn't believe what was happening. He'd seen this girl on the TV. She was immaculate, and here she was, smiling at him with piercing-blue come-to-bed eyes.

"Never mind about that, darling, I want you to meet two incredibly lovely friends of mine – Linda De Freitus and Michael Stott. Linda, Michael, this is Christina Lopez."

"Hello Christina, pleased to meet you." Linda's warm smile and air kisses were reciprocated with a mwah, mwah.

"Hello, pleased to meet ya," Mikey said in his deep northern brogue.

Mikey could barely believe his luck and decided to use Linda's greeting method. Christina's degloved hand was warm and smooth with a surprisingly strong grip. Mikey leant in holding her hip and brushing a kiss against her silky skin, drawing it out so that he could take in her aroma. He retreated with a smudge of her glittery pink lipstick splashed across his cheek. He knew it would be there and was more than happy for the world to see his badge of honour.

"Have we met before, Mikey?" Christina asked, slightly taken aback by Mikey's invasion of her personal space.

She craned her head and pouted at him. She knew she'd never met Mikey before. It was just an excuse to start a conversation. Her boyfriend would be hanging around with all his friends somewhere, getting smashed on free booze and acting like a complete knob. A day didn't go by when she didn't imagine ditching him once and for all. In comparison to the tall, fair-haired stallion standing in front of her, Marcus was well and truly in the carthorse bracket.

Holding onto his chin, deep in thought, he said, "Well, I dunno, Christina, quite possibly. Were you at Monaco this year? Or perhaps I saw you at the Chelsea Flower Show?" Mikey's bone-dry delivery hit the mark and Tarq, Christina and Linda doubled over, snorting and cackling.

Christina flung her arms around Mikey and kissed him on the opposite cheek. He now had a matching pair of smudges. "You are to die for, you really are."

Tarq took a sharp breath. "Christina, darling, you absolutely must interview Michael and Linda."

"Oh, absolutely darling, give me a couple of minutes." Christina transformed into work mode, as she talked to her producer through her earpiece.

"Linda?!" Mikey said in a fit of panic, his bravado evaporating at a rate inversely proportional to the sweat now pouring down his back. "They're gonna put us on the telly?" Mikey could feel his pulse quickening.

"Don't worry, darling, you won't get a word in if Tarq's being interviewed."

He began to embrace the situation, thinking it couldn't be any worse than having Hansie Van Heerden running at him full pelt.

Christina stepped over with her cameraman and cleared her throat. "OK, people, we are going live shortly. Please can I remind you not to swear."

Fuck me! Mikey thought, his heart thumping in his chest.

"Thank you, Mark," Christina replied absently to her colleague in the studio while looking into the camera.

"Yes, you join me in the parade ring with Tarquin Pendlebury, owner of Bagshot Flyer. Tarquin, you've been here several times before, and you never fail to disappoint us with your style and flamboyance. You epitomise what makes today such a special occasion for many."

Christina's non-question was met by a well-rehearsed dialogue where he thanked everyone for making it happen. Mikey was a little disappointed he had become so neutral and staid.

"And you have two friends with you today?" she asked.

Christina offered Linda the microphone to respond, "Linda De Freitus," she beamed and giggled excitedly.

"Are you having a bet on the race, Linda?"

"Oh yes, I've put my money on Baggy. He's going to win, I'm sure." Linda clenched her fist and punched the air unconvincingly, giggling and bouncing nervously from one foot to the other.

Turning to Mikey, Christina winked and stuck her tongue out at him off camera. "And you are?"

"Mikey Stott from Highfield, Tyne and Wear." Mikey's deep voice boomed his announcement, the lipstick battle scars clearly visible in high definition on every TV screen in the country.

"Gosh, you have come a long way. What do you think of Bagshot Flyer's chances today?"

"Well, Christina," Mikey started, "I'd be surprised if he didn't get a place at least. He's bred for the trip and has a great engine. Jayne's dispensed with the cheek pieces, which I think is the right decision – the race is too important to experiment. He's drawn well in four, and if Charlie can tuck him in upsides, he'll open him up two out. If he doesn't hit traffic, he has a good chance."

Tarq, Linda and Christina were stunned into silence.

"If he wins this, we'll be going to Meydan in the winter. Maybe I'll see you there, Christina?" Mikey winked at her, which set the crowd cheering and wolf-whistling their appreciation of his swagger.

"Well, you don't get invitations like that every day," she replied coyly to the camera. She signed off and turned back to Mikey, hitting him across the arm with her crop.

"You little sod," she said, half laughing. "I hope my boyfriend wasn't watching."

Mikey wondered if Joy followed the horse racing but was confident she would find his audacity funny in any event.

Tarq was hyperventilating with laughter and trying to compose himself to give his jockey his last-minute instructions.

"Charlie, you've heard all I have to say from Mikey the racing pundit."

"Jockeys mount! Jockeys mount!"

Tarq waved Linda and Mikey farewell and they headed off to their box to watch the race.

***

"Dude! I can't believe you were on telly! Where did you learn all that shit about racing?" Jake shoulder-bumped Mikey as he laughed in amazement.

"Ah, just titbits I picked up along the way." Mikey's modesty fooled no one and set off Linda and Lesley into fits of giggles.

"He was great, wasn't he? Did you see Christina's face?" Linda said.

"Come over here, Lesley," Jake said excitedly. "I want you to meet a friend of mine. I know you'll find him interesting … he reminds me of someone, but I don't know who." Jake grabbed Lesley's hand and pulled her towards the balcony.

"Lesley, this is my good friend—"

"Hello, Alan," Lesley said demurely.

"Lesley … how lovely…" Alan looked lost for a moment, as if dealing with a painful memory. He reached out for her hand and leaned in to kiss her tenderly on the cheek.

"You look lovely. I wasn't expecting to see you here. It's so nice to see you."

Jake stared quizzically at a completely different version of his new friend, who was fidgeting like a schoolboy.

"I was sorry to hear about your wife." Lesley's condolence was a respectful formality and nothing more.

"Thank you," Alan said a little awkwardly.

In truth, he hadn't loved his wife for many years, if ever. They had lived separate lives – she Lady Captain at her exclusive golf club and he Minister for Foreign Affairs and MP for Surrey Heath – a neutral existence that had served them both well. It was only when she was diagnosed with terminal cancer that she showed even the slightest affection for him. She soon found out who her friends were when she began vomiting blood on the 7th green.

Alan cared for her to the end. He knew from the onset of their life together he'd made the wrong decision in marrying her. His penance was her servitude.

"So, you guys know each other?" Jake asked.

They shrugged ironically.

"We used to go sailing together and water skiing on Lower Mere Lake. Those were the days, eh?" Alan said. He had years of experience being diplomatic and turning tension into excitement.

"We did, it was so much fun. I still go out now from time to time, though the water's a bit manky these days." Lesley's initial reticence seemed to have dissipated and a hint of a smile crept onto her face.

"You're still running and working out, I'd guess. You always did look after yourself." Lesley eyed Alan quickly.

"I'm still doing karate and martial art training – it's a great fitness regime."

Alan's words nearly knocked Jake on his backside, as the penny dropped. Alan's eyes, hair, size, attitude, personality, and now hobbies – he was clearly looking at an older version of himself. Was this why Lesley had taken a shine to him all those years ago? Had she seen in him what she had obviously lost in Alan?

Lesley released the grip on Jake's arm, her attention firmly held by his senior doppelganger.

Was he deluded or offended? He asked himself. He was an impressive man, Jake thought to himself, as the pair caught up on the last thirty-five years apart.

***

"Congratulations, Tarq. Are you happy with second place? It was a close race." Mikey wasn't sure how Tarq would react to losing and hoped he wouldn't be too disappointed.

"Absolutely, old boy! It's not every day you win a hundred thousand pounds, is it?"

Michael blanched at his response, remembering winners of the best in show at Highfield walking off with a £25 voucher for Strikes garden centre.

"Robin, dear boy, you have some adorable friends. I'm so glad you brought them. And I hear the BBC has asked Michael to appear on their next show."

With that, Tarq left.

"What was he talking about?" Rob asked, confused.

"He's talking about your idiot friend here appearing on TV. He was interviewed by Christina Lopez and made a fool of himself."

Rob's drunken sister appeared at his shoulder in time to mock his friend.

Mikey swigged his beer in silence.

"You and your little friend scrounging off Tarq these days … doesn't surprise me. The idiot will splash money on toyboys all week long."

Evie teetered in her heels, trying to overcome the effects of several bottles of champagne and three lines of cocaine.

"Fuck off, Evie, no one's interested in anything you have to say." Rob was less inclined to turn the other cheek.

"You're brave in front of your friends, aren't you? Too frightened to stand up to Daddy though. You're pathetic," Evie sneered and threw back her head as she turned to leave.

The delicate balance of fluids in her inner ear had taken a hammering from the cocktail of alcohol and drugs she had consumed, and she staggered into the back of Marcella Montreaux, spilling her wine.

"What are you doing! Are you drunk?" Marcella demanded in Italian, brushing her skirt with a napkin.

"Fuck off and go back to your own country, you stupid bitch!" Evie screamed in her face.

Marcella never looked that far away from punching someone, even on a normal day – Monty had seen her explode on several occasions for a lot less. He was usually quick to read a situation and step in to prevent bloodshed, but not today.

She swung a fist, catching Evie square on the jaw with a resounding thwack, which sent her spinning to the floor in a haze. Marcella calmly placed her glass on a table, nodded at Monty, then left.

The only two people who didn't hear the commotion were Alan and Lesley. They were busy picking up where they'd left off.

14

THE HEARING

"Mr and Mrs Van Heerden, after detailed deliberation, having considered the merits of your application for leave to remain, we regret to inform you that you have been unsuccessful. A report will be made in due course that explains our reasoning in accordance with the guidelines issued by the FCO."

Hansie looked on, confused. He understood what he was hearing, but he just couldn't believe it.

"No! This can't be happening!" Trixie held his hand tightly, and placed her other hand on his bulging forearm to try and calm him.

"I don't understand … why are you doing this? It's because of me isn't it, because of what I did? You asked me to explain what happened, and I did … I told you everything … I told you the truth. I was cleared by the courts in South Africa," he protested.

"Mr Van Heerden, please remain calm. I will issue the full report. You must understand we have our jobs to do. We are merely following the rules. Your circumstances leave us no choice."

The coward refused to make eye contact with Hansie, and his condescending tone drew the conversation to an end.

"Your application has been submitted automatically for appeal. The individual circumstances of your case may be looked upon sympathetically by the appeals panel. In any event, your UK visas will expire on 31 December 2021, at which time you will be forcibly repatriated, if you have not left the country voluntarily. If you fail to comply with the conditions of your visa, you will be held in contempt of court and imprisoned. Do you understand?"

"You're sending us to prison?" Hansie fumed.

"No, Mr Van Heerden. If you follow the rules, that will not happen. Your appeal date is currently set for 17 December, which I fear with the Christmas holidays fast approaching, may be delayed. If that is the case, you will be required to continue your appeal from outside the UK."

Hansie couldn't bear it any longer and jumped to his feet angrily.

"You have no idea what we have gone through!" Hansie snarled, through gritted teeth in Afrikaans. "And let me tell you, nothing you people have said would stop me from doing it again. Nothing!"

The memories of that day on the farm would haunt them for the rest of their lives. Now they were being forced to return to the horror of it all.

"Thank you for your help," Trixie said nervously as she stood to her feet.

Her crackly voice got Hansie's attention and calmed him down. He wrapped his huge arm around her to protect her. Without her, his life wasn't worth living.

***

The outcome of Jake's twenty-minute appearance at Fulwood Magistrates' Court was wholly predictable. Tamara told him how the day would pan out and she was proven right.

"What do you reckon?" Jake asked John as they exited court.

"There's not much to say in my view. The injuries are too serious – we knew that. I was interested to see who was in the gallery, though," John said with intrigue.

"Did you recognise any of them?" Jake asked.

"No, but I took photos."

John whispered his response, knowing it was against the law to have cameras in the courtroom. He took the risk of being charged with contempt of court anyway.

"There has to be something that links those attending and Ben Stockton. We've not found anyone he knew, and the one we do know of, Tracey Ingham, didn't turn up."

"Why risk taking photos?" Jake asked.

"We can cross-check them with known associates. There's always someone who gets flagged up. This will be no different."

"Did you see the meathead sat at the back? I wouldn't want to bump into him in a dark alley."

"I think we've seen him before. Molly visited Ben Stockton's girlfriend and someone matching his description turned up as she was leaving. She had a nasty feeling about him. I've texted her his picture for confirmation and asked her to do a follow-up visit. It may explain why Tracey wasn't here."

"Is that wise, if he's hanging around?" Jake asked.

"Good point." John kicked himself for not thinking of the danger himself.

"The police turned up in force as well – DS Cantly and the other fella. I suppose that's to be expected," Jake stated without interest.

"It isn't, though. I don't know why they both came. You'd think they'd have better things to do. The bundle will have been sent and summarised beforehand. The outcome was predetermined, so why attend?" John made a mental note to research the two officers.

Over the last four weeks, Jake's anxiety levels had crept steadily upwards. He was relying on Matsumoto's mindfulness techniques more than ever before. Unless he was with John, that is.

Tamara was right. He was a huge benefit to the investigation – but it was more than that. He wanted to be around him. He was like a safety blanket, a barrier to everything that was bad. After all the years of self-sufficiency, Jake now felt valued, in a way Mikey and Rob had never made him feel. He wasn't taking anything away from them – they were his best friends – but with John, it was different somehow. More permanent.

Bell and Sandringham Legal, Farringdon, London: 29 September 2021

"Report!" Morris Bell said irritably, snatching his burner mobile off his desk.

"It's gone to Crown."

"I know that, you idiot, give me the details!" he demanded. He was in no mood to drag the information out of the man.

"He requested permission to travel to Spain for a pre-booked holiday, which they granted."

"Excellent. Call me if you hear anything else."

"Hang on a minute, there is something else. Doda turned up to the hearing. I don't think that was a good idea."

"I don't pay you to think." He hung up and dialled Doda's number.

"Who's this?" Doda answered angrily. He'd have to get a new burner if someone had got hold of his number.

"What business did you have attending court? You've been seen," Bell snapped.

"By whom? The police? They don't know me, no one does. I'm clean. What's your problem?"

Bell hated speaking with him. The lack of respect in his voice grated him, but he was a necessary evil, in every sense of the word, and had no issues doing the dirty work, which Bell had to admit he was good at. He'd have to tolerate him a while longer.

"Listen to me, do not take any unnecessary chances. We are at a critical stage." Bell lowered his voice, fearing Deidre, his secretary, might hear him. "Did you visit Stockton? And the girlfriend? I want that laptop. I need to check his emails!"

"Yes, I have it, but Stockton needs to go. He's an idiot. He'll not answer the door again."

Bell thought he could hear him grinning. "And the girlfriend?"

"She had no respect for me. Now she's learned." Doda chuckled to himself.

Bell rubbed his forehead, trying to scrub the grotesque images he had conjured up. He didn't want to know the details. He hated the sight of blood, even the thought of it.

"Forget the girl. When it's over you can deal with Stockton. For now, I want Webster followed. Go to Spain if you have to. I'll get you his address – he'll have had to declare where he's staying to the court. Make sure he gets arrested. And Doda – do it quietly."

15

OUT WITH THE OLD

414 Ainsley Road, Hackney, London: 4 October 2021

Jake knocked on his mother's door after he tried the handle and found it locked. *Good*, he thought to himself. He'd spoken to her a hundred times about security. It had finally sunk in.

"Mum, it's me – are you there?" Jake peered through the grimy window into an empty room and saw a shadowy movement.

"One minute," Denise replied croakily, unlatching several deadlocks.

A gap opened in the door and a watery eye peered through. She stepped aside quickly and closed the door the moment Jake was inside, clipping his ankle, such was her urgency to keep the outside world away.

She led him through the hallway, wallpaper curling up from the skirting boards, which were laden with dust. Piles of junk mail carpeted the worn-out linoleum.

In the kitchen, the small dining table, where Denise spent most of her day, was covered in unwashed laundry. A glass ashtray mounded in cigarette ends teetered on the edge. The narrow galley resembled a war zone. Unwashed pots were stacked up in the sink, and a putrid stench of grease and rotting food filled the air.

A missing pane in the rear window had been replaced with a black bin liner that fluttered in the autumn breeze. Jake took in the scene. He'd seen it many times. Denise never worried too much about appearances, and it hadn't worried him that the house was a tip – it just was. There were no airs and graces in a six year old. He'd learned to live with it.

His stepdad's influence had changed all that, at least for a while. Stewart was intelligent and dependable. He had got her clean, turned her into a nice person. She'd put on a little weight and had begun to enjoy life. They spent holidays in Cornwall each year, having bike rides and being normal. She was on the straight and narrow, or at least Jake thought she was, until he arrived home from school one day when he was sixteen.

"He was too nice for me, Jake. I was holding him back. He can find someone better than me."

She led Jake to believe it was his decision to leave and that he had abandoned them. But then, during one of Stewart's visits from Scotland months later, he told Jake the real reason for his forced departure – he'd had to move to Glasgow to tend to his dying mother. And that he'd wanted Denise and Jake to go with him.

"It'll be like an extended holiday, Denise. You'll love it."

"It's me or her, Stew. You decide."

She told him not to come back, and didn't blink an eye, whereas Jake was devastated. He begged his mother to get him back, but it was no use. She returned to drugs, and like all users, gradually drowned in self-loathing and paranoia.

Six months later, Stewart's mother died, by which time the damage was done, not only to their relationship but to herself. Stewart knew Denise wasn't prepared to go through drug therapy and medication for a second time. He died in a road traffic accident twelve months later.

Jake looked at his mother with a mixture of pity and anger. There was no point asking questions he knew the answer to. He wasn't in the mood to listen to lies and excuses.

"Come here, I need a cuddle." He offered up his arms and she leant against him and began to sob quietly.

"I'm sorry, Jakey … I'm a mess."

He felt the cold sting of his mother's tears through his shirt. His temper flared. He should have been there to look after her, but he had tired of her selfishness and self-destructiveness and kept away so he didn't have to witness it. His body shook with rage. He breathed it down as he rocked her slowly in his arms.

"Come on," Jake said, with an air of authority. "Let's get the place tidied up. I'll order Deliveroo and get some shopping in. We can turn it into a game if you like?"

Jake remembered being brainwashed into chores by Stewart. His mother then used the same ploy for years. In truth, he didn't mind, so long as he was occupied. Denise smiled at the memory, something she hadn't done in a long time.

After three hours, moving from room to room, scrubbing and cleaning, the house looked presentable, although no amount of carpet shampoo and detergent was going to completely remove the funk of damp and cigarettes. Jake spent forty-five minutes in the back yard cleaning up the dog-ends and sweeping away the rubbish. He stacked some old timber batons the council had left behind after they'd repaired the roof, and cleaned the windows. The old shed had been fitted with a new padlock – he noted with curiosity – although the garden hadn't been mowed in a while.

He returned to the house, washed up and paid for the pizza when it arrived. Jake sipped at the sweet tea Denise brewed in an old teapot he remembered as a child. The meat feast provided long overdue sustenance that took its hold on Denise's stomach, which groaned in relief at having something to process.

They chatted openly and Jake updated Denise about the trips he'd taken to Newcastle and Ascot. It filled her with pride and happiness that he had such good friends and was making his way in the world. He paid her overdue utility bills online and gave her some money to get her hair done.

The sole purpose of his visit was to tell her about his prosecution, but he changed his mind when she began to relax.

"What's the score, Mum? I need to know where your head's at." Jake couldn't help asking. Leaving things unsaid worked to a point, but they were past that.

"I'm not back on the gear, if that's what you mean. I'm done with that. I made a promise to you and I'm keeping it."

She lit another Marlboro and sat up straight, as if daring him to question her word. Her lip trembled in unison with her hand as she took a drag on her umpteenth cigarette of the day.

"I take medication for my nerves, that's it." She handed him the bottle of antidepressants, which she fished out of her pocket, and he inspected it without comment.

"You look thin, Mum. I worry about you."

He knew antidepressants suppressed appetite, but his hug told him all he needed to know about how malnourished she was.

She shrugged and looked at the clock on the wall.

"Where's Lance?" Jake asked, guessing the cause of her anxiety.

She turned her head away from him, as if just stating Lance's name would make him appear. Lance had been on the scene for the last eighteen months. He was yet another one of her failed relationships that dragged on until the police arrived to throw them out for one too many beatings.

"He's not hurting you, is he?"

She took a deep breath and slowly shook her head. Just then, the front door opened. Her nightmare scenario was now reality.

***

"What's he doing here?"

Lance Anderson was an overweight, greasy-haired, sad excuse for a human being. Jake had disliked him the moment they met. The feeling was mutual, so much so they'd barely acknowledged each other more than once or twice. At fifty years old, Lance had achieved nothing in his pointless life, apart from an impressive criminal record and several stints at Her Majesty's pleasure for drug offences, theft and assault. Jake eyed him with utter contempt.

Is this who people will compare me to? The thought angered him.

"I asked you a question." Lance stepped forward menacingly, towering over her, his eyes dilated and his breathing irregular.

Two equally unpleasant-looking scumbags wearing garish red and orange tracksuit tops appeared at the kitchen door. Denise shook with fear under the eager eye of the orange-clad scumbag, a tubby, pasty-faced man in his forties fidgeting with his scrotum and rolling his tongue over his rotten teeth.

The penny dropped. This vile bastard and his mates were abusing his mother. She was a prisoner in her own home. They were using it as a doss house, if the state of the bedrooms were anything to go by, and she was too scared to do anything about it. He shuddered with rage.

In recent weeks, Jake's panic attacks had surged up from his stomach and into his lungs and throat, overwhelming his senses. If he didn't catch them early enough, he would literally pass out, drowning in fear for his own future.

Not now.

He could see what Lance and his guttersnipes were doing to his mum. He'd seen it a thousand times before.

Bullies.

They always wanted the high ground, the power, to exact dominance and cruelty. It's all they were capable of – inflicting misery on others - in an attempt to improve their own miserable existence by proxy. Their need for superiority had to be satisfied.

Jake stood to leave, avoiding eye contact. He had to get them out of the house. It was too cramped inside. He shuffled around them and walked to the front door, receiving a serenade of mockery and abuse.

He locked the door and put the key in his pocket, turned around and slowly walked back to the kitchen, jinking through the uninvited and now thoroughly confused house guests.

The chorus of abuse came to an abrupt halt. The three men gawped through the kitchen window at their object of derision.

Lance grabbed Denise by the hair, hoisting her fragile, cowering body off her chair, a look of pure evil on his face.

"Your boy thinks he can take us on."

Lance's sour breath washed over her as he laughed at her pleas to spare him.

"Don't hurt him, Lance … I'm begging you … please."

She dropped to her knees and pulled on his hoodie, which stretched over his pot belly. His cigarettes and lighter fell to the floor. In a temper, he struck her hard across the face. She hit her head against a cupboard and blood began oozing from her nose.

"Keep her here!" he snapped to orange scumbag, then jerked his head at red scumbag to follow him into the garden.

An early morning autumn shower had moistened the algae that had formed on Denise's dank patio where the sun never shone, giving it a bright-green hue. Two plastic chairs were backed up against a white brick wall, which formed the boundary to her narrow back yard. Weeds, nettles and invasive plants had made a decent attempt to claim back to nature what had once been Jake's play area as a child, defeated only by a narrow strip of trampled grass that led to the shed.

It was a secluded spot and suited Jake's purpose.

Lance and his pal sauntered out and stood opposite Jake with their arms crossed.

"I'd like a word with you about my mother," Jake said in a whisper, making Lance crane his head over the noise of the traffic passing by beyond the confines of the garden wall.

Lance looked towards his bemused sidekick, the green slime squelching beneath his feet.

"You hear that? He wants a word with us about his mother."

Red scumbag snorted a laugh.

Lance noticed a length of 2x2 conveniently propped against the shed behind them. He reached for it and weighed it in his hands to gauge its suitability for inflicting injury.

Perfect, he thought.

Jake moved to his right and shuffled towards him by half a step. He stood tall with his hands in his pockets, offering himself as a target. Lance swung for Jake's head in one fluid and entirely predictable motion.

Jake didn't need to look at the weapon. He knew where it was and how fast it was travelling. He didn't need to look at Lance's face. He knew it was bristling with hate. Jake's focus wasn't even on red scumbag, whose ability to breathe properly and see out of his right eye was half a second away from being irrevocably diminished.

Jake's full attention was on Lance's feet – or, more accurately, his balance – in the smooth-soled shoes he'd chosen to wear that morning.

The four-foot-long wooden baton whooshed over Jake's ducked head on its relentless orbit, its momentum taking it towards the bridge of red scumbag's nose. A spectacular mist of blood splashed across the whitewashed wall. Unfortunately for red scumbag, he could only partially see the pattern it made, his vision being obscured by the rusted nail protruding from the end of Lance's weapon of choice, which had planted itself squarely through his right eye.

Lance barely noticed what he'd done, or the screams emanating from his friend. He was already swinging in reverse, the return flight taking an identical path. This time, there was nothing to stop it, apart from Jake's head, which he had weaved out of the way.

The swing had shifted Lance's weight to his left heel, which Jake deftly swept out from under him, an action lubricated by the green scum underfoot. Such was the effort Lance put into the assault, his body lifted itself almost horizontally in the air and he fell to the ground with a loud crack, as his head and right elbow impacted the cement.

If Jake had to guess, he'd say his humerus was fractured and his vision seriously impaired by the whack to the back of his head. Only four seconds and one ankle tap later, there were two bullies lying on the floor - one bleeding from his face, one with a broken arm, both concussed. A feeling of déjà vu swept over him.

He stepped over and stamped on Lance's left shoulder with his heel, cracking and dislocating his collarbone. He deserved to be in a lot of pain for what he had done to his mum.

Red scumbag had got to his feet and stopped screaming. He was holding his hands over his eye. Jake could hear the rage building up inside him. Two seconds later, he fell to the ground, clutching another ruptured testicle. Jake felt not one ounce of sympathy for the man, who would likely never have children – which maybe wasn't a bad thing for the human race.

He walked calmly into the kitchen to find orange scumbag staring in horror at what he'd just witnessed through the window.

"Time to leave," Jake said evenly. "Take whatever you have stashed in the shed and piss off. If I see any of you here again, I won't be so gentle next time."

Orange scumbag didn't need telling twice. He ran to the shed, digging a key out of his pocket, and skidded on the algae mantrap, like Bambi on ice. He returned with a plastic bag, lifted Lance and red scumbag to their feet, and they left without a word.

Bullies. They're all the same.

Fulwood Sports Centre, Kentish Town, London: 4 October 2021

Mikey convened the 4M meeting in Euan's absence, having been told to 'get all the other rubbish out of the way' before his arrival. No one had complained, especially not Beverly Lancing, whose gag reflex would be spared another workout.

Will Halperson summarised the preparations that had been made for the squash competition in December, and the other department heads made short work of their presentations in a rush to get to the main agenda items: redundancies and budget cuts.

"What's going on, Mikey? What's Euan's game? There's no way we're losing money. There must be a problem at Head Office or at another centre… Why should we bear the brunt?"

Lisa was far from militant, but her question raised agreeable chuntering from everyone present.

"I wish I knew. Euan told me not to talk to you all about profitability or productivity. He said it's none of my business. Which leads me to believe he's hiding, or not telling me, something. He said he was going to make an announcement." Mikey shrugged.

"I think he's dodgy," Big G chimed in. "I saw him getting out of a brand-new Porsche at Tesco the other day. I don't know what he earns, but I doubt his salary's that good he can afford a new Cayenne."

"He drives a Porsche?!" Lisa exclaimed. "How does he get his lardy arse in and out of it?"

"It's an SUV. They go for well over a hundred grand." Big G had done his homework.

"He must have won the lottery or something," Carla said.

"You don't think we'd have heard? He'd be rubbing our faces in it … which begs the question why he isn't." Big G wanted answers.

"Maybe it wasn't his car?" Carla ploughed on with giving him the benefit of the doubt.

"I wondered that, Carla, then I noticed he has a private registration plate with his initials. Those aren't cheap either. He doesn't have a lot of family, but I'm sure those he does have hate him as much as we do, so it's not inheritance. No, he's bent. He's dealing drugs or something." Big G wasn't letting go.

"How much cash do we take a week in the restaurant, Jo?" Mikey asked.

"Not that much really … maybe £2,000 a week. I bag it all up and a security company collects it. It's the same with the class fees. Elaine would know if he had his hand in the till." She shook her head, dismissing Mikey's thought process.

Big G raised his eyebrow sceptically. "I trust her less than Fatboy."

Mikey's mind began to whirr. "Bev, last month, the net increase in numbers was 150 and this month it was 78. The membership fees are all done on direct debit or standing order, right?"

Beverly nodded.

Mikey continued: "Can you remember in the last meeting what he said about increases in memberships and classes? He said, 'No amount of swimming classes, membership uptake and sporting events is going to change anything.' I think Big

G's right. I don't know how he's doing it, but he's syphoning money somehow."

"There's no way, Mikey. Head Office would see it," Beverly said emphatically, while packing her paperwork away. She'd grown tired of talking about him. The whole thing had left her disheartened.

"Do me a favour and just keep this between us. If he finds out we're on to him, he might do something stupid."

Everyone agreed.

"I've stuff to be getting on with. I'm not waiting around for him any longer." Beverly started a stampede of legs, everyone using her excuse to avoid hanging around.

Mikey sat alone deep in thought. Something wasn't right, he knew it, but there was no way to find out. Euan and Elaine had the finances locked down. He wished he had Joy around to talk it through with.

"Michael Stott to the manager's office! Michael Stott to the manager's office!" Luke heralded the opportunity for Mikey to do some digging.

***

Mikey diverted to Beverly's office at reception for another brief chat before his meeting with Euan. There was something that didn't add up, and he needed Beverly to help him. Despite her doubts in the 4M, she readily agreed. Five minutes later, Mikey vaulted over the turnstile and diverted through the main pool area to check on Lisa, only to find Arthur fully clothed in the waiting area.

"Arthur, what's up, mate? You not feeling well?" Mikey dropped to his haunches and held Arthur's hand.

Arthur's eyes were red from crying. "Mr McArdle said I was banned because I was sick in the changing rooms last week. He said I shouldn't be here, and that I was a 'lying bilty'. Mikey, I promise I have never lied to anyone. You can ask my grandad."

Arthur sobbed his heart out till his breathing reached the point of hyperventilation.

"On your feet, Barracuda!" Mikey snapped Arthur out of his hysteria. "We are going swimming. Come on."

Mikey was furious at how cruel Euan had been and decided to put things right with Arthur, who needed no more encouragement. He grabbed Arthur's kit bag and led him to the staff locker room, where they put on their swimwear.

Mikey took the chance to ask him about how he was doing in class, his sickness and his diet. There was no doubt in Mikey's mind that he was overindulging, that his grandparents were allowing him to eat whatever he wanted.

"Listen to me, Arthur," Mikey said as they got ready. "It's very important you do not eat before you go swimming, OK? I would never do that, because it would give me a sore tummy and I'd be sick."

Mikey laboured the point, by rubbing his stomach and nodding with his eyes wide open. He saw how contrite Arthur looked and made a mental note to get Jules to reinforce the message.

They jogged to the poolside and Arthur jumped into the shallow end with the rest of the class. Mikey apologised to

Lisa for the disruption while all the class waded over to hug Arthur. They had heard Euan calling out their friend, and it had set some of them off crying in sympathy – and in terror they'd be banned too. Seeing him reinstated made everything better.

"Don't worry, Mikey, it's great to have you here. Is Arthur going to be OK? Euan said he wasn't allowed in any more."

"I'll deal with him."

With that, he leapt into the pool.

"Last one to the deep end's a horse's arse!" he shouted while swimming squid-like to the end of the pool, the whole class frantically trying to keep up with him.

Lisa watched on as her class plan was destroyed in seconds. She'd never seen them swim so fast and so hard. Every one of them wanted to impress Mikey and be near him.

He relayed up and down, fetching the stragglers and encouraging every single stroke until they all reached the end. He captivated their attention. Whatever he said, they all repeated. The class of twenty cheered and patted one another on the back when they finished his tasks.

He shouted out their nicknames, and they whooped and roared. The noise was off the scale. Towards the end, Mikey split the group into boys against girls – political correctness rarely featured in his thinking. He joined the girls' team and taunted the boys, calling them sea slugs and bottom-feeders. The hour-long class flew by, and Lisa was left wondering how she would cope with their disappointment at him not being at their next class.

She blew her whistle and received a universal groan of displeasure.

"Everybody out!" she shouted in her thick Scottish brogue. They filed out, laughing and joking, and streamed into the changing rooms. Arthur stopped and gave Mikey a hug and told him he loved him.

"I love you too, Barracuda. Now into the showers and make sure you dry off properly, OK? I'll meet you and Jules for a milkshake in Bannister's." Arthur cheered and ran to tell Jules the news.

"Mikey, I don't know how you do it." Lisa shook her head in amazement at the power he had over people. They would literally fall at his feet.

"Do what?" he asked, genuinely confused.

He gave her a kiss on the cheek then ran off to get changed and meet Euan. All this splashing around having fun had given him an idea.

***

"You took your time. My call went out over an hour ago." Euan's idea of a welcome didn't impress Mikey.

"I had a class and a few issues to sort out," Mikey said by way of an explanation.

"Such as?" Euan rolled his eyes patronisingly, as if whatever it was couldn't be solved in seconds by someone with his intellect.

"Carol Dewhurst, the council's Head of Sustainability, caught wind of a member of staff bullying a guest."

His lie took considerable effort to tell without cracking up.

"Why wasn't I informed?" Euan said indignantly. "Who was it? I need to arrange a disciplinary meeting with Personnel." His jaw wobbled and bounced as he shook his head in disbelief. "Do we know what happened? Did they make a complaint? What did Carol say?"

"It only happened a couple of hours ago. Arthur Soames in the special needs class said someone called him a 'liability' and banned him from the pool for being disabled. He's too frightened to say who it was. He thought they were going to hit him."

Euan's mouth gaped in horror.

"I just hope the press don't hear about it," Mikey said, twisting the knife. "That's all we need, someone being discriminated against for being disabled. What sort of arsehole would bully a boy with Down's syndrome? They should be locked up."

Mikey was met with terrified silence but carried on, gleefully. "I feel the same as you, Mr McArdle. I was shocked, let me tell you." Mikey shook his head and tutted out loud. "I spoke with Arthur and suggested we had a milkshake after I'm finished here. As yet, he's refusing to point the finger. Perhaps if you came along, he'd be more receptive."

Mikey was having fun watching him squirm.

"No!" Euan jumped in, hands raised. "You deal with him, Michael. You have a way with these people. Just make sure he doesn't make a complaint. I don't need it right now."

Even then, the disgusting bigot couldn't bring himself to show some respect. Beads of sweat hurdled over the wrinkles on his forehead. His soiled handkerchief struggled to absorb his liquid panic.

"You wanted to talk with me about something, Mr McArdle," Mikey said, handing him the minutes of the 4M he failed to show up for.

"It can wait," he said, without energy.

Mikey took that as his ticket out of there.

John Devlin Public Relations, London; 4 October 2021

John was first into the meeting room. Cakes and doughnuts were the order of the day, with fresh coffee, and green tea for Derek, at the ready.

Molly was first to arrive. Her eyes lit up. "John, marry me?"

"Ha, don't toy with my dreams, Moll," John said, playing along. "You got much to report?" He literally couldn't wait to find out.

"Yes. Let me have a cake first, will ya," Molly said, reaching for a vanilla slice. Her proposition was non-negotiable.

Justin and Derek arrived together and busied themselves linking their laptops up. Patrick was last. He thanked Molly for preparing him a coffee and securing him a Bakewell tart.

"Good work, John."

John grinned in response to Patrick's endorsement.

"Now we are all adequately smacked up on sugar, let's make a start, shall we," John said.

Justin stepped up and began his report in methodical fashion.

"Just a quick recap on our remit, which was to establish the credibility of Ben Stockton, his injuries, and, consequently, the veracity of what could possibly be a sizeable insurance claim. And the prosecution of John's friend, Jake. To do this, we are looking into Stockton's private life and work history. We are also investigating the events leading up to and including the night of 27 August 2021."

Justin took a breath and continued. "Ben Stockton is clearly not who he says he is, which is suspicious in itself and proves John's assertion that he's dishonest. The sophisticated lengths he's gone to hide his personal information leads me to conclude even 'Ben Stockton' doesn't know who Ben Stockton is. We have no record of who he's worked for, where he came from or where he lived before he moved in with Tracey Ingham in March 2021. Tracey confirmed to Molly he's never had a single item of mail delivered to his home."

Molly nodded. "My guess is it's redirected, to avoid a trail. Tracey's a beard, nothing more."

"The man calling himself Ben Stockton has the intellect of a slug – if we're to believe John – so he can't be operating alone. In fact, I'd go so far as to say this is a team effort. So, if we assume a vendetta against Jake is not the motivation here, then what's going on with the bloke?"

"Molly, for the benefit of everyone present, tell us briefly what you learned when you met Tracey Ingham."

Molly put an image of her on the screen that she took during their meeting.

"She's common. All-garden East End trash. Her relationship with Stockton was transactional. She kept the house, after a fashion, while he paid for it. She has a child from a previous relationship. I'm guessing his name was Lee Grassington, as there was mail addressed to him – I need to check that. There were no photos or evidence of his belongings, which was surprising, considering he's been there for six months. She met Stockton trying to score some drugs off him, and they consummated their whirlwind romance the same night. She thought she'd hit the big time – he'd regularly come home with plenty of cash. I assume he was dealing."

"Did you get his mobile number?" Derek asked, speculatively.

"It's a burner phone, Derek. I've already tried it."

"What about a laptop or tablet?" Derek thought he'd put on a lottery ticket at the weekend if the answer was yes.

"Yes, but we'll never see it. As I left Tracey's, a huge ugly guy turned up. He took it away, saying it was Stockton's ex-employer's and they wanted it back. It shook her up, though. When I rang her, she said he got a bit rough with her. He had blood stains on his shirt." Molly shivered at the memory of him.

"Do you think it was the same guy we saw in court?" John asked, pointing at an image on the projector.

Molly nodded. "That's him. Shockingly ugly. I do not want to see him again."

"He looks Balkan - maybe Albanian," Patrick offered. He was the best travelled and no one argued with his guess.

John lowered his tone to get everyone's attention. "It's safe to say, if we're dealing with people like this, we all need to watch our step. Do not use your own name in communications and make sure Project Fandango remains secret." He cursed himself for the danger he'd already put Molly in.

"Derek, what do you have please?" Justin was keen to keep the pace of the meeting going.

"In 2020 there was £1.2bn of fraudulent insurance claims made. The insurance industry knows this, as they've prosecuted the claimants. Best guess is this is the tip of the iceberg."

Derek hesitated to let the information sink in.

"Most claims are individuals who wish to gain some form of retribution from an employer, or an unsuspecting driver not paying attention at a roundabout. Many feel like they need payback from years of premium payments. They don't injure themselves in a way that can be detected – a bad back or neck due to whiplash, stress, etc. The claims are £10,000 here, £20,000 there … it soon mounts up. The scale of the problem is huge, apparently."

"So, are we proceeding on the basis this is all about an industrial injury claim? Do we even know if he *was* insured, or will he be claiming from Jake, or the club?" Patrick asked.

"No, we don't know any of that, but one thing's certain, if Jake *is* prosecuted, any future claim will be processed far quicker, as all the evidence would have been proven in a criminal court," Derek added.

"Mr Stockton's alleged injuries are significantly worse than those I mentioned earlier, so if industrial injury is the motivation behind all of this, my estimation is he'll be claiming injury payments of nearly £1m, which makes Jake's prosecution all the more important."

This grabbed people's attention. Derek went on.

"The doctor's reports are meticulous and extensive. They address every single detail of his injuries, including losing the sight in his eye, which would get him nearly £100,000 alone, depending on his age and occupation. If we assume Stockton *is* falsifying his injuries, on the basis no one would go out to intentionally break their own back and gouge out their eye, surely it stands to reason any self-respecting doctor would see this and raise the alarm, would they not? My GP told me Stockton's medical assessment report is one of the most detailed and exhaustive he's ever seen."

"So, his injuries are real?" Molly asked, sounding utterly confused.

"Or the doctor's bent as well," John put in.

"Exactly, dear boy." Derek knuckled the table. "I haven't completed my investigation into Mr Choudary yet, but I have looked into his finances. He's worth circa £52m, with holiday homes in Capri, Dubai, California and Cornwall."

"Ooh, I'd love a place in Cornwall." Patrick wasn't one to aim high.

"His house in Swiss Cottage is worth £9m alone. He holds a visiting professor's seat at City Medical, London, granted on the basis of his charitable donations. I doubt he's ever been there in his life. Something really doesn't stack up when the likes of Stockton are treated privately by someone like Choudary."

Molly spoke up. "Let's say his injuries are genuine, and he has private medical insurance, then surely Choudary is simply being paid a lot of money to treat him. I don't see what's wrong."

"Good point, Molly, but why has Stockton gone to ground? Why has he no past? And how has Choudary amassed such wealth at the age of forty-eight when he only arrived in Britain ten years ago, as a GP in Chichester?" Derek tried not to sound like he was putting Molly down; her question was valid.

"Is he an owner of Lexington Health? That would explain it," Patrick said.

"He is, yes. The company's been running for five years, but the turnover, although decent, cannot explain that level of wealth."

"Hold on a minute, gang." John buried his head in his hands trying to think. "Let's look at the facts here. An overweight, overpaid, anonymous bouncer from Sheffield, with a Cayman Islands bank account and flawless tax record, has an accident, gets rushed to hospital, is then transferred to a private hospital, is treated by a high-end surgeon with a chequered history, gets discharged, disappears, blanks his girlfriend, and has his work laptop removed by a bloodstained meathead who turns up at court to see Jake referred to Crown. This is a minefield."

"Erm, this might not help either." Patrick raised his notebook in the air.

John laughed out loud. "Surely this can't get any weirder?"

"None taken," Patrick sniffed. "You asked me to look into DS Cantly and PC Will Owens … well, it turns out they're cousins. Isn't that nice?"

"And?" Justin said sceptically.

"DS Stephen Cantly has been in the force for twenty-two years. He's worked all over the UK, transferring police force on fourteen occasions. His record's clean as a whistle. What's interesting is, in recent years, PC William Owens has moved with him at the same time."

"Not sure that makes them complicit." Justin played devil's advocate.

"No, this *is* relevant, Justin. On the night of the incident, I couldn't believe how quickly that cop turned up to arrest Jake. Stockton was still rolling around on the bottom step, when he charged up and slapped the cuffs on him. And when we were in the police station, they were extremely well organised and had no hesitation in charging him, as if they had it in mind the whole time. Then, they both turn up for a committal hearing. Why?"

"Isn't that their job, John? Do you really think those cops are involved with Stockton? More to the point, why?" Justin was struggling to buy it.

"I don't know to be honest, but they certainly wouldn't be the first bent coppers we've met. What I do know is, we now have more questions than answers. Derek, did you research the statistics on simultaneous back and eye injuries?"

"I did. It's not exhaustive, but I've got a hundred and twenty-eight cases to wade through for the last seven years." He looked tired suddenly.

"What?! There are that many? Can you narrow it down any? Males only, age group, industry type?"

"I've done that already. Don't worry, I'm on it. If Stockton has done this before, I'll find it." Derek had the bit between his teeth.

"If no one has anything else, let's meet again on Monday. We've a lot to be getting through. And children, watch where you step – there's a lot of rabbit holes with this one."

John was never more serious.

***

"DCS Thornley." Sarah Thornley answered her work mobile inside one ring. There were few people John knew who worked harder than he did, but she was a machine.

"Hey, Sarah, it's John Devlin. How's life treating you?"

"Better for hearing your voice, darling. You owe me a beer by the way. Forget the beer – I'll take a nice bottle of Puligny-Montrachet and dinner at Miguel's."

John owed a lot of beers. His life was consumed with chasing shadows in recent weeks. He had no chance of paying her back anytime soon.

"Deal. I need a favour."

Sarah heard his business-like tone and quit the small talk. "Go on."

"I've just text you an image. He is a person of interest to a client of mine. We think he originates from a Balkan state – Albania, Serbia. I'll take all you have on him."

John heard Sarah's phone let out a light ping as the message landed, followed by a minute of silence while she examined it.

"Jesus, John, you're not mixed up with him, are you?" Sarah asked, wishing she hadn't. She knew John Devlin well. He'd dealt with some high-profile cases and was utterly professional and very capable.

"You know him? Good. Who is it?" John was unrelenting. "And no, I'm not 'mixed up' in anything."

John wasn't overly happy about lying to a senior officer of the Met, but needs must.

She let out a deep sigh. "His name's Doda Kelemendi. He's an Albanian Serb and holds a UK passport. He's the person gangsters go to to make problems go away. He's very good at it apparently. We have nothing solid on him, other than we suspect he's involved with some very unscrupulous people. His last boss was found in the boot of his car with his testicles in his mouth."

John swallowed hard. A vision of Molly's brief encounter flashed through his mind.

"Who does he work for?"

"Are you listening to me, John? Do not get involved with this person or anyone he's working for."

John knew she meant business and would reverse the questioning very quickly if he wasn't careful.

"You know me, Sarah … I'm discretion personified. Listen, let's have that bottle of wine soon, OK? I've gotta dash."

He hung up. Sarah was right. He'd avoid the guy like the plague.

16

PARIS IN THE FALL

De Freitus Wealth Management, The City of London: 19 October 2021

Rob was sat fidgeting in his father's anteroom waiting for him to finish his Zoom meeting. His flight was in three hours, and he didn't want things to get off to a bad start with Maddie by keeping her waiting.

His break-up with Lauren hadn't gone to plan either, although the outcome was the same. The fact that she'd dumped him didn't matter – what did matter was that she had left DWM and taken one of their best currency managers with her. It was likely the reason his father wanted to speak with him. If not that, then it was the Montreaux account. Either way, he wasn't looking forward to it.

Evie hadn't made it to work since Marcella's glorious exit on race day. She had given his sister what she'd been asking for, for a very long time, and it hadn't put Rob off the Montreaux one bit.

It made Rob think hard about their interest in him. One of the most prestigious contemporary art galleries in Paris was praise indeed. *What is there to stay in London for?* He'd miss his friends that's for sure, but Larry had told him to jump at the chance. Mikey and Jake too: *"Maximise your true potential, Fruit what are you waiting for?"*

What am I waiting for? he asked himself. He knew the answer: he had become besotted all over again. He and Maddie had picked up where they'd left off, bar a few trifling details. He understood her reluctance to leave Jacob in the lurch. In fact, it was to her credit that she'd refused to move out immediately.

"I told him it's over, but I can't leave him with all the bills to pay. I need to see things through."

Credit where it's due, Rob thought.

"You can go in now, Robin." His father's receptionist, Maeve, invited him with a warm smile. He thanked her, dragged himself off his chair and trudged into Roger's palatial office.

His father offered him no welcome and didn't look up from his desk, where he was busy writing notes with a gold fountain pen. Rob shuffled through the shagpile carpet and slumped down on a soft leather armchair, which hissed and squeaked under his weight.

This will all be mine one day, he mocked.

He took in the view of London over his father's bowed head. The faceted windows of the Walkie Talkie building opposite glistened in the afternoon sunshine, bouncing rays of light on the rooftops below.

Around the room, huge paintings of De Freitus family members before him adorned the walls, the biggest being that of Roger himself, who looked younger and more athletic than he ever had. Rob admired the brushwork and depth of colour and wondered how he'd pose. With a sword perhaps, sitting on a horse.

"Off to Paris, I hear," Roger said into his notepad.

"That's right," Rob said after a few seconds, wondering who'd told him. As far as he knew, only Larry was aware of his plans, and he doubted he'd say anything.

"Travelling alone, are we?" Roger looked up and held his gaze. "I heard Lauren dumped you, that's all. Shacked up with Marlon from the Currency Office. Shame – I liked them both."

Rob knew stonewalling him got up his nose, so he said nothing in reply. Truth was, as much as he wanted the outcome, he was hurt by Lauren's sudden departure and the manner of it. Had he really treated her so badly? He knew she wouldn't be alone too long, but you couldn't slide a cigarette paper between his exit and Marlon's arrival.

"I assume you are going to meet those ghastly French people Larry knows. Evie still isn't right, you know. She's still going on about suing the woman for assault." Roger waved and pointed his pen in the air as he spoke.

He considered telling his father about Evie's cocaine habit, but nothing good ever comes from delivering bad news.

"I heard Evie was totally pissed, crashed into Marcella and was racist in front of everyone. She got a slap for her trouble. It's no big deal. You slapped me enough times when I was a child – hasn't done me any harm."

Being reminded of the abuse Rob had endured caught Roger off guard. He couldn't argue it hadn't happened. He blanked Rob in return. He had no intention of defending himself.

"I want you to visit François while you're there. Take him with you to meet them. He covers France, so I want him to manage the Frogs. You can get it off the ground, do a handover. Tell Larry I said so." Roger waved his pen again as if the conversation was over.

Rob walked towards the door. "I'll do no such thing. François is a fucking dope, and you know it. Plus, it's the UK office they want to deal with. They're planning to open a London gallery on Bruton Street – as part of their long-term tax plan. Did you read the investment strategy document I wrote? I'm guessing not."

He opened the door and turned to glare at his father. Roger couldn't help but admire Rob's strength of conviction. His intransigence and arrogance were infuriating – the apple hadn't fallen far from the tree on that score. There was nothing about his work performance he could criticise. He was an exceptional talent. Perhaps one day he'd tell him. He'd tell him how proud he was, how Robin is twice the man he was. He'd tell him how much he regretted hurting him and making him cry as a child, locking him in his room and mocking him in front of his friends. He'd tell him he loved him dearly and hug him, hopefully before it was too late.

"Have it your own way," Roger snarled, snatching his phone from his desk. "Now get out!"

City Airport, London: 19 October 2021

Maddie's irritation worsened with every passing minute. The lukewarm ginger tea she drank to calm her morning sickness hadn't had much effect, serving as a reminder of how real her situation was. She was going to become a mum, there was no doubting that, and Rob was to become the father. At least that's what the birth certificate would say.

This was supposed to be one of the most joyous times in her life, but nothing could be further from the truth. She hoped after the trip was over, it would be plain sailing from there on in. No more hiding and skulking around making excuses about her health and appearance. Rob would know he was going to be a father and he'd be ecstatic about the news – she was confident about that.

She'd return home and tell Jacob they were over – for real this time, not just a scene she'd played out in her mind and regurgitated to keep Rob happy. It would hurt Jacob, she knew that, but better now than years down the line. She'd hold back the news about Rob and the baby. Give things a chance to settle down.

She loved Jacob. He'd done nothing wrong, apart from getting her pregnant, but there was no way she could stay with him – they were chalk and cheese. He'd get over her and never know the baby was his. She'd never tell him.

Her mother would flip, especially when she'd tell her Rob's the father. Kim loved Jacob to bits and didn't hide her pleasure on hearing she'd broken free of the De Freitus family. Jacob had been exactly what Maddie needed when she returned from Malawi – someone who'd love and cherish her and help her feel normal again after the horrors she'd witnessed.

The money doesn't matter, she'd told herself at the time. It didn't. She earned a decent salary and had banked a lot of her wages while she was away. Everything was under control, until those two little blue lines changed everything.

Statutory maternity pay and a bricklayer's wage weren't going to cut it. They'd be living in a one-bed flat for years to come, relying on hand-me-downs. She could kiss goodbye to any chance of a holiday, let alone first-class travel. Jacob's family would become even more suffocating in their kindness. Well intentioned as it might be, the fact was, her life would be over.

The nausea rose in her stomach, setting her nerves on edge. She had to remain strong. She would get through this – the baby was part of her now, and it didn't really matter who the father was, did it? She was responsible for bringing a life into the world and she'd do whatever it took to secure their future.

If all those pregnant women in Africa can survive in forty-degree heat, walking miles for water, with no food, shelter or the right clothing, then I can manage. Difference is, they're not lying to everyone, are they? They're not manipulative and cruel – those women are desperate and trapped. They're not looking for easy street. They just want to live. Her inner resolve teetered.

She scrunched her eyes and balled her fists. Her pink nails dug into the palms of her hands, leaving small crescent-shaped punishments. Waves of nausea and guilt surged through her, competing for top spot – her dizziness a physical manifestation of her deceit.

"Hey! Are you OK, princess?" Rob dropped his bag and ran to her.

Maddie rose out of her panic, startled at hearing his voice. "I'm fine," she snapped, shrugging his arms off her. "Where have you been? You said you'd be here on time." Her sickliness had abated, but the tears wouldn't stop. Guilt had won.

Rob wrapped his arms around her again. "Hey, what's all this? I'm here now, don't worry."

She sniffled against his shoulder, rinsing her eyes against him. She inhaled her favourite aftershave, which had a settling effect on her nerves.

"I'm sorry … it's been a really tough day at home," she lied effortlessly.

"Jacob's not been difficult, has he?" Rob's voice hardened suddenly.

Maddie shook her head, wondering just how bad it would be when she did tell him.

"No, he's not. It's just me. This is all happening so fast, Rob, I just want to make sure in my own mind I'm doing the right thing."

She'd admitted the truth for once. She sighed and lasered her huge brown eyes into Rob's. He nodded imperceptibly. The sneaking around had taken its toll on him too.

"Come on, let's get through security. We can get a bite to eat in the lounge before we board. I want you fully relaxed. We are going to have a great time."

Rob yanked up her suitcase handle and held it back to back with his own. Maddie linked his arm and leaned into him. Panic over.

La Galerie Montreaux, Rue des Quatre-Fils, Paris, France:
21 October 2021

"So, you like what you see?" Monty asked.

Rob blew his cheeks in response. He was like a child in a sweet shop. He couldn't believe the size of the place, and the Rome gallery was better, if Marcella's bias could be set aside. He'd seen twelve separate spaces for sculpture, paintings and expressionist art exhibitions, covering 4,500 square feet. There was a steady footfall for a Thursday afternoon, and their private viewing appointments were full until the new year. Rich people out Christmas shopping, he supposed.

As part of their financial investment plan, Rob had been privy to their income streams, cash reserves and asset holdings, which were impressive, considering they'd managed without significant financial investment. Their lifestyle, although hardly frugal, was simple and elegant. They had no cars or holiday homes, they walked or cycled to work each day and spent a lot of their time perfecting their business model and leaving nothing to chance. They had the life he wanted with Maddie, and they were laying it on a plate for him.

"We want you and Paul to help make the Montreaux name the best in Paris, if not Europe. We want to find the newest talent and help them break through."

Marcella's enthusiasm was out of character. He'd hardly ever heard her say more than a dozen words without moving on to another topic of conversation. Clearly, this was what she lived for.

"It's truly breathtaking. You have some of the biggest names in contemporary art exhibiting here. I'm blown away. Your plans for Bruton Street are incredibly bold. To be involved in something like that would be a dream come true."

"You can stay in the studio flat on the top floor. This is a lovely area of Paris. It's where Marcella and I first came. We had a lot of parties when we were young, created some great memories, hein?" He nudged Marcella, who grinned, momentarily lost in the past.

"You and Maddie could build a beautiful life here. There is so much to see and experience. It's the perfect place to raise children," Marcella said.

"Is this where Paul grew up? Did he like it here in Paris?" Another piece of Rob's jigsaw puzzle was beginning to slot into place.

A family. Imagine that – raising a child here, in this environment, with Maddie.

"Certainement, il l'aimait!" Marcella dropped into French to make her point that Paul liked it.

"Let's have dinner tonight at our favourite restaurant. It's very near to your hotel. We want to meet Maddie again and hear all about her work in Malawi."

"That sounds great. She can't wait to meet you again. I hope she's up for it – she's not been too well since we arrived. Between her work and my sightseeing, I think I've worn her out." Rob couldn't hide his concern.

Marcella raised her eyebrows and took a deep breath. "Rob, can I—"

"Darling, we need to let Rob get back to Maddie. He has a lot to talk to her about. I'll text you the time, Rob. A bientôt, mon ami."

Hotel Shangri-La, 3rd Arr., Paris: 21 October 2021

"Hold on!" Maddie threw on her dressing gown and skipped across the room to answer the door. She opened it to find Rob with a large bunch of flowers.

"Hello. I'm looking for a beautiful princess called Maddie Parker," he said in French. He pretended to read the name card.

"That's me. Thank you very much," she replied in French. Maddie took the flowers and closed the door in Rob's face.

He took her playfulness as a good sign and waited patiently for her to let him in, which she did, with a huge smile and open arms.

"Rob, they're lovely, thank you." She kissed him tenderly and buried her head in his shoulder. Her perfumed damp hair chilled the side of his head, causing a shudder of electricity to run through him. He picked her tiny body up and flicked the door closed with his heel.

"We have dinner booked with Marcella and Monty for 8pm at a restaurant nearby. Are you going to be up to it, darling?"

He walked through the £2,500-a-night penthouse suite to the bedroom and kicked his shoes off as she nibbled on his ear and pushed her tongue inside. Her hot breath gave him goosebumps.

"That's not all I'm up for," she whispered seductively.

***

The remainder of the afternoon passed without too much conversation. Maddie's hormones had hit levels so high she barely recognised herself at times. Rob wasn't complaining

– a herd of wildebeest wouldn't have stopped him, although a woman in the next room tried her best, hammering on the wall in protest to the syncopated rhythm of their headboard.

Rob snapped out of a daydream and rolled off the huge emperor-sized bed to get a shower, before the sight of Maddie padding around the room naked set him off again. He had twenty minutes to get ready and, for once, he didn't want to be late. He shaved, towelled his wavy hair, put on his Armani suit and crisp white cotton shirt and slipped on his shiny loafers.

They'd gone shopping several times in the last three days and Maddie had been spoilt rotten. She wondered how she would fit everything in her suitcase, until Rob suggested he take her clothes home with him to begin populating her new walk-in wardrobe.

Excellent idea, she thought.

Her cream Dolce & Gabbana satin cocktail dress shimmered in the light as she applied the finishing touches to her make-up. The material clung to her slim frame, the silhouette of her body clearly visible through the thin fabric.

She purred as she stepped into her new Giuseppe Zanotti stilettos, watching Rob out of the corner of her eye while she fastened the snake-like diamante strap around her ankle.

"Do you like them?" She sashayed over to him and twisted her body to show him the whole collection.

He took a deep, shaky breath, wondering how he was going to get through the evening without having sex with her in a cupboard or cloakroom.

"You look sensational … although there's one thing missing."

He rose and pulled out a diamond necklace and matching earrings from his pocket.

Maddie gasped. Her dark eyes sparkled in awe. "Rob, you shouldn't have!"

She turned her back to him and he wrapped the necklace around her. The gems and setting felt heavy. A shiver ran down her spine in response to the cold metal on her warm skin.

She swapped the earrings Jacob had bought her for her birthday, tossing them on the dressing table without hesitation. The jewels blinked in the lights. She touched them with her fingertips, mesmerised by their radiance. She was speechless in wonder. She dreaded to think what the collection cost, so put it out of her mind. This was what she wanted, for her and her baby. This is what she deserved.

Rob grinned at her, reading her mind. "Anything for my princess."

La Vallée des Cygnes Noirs Restaurant, Paris: 21 October 2021

Rob and Maddie entered the ostentatiously named La Vallée des Cygnes Noirs (The Valley of the Black Swans) and were met in the doorway by a serious-looking maître d' standing behind a lectern. He eyed them up and down and nodded his approval.

"Monsieur, mademoiselle, s'il vous plaît."

He clapped his hands together, bowed and turned his back on them. They followed him to their table. Nonverbal communication the order of the day.

Marcella swotted Jean-Pierre with the back of her hand as he fussed with Maddie's chair and napkin. She embraced Maddie, kissing her left and right.

"Maddie, you look very beautiful. Robin is so lucky, hein?" Monty said softly in French, trying his best to put her at ease.

"Thank you, Monty, and yes he is."

Her playfulness got the laugh she was hoping for and put paid to any doubt that she had recovered.

"I hope you are feeling better. I hate travelling on the Métro – it is full of germs. I prefer to be poisoned on the street with carbon monoxide," Marcella said, trumping Maddie and setting the scene for what was to be a night to remember.

***

After five courses of the most exquisite gourmet food, Marcella and Rob excused themselves and headed out onto the smokers' terrace.

Two-stroke scooters zipped past, their high-pitched engines incongruously adding to the ambience. Across the street, a three-piece band was playing in the corner of a tiny, old restaurant, where the bourgeois elite would have once met to listen to salonnière music and drink wine. It appeared as though nothing had changed in the last three hundred years. In truth, everything had changed. The bourgeoisie were now the middle class, the music merely background noise; the food and drink now an art form rather than sustenance.

Marcella never tired of Paris. She was hostage to its elegance and sophistication. It inspired her. Her heart would remain in Italy, of course, but for Marcella, Rome's history seemed to block its future. There was no room for new life. People scurried between the ruins as if they were servants attending to their masters thousands of years ago. Paris, on the other hand, was different. It was old, used and run down in places, but scrape the surface and it was reinventing itself over and over again. No one seemed to mind. What's more, they demanded it. It was a place for the young and for the young at heart.

"Maddie is truly beautiful, Rob. She speaks French like a Parisienne."

Marcella let thick cherry-flavoured smoke ooze out of the side of her mouth, which then disappeared behind curtains of her auburn hair.

Rob nodded his head, as if he couldn't believe his luck.

"You have known each other a long time, hein? You've been through your ups and downs, no? After that, it is easy to know how the other thinks, n'est-ce pas?"

"You are well informed, Marcella."

Rob was not surprised; he was quickly coming to the conclusion that whatever Marcella didn't know was of no interest to her.

"Michael gave me a brief history when we were at Ascot. You have a big heart. It is clear to me Maddie has hold of it in both hands."

Rob smirked to himself. *To think I wanted Mikey to help learn about the Montreaux, an unlikely double agent.*

"I love her. I always have and always will. When she left for Africa, it was something she had to do. The distance ate away at our love. It's different now. We've both grown up," he added.

"It is, how do you say, 'a whirlpool romance'."

"Something like that… We've only been seeing each other a short time – it's early days."

"How did you meet again?"

"It was the week before you were in London. It was my birthday – 27 August. A day to remember, I guess. We've never looked back."

Rob went misty at the memory, while Marcella remained coherent and sceptical.

"What if she doesn't want to come to Paris – will you still join us?"

"We have a lot to discuss."

Rob's evasion tweaked at her patience. His infatuation was disappointing to her, if not unsurprising. Her own son was wrapped around his girlfriend's finger. A 'pathetic fool' – is how she described him. The overbearing mother had got the better of her.

That's men, she thought to herself. *Give them a pretty face and lots of sex and you can make them believe whatever you want them to. The optimism bias shutting out what it doesn't want to see, even when it's evident to everyone else. Maddie's sickness, her hot flashes, bigger breasts, and mood swings – obvious unless you're a blind, lovestruck idiot.*

"*Do not get involved!*" Monty had told her. He was right, of course. She decided she wouldn't, at least not directly. A little push and pull in the right direction would certainly help, though.

"This is a beautiful city, a place for the young and old. When Monty and I came here, we were poor. We rented a place not far from here and set up the gallery. I worked in fashion at the time and did a bit of modelling – it paid the bills. We had a wonderful life."

She inhaled the smoky memory and held onto it as long as she could. "Good times," she whispered, nostalgia warming her heart. "This is your time, now. This is the place for you. You can raise your family here. It is safe and full of excitement. You can be part of our family too, hein?" Marcella hooked her arm in his.

"A family? You may be jumping the gun a bit, Marcella." Rob laughed off her comment half-heartedly, despite a shiver running up his spine and his blood running cold.

"Maybe. Maybe not," she replied.

She bounced her eyebrows at him with each word. Ignoring the ashtrays attached to the balcony, Marcella flicked her spent Mehari onto the street below, the trail of sparks igniting the bomb exploding in Rob's head.

17

WHO WANTS BRAAI?

Mikey's flat, Holmes Road, Kentish Town, London: 28 October 2021

A month without seeing Joy was taking its toll. Mikey's night terrors had returned with a vengeance. Kaitlyn and Joy were now making regular appearances together, with the outcome becoming more traumatic. He knew it wasn't real – they could never meet – but his brain was cruelly bringing them together and snatching them away; the ending to their lives more gruesome each night.

He pinched his nose to rid his mind of the horrific images. She'd be here soon enough, and he'd forget about them then. Taking deep breaths to calm himself, he inhaled the aromas from the spices he was using to season his pork chops. It had a soothing effect. Mrs Yip from the Golden Wok had gone to considerable effort mixing her own blend for him and giving him instructions on how to marinade and cook the meat.

"You have Chinese girlfriend. She must be pretty girl. Mikey is very handsome man." She was a sucker for Mikey's charm, and he didn't spare her the rod.

"There's only one Chinese girl for me, Mrs Yip," he said with a wink. "My friend is Thai. Her name is Joy, and, yes, she is very pretty."

Everything was ready – the chops, the vegetables, a decent bottle of wine from Mustafa, a box of profiteroles and a tub of double cream, in case Joy had a sweet tooth. He considered trying out Renoir's again, but Joy's schedule of late had been more exhausting than ever, so a quiet night in was for the best.

With all bases covered, Mikey showered and did a rapid-fire tidy-up of his spotlessly clean apartment.

Maybe Joy will give me a cleaning job if Euan sacks me. The thought hung around in his head for a while. At least he'd be able to spend more time with her and shoulder some of the burden.

His home had a welcoming appeal, although decorated for a male inhabitant. A girl he dated briefly worked in IKEA and had a 40% discount. The soft furnishings and trendy wallpaper were the only positive outcomes from that brief interlude.

The intercom pinged. He leaned across from the stove and held down the respond button.

"Come in, beautiful. Up the stairs, flat four."

He pressed the unlock button and Joy's head ducked under the camera. He opened the door and stood like a sentry at the end of the corridor ready for her arrival. Joy rounded the corner in her Converse, stonewashed jeans, and chunky merino wool jumper. Her glossy, shoulder-length hair bounced as she ran the last few strides and threw herself into his arms. Ever ready to receive the ball, Mikey swept her up and span her around.

"Hello baby," he mumbled into her neck.

Joy said nothing. She hung there on her tiptoes, such was her relief to be with him. He rocked her in his strong, silent arms.

"I've missed you, Mikey. I've missed you so much."

Her grip around his neck and shoulders made him wonder if she'd thought about playing rugby.

"I've missed you too, darlin'. Come in... I've got dinner on the go and a lovely bottle of pinot grigio on ice, courtesy of Mustafa El Sharif."

He lowered her to the ground and cupped her head in his hands. He kissed her watery eyes and guided her into his home for the first time.

"Turn right and take a seat at the breakfast bar."

Joy did as she was told and hopped up onto a high swivel chair that Mikey had positioned in front of the tabletop to avoid creating a barrier between them.

Her loose-fitting top had slipped off her shoulder as she hoisted herself up, revealing her bare upper arm. She made no move to cover herself up, and Mikey made no attempt to hide his eyes.

He cleared his throat. "I'm fresh out of plane food, so I'm afraid it's prime rib pork chop, with broken mash and roasted spring vegetables. Sound good?"

"I didn't know you could cook, Mikey. You are so talented," Joy ribbed playfully.

Funny girl. He grinned to himself and mentally ticked another box as he placed the two chops on the griddle and set the heat to slow cook.

The open-plan kitchen was bijou to say the least, but it was modern, scrupulously clean and well organised. Joy admired his attention to detail and fluid movement as he reached every drawer and cupboard while hardly moving his feet more than half a step. Her eyes danced across his huge back and down to his butt. She absentmindedly bit the side of her mouth and took a slow breath.

He tugged open his American-style fridge and pulled out Mustafa's favourite wine, which he had already opened. He picked up two long-stemmed glasses from a work surface and walked a single stride to where Joy sat straight-backed and cross-legged, with a satisfied smile on her face.

She stroked her hand across the back of his as she took her wine glass. The hairs on his wrist stood to attention.

"Cheers," they said in unison as they clinked their glasses, maintaining eye contact. All that time wishing they were together and now they didn't know what to say. Small talk just didn't seem necessary.

Actions speak louder than words, Mikey thought to himself. He stepped towards her and leaned in to kiss her gently on the lips, the icy vanilla hit drawing an involuntary moan of approval from him.

Joy uncrossed her legs, hooked her thumb into a loop on the waist band of his jeans and pulled him in. She deftly placed her glass on the counter and grabbed a handful of his cotton T-shirt, all in one move.

A dozen thoughts ran through her head, none of which included food or wine. The kiss rapidly descended out of control as Mikey brushed his lips along her neck, his freshly shaven face causing her to arc her head back in pleasure. Mikey's hand found its way in through her blissfully loose open-necked jumper and down her taut back. A quick pinch of his thumb and middle finger unhooked Joy's strapless silky bra, which fell to the floor.

She hopped off the barstool, laced her fingers in Mikey's and led him towards what she correctly assumed to be his bedroom. Mikey reached over and spun the dials on the hob to zero and fell in step.

He wasn't hungry anyway.

***

Wrapped in one of Mikey's old fleece shirts, which just about covered her knees, Joy sat tucked in his arm with her toned legs stretched out over his lap. Nat King Cole crooned in the background.

"The very thought of youuu…" Mikey sang along as softly as his bass voice would allow. "I love this song. I'll never forget it now, will I?" He kissed the top of her head.

"I've had such a lovely evening, Mikey. You are a wonderful cook – my mum will be pleased."

Joy wasn't exaggerating. Between Mikey and Mrs Yip, they had created a feast for kings. She doubted she'd ever get to Renoir's at this rate.

Mikey was relieved to hear it, although he couldn't help wondering whether his cameo performance in the bedroom had had a sobering effect on her. His second and third act had made up for any shortcoming. He grinned at his own crudity.

"What's so funny? My mother was very impressed when you came to our house. The fact you know your way around the kitchen will seal the deal for her."

"He's a fine boy, with kind eyes, and the way he is with Jules is lovely. You have met someone special – hold on to him." Joy smiled at the thought of her mother's comments.

She tightened her embrace, burying her head against him, fearful he might disappear.

"Will you come to the game tomorrow? It's the cup final against the Boks. It'll be a bloodbath. I'll need a nurse to look after me..."

Mikey wasn't joking. Hansie Van Heerden would be looking for revenge after narrowly losing out to Camley in the league.

"I can come for the game but I've a flight to catch at seven. I've got a league match on Wednesday in Lyon. I was going to suggest bringing Jules and Arthur to the game to save you a trip."

"That's OK. I got the impression Jules wanted me to collect him. I was going to introduce him and Arthur to the team in the locker room. I hope to get him interested in training and helping out on match days."

"Mikey, you are so nice to my brother. I know he would absolutely love that. Just make sure he doesn't become a nuisance for you."

Joy was comfortable being honest about Jules. She knew him better than anyone.

"He'll never be that," Mikey said emphatically. "It's all arranged. They're going to help Jed the groundsman get the pitch marked out and bring on the drinks at halftime. There'll be a braai after the game, so they'll get fed as well. I'll make sure they're home for eight."

Joy closed her eyes. *How could one person take over her heart so quickly? How does he have all the answers to everything?*

"Is there anything I can help you with at work?" Mikey said, proving Joy's point in a matter of seconds.

"My work? No. That's sweet of you to offer though. Actually, yes, there is something you can help me with," Joy said, sitting up and tucking her feet under her. "I've had problems with my invoicing to Fulwood."

"What sort of problems?" Mikey asked, his interest piqued.

"We get paid monthly, on time usually, but I can't seem to get a copy of the remittance, which says who I was paid by and how much. Elaine said they don't provide them any more. I don't know why it's such a big deal." Joy shrugged and sipped the green tea Mikey had made her.

"No problem. I need to speak to Bev about memberships anyway. I asked her for a copy of the members database. I'm sure Euan's up to no good, but I'm rubbish at spreadsheets. I can't find anything amiss."

"Do you want me to have a look? I have a degree in business and accounting, and I was top of the class in maths."

Mikey rolled his eyes. "Why am I not surprised?"

"Seriously, let me take a look, it can't do any harm. I'll make sure the data's secure." Joy was keen to reciprocate his support.

"OK, it's a deal."

They sat with their limbs interlocked for another hour, Mikey's banquet taking its toll on their energy levels.

Eventually, Joy said, "It's late, I better be going."

"Please stay the night. I promise I'll not snore. You can sleep in my shirt … it suits you."

"My mother was expecting me home, Mikey," Joy said without much conviction.

"I don't know your mother that well, but I'm guessing she wasn't expecting you home, at least not until tomorrow."

He threaded his fingers through her hair, and she leaned into his hand. He was right, again.

"OK," she relented after some thought, and with some relief. "On one condition."

"Name it," he said excitedly.

"You carry me to bed again. I loved it when you did that last time."

Singleton Rugby Club, London: 29 October 2021

"Lads, can I have your attention?" Mikey stood in the centre of the dressing room to address the team.

"We have two special guests with us today. This is Jules Wong and Arthur Soames, who are very good friends of mine. I'd like you to welcome them in our time-honoured fashion."

Matt, the scrum half, stood up and orchestrated the team.

"Three cheers for Jules and Arthur: hip, hip, hooray! Hip, hip, hooray! Hip, hip, hooray!"

The noise was so loud in the crowded room, it made Jules duck in fright. The team of giants filed past, shaking their hands and patting their backs. Mikey nodded to his teammates in appreciation and led the boys out to where he wanted them to watch the game.

"Joy'll be here shortly. I need you to take care of her, OK?" They nodded, shellshocked at what had just happened in the changing rooms.

"Stay together at all times. You can buy drinks and use the toilets in there." Mikey pointed to the clubhouse. "If you're hungry, there's a burger van over there, but don't fill up because we have braai later don't forget."

Arthur raised his hand to ask a question.

"Yes, Arthur," Mikey said, expecting a question about food.

"What's a braai?"

Jules nodded, backing his friend.

"Trust me, big lad, it's your idea of heaven."

***

The Boks lined up in the corridor leading to the pitch, a wall of African muscle fed on buffalo, biltong and wurst. Mikey crabbed his way past them, leading his team from the front. The pent-up aggression from both sides bubbled in a fog of testosterone and eucalyptus VapoRub.

At the head of the queue, Mikey shook Hansie's hand and wished him the best of luck, receiving a curt nod in return.

Varkie was mid-queue, ranting in Afrikaans about how they were going to 'fuck them up', in a failed attempt at intimidating the opposition in a language none of them knew.

"Varkie! Hou jou bak, doos!" Hansie told him to shut up. He was in no mood for his antics.

The teams ran out onto the pitch and began warming up and stretching off. Mikey found Joy in the crowd next to the boys and gave her a quick wave, before rounding up his team for one last pep talk.

It was Camley's kick-off. With a blow of the referee's whistle, the game was under way. The ball was dropkicked to the stand side and collected in the air by a Camley second row, who dropped to his feet setting up a maul. Matt, the scrum half, fed the ball out to the backs and fifteen metres of ground was made in the first passage of play, before the touchline was found.

Hansie was lifted in the lineout and took the ball cleanly, filtering it back through the maul. Their fly-half kicked it high into the Camley half, where it was collected by the fullback, who ran forward to gain territory. He was tackled by the Boks' number 11 but he remained on his feet and offloaded to a teammate, who flicked it onto the outside centre. Mikey saw the start of a well-practised move and ran onto a reverse pass at pace, breaking through the Singleton backline and handing off Varkie with ease, leaving him flat on his backside.

Mikey picked up his knees and broke for the line, jinking into space and swerving tackles. As he reached the Boks' twenty-two metre line, he felt arms around his waist, which checked his run and turned his legs to lead. He managed to slip the tackle only to face a wall of orange and green. He ran straight into them, making no attempt to dodge them, and took the impact of three players thundering into his ribs and thighs. He spun his upper body and passed the ball to the waiting winger, who sprinted into the gap Mikey had created for a try. Mikey was mobbed by his teammates and returned to his half of the pitch in preparation for the inevitable onslaught.

When it came, it was relentless, as if the Boks were punishing them for making them look foolish in the first phase of play. The game finished 32-12. With the hip, hip, hoorays over, the Boks left the pitch in a corridor of bruised Camley egos.

"Well played, Hansie," Mikey said magnanimously.

Hansie shook hands dismissively and turned his back on him. Mikey put it down to exhaustion; the man had battled like a Trojan.

Jules and Arthur ran over to Mikey and threw their arms around him, randomly shouting 'Hooray, hip! Hooray, hip!' Joy appeared and kissed him on the cheek. She gave him a consolation hug, despite the mud, sweat and blood covering his shirt.

"You were amazing, darling, I'm so proud of you."

Mikey had never had a girl watch him play before. It felt euphoric, although he would have to call a fine on himself for inappropriate behaviour on the rugby field.

Mikey laughed off the battering his team had just taken. "They were just too good in the pack. Hansie's a monster when he gets going. I've never seen him so aggressive."

Joy shuddered as she glanced over at him. "He's enormous. Are you OK? You took some hard hits out there."

She brushed his face with her hand but didn't find too much to concern her.

"I'm fine – nothing a hot bath won't cure."

"Listen, I've got to go," she said reluctantly. "I'm going to miss you all so much." Joy hugged Jules and spoke to him and Arthur quietly.

She turned round and hugged Mikey. "Look after my boys. I'll be back before you know it."

"See ya soon, darlin'. I'll be waiting."

***

Jules and Arthur slid into their Uber and buzzed down the windows.

"Text me when you get home, and don't keep your mum awake all night playing video games."

Mikey's final instructions were received loud and clear. Jules and Arthur had eaten so many lamb chops, broodjies and roosterkoek they could barely move.

Mikey returned to the clubhouse bar and slumped next to Jake, halting what appeared to be a serious conversation between him and Rob. Mikey had no trouble in guessing it involved babytalk.

"Right! It's beer o'clock. Let's get wrecked."

Mikey didn't want to discuss babies. It had left him cold with anger when he heard the news and caused the first signs of rancour between them since the last time Maddie derailed Rob's life.

"You played a blinder out there, Mikey."

He took Rob's olive branch in good faith.

"Cheers, Fruit. The only good thing to come out of it was not getting killed by Hansie. He was full on today. Did you see the tackle he made on our tighthead? Nearly cut him in half—"

Mikey was cut short by the arrival of the goliath himself.

"Hansie, howzit Chyna? You were awesome today, bru."

Mikey tried to mollify him. He was clearly pissed off about something and in no mood for banter. He stared at the three smartly dressed Englishmen with hostility as he gulped down his beer. He slammed his empty glass on the table.

"Rob – three beers and a G&T, there's a good chap," Jake said with a sharp edge to his voice to convey the urgency.

Rob obeyed without delay, happy to be out of the way, as Jake wanted. If anyone was going to annoy Hansie further, it was Rob. They sat in awkward silence for a few moments, Hansie heaving up and down, like a dying animal during its last breaths.

Jake fixed his eyes on Hansie's. "It's hard to take, isn't it?"

"What is?" Hansie growled.

"When someone holds your life in their hands, there's nothing you can do about it, no matter how hard you plead."

Hansie's face reddened at listening to Jake's home truths for a second time. Déjà vu swept over Mikey, who wished for the first time in his life that Fozza was there.

"Wat weet jy daarvan," Hansie spat back at him.

"I know plenty," Jake said harshly as he held Hansie's gaze.

"Trixie told me your application had been denied. You have to go home, is that it? You're angry because you have to go back to South Africa and you're glaring at us like we are to blame."

Hansie shook his head, rebutting Jake's synopsis. "Your lives are so simple," he snarled. "You go to work, drink beer, play sports. You have no idea what other people have to go through – the pain and horror they endure."

Jake took a deep breath before responding. He didn't want a slanging match – he genuinely wanted to help him, even though he knew in his heart he couldn't. Hansie was hurting, though Jake suspected his deportation wasn't the only reason.

"Horror, you say?" Jake let out an ironic humph. "I'm meeting a five-year-old boy next week. His name's Razzaq. He doesn't eat for days at a time, and his nine-year-old sister's the same. She's as thin as a rake. She will more than likely be trafficked to be married to a sixty-year-old paedophile, if I don't act to prevent it. It's the only life he and his sister have ever known. He's too frightened to even speak about it. To date, he's been to hospital for 'accidental' injuries more than twenty times. The horror he's been through's unspeakable."

Hansie dropped his head in shame and sighed as the image of Razzaq took hold in his heart.

"There are horrible people out there, Hansie, make no mistake. They live their lives on the backs of others. They know nothing of hard work, empathy, or kindness, but I can tell you now, Mikey and I have had our fair share of hurt and we live with the consequences."

Jake's voice softened as Hansie's body language changed. "Two months ago, Mikey was assaulted by three bouncers in Fandango's. I stepped in to stop it and now I'm being prosecuted. There's a good chance I'll go to prison for protecting my friend from what would've been life-changing injuries. Let me tell you, Hansie, I'd do it again today, and I'd do it for you and Trixie. Don't doubt that. I don't want to be where I am. Who'll protect little Razzaq when I'm gone? Life has a tendency to kick you in the balls – it's how we take the knocks and what we do to prevent them from happening again, right?"

Hansie's jaw twitched in anger. His self-pity had a stranglehold on him that he couldn't shake free from. He buried his head in his hands.

Rob returned with the drinks. He'd added four double shots of single malt whisky to the round.

Hansie lifted his head and looked at the boys. "I had to do it. I had no choice. They would've killed everyone."

Gorriekoppen Farm, Mpumalanga Province, South Africa: 6 July 2017

Hansie kissed Trixie on her forehead and slid out of the bedroom in his slippers to avoid making a noise on the creaky wooden floor.

Their lodge sat high up on the banks of the Dulini River, a winding slow-flowing watercourse that irrigated the sugarcane crops and provided water to the sheep and goat kraals. Built in the 1940s by Trixie's grandfather, Arno Senior, its modest size suited their needs. It was cosy and took no time to clean.

On the weekend, they would head to their flat in Nelspruit, now known as Mbombela, the capital of Mpumalanga province, where they would party with their friends. Life was sweet.

At 55,000 acres, the Du Toit estate spread across fertile lowveld and low-lying escarpments, bordered by the Dulini, Sabie and Sand Rivers that meandered through their land. To the west, at a place called Hazyview, they grew sugarcane, barley, wheat and coffee beans, and in the north, Hansie had the responsibility of managing twenty-five river lodges that backed onto the game reserves.

Early morning was Hansie's favourite time of day. The night-time noises and aromas gave way, like a shift change in a factory working around the clock. The sun dried out the moisture and the winds stoked up the pollen from the veld grass.

He walked into the kitchen, where Louise, the maid, was busy making coffee and toasting bread. Alice, her sixteen-year-old daughter, was hanging out clothing in the laundry room.

"Good morning, sir," Alice said respectfully, turning to face Hansie.

"Good morning, Alice," Hansie said softly, attempting a smile to put her at ease but failing miserably.

"There's bacon and eggs in the oven, Hansie. I've warmed up the leftovers from last night's braai as well," Louise screeched, before giggling her nervous laugh that ended everything she said.

Louise was old school and still not used to casual interaction with white folk. She lived in the local township with Henry and their five children, four of whom worked on the farm. Louise's English was better than her Afrikaans, but she liked to practise both. Most lodge guests spoke English and Afrikaans; literally no one spoke Swati, Xhosa or Zulu.

"Dankie, ouma," Hansie said, dunking a beskuit in his coffee – an adult version of a buttermilk rusk.

"Where's Henry? I wanted him here early – we have a lot of work to do."

"He's gone to the yard to check on the men. Temba and his brother haven't turned up for work this morning. He is not very happy." Louise sung it and laughed, as if it was Hansie's fault and he was the one in trouble.

Hansie rolled his eyes. The time had come to say goodbye to those two fellows. They'd been trouble from the get-go. Henry had given them way more chances than he would have. Even Trixie didn't like them, saying they stared at her and laughed behind her back. He made a mental note to call the office and end their contracts.

After three cups of sugary coffee and a plate full of fried food, Hansie jumped in his bakkie and headed to the yard. On the dirt approaching the yard he passed four cattle trucks, their drivers squatted around a small fire at the roadside warming their hands and enjoying a cigarette. He buzzed the gate open and drove up to the office in the corner of the main shed. Dozens of farmhands clad in blue overalls herded sheep into external pens ready for market under Henry's watchful eye.

Three Jack Russell terriers raced around yapping excitedly, eyes peeled ready to catch a rat or dassie disturbed by the activity. Hansie wasn't really an animal lover despite his occupation, but those dogs were worth three farmhands each – their ability to round up a flock of sheep and goats in minutes was amazing. At night, they would raise hell if they smelt, heard or saw anything they weren't happy about, including snakes, all for the price of a tin of dog food, a bowl of water and a pat on the head.

"Boss Hansie!" Henry shouted above the din of the bleating sheep. "We need to trim the hooves on about three-hundred head, then we'll be ready to load. I'd say we'll be finished at ten. The trucks are on the lane waiting."

"I want it done by nine. This should have been done yesterday. We need to head over to the lodges and check on the building work. Make sure you bring more bait and scent bags – there are jackals in the traps. We need to shoot them and rebait them."

The quickest way to lose a hundred lambs was to allow the jackal population to get out of control.

"Once we're done, we'll head to market." Hansie's tone never required debate.

"Yes, Boss." Henry nodded.

"Temba and his brother have been sacked. If any of the men refuse to work, sack them as well, do you understand? Make sure the kitchen staff have pap, figs and fruit ready. The quicker they finish, the quicker they eat."

Henry remained motionless. He hated threatening his men – they never took it well.

"Put a crew on the fences. They're down again on the Sabie Sands Road. I've left three webcams I want you to set up. I think we have poachers – I saw two dead kudus at the Kloofis last week."

Poachers were Hansie's worst nightmare. There was literally nothing he could do other than chase them off. He could shoot them, of course, but any shot in the back or limbs would mean jail time. The courts looked down on retribution. It was their word against his, and besides, he wasn't in the business of shooting people for the sake of a kudu.

"Yes, Boss," Henry said, bowing his head and avoiding eye contact.

The chores Hansie had listed were nothing new to him – his days were long and arduous. But there was something else on Henry's mind, and he was worried sick about saying anything.

"What's up, Henry? Spit it out." Hansie had no patience for histrionics.

"I hear the men talking, Boss. They're worried about bandits … they hear rumours. They say it's not safe in the kraals, or down in the Klein Kloofis," Henry implored.

"What rumours?" Hansie said disbelievingly.

"The Muellers' farm was attacked last month. Men were killed, women raped…" Henry's voice trailed off. The idea of his daughters being defiled left him shaking.

Hansie could see Henry's apprehension and didn't want to dismiss his concerns glibly.

"OK, I'll speak to Mr Du Toit about hiring a security firm to do some patrols for a while. Word will get out we are serious about trespassers. They'll stay away."

Using Arno Du Toit's name was an easy way to allay Henry's concerns. In truth, Arno hadn't made a decision on the farm in years.

"Thank you. You are a good man, Boss."

***

"Hansie, my boy, you make an old man smile." Arno reached out his liver-spotted arm and winced under Hansie's vice-like grip.

Arno's maid, Thadie, scurried into the room. "Excuse me, gentlemen, can I make you some sweet tea?"

"Thank you, my dear, that's very kind," Arno said with grace.

At sixty-four, Arno had all but retired from the day-to-day running of the farm, leaving it instead to his son, François, and Hansie. Between them, they had made the last three years of his deteriorating health bearable. His crooked back, failing eyesight and advanced emphysema meant even the smallest of tasks left him in pain and gasping for breath. It was an ignominious ending to a life full of achievement.

"Have you been in to see Patricia in the office? She won't be happy if you ignore her."

Arno knew his daughter well, but he didn't know how cranky she could get when her concentration was broken.

Patricia, otherwise known as Trixie, had set up her website design business five years previously and bilocated between Nelspruit and Gorriekoppen. It was no surprise to Hansie she had developed a thriving business, which employed twenty people and made good money.

"Yes – she's fine," he lied. "Arno, why don't you come for a ride out with me today? I've a few errands to run then I'll be heading to Hazyview to meet François. We can stop for some lunch and have a beer or two."

Hansie sat as he spoke, allowing Arno to take the weight off his arthritic hip.

"Now that sounds lekker," Arno whispered with a grin on his face. They had gotten into a fair bit of trouble in the past getting wasted in dusty roadside bars, just for the hell of it.

"Trouble is, Elsa has her gang round later to play canasta. It'll be my job to fetch the brandy and sherry. Jeeeez, those women can drink." Arno blew his cheeks out and laughed along with Hansie.

"OK, next time then. You can't sit in this chair all day. You'll get fat like me."

Hansie's face crumpled. He knew Arno didn't have much time left. His days were spent doing literally nothing. He wondered how he would manage without Arno there.

Hansie's own father had died in a farming accident when he was only eight years old, and his mother of cancer shortly afterwards. His brothers were left to raise him. In their remote farm near Kirkwood, in the Eastern Cape, Hansie was often left to entertain himself, which usually meant shooting small animals with his .22 rifle, racing around on his motorbike, and attending army reserve weekends. He worked evenings and weekends at the farm, only stopping to play rugby and to study. At twenty-three, he left Stellenbosch University to move to the Transvaal to play provincial rugby for Nelspruit. He got a part-time job working on the Du Toit estate, where he met Trixie.

Hansie's awkward yet direct approach scared most girls he'd ever had the courage to ask out on a date, but with Trixie it was different. They became inseparable. It was no surprise to her that her father and Hansie had become very close – they were literally the same person a generation apart.

***

"Henry, come on, we are late!" Hansie bawled out of his bakkie window.

"Yes, Boss," Henry replied as he scurried over and jumped into the passenger seat.

"Boss, can we take the back road? I want to make sure the fences are mended." Henry joined his hands together in prayer, almost begging.

"Oh, for goodness' sake, Henry! Have they not got radios?" Hansie was losing his patience.

"Yes, Boss, I tried. The reception in the Klein Kloofis is bad."

The Klein Kloofis, or little valleys, were a series of shallow veld-covered valleys where the sheep congregated to eat the lush grass and spekboom leaf.

"You think there's a problem?"

"No, Boss, I just want to check, that's all." Henry's voice broke slightly as he fidgeted in his seat. The forty-five-minute detour would put an hour on their journey, by the time they'd stopped and inspected the work.

"OK, let's go," Hansie reluctantly agreed. It would give him a chance to check on the pasture and the river levels.

***

The route to the Klein Kloofis was circuitous, with eight gates to unlock and relock. The morning dew had burnt away hours ago, and each time Henry hopped in and out of the Land Cruiser, the cool interior was blow-dried and dusted in fine sand.

As they approached the work crew, Henry whispered, "Boss, stop! Look!"

Hansie slowed and then shut off his engine. He sat stock-still as the enveloping dust gradually cleared to reveal a gruesome scene. In the distance, at the peak of the dirt road, he could see a blue and red heap of clothing. He slowly pulled his binoculars out of the door side pocket.

"Take the gun out of the glove box," Hansie said quietly.

He didn't need binoculars to know what had happened. His eyesight was exceptionally well tuned to life in the bush. He focussed his attention on the distant horizon, to see if there was movement. There wasn't.

He loaded the chamber and removed the safety clip, holding the gun out of sight in his right hand. He started the vehicle and slowly drove forward. With the perimeter fence to his left and the veld to his right, they were visible. And the sound of the V6 engine could be heard from miles away.

"Boss, we should walk, they can hear us," Henry said trembling.

It was precisely what Hansie wanted. Stealth was not an option, even if he'd wanted to creep up unheard. The vehicle rolled towards the dead farmhand, who lay in a twisted, bloody mess. He'd been hacked to pieces.

Hansie looked for signs of movement, hoping the bandits would be fleeing from the scene eastwards. There were none. He brought the bakkie to a halt and got out, scanning the horizon in every direction. A metallic stench of blood oozed up from the mutilated body at their feet, recognisable only by the nametag stitched onto his pocket. Any signs of life had long since departed.

The man's hands had been severed and lay contorted next to his corpse. His eyes had been gouged out and his body was covered in angry slashes. Swarms of buzzing insects covered dark pools of blood, completing a grotesque circle of life.

Twenty feet away, a worker had been strung up on a fence pole naked, his genitals cut from his body. His lower abdomen had been sliced open, and his intestines dangled to the ground like an umbilical cord. Their radios were smashed to pieces.

Hansie began looking for spoor to determine which direction they'd gone. He found the trail soon enough, then his blood ran cold.

"Henry! Get in the bakkie! Now!"

***

Hansie thrashed the vehicle through the bush, cursing his own security measures, which had him stopping at each gate. Every mobile number at the yard and Arno's place rang out or failed to ring at all. He called the neighbouring farm thirty miles to the west. The number rang out there also.

After thirty minutes they rounded the hill to the east of the farm, when Hansie suddenly slammed on the brakes.

"They must be at the farm, Henry, which means they have access to the gun cupboard. Arno has a .308 in there and there's at least five handguns, including Trixie's Glock 42. If we drive up there, we'll be sitting ducks."

Henry shook with fear. He had no answers. He'd heard about this gang on the news – what they did to farmworkers, who, in the eyes of the marauders, were worse than the whites who they accused of stealing their land hundreds of years ago.

"Boss, please call Louise. Tell her to hide, I beg you."

Tears began running down his face. At last, a hysterical Louise answered the landline.

"Hansie, I can hear screams and gunfire in the main house. What's happening? Is Henry OK?" Louise's happy voice was in panic mode.

"Yes, listen to me carefully," Hansie said, returning to Afrikaans. "There are bandits at the house. Tell Alice to go into the pantry and hide behind the boiler. There's enough room for both of you, do you understand?"

"Yes, Hansie, yes!" she cried.

"Do not come out until I, or Henry, tell you to. Go now."

He hung up. Hansie turned to his assistant.

"Henry, listen carefully to me. You know how to use the gun, right?" Hansie flicked the safety on and off to remind him.

"Yes, Boss," he said, his hands trembling.

After going through his plan, Hansie said, "Right, let's go."

He gunned the vehicle as fast as he could and began blowing on the horn and flashing his lights to attract the attention of anyone at the farm. He stopped five hundred metres away from the whitewashed building. Three of the bandits in bright-red overalls were hoisting a body over a wooden frame with the pulley system used for stringing up game. It was Arno. From the amount of blood on his face, it was clear he was in a very bad way.

They stopped what they were doing when they heard the bakkie approach. A tall, bald man ran to the back door and into the house, returning seconds later with another two men, making five in total. Hansie assumed at least one would remain indoors to guard Trixie and the maids. His teeth grinded and his heart pounded in his chest.

"Henry, listen carefully. I want you to climb over me and get out of the truck. Get on the bonnet and begin shooting at the house, like I said. Make lots of noise. I want them to see you and come after you … do you understand? Now hurry up."

"Boss, we are too far. The pistol is too small, you must use the rifle!" Henry implored.

"I don't want them to know I'm here. If you shoot at them, they'll come running towards you, hopefully with the guns from Arno's safe."

Hansie slid his seat back and Henry climbed over him, his ripe body dripping with nervous sweat. Henry bounced on the bonnet like it was a trampoline, leaving a huge dent in the top. He shouted obscenities and let off 9mm rounds with the handgun. Hansie slithered to the ground commando style and crawled to a safe vantage point out of sight.

"I see five of them."

"There's another two inside, Boss. The leader is wearing Mr Arno's hat," Henry confirmed.

A scream pierced the late morning air, then stopped abruptly. Hansie raged inside.

"Henry, take two or three shots. Make sure they hit the building."

He took aim and half a second later they heard a ping on the corrugated roof as the round ricocheted into the sky. Three of the bandits hit the deck and began shouting and waving. The leader lined Henry up with a handgun from a standing position and let off a few rounds with zero chance of a hit. He strode back into the house and came back with two more handguns, which he threw to his men. They peeled off left and right, in Henry's direction.

"Boss, they're coming, what should I do?" Henry asked, quivering.

"Stop looking at me! Keep swearing at them and letting rounds off until I tell you to stop!"

The bald bandit and what looked to be the junior member of the team began stalking towards them, confident that Henry, who was shouting and goading them from the roof of the truck, hadn't seen them.

Hansie crouched on one knee and took cover behind a cactus, to track their movements. It was clear to him they had little hunting experience. As Baldy and Junior crested the brow in front of them, they regrouped and scurried down into a dip in the road. Henry hadn't seen them, which was ideal. If he had, he could have scared them into hiding, or run for cover himself.

"Keep shouting," Hansie whispered. He didn't need to hear their footsteps – he wanted them to think they had gone unnoticed and to step out, which they did.

Hansie's silenced .270 Winchester Magnum was by far the best weapon he had ever held. He couldn't remember the last time he'd missed an animal from three hundred metres. At a hundred and twenty-five metres, these vermin offered no challenge whatsoever. He looked through the sight and saw a human face for the first time in his life. It was decision time.

His first shot hit Baldy directly to the left of his nose. His blood and brain matter splattered onto his apprentice, who froze in horror. As he attempted to rationalise what had just happened, his short, violent teenage life was put to an end with round two entering his eye and obliterating the back of his head. Both bodies collapsed to the ground.

"Henry, be quiet now. Get down out of sight!" Hansie barked. He looked through his binoculars to see what was happening at the house. It was worryingly quiet.

He motioned Henry to get behind him and began stalking towards the house through the thick scrub. After a couple of minutes, Hansie stopped dead in his tracks.

The third member of the lynch party, in a bright-yellow baseball cap, returned from the safety of the house and made his way over to Arno, with a large kitchen knife in his hand. Arno hadn't moved or made a noise since being hung by his hands. He was dead – there was no doubting that in Hansie's mind. Adrenaline stopped his anger from overflowing for the time being.

Yellow Cap spat and cursed at Arno's lifeless body. He slapped his face and laughed at some sick joke he amused himself with, while holding the knife to Arno's throat.

Bullet three hit Yellow Cap square in the chest. The knife flashed in the sunlight as it arced in the air. He fell flat on his back, his legs rigid and his hands twisted as his nervous system sent the last and final confused messages to his limbs.

Fifty metres to the left, the leader darted from the house and hid behind an old filled-in well, now the base for Elsa's herb garden. He looked left and saw Yellow Cap's prone body, blood trickling from the large hole in his chest.

Hansie watched him carefully then whispered in Henry's ear and pointed west.

"Run!" Hansie ordered. Henry had no intention of hanging around.

The leader aimed Arno's Winchester at Henry as he ran for cover. He let off a shot and heard a long, agonising scream in return. He dashed into the house and returned with another red overall, this one in bright-white sneakers.

Pointing towards the patch of aloe bushes where he saw Henry go down, the leader gave him Trixie's Glock 42 and shouted what sounded like 'hurry up' in Zulu.

White Sneakers ran up the slope and around the outside of a dense clump of cacti, out of sight of his boss. As he ducked beneath a low-hanging branch, Hansie grabbed him by the throat and wrist, and wrenched the gun from his grasp while preventing any noise coming from his gasping mouth.

"Bangaphi endlini?" Hansie's rudimentary Zulu served him well as the bandit held up two shaky fingers to indicate the number of men in the house. Hansie jerked his shoulder and felt the man's neck snap. He lowered his body to the ground soundlessly and reshouldered his rifle. The leader stood in plain view using the scope to locate his man through the thick scrub.

Bullet four hit him through the neck, decimating his oesophagus and other vital body parts. Arno's stolen .308 bounced on its end and landed on his buckled legs. Hansie waited to see if the men on the inside would make a move to see what was going on. They didn't.

After thirty seconds, he whistled to Henry, who jumped to his feet unharmed and followed Hansie, who was sprinting towards the house.

Trixie's pocket Glock felt tiny in Hansie's hand, but he knew there was no point trying to use his rifle at close range in the house. Something much more compact was called for. He circled around the house from the east, skipping across Elsa's vegetable garden through the soft soil towards the back door, which led to the kitchen.

He slid his boots off silently and placed them to one side, allowing himself a few seconds to catch his breath. He heard muffled screams and closed his eyes to blank them out. The faded-green mosquito door was closed, but the double-hinged stable door directly behind it was ajar, snagged on the doormat, which had folded over. He crouched low on his haunches; the pressure on his joints from years of rugby pinched on his tendons. Tiny tetrahedron-shaped thorns known as dubbeltjies stuck in his feet as though he was walking on drawing pins, but he barely registered the pain.

He inched open the mesh door, silencing the screeching noise it had made for the last fifteen years. He crawled through the kitchen to find Elsa lying on the floor with a collage of playing cards beneath her body, a length of rope wrapped around her neck. She'd been strangled.

From the main bedroom he could hear faint noises and whimpering. He got to his feet and crept through the living area without a murmur, swerving the floorboards which he knew would creak beneath his tread. He turned into the corridor and nudged open the bedroom door.

Trixie was pinned to the bed by the errant Temba, her naked body covered in bruises. Blood trickled down her face from a cut on her head, and her blonde hair was matted and tangled. Thadie and Sandi, the maids, cowered naked in the corner, having been beaten and raped.

Temba's brother laughed and cheered next to him as he writhed on top of Trixie, oblivious to Hansie's presence. Until he turned.

Hansie shot him in the forehead, bringing an end to the fun. The sound in the confines of the room was deafening; cordite filled the air in an acrid blue mist. Temba jumped to his feet and bent down to reach for his weapon on the floor. Bullet six tore through his anus, shredding his bowel, bladder and lower intestine. A tall vase directly behind him crashed to the floor as the bullet came to rest in the skirting board. Temba screamed as he held his groin and rolled around on the shards of porcelain.

Hansie grabbed his hair and dragged him through the house, leaving a slimy trail of blood from the bedroom to the kitchen door in their wake.

Outside on the scorched earth, in the shadow of the trestle used to string up Arno's dead body, Temba writhed in agony as a stream of hot blood poured from his backside like red diarrhoea.

"Please, Boss, don't kill me. I'm sorry, Boss … they made me do it."

The bullet tore through the top of his skull, splitting it in half.

Singleton Rugby Club, London: 29 October 2021

"It took a long time before Trixie could go back to the farm, and it was eighteen months before we were exonerated by the courts. That's when we came to the UK. We couldn't walk the streets at home without being heralded as heroes or attacked by those sympathetic to the bandits."

The boys were dumbfounded. Mikey was right: Hansie took no prisoners.

"Trixie's the strong one," Hansie said, nodding. "She's the one who lost her folks and was raped by those pigs. She's getting on with life, making the best of it. It's me that hides away, too frightened to think about what might happen when we return."

Hansie shook himself into the present. Despite his harrowing story, the gloom and hostility that he had brought to the table had gone. It was the first time he'd spoken about that day in years. He felt unburdened, somehow released from his shackles. Reliving it all had allowed him to face up to his actions. The anguish he had locked up had been aired; the pressure valve opened.

"Sorry for what I said, Jake. You are a brave man protecting your friend." Hansie nodded solemnly. "And you were right. I wouldn't hesitate to do it again."

18

IT'S NOT WHAT YOU KNOW

Jake's flat, London: 8 November 2021

Three classes and two one-on-one sessions had been mentally and physically exhausting. Shin's opinion of Jake since his brush with the law had changed dramatically. He could barely look Jake in the eye and would leave written instructions in his locker rather than speak to him in person.

A taste of things to come, Jake thought to himself.

His phone buzzed on his desk. He looked down at the screen and saw a picture of Lesley Chesterton beaming back at him.

"Lesley, how are you, darling?" Just the thought of her gave Jake the lift he so desperately needed.

"Well, I can safely say I have never felt better … thanks to you," she said.

"Me?! What did I do to make you feel so pleased with yourself?"

"It was seeing you and Alan together. Meeting him like that after all these years, it was like a dream come true. You are very similar, you know?"

Jake raised his eyebrows in amusement. "You looked like you were having fun. You renewed old acquaintances, did you?"

"You could say that." She chuckled. "I've just picked up your voicemail. We've been in Singapore at a trade conference. Alan said it's the best one he's ever been to."

"I bet he did," Jake guffawed.

"He's such a charmer, Jake. He hasn't changed a bit."

"Singapore sounds nice. I need to hear all about it. Actually, it was Alan I wanted to speak to. Would you send me his mobile number?" Jake thought while she was in such high spirits, now was a good time to ask.

"Hold on, he's right here. And don't go – there's something I'm itching to tell you."

Jake heard Lesley call Alan, who must've been in another part of the house.

"Jake, dear boy! How the devil are you?" Alan said in his cut-glass accent.

"I'm fine and I hope you are too."

"Dear boy, I couldn't be happier – and it's you I need to thank. I hope you'll come to the wedding? We want you and the boys there."

"Wedding? What wedding?"

"I've asked Lesley to marry me … and she said yes! I'm the luckiest man alive."

Alan was then admonished by his new fiancée for letting the cat out of the bag.

"Well, congratulations, sir! I'm thrilled for you, I really am. For you both." Jake's face crinkled with joy.

"What did you say to me, Jake, that time at the races? You 'hope never to regret – if you hide away frightened of the consequences, worse things happen'. I should never have left Lesley all those years ago. I've regretted it all my life. Seeing her that day, listening to your advice, I wasn't going to let history repeat itself..." Alan's voice softened and trailed off.

"This is the best news I've heard in a very long time. I'm thrilled for you both. Of course we will all be there," he said, ignoring the elephant in the room. He couldn't let it spoil a wonderful moment.

"Jake, my boy, if there is any way I can repay you, let me know. I owe you my eternal thanks for what you did."

"Well, as a matter of fact, Alan, there is a trivial matter you could use your influence to resolve."

Bates & Chandler, Gray's Inn, London: 11 November 2021

"John, it's lovely to see you."

Tamara hugged John then led him into her office, where coffee and cakes were laid out next to her notes.

"Help yourself," she said, waving at the plate of cholesterol.

"Jake will kill me if I break my healthy eating plan."

Tamara slid a slice of Bakewell tart off her plate and into her mouth without the slightest pang of guilt. "So, what have you got for me?" she asked through a mouth full of frangipane and jam.

"It's more what we haven't got. You've gone through the notes, right – what do you make of it?" John wanted Tamara to steer the conversation.

"Seems to me the guy has some very questionable friends in this Doda Kelemendi fellow, but there's no law against knowing people. He's split up from his girlfriend. It happens. He's also been very astute with his medical insurance, his income declaration's accurate, and he's paid his taxes to the penny. What more is there to say? None of it makes the guy a criminal."

"Are you not suspicious at all? He's changed his name, we have no record of his existence beyond eighteen months ago, and he seems to have been reincarnated in the form of a blobby bouncer from Sheffield."

"Quite frankly, John, no. It's not a crime to change your name – half of your celebrity client base have – if that is indeed what he's done. The fact you don't know isn't proof that he has. To be honest, the more I read, the more worried I become for Jake. The doctor's notes and medical evidence are irrefutable. The occupational therapist's report is exhaustive and has been carried out by a reputable firm."

John shook his head. "A firm owned by an offshore trust – the same trust that owns Lexington Health, who Dr Choudary works for. The same Dr Choudary who is worth over £50m."

"John, this isn't some scandal being ousted by the Daily Mirror. We require salient facts. Was the man injured? Yes. Is there evidence of my client's involvement? Yes. Is there proof that Mr Stockton is lying and this is some elaborate insurance scam? No." Tamara lifted her arms out as if proving her point.

"Our case will be centred around self-defence, irrespective of what might or might not have happened to Jake's friend. We'll argue he feared for his life and used his martial arts skills to avoid being beaten up, the outcome of which was accidental injury to Stockton. I've spoken with Jake and told him we'll need a guilty plea to a lesser charge in abeyance. Nothing you have given me will stand up in court – and you know it." John buried his head in his hands.

"What I need is evidence to refute the charge of assault, or proof his injuries are false – and from what I've seen they are very real. Your investigation is interesting, but do you honestly believe the police, a doctor, a solicitor, a bouncer, and God knows who else are in it together? It just doesn't stack up, I'm afraid."

"I do believe that, yes, and it does stack up. I'll find your smoking gun if it kills me."

He snatched up his notes to leave.

"I think you're wasting your time. If we take a plea, he'll get three years and be out in twelve months."

"That's not going to happen," John said, without turning round.

John Devlin Public Relations, London: 11 November 2021

Justin leaned against the door frame to John's office and blew on the back of his fingertips.

"Would you like the good news or the very good news?"

It had been a long day and John had absolutely zero to show for it.

"Go on," John said, without confidence.

"Lee Henry Grassington. Born 15 January, 1984, in Rotherham. Attended St Patrick's Comprehensive in Rawmarsh." Justin nodded knowingly and widened his eyes.

"Who's Lee Henry Grassington?" John asked, bored with Justin's grandstanding.

"Molly noticed a redirected letter when she was at Tracey Ingham's house, so she did a search on the name. There was an article in the Rotherham Gazette in September 1995."

Justin tapped his iPad into action and began to read:

'Lee Grassington, aged ten, from Moorside Road, Rawmarsh, was rushed to hospital with a suspected broken leg and severe trauma to his right eye. Witnesses say they had seen Lee and his friend climbing chestnut trees looking for conkers when they heard a scream. Paramedics attending the scene found Lee unconscious with blood pouring from a facial injury. A spokesman at the Sheffield Eye Infirmary confirmed his eye could not be saved.'

"It looks very likely that Lee Grassington is the original Ben Stockton."

"You are kidding me?!" John exclaimed, jumping to his feet. "That changes everything! If we can prove Stockton is Grassington, it means his eye injury's bogus, which means his back injury's probably bogus as well."

"There's more. His mother's still registered at their home address in South Yorkshire. I'll ask Molly to pay her a visit."

"Are you crazy? Under no circumstances send anyone anywhere, least of all Molly. If that lunatic Kelemendi sees her, there's no telling what he'll do."

"Are you going to tell Tamara Norazu? Maybe she can get the case kicked out."

"No, we need to tread carefully here. Tamara will want irrefutable proof Stockton's Grassington, and that his eye injury's a fabrication. A stray envelope on Ingham's sideboard won't be enough. It could even be a coincidence, as unlikely as that sounds."

John held his forehead deep in thought. "Something else that's just occurred to me – find out who treated Stockton in hospital. Did Choudary examine Stockton, or did someone else? And check if Cantly and Owen ever served in South Yorkshire Police."

Justin nodded as he typed frantically on his iPad. "Leave it with me. What are you going to do?"

"I'm off to Rotherham."

Fulwood Sports Centre, Kentish Town, London: 15 November 2021

"Beverly, have you got a minute, darlin'? I need a chat before the 4M," Mikey asked.

She smiled back. How could she refuse?

"I've been looking through the membership database and found a few points of interest."

Beverly rolled her eyes and her smile disappeared. "I think you're barking up the wrong tree here, Mikey. There's no way Euan can get money out of the business without Head Office seeing it. It's impossible."

"Hear me out, please … I don't need much information." He raised his hands as he took a seat in front of her desk.

"Am I right in saying that we calculate total income from memberships on the basis of numbers of members and subscriptions?"

"Yes … how else?" Beverly said impatiently.

"The memberships are classified by membership account number, concession and type, correct?" Mikey nodded wide-eyed at her.

"I gave you the database, Mikey," she replied condescendingly.

"There were no names on it."

Beverly fell silent for a moment. "It's data protection. Only certain people have access to names, addresses and bank account details."

Mikey's suspicions had been aroused by Joy's interrogation of the data. She had asked him to forward additional information so she could analyse it in more detail. He had no clue what a pivot table was, but he understood her findings easily enough.

"Says who? Seems a bit strange. I know literally everyone who walks through the door."

"Elaine – she's responsible for accounts."

"So, when new members sign up, they're given a membership number, which is added to the list on the database, right?"

She nodded, witheringly.

"Who assigns the membership numbers and takes bank account details?"

"Elaine."

"What's stopping the same membership number being issued twice?"

"There's a check code for duplicated membership numbers. The turnstile system would prevent access," Beverly said without conviction.

"You know that for sure, do you? Can the check be turned off? How reliable's that turnstile system – has it ever worked properly?"

Beverly scratched her head. *He has a point there*, she conceded to herself. The system had been playing up for years, and the maintenance company had no answers. They'd come out, plug in their computers and make positive noises about finding the problem, then leave, only for it to reoccur weeks later.

"Exactly," Mikey said in response to her silence. "What if there are members with duplicated membership numbers who pay subscriptions into other accounts? How are we to know?"

"I still don't see what you're getting at, Michael. How is that even possible? You need to be very careful who you make accusations against." Beverly's voice turned to a whisper as she pointed her pen in the direction of Euan's office.

"What I'm saying is, we have more and more members, and all I hear from Euan is we aren't making any money. I don't care who I make accusations about. If this blows up, I don't want to be in the firing line. If we all sit around blindly obeying his orders, we'll all go down with him. What I need is a list of members' names, membership numbers and bank account details so that I can reconcile them with income."

Beverly scoffed. "There's no way Elaine's going to give you that, and I'm not going to ask her. Keep me out of it."

She picked up her notepad and documents. "It's the 4M now … why don't you ask her yourself?"

***

Mikey's presentation on productivity was nearing its conclusion, when Euan and Elaine joined the meeting – twenty minutes late. He ignored their noisy arrival and continued unabated.

"As you can see from the new member uptake data, we have a net increase of twenty-two, which is less than previous months but shows our continued increase in market share. The manager at H&C Leisure's a mate of mine, and he says they've lost over a hundred members to us since January."

"He won't be your friend for long, Mikey," Big G said, laughing.

"Jo's new vegetarian cookery classes have gone down a storm. We've got members asking if you can put them on in the evenings. We need to talk about that, Jo. I'll pop up for lunch and we can look at a plan." Jo gave him the thumbs-up.

"Vegetarian? Ugh, no thanks," Euan sneered, having finally sat down.

Mikey stopped and the whole room stared at Euan, with his stomach ballooned over his belt and his shirt buttons at breaking point. After ten awkward seconds, Mikey cleared his throat and continued his summary of events, ignoring Euan's huffing and exaggerated displays of impatience.

"Will, give us the update on the squash competition, please."

Will picked up the projector control and flicked to slide one. "Not much to say really … we have 75% of tickets sold, with four weeks to go. Four gold sponsors. Sky Sports and BBC Sport contracted to cover the event online. And the Deputy Mayor of London's agreed to hand out the trophies to the winners. We anticipate a direct net profit of £45,000, with indirect income conservatively estimated at £30,000."

He sat back down to a stunned silence.

"Oh my God, Will, that's amazing!" Carla Umwhezi fist-bumped him across the table, while the rest of the group burst into spontaneous applause. Everyone apart from Euan.

"We're not in the least surprised you've made this happen, Will. Well done on all your hard work and commitment," Mikey gushed.

It didn't escape anyone that the amount matched Euan's shortfall in profits to the penny.

Once the applause had receded, Mikey opened the floor. "Any other business, guys?"

The blank faces told Mikey that Euan's presence was having its usual impact.

"OK. I've one or two minor points," Mikey said. "We've had a complaint that a member of staff has verbally abused a special needs patron. The boy's so upset he's unwilling to talk about the incident. I've spoken to his grandparents, who, mercifully, don't want the matter to be taken any further. Can I ask you all to reiterate to your teams to be courteous. Always."

Mikey could see Euan's spongy forehead beading with sweat. Lisa and Carla glared at him with uncontrolled hatred.

"On another matter," Mikey moved on, "I spoke with Luke in reception earlier about the ongoing problem with the turnstile not swiping people in. Camden Leisure use the same system, and I've contacted their security company, who are willing to come and have a look. They won't charge us if they can't fix it."

He looked directly at Euan to see his reaction. He wasn't disappointed.

Horror swept across Euan's face, and Elaine choked on her green tea.

"Michael!" Euan snapped. "You have no right to change one of our suppliers without consulting me first. I will deal with the turnstile issue personally."

He wrestled himself to his feet in a fluster and bounced past his employees, leaving Elaine stranded in no-man's-land.

Mikey wasn't the only one surprised by his overreaction. Beverly saw it too, and alarm bells began ringing in her head.

Hackney, London: 16 November 2021

Jake exited Hackney Central tube station with Irene and headed up Amhurst Road. Bohemia Market was in full swing and would be for the next eight hours, on into the evening. The tinny sound of a reggae band playing and a heady aroma of jerk chicken and marijuana filled the air.

Irene was well known in the neighbourhood. As they meandered through the crowds, she hugged and kissed people, leaving Jake isolated in a fog of déjà vu. As contagious as it was, her cheerfulness did nothing for his mood. His caseload was mounting, and the stress of his impending court case had left him distracted, irritable and short-tempered.

His mind drifted to John, who'd taken the brunt of his mood swings recently, and done so without argument, which both infuriated Jake and pinched at his paranoia.

Why did he care so much? What did he want?

The conveyor belt of boyfriends his mother had when he was younger came across the same way. They were best friends in the beginning. *"Whatever the boy needs, Denise.' 'Hey, Jake, do you want to come to the football? Play video games?"*

Then that would quickly change. *"Get out of my sight!" "Shut your fucking mouth!" "Go to your room!"*

He became wallpaper, a background noise they couldn't hear any more. He thought about the loud intercourse he would have to listen to in the honeymoon period, quickly followed by crying, screaming, black eyes and bruises. The indiscriminate injustice life handed out to innocent people left him cold with anger.

He had survived it, taken his opportunity, and thrived, only to become emotionally bereft and detached. He doubted he'd ever feel the love Mikey had for Joy, or what Rob had for Maddie. Then there was Bernard – he'd lost his beloved son, a war hero, and had cared for his crippled wife and he thanked God for the memories he had.

That was the problem for Jake – the memories. He had none. Only bad ones that tormented him. He only ever looked forward, and what he was looking at now was worse than looking back on his childhood of misery. His hands shook and his heart fluttered. He closed his eyes to clear his mind, to think of positive things.

Lesley and Alan were to tie the knot, Mikey had met Joy, and Rob was to become a father. His clean-up operation at his mother's house had had no repercussions, and John had found some very interesting background on Ben Stockton, which had given him a glimmer of hope.

His long weekend in Marbella at Rob's uncle's villa would be his first holiday, and likely his last, for many years. Still, it was something to look forward to. The *now* had rarely let him down, mainly thanks to his friends. If he concentrated on them, he'd get through it. He hoped.

***

The aromas and sounds of the marketplace had intensified in tandem with his trepidation of what they would find at the Khans'. Kelly Middlecroft's reports had been positive over the last three weeks. *A good sign*, he thought. Willing to accept improvement.

Irene set a slow pace as they walked the remaining quarter mile along Dalston Road, rehearsing their questions and what to do in the case of an emergency. They walked through an underpass and turned down a pedestrian access into the Pembury estate. Tolsford Road was mercifully quiet and reasonably free of traffic.

They arrived intentionally early for their appointment. Jake liked to see the last-minute window dressing people carried out. He rapped on the Khans' door and heard footsteps in the corridor of the 1920s mid-terrace house. Ebrah, the mother, answered the door wearing a simple green shalwar kameez and blue hijab. Jake introduced themselves and she beckoned them into the house.

"Please come, please come," she said in a whisper, directing them into the living room, where Muhammed Abdulla Khan was stood in his tan kurta pyjamas and suit jacket.

He was of medium build with signs of a well-worked pot belly. He had a long unkempt beard, bloodshot eyes and a bulbous nose. At thirty-three, Ebrah was eighteen years his junior, and, at first glance, utterly subservient to him.

All four huddled in the centre of the chilly and unwelcoming sitting room. There was no television, no reading materials and no toys in the spotlessly clean, eerily silent house. The only noise was the distant rumble of what sounded like a washing machine mid-cycle. The curtainless windows, spartan furniture and worn-out carpet told Jake this wasn't a room they used regularly, other than for Muhammed to lock up his children, or Ebrah, in for some minor transgression.

"May we sit?" Jake asked politely.

Ebrah ushered them onto a green and brown velour-covered couch, where they propped themselves on the edge, before removing clipboards and iPads from their bags. She sat opposite them on a dining chair positioned to Muhammed's left, like an Edwardian couple awaiting a family photograph. He remained standing, in front of a disused gas fireplace, staring malevolently at Irene.

Ebrah bunched her bony hands on her lap. Her knees and shoulder blades created knobbly bumps under her clothing. A bare 100W bulb hanging from the ceiling cast a hard glare on the undecorated white Anaglypta wallpaper.

"Are Razzaq and Haniya enjoying their new school?" Jake offered to both parents with a smile. It was a question to exert a little dominance, if for no other reason than to get some verbal communication under way.

"Yes, very much, thank you," Ebrah said, betraying a mixture of enthusiasm and relief. "It has been difficult for Haniya to adapt. She is loving it, though, especially her maths. She would like to be an engineer."

Irene joined in. "My father's an engineer. I'm sure she will do well. And little Razzaq – how is he getting on? Is he playing football or crick—"

"What do you want from us?! Why are you people here?" Muhammed's interruption was laced with venom and impatience.

Jake and Irene had agreed for Jake to deal with Muhammed if he became confrontational.

"We are here to ensure the health and wellbeing of your children, Mr Khan. Our health visitors, intervention officers and other colleagues have good reason to suspect your children have been subject to significant abuse and neglect." Jake spoke with quiet authority.

Muhammed crossed his arms defiantly and stared Jake down. Ebrah's eyes were firmly planted on her scuffed slippers, hiding her fear and shame.

"Our role is to protect children from harm, to assess their needs and to support you, the parents. We are also required, by law, to intervene in crisis situations and make decisions to safeguard them."

Jake didn't need to ask if he understood. His dismissive attitude said it all.

"My children are mine, do you hear! Mine!" He jabbed his chest possessively.

Jake allowed a moment to pass, while Muhammed took a breath.

"Mr Khan, we understand you may find our involvement in your family an invasion of privacy, but we do not consider that a priority where child safety is at risk. Your children have attended hospital on many occasions, and the police have been called out to find you drunk, aggressive and uncooperative. This is a situation we cannot allow to persist. If necessary, we will be forced to take your children into care."

Jake laboured his last point. Talking to the man about care and support was pointless. Numerous meetings and countless assessments had proven that.

Muhammed rubbed his head and bunched his fist, as if weighing up his options to agree or fight it out.

"I'm sorry, Mr Webster. In our culture, we don't have these things. You are right. We are in the UK now. Things are done differently. It is difficult for me, being the man in the house."

Jake and Irene were unconvinced.

"As you can see, Razzaq and Haniya are at school now and we have no more police coming to the door. I have stopped drinking and I'm working for my brother now, earning good money. Life can be difficult sometimes. We are trying our best."

He dropped his arm around Ebrah, who flinched at his heavy-handed affection.

"Ebrah!" he snapped. "Get our guests some tea."

Jake wasn't fooled by manipulative thugs like him. Whatever they said, they always had that look in their eye that betrayed a disingenuousness. A blind man in another room could see it.

***

After the visit, Jake and Irene went to a side street café to exchange notes and their take on how the visit went. The uplifting music and atmosphere of the market seemed macabre after what they had just witnessed. It reminded Jake of the band playing on as the Titanic sunk in the icy Atlantic waters.

"He's lying. It's a front. When I helped Ebrah with the tea she couldn't stop shaking. I never saw her pick anything up with her left arm. It may be broken or dislocated."

"Agreed," Jake said anxiously. "I'm going to recommend a protection order. There's no way we can leave them there. Maintain the health visits and IO work. I want feedback from the school – make sure the Head understands the seriousness of the situation."

I've got four weeks to save this family, Jake thought. He swallowed hard. His race to the precipice had begun.

19

JEZZABELLE

17 Moorside Road, Rawmarsh, South Yorkshire: 25 November 2021

He parked his car fifty yards from the Grassington house and waited for any sign of life. A milkman, postman and paperboy all came and went without stopping. No lights came on and no curtains were undrawn. Even the neighbours walked past without the slightest interest. This wild goose chase was beginning to annoy him. He hated his time being wasted.

Just then, as if God was answering his pleas, a man approached Lee Grassington's mother's door. He paused, looked around and rang the doorbell. He rang it three times and waited patiently between rings. But there was no answer. The neighbour at No. 19 leaned out his front door in his pyjama bottoms and soiled vest and began a conversation that lasted about two minutes. His anger at being disturbed at 10.30 in the morning seemed to disappear as the conversation developed.

The guy turned and looked directly at him as he left.

"Shit! It's the guy I saw at court."

Bell and Sandringham Legal, Farringdon, London: 25 November 2021

"Report," Bell snapped as he answered Doda's call.

"I still need paying! You wasted my time," Doda said through gritted teeth.

"*I* wasted *your* time?" Bell asked with surprise. "You work for me, remember – I pay you to do what I say. What's your problem?"

"The woman died three weeks ago. She was buried last Tuesday. You asked me to kill her, but she's already dead. I still want paying."

Morris hated surprises but he was happy about this one and had no problem paying the man the £4,000 for a wasted visit.

"Yes, yes, you'll get paid. How did she die?" he asked impatiently.

"I have no idea, I'm not a doctor. She was an old woman – maybe heart attack."

Morris had a good feeling. Stockton's mother was a stumbling block. With her out of the way, and his girlfriend and sister too frightened to say anything, there'd be no one left to worry about Stockton's disappearance after the insurance was paid.

"OK, good. You need to get on that flight. I want Webster in a prison cell before Sunday. Are you able to find enough heroin in Spain?"

"I have many Albanian brothers in Puerto Banús." Doda's familial allusion to the Albanian drug cartel ensconced in the Costa del Sol sent a shiver up Morris's spine.

"I've sent you the number of the police chief there. Send him a text and a photo of Webster once you've planted the drugs on him. Don't hang around, understand? He must be arrested before he returns."

Bell knew the insurance payout would be cut and dried with further proof. Drug dealing in Marbella would be perfect. He doubted he'd see the man ever again, which was fine by him.

"Wait … I have more information." Doda sensed his boss was about to hang up.

"Get on with it, man!" Bell demanded.

"I've sent you a photo. This man was at the courthouse for the hearing. He is a friend of Webster. I saw them together – they had drinks after." He waited until he heard the beep on his phone indicate the message had been opened.

"I parked at the old lady's house this morning. He spoke to her neighbour."

Morris's blood ran cold. "Jesus, that's John Devlin," he murmured to himself.

After several minutes listening to his boss's heavy breathing, he asked, "What do you want me to do?"

"Change of plan. Take Webster out. I want him in a body bag by Sunday – do you hear me?"

John Devlin Public Relations, Camden, London: 25 November 2021

"Well?" Justin picked up John's call, his curiosity getting the better of his manners.

"The good news is Grassington is definitely Stockton. I spoke to her neighbour, who described him to a tee."

"And the bad news?" Justin closed his eyes.

"The neighbour told me about another guy who paid a visit the previous day – 'a huge bloke, looked like he'd returned from a war zone, sunken eyes, yellow teeth'."

"Doda Kelemendi?! You're kidding?!"

"I wish I was. He didn't want to speak to him, as you can imagine. Told me the guy was asking questions in the post office. I have no clue why he was there, though I assume it wasn't to deliver early Christmas presents."

Justin shook his head, ridding the image of Molly being strangled by the monster.

"This is getting serious, John. We should hand this over to the police."

"That's a great idea – let's ring DS Cantly and PC Owens, shall we?" John's voice dripped with sarcasm, which he regretted immediately.

"I did learn something interesting from the neighbour... Aside from Margaret Grassington dying of cancer three weeks ago, Lee Grassington changed his name in 2008. Margaret told him one time when he took her shopping round. His new name was David Carlisle, not Ben Stockton. Give it to one of the team to investigate – see if they can find out where he went."

"Roger that. Speaking of DS Cantly, he transferred from South Yorkshire to Humberside in 2010. We have a copy of his work record, thanks to Molly's brother."

"Interesting. Make sure we do criminal record checks on these aliases, OK," John said. "Anything back about Choudary?"

"Not yet. I think it's best if Tamara asks about Choudary's credentials. They'll have to answer her questions and it's standard practice."

"No. I don't want them to suspect we're onto them. If they do, they'll shut up shop – or worse. If I'm right, these people shoot first and ask questions later."

Jezzabelle Villa, Marbella, Andalucía, Spain: 27 November 2021

Jake and Mikey ran along the coastal boardwalk at an easy pace, deep in thought, the early morning sun beating on their backs. Jake could see the ridge of the Baroque roof of Villa Jezzabelle in the distance and the whitewashed walls glimmering through the olive groves.

Jeremy, or Jezza as he preferred to be called, had remodelled the house over the last two years, spending over a million euros, which was as good a reason as any for a housewarming party. Arabelle De Freitus, his wife, knew how to lay on the style with champagne, fine wine, cocktails, caviar, lobster and the best steak money can buy. And that was only the welcome party – the real party had yet to begin.

John's lecture about looking after himself and being aware of those around him had overtones of Jasmin about it, with a more personable parental quality, which Jake appreciated, and ignored.

He and Mikey had spent the previous night on a massive yacht in Puerto Banús harbour in the company of two Russian oligarchs and several Russian ex-special forces henchmen.

Sergei and Igor were clients of Rob's and spent most of their lives jetting from place to place avoiding the gaze of the press. Jake had volunteered to train with Sergei and his henchmen using close quarter clinch techniques they hadn't seen before. Mikey volunteered to be their stooge and human punch bag. At one point, he was choked so hard by Vlad, Sergei's personal bodyguard, he passed out.

It was safe to say they had met two friends for life in Sergei and Igor, as well as several minders the size of walk-in wardrobes.

"Perhaps if you got into trouble in jail, you could name drop Vlad into the conversation. Every cloud."

Mikey's gallows humour got a belly laugh from Jake – a sure sign he was coming to terms with his fate.

Jake was almost willing the end to come, like some death row inmate awaiting execution, and despite John's optimism, nothing gave him confidence the outcome was going to change.

The more John dug into Stockton's past the less it made sense and the easier it was to dismiss his proposition that it was a conspiracy. He and Tamara saw things a lot simpler, although as much as he wanted to believe the argument of self-defence, he didn't believe it would wash with the judge.

Twelve months wasn't that long. He could deal with it, he told himself. It was the threat of a civil suit afterwards that didn't appeal to him. He'd be bankrupt with a criminal record, his career in social services over.

At least Razzaq would be safe. Last week's application to the family court was successful and on 7 December Razzaq, Haniya and Ebrah would be free from Muhammed Khan's cruelty.

Mercifully, Jake's last visit with Irene was the last time Ebrah saw Muhammed. Her broken collarbone had healed, and the children were beginning to catch up at school. Jake wasn't taking any chances, though. Many Asian men had multiple families, and he could return at any time. The plan was to rehome them and put in place an exclusion order on the father.

Thinking about Razzaq's bright future gave Jake a spring in his step. His feet skipped along the boards as he counted the beat frequency when his and Mikey's tread aligned. A physical alignment that matched their mental one. A closer friend he could never imagine having, until John's arrival on the scene.

Mikey bounced along at a pace just beyond comfortable, hoping Jake would feel a little of the pain he was feeling, having been mauled half to death by a squad of Russian assassins. His mind wandered to Joy. She was all he could think about these days. She was even on his mind when he lapsed into unconsciousness when being choked by Vlad the Strangler.

He'd called her a few times the week before and texted her just to check she was OK. He sensed something wasn't right, despite her stoic response. Panic had set in for a couple of days, when he thought she was giving him the kiss-off. That was until he received a teary FaceTime call in the middle of the night. She told him how much he meant to her and how badly she was missing him. The tears flowed in torrents on both ends of the phone.

He responded the only way he knew how: gatecrashing her mother's house and making pork chops, Mrs Yip style, for Lawan and Jules. He FaceTimed Joy from the kitchen in her mother's apron - along with Jules in a chef's hat - which prompted yet more tears. Happy ones this time.

Jake's rhythmic tread behind him was a comfort. He was an ever-present part of Mikey's life. How many times had Jake come to his assistance over the years, cheerleading, nursing him out of his panic attacks, and ultimately saving his life?

Jake ankle tapped Mikey, who crashed to the ground. He sat upright and combed his fingers through his sand-filled mop of hair while Jake ran off laughing.

If anyone could survive, it was Jake.

Holmes Road Antenatal Clinic, Kentish Town, London: 27 November 2021

Maddie left her first antenatal appointment with a clean bill of health. She had told the midwife the father was on remand for murder. That had killed the happy father conversation stone dead, which suited her perfectly.

"It's the size of a lemon" she was elated to hear. She was convinced her tummy was bulging.

Too late to turn back now. It's got a head, limbs and fingers.

She had no intention of turning back. Her plan was coming together nicely, apart from Jacob.

His unending empathy and helpfulness were a problem. She'd been so close to finishing it many times, only for him to do something sweet – like surprising her with a poem he'd written or preparing her favourite dinner.

He'd put her loss of libido down to a multitude of women's problems, from cystitis to chronic period pain. When she blamed her mood swings on the trauma she'd seen in Africa, he found the best psychiatrist in town and offered to pay for a consultation, once he'd worked extra shifts.

It would destroy him to lose her, and when he'd find out she was having Jake's baby, God knows what he'd do.

Rob had been great since Paris. He didn't doubt it was his baby. He held her in his arms and cried the happiest tears. She cried too. In years to come, when he'd inevitably find out, she would blame it on 'timing' or a 'mistake'. He'd not leave her – he loved her and he'd love his child too.

It wouldn't matter by then. It wouldn't.

He'd offered to cancel his trip to Spain and stay at home. He wanted to begin converting the spare room into a nursery. She'd insisted he go, telling him she'd call him before bedtime to fill him in with what the midwife had said. She needed time to think. She had a plan, and it wasn't complicated – she was moving to Paris and she couldn't face a long-distance relationship.

It had worked before; it would work again. Jacob would understand, just like Rob had. He'd be devastated, but he'd understand.

He really would.

Jezzabelle Villa, Marbella, Andalucía, Spain: 27 November 2021

Rob ended his call with Maddie and turned to join the party. It was going to be a mad one if the previous night was anything to go by. It wouldn't be long before weekends with the lads were a distant memory, which didn't bother him one bit.

He would be the best dad in the world. The places they'd go and the experiences they'd have together as a family – he couldn't wait. Whatever it took, he'd be there for them.

Rob slowed his pace through the gardens, enjoying his cigarette – another sacrifice he'd make willingly. The crickets chirped their incessant one-word conversation in the carob trees, competing with the noise of the music coming from Jezzabelle.

"Don't let your mother catch you smoking those things, or we'll both be for the chop." Roger puffed on a huge cigar, blowing the light-blue smoke above his head to chase away the mosquitos.

Rob was startled. His eye twitched in amusement. He hadn't heard his father's voice sound so empathetic before. He didn't know what to say, so he said nothing.

"I've always fancied owning a boat. You know, for me and your mother to sail away into the sunset together." He nodded forlornly as if he knew what Linda's reaction would be to such a preposterous idea. "You'd have to show me how to drive the thing first, I suppose."

"Me?" Rob said with surprise. "I don't know how to drive a boat."

"You're a bright fellow. You could do it." Roger's voice was playful, but the light from the tip of his cigar was too dim to reveal his smiling face.

Rob shrugged, confused. Minutes before he'd mused to himself how fantastic he would be as a parent, only to find how awkward it felt to talk to his own father. He racked his brains thinking of the last time they'd had a civil conversation.

A piercingly loud whistle came from the pool area. "Fruit!" Mikey shouted. "Come on, we're going clubbing! Sergei's got VIP passes."

The memory would have to wait, Rob thought. And he left his father alone, staring out to sea.

Pedro's VIP Lounge, Puerto Banús, Andalucía, Spain: 28 November 2021

Doda's stakeout ended at half past midnight when his mark appeared out of the wrought iron entrance in a parade of black BMWs. He tucked in behind at a safe distance and followed them into Puerto Banús.

He dumped his car in a side street and ran as quickly as he could to the strip, where the queue of cars dropping off the rich and famous encircled the quayside. No one seemed to mind the delay too much. It was the place to be seen and heard. It didn't take long for Doda to spot the cars outside a nightclub popular with Russians.

He considered his approach. It wasn't the ideal place for an Albanian to hang out, but what choice did he have? He had a job to do. The flick knife he had secreted in a pouch, taped into the small of his back, was all he dared carry. A man his size would almost certainly be frisked on the way into the club.

He walked down a side street and sat in a local pick-up spot weighing his options, finally selecting a leggy brunette in a pink body stocking with impossibly pert breasts as his escort for the night.

Natalia was Ukrainian with decent English, and likely to be well known to the doormen. He agreed a price for the night and paid her half up front. Doda had scrubbed up as best as he could, although at nearly two metres tall and looking like most people's idea of hell, he would always look conspicuous. He'd pinned his hopes on the whore attracting more attention, allowing him to blend into the background.

After a brief conversation, Natalia paid the doorman with cash Doda had given her and followed him to a spot at the bar where he sat side on to the room, with his back to most of the cameras.

He began fondling his date and plying her with champagne, playing the part of a grubby kerb crawler. From his position he could see most of the dance floor, the entrance to the VIP lounge, as well as the bar and an emergency exit at the end of the corridor, which led to the restrooms.

"Wait here," he ordered her.

He walked to the restrooms counting his steps and noting the position of the CCTV cameras, exits, number of security staff, lighting, blind spots and general flow of people and bartenders.

The restrooms were out of the question as a kill zone. There was an attendant on duty the whole time, handing out wipes and aftershave. Just before the entrance was a cleaning cupboard, which had been left unlocked. The cupboard door swung inwards, so using his left hand on the handle would mean leaving his knife hand free. He returned to his seat and timed how long it took people to walk along the corridor, counting each one in and out.

The quantity of cocaine being consumed on the tabletops astounded him. He doubted people would use the restrooms for that purpose.

"You vanna dance with Natalia, hmm?" Natalia asked as she swayed to the rhythm of the music, holding onto Doda's shoulders.

"Sit still, bitch, and drink your champagne. We'll be leaving soon," he growled.

After ninety minutes of waiting, the club began to fill, making his task more difficult.

The octagonal VIP area had booths set back around the outside. Bar staff passed by with a never-ending supply of booze and snacks. Doda had a perfect view of Jake's booth. He'd been on the dancefloor with his friends four times so far and had yet to venture to the toilets, which made him wonder if there were others he had missed.

Unlikely, he thought to himself, confident he had every aspect covered.

He watched Jake return alone to the booth, his shirt stuck to his back with sweat. He emptied his glass and motioned to the waiter for more cocktails. The waiter pointed towards Doda, and Jake headed for the restrooms.

This is it, Doda told himself, encircling the knife handle in his jacket pocket. He slid off his bar stool and tried to stay out of sight behind his date.

"Stay here," he told the hapless Natalia, who was slouched on her elbows bored to tears.

Doda looked past her shoulder as Jake meandered towards the restrooms. He walked towards him almost facing backwards to hide his face. His timing was perfect. Jake rounded the corner into the corridor, Doda one skip step to his rear.

Doda fell in line with Jake as he staggered towards the gents, holding his arm out to steady himself – for once, not a care in the world, oblivious to his surroundings, living his best life.

Doda was six feet from the cupboard door when the impact hit him in the back like a bolt of electricity. His body went rigid, and his world went blank.

On Board the Baltic Prince, Puerto Banús, Spain: 28 November, 2021

"Who is he?" Sergei asked Vlad the Strangler, staring at their prisoner, who was tied naked to a chair in the bowels of his super yacht.

"His name is Doda Kelemendi. He's an Albanian Serb. A mercenary."

Vlad didn't need ID. He'd come across him before.

"That name sounds familiar." Sergei rubbed his stubbly chin.

"He used to work for Agron Krasniqi, until he left Serbia for London. Rumour was he changed bosses and Krasniqi was killed."

Sergei stepped back and nodded at one of Vlad's men, who threw a bucket of water over Doda.

Doda opened his eyes groggily and looked around, the sharp pain in his wrists and ankles telling him not to bother trying to move. His head lolled forward when Vlad slapped the back of his neck. He saw two barbs attached to his testicles, with wires leading to a yellow taser. He sighed, realising what had hit him in the back.

Sergei gave another nod, and Vlad swung a hammer down on Doda's big toe, cushioning the ringing sound on the metal decking.

Doda screamed the pain out of his eyes, the duct tape preventing it coming from his mouth. After a few moments, his breathing settled, and Vlad tore away the tape.

"Mr Kelemendi, pleased to meet you. I hope you find our hospitality to your liking."

Sergei nodded at Vlad, who picked up the taser and gave it a five-second burst. Doda's body convulsed against his restraints, and his balls began to smoulder.

"You will answer my questions, or your life will end slowly and painfully."

Sergei turned a chair to face Doda and sat down and folded his arms.

"You parked outside my friend's villa for two days watching our movements, then you followed us to the club. Poor Natalia had to put up with your bad breath for a few hours while you cased out your kill zone, sizing up how you were to kill me."

Doda looked up out of the top of his eyes and shook his head. His attempt at correcting Sergei got him another 50,000 volts to his scrotum.

Once the screaming had stopped and one of Vlad's men had mopped up a puddle of Doda's urine, he continued.

"You then picked one of my guests to kill? Why? He means nothing to you?" Sergei gave him an opportunity to speak.

"He was my mark. I was paid to kill him." His throat felt like it was lined with razorblades.

"Who by?"

Doda wavered and had his left big toe flattened for his misplaced loyalty.

"Tell me now!"

Sergei looked at his watch. The party was still in full swing, and he was missing out.

"Bell, Morris Bell." Doda gasped for breath, his body shaking in pain. "He's in London. He's small time ... does insurance fraud ... he's a nobody."

Blood dripped out of Doda's mouth, having bitten a chunk of his tongue off.

"What has my friend done to warrant him being killed?"

"Nothing, he's a patsy ... I don't know all the details ... I just do what he asks me to." Doda dropped his chin to his chest. He knew what was coming.

Sergei thought for a moment and paced around the cabin. He nodded at Vlad a third time, who drove Doda's own knife into the base of his skull.

20

THE JOY OF LIFE

Tolsford Road, Hackney, London: 7 December 2021

"If Khan is there, we need to get the kids out as quickly as possible, OK?"

Irene nodded nervously. She hated this part of her job – it never went according to plan; a point she liked to repeat out loud, much to the irritation of Bernard Bradshaw. It was why he had promoted Jake, and not her.

Jake expected the best but prepared for the worst. A health worker, two community liaison officers, a triage nurse and an education officer huddling to keep warm in a crew bus with a malfunctioning heater. The police were on standby too, but with Muhammed Khan out of the picture, it would make the whole procedure an elaborate house move.

He knocked and heard movement on the other side. Ebrah opened the door and stepped aside without a word, as if obeying unspoken orders. Jake thanked her and walked into the same barren room from his previous visit, which was even less welcoming than before on account of it being at least ten degrees colder and Muhammed Khan glaring at him with a look of pure hatred in his bloodshot eyes.

"Mr and Mrs Khan," Jake began, level and calm, despite being at DEFCON 5, "I have a court protection order for the removal—"

"You have come to take my children, am I right?" Khan said casually, leaning to within arm's reach of Jake, his extra four inches in height empowering him with the illusion of physical superiority.

Jake smelt his sour whisky breath. He knew it all too well – the rotten odour of bile and alcohol that addicts carry with them. No amount of mouthwash or toothpaste could ever remove it, and, judging by the colour of his teeth and the gum disease prevalent below his incisors, he hadn't used a toothbrush in years.

Khan scratched his bearded chin with his grimy fingernails, evaluating just how he was going to beat up his unwanted house guests.

"Would you like to sit down, Mr Khan? I'll explain what is going to happen," Jake said, taking half a step back while inviting Khan to sit.

Khan declined Jake's kind offer and instead swung a vicious backhander at him.

"Muhammed! Please, no!" Ebrah reached forward to stop him and received the full impact of the blow in her face, sending her crashing through the open doorway into the hallway and cracking her head against a wall. Irene ran to her aid.

Jake heard a child scream from the floor above, followed by the sound of little feet running down the stairs. He quickly slammed the door shut. Having Razzaq in the room would not help one bit.

"Please, Mr Khan, restrain yourself. There is no need for violence." Jake's words were meant for those in the crew bus watching the live footage via his bodycam. He assumed the police were now being mobilised.

Khan pulled a knife from his jacket pocket and opened it with a practised flick of his wrist.

"You will not take my children! Do you hear me?!"

Khan lunged the blade at Jake's chest. Of all the fights Jake had had in recent months, this had to be the easiest to contend with. One on one with a man who was untrained, inebriated and weak. Even so, he took no chances.

Jake stepped and turned his body inside Khan's outstretched right arm. He gripped his wrist, ducked and threw Khan over his back, similar to the Scott the usurper move, but without the knife or trough of urine.

A combination of pulling and twisting loosened Khan's grip on the weapon and sent him toppling onto the arm of the sofa, which snapped under the impact of his coccyx. Jake twisted Khan's wrist further and felt his elbow dislocate, and even though he was winded, he stamped down hard on the man's left shoulder. A very loud agonising scream followed the muffled crack.

Five seconds after the door was slammed shut, Irene burst through to find Khan prostrate at her feet and Jake with his palms up, to say the emergency was over.

As if Khan's day couldn't get any worse, Irene dropped her butt on his chest while they awaited the police, breaking several of his ribs in the process.

Fulwood Police Station, Kentish Town, London: 7 December 2021

Tamara Norazu held her ID up at the camera and announced her arrival to the custody sergeant, Nick Lynch.

"Miss Norazu, how nice to see you again." He smiled welcomingly.

"I wish I could say the same, Sergeant."

Tamara signed the register and made her way into interview room four. Jake arrived shortly after in handcuffs, looking more bored than tired. PC Jones uncuffed him and he sat down opposite Tamara.

"Let me know when you are ready for interview."

She blanked Jones again and waited patiently for him to clear the room.

"Are you OK, Jake? I heard you were attacked with a knife." Tamara looked genuinely concerned.

"I'm fine, honestly." Jake shrugged and shook his head, bemused as to how he'd ended up in the exact same predicament.

He could at least understand being pulled up for drowning Scott in piss, or for a spot of kendo with Lance in his mother's garden, but given he had witnesses and a video for Khan – who had a knife – it didn't make sense him being arrested.

Tamara seemed very relaxed about it, like it was a big waste of her time.

"The police have viewed the bodycam footage and found nothing to indicate you used excessive force in restraining Mr Khan. They'll drop the charges, I'm sure about that. Your boss has been in touch with the Chief Constable to complain about police brutality, and your department's organising a walkout if you aren't released without charge. There are newspaper reporters outside. They're calling you the 'Hackney Hero'."

After a few seconds they laughed, united in the absurdity of it all.

"I'll need a good PR guy. Do you know any?" Jake asked.

Tamara shook her head and laughed. "John thinks there's more to it," she said dryly, grinning.

"I don't know how he sleeps at night with all these conspiracy theories running around in his head." Jake laughed again.

Tamara had seen a different side to Jake in recent weeks. He seemed tougher. More phlegmatic. Resigned to his fate. John had regressed. She'd never seen him emotional or angry until now. His vendetta against Ben Stockton had given Jake hope for a while, but now, even he was sceptical.

"You're taking this very well, Jake."

He took a deep breath as if a weight had been lifted off his shoulders. A satisfied smile spilled from one side of his mouth.

He didn't shirk his duty to serve and protect – quite the opposite. He went above and beyond what was expected of him. Who knows what the man would have done if he hadn't dealt with him. He wasn't comparing himself to Niall Bradshaw, but he had no doubt Bernard would be proud of his actions.

"The Khan family's free from that horrible bastard. What more is there to say?"

PC Jones walked in without knocking. "The charges have been dropped. You're free to go." The words jarred in his mouth.

Jake got up to leave, his route to the door barred by the pock-faced constable.

"See you soon, Jake."

Bell & Sandringham Legal, Farringdon, London: 7 December 2021

"Report!" Bell was in no mood for bad news.

"The charges have been dropped. I told you they wouldn't stick. This was a mistake."

"Be quiet, man. I didn't expect them to. If you throw enough mud, it sticks. He goes to trial a week on Monday. There's no doubt the judge will remember him from the TV coverage."

"Webster's being hailed a hero. We should pull out. I have a bad feeling about this one. Have you seen Stockton recently? He's a nervous wreck. He keeps soiling the bed, thinking if Doda catches him going to the toilet, he'll kill him. I told him he's quit and moved back to Serbia, but he's not having it."

"He's yours to manage," Bell said dismissively. "Make sure he's prepared and knows the score. The worse he looks, the better. Make sure he's wearing the eye patch. They'll call him as a witness late on, I'd guess."

"So, where's Doda?"

"I don't know, and I don't care. We can handle it from here on in," Bell said.

Doda was dead. There was no way he would leave money on the table. His membership to the Balkan boys' club had obviously expired. His absence was an inconvenience, not a showstopper.

There was no going back now – there was too much invested. The issue of John Devlin was a worry. He was obviously involved and had somehow linked Ben Stockton to Lee Grassington. Then again, if he suspected they were one and the same, he would have said something by now. He clearly wasn't that clever.

Bell's logic gave him confidence. And if push came to shove, he'd have Stockton killed.

"Get Stockton ready. Tell him I'm doubling his money to make up for the injuries. That should cheer him up."

John Devlin's Flat, The Docklands, London: 7 December 2021

The thirty-minute journey to John's flat had immersed them in déjà vu. Jake had thought hard over the events of the afternoon. He'd always had a good relationship with the police, but these days, it was like they had it in for him.

"What does the Hackney Hero fancy for dinner tonight?" John asked from his pristine kitchen counter while opening a bottle of Sancerre.

"I don't care, so long as it's not porridge," Jake joined in, fist-bumping his friend from the other side of the counter.

John tapped on his phone for a few minutes and slipped it back in his pocket. He couldn't be bothered cooking, so he ordered sushi and tempura prawns. There was no argument from Jake.

"You did a brave thing today." John raised his glass in a solo toast.

Jake shrugged. "You would have done the same."

John blew out his cheeks. "No, I'd have run over the back of Irene to get to the door. And even if I had tried to stop him, I'd probably be dead by now, along with everyone else."

"Irene was amazing. If she gives up on social work, she could always become a WWE wrestler. She broke four of his ribs. The poor guy needed oxygen. I've taught her all the killer moves."

They burst into laughter.

"Seriously, it takes a special kind of person to stand while everyone else runs … to protect others while risking your own life."

John patted Jake on the shoulder. An image of Niall flashed through Jake's mind.

Thirty minutes later, they'd demolished their food and were sniffing away the residual effects of a pot of very fresh wasabi.

"I can't imagine prison food'll be as good as that." Jake's humour fell flat. John's face hardened.

"I'm not going to let that happen. Stockton's bent – I'll prove it." He sounded more irritated than determined.

"I spoke with Tamara earlier … she isn't convinced. We have a last-minute guilty plea at the ready. Hopefully the CPS will accept it."

John shook his head in denial, while Jake talked. "She doesn't know what I know. For instance, she doesn't know Ben Stockton's changed his name eight times in thirteen years."

"And?"

"Lee Grassington, David Carlisle, Neil Bradford, Timothy Batley, Christopher York, Ian Sunderland, William Derby and Ben Stockton. He uses northern towns for some reason. I suppose it helps him remember who he is."

He sipped his wine while Jake tried to work out the relevance of what he'd been told.

"Each of these personas existed for eighteen months or so. They paid their taxes, they had no bills and they lived in other people's houses the whole time, eventually disappearing without a word. Like some human cuckoo."

"How do you know this?" Jake shook his head, not expecting an answer to a stupid question.

"Read this." John handed Jake the newspaper article Justin had found.

"Are you telling me Grassington is Stockton and that he lost his eye in 1995?"

John nodded slowly. "I haven't got proof as yet, but his mother's neighbour described him to a tee."

"Have you told Tamara?"

"Not yet. I know she'll want proof … we're in the process of confirming it."

"That changes everything, doesn't it?" Jake asked, excitedly.

"Not unless we can prove it, no. It'd be easy for us to throw in a random curveball like this to buy time. Without proof, our defence would be discredited, and we can't afford for that to happen. I have the whole team working the weekend."

Jake looked dejected.

"I want to tell you about the details and what we're investigating, but it's complex. I've found the smoke … I just need to find the gun. You're just going to have to trust me."

Rob's Flat, Primrose Hill, London: 10 December 2021

"I've made you some space in the walk-in wardrobe," Rob said, while preparing dinner.

Maddie had a suitcase packed for yet another trip to Paris. At least that's what she'd told Jacob when she left for work that morning.

Her boss in Paris was elated at the prospect of having her so close. 'Is Jacob coming with you?' he'd asked. She couldn't remember what she'd said to that. She'd lied so much to so many people, she was struggling to keep track of it all.

That's my life now – a lie. A despicable lie.

She showered away the guilt and put on some jogging bottoms and a vest top. She didn't intend moving off the couch all night. The sooner she planted her new roots with Rob, the better. She'd told Rob that Jacob would be gone by the seventeenth.

Rob had been very understanding, even offering to pay off the lease. Forty pieces of silver, Maddie thought – the cost of stealing his girlfriend away from him.

She felt sick, torturing herself with the pain and upset she was about to cause. It wouldn't be for long – Jacob would meet someone else and never see her again. She'd soon be in Paris building a life for her new family.

It's just like an adoption. The baby will grow up in a happy, cohesive family full of love and security. Time's a healer. It won't matter.

"Hey Princess, do you want a little glass of wine? I'm sure Junior wouldn't say no?" Rob sipped his glass of pinot grigio and waved an empty glass in the air.

"OK, just a small one," she relented, without a second's hesitation.

Rob brought her wine over and, with it, her vegetable stir-fry on a tray, which he set down on her lap with a napkin and some cutlery. He returned to get his own meal, which he'd smothered in king prawns, scallops and sweet chilli sauce.

Maddie munched her way through the mound of food like she'd not eaten a decent meal in weeks – which she hadn't. Her appetite was shot. Between her hormones, stress, workload and the incessant lying, she had struggled to maintain the healthy eating regime Michelle the midwife had advised.

"I told Larry today," Rob said, once he'd cleared the plates and assumed his position on the couch.

"Told him what?" Maddie said sleepily, her head tucked into his neck.

"That I was resigning. I got the impression he knew already. He and Monty have known each other for years. I think he must've called ahead to ask for his approval."

"Was he OK about it?"

"He was to be honest. He came up with a great idea. He offered me a part-time position in the Paris office, which is a total basket case. I said I'd mull it over."

Rob hadn't told Roger. He didn't know what he was going to say. The Paris move wouldn't bother him, or the Montreaux part, but the baby announcement would send him over the edge. That he was certain of.

"When will you tell your parents ... about the baby, I mean?" Maddie couldn't look him in the eye. The enormity of her deception seemed to grow every time she thought about people's reactions.

Roger was a brute of a man, but Linda was lovely. She hated causing her pain when she finished with Rob three years ago and was dreading how she'd react to the news.

"It's our family Christmas lunch next Friday. They're having it early because they're heading to Marbella. They'll ask us to go, I'm sure, especially when they hear the news."

Rob's statement was totally unfounded on fact. In truth, he had no idea what they'd say, but a positive spin made things seem better for now.

"Do you think?" Maddie perked up.

"They both worshipped the ground you walked on. If they see me happy, they'll be happy."

As far as his father was concerned, Rob didn't believe a word of what he'd just said.

"Do you think we should go?" Maddie was intrigued.

"Sure, why not?" He'd given up second-guessing people. It hurt his head. He decided to follow Mikey's lead and go with the flow.

"I'll not be staying at my parents for long. I want to be at court for Jake. His trial starts on Monday and is due to end late Friday afternoon. I'll come to your house and help you pack afterwards. The sooner you're settled here, the better."

Rob pulled her in tightly, taking possession of his prize. Maddie squeezed her eyes closed and held her breath to quell the all-consuming panic surging through her. It didn't help.

She vomited her stir-fry onto the floor.

Renoir's Restaurant, Kentish Town Road, London: 10 December 2021

Mustafa loved Christmas.

He had Renoir's decked out from top to bottom in tinsel and streamers. His cousins Emyr and Mehmet were playing Jingle Bells on their violin and accordion while getting gradually slaughtered on Raki and beer.

Mikey and Joy's entrance descended into a sideshow the moment Mustafa saw them. He made no attempt to hide his approval.

"Mikey, where have you been hiding this beautiful princess?"

Mustafa took Joy in his arms and hugged her like a long-lost sister. He swotted Mikey away and took her on a tour of his tiny bar and restaurant, as if it had three Michelin stars. In the kitchen, he introduced her to his chefs, who began singing in Turkish for some reason. It didn't matter to Joy; she loved it. She would never grow tired of being with Mikey, especially if this was where he brought her.

What Mikey didn't realise, which she had, was how special he was to people. He wouldn't believe Mustafa's hospitality was because of him, but it was – a simple reciprocation of the unbridled affection Mikey had for everyone he met. She watched him shake hands with the staff and acknowledge most of the patrons, whether he knew them or not.

She sipped her glass of Prosecco and swallowed down a wave of emotion. He was ridiculously handsome and just so lovely.

How has this happened? She told herself to stop asking that question, as if knowing the answer would bring it to an end.

"Did all your girlfriends get a tour of the kitchen, Mikey?" Joy asked once seated, reeling from Mustafa's stubbly treble kiss.

"No. I think he likes you," Mikey said, stating the blindingly obvious. "I can't blame a man with excellent taste." He flashed his brown eyes at her, and she giggled with faux modesty.

"Here's to us." They clinked glasses and leaned over the table for a kiss, which got them a roar of approval and wolf whistles from the kitchen staff. Emyr joined in on the violin with Mendelssohn's 'Wedding March'.

"I love this place," Mikey said, ignoring them. "They do great food as well. Don't bother looking at the menu, Mustafa will have a special dish lined up for us – and I never have the heart to argue with him."

"I hope it's as good as your chops. My mum was so impressed with the effort you went to. That was so sweet of you." She squeezed his hand, and his knuckles cracked under the pressure.

Mustafa did exactly as Mikey had anticipated, bringing them a banquet fit for royalty. He paired the wines for each course and gave them plenty of time to talk. He quit with the bar antics from earlier and made it a night to remember.

Mikey sipped his Raki at the end of a wonderful night. They'd covered every topic from Russian oligarchs to giant marrows, and eclectic racehorse owners to bandits in the Transvaal.

Mikey relayed Hansie's harrowing tale from the veld and the prospect of their deportation and facing the trauma all over again. Joy's first impressions of Hansie weren't the best. She made a mental note to give him a hug the next time they met.

Mikey struggled to hide his true feelings about Maddie when he reported the baby news, sceptical of her motivations. Joy had missed the news feature on TV where Jake, the Hackney Hero, walked out of the police station a free man. She hoped it was a good omen and the outcome of his trial would be the same.

"It's been a busy couple of months for us both. I'm glad I'm home, though. I miss you so much when I'm away." Joy hadn't let go of Mikey's hand all night.

"Ha, your mum said the same thing. You're very much alike, you know." Mikey flicked forward thirty years, imagining Joy in later life.

"She was telling me about your squash... I didn't realise you were so good. Why haven't you told me? Why don't you enter the competition at Fulwood? Shall I speak with Will Halperson?"

Joy grinned at him. "It doesn't work like that, Mikey. The entries went into the PSA months ago."

"Oh well, maybe you can watch then. I'll get him to sort us a few tickets, shall I?" Joy decided to let Mikey find out for himself that she had already registered and was second favourite to win.

"Did you see the email I sent about the memberships? I did a bit more digging and was able to unlock a fair amount of information," she said, changing the topic to avoid talking about herself.

"I did," Mikey said sheepishly. "I may need some help explaining what you wrote. I'm hopeless at spreadsheets."

"It's basic really. What you have is 306 more members than membership account numbers, so I assume you have multiple family passes on the one membership number?"

"What? No! We don't do family memberships. Euan stopped them years ago. How did you arrive at 306 extra members?"

Joy's synopsis of her report was having a sobering effect on Mikey, who sat up on the edge of his chair and leaned forward. Joy made the same forward motion and kissed him on the lips. His head span.

"Imagine the database to be a series of floors, rooms and filing cabinets that are linked together. Now, imagine some of the floors don't have lights, so it's hard to find your way around. Also, some of the rooms have a hidden door, with secret locks for the cabinets – locks you don't have the keys to."

"Go on," Mikey said, trying to follow her line of thinking.

"Well, that's your database. The knack is knowing how to unlock the doors. All the data comes from calculations and formulae that is nested deep in huge tables. The formulae create information that is useful to Fulwood, like attendances, age, what they spend their money on..."

"Ahh, yes, we use that information from Beverly to determine the viability of the courses we put on."

"Exactly. But not all the formulae are visible, unless you know what you're looking for. I uncovered 306 instances where membership numbers have been duplicated, which is what you asked me to do, right?"

As she told him everything he wanted to hear, he was in no doubt he had fallen head over heels. She hesitated and they kissed again, their noses literally touching while she spoke.

"When a member swipes in, if they have the same membership number as someone else, the system rejects it. It's called a check code. In your database, I found a nested IF formula, which automatically renames it with a suffix, concatenating the number on a hidden ID string, so #001, #002, etc. It doesn't change the original number, but it does store the new ones in a nested table you can't see."

She looked at Mikey's spiralling brown eyes and realised she was losing him again.

"It makes a note and stores the information where no one can see. Unless you know what to look for. Which I do. It also stores the members' names and bank details."

"Are you kidding me?" Mikey's mouth dropped wide open. "Does it say where they pay into?"

"No, but I'd assume Fulwood's bank acc—... Ah, I see ... you think they're paying into a separate account."

Mikey snapped his fingers and pointed at Joy. "Bingo! What if someone is duplicating membership numbers and has given the member different bank details to pay into? Who would know?"

"The member would know, of course, but who looks at account numbers? If their pass gets them in on the second attempt, why would they care, right? Also, if you do a search of their name, the short version membership account number comes up, not the suffix. That's hidden. For all intents and purposes, they're a paid-up member."

Joy's lonely nights in hotels between games had been put to good use.

"I might need your help explaining this to Amanda."

"Not sure how happy she'd be with you sharing this information with me, so I've written a report in your name explaining it all."

She sipped her espresso martini and raised her eyebrows. "What?" she asked, pursing her lips mischievously.

"My mind is blown!" he said, shaking his head.

Joy leaned over to whisper in his ear. "It will be when you see my new underwear."

Mikey waved towards the bar. "Mustafa! Can you order us a taxi, please?"

21

THE END OF THE LINE

Fulwood Crown Court, London: 13 December 2021

"All rise!"

Jake was stood in the dock, isolated and alone, as the wiry, stern-faced judge walked solemnly into court. The court clerk begged those attending to be seated and began purposefully organising his notes and tapping into a laptop.

Jake had expected more people to be there but was quite pleased there weren't. The judge had acceded to a closed doors trial to avoid unnecessary distress to the injured party. Jake was missing his friends. Just having them there would have been a huge lift.

In fairness, they had come to court, wished him the best of luck, then turned away. John had called from Manchester, where he was following up on information received over the weekend, but it wasn't the same.

He hadn't told his mother – she had gone AWOL. He suspected the next loser had moved in and she'd taken up drugs again. She was the least of his worries.

The clerk went through the formalities, and Jake played his part answering as required. Tamara watched on, giving him subtle nods of encouragement.

The prosecuting barrister, a Mr Stansfield QC, introduced himself and sat down. Jake tried to read him but gave up immediately. These people were there to do a job. It didn't matter to them if he was guilty or not – they got paid lots of money either way. What's more, the sight of the odious man fidgeting with his trousers was making him ill.

Mr Philip Carmichael-Prowse QC rose and introduced himself as Jake's defence barrister. He was a tall, athletic-looking man in his early fifties, with salt and pepper wavy hair, which was thinning on top. His balding pate poked out beneath his wig.

After two hours of initial statements and legal process, the judge adjourned for lunch, stating the court would reconvene at 1:30pm, when witnesses would be called. It was excruciatingly slow and laborious, just as Tamara said it would be.

John Devlin Public Relations, Camden, London: 13 December 2021

It was Derek's turn to organise coffee and cakes, and as normal, he'd forgotten. Or couldn't be bothered, more like, much to Molly's annoyance.

"We take tea, coffee and cake extremely seriously around here, Derek." Molly berated him while reaching into her bag for her emergency blueberry muffin.

"Guys, let's focus. This is seriously time critical. Justin, go ahead, please," John crackled from his Manchester office over Zoom.

"What we are trying to establish is where Ben Stockton or any of his suspected aliases have ever lived or worked and whether they've ever been involved in an industrial injury. If so, what were the details, and do we have proof? On the basis he still uses 'Lee Grassington', it's safe to say he hasn't claimed using that name, so to save time, we've concentrated on the others. Please object if you don't agree." Justin heard silence both in the room and on Zoom.

"Good. So far, we have information on three aliases, including NI numbers, tax records, last known addresses and employers' details. I suggest we start there. I've emailed their details to you, John."

"Question," John said. "They're all common names ... how do you know they tie in with Stockton?"

"We didn't to begin with. We had to check every one that fitted the profile – no ID, no passport, no driving licence, accurate tax returns, etc. It wasn't difficult, but it was time-consuming. It did help, though, as we've been able to list them chronologically. Christopher York's the one with the most information – he won £5,000 in a competition held by a local newspaper in Bolton. I guess he couldn't help himself, collecting the cash when he was supposed to be keeping his head down."

"Jammy bastard." Patrick's only contribution received resounding grunts of agreement.

"It's not far from me. I'll go there first. Check with the editor of the local rag, Patrick – he may have a photo if they did a piece on him."

John's video feed froze as he jumped in his car with his iPad.

"There's someone else you can visit while you're there," Molly put in. "To be a security guard or doorman, you need a 'blue badge'. It's like a CRB check – it proves you are who you say you are. I called Fandango's and spoke to your friend Jamal. He told me they use a company called ElectronPass Security. In fact, a lot of companies do. They're a huge outfit and run a nationwide database. When I called and asked about Ben Stockton, they put me through to a lady called Jennie Peacock. She told me she was new and that the previous girl just quit one day for no reason. Her name was Marie Grassington – she's Lee Grassington's sister."

"Go on," John said eagerly.

"Marie had signed off the EPS passes of three of the aliases. This gives us more proof, as the passes have photos of Stockton on them. She must be in on it. She lives in Bury, which is fifteen minutes from Bolton. I've forwarded her last known address and photo IDs."

"Molly, you are amazing." Patrick high-fived her sticky hand.

"Derek, what do you have?" John's head was spinning, and the rush hour traffic was not helping his concentration.

"Because of Molly's scoop, I've been onto the Health and Safety Executive and made an application for details of accidents at each of the three employers we know of. They have reports and data on successful prosecutions. I should get something back today."

"Chase them up, please, and call the employers. I'll pay them a visit," John said, as the sound of horns came blaring over his speaker.

"Are the other addresses in the North West?" he asked in hope.

"I'm afraid not, John. Neil Bradford lived up in Newcastle upon Tyne, and Tim Batley in Hull," Justin said with dread.

"This Stockton bloke was a lazy bastard. I bet a hundred quid he lived in a town with the same name as his. Narrow your search and cross-check with the other towns. Let's hustle, guys. We've no time to lose."

Fulwood Sports Centre, Kentish Town, London: 13 December 2021

Mikey was sat in front of his computer struggling to understand his own report. Pivot tables, nested IFs, concatenation, hyperlinks, track precedents – he had absolutely no clue what it meant. He doubted Amanda would either, although he admitted to himself that he had form for underestimating people. Joy was the latest case in point.

Friday night was a night of surprises, that was for sure. He hadn't stopped thinking about Joy. He played his worst game of rugby in months the following day, barely scraping a win against the bottom of the league. The lack of sleep was taking its toll.

What he did realise was that his night terrors didn't happen when Joy stayed over. That was a win-win he could handle every night of the week.

He picked up his mobile to text Amanda. Safer than email, he thought.

> Hey Amanda, I wondered if you could give me a buzz. I need to discuss something with you.

Mikey pressed send and watched the black tick turn blue immediately, followed by 'typing'.

> Sure thing. Just in the Lakes on holiday. I'll be back in the new year. What's it about? Is it urgent? Please don't tell me you're leaving.

Mikey smiled and cursed his luck.

> No, you're stuck with me. It's not urgent, but it is important. I have a report I want you to read. It's confidential, for your eyes only. I'll drop it on your desk. Have fun. M. x

Mikey tucked Joy's report in a blank manilla A4 envelope and marked it confidential. He had to go and see Will Halperson later that day, so he'd drop it off then.

> Thanks Mikey. A. x

Bolton Road, Bolton, G Manchester: 13 December 2021

John parked his car next to a working men's club in a part of Bolton called Tonge Moor. There were no yellow lines and no places to pay.

He was sure he'd been to a less salubrious place, but he couldn't remember when. No. 756 Bolton Road was on a hill so steep the front doorstep seemed to be half buried into the pavement.

He paused. His hand hovered over the door, wondering what was on the other side. Doda Kelemendi may have second-guessed him again. He was becoming paranoid, which was maybe not a bad thing.

There were a dozen ways to get people to talk. Hard-nosed northerners on the other hand, they were another breed. They could smell bullshit a mile away. He breathed out a foggy breath and knocked on the door.

A tubby, greasy-faced woman with dank hair wearing creased pyjamas sprung into his vision.

"Who the fuck are you?" she snarled.

"My name's John Devlin. I'm looking for a Christopher York," he dispensed with civility. A direct approach was called for.

"Huh?" she scoffed. "I haven't heard that name mentioned for a while. He doesn't live here any more."

She turned to slam the door in his face.

"Did he leave a forwarding address or contact?"

"No, he fucking didn't. All he left was his dirty laundry and me in the lurch."

She took the last drag on her cigarette and flicked it over his shoulder onto the pavement.

"It's with regards to the accident he had at work. I'm from the insurance company," John gambled.

"Yeah, well, he deserved it. The bastard dropped me quicker than a hot brick when he got his payout from Livermore's," she said bitterly.

A nugget of an idea suddenly formed in her greasy-haired head.

"Hey, do you think I could claim 'owt? He was living here for eight months, rent-free."

The second part of John's hook hit the mark.

"I'm not sure, madam, I'll gladly ask. Let me take your details."

John took out a clipboard and held it in her direction while she wrote, a recent picture of Stockton clipped to the corner.

"Can you just sign here to say this is a true likeness of Christopher York, and you were his common-law spouse at the time, and I'll see what I can do."

"He's put weight on and got rid of that stupid beard," she said, remembering a slimmer, trendier version of Stockton.

"It's lovely to have met you, Mandy," John said, reading his notes. "I'll be in touch."

He scurried back to his car and called Justin.

"Hit me," Justin answered abruptly.

"Christopher York worked at Livermore's Plastics in Trafford Park. Give them a call. He had an industrial injury. If you can, find out what happened and the details of the settlement. Chances are he was admitted to hospital and transferred immediately, just as Stockton was. Get Derek to check the admission records at Manchester Royal Infirmary, and others."

"Will do. And you were right, John. Ian Sunderland lived in Derby – one of his previous aliases. I've emailed you the details."

John's Flat, The Docklands, London: 13 December 2021

Instead of going home, Jake made his way to John's flat to avoid the glare of the press, who were camped out at his house, wanting the next episode of the Hackney Hero.

Jake walked out of court after three hours of prosecution testimony, exhausted and depressed. He hadn't realised Shin Matsumoto would be a prosecution witness, which perhaps explains him being so distant, especially in recent weeks with the trial approaching. He couldn't blame Shin – he was an honourable man – although a heads-up might have been the decent thing to do. The evidence he gave was factual and accurate. There was nothing his barrister could say to refute it. He figured he'd spent his last night training at Matsumoto's.

Calum Wittingham and Delroy Bance gave evidence despite neither pressing charges of their own. Bance limped into the dock with the aid of a walking stick and Wittingham repeatedly wrung his wrist, having likely been told to ham it up by the prosecution. He was surprised how well they described the events of the night, even though they were writhing in agony on the floor and had no view of Stockton's nosedive down the stairs, not to mention their initial statements claiming they'd seen very little – a point which Philip Carmichael-Prowse laboured to the point of tedium.

Jake checked his voicemail:

"Jake, this is Sergei Romanov, your friendly Russian oligarch. How are you, my friend? I wanted to thank you for your training of my bodyguard, Vladimir Tupov. He is happy you are his friend."

Homicidal maniac more like, Jake thought.

"I need to speak with you about a delicate matter. Please call me when you have a moment."

Jake closed his eyes and shook his head in disbelief. *"What on earth could a Russian billionaire think was delicate enough to need my help?"*

He poured a large G&T and called him back.

"Allo," Sergei barked into the phone.

"Sergei, it's Jake Webster, from England." He felt stupid the second he added his geographical locator.

"Jake, my friend, how are you? And how is Mikhail? I hope we didn't hurt him too badly." Sergei roared with laughter.

"We're all fine ... you wanted to talk to me?"

"Yessss," he drawled. "We had an incident at the club when you were here. My security guards dealt with it. There was a man ... we talked to him for a little while ... he mentioned your name."

"My name? Are you sure? I don't know anyone in Marbella."

"I'm quite sure," Sergei assured him, unaccustomed to having his word questioned.

"The man watched the Jezzabelle house for two days. He followed us to the club, met a prostitute to blend in ... he planned to kill you. He had a knife taped to his back."

Jake's blood turned to ice.

"He was an Albanian Serb, called Doda Kelemendi. We interviewed the man ... he told us he was being paid by a man in London called Morris Bell."

Jake didn't fail to notice Sergei referred to Doda in the past tense.

"Morris Bell? I don't know who that is. What the fuck? Why? I haven't hurt anyone..."

Did Ben Stockton hire a guy to carry out revenge on me?

"He said something about insurance. They were targeting you for some reason. I'm sorry to tell you this, Jake, I know it must be a shock." Sergei spoke with surprising tenderness.

"Where is this Doda guy now? Is he coming to the UK?" Jake suddenly felt exposed and frightened.

As if sensing his fear, Sergei said, "He will not be a problem any more. Vladimir is your friend." Jake closed his eyes, relieved and sickened in equal measure. "You must come to visit Igor and me in Russia. We have many places. Let's keep in touch, my friend. Do svidaniya."

He hung up.

Jake jumped to his feet and applied the deadbolt on the front door. He finished his G&T in one gulp and poured another, then reached for his phone.

"John, it's me. Do you know a guy called Doda Kelemendi?"

Fulwood Sports Centre, Kentish Town, London: 16 December 2021

"We all set for Friday?" Mikey dropped by the pool to check on the arrangements with the superheroes. It was the last class of the year and most of the group had proficiency tests coming up that they had been training for.

"Hell yeah, we were born ready! You're going to be here, right?"

Lisa looked worried for a minute.

"Try and stop me," Mikey said. He wouldn't miss it for the world.

He walked past the line of swimmers, fist-bumping each one, until he noticed Arthur was missing.

"Where's Barracuda?" he asked of the group.

Susan, aka Marina, threw her arm in the air to answer the question: "He felt dizzy and went home."

Mikey began to worry, then stopped. He had a million things to think about – he was glad Arthur decided for himself to miss class if he felt poorly.

"Michael Stott to the manager's office! Michael Stott to the manager's office!" Luke bellowed from the speaker above the pool.

"Fucking great," Mikey grumbled to himself.

***

Mikey knocked on Euan's door, which Elaine swung open, with a supercilious smirk on her face, as usual.

"Sit down, Michael," Euan ordered, pointing with his pen to an empty chair next to Beverly, who was sniffling into her handkerchief.

"Beverly! What's up darlin?" Mikey asked, full of concern.

"Never mind that," Euan said. "Elaine has drawn my attention to an extremely serious security breach. Beverly here, in her wisdom, decided to make an uncontrolled copy of our members' database system. She did this in contravention of the Data Protection Act 2018, which states, 'Personal records must be handled in a way that ensures appropriate security, including protection against unlawful or unauthorised processing, access, loss, destruction or damage.'"

He paused theatrically. Mikey could see the beginnings of a smile on his chubby jaw.

"Apparently, you authorised this. Is that correct?"

"Yes," Mikey said, trying to keep his nerve.

"For what purpose? And why make a copy? Have you distributed it?" Euan demanded.

"No, of course not." Mikey took a USB stick out of his pocket and handed it over.

"I haven't even looked at it," he lied.

"The information on that data is strictly confidential. You have no authority to do what you did. We as a company could be fined many hundreds of thousands of pounds for this. I'm left with no alternative than to dismiss Beverly for gross misconduct. Elaine, escort Mrs Lancing off the premises."

"Hang on a fucking minute!" Mikey protested, jumping to his feet. "It was me who asked her to do it – you can't fire Beverly!"

"I'm left with no choice. She was the one who committed the offence. You need to think twice before asking others to do your dirty work. You are responsible for this, Michael, you alone. If you had any integrity, you'd resign."

He's won, Mikey thought to himself. He's finally got me.

He glared into Euan's spiteful eyes. A more hateful bastard he never knew. He'd spent too many years covering his fat arse, making him look good. Perhaps this was destined to happen. Euan wanted rid of him – his comments and actions in recent weeks told him as much. Well, so be it, the Shinewell Group could go to hell.

"I'll resign, only on the condition that Beverly keeps her job, and no mention is made on her work record. I'll work until the Christmas break, then I'll go."

Euan closed his eyes, laced his grimy fingers across his gut and leaned back on his chair, which groaned under his shifting weight. He'd savoured this day for years. No more smart-arsed comments, impertinent questions, or do-gooder charitable events, where everyone fawned over him.

"Resignation accepted. Now get out."

Kedleston Road, Mickleover, Derby: 16 December 2021

John's list was growing shorter, with little to show for nearly 1,200 miles navigating the Pennines and the northeast coastline.

Marie Grassington had vanished, spooked by something, or someone. He guessed Doda Kelemendi had paid a visit, to clear up loose ends.

His journey to Liverpool to track down David Carlisle turned out to be a dead end. The company he worked for had closed ten years ago and was now the site of an affordable housing scheme.

His trip to Chester was equally as fruitless. William Derby's ex-employer had gone into liquidation, although a doorman in a local pub recognised his picture and said he'd fallen down some freshly mopped stairs.

As much as the hearsay was incriminating, it wasn't the solid proof he needed. No judge would accept a chat in the pub with a bouncer as evidence. He was running out of time, and he knew it. Ian Sunderland was one of his last remaining leads, and with only two days until judgement day, something had to give.

He knocked on Cindy Leeming's door, Sunderland's last known address.

"Shut the fuck up!" The barking stopped as soon as the door swung open.

"Hello … Mrs Leeming? I'm looking for Ian Sunderland. I understand he resides here." John smiled.

"You understand wrong. I've not seen him in four fucking years."

Cindy Leeming and Mandy Timpson could have been sisters. *Stockton certainly knew how to pick 'em*, John thought to himself.

"Ah, sorry to have bothered you, madam. If you hear from him, will you ask him to contact his insurance broker? We need to organise the collection of his last compensation payment from his accident. Thanks for your help. Sorry to have disturbed you."

He turned to leave, when Cindy stopped him. "I heard he was already paid out – is he going to receive more?"

"It's for his ongoing living expenses. I'd like to discuss it with you, madam, but as you can imagine, it's confidential." John held his arms up submissively.

"I know all about it." Cindy pointed at her enormous chest. A swathe of fat flopped and bounced under her invisible tricep. "I'm a nurse."

"Erm, well, I'm not supposed to divulge private information, Mrs Leeming," John patronised.

"I just told you, didn't I? I know everything. He had a compound fracture of his fourth and fifth lumbar vertebrae. He was paralysed from the waist down."

"Ah, I see. You must have been close. I'm so sorry, it must have been a terrible shock."

John was on Cindy's side. The poor girl was bound to be lost without him in her life.

"Well, I liked him, yeah, but I didn't want him back here shuffling around in a wheelchair. I've enough to look after with these little bastards. I didn't want to get stuck wiping his arse as well."

Two toddlers hung from her legs, green trails of mucus pouring from their noses.

"I understand totally, Mrs Leeming. You have a lot of responsibility. Ian's injuries, as serious as they were … it can't have been easy splitting up."

"Humph, you're joking. I didn't see or hear from him afterwards. I was glad. I got a surgeon friend of mine to look at his X-rays. He said he stood no chance of recovery. They admitted him to a specialist hospital in Belper – Lexington Health. We send basket cases there from time to time."

"The damage was that bad, was it?" John said, keeping the flow of information coming from Derby's answer to Mother Teresa.

"Oh aye, he was fucked. Hold on, I've still got a copy of the X-rays in a drawer somewhere. You can have 'em if you want."

John Devlin Public Relations, Camden, London: 16 December 2021

"Talk to me," Justin said, stubbing his twentieth cigarette of the day out on the pavement. It wasn't even lunchtime.

"Justin, hi, it's me," John said pointlessly. "I met Cindy Leeming in Derby. She signed an affidavit to state Ian Sunderland lived with her in 2017. It proves Stockton and Sunderland are one and the same person."

"That's good, but we have others who've done that," Justin said.

"It gets better … she's given me the scans he used to make his claim. She was a nurse and got copies made. It's a long story and it doesn't matter – what's important is it shows spinal injuries of the lumbar vertebrae. I've had them couriered to you. Get Derek to do a digital forensic analysis and report back to me, OK?"

"Shall I contact Tamara?"

"Not yet. Jake's giving evidence today – she'll be busy with that. I want to get everything together. I'll be heading back this evening … I've one more stop to make, in Hull."

Zanzibar Nightclub, Hull: 16 December 2021

John peered through the gloom of a dirt-caked window at the front entrance of what used to be Zanzibar Nightclub. A putrid smell of urine and mouse shit filled his nose.

"Fuck," he said, kicking the door in frustration.

"You're starting early, mate," a tramp muttered from a pile of blankets at one end of the covered entrance. John was in no mood for jokes, so ignored him.

"It closed a few months ago. Had their licence revoked. Wetherspoon's open if you need a beer." He hesitated a few seconds. "I wouldn't mind one myself, if you can spare a few quid?"

John turned to face him, embarrassed he was being so ignorant. "Sure, here you go, mate," he said smiling and handing over a tenner.

"That's very decent of you, much appreciated."

The toothless man's face peeked out over the opening to a very damp-looking sleeping bag. John couldn't discern his age, such was the weathered appearance of his face and hands, but his voice told him late forties.

"You a local guy?" John asked.

"Aye, lad, born and bred from 'Ull. My name's Kevin. Pleased to meet you."

John looked down at him pitifully. "John. Likewise."

"You sound like a Cockney. You're a long way from home," Kevin said, hitching himself up and rubbing his hands to keep them warm.

"I'm looking for a friend of mine, Tim Batley. He used to work here on the door at this place."

"Never heard of him." Kevin snorted and wiped his runny nose on his filthy sleeve. "I don't much like doormen, anyway, and the bouncers in this place were the worst. I had a proper kicking off them, just for trying to tap a few quid."

John felt sorry for the man and his wretched existence and wondered what could have happened to land him in such dire circumstances.

"Nice to meet you, Kevin. Take care." He turned to leave.

"It was a bad do that time when the guy broke his back. Awful. Wouldn't wish that on anyone."

John stopped dead in his tracks. The hairs on his neck stood on end. He turned to face his grimy friend.

"About ten years ago. Got into a fight, didn't he? Fell down the stairs … landed right here on the ground. Blood everywhere. They reckon his eye was gouged out. 'Orrible. The guy who beat him up got ten years for that. Serves him right."

Kevin got to his feet and walked off for his liquid breakfast.

Fulwood Crown Court, London: 16 December 2021

Jake's heart pounded. He had nowhere to run. It didn't matter how he positioned his legs or bent his knees, or who he predicted would throw the first punch or kick, his fighting skills and understanding of the human condition at this precise moment accounted for zip.

"Mr Webster, please relay the events of the night of 27 August 2021 as you remember them."

Philip Carmichael-Prowse had gone through his questions in detail the previous afternoon, including why he was asking and what he wanted Jake's answer to be. Tamara had coached him in the evening and helped him with his body language and delivery.

"When you saw Mr Stott being beaten by his two assailants, how did you react?"

Jake addressed the judge and tried his best to sound respectful, but was nervous and overwhelmed. Remembering the night was as traumatic for him as anyone else.

"When you were helping your stricken friend to the exit to receive emergency first aid, you were viciously attacked by Mr Stockton, were you not?"

Tamara had been insistent on not using any technical terms to describe how he defended himself. She'd asked him to stutter and struggle with his words on purpose, to sound weak and unpolished.

"Did you fear for your life, Mr Webster? When the enormous doorman came screaming at you, ready to beat you up, like he had your friend?"

He had never feared for his life before Sergei's call. That was fear on a different level.

His barrister went through every single detail of the night and of Jake's life in general: the doting son from a single-parent background, who'd defied the trials of an upbringing in destitution to become a senior social worker in the Fulwood community, blah, blah, blah. He made no mention of his martial arts skills and other abilities. He knew Stansfield would be all over that. And he was.

"Mr Webster, it is safe to say, killing a man with your bare hands is a skill you have been taught by Mr Shin Matsumoto, is it not?" the prosecution asked. "You executed a tai otoshi body drop on Mr Stockton, did you not? If not for my client's athleticism, we could be here on a murder trial, rather than a charge of grievous bodily harm."

They broke for lunch, and he checked his phone. The cut-off for a plea was fast approaching and John was nowhere to be seen.

Bannister's Café, Fulwood Sports Centre, Kentish Town, London: 16 December 2021

"Mikey, you can't let him do that, you've got to fight this." Joy gripped his hands and craned her face to meet his gaze.

"It's my own fault. I shouldn't have had Beverly copy that database. You said it yourself. I put her in a very bad position and that was wrong of me. Anyway, don't worry, I've been in touch with H&C Leisure ... looks like they're going to give me the Assistant Manager's post. The money's OK ... I'll be fine."

Mikey's positivity gland was struggling to keep up with the sense of dread eating away at him. He blanked out the reaction he would get from the superheroes class and others when they found out.

"What did Amanda say when you showed her the report? Surely she can see what Euan's doing?"

"I've thought about that. It wouldn't surprise me if she isn't in on the whole thing. How could she have missed what took us only a few days to find out? It makes sense now. At my interview, she did everything apart from tell me I should leave and go somewhere else."

He scrubbed his face in his hands. "Come on, let's have lunch. What can I get you?" Mikey tried a smile, but it came across as a grimace.

"Mikey, darling, I have a match … I can't stay. I'll call round later, OK?"

She kissed him then left.

"I'm training tonight, sweetheart." She'd gone, and with her, his appetite.

Melinda Linton's House, Hessle, Humberside: 16 December 2021

Hessle was a small town on the banks of the River Humber, nestled under the shadow of Humber Bridge. It took John thirty minutes to drive there following his serendipitous meeting with Kevin.

After a call to Justin, it didn't take long to find coverage of the incident and subsequent court case in the Humberside Tribune. The guy who assaulted the doorman was called

Mark Linton. He was arrested at the scene, charged and convicted. He killed himself in his prison cell, leaving a wife and two kids.

John knocked on the door. A fit-looking woman in her late thirties opened it.

"Mrs Linton, my name's John Devlin. You spoke with my colleague on the phone." John smiled genially.

"Yes, please come in. Head into the dining room and take a seat. Would you like a tea or a coffee?"

"No, thank you, I'm good."

John pulled a chair out and sat down, his mind doing somersaults as to how he was going to explain what really happened to her then husband.

"It's a lovely house you have, Mrs Linton. The views of the bridge are stunning."

Melinda had shoulder-length brown hair, alert blue eyes and a sun-kissed complexion. There was a spring in her step and a straightness in her shoulders. She exuded a confidence that told him she had perhaps got over losing Mark and rebuilt her life. A framed photo on the sideboard of Melinda and a dark-haired man about to take on an alpine slope was all the confirmation he needed, which made what he was about to tell her even more difficult.

"You can call me, Mel. That's my partner, Dan. We were in Chamonix last Christmas. The snow was amazing." She stalled and grinned as the memory bounced around her head.

"I appreciate you meeting me at such short notice, Mel. I've a few questions to ask you about what happened to Mark."

"Sure, it seems a long time ago now. It's nearly ten years since he went to prison, which was the last time I saw him … before he took his own life."

The tears were all cried out, although the love hadn't gone completely. A small twitch in her eye betrayed the fondness she still had for him.

"What I'm about to tell you may come as a bit of a shock. I want you to know I wouldn't spring this on you if it wasn't hypercritical to someone very dear to me."

Mel swallowed in surprise and took a deep breath. "Go on."

"Is this the man who your husband assaulted?" John slid Stockton's picture over the table towards her. She didn't move to pick it up or hesitate to answer.

"Yes, that's him. Tim Batley," she said breathing deeply, her eye twitching faster.

John took a breath of his own in readiness for what he was about to say.

"This man is currently going by the name of Ben Stockton and is giving evidence at Fulwood Crown Court in London, in the prosecution of my friend, Jake Webster."

Mel looked confused and shook her head.

"My friend is accused of assaulting this man in a London nightclub five months ago. Stockton, or Batley as you knew him, was working as a doorman. He had a scuffle with Jake and fell down a flight of stairs."

Mel shook her head disbelievingly. "You're mistaken. This can't be the same person. Batley had life-changing injuries … there were doctors' reports … he was in a wheelchair in court. They said he'd never walk again."

John shook his head slowly with his eyes closed.

"He was born in 1984 by the name of Lee Grassington. He lived in Rawmarsh in Yorkshire. We have established eight different aliases so far. He has made many insurance claims for major life-threatening injuries in the last twelve years. Five since the death of your husband and two prior to that date that we know of."

Mel picked up his picture, her eyes filling with tears. "I don't … I can't believe it."

"We believe he's not acting alone. Can you remember the name of the police officer in charge? Is the name Steve Cantly familiar to you?"

Melinda's head lifted on hearing his name. She knew him well it seemed.

"This can't be. Mark killed himself over this bastard. Are you telling me he faked the whole thing, and the police were in on it?"

"Yes. I'm afraid it was an elaborate scam, and it's about to happen again. I'm so sorry."

Her bottom lip trembled, and her breathing became erratic as she took in the horror of what he was saying. She shook her head in denial. "No, no, this can't be. You're lying. There must be some mistake!" she screamed hysterically.

She broke down. Ten years of guilt and anger tore through her. Her hands shook with rage.

"He wouldn't hurt a fly. I told everyone at the time. They had witness statements and CCTV. The judge called him 'a violent thug'."

Tears streamed down her face, then anger took over. John could see her jaw clenching as she tried to make sense of it. She snatched the picture, scrunched it in her hands and threw it against the wall, followed by her coffee cup.

"Bastard! You fucking bastard! You took my Mark!" she screamed at the top of her voice once more.

John held her while she cried her heart out, rubbing her back and rocking her in the safe refuge of his arms. He felt the emotion stinging his eyes and nose, then the anger boil in his blood.

"Come on, sit down. I'll make us a cup of tea and we can talk a little more."

***

John went through what happened in Fandango's and the events of the last five months. After a few more outbursts, Mel seemed to gain strength from within and sat up straight, with a determined, vengeful look on her face.

"So, what do you want me to do?" she asked.

He blew out a deep breath. "I want you to come to London and give testimony at Jake's trial tomorrow."

"I'll get my coat. Let's go."

22

YOU GET WHAT YOU DESERVE

Judge's Chambers, Fulwood Crown Court, London: 17 December 2021

"Mr Carmichael-Prowse, this is highly irregular and a fairly desperate tactic on your part, but I'm not so disagreeable as to offer you a cup of coffee while you present your argument."

Judge Hamlin scowled as he took his seat behind his leather-clad desk.

"No, thank you, my Lord. I'll get straight to the point if I may."

"Please do," he said witheringly.

"Evidence has come to light as to the veracity of Mr Stockton's testimony, and we wish to call upon an additional witness."

"And why the secrecy? Mr Stansfield has every right to object should your request prove to be a delaying tactic or an obfuscation."

"You would be correct in that assertion, my Lord, if not for the seriousness of the witness's testimony, which will likely warrant the arrest and detention of several prosecution witnesses, police officers, and legal professionals, as well as

Mr Stockton himself. To that end, I recommend additional court security and a representative from police internal affairs be present."

"Are you suggesting the CPS is complicit in whatever scenario you are alluding to, sir?" Judge Hamlin whipped off his reading glasses and leant on his elbows.

"No, my Lord. What I will say is evidence has come to light that suggests one or more police officers have aided and abetted a serious crime, and furthermore, they are complicit in a complex organised crime syndicate. My recommendation is that internal affairs are requested to detain them, to avoid any flight risk, which may bring unwarranted embarrassment to the court."

"Is there anything else? Perhaps a red carpet or a fanfare of trumpeters? Are you trying to make a fool out of me, sir? If so, I would suggest that was a serious error of judgement on your behalf." Judge Hamlin's patience was wearing thin.

"My Lord, it is precisely that outcome I am determined to prevent."

Montrose Gardens, Bagshot, Surrey: 17 December 2021

Hey princess, I've been trying get hold of you. I'm at my parents' for this bloody Christmas dinner. I'm not looking forward to it to be honest. I'll be at yours for 5pm. I can't wait to get you both back home to begin our new life. I hope all's well with Jacob. Let me know if he's being a dick and I'll be straight there.
Love you. xx

Rob sent his text and buzzed himself in through his parents' enormous cast iron gates and freewheeled his Audi Q8 down the drive. He parked next to Evie's Porsche.

"What a waste," he mumbled to himself and walked in through the front door, which was flanked by two of Santa's reindeers, immortalised in bronze.

"Robin's here!" his mother shouted to no one in particular.

She hugged him and kissed his face, feeling his shoulders and chest. "That Mikey Stott has you doing too many weights. Look at the size of you."

Rob hadn't been to the gym in six months, but he wasn't prepared to argue with her.

"Your father is in his study. He said for you to pop in and see him when you got here," Linda whispered, for some reason, as if talking about Roger required quiet reverence. "Don't be long, darling. Lunch is nearly ready."

Rob made his way across the marbled hallway floor and along the corridor leading to Roger's inner sanctum. He knocked and waited for once.

"Come in," Roger said cheerily.

"Hey, you wanted to see me." Rob strolled over and sat on the chair in front of his desk.

"So, you're off to France, I hear." Roger looked up with a curious grin on his face.

"Yes, I'm going to work part-time in the Paris office … get François licked into shape. You OK with that?"

"Of course, why wouldn't I be? You are your own man. I've never doubted any of your decisions before. I'm sure you'll make a fist of it. Besides, you love your artwork. It will be like a busman's holiday working in a gallery."

Rob was utterly flabbergasted. Where was the Roger he'd known all these years – the sceptical, arrogant, disingenuous bastard he'd loathed his whole adult life?

"I was expecting a bit more pushback from you, if I'm honest," Rob said, sounding relieved.

"I'm trying my best, Son. We only get one chance at life … let's make it count, shall we?"

Roger smiled awkwardly. His fatherly love needed a little practice yet. "Come on, let's have lunch. We all want to hear about your plans."

Fulwood Sports Centre, Kentish Town, London: 17 December 2021

Mikey was standing at the poolside in his swim trunks, perhaps for the last time, admiring a full contingent of superheroes being given a raucous introduction by Lisa on the microphone and receiving applause from their parents.

A lump caught in his throat as the prospect of leaving them behind began to dawn on him. He'd taught some of them for years. He'd become an integral part of their development and lives.

He'd decided not to tell them until the end of the class. Chances were, he wouldn't tell them at all. They'd feel betrayed and abandoned, as would their parents and siblings. He'd become a household name. They didn't attend swimming classes – they went to *Superheroes.*

The spectator gallery was packed with expectant parents, watching eagerly as each class member took their positions for the relay race and freestyle exhibition. Joy and Lawan sat front and centre, proud grins on their faces on seeing Jules lead the line.

Lisa announced the first race: "Barracuda, Thunderbird, Marina and Ironwoman – take your positions!"

Jules, Arthur, Susan and Rebecca all slid into the shallow end, faced the poolside and held onto the rail, ready to push off into backstroke.

"On your marks!" Lisa blew her whistle and they set off, weaving left and right across their double lanes.

Jules reached the end first and handed off to Dean, aka Captain Chaos, who belly flopped into the water, kicked up to the surface and took up front crawl. Arthur was in lane two and plodding slowly towards his handover.

Mikey noticed he'd started to slow, so started a chant on Lisa's microphone to urge him on.

"Bar-ra-coo-da! Bar-ra-coo-da!" The crowd took up the chant with him, creating a deafening chorus of encouragement.

It didn't help. He seemed to be swimming on the spot and making no forward progress. Then he slipped beneath the surface in the blink of an eye and sank to the bottom of the pool like a stone.

Mikey blew short sharp blasts on his whistle while running towards the deep end, where he dived in barely making a splash. He opened his eyes, enduring the sting of the chlorine, which blurred his vision temporarily.

He caught sight of Arthur face down, motionless, at the bottom of the pool. He swam down to him and quickly wrapped his arms under his armpits, then launched them both upwards, kicking as hard as he could.

Arthur's huge bulk hardly moved, their combined weight anchoring them to the bottom of the pool.

Mikey's lungs burned as the oxygen in his bloodstream was consumed with every kick. His arms were barely long enough to reach around Arthur's chest, and he felt his grip begin to give way.

He looked up to see the distorted shapes of spectators dancing cruelly above his head. He felt his teeth grind in effort. Fear began to take over. They were sinking back down, and there was nothing he could do about it.

He heard the faintest of cries for help, which became louder and louder.

Kick, Mikey, kick! Please save me, please.

Kaitlyn? Mikey looked around, shaking his head in confusion and horror. *No, it can't be!*

The cries for help became more distinct. There was no mistaking her voice.

He looked down to find Kaitlyn's emaciated body hanging limply in his arms, her face tilted towards his in a stare of desperation.

Mikey froze in the water, too traumatised to move. He shook his head in disbelief.

No! Kaitlyn! No! How can this be?

Mikey don't let me die, please, I beg you. Don't let me die again!

Her blackened, lifeless eyes bored into him accusingly.

Her body began to turn to sand, disintegrating before his eyes, slipping through his grip once more. He was powerless to stop it.

He screamed her name and the words bubbled from his mouth: "Noooo, Kaitlyn, noooo!"

Mikey roared and threw his head back. He thrashed his legs and groped at the water with his free arm, pulling them up in rapid surges. He felt his limbs go numb and his pulse pound in his eardrums, while the macabre dancing shapes celebrated above him.

He wouldn't fail her again. She had to live.

That's it, Mikey, kick! Kick! Please, save me, Kaitlyn urged, her voice becoming clearer with every stroke. *You can do it, Mikey.*

He broke the surface and launched himself against the poolside as Big G's gorilla-like arms reached in to lift Arthur out of the water and lay him down.

"He's not breathing," Big G said as Mikey jumped out of the pool. He flipped Arthur onto his front, cradling his face.

"Carla, call an ambulance and get the defib! Lisa, clear the pool! Jules, bring towels ... lots of them ... go!"

Everyone scattered.

Mikey pushed on Arthur's back in hard lunges as the water gushed from his mouth. He and Big G flipped him onto his back and Mikey tilted his head to check his airways were clear.

He gave two rescue breaths.

Nothing.

He crossed his hands and laced his fingers together and pushed his weight through his shoulders onto Arthur's sternum and began counting double time to thirty.

Nothing.

He repeated the process.

Nothing.

Carla returned and debagged the defib, which automatically burst into life, informing the uninitiated it was ready for use.

Big G dried Arthur's chest and body, before Mikey peeled away the covers and applied the shock plates. The defib beeped and began assessing Arthur's heart rhythm. A couple of seconds later an audible message rang out.

"Stand Clear! Shock Advised!"

Mikey pressed the orange button and Arthur's body convulsed. He repeated it a few times until the machine relayed a new message.

"Shock Not Advised."

He lowered his ear to Arthur's airways and felt a shallow breath. He held his wrist to find a weak pulse had returned.

Big G rolled him into the recovery position, onto the towels Jules had fetched, and wrapped him up.

Jules stayed at Arthur's side.

***

Joy made her way to the poolside and ran into Mikey's embrace.

"Mikey, I'm so proud of you! You saved Arthur's life."

He would never tire of holding Joy in his arms. It was as if she had grown into a shape that fitted his body to the millimetre. He could travel the entire globe and hold every woman, but the only one who would fit perfectly was right there. The only one who truly knew him.

He broke down, the enormity of what had happened crashing into reality.

"She was with me, Joy, she saved him. Kaitlyn saved him."

"It's OK, Mikey, I'm here now. I love you so much."

Big G wrapped his ridiculously long arms around them both.

"You guys kill me." He sobbed like a baby on top of both of their heads.

"Gordon, you were amazing too. I'm so proud of you."

Joy released her grip on Mikey to include Big G, who winced at the force she applied to his abdomen.

An elderly couple scurried over to them. "We are Arthur's grandparents. We owe you a debt of gratitude. You have no idea what that boy means to us. He is all we have in the world."

Arthur's grandad offered Mikey a shaky hand. Mikey shook it tenderly.

"He means the world to me as well, Mr Soames. He is a fine boy ... you should be proud. He swam until he couldn't swim another stroke. I wish I had his determination."

Even then Mikey knew exactly what to say and how to say it. Joy burst into tears all over again.

"Michael Stott to meeting room three!" Luke's voice rang out over the tannoy, spoiling the moment.

Fulwood Magistrates' Court, Kentish Town, London: 17 December 2021

Hansie and Trixie held hands, void of all hope. The appeal committee had returned to their seats following a five-minute recess, which told Hansie everything he needed to know.

An officious-looking man in rimless glasses lifted his head and said impassively, "Mr and Mrs Van Heerden, after considering your appeal for leave to remain, and in accordance with Foreign Office guidelines, I regr—"

There was a knock at the door. He slammed his pen on his notepad.

"Can't you read? It says court in session."

A tall lady in a tweed suit shuffled over to their desk nervously.

"I'm sorry to interrupt, Mr Turner … there is an urgent call from the Foreign Office." She handed him a mobile phone.

"Andrew Turner," he said, followed by a short one-sided conversation.

He hung up the call without speaking and handed the handset back to the woman, who retreated and closed the door with a soft click.

Turner spoke furtively to his colleagues, who shrugged and shook their heads confused. After several moments, he collected his notes and placed them in his file, and zipped it shut.

"Mr and Mrs Van Heerden, after considering your appeal for leave to remain, and in accordance with Foreign Office guidelines…" – he paused and took a deep breath – "I am pleased to inform you that your appeal to remain has been successful."

Fulwood Sports Centre, Kentish Town, London: 17 December 2021

Mikey knocked on the door and entered, surprised to find Amanda Knowles and Cheryl Neaves sitting at the meeting room table.

"Take a seat please, Michael," Cheryl said without looking up.

Mikey slumped on his seat. It didn't matter what they said, or if they fired him. He didn't care. He'd saved Arthur's life, and with it, the remainder of his grandparents' lives. Nothing would spoil that moment. The trauma Jules could've endured witnessing his best friend dying wasn't worth contemplating.

For ten years he'd battled with the grief of Kaitlyn's death. But not any more – he'd saved her too. She was there, pushing him, crying out his name. Without her, Arthur would have died, of that he had no doubt. These people could say what they liked. He couldn't care less.

"Firstly, Michael, tell us about Arthur Soames. I understand he's been rushed to hospital after an incident in the swimming pool," Amanda asked in a business-like manner.

"Yes. He'll be fine … he may have had a seizure … we aren't sure." Mikey sounded exhausted.

Amanda closed her eyes with relief. She nodded as if to reset her train of thought.

"You sent us a report last week. I have to say I'm rather embarrassed by it."

I bet you are, Mikey thought.

"Euan McArdle and Elaine McIlroy have been embezzling funds from Fulwood for over three years … and we hadn't noticed. They've stolen over half a million pounds."

Mikey's jaw dropped open.

"They have both been dismissed and will be subject to a police investigation."

Mikey blew out a half whistle.

"We should have been watching, and we weren't. This is my responsibility and mine alone. I know how patient you've been working alongside Euan. His methods and management style left a lot to be desired. I'm truly sorry."

Amanda tore up the corporate playbook in favour of an unequivocal apology.

"What for?" Mikey asked in all sincerity.

"For allowing that man to remain in post for so long," Cheryl put in. "Your report has enabled us to put an end to his shoddy practices, and we hope to recoup the monies he's stolen. And for the record, we had not authorised any redundancies at Fulwood."

"Does this mean I get to keep my job?"

Montrose Gardens, Bagshot, Surrey: 17 December 2021

Rob had had a wonderful afternoon. His father seemed to have turned over a new leaf. Even Evie had been civil. It may have been easier to tell his news with half a dozen pints of Guinness in his system, but, hey, it was now or never. He had a good feeling about what he was going to tell them.

"I hope you are going to visit us in Paris," Rob said to his father.

"Please don't make me. I can't abide Frenchies." Roger chuckled, missing his point completely.

"Us? Who is us? Have you met someone new?" Linda asked, in the forlorn hope it wasn't Maddie.

"Not quite. I'm back with Maddie. She's coming with me … I thought you should know."

A stony silence enveloped the room. Roger's face folded in on itself.

"We've been seeing each other since August. I'm not proud of myself for two-timing Lauren, but when you love someone … you know how it is." He gave up explaining himself.

"Are you sure this is what you want?" his mother asked, squeezing his hand. "She let you down badly before. I don't want you hurt again."

"It is, Mum. I love her, and she loves me. It's going to be a great place to raise our family."

Roger dropped his cutlery. "She's pregnant?!"

Rob nodded defiantly.

"You idiot! You total fucking idiot!" Roger stood and knocked his wine over. "That little slag is playing you for a fool, and you are falling for it."

"Fuck you," Rob said, standing up to leave. "I knew you would react this way. Well, I couldn't give a fuck what you think. I love Maddie, and she loves me. We are having a baby and that's that. You can choose to support us or not, I don't care. I don't run away from my responsibilities. I see them through, no matter what. I'll be a proper father, who doesn't beat his kids and lock them in cupboards."

He snatched his coat off his chair and kissed his mother on the cheek. "Sorry, Mum … I'll call you."

His sister sneered at him as he left. "Dad's right. You *are* an idiot."

123 Kilkenny Road, Crouch End, London: 17 December 2021

Rob pulled up to the kerb twenty metres from Maddie's house and killed the engine. The hour he'd spent driving had allowed him to calm his nerves.

Dad's reaction was wholly predictable. Why I thought it would be any different, I don't know. That show of parental kindness and encouragement about my career move was a sham. What does he care of my happiness? What does he know? Nothing! He can go fuck himself. It doesn't matter – my future's set, with or without his approval or his money. I just don't care.

He flicked his fifth cigarette butt to the curb, just as a black cab pulled up outside the house. A large guy with short brown hair got out, followed closely by Maddie. He held her arm as she stepped onto the icy footpath.

Rob made to get out of his car when something stopped him.

The guy turned to Maddie, cupped her face and kissed her on the lips. He brushed his hand over her stomach and bent down to put his ear to her navel. Maddie laughed and stroked his head. Even in the dim orange streetlight, he saw in her eyes what he meant to her. He saw the look of love he'd hoped to see himself. He realised there and then he'd been duped.

Maddie looked up and saw Rob staring straight at her. Her happiness disappeared into panic. She spoke to Jacob briefly. He picked up her shopping and headed into the house. Maddie made her way over to Rob's car.

"It's not mine, is it? The baby. It's his!" Rob's bottom lip trembled.

"I'm sorry, Rob. I ... I don't know what to say." She buried her face in her hands.

"It was all a trick, wasn't it? You conned me. You made me think…"

He didn't know whether to laugh or cry. His father was right. Evie, Lauren, Mikey, Jake, Marcella, even Beryl – they all saw what he refused to see. What was staring him in the face.

She glanced over to her front door, fearful Jacob would join the party. "I so wanted the baby to be yours, I fooled myself into thinking it would work. I couldn't follow it through … I couldn't do it to him."

"Don't you dare cry! Don't you fucking dare!" Rob shouted through gritted teeth, tears stinging his eyes.

He turned his engine over and drove off, leaving her and Jacob's unborn baby standing in the middle of the road.

Fulwood Crown Court, London: 17 December 2021

"You are Mrs Melinda Linton of 193 Hull Road, Hessle, Humberside, are you not?" Carmichael-Prowse smiled at Melinda to put her at ease.

"That's correct," she replied nervously.

"In your own words, can you tell the court what happened on the night of 4 April 2011?"

"Yes," Mel said solemnly. "It's a night that changed my life forever. It was a Saturday, and my husband, Mark, had gone into Hull to celebrate the birth of his friend's son. He spent the night drinking and went to Zanzibar Nightclub."

The journey south had been gruelling. John had given her details of the incident at Fandango's months before, which had triggered many of her dark thoughts following Mark's death. She'd hated him for 'ruining their lives'. *"You did this. You made this happen."* She'd placed responsibility firmly in Mark's hands, which had contributed to him taking his life – she was certain of that. She was forced to live with the guilt for the rest of her life.

"Did he make a habit of frequenting nightclubs, Mrs Linton?"

"No. He wasn't a big drinker, and he couldn't dance." She laughed absently. "He went along because his friends asked him to … to make sure they got home safe."

"Please carry on."

"It was the end of the night. Jamie, his friend, was drunk … he could barely stand up. Mark was carrying him out of the club to get him a taxi home, and he bumped into one of the doormen. It was an accident, nothing more. He wasn't a violent man … he really wasn't … he apologised, but the bouncer began hitting Jamie around the head. Mark tried to stop him, but he was too big."

Melinda's tears began to flow, dragging her mascara down her face.

"He tried to get him away from Jamie, to stop him hurting him," she sobbed.

"Please take your time, Mrs Linton. In your own words, what happened next?"

"The doorman fell backwards down the stairs leading to the exit. He broke his back and suffered a serious eye injury," she said in a quiet but audible whisper. She cleared her throat and looked up, rage gripping her suddenly.

"Is it true your husband was prosecuted for assault, Mrs Linton?"

"Yes."

"Is it also true he took his own life in prison?" Carmichael-Prowse lowered his voice respectfully.

"Yes, he did." Melinda gritted her teeth as she replied.

"Mrs Linton, the injured party that fateful night – can you recall his name?"

"Tim Batley."

"Mr Timothy Batley, is that correct?"

"Yes."

"Mrs Linton, is Mr Batley in this courtroom today? If so, please point him out to the court."

"Him! In the wheelchair. That bastard caused my Mark to kill himself."

Ben Stockton shook his head. "She's lying! I've never been to Hull!"

"Order!" the judge demanded as the courtroom noise level went up a notch.

"My Lord," Carmichael-Prowse persisted, "please may I draw your attention to document B4, which shows on the lefthand side an X-ray of Mr Stockton's injuries, taken by a Dr Choudary of Lexington Health on 29 August, 2021. On the righthand side, it shows an X-ray taken by Dr Choudary of Lexington Health in 2017 of an Ian Sunderland, from Kedleston Road, Mickleover, Derby."

Judge Hamlin studied the document.

Carmichael-Prowse continued. "My Lord, a digital forensic analysis has been carried out on the scans. They are an exact match, down to the last pixel."

Jake was in awe of his barrister incinerating the prosecution's case.

"Indeed, not only are the scans a match, but Mr Stockton himself is an exact match for Timothy Batley also, as testified by Mrs Linton."

Carmichael-Prowse allowed the judge time to catch up.

"My Lord, our investigations have found a further six aliases used by Mr Stockton and his accomplices in a complex and far-reaching scam to defraud insurance companies for personal injury claims, involving the police, medical practitioners and senior legal professionals."

Stockton leapt to his feet, making a miraculous recovery from his life-threatening injuries. "It's not my fault! I was forced to do it! They were going to kill my girlfriend and my sister! He's a maniac – you don't know what he's capable of!"

Stockton stumbled towards the exit of the courtroom, where he was restrained by security staff.

"Order! Order!" Judge Hamlin demanded, banging his gavel on his desk.

"I'm not taking the rap for this!" Stockton screamed, yanking the bandage from his pink head to reveal the grotesque sight of his sagging eye socket.

"It was Bell and Cantly, and that crazy bastard Doda! They've been doing it for years!" Stockton yelled, pointing at DS Cantly and PC Owens, who were being handcuffed by an internal affairs inspector who had been called in on Carmichael-Prowse's request.

"Order! Order! Security, detain that man. Order! Order! Court will take a thirty-minute recess."

Judge Hamlin glared at Carmichael-Prowse, who was gathering his notes with a serene grin on his face.

23

A NEW BEGINNING

The Swann & Key, Kentish Town, London: 17 December 2021

Mikey's entrance to The Swann & Key had never failed to grab people's attention, and this Payday Friday was no different.

The politician's backslapping arrival had gone. Mikey's new persona resembled that of a film star, modestly absorbing the applause of his adoring fans, Joy playing the part of leading lady like a seasoned professional.

Her gleaming white evening dress clung to her athletic body, visible through the sheer satin. Her hair was tied in a curly top knot that looked like a fountain of jet-black oil, speared by a pair of amethyst hairpins.

Joy's trademark vanilla lip gloss glistened, framing her perfect white teeth. She'd had plenty of practice applying it in the taxi with Mikey.

She linked her arm through Mikey's and smiled warmly at the sea of captivated faces blinking silently at their arrival. She moved with the confidence of an athlete, and just like Mikey only a few hours previously, her audience was blissfully unaware of just how capable she was, in every facet of her life, which was just how she liked it.

Mikey had watched Joy destroy her opponent in straight sets to claim the London Open and a £50,000 winner's cheque from the Deputy Mayor of London. She had insisted on being interviewed with Mikey next to her. He had found sporting fame at last.

Her eyes shone, smiling in a nonverbal, dreamy welcome. She buzzed with excitement having Mikey next to her. The uncontrollable exhibition of love and devotion in his eyes made her want to cry with delight.

"Champagne?" he offered, and she nodded eagerly.

Mikey glanced right towards the bar and mouthed, 'Champagne please' in Thea Horgan's direction. Even from that distance he could see the sparkle in her green eyes. Tonight though, in place of the mischief that normally resided there, she showed genuine affection and happiness for him, and maybe a little regret. She didn't need to be Sherlock Holmes to see what the Asian beauty queen meant to him.

As they glided through the bar area, he came face to face with Alexa and Welsh Ian, who were holding hands at their usual table. This time, instead of making a bolt for him, Alexa waved and snuggled into the crook of Ian's arm. Ian had a curious smirk of victory on his face, a warning for Mikey to stay away. He was happy to oblige.

They stepped into the taproom and were greeted by Jake and John, who sprang to their feet. Mikey dispensed with introductions and threw his arms around his friend, burying his head into his shoulder, hugging him like it was for the last time.

"Jakey boy, this has got to be one of the most fucked-up days of our lives, and I've never been happier! I need to hear all about court … what happened in there?" Mikey's eyes were glassy from sheer relief.

"All in good time, Mikey. We want to meet Joy first, don't we, John? I seem to remember the last time I saw her you sprinted off in a sulk."

Jake nudged his mate but didn't take his eyes off Joy.

"This is Joy Wong. She is truly the most beautiful woman I've ever met, and I'm proud to say she is my girlfriend," Mikey declared.

"She's Thailand's number one squash player and is ranked fifteenth in the world. I didn't even know… And as of this afternoon, she's the All-England Squash Champion!"

Jake slapped him on the chest with the back of his hand. "Step aside," he said, bearing down on her. He held both of Joy's hands and kissed her tenderly on the cheek.

"Joy, I have never seen my mate looking this happy in all the years I've known him. I'm so pleased for you both."

"Thanks, Jake, you're so sweet. Is this your partner, John? Mikey's told me a lot about you both."

"I .. er … yes, I guess he is," Jake said hesitantly and held out his hand. John did the same.

"Joy, this is John."

Jake looked at his friend and came to the same conclusion that many had made silently for months. He'd just refused to admit it.

What's the point in holding back? he told himself – and perhaps the whole world. A quiver of excitement ran up his spine and a grin spread across his face.

"Hello, Joy. I'm so pleased to meet you. Mikey is a lucky boy."

John kissed her gently on the cheek as Jake had. She wondered how many more gorgeous guys would be joining them tonight.

Mikey stepped over and wrapped his arms around John. "You're a lifesaver, mate, truly you are. What you did for Jake, I can't thank you enough."

"Well, that makes two of us." John shook Mikey's hand, full of respect and admiration.

"We heard on the radio on the way over that you managed to save a boy's life today, and you did it using a defibrillator that *you* raised the money to buy. *That* is truly heroic, Mikey. You should be proud of yourself."

Mikey smirked modestly and laughed at his description of Arthur as a boy. The lad was a man mountain.

Joy leaned into him and hooked his arm. "He's my hero. It was my brother's best friend he saved. Without Mikey, Arthur would've died. You should've seen him, he was amazing."

"You would've all done the same, and besides, Jake's the real hero here. If he hadn't battered those guys at Fandango's, I'd be brain damaged. Or worse. Not only that, but he was prepared to go to jail for me." Mikey welled up and swallowed it down.

"He also disarmed a drugged-up nutcase who was going to kill his wife and children last week, don't forget. That's a true hero right there. I think he deserves a toast," John said.

They turned to find Thea had already set out six flutes and a bottle of Moët in an ice bucket, which Mikey began to pour.

"Mikey, shouldn't we wait for Rob?" Jake asked.

He didn't have to wait long for his answer, as Rob made the timeliest arrival of his life. Mikey delegated champagne pouring to John and turned to hug his lacklustre friend, who was clearly upset. It didn't take a genius to work out why.

He sat him down next to the newest members of the Payday Friday Club. There was no mistaking the despair on his face. It had killed the atmosphere stone dead.

"Come on, spit it out, Fruit. What's happened?" Mikey had no time for drama. Tonight was a night of celebration.

"I've been a fool. She had no intention of being with me. The baby's not mine." He dropped his chin to his chest.

Mikey didn't wait for Jake to speak this time. "Yeah, you have. So what? We're all foolish from time to time. I tell you what though, mate – you're not a conniving bitch who'd lie to her unborn child just to secure an easy life. You're a sensitive, loyal, intelligent man who, I am proud to say, is one of the best friends a guy could have. You've been there for us when we've needed you the most, and we're here for you now. Aren't we?"

He turned to Jake for support.

"Fucking right, Mikey," Jake said, before immediately apologising to Joy for his coarse language.

"You've decided, and not a moment too soon in my opinion, to live a life in Paris, a place you adore, doing what we all know you do best. Working with the Montreaux family's going to be a massive adventure. We're stoked for you, aren't we?" Jake received resounding nods.

Mikey joined in again. "I'm chuffed for you, Fruit, and I can make a cast-iron guarantee to you now, the first Payday Friday you have free, we'll be coming to Paris."

"You'll love it, Rob. I've just been there … I can recommend some lovely restaurants," Joy chipped in.

Rob turned to face her. She didn't know he'd lived there. She just wanted to make him feel better.

"You must be Joy," Rob said, a flicker of a smile creeping into the side of his mouth.

He could only dream of finding someone as lovely as her, and being as happy as Mikey clearly was.

"Nice to meet you, Rob. I'm sorry it didn't work out for you and Maddie … that's so sad. I'm sure you'll find someone who will make you happy and you'll look back and thank your lucky stars." She kissed him on the forehead, brushing his face with her hand.

Rob lifted his head to see a tidal wave of contentment. His two friends were the happiest he'd ever seen them. They'd become that way by helping others, despite their own problems. He still had a lot to learn from them.

Jake's matchmaking of his Auntie Lesley with Alan Willoughby was pure selflessness. Playing his double jeopardy card to get Alan to pull strings for Hansie and Trixie with the Foreign Office was a stroke of genius. Even with the threat of incarceration hanging over himself, he thought of those less fortunate.

Why didn't I think of doing all those things?

Hansie's and Trixie's lives had been transformed because of a simple telephone call, with no apparent benefit for Jake, other than seeing the smiles on their faces and knowing he'd done the right thing.

Rob's own showboating at Highfield had given him a taste of humanity, and he liked it. He told himself it was time to step up, and that time was now. The pain of Maddie's deception and rejection was his punishment. Unlike Jake, he deserved it.

He'd willingly conspired to coax Maddie away from Jacob because he wanted her, and what he wanted he bought, just like Roger did.

He had battled against his father his whole life – his greed, conceit and ignorance – only to identify the same attributes in himself. Now he owed him an apology. The effort his father had gone to in recent weeks showed he was learning how to love. And Rob had gone and thrown it in his face.

If he were to ask himself truthfully, he could have seen through Maddie's treachery, just like Roger had. The signs were there – perhaps more apparent now – but they were there and he'd chosen to ignore them.

He remembered her sickness on the night they met Marcella and Monty – her insatiable appetite, like she was eating for two – and how when she told him the news, she could barely look him in the eye. He believed it to be reluctance on her behalf, worried about his reaction. In truth, it was her conscience eating away at her.

She had no intention of leaving Jacob. Or perhaps she was exhausted by the prospect of lying for the rest of her life. Either way, she'd tired of him, and just as quick as the idea had entered her pretty little head, she'd stubbed it out. She was a self-serving schemer, and he'd been played.

Joy was right. He should be counting his lucky stars. He'd escaped a life-changing event of crippling magnitude, the ramifications of which made him sick to the stomach. And through it all, his friends had stuck by him when he needed them most.

Leaving them behind was going to be difficult, but he knew this was the time to cut free of the catch net they had always had ready for him. They'd found happiness. Every moment spent away from that was a moment wasted for them. They wouldn't see it in those terms, but he did. He had to give them room to go their own way.

***

Jake and John were sat huddled up. John didn't want to let him out of his sight and Jake didn't want to be anywhere else. The last three months had been a rollercoaster ride he didn't want to take again.

Poor Bernard decided to walk away from Fulwood Borough Social Services with literally nothing to show for his twenty years of hard work. He'd lost his son to the war in Afghanistan and his wife to the ravages of motor neurone disease. He had nothing left. Heading back to Yorkshire was the only place he'd find solace. A place to remember the good times.

"Cut out the bullshit, lad. Live the best life you can. Don't make excuses, and don't lie to yourself."

Jake had felt something for John from the moment they met. He just didn't know what it was, or why he felt the way he did. He was in denial. He laughed at the cliché, but it was true. And when push came to shove, John was there making things happen, pushing away those intent on harming him. Tonight, he was free, in every sense of the word. No more hiding, no more blocking out what he didn't want to hear and what he didn't want to feel. Jake knew his future was now with John Devlin, and he'd never look back.

This beating of his heart and excitement for the future was new to him. He'd revel in it. Why not? He deserved a little happiness. He'd conceded his friendship with Mikey and Rob had come to an impasse. Even in the last five minutes, Rob's spine had straightened and his jaw clenched in determination. He had the inner strength to overcome Maddie's deception, and he'd be back twice as strong.

Rob's journey had started with just one kiss on the forehead from Joy, such was the power of love. Jake imagined what Mikey's future held in store. If he could bottle the euphoria he was experiencing, he'd make a fortune.

It was no surprise to him that Mikey had found someone as attractive as Joy. She was breathtakingly beautiful, even when she belly laughed at his goofy humour. Her smile and girly cackle were contagious.

***

As they recounted the day's events, toasting one another's heroics, Mikey remembered the picture Joy had sent him months earlier of her holding a champagne flute and laughing at something. He'd wished then she'd be laughing with him one day. Now here she was.

The last three months had had a profound effect on Mikey: the threat of redundancy, Euan's corruption, feeling guilty about Jake, his panic attacks, and then 'little' Arthur – the poor guy could have died. If it weren't for Joy, he doubted he'd have made it. Even in her absence she had held him together. He'd fallen in love with her the first day he'd met her. He realised that now.

He stared into her face, and the rest of the world receded into blurry slow motion. Puddles of happiness welled up in his eyes. She brushed them away, holding her fingertips against his lips, making everything right again.

They had a lifetime of memories to make, and they couldn't wait.

ACKNOWLEDGEMENTS

My thanks go out to all those who have helped me on my journey to authorship. In particular, I'd like to thank Alia Coster of Coster Content, who never spared the rod and put me on the right path. Latterly, I owe a debt of gratitude to Yasmin Yarwood from Meticulous Proofreading for turning my manuscript into something worth reading, and to Alexa Whitten of The Book Refinery for her awesome cover design and flawless typesetting.

As a group, the writing community is one of the most welcoming kind-hearted bunch of folk you'd wish to meet. Their encouragement and feedback have been heartwarming. A special thanks to John Chambers, author of the best-selling *A Belfast Child*; Tina Baker, author of *Make Me Clean*; and Scott Blackburn, author of *It Dies With You*. Their advice and encouragement means so much to me.

To all my beta readers, I doff my cap to you. Without your effort, I feel certain I would have missed the mark. I thank you from the bottom of my heart. A special thanks to Kerry Shelley, Chris Green, Julia Kett, Tordy Bateman and Ady

Shelley for their never-ending stream of observations and feedback.

My sincere thanks go out to my good friends Dr Johan and Dr Ronette Goosen. They graciously conceded to allow me to loosely base Hansie and Trixie on them, for no other reason than that they are lovely and South African, which is where the similarities end. Thanks to Jenny 'Ma' Goosen for allowing me to base the farm scene at Gorriekoppen in the Eastern Cape, a wonderful place with special memories.

Big G, aka Gordon Watson, is the finest PT instructor I know, and if you were to meet him, you would know one of the kindest and most gentle giants. Thanks for being yourself.

My appreciation goes to Claire Rushton for her advice and guidance on the UK social care system, and to Elizabeth Bird for her mind-blowing knowledge of the world of investment and finance.

My thanks to Julian Shawcross of Peter Hattersley and Partners, who has been my insurance broker for many years. Without his expert help, I doubt my success in business would have happened. His experience of the world of insurance has been invaluable, and an eye-opener.

As a regular visitor to the Queen's WMC in Thornaby-on-Tees, I felt it stood in very nicely for the Highfield WMC, as did The Marble Arch pub in Manchester, and The Clarence in Bury.

A massive thanks goes to my lifelong friend Nick Lynch, who got his own character (and promotion) and played him to perfection. 'I don't believe you wrote that!' he said, on reading it. A backhanded compliment if ever I heard one. We all need a true friend in our lives, and Nick has been there for me through thick and thin. Thanks, mucker.

It was heartbreaking that my mam, Sheila O'Rourke, passed away before seeing the book published. I'm sure the Queen of Sheba is watching down on us all with Dad, enjoying a cuppa and a nice sponge cake. She was the inspiration behind the eponymous Beryl Stott, and a huge influence in my life.

A final nod to all my teachers and mentors who I have been lucky to have guide me through life. I owe you all a debt of gratitude.

ABOUT THE AUTHOR

One of five siblings, Rory O'Rourke was born and raised in the Northeast of England in a town called Thornaby on Tees. He studied Civil Engineering at Bradford University in West Yorkshire and went on to work for British Rail until 1996. At 29 he set up his own engineering business which he expanded into Europe and the USA, eventually selling his group of companies in 2018. Rory began writing fiction immediately after and completed his debut novel *Memories Can't Wait* in 2023.

He now lives in Lancashire with his wife Tammie and daughter Scarlett.

Printed in Great Britain
by Amazon